THE FACTS ON FILE
COMPANION TO

AMERICAN
POETRY

VOLUME I
BEGINNINGS TO 1900

RANDALL HUFF

Facts On File
An imprint of Infobase Publishing

The Facts On File Companion to American Poetry, Volume I: Beginnings to 1900

Copyright © 2008 by Randall Huff

Facts On File, Inc.
An imprint of Infobase Publishing
132 West 31st Street
New York NY 10001

Library of Congress Cataloging-in-Publication Data

The Facts on File companion to American poetry / [edited by] Burt Kimmelman, Temple Cone, Randall Huff.
    p. cm.
  Rev. ed. of: Facts on File companion to 20th-century poetry. 2004.
  Includes bibliographical references and index.
  ISBN 978-0-8160-6950-7 (alk. paper)
  1. American poetry—History and criticism—Handbooks, manuals, etc. I. Kimmelman, Burt. II. Cone, Temple. III. Huff, Randall. IV. Facts on File, Inc. V. Facts on File companion to 20th-century poetry.
  PS323.5.F33 2007
  811′.509—dc22   2006035417

Text design adapted by James Scotto-Lavino
Cover design by Salvatore Luongo

Printed in the United States of America

VB Hermitage 10 9 8 7 6 5 4 3 2 1

This book is printed on acid-free paper.

For Millicent Huff
A lover of horses and poetry

CONTENTS

Introduction to
The Facts On File Companion to American Poetry

The two-volume *Facts On File Companion to American Poetry* is designed to accompany readers on their journeys through the landscape of American poetry. It is divided in two parts to reflect the two semesters typically devoted to the subject in introductory courses, with the break usually coming at the start of the 20th century. Together, the volumes have the goal of whetting rather than satisfying a reader's intellectual curiosity. The entries point toward the many unique features of individual poems and the challenges faced by individual authors as they struggled to find their voice and, frequently an even more daunting challenge, to make their voices heard.

The major differences in the two volumes were dictated by their varying subject matter. Today's anthologies of American poetry typically include more poets from after 1900 than before, and in addition, literary criticism has solidified the reputations of more of the major pre-1900 poets and poems. The author of the pre-1900 volume has, therefore, chosen to include

many more entries on poems, including a large percentage of those normally found in poetry anthologies today. Readers will note that the dominant authors of the pre-1900 period, including Walt Whitman, Emily Dickinson, and Edgar Allan Poe, have many entries devoted to their individual poems.

The second volume presented a much more difficult problem of selection. This volume was first published in 2005 as *The Facts On File Companion to 20th-Century American Poetry* and is presented here in significantly expanded form. In his introduction to the volume, Professor Burt Kimmelman discusses the difficulties of the selection process, and his decision to "err on the side of caution" and include more poets. The 20th-century literary canon has not yet been so firmly established, and the flowering of poetic voices and schools since 1900 necessitated a different critical approach. Furthermore, in order to cover adequately the many specialized schools and styles of poetry that have sprung up, and the many varied voices of today's multicultural poetic world,

Professor Kimmelman employed a variety of experts in the field to write many of the volume's entries.

For this new edition of the post-1900 volume, Professor Temple Cone has added more than 100 entries, mostly on important poems from throughout the period of 1900 to the present, but also a handful of poets who have emerged in recent years. The resulting volume brings the story of American poetry up to the present day.

Each volume in *The Facts On File Companion to American Poetry* contains not only entries on important poets and poems but also on movements, journals, and subjects. Some of these subjects—such as war and anti-war poetry, European poetic influences, and many more—have entries in both the first and second volumes, so that readers can track the importance of the subject throughout the course of American poetry. Each volume also contains an appendix with a selected list of useful secondary sources. Volume II contains an appendix defining important poetic terms.

Together, Burt Kimmelman, Temple Cone, and I unite in wishing you bon voyage! We hope that this companion will assist you in many ways as you begin your own journey through American poetry.

Randall Huff

Volume Introduction

American poetry began life as an immigrant, closely bound to the Old World in its language and culture but energized by the seemingly unlimited potential of the new land. The daunting landscape it faced presented barriers that would take more than three centuries to overcome, beginning with the arduous tasks of physical discovery and exploration. More than two centuries of intermittent warfare among the western European powers were required to determine not only the political control but also the language that would dominate and define the geographical sectors of the Western Hemisphere. The treaty ending the French and Indian War in 1763 brought an end to the serious French military threat to British rule in what became the conterminous United States and determined that English would be the major language of subsequent American poetry.

The infant American poetry found itself in the hands of a very domineering mother, since the English poetry within which it identified itself had already produced the several centuries of masterpieces that still maintain their importance at the center of the world's cultural heritage. Throughout the colonial era, American poets were generally held at the mercy of the British printing establishment, for whose attention they had to compete against some of the best poets in the world. In the 17th century, Anne Bradstreet and Edward Taylor made important contributions to American poetry, but each was born in Britain and their work was limited in its influence. Bradstreet's work was privately published, initially without her consent, and Taylor's poetry remained unpublished, probably in accordance with his own wishes, until the 20th century. The best American minds of their century were devoted to survival, agriculture, trade, and religion, with religious devotion producing the best poetry.

Inadequate copyright protection, an absence of mass-market journals that could provide their most important contributors with a sustainable income, war, and a general shortage of funds in the new nation's economy damaged the careers of even such notable poets as Phillis Wheatley and Philip Freneau in the 18th century. In fact, America lacked the population and literary infrastructure necessary to produce and sustain first-rate poetic talent until at least 50 years after it attained political independence. The best American minds of the 18th century were devoted to science, commerce, political theory, war, and nation-building, and although poetry pulled its weight in the propaganda war by satirizing the Loyalists and the British war effort, most of it was ultimately of mere passing interest. Celebrations of the rising glory of America were produced during the Revolutionary War era and were joined during the postwar period with poems raising George Washington to the level of a secular saint, but the land had yet to produce a native son or daughter who could be heralded as the authentic poetic voice of the people.

American pride and prestige soared following the War for Independence and the nation's survival of a second war with Britain in 1812. By 1825, American boosterism, fueled in part by a very accurate sense of its cultural inferiority, called for advancements in poetry and all other aspects of human endeavor that could place the United States on an equal footing with countries as old as those of Europe. Although poetry books were rarely published before that year, general magazines were gradually becoming profitable, and in time would afford respectable livelihoods for poets like Maria Gowen Brooks, who could satisfy the seemingly limitless demand for romantic and sentimental poetry. The change came too late for the ill-starred Edgar Allan Poe, but by mid-century, America had produced, in William Cullen Bryant, John Greenleaf Whittier, and Oliver Wendell Holmes, three poets who, while they cannot be considered the equal of their British peers, at least were providing their country with a very respectable tradition. Henry Wadsworth Longfellow's sparkling professorial career could serve as a model for the successful academic poets of the 20th and later centuries.

The poet whose voice for cultural independence became the loudest was Ralph Waldo Emerson, and the two greatest poets in America to date, Walt Whitman and Emily Dickinson, soon answered his call. In a series of lectures that he subsequently published as books of essays, Emerson called for a new brand of American poetry worthy of the richness of the country and the astounding productivity of unfettered men. Henry David Thoreau developed the persona that would make him famous under Emerson's tutelage (and often, under Emerson's roof). Whitman, with his insistence on an organic development that relied on its natural rhythms instead of traditional meters and rhymes, was also indebted to Emerson's insights. By the start of the Civil War, Emily Dickinson had also set up shop with her own house rules, breaking many of the traditional poetic norms in order to create lasting memorials to her private moments. The work of both Whitman and Dickinson was so radically different in structure from that which preceded them that it took the poetry of each considerable time to reach a wide audience, but after them, no poet could be dismissed as second-rate merely on the basis of being American.

The Civil War redefined America, carrying off many of her ablest young men and leaving scores of potential poets, perhaps even a few great ones, rotting in the trenches at Petersburg, on the field at Gettysburg, and in the Wilderness, with their scribbled notes tossed to the wind by the human scavengers who ransacked their pockets after the battle. Their lips were forever sealed, but the conflict engendered a few of the nation's more enduring patriotic songs and cured the slavery that was searing the country's soul. The two most famous southern poets to survive the war, Sydney Lanier and Henry Timrod, soldiered on without their health, never achieving the full poetic careers they might have had in better times.

Throughout the 19th century, women were making their voices heard both in broad public forums as they effectively engineered a kaleidoscope of progressive social reforms and in their poetry, which they produced, published, and read in startling quantities. Dickinson was merely the most accomplished poet of their gender, but in her time she was virtually unknown while others were far more popular. A few of the poems by Frances Sargeant Locke Osgood, Sarah M. B. Piatt, and Lydia Huntley Sigourney indicate an identification with others of their gender that crossed racial, national, and religious lines.

The closing decades of the 19th century witnessed triumphs of human greed, as many great fortunes were amassed by individual capitalists at the apex of their varied industries; engineering marvels were accomplished by the new combinations of money and technology at unprecedented speeds that forever changed the landscape; and slums spread in the cities. These slums were peopled by successive waves of new immigrants and other disadvantaged people, a population occasionally spiced by the presence of those who had lost almost everything in the slumps that intermittently shook the economy of the nation like a malarial fever. The uncertain times produced in some cases desperate men and women whose lives were eagerly depicted by the poets of the new literary style of naturalism.

Even as echoes of the last Native American war fell silent on the American Plains, voices suggesting their rich spiritual lives were slowly making their way into English translations. In later centuries, denizens of the increasingly urbanized, secularized, and, ultimately, cubicled, mainstream culture turned nostalgic eyes to their recent past with unbridled fascination and a deep-seated longing for the feeling of being free. A survey of pre-1900 American poetry has the potential to recover some of those lost sensations, even as it chronicles many of the milestones that determined the subsequent course of the nation.

Equally poignant are the poems dedicated to conveying and ultimately ending the experience of slavery and the racism upon which it was founded. Despite the many filters through which it had to pass, the 18th-century poetry of Phillis Wheatley proved that race was no bar to inspiration and intelligence. Later poets helped bring pictures of the agony of slavery alive for their readers and helped stir the emotions that led to its demise in the Civil War. Paul Laurence Dunbar and other late 19th-century African-American poets first voiced many of the concerns about America's enduring racism and the horrendous insult of the color line that invigorated the black poetry of the next century.

Like the nation that produced it, American poetry entered the 20th century with seemingly unshakable confidence founded on a track record of increasing success and remarkable achievement. As part and parcel of the cultural imperialism that followed in the wake of the country's military and economic success, the work of Poe, Whitman, Dickinson, and others continues to inform the rest of the world of the benefits, and many of the disadvantages, of being American.

ABOUT THIS BOOK

This book represents a survey of pre-1900 American poetry designed to provide insights into the poets and individual poems that are most often included in the major anthologies and on the reading lists used in high school and college classrooms. Basically, the author acquired anthologies of American literature from the major collegiate and scholastic presses and marked for inclusion those poems that were most often chosen by their editors. I have generally tried to include at least two poems by each writer and also included work by such once-popular but now largely marginalized poets as Maria Gowen Brooks and Julia Ward Howe.

Once the entry list had been determined, my initial approach to each poem resembled that of a New Critic

of the mid-20th century. With an eye toward fulfilling the needs of the target audience, I have performed a close reading of the text and attempted to create a solid introduction to each poem presenting its essential elements with a minimum of distortion. I also felt that the most useful companion for a student in a college-level introductory survey would also sometimes be willing to assume the role of guide, and in many instances I have attempted to point out the excellence of an artist's technique and a few of the reasons for a poem's enduring popularity. For each poet, I also wrote a biographical entry designed to stimulate interest in his or her work. Note that entries on poems give the date of the poem's first publication in parentheses, just after the title. Because many important pre-1900 poems were published long after they were written (such as much of the work of Emily Dickinson and Edward Taylor), these dates are sometimes well into the 20th century.

Ideally, this book demonstrates how a poem can invigorate an active intellect by challenging it to anticipate the likely questions raised by a text. I also attempted to smooth any barriers arising from the distance between the 21st-century reader and the language and aesthetic taste of far earlier eras in American literature. Biblical citations refer to the Authorized (King James) Version. The name of a book is followed by the chapter number and then the verse number. Thus Genesis 1:1 refers to the first verse of the first chapter of Genesis. Unless the gender of a speaker is announced within a poem, the speaker is referred to as *s/he* or *him/her* the first time a pronoun is used, then the gender of the poet is used for pronouns referring to the speaker throughout the rest of the poem.

The individual entries you are about to encounter are not intended to be definitive; much of the work discussed below has defeated every attempt to fully explain all that it contains. Instead, the entries are intended to be suggestive of the richness and variety of the poetic experience. They are also meant to convey the author's pleasure at the worlds of new emotion, intellect, and experience that they have opened up for him, and encourage additional readers to advance on their own from this start. May you all grow as much from this exposure as I have, and may it bring you as much happiness as it has brought me.

A

"ABRAHAM DAVENPORT" John Greenleaf Whittier **(1866)** Meteorological phenomena occasionally take unusual shapes that cannot be
explained by the science of the day or perhaps ever.
On May 19, 1780, a freak cloud formation darkened
the sky over all of New England except where the
sunlight fringed its edges, giving it a dull red glow
as if lit by the "red hell" at the bottom of a volcanic
crater (lines 16–19). Birds, cattle, and bats all acted as
if night had fallen, but the most pronounced effects
were evident in the human population. Although
elsewhere in America people were priding themselves
on living in the Age of Enlightenment and seeking
scientific explanations for such things, religion still
dominated life in the western Connecticut backwa-
ters the poet identifies (lines 4–6). All labor stopped
as men prayed and women wept in anticipation of the
trumpet heralding Christ's return as the stern Dooms-
day Judge.

At the State House, the legislators wavered until
Abraham Davenport steadied them. After acknowledging their fears, he argued that even if it were Judgment
Day they should attend to their business in accordance
with the Lord's command (line 40), behaving more
like the dutiful servants in the Bible who providentially
invested the funds that had been entrusted to them
instead of the unimaginative servant who merely held
the money (Luke 19:12–26). He then called for candles, listened as the Speaker read a proposed amendment regulating the shad and alewife fisheries (line

52), and calmly delivered his speech on the question
despite the intermittent thunder of the storm.

John Greenleaf Whittier evidently envisioned this
anecdote as a profile in courage, for his last stanza is
a virtual portrait of the "erect, self-poised" man with
his "rugged face half seen against the background of
unnatural dark" (lines 62–63). The poet also appended
a suitable moral: "simple duty hath no place for fear"
(line 65).

Such a figure would have seemed especially heroic
to mid-19th century Quakers like Whittier, trained to
silence even in their religious meetings as most members of that sect were until they felt prompted to speak.
They were also resolute in their opposition to violence
in general and especially to war, and the Revolutionary War had already lasted five years and would continue for a year and a half after Davenport made his
courageous stand. Because the poem appeared just a
year after the 1865 conclusion of the American Civil
War, Whittier may have felt that the country needed a
less bloodstained hero than those whose exploits had
been filling the newspapers for four years. Although
the daily carnage experienced in all forms of media by
early 21st-century readers may render it difficult for
them to fully appreciate the courage of merely standing up to speak, many painful incidents in the 20th
century and even more recently demonstrate that there
are times when that simple act requires more fortitude
and exposes one to far more deadly danger than facing
a volley of musket fire or a lightning storm.

On the other hand, by 1780, long after Benjamin Franklin's experiments with electricity had robbed stormy skies of much of their supernatural terror, it seems unlikely that the inhabitants of most American communities would have reacted in quite the uniformly fearful manner described in the poem. Late 18th-century governments were very interested in the laws regulating the important fishing industry, however, as indicated by the numerous clauses in international treaties guaranteeing access to fisheries.

"ABRAHAM LINCOLN" WILLIAM CULLEN BRYANT (1865)

This eulogy, written by the 70-year-old poet in the 10 days following Lincoln's assassination on April 14, was delivered in New York City's Union Station for the largest audience WILLIAM CULLEN BRYANT ever addressed. Because of the public nature of the event and the fact that Bryant was invited as a public figure to read the poem, the speaker's voice is probably closer to that of the author than it is generally safe to assume in a poem. The internal audience is Lincoln himself, and as Bryant took the opportunity to thank the great man he assumed the voice of the grateful nation, or at least of the New England elite who had favored most of the president's policies.

Bryant's praise of the president as "slow to smite" (line 1) arose from the fact that Lincoln had been wise enough not to take the first military action of the Civil War by immediately invading those southern states that seceded following his election to the presidency. By waiting for the shelling of Fort Sumter from the South Carolina mainland, he partially forestalled those critics who otherwise could have argued against the conflict as Mr. Lincoln's War. The second half of Bryant's first line was even more topical; upon the cessation of hostilities, Lincoln had been "swift to spare" by advocating that the former states of the Confederacy be readmitted to the Union fairly easily.

Bryant's praise of Lincoln as gentle also may refer to his roles as the indulgent parent and tolerant spouse at the White House. His mercy was evident not only in his relatively benign policies toward the former Confederacy, but also in his willingness to occasionally commute the sentences of his military courts in an environment where falling asleep on guard duty

could be viewed as a dereliction of duty punishable by death. By "just," Bryant may have been referring to Lincoln's career as a practicing attorney; his legal training helped him make a measured response to a crisis instead of overreacting. Bryant was justified in mentioning Lincoln's fear of God because of the president's many invocations of God in his most important public addresses. Lincoln did bear "the sword of power" (line 4), taking an active role in the war by assigning the most competent officers available to lead his various armies, and returned the nation's trust by keeping the United States together under the most trying of circumstances.

The second stanza speaks of the nation's reaction to the shock of the assassination, and the third stanza, the most controversial at the time and place of the poet's public reading, correctly predicted that his freeing of the slaves would serve as Lincoln's "proudest monument." Lincoln's freeing of the slaves of the Confederacy in his Emancipation Proclamation added moral force to the Union cause, but there not only had been a strong southern presence in New York City but also antidraft riots. Many of the city's newest immigrants and other urban poor feared the wage competition from freed black labor, so the crowd on that day would have been far more ambivalent on this issue than the New Englanders or later generations of Americans would be. The reference to the "broken fetters" was more than a metaphor for the destruction of the institution of slavery; most Americans would have at least anecdotal knowledge of the chains in which the slaves were ferried across the Atlantic and sold in the marketplace. The image is as provocative and ultimately as unassailable as the Cross.

The purity of Lincoln's life (line 13) is difficult to fathom by later generations because the blood of his martyred death rinsed away any objections that might have been raised by his contemporaries. Suffice it to say that his reputation for integrity has remained untarnished even when it was fashionable among some later generations to publicize whatever shortcomings they could find in the personal as well as professional lives of the most important public figures in the nation's history. Bryant's contemporaries would have taken his reference to "the sons of light among the noble host of those who perished" (lines 14–15) on a deeply personal level since few of them would not have been touched by the war, and the poet's New England bias is evident in his insistence that Lincoln and the other casualties perished in the cause of Right.

"ACCOUNTABILITY" PAUL LAURENCE DUNBAR (1895)

A heritage of more than two and a half centuries of slavery and then an additional half century of open oppression forced many black Americans of PAUL LAURENCE DUNBAR's day to assume stereotypical roles as a means of survival. On one level, the speaker in this poem has the difficult task of getting his woman to accept stolen goods, but he also means to impress her, as he does the modern reader, with his linguistic virtuosity. While the title of the poem suggests that he may be working out the moral implications of his theft, he is also accountable to his wife for fulfilling the traditional male role of provider. In this connection, note that the flesh of each of the animals whose qualities he contrasts (squirrels, rabbits, and various types of fish) are considered regional delicacies. Part of the fun of the indirectness of his speech is the way that it prolongs the delivery of an answer to the very crucial question of what, if anything, he has brought for dinner. The hungry wife must have savored the names of the animals with the appreciation of a gourmand reading the menu at his favorite restaurant.

Like any good salesman, the speaker begins with a statement with which his auditor can agree: only God has the right to judge people and their habits. God gave squirrels longer tails than rabbits and created valleys as well as mountains. Notice the speaker's humorous shift from the divine and majestic to the artificial and increasingly less grand objects he compares in the fourth line. On some level, the speaker's argument that the divine maker of streets and driveways was not ashamed to make alleys reveals an acute awareness of the inferiority of the alleys. He also may be identifying the route he took to obtain the food and implying that his crime was not against God, who as his Maker was responsible for his habits, but against the power elites of the city or town, who may be even more responsible for them.

In the seventh line, the moral confusion of the poem extends to the point where the speaker seems to be counseling himself against showing off while doing good (that is, pulling off a lucrative crime): He should not take credit for such good results because his behavior was channeled in that direction by outside forces. The ninth line may contain a hint as to how he pulled off the endeavor; he may have fit through places that larger men could not. Mindful that this might paint a picture of the crime too realistically in his wife's mind, he quickly explains that the places he has in mind were like the roles only he could fill since no two people (and no two species of fish) are alike. He may also hope that the comparisons he makes throughout the poem may prompt his wife to compare him to other, less resourceful (and humorous) men.

In the fourth stanza, he admires the way his unconventional belief in predestination (or a behaviorism based entirely on factors outside of his control) frees him from all moral responsibility. Then, almost like a magician, he produces the chicken he stole from the "master." Slavery had been outlawed for 30 years by then, but many former slaves continued working for their prewar masters and retained the traditional form of address. However, the whole tone and temper of this poem suggests that the speaker is using *master* ironically and probably even derisively.

"AN ADDRESS TO MISS PHILLIS WHEATLY, ETHIOPIAN POETESS, IN BOSTON, WHO CAME FROM AFRICA AT EIGHT YEARS OF AGE, AND SOON BECAME ACQUAINTED WITH THE GOSPEL OF JESUS CHRIST" JUPITER HAMMON (1778)

Of all the many profound and enduring ways the Christian religion served American slaves, the two that are most evident in this poem are the fostering of a community identity and, for an extraordinarily fortunate few, an opportunity to obtain basic literacy. JUPITER HAMMON, "a Negro Man belonging to Mr. Joseph Lloyd" as he was identified as the "composer" of this poem, was one of the first black American poets. Upon learning of Wheatley's work, Hammon published this poem as an open letter to convey his regard for PHILLIS WHEATLEY as a black American who shared the transatlantic transportation experience, as a fellow poet, and as a coreligionist.

Calling Miss Wheatley an "Ethiopian" merely identified her as African-American and was not meant to indicate or suggest her precise country of origin. Equally quaint is the term "poetess;" modern writers use the term "poet" for both genders. Referring to her as "Miss" would have been controversial in some parts of the country, and for those slaveholders everywhere who would deny the basic humanity of their "property." His misspelling of her surname in his title resulted from the brevity of his exposure to her work and not from carelessness.

Hammon characteristically expressed himself in devotional poetry, and his use of ballad meter in this poem and the biblical citations he attached to each stanza enshrine Wheatley's experience as she expressed it in such poems as "On Being Brought from Africa to America." By placing certain aspects of the slave experience in a religious context and adapting it to fit the melody of many popular hymns, Hammon may have been suggesting that his were the chosen people. In asserting that Wheatley herself might be "a pattern" (that is, an example) for the youth of Boston (lines 21–22), he places her on a higher plane than the Harvard undergraduates (exclusively privileged white males at the time) whom she admonished in another of her poems, "To the University of Cambridge, in New England." In this regard, the most salient of his biblical citations accompanies stanza 19: Matthew 5:3 blesses the humble and promises them heaven.

The fourth stanza requires the greatest leap of faith in the poem, for it suggests that it was "God's tender mercy" and not slavery at its worst that brought Wheatley and her fellow sufferers "over the raging main." This line suggests that Hammon read Wheatley's "On Being Brought from Africa to America," but Hammon also echoes familiar church doctrine in asserting that the salvation offered by Christ is worth all the gold of Spain (lines 15–16).

The most painful line of the poem for a modern audience congratulates Wheatley on having left "the heathen shore" (line 41). This putdown of her African heritage is ameliorated to an extent by his suggestion that she live no more among the heathen (line 43), a line implying, by its verb tense, that even America has its heathen. Unfortunately, all too often the slave experience in America was marked by hunger, suffering, and thirst (evoked in lines 49, 50, and the biblical reference for stanza 16), during which Hammon reminds her to turn to Jesus for solace. The last four stanzas remind his audience of the Judgment Day, here rendered as a moment of triumph if she follows his earlier advice (line 36) to perfect herself in God's word.

"ADVICE TO A RAVEN IN RUSSIA" JOEL BARLOW (published 1938)

Although sent to France to make history, or at least to represent American interests in the French court, JOEL BARLOW instead found himself a witness to the aftermath of a military debacle. The great emperor Napoleon Bonaparte, having seduced France with his generalship and pushed his power and influence to the Russian border through a series of brilliant military campaigns always culminating in a decisive battle, thought that he could annex Russia in the same way. He found the Russian Czar Alexander I unwilling to negotiate, however, even after the French were able to occupy the Russian capital. When the winter of 1812 arrived early and ferociously, and when his thinly guarded thousand-mile supply line proved inadequate to the task of feeding half a million soldiers, he had no choice but to withdraw. The retreat turned into a rout, and although Napoleon was able to escape, his Grand Army was destroyed.

Much of the world had been enchanted by the 10 years of Napoleon's brilliant successes and largely ignored the butchery by which he achieved his ends until this decisive defeat. Suddenly it became fashionable to question the human cost of his victories, and Barlow was not alone in focusing on the cadaver-strewn battlefields as a way of bringing out the human cost of the Napoleonic wars.

Since the scavenging birds seemed the chief beneficiaries of the carnage, the speaker of the poem addressed himself to one of them. Notice how deftly the poet paints his winter landscape as a place of frozen skies broken only by the black wings of the raven and its cries. He exaggerates in imaging the French army and its allies so far north that the daylight does not interrupt the night in December (lines 3–4), but not in listing the various European nations that, previously having been subjugated by Napoleon, were forced to add their armies to his ill-fated attempt to conquer Russia. Reaching out to his avian internal audience, the speaker informs it that the emperor's presence in the north did not mean the end of war in warmer climes. His reference to Napoleon's "feathered cannibals" (line 16) not only refers to the plumed generals who led hundreds of thousands of men to their deaths in his Russian campaign alone, it foreshadows the grisly details of the raven's scavenging of the corpses of these cannibals (an appellation earned for their participation in the uncivilized practice of war) which is to follow in the poem.

The French excursions into Spain were turning out as badly as Napoleon's Russian campaign, a fact which Barlow acknowledges when he points out that more French blood is being shed than that of Napoleon's enemies (lines 18–24). Napoleon's far-flung adventures had taken him to Egypt, and his minions sought to increase his empire with similar adventures as far away as India and the West Indies. It almost seemed as if a raven might choose a climate and just wait for Napoleon to bring destruction and blood to it (lines 31–32).

As an honorary French citizen before he became the American minister, Barlow knew of the three levels enumerated by French draft laws. He compares the security of their grip on successive crops of French youth with that of Cerberus, the three-headed dog that guarded hell in Greek mythology (line 40). Thus the ravens need not fear a food shortage, for Napoleon will keep them fed in appreciation of their cleaning up the dead. Barlow sees a problem with this arrangement on the battlefields of Russia, however, since the dead are so deeply frozen that the ravens won't even be able to pluck out their open eyes (line 58). Instead of being "marbled" with fat, which greatly improves the flavor of the choicer cuts of meat, the dead soldiers are "marbled through with frost" (line 51). The best hope is to winter in Spain, then wait for Napoleon to raise another army against other Spains. Large districts of Moscow had been burned while under French occupation, a fact to which Barlow alludes in his prediction that "other Moscows (will) suffocate the skies" (line 76).

Barlow predicted that "the monster" would continue campaigning until "men resume their souls" (line 79) and hurl the "king of woes" from his blood-built throne (line 81). Although the poet hoped he would be dashed to dust, Napoleon's mystique helped earn him a kinder fate. He was back in Paris before Christmas and, with yet another army, defeated several allied armies the next year. In 1814 the allies managed to reach Paris, and Napoleon was exiled to Elba near his ancestral home of Corsica in the Mediterranean Sea. He escaped in 1815 and for a hundred days terrified Europe with the specter of his return at the head of a rejuvenated French army. It was this rebuilt army that the British general Wellington and allied armies defeated at Waterloo, and even after that Napoleon was only exiled to the far more distant isle of Saint Helena off the African coast. He died in 1821. Barlow did not live to see any of that, however, for he died of pneumonia even before he could return to Paris.

"THE AEOLIAN HARP" HERMAN MELVILLE (1888)

Although HERMAN MELVILLE found it expedient to quit sailing more than 40 years before he wrote this poem, after his adventures on a South Seas whaling vessel and service on a U.S. Navy ship, the sea remained his muse throughout his life, as this poem indicates. Just listening to the chimes at a seaside inn could bring back vivid memories, and for one whose life and possible death once depended upon the force of the winds, a seaside gale could sound like a shrieking "mad crescendo" (line 3). Even when it died down, its melancholy voice could speak to him in ways only an old sailor could understand.

In the second stanza, the speaker offers to translate the message he just received from the winds, although he promises it will be less fantastic than "Ariel's rendering of the Real" (line 6). In the second scene of the first act of William Shakespeare's *The Tempest*, the spirit Ariel reports to the master magician Prospero that he has frightened everyone off the king's ship then passing except for the real sailors. His chief weapon had been something like Saint Elmo's Fire, a visible discharge of static electricity during an electrical storm, although the spirit enhanced this effect as he did all aspects of the storm until the king's men thought that hell had dumped all its devils on board. In contrast with these fantastic elements, the speaker in this poem promises a picture as real as a coin "stamped in memory's mint" (line 8).

On a yardarm (each side of a spar attached at right angles to the mast of a ship and from which the sails are hung) of the *Phocion,* a vessel bound for Baltimore from Spain, comes the authentic-sounding cry of "Wreck ho, a wreck!" (line 14). All its masts and other structures that once stood above the sea have been swept away until every wave washes over it like a slumbering kraken (line 18), a mythical Norwegian creature now thought to have been inspired by giant squid or a large octopus because it could overwhelm a ship with its arms or use them to pluck off individual sailors from high in the ropes. The hull of the derelict ship is nearly as terrifying as the mythical monster because the midocean currents, winds, and waves can drive it into the shipping lanes. Collision with only an empty hull could be devastating enough to sink a ship, but the wreck in question was once a lumberman. If its hold is filled with wooden timbers, it could have the same effect on any ships striking it as if they had hit a reef.

It has drifted so long that weeds (perhaps long strands of sargasso, a seaweed typically drifting in the tropical Atlantic) trail from it. Each of its formerly solid planks is now as "oozy as the oyster-bank," a simile probably suggested as much by the other animals and plants that thrive in and around their cluttered stacks of shells as by the oysters themselves. In addition to its somewhat unpredictable drifting, the wreck is dangerous because it never has a light or bell to alert other ships of its presence at night or in a fog (lines 33–36).

Every sailor must have, at some level, a fear of drowning at sea, some of the horror of which Melville conveys by using the term "darksome smother" (line 38) to indicate the ocean. Also worthy of note are his unconventional conjugations of "shifteth" and "drifteth" (lines 42 and 44); perhaps the verbs help the reader share the speaker's fear of such a deadly snare "torpid in dumb ambuscade" until "waylayingly it drifteth" (lines 43–44). While the "-eth" endings recall the antiquity of sailing (and perhaps of the derelict vessel) by echoing the grammatical constructions popular

in Chaucer's 14th century, they may also suggest the speaker has such dread that he is having trouble communicating. *Waylayingly,* an adverb one meets here for probably the first and last time, may have been chosen for the same reason. To "waylay" is to lie in seclusion in a remote or deserted location and then to violently rob a surprised passerby.

In his final stanza, the speaker bemoans the lost sailors, ships and crews. Note how by calling the wind chime "the harp of Ariel" Melville artfully returns the reader to the Shakespearean reference of the second stanza. In the same way, the wails of that harp convey "Thoughts that tongue can tell no word of" (line 48) partly because there are no survivors after a truly cataclysmic collision, and partly because, as the previous stanza indicates, those who know of such things find it exceedingly hard to convey them.

AFRICAN-AMERICAN POETRY More than a century passed from the first sale of enslaved Africans in the territory that became the United States before one would be credited with authorship of a poem. In 1746, a slave named LUCY TERRY composed a ballad called "BARS FIGHT" that so well described the aftermath of a Native American ambush of the white settlers in western Massachusetts that it became part of the oral tradition of the region.

JUPITER HAMMON'S "AN EVENING THOUGHT: SALVATION BY CHRIST, WITH PENITENTIAL CRIES" (1760) is believed to have been the first poem by an American slave who was allowed to see his work published. Although its religious thought can seem rather conventional for the 18th century, the poet's passion for and identification with his subject still maintains its force into the 21st century. Another of his few surviving poems, "An ADDRESS TO MISS PHYLLIS WHEATLY" (1778), counsels the younger poet to seek her salvation in Jesus Christ.

To PHILLIS WHEATLEY'S *Poems on Various Subjects, Religious and Moral* (1773) belongs the honor of being the first published book by an African American. Unlike Terry and Hammon, Wheatley enjoyed the privilege of having her prodigious poetic talent nurtured early in her childhood. Her "An HYMN TO THE EVENING," its companion piece ". . . TO THE MORNING," and "ON VIRTUE" reveal not only her religious inclination but also her exposure to the classical literature so esteemed by the educated readership of her day. Of even more interest are her poems with autobiographical content, especially "ON BEING BROUGHT FROM AFRICA TO AMERICA," "TO S. M., A YOUNG AFRICAN PAINTER, ON SEEING HIS WORKS," dedicated to the artist who created the portrait printed in her book, and "TO THE UNIVERSITY OF CAMBRIDGE," which urged the undergraduates to make the most of their privileged status while remaining mindful of their religious responsibilities. All of the above were published in 1773, but three years later another poem, "TO HIS EXCELLENCY, GEORGE WASHINGTON," gained her an audience with that worthy.

By the first half of the 19th century, increasing numbers of former slaves and their descendents were making their voices heard in the northern states. SARAH LOUISA FORTEN might be taken as a representative example of the black children of privilege who created such poems as "The SLAVE" (1831) and "The SLAVE GIRL'S FAREWELL" (1832) to inform white audiences of the plight of their less fortunate brethren. FRANCES ELLEN WATKINS HARPER, a more accomplished poet, served the same ends with some of the same means in poems like "The SLAVE MOTHER" (1854). Shortly before the Civil War, she could also remind northerners of their complicity in slavery if they used the cotton produced by it ("FREE LABOR," 1857) and the unfulfilled promises of the War for Independence in "An APPEAL TO THE AMERICAN PEOPLE" (1858). "BURY ME IN A FREE LAND" (1864) revealed her fear that the war might end in a compromise that left slavery intact. Her postwar jubilation at the extension of voting rights to male former slaves became almost tangible in "FIFTEENTH AMENDMENT" (1871).

It remained for PAUL LAURENCE DUNBAR, one of the most outstanding American poets prior to 1900, to create the strongest poetic voice for the black experience up to that point. Despite dying of tuberculosis at the relatively early age of 33, he produced 11 volumes of poetry and five volumes of fiction. He first gained notoriety with such dialect poems as "ACCOUNTABILITY" (1895), "An ANTE-BELLUM SERMON" (1896), and "The REAL QUESTION" (1896); their common thread is a speaker's struggle to survive against the economic pressures caused by a racial prejudice that presented very

real barriers. In the aggregate, such poems argued for the humanity, practicality, common sense, and essential goodness of an oppressed people. Poems like "WE WEAR THE MASK" (1896) and "SYMPATHY" (1899) harrowingly reveal the incredible pain of the black experience of American history even in what were the best of times for the mainstream community.

However, some of the finest examples of African-American poetry were not published poems by named poets but folk songs. The same duality that becomes evident when Dunbar's dialect poems are juxtaposed with his protest poetry was long a feature in African-American songs. The closest thing to a Rosetta stone that would allow readers from other communities and later centuries to decipher the true despair, defiance, and hope that often lurked beneath even what seemed the most innocuous folk songs is the second chapter of the autobiographical *Narrative of the Life of Frederick Douglass, an American Slave* (1847).

A few of the pre–Civil War African-American folk songs acknowledged the suffering of the people while divorcing them from any religious context. Both "The BLUE-TAIL FLY" and "MASSA'S IN THE COLD, COLD GROUND" refused to mourn the passing of the slaveholders, and the speaker in the first may have been complicit in the master's death. Others, like "DERE'S NO HIDIN' PLACE DOWN DERE," reinforced belief in a biblical literalism in which hell was as real as a rock.

Many of the most popular songs counseled members of oppressed communities to remain patient while they trusted in the Lord ("DIDN'T MY LORD DELIVER DANIEL") and hoped for deliverance by a savior like the biblical patriarch who delivered the Jewish slaves from Egypt ("GO DOWN, MOSES"). Others acknowledged the suffering of the people but encouraged them to identify with Christ's suffering on the cross ("NEVER SAID A MUMBALIN' WORD") and His promise of redemption ("NOBODY KNOWS THE TROUBLE I'VE HAD").

Several of the widely anthologized folk songs discussed in this volume may once have carried hidden messages, including such classics as "SWING LOW, SWEET CHARIOT" that still remain popular with church choirs. The most obvious of these was probably "STEAL AWAY TO JESUS," which appeared to offer community support for an escape attempt. The "angel march" described in

"ROLL, JORDAN, ROLL" might be construed as a flight to the nonslave states or Canada. In this context, its suggestions to fear the Lord, to let your days be long, and to avoid spiteful or false words could be viewed as tactics designed to allay suspicions prior to one's flight. "LAY DIS BODY DOWN," while a seemingly straightforward expression of weariness with this world, could also provide the specific tactics (traveling by night and hiding in graveyards by day) that a slave could use in an escape attempt.

"MANY THOUSAND GO" lists several of the specific grievances that a group of slaves voiced in song as they were being freed en masse by Union soldiers in the Civil War. These included inadequate rations of food, exposure to the driver's lash in the field and the "hundred lash" as a severe form of corporal punishment, and personal attendance at the whim of the mistress.

BIBLIOGRAPHY

Bloom, Harold, ed. *African-American Poets: Phillis Wheatley through Melvin B. Tolson.* Philadelphia: Chelsea House Publishers, 2003.

Gray, Janet. *Race and Time: American Women's Poetics from Antislavery to Racial Modernity.* Iowa City: University of Iowa Press, 2004.

Leonard, Keith D. *Fettered Genius: The African American Bardic Poet from Slavery to Civil Rights.* Charlottesville: University of Virginia Press, 2006.

Sherman, Joan R. *African-American Poetry: An Anthology, 1773–1927.* Mineola, N.Y.: Dover Publications, 1997.

"THE AFRICAN CHIEF" WILLIAM CULLEN BRYANT (1825)

One of the sorrows visited upon victims of the African slave trade was their immediate separation from all the tribal ties that had previously kept them alive. Several poets focused on the separation of babies from their mothers in the American slave auctions, but in this poem WILLIAM CULLEN BRYANT tries to establish the noble humanity of a prince to counteract the assumptions of racial inferiority that grew out of the despicable conditions in which many slaves were held. The poem also brought home the fact that foreign demand for slaves was responsible for the wars fought to obtain them in their native Africa.

The situation of the poem is that the huge man held in chains in the African slave market attracts a crowd because of his reputation. Several battle scars attest to his warrior spirit, and like a chained lion (line 8) he is constitutionally unsuited to be a slave. In the third stanza he informs his captor that his brother the king would ransom him with ivory and gold, but his offer is rebuffed because he is worth more if sold to a foreign Christian as a slave.

As if reasoning that the refusal was based on the inconvenience involved with ransoming, he orders his locks shorn. Within them are wedges of gold with which he tries to purchase his freedom, and he also tries to move the slaver to pity by pointing out that his wife and young children weep and wait for him. Bryant probably erred in placing a cocoa tree, a native of Central and South America, in the scene (line 46).

The slaver picks up the gold but tells the prince that his wife will wait for a long time. The prince's demeanor changes to mortal fear. Heart-broken and brain-crazed, "his eye grew wild" (line 58). He experiences a quick succession of emotions from anger to weeping, but is soon whispering and even smiling. Preferring death to slavery, he evidently gave up the will to live because before they even left Africa they had to drag his body out on the sands for the hyenas to scavenge.

Although the poet meant well, his depiction of the chief's emotional instability probably undercut his attempt to show him in the noblest light.

"AFTER GREAT PAIN, A FORMAL FEELING COMES" EMILY DICKINSON (published 1929)

This poem conveys some of the shocking effects of the profoundest grief and the process by which, very gradually, it can be outlived if not entirely overcome. After EMILY DICKINSON announces the situation in the brilliant opening line, the first stanza deals with the stunning effects of the blow and the way it has drained the life out of the speaker. This victim's former vitality is evident not only in the depth of the feelings she describes here, but also in the freshness of her imagery and in her repeated attempts to use her intellectual and emotional resources to regain her footing. Each stanza begins with an unforgettable opening line that attempts to probe the depths of her misery, as if the wound could somehow be cauterized at its source, and the poem gains additional coherence in its continual but beautifully understated references to the time it really takes to heal. Each stanza also marks the speaker's returning vitality by tracing her gradual return to physical movement.

The most profound change the speaker notes is the closing down of her nerves, described as sitting "ceremonious, like Tombs" (line 2), perhaps the deadest image possible for what are usually the most vital aspects of human physiology as well as the only way we have of receiving information from the outside world, since all the senses depend on nerves (for instance, the optic nerve) to convey information to the brain. Of course the heart is affected; formerly a ceaseless, uncomplaining pump, it seems to have developed an awareness of its own or at least has made the speaker aware of its existence. "Stiffness" (line 3) is the last thing you want in the muscle that keeps you alive, and the strain is evident in its question as to whether it bore the pain of loss yesterday, or countless centuries ago.

The second stanza has the speaker moving around in the world again, albeit in a peculiarly "wooden way" (line 7). As soulless and detached as a mechanical toy, she knows that her feet make their rounds, but the motion seems as meaningless as if they were touching ground, air, or nothing at all (line 6). The mourner appears to have no emotional attachment with or intellectual stimulation from anything, having "grown regardless," but the phrase also introduces the slightest indication of recovery since it also suggests that the speaker has continued living and growing despite the bitter blow so recently received. In an image vaguely reminiscent of the tombs of the first stanza, her false facade registers "Quartz contentment" like a stone (line 9). Unlike ordinary rocks, however, quartz is a crystalline mineral capable of resonating at consistent frequencies given the right impetus, and it tends to be translucent instead of opaque. Although the speaker is still emotionally withdrawn, on a metaphorical level the poet is suggesting that the process of returning to her normal rounds is beginning to involve her in life again.

Referring to the troubled times as the "Hour of Lead" (line 10) conveys not only the weight, density, and immobility of that ponderous element, it also sug-gests that, because like lead the period of bereavement is relatively worthless, it can be left behind. Scientists now know that the sensation of warmth experienced by people as they approach death by freezing is produced by the body's reducing the blood flow to the extremities in order to maintain its core at a temperature from which the vital organs can recover. Such victims lapse into unconsciousness before they die, hence "the letting go" of the last line. That phrase is also idiomatic as a description of the process by which survivors overcome the debilitating aspects of bereavement and return to regular life.

"AFTERMATH" HENRY WADSWORTH LONGFELLOW (1873) At 66 years of age when he wrote this poem, HENRY WADSWORTH LONGFELLOW had seen many summers come and go. Although in its seventh line the poem states that its title refers to the gleanings of a single year's last mowing, the poet also may have been thinking of his life after he reached retirement age, the so-called golden years. The word "aftermath" is most often used in reference to the events following a tragedy, and this poem may be a testament to how, many years later, a few tragic incidents irredeemably darken the speaker's perception of his entire life.

Mowing a summer field in the mid-19th century usually required much physical labor, but it also kept the farmers more closely in touch with nature for a longer period than would be the case with the more efficient, mechanized farming of later centuries. The poet also may have been thinking of his own children when he pointed out that "the birds are fledged [that is, they have grown all their feathers] and flown" (line 2); in later centuries, older married couples sometimes felt lonely after their children left home, a situation so common it is referred to as the empty-nest syndrome. The poet may have been thinking of love letters or even business letters when he wrote of the dry leaves that strew the path in line 3, but the leaves are also as dead as the loved ones who passed before him. The snow may refer to the chronic ill health with which most elderly are eventually afflicted, and the crow, because of its scavenging habits and funerary hue, has long been associated with death. When the fields were mown for the last time each fall, it signaled the end of the immediately productive labor a farmer could put into them, and this harvest was less advantageous than the earlier ones had been for reasons which become apparent as the speaker examines the proceeds of this late harvest in the second stanza.

He begins by focusing on the missing blooms which sweetened the early or mid-season crop, whereas the rowen (a New England term for the year's second, and usually final, mowing) picks up far more weeds than had been apparent earlier in the year. The drier conditions of late fall enable a farmer to mow more marginal land, such as the marsh and less-tended meadows of line 12, so of course the harvest is more mixed. It may include poppy seeds, dropped far earlier in the year "in the silence and the gloom" (line 14). The poppy has long been associated with remembrance and consolation, hence its adoption as the quasi-official flower of Veteran's Day in the United States. By focusing on the poppy in his last two lines, the speaker may be implying that, as he thinks back over his life, several traumatically painful incidents pepper his memories. They brought the painful knowledge that life is not as sweet as it once seemed, and with all his most productive (and reproductive) years behind him, it is beyond his power to remedy them.

"AFTER THE PLEASURE PARTY" HERMAN MELVILLE (1891)

This is HERMAN MELVILLE's study of the complexities of love as it manifests itself in the breast of a woman who seemed to think she was immune. Sophisticated, well-educated and affluent, her chief shields against Cupid's arrows had been the intellectual detachment with which she viewed herself and her indolent satisfaction with her placid and lovely but unchallenging life.

The poem begins with a picture and an epigraph that introduce its theme as well as its central conflict. A succession of subsequent cartoonists have found the image of Cupid so irresistible that he has become universally recognizable as a stock figure of comedy, but in 1891 he would have been taken more seriously. The sentimentality of that late Victorian age might have prompted a society woman such as the central figure of this poem to place such a picture on her wall as a decidedly feminine touch, since Cupid was typically depicted as a cherubic infant despite his wings and bow.

One of the earmarks of Melville's thinking has always been his preoccupation with the multitude of possible meanings one might find in a symbol. The epigraph lends a voice to Cupid, whose pronouncements on love reveal a more confrontational attitude than his angelic face might lead one to expect. The term *amor* suggests an abstract, exotic, and romantic experience, but this Cupid is more threatening than sweet.

A problem of the poem proper is the difference in voice and tone between the second, 14th, 15th, and 17th stanzas (if the epigraph is taken as the first stanza) and the rest of the poem. This voice serves as a frame in which to present the chief character's interior monologue. It provides the reader with an objective view of the white marbles and green halls, the terraces and the sea which the speaker is less likely to convey because of her greater familiarity with the scene.

In the third stanza the speaker begins reflecting on the discrepancy between the enshrined beauty with which she has surrounded herself and her inner turmoil. She is so disturbed that her accustomed bower cannot provide the balm she desires, and her pent-up emotion leads her into mangled, almost incoherent, syntax.

Although she lives along the Mediterranean, she seems to identify more with the shore (the "iron-bound verge" of line 21) that resists the ocean's billows rather than the sea that so impulsively sends them in its direction. In the fifth stanza, she counsels herself to forget the glade in which "Fate sprung Love's ambuscade" (line 26). Likening herself to a nun, she dislikes the sensuous strife that can cause a virgin to behave like the love-mad Sappho who passionately killed herself. She thinks she would do the same if she had more cause. In the meantime, she will try to sleep it off.

For the first time in her life, she feels her sexual nature asserting itself. Because she has ignored the impulses before, they will finally escape with geyser force, a sexually suggestive, even ejaculatory image. The "winged blaze that sweeps [her] soul" (line 42) seems to burn like an uncontrollable prairie fire.

The seventh stanza reveals the pride she formerly took in comparing herself with the distant stars (especially those of the constellation Cassiopeia). In reality she was only fooling herself like "an idiot crowned with straw" (line 52), a reference to the way the insane were inhumanely imprisoned at the time. The next stanza reveals her confusion at the dubious nature of her new discovery, which has led her to the envy and ill temper (the "spleen" of line 59) she did not know she possessed.

She finally reveals the cause of her discontent in the ninth stanza. An unexpected rival for an admirer she had not realized that she fancied sparked her jealousy. The challenger is a maid, fresh and young as May, such as makes strong men weak (line 69). She possessed innocent bare feet, a meek demeanor, and a "blossoming rod" (line 62), a stick with its leaves and flowers still attached to it that suggests that its bearer may be similarly fertile. Notwithstanding the pain, she feels compelled to continue as if each element of the tale were a painful bead on a rosary.

After lunch the group had gone outside, but the gentleman in question apparently did not realize that the speaker, although her cheeks no longer bore the roseate blush of youth, had been touched by the sun and other delights of spring. She feels frustrated because all her intellectual accomplishments and refined sensitivity have little chance of removing his arm from the "radiant ninny" (line 82). She would trade all her "starry lore" (line 83; notice how deftly the phrase conflates her advanced learning and her private mythology in which she identified with the distant stars) for the truest wanton's rose if her bee could repose in it. Such imagery probably does not require Freudian analysis for most readers.

Feeling somewhat enslaved by her sexual urges, she ponders whether indulgence would free her from its spell. The problem lies in the way we are made; as a consequence of a cosmic jest or an anarchist's blunder, humans seem incomplete (in her opinion!) until they chance upon the matching half whom they can meet and mate (line 97). Even the stars fail her now; she has stayed up so late in her misery that dawn begins to weaken their light.

The narrator resumes speaking in the 14th stanza. No one knows if the former speaker settled her turbulent heart and rebellious brain and survived (line

114). Love (or Amor, the Latin version of Cupid) may have tormented her beyond endurance in retribution for her former disdain. No one knows, that is, except for the narrator; in the next stanza he reveals he saw her in Rome. Like a Christian pilgrim or monk before a venerated object, she had stood in awe before a huge pagan carving in a private villa.

Eventually she began to rally under the influence of her Christian principles. In the 16th stanza, she reveals that she almost took the veil. Instead, she asked the pagan goddess of wisdom, Athena, to raise her and arm her.

This, the narrator reveals in the penultimate stanza, was foolish. Passion will never bring peace, nor will inanimate art long inspire (lines 147–150). Amor, incensed, will be even more vindictive, even to the point of blaspheming and betraying himself.

The final stanza consists of a single couplet containing a warning for virgins everywhere. They are to pray for the speaker, learn from her example, and take care.

This was a strange note for the poem to end on; it seems to imply that passion will eventually overcome even the most chaste woman. While this may or may not be true (21st-century readers have been schooled against believing that biology equals destiny), one might be able to extrapolate a sound bit of advice from it. The speaker's mistake was to deny her passion until, sparked by pangs of jealousy, it overwhelms her. Perhaps a wiser policy would be to acknowledge and understand one's feelings and to cope with them from within a matrix of intelligence, experience, and one's personal belief system or formal religion. Everyone may have primal urges, but not everyone has to act on them.

"AFTER THE SUPPER AND TALK" WALT WHITMAN (1887) One of the things that seem to separate our species from others is our consciousness of our own looming deaths. Even if we are blessed with the retention of our mental facilities and enough good health to get out and visit friends right up to the end, there must unfailingly come a day when we have to recognize that we are enjoying each of our pleasures for the last time. WALT WHITMAN's poem captures the poignancy as well as the awkwardness of the final meeting between a dying man and his close friends, and the speaker is one of those people from whom the old man is reluctant to leave.

The images of the poem are organized logically as well as chronologically if one thinks of the supper as representing not just all the good meals enjoyed in the evening of the speaker's life, but also all the things he once enjoyed to the fullest. In his declining years with his workday done, there came a period of reflection and conversation, with talk increasingly assuming the role once filled by action. Both the supper and the talk passed through his lips, now rendered so ineffectual by the inroads of time that, although he is intensely emotional, they can only repeat his good-byes.

If his words fail him, the burden of communication falls to his hands, formerly so efficient in fulfilling his desires, but now all they seem capable of is holding onto the hands of his hosts as if he could somehow hold onto life. Evidently he has arrived at that stage of coming to terms with his death in which he hopes to bargain for more time, for he seeks any slight pretense to delay his departure, thus gaining "something to eke out a minute additional" (line 9). Note how the poem had earlier shifted from emphasizing his lips to focus on his hands, and now just his intellect might keep him in this life. In line 6 he had tried to avoid "the last word ever so little," with the phrase conveying the double meaning of his gaining a minor delay in time at the same time that it suggests that even his words were losing their force until the very last one seems minuscule. Similarly, in the 10th line the messages (both those he is sending and receiving) are "lessening" in number as well as purport, and both his visage and form also seem to be becoming inconsequential. They will soon be lost forever in the darkness of the grave as well as in the fading memories of those who survive him. He is reluctant to leave this world and his hosts, but notice how, with a single word in the last line, the poet drains all the sentimentality from the poem. To be "garrulous" is to be excessively rambling and loquacious; the old man has grown burdensome to the speaker. He remains immersed in his own joy and youth, which he had earlier contrasted with the old man's sorrow and age (line 5).

Because the poem deals with what is essentially a last supper, the old man's worth is enhanced by the inevitable comparison with the Last Supper of Jesus Christ and his disciples. This makes the speaker, so begrudging of a few extra minutes of his company despite its being the last time he will see the old man, seem self-absorbed and selfish. However, the point may be that a true "communion" (the word is used in line 5 as well as in Christian rituals) of souls is impossible, and that an individual must remain isolated as he faces the largest mysteries and challenges of life.

"ALONE" EDGAR ALLAN POE (1875)   This fragment is another of EDGAR ALLAN POE's first-person investigations of aberrant psychology, and the most interesting thing about it is the way Poe tweaked poetic conventions to reinforce the sense of alienation in the speaker's voice. For example, a poet might use a single day to represent an entire life, but even for a condensation that dramatic, reducing one's childhood to a single hour, as the speaker does in the first line, suggests that he was almost entirely cheated out of the full benefits of this important developmental stage.

Most poets agree that iambic pentameter is the traditional rhythmic pattern that most closely replicates English speech, but this speaker opens with, and generally prefers, an eight-syllable, iambic octameter line. This could make him seem rather short of breath, although he jumps to nine syllables when the thought expressed in a particular line seems especially troubling or seven syllables when the beauty of a natural phenomenon takes his breath away. However, his lines are enjambed and not end-stopped as they are in most poems. All this means is that he does not use punctuation at the end of each line, a convention that poets sometimes use to indicate the speaker's breathing pattern and perhaps even the pace that should be used when a poem is to be read aloud. As if to reinforce his assertion that he is not like other people, his lines are a foot shorter but his breathing is a foot longer than the norm. Even the punctuation of this misfit is irregular; he uses dashes in place of more conventional symbols and sometimes in place of conjunctions as if he were unable to put his thoughts together like other people.

As if to back up his assertions that he is not like other people and does not even see things as they do (lines 2–3), he at once begins talking about his passions and his sorrows. Although he evidently tried to fit in (his assertion in lines 3 and 4 that "I could not bring my passions from a common spring" suggests that he at least made an attempt to do so), notice how his metaphorical language illustrates the impossibility of his task. He seems too forceful, too literal in attempting to wring passion from the common spring of human experience and, even more telling, he tries to awaken joy (lines 6–7), whereas at its best that emotion is more spontaneous for most people. Another sign of his befuddlement is that to awaken joy he evidently listened for a "tone" that evoked the emotion in other people instead of more closely searching for its causes (although the same word also implies that his reactions were pitched at a noticeably higher or lower level than theirs). His complete isolation is indicated in the eighth line, for he could not share a single thing out of all the things he loved.

These ruminations bring him to the point in his childhood (at the dawn of what would prove "a most stormy life," line 10) when everything changed. The nature of this momentous event is not revealed, but the speaker remains perplexed as to whether it was a blessing or a curse. He uses the same water-drawing metaphor to describe the origin of this feeling as he had earlier, but in place of his earlier impotence at the benevolent and tranquil spring, he now draws "from every depth of good and ill" (line 11). The force by which he is still bound is so mysterious and powerful that he does not even know if it is destructive and potentially deadly (like the torrent mentioned in line 13) or constructive and sustaining (like a fountain). It also brings to mind a contrast between the solidity of a red cliff (an image that also hints at suicide) and the equally enduring but enriching gold sun. Perhaps driven to distraction by the inherent duality of his gift, he evidently (or at least metaphorically) ascended a cliff, for he next describes the lightning that flies by him in a thunderstorm (lines 17–19). There is a final, sinister note to the fragment before it trails off into silence. With the exception of the thundercloud that the speaker views as a demon (lines 20–22), the rest

of the sky appears blue. This is the final bit of ambiguity and perhaps irony in the poem as it comes to us, for the traditional meanings associated with that color range from piety (because it was used so extensively in religious paintings for the gown of the Virgin Mary) to the oppressive emotional state of dreary depression. The statement "Heaven was blue" (line 21) may either be an objective indication of the sky's appearance or a suggestion of divine displeasure that the speaker is paying such close attention to his personal demon. Although he remains ambivalent about its source and true nature, the speaker seems poised to act in accordance with the whims of this mysterious force because nothing else seems to reach him.

"AMPLE MAKE THIS BED" Emily Dickinson (1864) This odd poem belongs in Emily Dickinson's canon because it combines her domesticity and her spirituality. Thinking of the poem as an interior monologue—perhaps as a revelation of the speaker's thoughts as she performs a routine chore—reveals a sense of the divine in everyday life. Like a cloistered nun in an order emphasizing humble physical service and toil, the speaker performs her allotted task with transcendent devotion. Making the bed and performing other chores might be part and parcel of the whole outward fabric of her life, and she exhorts herself to live in such a way as to merit salvation on Judgment Day. Thus, the bed represents more than the grave, although that is the surprise and central image of the poem. Making the bed is a metaphor for how she should conduct her life in accordance with God's will. Her strategy also seems to involve living fully while storing up good works, thus amply making her bed will insure her soul's lasting ease.

Proper care in the conduct of one's life will leave no fear of Judgment Day, described in line 4 as though it were a fine day for a picnic. A modicum of doubt seeps into the second stanza, however, for if the bed is not properly (perhaps perfectly) made, "yellow noise" (the howls of the damned? an indictment of her inadequate life? sin in one form or another?) predicts a far different experience on Judgment Day. Emily Dickinson was too intelligent not to have realized the fun lesser minds could have with her choice of color in connection with the sheets that have to be changed, but the reader is cautioned against taking the image too literally.

The poet's unconventional use of an apostrophe but no terminal s to indicate the possessive nature of "sunrise' yellow noise" helped her keep up the syllabic pattern she established in the first stanza (two lines of five syllables are followed by one of seven and then one of five). It may also suggest the miracle of divinity; her distorted punctuation may represent a disjuncture between our rational world and the suspension of all the physical laws based on our scientific knowledge.

Ground was a fine word for her to end with as it not only refers to her good works but may also touch upon the philosophical or religious grounds on which the speaker has built her belief system. We know from other of her poems that Dickinson usually was not so adamant in asserting the infallibility of her beliefs as the speaker of this poem appears to be. Since we would not usually expect blatantly ribald humor from such a reticent author, advocates for this interpretation of the poem might praise the author for simply being true to the more earthy nature of a less refined but no less devout chambermaid. Viewed in this light, the poem may represent the speaker's prayer that her physicality will not undermine her spirituality. Desperately troubled, the speaker might be trying to focus on the domestic task before her before bringing religious doctrine to bear on her concerns. As a last resort, she may be focusing on the repulsiveness and banality of sin in hopes of coming to terms with, and in some way controlling, her sensuality.

"AND CHANGE WITH HURRIED HAND HAS SWEPT THESE SCENES" FREDERICK GODDARD TUCKERMAN (1860)

The vitality of this poem stems from the contrast between the passive verbs used to describe the present stasis of the land and the active verbs that suggest the continual flux when untamed nature held sway over the same area. One must also admire FREDERICK GODDARD TUCKERMAN's objectivity; in lesser hands, nostalgia tends to lead a poem into the puerile sentimentality that is one of the hallmarks of the minor artist.

Note that change and not nature or man's influence on nature is the speaker's chief concern, although at first he seems to favor the virility of the bygone age over the domesticity of the present. The "hurried hand" which "swept" the land (line 1) seemed intent on taming or even eradicating nature rather than harnessing or harvesting it, and human nature did not escape the same treatment. In place of the hunting and trapping trails (line 3), once the means as well as the scene of free movement within the woods, he now finds the sterility of a marble mantel with its cultivated rosebuds (and not blooms, for the inhabitants of the well-appointed cottage do not care for nature at its fullest). Even this remembrance of nature is temporary; eventually only the cold, beautifully artificial violet vase will remain (lines 11–12).

Some of the changes and loss the speaker observes in nature hold implications for his own experience. He can still remember the wildness that passed from the area within his lifetime. In sharp contrast to golden natural light that once illuminated the abundant game found amid autumnal leaves, the only light admitted to the cottage is filtered at least twice, by the window pane and the curtains. Human life was once more closely linked with nature and in many ways it was more interesting in those days.

The speaker seems somewhat ambivalent as to whether these changes are entirely bad, however. Few modern readers can share the equanimity with which he treats the final image of the poem, the nonspecific "wolfbait" which "hung blackening" (line 13) beside the stream. Unlike the denizens of the sheltered cottage, the speaker was once in close enough contact with nature that he has a clear vision of the color changes meat undergoes as its bloody freshness dries.

"ANNABEL LEE" EDGAR ALLAN POE (1849)

EDGAR ALLAN POE's poem begins innocently enough. The speaker is an elderly man who asks his internal audience, evidently a man of about the same age, to recall Annabel Lee. He does not provide many aids to jog the memory; the eponymous character was a beautiful maiden who devoted her life to the love she shared with the speaker. The events he is about to relate are not only remote in time but perhaps also in space, for he keeps insisting that they happened in a kingdom by the sea.

They were both very young, but the magnitude of their feelings is suggested by his assertion that they "loved with a love that was more than love" (line 9); even the angels envied them. Everything seemed to be going well, but their love could not last.

Exactly what happened is hidden by the diction of the third stanza. She may have become ill, which led her relatives to take her away as a health measure. The speaker's language is so convoluted, however, that it begs other interpretations. His obfuscation suggests that her ardor may have cooled; this might have been so baffling to the young lover that he can only blame her sudden chilliness on a wind from a cloud (line 15). He provides sufficient evidence to suggest more pragmatic reasons for this change in addition to the lovers' youth and inexperience. His notice of her highborn kinsmen (line 17) suggests that he was not a member of the nobility; perhaps the gulf between their social backgrounds influenced her decision. However that may be, she was so effectively isolated from him that she might as well have been dead; he refers to the buildings where they "shut her up" as a sepulchre (line 19).

He could not admit the death of their love, however, and when she died he could only attribute her final illness to the jealousy of angels. Theirs was a love that transcended death to the extent that their souls remained linked, or at least it seems that way to him. He was so committed to their relationship that he is constantly reminded of her, and the elegance of his praise in lines 34 to 37 attests to the depth of his feelings, especially: "And the stars never rise, but I feel the bright eyes of the beautiful Annabel Lee" (lines 36–37).

If he could not have her in life, at least they are wedded in his dreams, where he sleeps by her side. This is hopefully not literally in her tomb, but in the rich establishment of her relative for which he had earlier used the term "sepulcher." Either way, he still has the sea that served as the backdrop for their young love.

"ANOTHER (LETTER TO HER HUSBAND, ABSENT UPON PUBLIC EMPLOYMENT)"

ANNE BRADSTREET (1678)   Although not until the early 20th century would the popular and public conception of femininity include frank discussions of sensuality, in identifying with a succession of increasingly lower animals the speaker in this poem comes close to admitting the animal aspects of her nature. At the same time, however, the animals are advanced as symbols of fidelity, and the speaker repeatedly affirms that such delights of intimacy are meant only for her husband. The poem was probably intended only for her spouse's eyes, for it begins with enough puns to suggest that she may have been playfully aiming at filling her absent husband with ribald laughter in addition to longing.

ANNE BRADSTREET's British birth is immediately evident in her diction; an American of a later generation would more likely call the "hind and hart" a "doe and buck." But *hind* also refers to the posterior or behind, an image as provocative as the implied comparison of her husband with that emblem of virility, a fully antlered deer. The image of the "hartless" hind wanting her deer is suggestive enough, but if the word is accepted as an obvious pun on "heartless," the implication is that no sentiment will keep her from her desired goal. "Scuds" (line 2) sounds rather risqué in this connection although it only means to quickly scamper, but reference to her "harkening ear" definitely underscores her eagerness to be reunited. When prying around "in every bush or nook" (line 3) proves unsatisfactory, she again misses her "dearest dear" who might answer ear or eye, and "eye" probably puns on "aye," a verbal assent. In contrast with the bodily desires of the woodland mammal, it is the speaker's soul that misses her "dearer dear" and his far dearer heart (line 6). She also tones down the sexuality expressed in the poem by removing some of the ambiguity inherent in her prior language; now she only wants to hear his voice and see him (line 8).

Greater familiarity with American birds might have encouraged her to substitute the native mourning dove for the turtle dove (line 9); like the European species, they suggest fidelity because they supposedly mate for life. To identify with the bird's "uncouthly" bemoaning her absent mate (line 10) may suggest that she was well aware of possible censure for revealing her unrefined longing in the poem, although for such relatively highborn leaders of the colony, deep sad groans, "doleful sighs and mournful coos" (line 16) could seem equally ungraceful.

Since she was not a marine biologist, it was OK for her to interpret a mullet's apparent willingness to swim ashore when its mate is caught as devotion to the pair bond, although a naturalist professionally trained to avoid anthropomorphizing his subjects might attribute it to the animal's schooling instinct. Turning again to her own circumstances, she seems to lead a joyless life despite her social advantages; a tinge of class consciousness is revealed in her assertion that she has "a loving peer" (line 22). Although the term suggests their equality with each other, it also recognizes that the high governmental post held by her husband qualifies them as nobility. They are kept apart by the "force" (line 24) of circumstances; he must stay away until his official responsibilities have been met, she must maintain her household and attend her domestic duties, and both suffer from the tyranny of distance imposed by the colony's underdeveloped roads and reliance on primitive transportation alternatives.

Lines 24 through 27 contain the most charming statement in the poem; to reveal how worthless her life seems without him, Bradstreet juxtaposes conventional terms of endearment for him ("my joy, my only love") with her fresh but relatively disparaging terms for herself ("thy hind, thy mullet, and thy dove"). In summing up the meaning of the poem, she finds herself unable to enjoy pasture, house or streams without him. The rhyme scheme seems to have dictated the order of the animals and their environments; the lists could have been more pleasing if the elements in each series had been parallel, that is, pasture, streams, and house, so that each species is aligned with its habitat.

Like these animals, she would like to browse, roost, and glide with her husband. It would take a Freudian critic to decipher the sexual implications of her desire to "browse together at one tree," but her final wish "to remain one, till death divide" (line 32) echoes key phrases of the traditional wedding vow.

In keeping with her title, Bradstreet ends the poem with the formal closing one would expect in a letter. The pairing of "dear" and "everywhere" strikes the modern ear as unmusical, but they were a perfect rhyme when the poem was written.

"AN ANTE-BELLUM SERMON" Paul Laurence Dunbar (1896) The title promises a sermon from the pre–Civil War days, and Paul Laurence Dunbar's phonetic rendering of a thick southern dialect suggests the presentation of a voice from within the shackles of slavery. The speaker had to be aware of two different audiences, the slaves who made up his congregation, and their masters. To be effective, he had to deliver a message that was relevant to the suffering of the people, but to be allowed to speak at all, he had to deliver it in a way that would not threaten the power of the slaveholders. His choice of text, the story of Moses and his leading of the chosen people from their Egyptian bondage, could not have been more incendiary, from the standpoint of the oppressors.

They may have been forced to meet outside, for the preacher refers to "this howling wilderness" in the second line, but the phrase may also contain an indictment of an ungodly land that permits slavery. Theirs is a very personal God, as evidenced by the direct dialogue between Moses and the Lord, which is delivered in the slave's own patois. To support his claim that the pharaoh is the worst man ever born (line 8), the speaker mentions that he had his Hebrew children working in his corn, an agricultural pursuit to which most of his audience could easily relate. Against the Lord's power, however, the pharaoh's army "wasn't worth a half a dime" (line 22), and you can trust the Lord to help his children every time (line 24). The Lord will bear the battle's brunt (line 28), and even if you are chained and shackled, He will send some Moses to set his children free, and back it up with His thunder.

Thus far the preacher has been exceedingly courageous, but he begins to back off by speaking of his fear (an emotion to which his entire congregation could relate) that someone would mistakenly think he was not "a-preachin' ancient" (line 39). He hastens to reassure them that "I ain't talkin' 'bout to-day." Fear for his personal safety was probably not the only motivation for his backtracking on this important point, however, or he probably would not have chosen such a provocative subject. He also had to be careful not to incite his followers into foolish acts of open resistance that might lead to their being subjected to corporal punishments sometimes as severe as torture. He counsels them to wait for the Lord to free them, for all the love He showed Israel was not spent on Israel, and not to tell their masters that he was preaching discontent (lines 45–48).

He claims only to be judging Bible people by their acts, and the Lord let the pharaoh see that of the people he put breath in, every mother's son was free (lines 49–56). Other people may believe in slavery, which he criticizes as unbiblical since the Bible states that "a servant is worthy of his hire" (line 60). The Lord's intention was that His almighty freedom should belong to every man, but the speaker reminds them that he is only talking about their freedom "in a Bibleistic way" (lines 71–72).

A Moses is coming to free them, a belief so fervidly expressed that its exuberance fairly jumps off the page even a century and a half later:

> ". . . he's comin', suah and fas' (he's coming,
>   sure and fast)
> We kin hyeah his feet a-trompin,' (We can hear
>   his feet a-tromping)
> We kin hyeah his trumpit blas.'" (We can hear
>   his trumpet blast; lines 74–76).

Immediately, however, he must again caution them against becoming "too brigity" (line 78). Instead of bragging (or becoming brigands), they should wait to see this change come about. When Moses comes to set them free, they will praise "the gracious Master, who has given them liberty" (lines 83–84). They will sing hallelujahs on that Day of Reckoning, let us pray!

ANTISLAVERY POETRY
Well-documented slavery arrived in the New World with the Spanish conquistadores, who forced many native people to labor in agriculture and their dangerous gold and silver mines. In 1619, a year before the first pilgrim's foot touched the rocky shore of Massachusetts, the first Africans sold in British North America were purchased from a Dutch ship in Jamestown, Virginia. Native Americans captured in their wars with the New Englanders also were sometimes forced into slavery, and later British colonists became increasingly acquainted with slavery since the international trade in misery proved a profitable source of wealth for the home country. Soon the important, labor-intensive cash crops, first of sugar and tobacco and eventually of cotton, created an insatiable demand for all the Africans who could be kidnapped from their home shores and forced to labor in regions where the climate supported those crops.

Poetry, especially that of William Cowper (1731–1800), played an important role in mobilizing British popular sentiment against slavery. As early as 1782, sections of his poem "Charity" protested his country's loathsome trafficking in cargoes of despair. In "The Task" (1784), his most famous antislavery poem, Cowper argued that he would rather be himself a slave than to place others in shackles in the West Indies and other British colonies. In such poems as "Sweat Meat has Sour Sauce or, the Slave Trader in the Dumps" (1788), he focused on the cruel punishments, including the use of thumbscrews and other torture devices, that could be used to end hunger strikes and other protests. Other British poets also voiced their objections to slavery on moral grounds, including Ann Cromartie Yearsley (1752–1806, author of "A Poem on the Inhumanity of the Slave-Trade" in 1788) and Hannah More (1745–1833, author of "Slavery, a Poem" in 1788). The American poet PHILIP FRENEAU personally observed the excesses of British slavery in Jamaica and created "TO SIR TOBY" in protest. By the start of the 19th century, public opinion had so swung in the right direction that the British were able to ban the African slave trade in 1807, although slavery was not officially stopped throughout the British Empire until 1838.

In the American colonies, slavery quickly became a racial issue because new laws mandated perpetual slave status for the African prisoners and their descendents. Then the perfection of the cotton gin by Eli Whitney in 1793 removed the processing bottleneck that had earlier limited the production of that valuable cash crop, greatly increasing the demand for slave labor in the South. The British-enforced ban on the international slave trade (the Royal Navy classified the slavers as pirates and actively intercepted their vessels) had the unfortunate consequence of driving up the price of those slaves already on American soil. These developments drove a wedge between North and South that defied an easy economic solution: any large-scale measure freeing some of the slaves would have dramatically increased the market price of those still held in bondage. Thus the slaves continued to represent such a store of wealth that the southern economy (and sometimes the entire national economy) depended upon their labor in the plantation system, and the entire culture of the South was soon unthinkable without them. Only a Civil War could root out the evil on every level.

Inspired by the British example, American poets strongly voiced their moral objections to slavery. One of their more important strategies was to engage the reader's empathy for the slaves by dramatically portraying the latter's suffering. These poems sometimes featured either a mother's agony when separated from her child on the auction block (as in FRANCES ELLEN WATKINS HARPER's "The SLAVE MOTHER" [1854] and "The Slave Auction" [1854]) or the physical suffering resulting from the lash and other tortures. Other poets dramatized the innate nobility of the African prince reduced to slavery by the fortunes of war who would not permit himself to live under such oppressive circumstances, a motif central to WILLIAM CULLEN BRYANT's "The AFRICAN CHIEF" (1825) and HENRY WADSWORTH LONGFELLOW's "The SLAVE's DREAM" (1842). Both of these poems also hint at the destruction of African culture caused by the slave trade. SARAH LOUISA FORTEN tried to reduce the distance between her external audience and the slaves by focusing on the latter's human attachments in "The SLAVE GIRL's FAREWELL" (1832). Both Forten's "The SLAVE" (1831) and Harper's "An APPEAL TO THE AMERICAN PEOPLE" (1858) argued that many African Americans fought for the freedom of the country during the American Revolution but were still denied the promised liberty.

In "FREE LABOR" (1857), Harper pointed out the connection between fine clothing and the slavery that produced some of it. Many of the arguments advanced throughout the long course of antislavery literature can be found in the same author's "BURY ME IN A FREE LAND" (1864); its very title questions whether America was living up to its promise, and its imagery extends to the bloody gashes inflicted on a mother as her babies were torn from her breast. The same poem also attacks the licentious nature of those slaveholders who bought slaves for their youthful charms, a charge that did much to inflame even reticent New Englanders with

indignant passion, although the vast majority of southerners rejected it as unwarranted calumny.

Other writers were also willing to lend their fame to the antislavery movement; such major poets as JOHN GREENLEAF WHITTIER (Voices of Freedom, 1846) and Longfellow (Poems on Slavery, 1842) produced volumes (of 192 and 31 pages, respectively) of poetry on the subject. Many poets conveyed their elation at such important milestones on the road to racial equality as the Thirteenth Amendment (Whittier's "LAUS DEO," 1865) and Fifteenth Amendment (Harper's "FIFTEENTH AMENDMENT," 1871) to the United States Constitution. These laws banned slavery and extended voting rights to male former slaves (like their white counterparts, black women had to wait for the 19th Amendment in 1920 for the right to vote).

BIBLIOGRAPHY

Basker, James G. Amazing Grace: An Anthology of Poems about Slavery, 1660–1810. New Haven, Conn.: Yale University Press, 2002.

Leonard, Keith D. Fettered Genius: The African American Bardic Poet from Slavery to Civil Rights. Charlottesville: University of Virginia Press, 2006.

Morgan, Kenneth. Slavery, Atlantic Trade, and the British Economy, 1660–1800. New York: Cambridge University Press, 2000.

Wood, Marcus, ed. The Poetry of Slavery: An Anglo-American Anthology, 1764–1865. New York: Oxford University Press, 2003.

"THE APOLOGY" RALPH WALDO EMERSON (1847) Although the sentiments found here would find their fullest expression in HENRY DAVID THOREAU's Walden, this poem illustrates the creative cross-fertilization that frequently enriched the work of both writers. Both men valued their isolation and were fond of long walks on which they would commune with nature. The more civil RALPH WALDO EMERSON, shaped by his divinity school experience and status as a wealthy landowner and public figure in Concord, issued this apology for occasionally turning his back on his neighbors' fellowship in order to fetch the word of "the god of the wood" (lines 3–4). An even greater sin than this apparent misanthropy, however, was the evident idleness necessary for this pursuit.

The necessity of work in the Protestant ethic was closely tied to a belief in striving for self-perfection, but the relative harshness of their climate meant that the earliest New Englanders also needed to work for self-preservation. Sloth was considered not just one of the seven deadly sins, but the open door that led directly to other sins. Thus the images of the poet's leisure in the poem could seem incendiary to "the laborious band" (line 9) who were forced to harvest their crops by hand before their strong oxen could bring them home (line 18). The spectacle of the speaker's folded arms and the flowers he gathered (lines 6 and 9) must have been especially exasperating during harvest time, when every extra hand could be a blessing.

To avoid being taxed by public opprobrium, the speaker comes up with three roles that are dependent upon quiet contemplation: the philosopher (who tries to fetch the word of God, lines 3–4), the writer (for whom each passing cloud writes a letter, line 8) and the naturalist (note not just his interest in flowers and birds in the third and fourth stanza, but in the mystery of their secret history, line 15). He also hopes to diminish the distance between his pursuits and theirs by appropriating their language; he refers to the products of his work as the "second crop" from their acres (line 20).

Although Emerson's wealth shielded him from the necessity of manual labor, it is worth noting that he worked hard at all three of the intellectual roles he mentions in this poem for as long as he possessed the capacity to do so.

"APPARENTLY WITH NO SURPRISE" EMILY DICKINSON (1890)

Through its use of personification (the attribution of human characteristics to inanimate processes or things), EMILY DICKINSON's poem implicitly contrasts the speaker's sentimentality with the detachment of the sun and (more chillingly) the God who approves assassination.

Like every poet, every gardener has probably thought of flowers as having faces at one time or another. The speaker of this poem not only thought of some flowers as playful and happy, she cared enough to examine them after a killing frost had done its damage. To her evident wonder, the flowers registered no surprise at their sudden beheadings (line 3) and no protest (since their deaths occurred as a result of the frost's accidental power, line 4). The speaker's conception of the frost as "the blonde Assassin" suggests that she is aware of even its beauty. Like the flowers, the frost "passes on," a common euphemism for death, and the sun is as unmoved by the frost's demise as it was by that of the flowers. Perhaps it is this sense of fitting retribution that meets God's approval, for everything has seemingly gone down in accordance with His design. Note how the poem began with nearly incendiary language as the speaker indicts the frost as a beheading assassin, but how its tone changes as the "unmoved" (that is, emotionally detached) sun mechanically fulfills its function. This change in diction suggests that the speaker has come to an acceptance of the naturalness of death and no longer takes it so personally. Although she is still a long way away from approving of the death of her happiest flowers as God evidently does, at least she has come to a clearer understanding of the workings of natural processes.

"AN APPEAL TO THE AMERICAN PEOPLE" FRANCES ELLEN WATKINS HARPER (1858)

A propaganda piece, FRANCES ELLEN WATKINS HARPER's poem effectively combines lurid imagery with half-truths and distorted history to push abolitionists toward taking up arms against slavery. Its appeal is entirely emotional; it begins by suggesting that the nation owes it to the black soldiers who fought in the Revolutionary War to help free their descendants, reminds them of the hated practice of hunting runaways in free states, and portrays the enemy as a brigand with a knife aimed at the nation's life. Finally, it appeals to their manhood and patriotism, asking if they will let a traitor grind up the nation's freedom. The poem appeared three years before the start of the Civil War, in the year when John Brown tried to incite a violent slave rebellion.

The two opening stanzas vaguely recall the very real contributions black Americans made as Revolutionary War soldiers. While no specific battles or accomplishments are listed, it does present the image of the black community's faithful friendship even as a traitor "plunged his steel" into the "quivering hearts" of the nation (lines 3–4). The second stanza is more abstract;

the black soldiers faced "fiery storms of death" (line 8), never losing their courage. Lost in this bombast is the fact that the plantation slaves hastened to join whichever army offered them freedom in exchange for their service. Since the British army was the first to seize upon this expedient, more former slaves fought for the Crown than on the other side. Historians might also quibble with calling the enemy in that war "traitors" since the patriots were the ones rebelling. Similarly, the only rebel flags (line 22) in that conflict belonged to the units fighting against British domination, and the "rebel flag" that would fly over the Confederate States of America was still three years away.

The third stanza is more topical and in many ways more inflammatory. Many northerners resented the fact that the Fugitive Slave Act of 1850 authorized pursuit of escaping slaves into the states that had already banned slavery. Under federal law, northern officials were required to assist slaveholders or their representatives in the return of their "property." The image of a human being hard-pressed by bloodhounds while seeking only to fill the most basic needs (crust, trust, and liberty) had been brought to the forefront of the nation's consciousness by a widely popular novel, *Uncle Tom's Cabin,* completed by Harriet Beecher Stowe in 1852. The scant details provided here were probably enough to rekindle the anger generated by that book.

An important objective of the poem was to unite the American people behind the use of violence to overcome slavery. Notice how the author's pronoun use moves toward this goal; in the third stanza, both speaker and audience are united in the "we" that aids the fugitive slave. Elsewhere in the poem, the speaker serves as a representative of the black American soldiers who, by virtue of their service, have created a debt that the American people can only repay by fighting to obtain freedom for their people.

The use of the second-person pronoun in the rest of the poem unfortunately divides the interests of black America from those of the majority of the citizens, but it also serves to bring the issue to a more personal level. Earlier in the poem, "we" fought with your soldiers, but now "you" are confronted by a traitor with

crimson hands, blood on his knife and a scowl on his brow (line 27) who would force you to renounce all that "we" won on the battlefield (line 32) and subject the name of freedom to bitter mockery.

Slavery was an abomination, and Harper and other writers put all their skill into trying to achieve its end. Aside from its rhetorical force, this poem is interesting in that it suggests a growing awareness, long before the first shots were fired at Fort Sumter, that only the violence of the Civil War could settle the issue.

"ARMISTICE" Sophie Jewett (1892)

The initial audience must have been greatly surprised when Sophie Jewett's poem with such a martial title turned out to be more concerned with marital issues than with the late Civil War. Most of them could also appreciate the irony of the speaker's emphasis on the unresolved issues of yesterday's arguments that still tremble beneath the surface despite the quintessentially romantic setting of a couple's boating party. Like a placid river, the stereotypical Victorian household was supposed to be utterly tranquil and rejuvenating, with the husband as its unquestioned head. By the last decade of the 19th century, however, the increasing success of a wide variety of women's movements was helping individual women find their voices on domestic as well as public issues.

Each of the three stanzas of this poem begins with an attempt to fully appreciate the landscape in traditionally romantic ways, but the mood dissolves as memories of yesterday's strife surface in the concluding two lines. By the third stanza, the most the warring parties can pray for is that their truce will last through that day.

How beautifully the two opening lines evoke the spirit of peace that permeates the place and the happiness of carefree boating. The third and fourth lines celebrate the traditional strength that marriage was supposed to lend each partner, rendering the husband fearless before his enemies in the business world and the wife totally secure behind such a worthy protector. The romantic ambience of the poem receives its first shock in the speaker's mention of "the losing strife of yesterday" (line 6), which suggests that a "fear of life or death" (line 4) relates to the circumstances within the couple's relationship instead of their reaction to stimuli external to it.

The "swallows" of the second stanza are not much bigger than sparrows, but their high-speed turns and dexterous dips to drink from the surface of the water while on the wing are familiar to most frequenters of North American lakes and ponds. They seem magic, but in sharp contrast to the gentle counsels of life and love that would be more in keeping with the scene, the speaker recalls the hearts that bled and tears that burned (line 11) in the recent past. Only the river "floweth unconcerned," and such quasi-biblical phrasing suggests that the conflict we are viewing is at least as old as Western civilization.

Note how careful the poet was not to reveal the gender of the speaker or to attack either side. Such objectivity suggests that the theme is universal, and the poem serves as a warning for those men and women who would enter marriage with the unrealistic expectation that their relationship will unfold without disharmony or recriminations. By the third stanza, both partners seem united in praying for the evident impossibility that "the fickle flag of truce" will continue "floating deceitfully and fair" (lines 13–14). The most they can hope for seems an hour without a fight (line 16). Both know that tomorrow will bring them again into combat, and familiarity with each other's weapons leads them to expect another fierce battle.

"THE ARSENAL AT SPRINGFIELD" HENRY WADSWORTH LONGFELLOW (1844)

This poem was evidently inspired by the similarity between the rifle barrels in their uniform rows on shelves and the extensive pipes of an organ, which also reached from floor to ceiling in some churches. Despite its destructive potential, the arsenal is quiet, while churches can startle villages with strange alarms (line 4), a reference to the time when smaller communities often used church bells to spread notice of fires or other calamities. When the death-angel begins playing the martial pipes, choruses will mingle their laments and cries for mercy with the tune (lines 6–8). This leads the speaker to contemplate the sounds created by other instruments of war among peoples historically notorious for their aggressiveness; note that each of the following words

(reverberations, rings, roars, clamor, din, beat, bursting, rattling, and crashing; lines 11–20 and 25–26) uses onomatopoeia (words that imitate the sounds they indicate) to achieve their effects. He also imagines an arsenal or museum of martial instruments (hammer, gong, battle-bell, and drum) that were used to rouse fervor among warlike tribes.

HENRY WADSWORTH LONGFELLOW may have missed an opportunity by not extending the list to those instruments actually used on the battlefields at the time. Earlier in American history, fifes were used to help keep up the cadence as well as the spirits of marching men, and bugles were replacing drums as effective means of orchestrating troop movements. Instead, he immediately turns our attention to the merciless burning and pillaging that represent the face of war. A "beleaguered town" (line 24) has been completely surrounded by a hostile army, a circumstance inevitably leading to famine unless the siege can be lifted.

The "music" of the weapons will drown out nature's sweet voice and jar "the celestial harmonies" (line 32). The phrase recalls the theories of the ancient Greek philosopher Pythagoras, who believed that planets produced "the harmony of the spheres" as they orbited. In the early 17th century, Johannes Kepler, a German astronomer, used the phrase "celestial harmony" to suggest that planetary motion was the work of the same divine force that made musical harmony possible. In this poem, the line suggests that modern weapons of war will upset God's design.

The ninth stanza contains an economic argument for world peace. If half the money and power devoted to fighting wars and crime were diverted to "redeem the human mind from error" (line 35), there would be no need for armaments. Such an argument seems based on a belief of human perfectibility through education that seems characteristic of the optimism of the 18th-century Enlightenment philosophers.

The 10th stanza personifies countries based on biblical precedents; any country lifting its hand against its brother would forever bear the curse of Cain (line 40) just as in *Genesis* (4:8–15) God brands the murderer. The speaker's optimism reaches its zenith in the next stanza; he foresees a time in the distant future in which the echoes from the thunderous organs of war will end, and like a bell, the message of "Peace!" will again be heard in the clear voice of Christ (line 44). Similarly, "the blast of War's great organ" will no longer shake the skies" (line 46) but will be replaced by holy melodies of love. Although this last stanza seems to cry out for Freudian analysis, such an interpretation would do a grave disservice to the earnestness of the poet.

ARS POETICA (THE ART OF POETRY)

Horace (the name by which Quintus Horatius Flaccus, the Roman poet [65–8 B.C.], is commonly identified) was the first great poet whose extensive comments on his art have been preserved. In homage to his precedent, the title of his seminal work (*Ars Poetica,* c. 18 B.C.) has come to represent the best public commentaries on their own practice of poetry that modern poets have produced. The term "Ars Poetica" was not used for this specific purpose until the 20th century, however.

In an essay called "The POET" (1844), RALPH WALDO EMERSON called for a new type of poetry worthy of representing the magnitude of America's greatness. For this to happen, poets had to move away from the old European models. The public also had to be made receptive to their experiments and recognize the true poet as the man of beauty who can awaken them to the spiritual nature of his (and their) existence. Emerson argued that the content (or "meter-making argument") is what makes poetry, not its meter, and a true poem must reveal something new.

In dealing with American materials, Emerson urges the poet to consider whether any true depiction of life can be considered pornographic, and if an object in a factory town can be as worthy a subject as a spider web (or presumably, any other natural object). It is only necessary for the poet to open up to nature but to avoid any artificial stimulants in seeking a sublime vision. Like a god, a sober poet can liberate other men by showing them the connections between words and natural objects, and also between man and nature. Emerson's new poet will create the original and beautiful, but Emerson cautions that he should not expect to be appreciated beyond his immediate circle. Only with time will all the separate parts of America belong to him.

EDGAR ALLAN POE defined poetry as the rhythmical creation of beauty in "The POETIC PRINCIPLE" (1848). He would have poetry judged on its beauty and not its moral lesson or length, and insists on the superiority of shorter poems that elevate a reader's soul because they preserve the unity of effect that longer works cannot maintain. To illustrate his point, he examines a number of works by both famous and relatively unknown poets, typically praising the naturalness of their meter, the accuracy with which they reveal human nature, and the intensity of their conveyed emotion. He ends by defining the poetic principle as the human aspiration for supernal beauty. Poe argues that love is the purest and truest of the poetical themes, and making a list of things with the most powerful poetic effect leads him to dwell on the beauty of a woman and the divine majesty of her love.

Perhaps in an attempt to educate the public into fully appreciating the mastery of "The RAVEN," Poe produced "The PHILOSOPHY OF COMPOSITION" (1848). His stress was on the conscious choices a writer makes while working as an artist to create a specific effect that could reach the largest possible audience, and among his chief concerns was maintaining the poem's unities of impression and of effect. Determined to reach the heart of his audience, he sought a monotone expression which could convey the most mournful tune and then contrived a situation in which it could be repeated. The death of a beautiful woman as experienced by her lover seemed to him the most dramatic and poetic subject for a poem. Applying the psychological insight that even the most melancholy experience also contains a bit of pleasure, he created the most painful circumstance to which the monotone reply would be appropriate. He then worked backward to create the stanzas leading toward the last one but weakened each one enough to preserve the "climacteric effect" of his ending.

Poe implies that, as artists, poets should strive for as much originality as they can muster for their work. Thus he chose a novel combination of metrical lines that not one 21st-century reader in 50,000 would be able to identify correctly without Poe's prompting. His real aim in choosing such a repetitive metrical pattern was to prolong the suspense until delivery of the deepest pain satisfied the human thirst for self-torture. He rendered all the elements realistically until the end, when he concluded with a metaphorical expression he hoped would lead readers into seeking a moral to the poem. This process and their satisfaction with the emotional impact of the poem will eventually lead them to appreciate the poem's complexity.

In a rambling "PREFACE TO THE 1855 EDITION OF LEAVES OF GRASS," WALT WHITMAN furthered the agenda advanced by Emerson's "The Poet" by acknowledging the roles other cultures have played in shaping America. In his opinion, their chief contribution has been the immigrants whose flourishing in the freedom of the new country will lead it to greatness.

Whitman advances a broad definition of poetry that extends to such gestures as the president's doffing his hat (removing it as a salute) to the people, its full-sized, unconquerable simple men. The scope of the American experience requires a bard whose great psalm for the republic must not be limited by traditional poetic forms or received notions about decorum. His chief functions are to realize the grandeur of the universe and to enable others to see it, and Whitman argues that artificial notions of propriety must not inhibit his search for beauty. Nor should he let conventional forms dictate his expression, or spend his time in other unnecessary work.

While agreeing with Emerson that the pleasure of poetry does not lie in its handsomest tropes (poetic devices), Whitman argues that it rests in the passion it brings to the individual auditor. Like Poe, Whitman asserts that the greatest poet does not moralize. Whitman adds that the greatest poet knows the soul, and is the "non-distorting channel" of thoughts, things, and himself. His great poet will love and express the whole of America, including its science. Supernatural elements will depart like a dream because, Whitman asserts, there is nothing more divine than men and women.

Political liberty is essential to the great masters of poetry, and the instinct for it and for the truth is an essential part of human nature. Thus great poets are known by their perfect personal candor, and their fidelity to truth makes them superior to writers of history, fiction and romance. Like HENRY DAVID THOREAU, Whitman bemoans the years men spend moneymaking and the underhanded dodges that lead to surplus while others starve. Only truth satisfies the soul, and the direct trial for the greatest poet is whether he focuses on his own body and soul instead of only flooding himself with current events.

Whitman argues that the work of priests is done, and that poets will assume a leadership role. This will lead to a superior breed of prophets when every man becomes his own priest. The English language is brawny enough for their work, and American standards of perfection will eventually lead to producing goodly men and their perfect mates. Only the demeanor of the vital and great will satisfy the expectation for the vital and the great; the polite and timid leave no mark. An individual can become as superb as a nation if he possesses the qualities that make a superb nation, and the eventual test of a poet is whether his country has absorbed him as affectionately as he absorbed it. All three of these writers felt that their readership was retarding the advance of poetry because of their preconceived notions about the art. Although Emerson never carried out the experiments necessary to fully develop the new verse forms he advocated, he paved the way for a friendlier reception for Whitman's development of the free verse that was to become the dominant form of poetic expression in the second half of the 20th century. Each of the three writers hoped to create a new audience that could appreciate their effort for its aesthetic appeal instead of applauding its attempt at conveying a didactic morality lesson or censoring its (or the poet's own) improprieties.

"ART" HERMAN MELVILLE (1891) This poem is more than just a list of juxtaposed opposites adding up to a complaint about how difficult the poet's job is. In addition to being generally skillfully rhymed and metered, the energy the poem celebrates is based not just on the creation of a single work of art, but on the poet's having a devotion so thorough that it takes everything that he or she has, including the superhuman courage to wrestle with an angel. The speaker seems intent upon a creation as miraculous as that in the ancient Greek myth of Pygmalion, who made a statue so beautiful and who loved it so devotedly that Aphrodite brought it to life. HERMAN MELVILLE here provides a recipe for those who would follow in his footsteps, and like the myth of Pygmalion, its imagery generally centers on the plastic arts, especially sculpture.

The first four lines begin contrasting the idle dream of success with the effort it takes to bring art to life, in language vaguely reminiscent of Mary Shelley's *Frankenstein:* the goal is no less than the creation of "pulsed life" (line 3). The list of juxtaposed opposites begins with the two verbs "meet and mate," activities that usually involve the scantest and the most intimate connections, respectively. The next pairing is among the most interesting in the poem because it suggests the speaker is working as a sculptor. Under normal conditions, most earthly metals, glasses, and some solids (such as ice) melt in flame instead of burning, and solidify (or "freeze") when chilled (line 5). Note that even the verbs, as well as the nouns, represent opposites, but that flame (if only its heat is considered) is strikingly similar to wind (if only its freezing capability is considered). Since these phenomena are valued here only for the changes their temperatures effect in the material to which they are applied, their juxtaposition represents a unity instead of a dichotomy. This metaphysical insight is usually more celebrated in Eastern religions (and by those who studied them, such as the American transcendentalists who were Melville's contemporaries) than in Western science or theology.

An artist might think "patience sad" because his natural inclination is toward expression, but a lengthy period of serious study must be endured before his "joyous energies" (line 6) can profitably be employed for the desired effect. Humility is necessary because of the lengthy learning process, yet pride is also necessary if one is to have enough confidence to persevere. Scorn is best reserved for the shortcomings of one's own work, and for anything that prevents one from achieving it. "Instinct and study" are like "Audacity (and) reverence" (lines 8–9) in that an artist must attempt something new while still remaining in awe of his craft, its traditions and its history. All these things must mate (line 9) before the mystical transformation that leads to the artist's discovery that he has Jacob's heart and, like that biblical patriarch, is worthy of wrestling with an angel—in his case, Art. Throughout, the poem has

stressed how arduous is the challenge of acquiring the necessary skill; ultimately, it seems that the process is more important than the product.

"THE ARTILLERYMAN'S VISION" WALT WHITMAN (1865)

Among the poet's many duties while he served as a volunteer nurse with the Union Army was writing letters for the illiterate and those too badly injured to write by themselves. While the poem was not based on his firsthand experience, he had constant access to those who did have it.

The vision of the title is really twofold as the poem commences at least nine months after the artillery veteran's return home. Although his wife is by his side and he can hear his child's breathing in the same room, the speaker experiences what veterans of another American conflict a century later would call flashbacks, vividly painful scenes of battle that probably had been repressed during his waking hours. This phenomenon, later identified as a symptom of what was called shell shock, battle fatigue, and eventually posttraumatic stress disorder in the successive wars of the 20th century, was largely undiagnosed in the 19th century.

In keeping with the dreamlike quality of his vision, the speaker is strangely detached from the major incidents of the battle he describes, although some of the strain he experiences is revealed in his diction. The battle unfolds in the classic Civil War pattern. Lacking aerial reconnaissance, armies would send out detachments of soldiers as skirmishers in a maneuver designed to detect the enemy's strength at various positions on the battlefield. In line 6, notice how skillfully their motion is described as a cautious crawl. They have been spotted, however, and the speaker uses onomatopoeia (words that mimic the sounds they represent) to begin conveying the sounds of battle: rifles "snap" when fired (line 6) and the great shells "shriek" as they pass (line 8). He also tries to convey the "t-h-t" sound made by passing rifle balls by transcribing the letters needed to replicate it (line 7). The ordnance of the day included round rifle balls instead of more cylindrical bullets, cannonballs, shells that would explode overhead in order to send fragments over a targeted area (hence the "small white clouds" of line 8), and grape shot (line 9; grape-sized iron balls often mixed with assorted pieces of metal and fired at close range from a cannon in order to wreck havoc on any infantry advancing upon the guns). The "batteries" (line 10) are artillery units placed in firing position on the field. To anyone familiar with Civil War battles, the successive employment of the weaponry described in lines 6 through 9 renders the phrase "tumultuous now the contest rages" superfluous.

The sights ("smoking") and sounds ("crashing") of the battle are combined in line 11 with a shift in focus to the individuals engaged in the fight, beginning with the gunners who take pride "in their pieces" (that is, cannon). Individuals such as the methodical chief gunner (line 11) and the young colonel who leads an infantry assault with his drawn sword (line 13) behave bravely despite the chaos of the battle and its implications for their own danger. "Volleys" (line 14) are simultaneous discharges of every available rifle by a line of soldiers designed to concentrate firepower on an advancing line of enemy soldiers. Because the cannon relied on black powder to propel their shells, flat clouds of suffocating smoke soon limited visibility (line 15). A "strange lull for a few seconds" was necessary to reload the cannon and sometimes to assess the effectiveness of the last shot in order to adjust the aim of the next. Because of his occupation, cannon fire rouses "devilish exultation" and "the old mad joy" in the soul of the artilleryman (line 20); the line reflects the pride each branch of the military takes in its special province and the strange sensations attendant upon the adrenalin rush accompanying such imminent danger.

From the close-up views of the two professionals acting so coolly under pressure, the perspective has shifted to groups of men moving in their infantry, artillery, and cavalry units. Evidently engrossed in his own professional responsibilities, the speaker ignores the casualties, even though on some level he registered the red dripping wounds and noticed a few men hobbling to the rear (line 22).

This "fantasy unreal" (as he described it in line 5) includes the dirt, heat, and disorder of the battle, but as it winds down, he again becomes aware of the scattered small-arms fire that began it. The poem ends with rockets and bombs bursting in air; by echoing the well-known lines of the "Star-Spangled Banner," the speaker succeeds in placing all of his extraordinary experience in a patriotic context. Given the manifest patriotism that permeated American society after the Civil War, this last line suggests that, rather than being tortured by recurrent nightmares of horrific scenes of slaughter, the veteran artilleryman takes pride in having so admirably performed his duty.

"AS ADAM EARLY IN THE MORNING"

WALT WHITMAN (1861)   In striving to encompass all of human experience, WALT WHITMAN reached back to the prelapsarian Adam to express his feelings about a fresh new day. Like the biblical patriarch, the speaker of this poem is probably nude and evidently felt no shame about it, for he summons the internal audience to behold him, listen to his voice, and touch him with the sensitive palm of a hand "as I pass" (line 4).

It is a voice unlike that of Adam, however, in its use of the imperative mood. In commanding his audience with biblical language to "behold," he sounds more like a god than an innocent. With his final command for the internal audience to "not be afraid of my body," he is implying that he himself is comfortable with it, and with his sexuality.

"AS I EBBED WITH THE OCEAN OF LIFE"

WALT WHITMAN (1860)   An ebb tide begins immediately after a high tide crests. As the water recedes, it reveals things that had been hidden or forgotten as well as the flotsam or jetsam (things dropped into the water accidentally or intentionally, respectively) left by man and rotting pieces of animal and vegetative life washed ashore. Since WALT WHITMAN was approaching 40 as he wrote this poem, he may have felt that at least physically, his best years (representing the high water mark of his life) were behind him. Taking extensive walks in the solitude of the shore of still underdeveloped Long Island, as Whitman was wont to do, gave him the opportunity to reflect on the meaning of his life, including his personal flotsam and jetsam. The poem's numbered sections are generally divided into an opening stanza that deals more directly with the experience of walking on the beach and subsequent, more subjective stanzas that reveal how these new sensations prompt his thoughts on his own life.

The speaker sets the stage in the first stanza by identifying the island as Paumanok (line 3) and himself as one who frequently walks on its shores. The speaker's use of the Indian name avoids confusion with other Long Islands, establishes his knowledge of the island's history, and conveys his fondness for the locale. Almost as soon as his feet hit the sand his senses become fully engaged; he invites the reader to hear the "hoarse and sibilant" (line 4; *sibilant* means extremely high-pitched, like a hiss) sounds of the waves as they "rustle" up the beach. Note the elegant specificity; the poet does not just refer to the sound of the waves, but uses onomatopoeia to convey the two distinct tones that each one makes. He proceeds to personify the ocean as a "fierce old mother who endlessly cries for her castaways" (line 5), thus adding a subjective interpretation of the sounds. All of the above is so unforgettable that he echoes it in the last section (lines 51–54), thereby not only providing the poem with a pleasing frame, but also returning the reader to the starting point, where most beach walks end.

The speaker was held by his "electric self" (line 7; the phrase not only captures his vitality but also may refer to the miracle of the human nervous system, including the brain) until the trails underfoot reminded him of all the land and water in the world. This brings him to a list of things cast on the shore, presents of the fish-shaped Long Island (line 15; perhaps appropriately for this poem, its shape most closely resembles a decaying fish). He sought "types" (line 17); to a writer the term suggests things that he can use in his poems either because they intrinsically merit such consideration or because they remind him of something else. The word puns on the fonts used by printers at the same time that it suggests representative specimens, valuable to an artist for their perfection and/or their universality.

In the second part, he passes on to a section of the beach he had not previously explored, or on a less literal level, his thoughts wander to the men and women lost at sea. He, too, is made up of sand, and acknowledges an urge toward self-destruction that would enable him to merge with nature. Recognizing that he has no real idea of who or what he is (line 27) despite all the "arrogant poems" (line 28) that boisterously proclaim his importance to the world, "the real Me" mockingly contrasts his words with the reality represented by the sand beneath his feet. It seems as though he has not understood anything and that no man can, and that nature darts in and stings him for daring to sing at all (lines 32–33).

In part 3, he "closes" with both oceans (the Atlantic and Pacific bordering America? Or do his thoughts make up one ocean and the reality of the things upon which he stands make up the other?), merging his murmurs against the rolling sands and drifts with theirs (lines 34–36).

This leads him to consider the land; identifying with the debris washed ashore, he throws himself upon Long Island, his "father," pleading for a kiss and the secret of the murmuring that he envies (line 50).

In the last stanza he pleads for the ocean of life not to fear or deny him. He gathers for himself and "this phantom looking down where we lead" (line 56). He and all that belongs to him (including those people he loves) will become mere corpses, and the sea's froth and bubbles suggest the "prismatic colors glistening and rolling" (lines 59–60) that will ooze from his own dead lips. He lists the things both tangible and intangible (his musings that he has so carefully preserved, and breaths; line 64) that will remain like debris on the shore. The dirge for the drowned that he thought he heard from the ocean sounds equally for all men. We all will lie like debris at the feet of whoever is up there, walking or sitting.

"AS I LAY WITH MY HEAD IN YOUR LAP CAMERADO" WALT WHITMAN (1865) It is probably necessary to read this poem as a declaration of homosexual sentiments since the title is rather suggestive and the male poet evidently went out of his way to add a masculine ending to the Spanish word for comrade, *camarada*. It could also be viewed as a general celebration of that aspect of the human spirit that refuses to compromise its essential nature or moral principles despite enormous social pressure to conform, or as a protestation of a love so strong that the speaker is willing to renounce heaven and face hell for it. Readers who absolutely cannot permit themselves

to admit the possibility of homoeroticism in the poem might try to imagine it as an address from someone in a situation like that of the Reverend Mr. Dimmesdale of Nathaniel Hawthorne's *The Scarlet Letter,* who privately brings himself almost to the point of publicly confessing his affair with Hester Prynne. The reality remains, however, that our foremost great gray poet was also our first great gay poet. The interminable wait for public acceptance of his sexual orientation made WALT WHITMAN "restless" (line 3), and he was aware this public admission would make others also restless.

Unlike Dimmesdale in the Hawthorne novel, who would only profess his love for Hester in the woods where he ran little risk of being overheard, the speaker in this poem is willing to repeat his assertions once they have returned to everyday life. The most interesting word he uses is "confession" (line 3), for it not only suggests that love is compelling him to speak, it also employs language usually used for public admissions of guilt for perpetrating a crime.

Note that the poem consists of a single sentence, as if the speaker's feelings force him to get everything out before he can be interrupted. He also tries to anticipate the arguments against their love, including a social climate in which his "words are weapons full of danger, full of death" (line 4) that can be used against them. Although homosexuality in America generally was not legally punishable by death in 1865, individuals convicted of "homosexual acts" faced prison terms and social ostracism, and even late into the 20th century, public opinion seemed to condone violence against gays, which could sometimes result in the victim's death.

Having accepted the naturalness of his own sexuality, the speaker became more resolute in his identity "because all have denied me" (line 6). He makes a short list of the means society employs to coerce his silence: "experience, cautions, majorities and ridicule" (line 7). He adds religion to the list in the next two lines, adding that neither the threat of hell or the promise of heaven will motivate him to change.

Only his "dear Camerado" seems to matter to him, and he admits urging him on without knowing their destination (line 10). Even a century later, they might face hate-crime victimization, incarceration, and public

humiliation, or find a redemptive love that might allow them to transcend all of society's fears. As with any struggle, it is impossible for them to predict if they will end up victorious, or utterly defeated (line 11). The struggle for broad public acceptance of homosexuality in America has even lasted until the 21st century, but recent developments seem to indicate that eventually even marriage or at least fully legal domestic partnerships will no longer make it the curse it once seemed. Whitman would have been pleased.

"AS IMPERCEPTIBLY AS GRIEF" EMILY DICKINSON (1891)

This poem seemingly mocks the language used to assuage the suffering of the bereaved by using the same language to eulogize the passing of a summer. On another level, it criticizes the inadequacy of the lackluster, even dismissive, obsequies typically delivered over those quiet people (such as the virtually unpublished EMILY DICKINSON who penned these lines) so little valued by society that their lives seem only a sequence of sequestered afternoons.

The most striking feature of the first line of this poem is its inverted metaphor. Instead of the usual poetic practice of using something familiar to introduce the audience to a particular aspect of a new thing, the speaker evidently assumes that grief is a more pervasive experience than summer, or at least the way that summer weakened and passed away that particular year. The verb "lapsed" (line 2) reinforces this effect because of its use in phrases such as lapsing into a coma or lapsing into death; in each case the word implies that the change occurs without a struggle. In fact, the change can be so imperceptibly slight that it does not seem like treachery (the "perfidy" of line 4) to the survivors left behind. Instead, it seems a moment of "Quietness distilled" (line 5).

Similarly, the summer imperceptibly passed into autumn, with the latter's shorter days and relatively dim sun seeming like a long twilight. It seems as though Nature, personified as middle-aged woman, was merely spending a "Sequestered Afternoon" with herself (lines 6–7); the capitalization in and beautiful wording of that phrase suggest that the speaker valued the tranquility and solitude she would experience on such occasions. Yet dusk's early arrival reminds her that "Morning foreign shone" (line 10) before departing like a courteous yet too formal guest whose Grace at parting is disturbing (even traumatic, her use of "harrowing" implies) because it so poorly disguises how happy it is to leave. In retrospect, the relative weakness of the morning sun might have alerted her to the passing season; the shortness of the morning was another missed clue.

Thus, summer escaped "without a Wing" (line 13). Since this poem was written before the advent of air travel, the phrase contrasts the torpor with which the season departed with the speed of the birds. At the same time, however, the speaker may be noting the absence of biological clues such as the arrival or departure of certain birds that the poet elsewhere celebrates as the heralds of spring. Noting that the escape was made without "service of a Keel" (line 14) achieves the same ends; a keel is the bottommost support of the frame of a boat, and certain boats were among the fastest means of sustained human travel at the time when the poem was written. Use of that nautical term also puns on "kill;" unlike winter, the more tranquil arrival of summer is typically not announced by killing frosts and other threats. Instead, that summer made a "light escape into the Beautiful" (lines 15–16), an ending that mimics the optimism of the Christian sects with their confidence in the promise of heaven.

"AS I SIT WRITING HERE" Walt Whitman (1888)

The most valuable lesson a nascent poet can learn about his craft from this short poem is that despite his decrepitude, including all the indignities that aging has forced upon him, Walt Whitman still sat at his desk to compose his "daily songs" (line 4).

This poem may have been written as therapy, or at least as a means of overcoming the distractions he lists in the first three lines. By recognizing his problems and relegating them to a work so insignificant that he only annexed it instead of integrating it into his *Leaves of Grass*, Whitman may have hit upon a means of categorizing his potential distractions so that he could continue with the task at hand. The most interesting item in the list is probably "ennui"; it was originally a French term signifying terminal boredom.

Throughout his career Whitman often seemed a brutally honest autobiographical poet, but he always seemed to be in command of his material and confident of his potency. In "After the Supper and Talk," another poem of about the same vintage, Whitman studied how boring the elderly can be to an audience more interested in their own lives. Perhaps this insight has put him on his guard against letting his purely personal complaints "filter" (a modern writer might say "ooze") into his serious poetry.

"AS ONE TURNED ROUND ON SOME HIGH MOUNTAIN TOP" Frederick Goddard Tuckerman (1931)

Poets and other writers are fond of using mountain trekking as a metaphor for an individual's life because each can present a series of increasingly difficult steps. Frederick Goddard Tuckerman's poem is original in not focusing on the struggle, stressing the speaker's pride in having separated himself from the meaner life of the nonartist, or in marveling at the perspective gained from a lifetime of hard work. Instead of elation, this speaker feels disoriented and confused about how he got there. The perspective is similar to that of a senior citizen so old that his passions have burned out, and his symptoms (such as not recognizing familiar landmarks in line 5) may suggest the onset of senility.

The chief advantage the speaker gained for his trouble is making the acquaintance of someone who arrived at the place from the opposite direction. At first the new acquaintance sounds like he came from south of the equator, where hot winds can blow from the sultry north (line 10), but his account soon turns into a seemingly fanciful collection of oxymorons and opposites.

Closer examination of the phenomena he lists suggests that they may be based in reality, however. The phrase "forests that give no shade" (line 11) may merely refer to a winter landscape, a recently burned woods in which no leaves and few branches survived, or even a petrified forest. Quicksand might as well be bottomless, and in the right conditions a plummet or other weight would sink in it as it does in the sea (line 12). Modern meteorology recognizes reverse lightning as just one instance where the lightning jumps from the earth to the sky, and tornadoes over salt beds could easily produce rain as salty as blood (line 14). In the right light, perhaps at sunrise or sunset, falling or blowing snow might be illuminated in such a way as to appear fiery, or the still glowing sparks amid the falling ashes of a wood fire may have brought fiery snow to mind.

Extreme mountaineers may experience hypoxia-induced disorientation similar to that described in this poem. Modern sportsmen might thus be content to interpret the poem as a celebration not of the unique views one obtains from great height, but of the unique perspectives the exertion provides into the psyche. Because transcendentalism was the most exciting intellectual trend while Tuckerman was in his prime, however, the poet may have expected some of the phenomena he describes to remain inexplicable mysteries.

"AS TOILSOME I WANDER'D VIRGINIA'S WOODS" WALT WHITMAN (1865)

Because it was a border state in the Civil War, because Richmond served as the capital of the Confederacy despite being very close to Washington, D.C., and because its superb generalship and generally fine fighting spirit throughout the ranks enabled it to repulse invasions by larger armies for four years, Virginia was the site of more hastily dug graves than other states.

The awkwardness evident in the grammar of the title and first line of the poem reveal the troubled spirit of WALT WHITMAN's speaker; the oxymoron of "wandering toilsomely" makes sense only if he were walking to work out the trauma experienced as a soldier or volunteer nurse (like Whitman), or if, also like Whitman and numerous other writers, he composed as he walked, often encountering new images like that used in this poem.

The dead leaves that he is so musically kicking as he walked (line 2) connect the speaker with the discovered grave at the same time that they symbolize the soldier's fall. Whatever his role in the war has been, the speaker is familiar enough with the movements of a retreating army that he understands how the stricken man was evacuated and hastily buried. The exigencies of the moment forced his comrades' quick withdrawal, but one still penned a quick note to his "bold,

cautious, true and loving comrade" (line 7). As these are attributes the speaker admires, the grave and its accompanying words often occur to him at "changeful seasons and scenes" (line 10); thus the hastily penned words became something like a mantra for the speaker as well as the refrain of the poem. The phrase encompasses much of what a soldier can take from the war: confidence in his own demonstrated courage, the technical survival skills of which caution is foremost, and the revelation of his "true" self after the combat experience has eroded the more superficial aspects of his personality. Combat soldiers may also meet comrades for whom a mutual reliance in circumstances where their lives depend on each other frequently forges a love that is stronger than that between brothers.

"AS WEARY PILGRIM" ANNE BRADSTREET (published 1867)

As she lived out her final years, ANNE BRADSTREET, ever the good Puritan, struggled to place her inevitable decrepitude into a religious context. She begins by considering the plight of a wandering pilgrim who painfully endured traveling from one holy site to another in search of salvation. The author probably desired the same happy ending, a sense of having fulfilled her religious obligation and a joyful certitude about her destiny.

The pilgrim, having satisfied whatever impulses drove his peregrinations, now rests triumphant, for he hugs his silent nest with delight (line 2). The implication is that he undertook the pilgrimage as a devotional duty, and having completed it, he feels that he cannot (and probably need not) do anything more to ensure his salvation. He evidently led the life of a hermit, for he recalls facing the burning sun, storms, briars, stones, stumps, wolves, and a wild-fruit diet. He also achieved a victory over himself; he recalls taking "mirey steps" (line 4) but evidently never fell into a moral quagmire. He is now out of danger (line 6) not only because his travels are over, but also because his limbs are wasted (line 3). The phrase suggests he has mortified his flesh to a point beyond temptation. He intends to dwell in heaven; it is the only place of safety (line 18) because only there can he obtain eternal bliss.

In line 19, the point of view shifts as the pilgrim takes over from the erstwhile speaker of the poem and continues in first person to the end. It was fashionable in Puritan theology to denigrate the body as mere clay, since God fashioned Adam out of the substance, so the moldering "clay house" of line 22 refers to the pilgrim's body. Life was still hard enough in New England that most people of Bradstreet's age (approximately 57 at the time the poem was written) could relate to the fainting fits, grinding pains, cares, fears, losses, and sorrows mentioned here, and the promise that heaven would be free of them. The resurrection from corrupt carcass to glorious body (lines 35–36) followed from Christ's sacrifice on the cross.

Unlike the more famous British Puritan poet John Milton (in *Paradise Regained*), Bradstreet rarely tried to describe the delights of heaven (lines 40–41). The poem ends with the pilgrim's prayer to Christ to make him ready for Judgment Day. The final line, in which the male pilgrim asks Christ to come to him as a bridegroom, recalls a biblical passage (Mark 2:19) in which Christ essentially promised to care for his followers as if they were his children.

"AT THE TIME OF THE WHITE DAWN"

ANONYMOUS (1908) This extraordinary song of the Pima Indians of southern Arizona comes across as exceptionally sophisticated poetry even in translation. The double surprise of the poem is that it is written from the deer's perspective even after the animal has been killed.

Tribal people often believe in a mystical connection between the word and the flesh, as if saying something or dreaming up an image could have an impact on subsequent events. Mainstream American culture tends to dismiss any perceived connection between the two as mere coincidence, but in so doing it denies the powerful spiritual and emotional forces that can have an important impact on human life. The magic of song, ritualistic chanting, or dancing can seem apparent to those who believe in it, and even from a modern psychological perspective, visualizing a positive outcome has been proven to influence and enhance athletic performance, to cite just one scientifically verifiable modern example.

The formulaic repetition of the first line in the second one focuses audience attention and suggests that the speaker is getting in touch with the memory he is about to relate. The White Dawn of the title may refer to the time of day at which he started or to a newly fallen snow, which would make tracking a deer easier. For an American of the 21st century, the color may also suggest the speaker's ignorance of the catastrophic events to befall the speaker later in the day just as the Blue Nightfall might suggest death. One of the exceptional delights of this poem is that its repetition of key phrases always enhances its meaning; note the shift between the mere act of moving away as it is expressed in line 3 and the implications of the same phrase ("I went away") in the next line, where it can be read as yet another euphemism for death. The first stanza promises that the speaker will relate the major events of the day on which he died.

The second stanza suggests that the speaker was somewhat complicit in his own demise since his indulgence in thornapple leaves and flowers left him with the diminished capacity of a drunkard; he became so dizzy that he staggered. Instead of serving as a bad example such as one might find in a temperance tract, however, the poet may have been showing the deer's consciousness of its own actions, a capability modern man usually tends to ascribe only to members of our own species. Similarly, the stanza reads as if the speaker were providing an excuse for being taken. Not only has he provided an amusing sketch of his tipsiness, but he also has conveyed his pride in his natural abilities. The notion that animals have personalities may be disquieting for those modern readers who prefer to purchase relatively bloodless meat after it has been wrapped in plastic and refrigerated, but people who subsist on the game they kill tend to develop a more personal connection with the animals.

The third stanza reveals the deer's death and, because he fell to a meat and not a trophy hunter, how his horns and feet were thrown away. Like Native Americans in many tribes, the deer names the hunter according to his attributes or actions during a singularly memorable event, hence he is called Bow-remaining and Reed-remaining.

The last stanza is intelligible only if the reader is willing to attribute something like a soul to the animal, for the speaker remains conscious despite his obvious death. One nice touch is that the speaker seems to relate to the mental states of the flies (they "become crazy" in line 15) and butterflies in the same way that the poet identified with him, and the greater acuity of his deer eyes enables him to see the flapping wings of the flies. Especially fortuitous is the implied link of the drunken butterflies to his own drunkenness in the second stanza.

The beautiful final image of the poem, butterflies opening and shutting their wings, suggests the speaker's acceptance of the naturalness of his death. He evidently feels no more ill will toward the hunter than he does toward the flies and butterflies that have come to feast on their sudden bounty.

"THE AUTHOR TO HER BOOK" ANNE BRADSTREET (1678)

After her father had supplied her with the tutors needed for her education, ANNE BRADSTREET continued experimenting with poetry. She circulated her poems within her family circle until, without her knowledge, her brother-in-law had some of them printed as a book. This poem relates her feelings upon being presented with the resulting volume, and she relied on the complex feelings of motherhood to express her reactions.

Just as a human infant needs many years of additional care after its birth before it is ready to enter the larger world, she thought she would have more time to get her brainchild ready. In stating that the manuscript was "snatched" (line 3) from her side, she likens the experience to kidnapping. Having thus expressed her anger as strongly as possible, she immediately softens the blow by stating that her true friends were responsible (though she cannot resist the parting shot of calling them unwise). Even more graciously, she implies that she could not have corrected the flaws in her poems even had she had the opportunity to do so by a final proofreading and editing of the manuscript just before it was published, as authors are wont to do (lines 11–16). A similar concern for the impact of her words on those around her becomes evident when she makes it clear that the term "rambling brat" (line 8) does not refer to her biological children, but only to the book. Her nurturing instinct becomes apparent in her eventual acceptance of the child (that is, the book) even

despite its shortcomings (lines 11–12), in her attempts to manipulate its joints to remedy its uneven feet, and again in her final instructions to the child concerning his place in society.

Having dealt with her annoyance, she examines the book as it will appear to the public. Note how deftly she found words from the world of poetry, books, and publishing, which also had meaning when applied (alas!) to a repulsive and unwanted child left to fend for itself. She was probably close enough in time to the origin of the word "brat" to have noticed its derivation from a coarse medieval garment; the 17th-century equivalent was "homespun cloth" (line 18). In both eras, such inexpensive raiment could signal, to a relatively high-born, affluent, and privileged woman such as the author, that the child may have come from a vulgar home of limited financial resources and perhaps even neglect. The "rags" in which the child was hauled to the press (line 5) may also refer to the high rag content of most paper at the time; it was the expensive product of a labor-intensive process and usually superior in many ways to most paper produced today. The speaker is probably not thinking of the relative elegance of colonial paper in this poem but may be letting one of the materials from which it was made stand for the entire paper.

The unevenness of "feet" (line 15) concerned the speaker because part of the creative challenge facing a 17th-century poet was strict adherence to a metrical pattern once it had been established in a poem, or adopted in accordance with its conventional use in a specific type of poem. Note, for example, that each line in this poem contains 10 syllables and that an unaccented syllable typically precedes an accented syllable, a pattern known as iambic. This two-syllable pattern is generally repeated five times in each line, so Bradstreet chose to create the verse in iambic pentameter, generally considered the rhythm closest to the natural pattern of conversational English. Lines failing to meet this standard (or the different standard accepted for the other poems) could be dismissed as "hobbling" like a crippled child.

In finding only homespun cloth in her house (line 18), the speaker not only implies a lack of resources in her brain but also offers a plausible excuse for her lapses (of which there are few in this poem). As was the case for almost all women in her era, her lack of advanced academic training left her to her own "homespun" devices. The poem's lack of a father (line 22) may refer to the absence of an intellectual father like a college professor or other mentor schooled in poetics in the speaker's life. The poem ends with a plea that it not be judged as a masterpiece of fine art bred by years of formal instruction, but more privately enjoyed by ordinary people. Despite this special pleading, however, the final line acknowledges that as the mother of the poem she is ultimately responsible for it. In developing such maternal analogies, Bradstreet demonstrates that poetry, and especially its creation, is something that women can do. The poem's title may thus not only indicate the poem's internal audience, but also stands as an assertion that poetry is within the province of women. Separated from the poem, it could be an imperative slogan with revolutionary implications: it calls for the author to take up her work.

B

BARLOW, JOEL (1754–1812) On March 24, 1754, Barlow was born into a farm family in Redding, Connecticut. He graduated from Yale in 1788 and served with the Continental Army during the Revolutionary War. He began practicing law in 1786, but with five other young writers he created the Connecticut Wits, an informal group determined to provide the new nation (the United States Constitution was ratified in 1788) with an American tradition in literature. He traveled to France as an unwitting employee of the fraudulent Scioto Land Company, survived the scandal, and eventually made a fortune investing in European securities. He lived abroad for about 17 years in all, becoming a French citizen and helping save Thomas Paine, an ideological hero in America, from the terror of the French Revolution. From his college years onward, he cultivated friendships with other remarkable men, collected fine wines and steadily grew wealthier. Eventually becoming a diplomat, he successfully negotiated treaties with the Barbary states and was on the verge of similar success with Napoleon when he met an untimely end.

As a poet, Barlow first gained a national reputation for "The Vision of Columbus" (1787). He ill-advisedly expanded it into "The Columbiad" (1807), which is rarely anthologized because of its length and labored style. "The HASTY PUDDING," a mock heroic poem, brings to mind "The Rape of the Lock," a famous poem by the early 18th-century British writer Alexander Pope. Perhaps only a man grown accustomed to much richer fodder could so nostalgically savor the plain breakfast dish of his youth.

The most painful irony of his "ADVICE TO A RAVEN IN RUSSIA," a rather grisly poem that advises the winged scavenger that fresh meat will be available wherever Napoleon goes, is that Barlow himself might be considered one of the victims. As American minister to France, he was summoned to meet the French emperor in Poland during the latter's disastrous Russian campaign. Recognizing the necessity of making his own retreat, Barlow died of pneumonia on December 24 (or December 26; accounts vary), 1812, in Zarnowiec, Poland.

Nothing remains of the mansion Barlow purchased and renamed Kalorama in 1807, but its 30 acres now support many other most glamorous homes in the Washington, D.C., suburb that retains the name. The Houghton Library at Harvard holds several boxes of Barlow manuscripts, notebooks and other material. The University of Virginia holds several of his letters and manuscript diaries.

BIBLIOGRAPHY

Barlow, Joel. *The Works of Joel Barlow,* edited by William Buttorff and Arthur Ford. 2 vols. Gainesville, Fla.: Scholars Facsimilies, 1970.

Bernstein, Samuel. *Joel Barlow: a Connecticut Yankee in an age of revolution.* New York: Rutledge Books, 1985.

Douty, Ester Morris. *Hasty Pudding and Barbary Pirates: A Life of Joel Barlow.* Philadelphia: Westminster Press, 1975.

Woodress, James. *A Yankee's Odyssey: The Life of Joel Barlow.* Philadelphia: Lippincott, 1958.

"BARS FIGHT" LUCY TERRY (1746)

The sole surviving work attributed to the first African American credited with creating poetry, this poem remained part of the oral tradition of western Massachusetts until it was published in 1855. Its dominant rhythm is tetrameter, and the simplicity with which it relates the essential elements of the raid helps convince the audience that the poet's account is as accurate as her careful recording of the date in the first two lines would indicate. Its other aesthetic virtues include the ease with which the victims' names and fates are woven into its fabric, and its organization of the materials according to their shock value.

Compared to earlier battles in Deerfield, Massachusetts, the events of August 25, 1746, were minor. In 1675, 60 colonists were killed south of the town during King Philip's War, and several hundred Native Americans were killed in a retaliatory attack on a nearby village in the next year. There were several smaller skirmishes, such as the one Terry describes, over the intervening years until February 29, 1704. The town was abandoned after the Deerfield Massacre, in which about 50 more settlers were killed and more than 100 were taken prisoner, but it was rebuilt three years later.

The poem stacks the rhetorical cards against "the Indians" waiting in a meadow (the "bars" of the title) to slay "some valiant men" (line 4) in an ambush. The first victim the speaker mentions is Samuel Allen, whose "face no more shall we behold" (line 8). This is an effective euphemism for death, but for the poem's initial audience it may have suggested mutilations such as scalping or other grievous injuries. Still, he had managed to fight "like a hero" (line 6).

Eleazer Hawks was shot and killed without having seen his assailants. Oliver Amsden, much missed by his friends, was also slain, and the body of Simeon Amsden was found not many rods (a "rod" is 16.5 feet, or 5.03 meters, long) distant from him. The colorful phrase "distant from *his* head" is ambiguous because the pronoun could possibly refer to Simeon Amsden instead of Oliver. This would imply that he was beheaded and that a grisly trophy had been tossed or carried a short distance before being discarded. In the work of a more literary or ironic poet, the reader's discovery of this possibility and the discrepancy between that horrible act and this rhyming description might send the same shiver of pleasurable incongruity up the spine that is much beloved in macabre tales.

By announcing that the speaker had only heard of Adonijah Gillet's death (lines 17–18), she implies that she actually saw the other bodies. John Sadler escaped "the dreadful slaughter" by fleeing (perhaps by boat or canoe) across the water. Eunice Allen was less fortunate. Her attempt to run away was foiled by her own petticoats, and the Indians caught and tomahawked her on the head. She probably survived; they left her on the ground "for dead" (line 26). Samuel Allen, a boy, was taken as a hostage to Canada.

Her initial audience would probably have appreciated Terry's listing of the dead before turning to the living. They also would have viewed the assault on a defenseless woman (trapped by her own petticoats, a detail that further emphasizes her gender) as an atrocity worthy of the additional space and provocative diction (the "awful creatures . . . catched [and] tommy hawked" her; lines 24–25) the poet devotes to it. Both colonists and Native Americans perpetrated deadly attacks on women and children in their frontier fights, but in this poem falling prisoner to the Indians was considered a fate so gruesome that it provokes the speaker's only emphatic remark (the "Oh, lack-a-day!" of line 28). Captives often faced a grueling trek through the roughest terrain at a pace calculated to outrun any pursuit. At worst, they could face torturous deaths, but survivors also could be ransomed by the British authorities in Canada. Children were sometimes adopted into the tribes, and a few adult survivors willingly chose to remain with their captors.

"THE BAT IS DUN, WITH WRINKLED WINGS" EMILY DICKINSON (published 1896)

This poem reveals the process by which a poet can examine nature. Although she begins by naming the creature, immediately she relies on her own perceptions, noting its color ("dun," a dull dark brown) and texture (its wings are wrinkled). Sometimes Dickinson's capitalization can seem haphazard, but the capital *W* could almost represent the wings on the page, and the sudden, almost shrill sound of the *i* in "wings" can suggest a rising inflection or other change in the speaker's voice as she considers the meaning of these appendages. The dash at the end of this line provides the best introduction to Dickinson's frequent use of unconventional punctuation. It could serve as a change in time—as if everything were being held in abeyance as she came in for a closer examination of the animal. It invites the reader to imagine the situation and the reactions the speaker (and perhaps even the reader) would have at such a moment. It may signal the pause required as she sought precisely the right word, or a pause in her voice of similar duration for dramatic effect. It also reveals her turning from objective description to a mental search for something with which to convey her overall impression.

Without its qualifying adjective, the simile she devises would disappoint because it relies on an abstraction instead of a concrete noun. In comparing the bat to a "fallow Article" (line 2), she may have been suggesting that it looked dead (thus reinforcing the earlier pun on dun/done); the term is typically applied to fields that are not cultivated for a season to allow for natural replenishment of the soil or to prevent a buildup of harmful insects such as might occur if the same crop is always planted in the same field. Dismissing the bat as a fallow Article suggests that she is nearly through with it; because it is dead, it lacks interest and is again relegated to those things that are not mentioned in polite society. Having introduced the subject of death, the poet toys with a euphemism for it, noting that "not a song pervade his Lips." This phrase serves as a transition back to examining the animal, which we see in motion for the first time. A discovered bat will typically show its teeth in a threat display, as this one may have done: the speaker's comparison of the bat to a singer reveals she is not afraid of it, and she returns to the objective, almost scientific tone with which she began the first stanza. She cannot hear any sound from it.

In the second stanza we see the bat extend its wings (beautifully described as a "small Umbrella quaintly halved" in line 5) and take flight. Dickinson preserves the transcendence of that moment by referring

one mystery to another: both the bat's wings and its path through the air are "alike inscrutable" (line 7). The same duality is apparent in her unidiomatic use of "elate" in the eighth line: it seems to either modify "philosopher," implying that the bat may be "elated" like a human theorist by its intellectual flights, which no one else can follow, or, as a transitive verb, it may imply that a philosopher would exalt as if the bat provided tangible physical evidence of another level of being. The latter interpretation seems to fit better with the third stanza.

Like the early New England theologians, the speaker is intensely interested in such relatively rare occurrences as finding a bat in the house because they may hint at the nature of God. She questions whether such a messenger is from Heaven or Hell (or some other "Firmament," line 9) and hedges her bet by merely referring to its origin as an "Astute Abode" in the next line. It does seem more likely a demonic rather than an angelic deputy, which leads the speaker to ponder the potential power of its Malignity, "Auspiciously withheld" (line 12). The dash with which the stanza ends may be an invitation for the reader to ponder the many metaphysical questions such speculations engender.

For the speaker, the fact that the bat has been so cleverly wrought merits praise for its Creator. Although the bat may seem a doubtful addition to life on earth, she is confident that the Creator's eccentricities are beneficent (lines 15–16). On a theological level, the argument is that although the ways of God (such as the reason for His creation of such repulsive animals) must remain a mystery, the very variety of life on earth argues for the divinity of the Creator.

"THE BATTLE HYMN OF THE REPUBLIC" JULIA WARD HOWE (1862) One way of dealing with the problem of meter is to develop new lyrics for a popular tune, as the poet did after hearing a group of soldiers singing "John Brown's Body." It was an immediate hit, for it not only insisted on the righteousness of the federal cause in the early days when the outcome of the American Civil War was still in doubt, but it even promised divine aid for those soldiers so clearly doing God's work.

From the very first phrase, the language is occasionally enlivened with intentionally biblical grammatical constructions and religious imagery. Virtually everyone in America had heard of the Second Coming of the Lord, but in this song he might as well appear in the uniform of a Union soldier. Unlike other well-known portrayals of Judgment Day, Christ is more concerned here with improving life by trampling the vintage where "the grapes of wrath are stored," the most famous phrase of the song. It seems appropriate for the Prince of Peace to prevent the fruits of anger from reaching the consumer, but then he also unleashes "the fateful lightning of His terrible swift sword." Like the millions of men eventually mobilized in the conflict, His truth is on the march. His day will join the march at the end of the second stanza, and even God will get in the act at the end of stanzas 3 through 5.

Perhaps because she visited the Union Army in the company of a minister, Howe evidently saw the conflict as a battle between the forces of light and darkness, imagery that was reinforced by the spectacle of the "watch fires of a hundred circling camps" and their sundry "dim and flaring lamps" by which she reads His righteous sentence. The same fiery gospel is also "writ in burnished rows of steel" in the third stanza; Christ urges them to treat the enemy as they treat those who condemned Him, pointing out the serpent crushed under His heel as an object lesson.

In the fourth stanza, the army's trumpets are linked with those announcing Judgment Day, with the important distinction that the latter will never sound retreat. Christ finally assumes His traditional role of judge, but in this song he is especially keen to judge those who do have not joined His march.

Only in the fifth stanza does the poet recall Christ as the Redeemer and His promise of transfiguration, but she recalls His model of sacrifice in asking "us" to "die to make men free." Notice how this antislavery message is almost tacked on at the end of the last stanza, soon to be followed by yet another interminable chorus of "Glory, glory, hallelujah," etc. It took even President Lincoln a couple more years to say that the war was about slavery, and public opinion among the song's original audience, the northerners who believed in the Union cause, was far from unanimous on this issue in 1861 when it was written.

As propaganda, the song succeeds in demonizing the enemy, in justifying the war as divinely sanctioned, and in calling on individuals to sacrifice themselves for its cause. It also commandeered the familiar language and images of the Christian faith to further its own ends.

"BEAT! BEAT! DRUMS!" Walt Whitman **(1861)** It would be difficult to overestimate the importance of musical instruments to the armies of the Civil War. Their most vital tactical role on the battlefield was the coordination of troop movements; despite the din of a major battle, drums and bugles formed the most reliable communications link by which officers could convey their simplest but most urgent commands (Attack! Retreat!) to far-flung units. Unlike hand-delivered written messages, which could travel no faster than a galloping horse, the drums could get an entire army moving at once.

Before, during, and after a battle, they were used to facilitate unit cohesion. Properly trained and motivated soldiers would fall in with the cadence of drums while marching, and their daily use to announce such rituals as reveille and formations helped everyone understand exactly what was expected of them at a certain time. During a battle, they could be used to signal a short cease-fire in order to negotiate with a hopelessly surrounded enemy. After a battle, a similar parley could facilitate each side's removal of its dead and wounded from the field.

Drums were also immensely valuable for recruiting purposes; the heart of every hot-blooded youth tended to beat faster in unconscious syncopation with their exciting rolls as the soldiers trooped past or an honor guard announced the arrival of a recruiter. Whitman heard the drums, and lent his words to the war effort.

From a historical perspective, the poem may demonstrate how quickly Walt Whitman realized that the Civil War would have a major impact on all aspects of American life. The sounds of war (and often, the war itself) would intrude "like a ruthless force" (line 2) on the churches, the colleges, and even the honeymoon suites (line 5). Even farming would be changed.

If the speaker of this poem had his way, the drums would be heard over the noise of traffic in the city, preventing inhabitants from sleeping and bringing commerce, entertainment and legal proceedings to a halt. They would not stop for negotiation, explanations, sentiment, or prayer, nor pause for the old to counsel the young or for the begging of mothers and children. The din would be so loud as to shake the supports ("trestles," line 20) beneath the coffins at funerals. This is as close as he comes in this poem to admitting that war must inevitably lead to death.

Although the speaker recognizes the cost of the war in terms of the suffering those closest to the soldiers must endure, its staggering economic costs and the threat it poses to the American social fabric even at the level of the nuclear family, he would have the "terrible" (line 21) drums and blaring bugles do their work.

"BECAUSE I COULD NOT STOP FOR DEATH" EMILY DICKINSON (1863)

The surprise of this poem lies in the stunning reversal of its portrayal of Death; few images are chillier than its popular caricature as a skeleton in a mysterious cowl with a scythe over his shoulder. Most people shudder at the thought of being "taken" by him; the verb suggests robbery. Death held no terror for the speaker in this poem, however. She evidently led a sheltered life of genteel civility rather like that of the reclusive EMILY DICKINSON, and death comes to her with a carriage (line 3) like a not-unwelcome suitor. Instead of "taking" her, Death kindly stopped, graciously allowing her to set the pace of their encounter.

The immortality which the speaker encounters in the carriage is not the lasting literary fame of the author; the dates are wrong, for one thing, and such a reading diminishes the universality of the poem's application. Note that immortality does not merit capitalization, which indicates that it is not personified as is Death. There are only two figures in the carriage.

In listening to such a speaker, three important questions spring to mind. What was the experience of death like for her? How did the conduct of her life enable her to accept death so magnanimously? Is there life after death? The entire poem is devoted to answering the first question, but it touches on the other two as well.

The speaker meets Death on such agreeable terms that she willingly put away the concerns of this world, her labor and her leisure, "for his civility" (line 8). The word *for* invigorates this phrase; it might be read as "as a reward for his civility" or "to make things pleasant for him," which suggests a reciprocal relationship. The speaker was a very willful woman, probably not the kind to be so swept away by a debonair suitor that she would give up her life without a backward glance. She was so centered that, as the title indicates, she could not give up her active life even as death approached. This interpretation suggests that she was a woman who accepted life on her own terms.

The carriage ride she shares with Death does more than follow the route of a funeral procession from her home (professional funeral parlors were still in the future), through the town and to the cemetery. It also carries her past several important places in the order in which they played a role in her life. Her childhood may not have been especially happy, if one listens closely to the third stanza. That children "strove" during recess in the schoolyard suggests strife as well as the earnest pursuit of living. The "ring" of line 10 recalls boxing or wrestling rings, or the social circle in which everyone must find a place. It also suggests the most popular children's circle game of Ring Around the Rosy; that the activity arose in response to the bubonic plague seems in keeping with the central theme of the poem. The medieval children's satirizing of the Black Death, turning it into a joyous opportunity for healthy socializing, was as unconventional as the speaker's thinking of death as a date in the present poem.

They also pass fields of "gazing" grain, an adjective hinting that the speaker's unconventional thinking may include a trace of pantheism. The image suggests that the speaker's recollections of her life have now passed into the fullness of late summer or even autumn, and the speaker has condensed her entire adult experience up to the time of her death into a single line. The line may also suggest how self-contained the speaker was; all the usual societal pressures meant no more to her than if she were conducting her life before grain instead of people. More conventionally, the line may imply that God is everywhere and sees everything. Alternatively, the grain might be viewed as the fruition of her lifetime of good work, not itself capable of sight but readily manifest for the gaze of any man or God.

The use of the setting sun as a euphemism for death (lines 12–13) suggests yet another view of the end of life as a beautiful thing. In keeping with the central conceit of the poem, in which Death is presented as a date, the speaker reveals what she wore. Her ensemble is delightfully ambiguous. The elegance of a gossamer gown might be viewed on a modern red carpet, or the phrase may refer to the light bedclothes designed to reduce the fevers of a deathbed patient while still maintaining her modesty. A tippet (line 16) was a wrap placed around a woman's shoulders for warmth while traveling. That her tippet was made of tulle (an exceedingly loosely-woven net of fabric, such as a wedding veil) suggests either that she was very comfortable with her gentleman caller or, now insensate, that she was indifferent to cold. The airy, liquid qualities of her flimsy attire unite her with the quivering and chill dews (line 14) outside the carriage. It is almost as though she was becoming cloaked by the nature to which corporal decay would return her corpse.

She viewed her final resting place as the house that seemed a swelling of the ground in the fifth stanza, with perhaps the tombstone serving as the cornice of this final dwelling. Her language cloaks even the grave with a comforting, familiar domesticity.

The assertion in the last stanza that her death occurred centuries before this rendition of it reveals that for her there was life after death. Eternity is so pleasant for her that the time passes quickly, and this exceedingly optimistic poem shows that her personality (the most important aspect of her individuality) has been kept intact. Even her intellect survived, as revealed in her surmising that the horses' heads were turned toward Eternity (lines 23–24).

"BEE! I'M EXPECTING YOU!" EMILY DICKINSON (1890) Of all EMILY DICKINSON's poems, this one furnishes the best reminder of the difference between a poem's speaker and its author. In form it most closely resembles a telegram because of its use of short ungrammatical phrases (a useful approach when the cost of sending your message is based on the number of words you use) and because the speaker announces that s/he has also sent a letter (lines 9–10).

Notice that she begins and ends the poem with an assertion of her desire to be reunited with her audience. Her tone is familiar and confidential (perhaps even conspiratorial), as she not only announces that she is expecting her correspondent to arrive, but that she and an unnamed "Somebody you know" (line 3) have been talking about the correspondent being overdue.

In the second stanza she conveys the local news, beginning with the item of most concern to her: the frogs "got home" the prior week. Line 6 is the best and most humorous of the poem because she takes a statement that is unexceptional in its usual context: like any returned vacationer, the frogs are "settled, and at work." The phrase accurately conveys a picture of the amphibians in their natural habitat. Then she moves on to items of particular interest to her correspondent: most of the birds (the traditional coworkers of the bees whenever the difficult subject of sex is to be broached by a parent) have returned. She saves the best news (from her correspondent's perspective) for the last; the clover is warm and thick (line 8).

Her closing ("Yours") could be dismissed as a mere formality were it not preceded by the heartfelt plea of "be with me" (line 11). Like a good comedienne, the poet has saved the punch line until the very end, when the message is signed by "Fly." Assuming that "Bee" and "Fly" are not pet names (as this poem demonstrates, Dickinson would probably have appreciated even such a weak albeit unavoidable pun) used by human correspondents, the poem suffers because the implied relationship between the two animals has little correlation with their behavior in nature. This disappoints because Dickinson was so adept at closely observing animals and accurately conveying their essence in her poems (for example, the "settled" frogs). Of course, in a fable the animals are supposed to be more like people (just as these insects correspond and develop personal relationships). In the hands of the true masters of the genre, however, the hybrid human/animals frequently reveal basic truths about both sides of their natures.

"BEES ARE BLACK, WITH GILT SUR-CINGLES" EMILY DICKINSON (1945)

This is EMILY DICKINSON's paean to the bumblebee, which is larger, louder, and more ostentatious than the honeybee with which it shares black and gold stripes. The key to understanding the poem lies in the speaker's use of "surcingles" (line 1). In modern times this arcane term refers to the girth straps around a horse's belly, normally only partially visible from the side when a saddle is in use; unfortunately, the fact that the bee's stripes cover the animal's back ruins the imagery suggested by this analogy. Instead, Dickinson may have used the word to designate the belt worn by the clergy of some churches to fasten the cassocks worn for church services. Such diction, although archaic, does not merely describe the insect more accurately and unforgettably; it introduces the central comparison of the poem and its theme. Comparing insects to clergy comments on both sides, and the challenge the poet set for herself was to discover how far she could meaningfully extend the analogy.

At first, referring to the bees as pirates seems a departure from the central comparison, but the "Buccaneers of Buzz" (line 2) is appropriate on the one side because the coloration of the insect and its flamboyance suggest the famous striped shirt and devil-may-care attitude so characteristic of pirates in illustrations. Applying the latter half of the phrase to the clergy captures the sonorous tones used by the best speakers among them in moments of rapture, although it also calls their morality into question by suggesting that some may use the sanctity of the pulpit to conceal their acquisitive natures. Both bees and prosperous clergy might "ride abroad in ostentation" (line 3). It is clear that bumblebees are hairy or fuzzy, but when applied to the clergy (or at least their messages), the term *buzz* may suggest that they use insider terminology and knowledge. The term *fuzz* (line 4) implies that they may sometimes obscure or blur their message (perhaps to mystify their followers and thus maintain the necessity of their jobs as interpreters of divine secrets, since the speaker asserts that they subsist on fuzz).

The comparison becomes much more clear when the poet uses religious terms in the second stanza. In Puritan theology, God "ordained" that a few divinely selected people would enter heaven, while theologians of other sects argued that the promise of heaven was "contingent" upon one's behavior in this life. On a sartorial level, "fuzz ordained" suggests that God (or perhaps only the poet) may have a low overall opinion of the human race, but a relatively few people have been elected (an important term for the Puritans) to serve Him. Like bees that are genetically programmed to do the things they do, those chosen to receive God's grace must behave in accordance with that high calling. Whereas the poet seemed to be having fun at the clergy's expense in the first stanza, in this one she begins to celebrate them.

Their rich colors and the fact that they make their nests underground may have prompted Dickinson to call bumblebees the "Marrows of the Hill" (line 6), but applying the phrase to the clergy underscores their necessity; it places them at the core of the community as well as of the church (just as marrow is found in the center of bones). On both sides of the comparison, the subjects of the poem create "Jugs" (line 7) that not even "a Universe's fracture" could jar or spill. On one hand, this celebrates the seeming single-mindedness with which bees act in accordance with their instincts. On the other, the terminology of the "fracture" recalls that of Judgment Day, when Christ returns to earth and the universe as we know it ceases to exist. The truly faithful will remain sublimely confident in their "Jugs," their repositories of faith, even in those otherwise horrendous circumstances.

"BEFORE I GOT MY EYE PUT OUT" EMILY DICKINSON (1951)

This poem by EMILY DICKINSON reads like a dramatization of Mark 8:36 (a variation of the same statement was recorded in Luke 9:25): "For what shall it profit a man, if he shall gain the whole world, and lose his soul?" The speaker had an eye put out (line 1) either literally or figuratively (perhaps he turned a blind eye to the splendor of this world after religion taught him its limitations). Prior to that time he was as fond of seeing (and of living) as other creatures with eyes that "know no other way" (line 3; this stanza implies that his spiritual awakening was of such magnitude that his former life seems bestial in comparison).

If promised the sky, he would answer that it would split his heart because of how large that would make him. This answer is delightfully ambiguous. It not only remains unclear whether he would accept such a gift or not, it introduces a new riddle: does the phrase "splitting my heart" convey an expression of his gratitude, does it also suggest that he might abandon his spirituality for such a prize, or does it imply that it would kill him? Similar possibilities surround the meaning of "for the size of me" (line 8); it might be another expression of his happiness, or it could reveal his greed.

In the third stanza he contemplates ownership not just of the sky but also of the meadows, mountains, all the forests, the "Stintless" stars (so indicated because their lights always stay on), and as much of noon as he could "take between (his) finite eyes" (line 13). This is another troubling phrase because like a split heart, a blow between the eyes can be deadly, an interpretation furthered by the emphasis placed on the "finite" aspect of those organs. They are not only limited in their ocular power but also by time, since they will perish when the speaker dies. He later offers a solution of this aspect of the riddle when he states that the news of his restored sight alone would be enough to strike him dead (line 17).

A third ambiguity arises from the notion of possession. Is he somehow being promised a quitclaim deed to all that he sees, or is sight alone a type of possession? The fourth stanza clarifies this point. He would also have possession of "the motions of the dipping birds" (certain members of the swallow family spring to mind since they take occasional drinks from a pond while catching flying insects with high speed turns just above the water's surface) and that moment when the morning sun turns the road amber. They would be his "to look at when he liked" (line 16).

In the final stanza, he expresses a preference for having just his soul on the window pane "where other Creatures put their eyes" (line 20). Calling them "Incautious" of the sun reminds us that prolonged staring at its surface can destroy vision, but it also suggests a condemnation of sight because it can lead to desire. Up to this point the reader has probably been admiring the speaker because of his evident acceptance of his misfortune in losing his sight, but the final stanza

introduces the ultimate irony of the poem by directing our attention back to the opening line. When the speaker said "I got my eye put out," was he merely stating his affliction or was he describing a willful act in accordance with Matthew 5:29: "if thy right eye offend thee, pluck it out, and cast it from thee." Such an extreme mortification of the flesh seems especially gruesome.

"BEFORE THE BIRTH OF ONE OF HER CHILDREN" Anne Bradstreet (1678) The chief surprise of this poem is that it is addressed to Anne Bradstreet's husband and not the child of the title. Contemplating the possibility that she would not survive the coming ordeal of childbirth led her to pen her farewell to her husband.

Bradstreet began the poem by reminding him that all things must end and that all joys have an undercurrent of sorrow. Their marriage was evidently an exceedingly happy one, for in contemplating her death, she refers to their strong ties and dear and sweet friendship (line 3).

Because both her husband and her father had been involved in governing their colony, one of the potentially rich veins of Bradstreet's diction arose from her exposure to court matters. She combines this with a biblical reference in the fifth line; the irrevocable 'sentence past' is the divine punishment meted out to Adam and Eve. Their original sin of eating the forbidden fruit of knowledge not only led to their expulsion from paradise, but to their descendents being forced to endure physical labor, painful childbirths and, inevitably, death. Although Bradstreet and her husband are ignorant about how soon she will die and he will lose his friend, she hopes that she will still seem his, although she has passed.

Most 17th-century Americans lived less than 40 years, but she notes that her age is less than half the three score and 10 (this equals 70) years promised in the Bible (line 13). She prays that God will grant all of nature's favors to him and his remaining family, and pleads that her husband should forget her many faults. Note the humility with which she phrases her next request; she does not state her own claim to virtue, but disingenuously phrases it conditionally: "if any worth or virtue were in me" (line 17). She asks him to keep this part of her memory fresh even after he no longer grieves for the loss of one who for so long lay in his arms.

It is curious that in contemplating her husband's remarriage she refers to it as a virtual certainty ("When thy loss shall be repaid with gains;" line 21) instead of conditionally, which she might easily have done by replacing "when" with "if." If her husband finds this poem after her death, he need have no qualms about joining another union. She does instruct him to look after their children, her "dear remains" (line 22), and to protect them from possible injury at the hands of their stepmother. Having settled the practical problems attendant upon her death, she is free to engage in sentimentally envisioning his sad sighs if he reads these last words. She even orchestrates the stage gesture of having him kiss the paper upon which this last farewell is written, and only then permits the free flow of her own salt tears.

"BEGINNING MY STUDIES" WALT WHITMAN (1865)

Poets are typically more aware of their sensations and emotions, or at least the compulsion to write, than other people. In this poem, WALT WHITMAN implies that he did not begin his studies by focusing on the work of other poets, but by turning directly to nature. His pleasure in his own consciousness, form, movement, and even simple animals was so great that he did not wish to progress beyond the first step, but to "loiter all the time to sing it in ecstatic songs" (line 6).

All this suggests that his poetry came as naturally to him as the songs come to a bird, and despite the process of continually representing his daily life and the communal experience of the American people in his poems, he rarely admits reading a book or admiring another poet in them. The sophistication of his diction in the poems that followed this one reveals his intense devotion to reading, however.

"BEHIND ME DIPS ETERNITY" EMILY DICKINSON (published 1951)

EMILY DICKINSON's poem emphasizes the limits of this life and the miracle it represents by comparing its brevity to the few moments before dawn and its scope to the narrow limits of an ocean wave with precipitous drops on both sides. The lifespan of the speaker is the highest feature of this seascape, offering a perspective so high that the plunge into immortality can be seen to the west. Eternity, a seemingly bottomless abyss, yawns behind the speaker to the east. If death is "the Drift of Eastern Gray" dissolving into dawn (lines 4–5), then Immortality would be sun-drenched, and Eternity would be dropping into a featureless dark. Lest this make our present life seem too grand a prominence, the speaker points out that the West has not yet begun (line 6).

Although she lacks the power to see that far, she has been told (by "they" [line 7], a group presumably including religious authorities, the authors of the Bible and others) that the kingdoms after death are ruled by perfect, unceasing monarchy. The ruling prince seems the most striking oddity of this new land; the mysteries or legends surrounding Him lead to his being called the "Son of None" (line 9; this probably refers to the tradition of the Immaculate Conception of Jesus; in keeping with the patriarchal prejudices of the authorities on such matters, this moniker disregards the rather important role of His mother). Since the Son is part of God, the speaker seems to have reasoned, that makes Him His own father (lines 9–10) as well as His own dynasty. In a process unlike human reproduction, He "Himself diversify" (line 11) in "Duplicate divine" (line 12; these lines recall that the Trinity of God, Jesus and the Holy Spirit are essentially one).

Surrounded by such limitless miracles, this life seems as ephemeral as a "Crescent in the Sea" (an image suggesting a reflection of the moon, line 15). Midnight reigns to the North and South of Her (a pronoun referring to the speaker's soul, presumably, as well as to the Crescent), and a "Maelstrom in the Sky" (line 18), a dangerous cloud or water swirl, portends the destruction of even this illusion.

"BEHOLD THIS SWARTHY FACE" WALT WHITMAN (1860)

Before mainstream America developed its phobia about homosexuality in the 20th century, it was common for straight men to be much more open in publicly expressing their fondness for each other than would later be the case. Although laws against "unnatural acts" (among which kissing had never been categorized) carried stiff penalties in most states, the chances of actually meeting an avowed homosexual were considered so remote as to be practically nonexistent for most people. Thus the initial audience for this poem would probably have been more shocked by the speaker's inference that he was of African descent and hence that the kiss might have been biracial than at the possibility of its being homoerotic.

WALT WHITMAN skillfully used some of the language then current to designate people of color (especially the word *swarthy* and the description of his hair as unclipped white "wool" in the first two lines) to identify the speaker as probably black. Although beards were more common among white Americans, they were not exclusively so. Of course, he could have acquired "brown hands" (line 3) as a consequence of being a sailor or from other outdoor pursuits, but in the racially charged environment of some American communities on the eve of the Civil War, properly identifying (or at least thinking that you had identified) the race of the person you were encountering could be of paramount importance. The dominant American culture of the time insisted that all of the stereotypical black features were "without charm" (line 3), hence the speaker is surprised that someone from Manhattan would kiss him "with robust love" (line 4).

That they could openly kiss on the street or on a ship's deck (line 6) as a "salute of American comrades" (line 6) suggests that the custom may have been as socially acceptable as the similar same-sex greeting is among the women of modern France, and the fact that their lips touched may not have raised any eyebrows at the time. All could indeed seem "natural and nonchalant" (line 7).

A 21st-century audience is more likely to react to the poem's homosexual overtones than its racial implications. Although mainstream American culture still finds such overt expressions of same-sex affection as a public kiss to be repugnant, readers of poetry are more likely to mark the ennobling quality of love without feeling threatened.

"THE BERG" HERMAN MELVILLE (1888) Although HERMAN MELVILLE subtitled the poem "A Dream," a similar scenario became all too real on the night of

April 14, 1912, when the *Titanic,* a gigantic transatlantic passenger ship, sank after colliding with an iceberg. Here, the luckless vessel is a warship, and although a certain amount of hubris played a large role in each disaster, in the poem the vessel is deliberately steered into the hazard "as if by madness" (line 4). Although the "infatuate" (that is, inspired by a foolish love to the point of madness, line 5, the captain or pilot may have been so infatuated with modern technology that he thought he could power his way through the iceberg) ship went down, the collision caused only tons of ice cubes to fall on the deck but no other movement besides that of the sinking ship.

The second stanza consists of a damage assessment report on the berg. None of its ridges, spurs (a lateral ridge projecting from the side of a mountain [or mountainous iceberg]), shafts, prisms over glass-green gorges (icebergs come in a variety of colors depending on how recently they calved from a glacier, whether or not they contain mineral sediments and dirt rubbed from a distant valley floor, and the ambient light) were damaged. The berg showed no additional cracks in its ice (that is, no "lace of traceries," line 13), and no ice pendants in its hidden valleys and tunnels (the grottoes and mines of line 14) were jarred. Neither the distant gulls nor the closer fowls felt the collision, and the very fragile "jack-straw needle ice" (probably thin icicles) remained firmly attached to the ceilings of its caves. Even the towers and giant blocks seemingly on the verge of tumbling by their own weight remained stationary. The seals ("dozing sleek on sliddery edges," a very nice description in line 24) were unaffected even though the overthrown ship went down.

In the last stanza the speaker marvels at the berg's emotional indifference to the fate of the ship and its own destiny ("adrift dissolving, bound for death," line 31). Although the iceberg is only a lumpish, lumbering, loitering lubbard (oaf), impingers (encroachers) lament their action and sink, "sounding thy precipice below" (finding out how deep the water is beneath it; line 35). Not even the slimy slug was stirred as it sprawled on the dead indifference of the iceberg's walls (the iceberg slug may be part of the poet's dream imagery, but ice worms [maximum length of approximately one inch] inhabit many Alaskan glaciers). An alternative reading would attempt to understand the unnamed antecedent (if it is not the "berg" of line 28) of the antiquated possessive pronoun *thy* (line 37) as either nature or at least the ocean. Even though the massive ship was steered directly into the iceberg to demonstrate the awesome impact man's ingenuity could have on nature, not even the simplest slimy slug on the submerged canyon walls was stirred by its passing.

"A BIRTHDAY SONG FOR KING'S BIRTHDAY, JUNE 4, 1777" JONATHAN ODELL (1777)

The institution of the monarch was (and remains) an important source of national identity for the people of the United Kingdom. Prior to the American Revolution, it was celebrated on both sides of the Atlantic with fireworks, cannon fire, speeches, toasts, and flags. From 1760 to 1820, the reigning monarch was George III (born in 1738).

JONATHAN ODELL's poem tries to drum up support for the Loyalist cause by contrasting the freedom, peace, prosperity, and pride enjoyed when British America was united by its joyful chants of "God Save the King" with the troubling times of the Revolution. Nothing could check the growth of the people while they shared that chant, and had they continued upholding the same honor and truth, they would have been blessed beyond measure.

Now that rebellion has "lifted her head" (line 17), loyalty, honor and truth have also fled. The speaker feels s/he is in the minority now that the deluded multitude flies to a cause built on a lie (line 22). The "lie" is probably either that the king intended to enslave the colonists, or that ultimate victory over the strongest military power on earth is possible. He is confident that although "faction by falsehood" can hold loyalty a prisoner for a time, Britain is roused and the rebellion is failing (line 27; in fact, the British army had nearly won the war in the Battle of Brooklyn in August of 1776. Despite the surprises of Princeton and Trenton near the end of that year, on June 4, 1777, the British were building up for the push that enabled them to capture the congressional city of Philadelphia on September 26, 1777). Military conquest, the speaker asserts, will restore the colonies to Britain and release the captive (Loyalty, identified in line 26) from its chain.

"A BIVOUAC ON A MOUNTAIN SIDE" WALT WHITMAN (1865)

In trying to embrace all of the soldiers' experience of the Civil War, WALT WHITMAN was not insensible to the fact that their service would not only expose them to the horrors of bloody combat and its aftermath, but also to areas of the country of such surpassing beauty that they could never have dreamed of them had they stayed at home.

A bivouac is an encampment so temporary that it sometimes involves sleeping under the stars instead of setting up tents. On this night the speaker, evidently attached to an army on the march, finds himself settling down for the night on a delightful mountainside from which he can see the barns and summer orchards of a fertile valley. The sight must have reminded many of the soldiers of the comforts of home and the promise of their postmilitary careers, but the speaker merely views the sight without connecting it to any other aspect of his life.

For all its surpassing beauty, the mountain may itself carry reminders of the harshness of their present service. By now they would be very familiar with the effort it took to climb up its broken terraces and past its clinging cedars, and they would be reassured by the knowledge that the numerous campfires above and beyond them support their fellow soldiers.

There is something unsettling in the speaker's description of the "shadowy forms of men and horses, looming, large-sized, [and] flickering" (line 6) as they pass in front of the fires, but the speaker's attention is absorbed by the sky. His objectivity is striking; although the stars are unquestionably beautiful, it is their isolation ("far, far out of reach") and seeming immortality ("the eternal stars") that he notes. Perhaps the speaker's emotional distance (he never reveals what, if anything, he feels about these scenes) is symptomatic of the trauma attendant upon the harsh realities of his existence.

"BONNY BARBARA ALLEN" ANONYMOUS (19th century)

In a small community, it may be difficult for nontraditional people to live according to their own lights. Thus it happened that although Barbara Allen chose to live with another maiden for whatever reason, a young man (William) on his deathbed sent her his servant with flowers in May, arguably the best month for young love.

Perhaps skeptical about his condition, she went to his bedside and saw that he was not faking his illness. Although he stretched his pale hand to her (line 17), she "hopped and skipped" away (note the fun with which the unknown author juxtaposed his weakness and her vitality).

She "won't have him" (that is, accept him as a suitor, line 20) because he drank a toast to all the ladies except her. He turned his face toward the wall (perhaps so she could not see how much this pained him) and said he would not see her again.

No sooner was she on her way home than she heard the church bells ringing (as they traditionally do to mark the passing of a member of their congregation). For some reason his corpse was being transported already, and she asked to see it. Taking responsibility for his death (she might have saved him if she "had done [her] duty;" line 36), she tells her mother she will die the next day to atone for it. And she did.

Her mother died (on Easter Sunday, no less) for the love of them, and although William was buried in one graveyard and Barbara Allen in another, the rose and briar that grew from their graves reached enormous heights and finally entwined in the church steeple, with his rose clinging to her briar.

As a folk song, a principal attraction of this story is its accessibility. Each of the main characters is one-dimensional and their maudlin deaths transpire because they did not take each other's love seriously. Although decency demands the separation of their graves, nature (that is, a nature that acts as if in sympathy with the human action of a story or sentiments in a poem) enables them to transcend their deaths, at least symbolically. Each plant shares a key trait with the person whose grave nourished it: the briar's thorns tend to keep people at a distance as Barbara Allen was wont to do, while William's grave continues to produce flowers reminiscent of those he sent to his love during his life.

BRADSTREET, ANNE (c. 1612–1672) In the 21st century, Bradstreet is honored as the author of the first book of poetry by a British colonist, and

her work frequently informs historical studies of Puritanism and the status of women in early America. Perhaps the best short introduction to her life is the letter she wrote, "To My Dear Children," in the year of her death. She was born into a life of privilege in Northampton, England, as the daughter of Thomas Dudley, a law clerk who soon became the steward on the Earl of Lincoln's estate. In 1634, her father became the first elected governor of the Massachusetts Bay Colony. Although like most girls of her time she could not attend school, her father provided her with tutors, and she took great comfort in reading the Scriptures and joy in creating her poems.

At 16, Anne married her father's assistant, the Cambridge-educated Simon Bradstreet, and in 1630 she joined husband and father on the *Arabella* for their pilgrimage to America. Emigration was necessary if they were to live in accordance with their religious beliefs, which they considered a more direct, purified connection with God than the English king Charles I was willing to allow. Upon their arrival they discovered, in Bradstreet's words, "a new world and new manners, at which my heart rose." In place of the elaborate church architecture and elegant manor houses to which she had become accustomed, she suddenly found herself in circumstances where basic survival was an issue and starvation a real possibility for most of the less well-connected colonists. In 1633 she gave birth to her first child, and their marriage was blessed with seven additional children, with the last one being born in 1648. In the meantime, her extended family had moved to Ipswich, Massachusetts, in 1635 and to Andover in 1645.

In the letter to her children cited above, she records having wavered in her faith at various times in her life, but God graciously smote her or her children with illness or material reverses (including the burning of their house in 1666) to keep her focused on the state of her soul. Eventually she found her heart enlarged in thankfulness to Him.

In 1650 her brother-in-law secretly had her poetry printed in London under the title *The Tenth Muse Lately Sprung Up in America*. Her reaction to this surprise can be read in "The Author to Her Book"; its appearance without her consent initially brought to mind a kidnapping, and she especially regretted not being able to proofread the printer's copy before it was published. Like a good sister, she pardoned the transgressor, however, and like a good mother, she accepted it as the natural offspring of her mind despite its faults. The poem appeared in her second, posthumously published (1678), corrected and expanded version of *The Tenth Muse*. The book now bore the title of *Several Poems Compiled with great variety of Wit and Learning, full of Delight . . . by a Gentlewoman in New England*.

Although "The Prologue" (1650) initially appears wholly deferential to male dominance, the poem can be viewed as an assertion of 17th-century feminism. Bradstreet anticipated criticism of her book as the mere product of a woman's mind that did not deserve the exalted title of poetry because of her emphasis on domestic matters instead of the noble subjects preferred by the aesthetics then in vogue. She effectively disarms such criticism by arguing that her work is so far below the highest standards that it should probably be read (and valued) as an entirely different kind of poetry: that written by women. That she would create such a double standard to benefit her gender is a remarkable adaptation, and the bulk of her work after the publication of *The Tenth Muse* would forestall criticism suggesting that her excellence in verse indicated neglect of the domestic duties (a more pernicious double standard). Such poems as "A Letter to Her Husband, Absent upon Public Employment" and "Before the birth of One of Her Children" demonstrate her devotion to her spouse. "In Reference to Her Children, 23 June 1659" reveals her obvious pride in and care for her offspring.

In her early poems, Bradstreet tended to deal intellectually with the problems of the human condition. In "The Flesh and the Spirit," she imagines a dialogue in which two sisters debate the relative merits of each source of identity. The spirit's victory is a foregone conclusion given the parameters of the debate. "Contemplations" presents a Puritan soul bringing all her faculties to bear in appreciation of nature. She is grateful for the insights that her education, science, and religion provide her, but recognizes that lasting honor, wealth, and safety are possible only in heaven. Such poems reveal that her faith had adequately prepared her to deal with loss as an abstract idea, but a slowly unfolding series of personal crises would put it to a real test.

"To the Memory of My Dear and Ever Honored Father, Thomas Dudley, Esq . . ." and "An Epitaph on My Dear and Ever-Honored Mother" show that Bradstreet was also a dutiful daughter. Each presents an idealized portrait of a Puritan of their respective genders. Her father was a four-time governor of the colony and gave unsparingly of his time and wealth to insure its success. Notwithstanding his personal modesty in attire as well as manner, he could unleash terror on those who did not share his beliefs, but his daughter remained grateful for all that he had given her. In her epitaph for her mother, Bradstreet portrays a society matron who lives a public life beyond reproach while privately filling her home with love, wifely obedience, and charity. She also kept up the discipline of her servants, preventing their lapses into immorality, and instructed her children on the proper moral and religious principles. Despite the social perks of being the governor's wife, she lived with the consciousness that her death was coming, and her soul would be ultimately judged by Jesus.

The Puritans typically believed that God took an active role in human life and an interest in each individual's destiny. That raises questions about why man must suffer, and the Puritan answer is evident in Bradstreet's reaction in "Here Follows Some Verses upon the Burning of Our House." The catastrophe reminded her to be even more grateful for everything that survived the fire, since everything really belongs to God. The loss reminded her not to value the possessions of this world but to stay focused on heaven. Nor was her health to be taken for granted. Although she prayed to God for relief in "For Deliverance from a Fever," she wondered if her affliction might have indicated divine displeasure. Crying out for Jesus saved her, and she was grateful for her recovery and for the chastisement that helped her focus on the condition of her soul. The deaths of her grandchildren in earliest childhood were equally troubling, but she tends to place the blame for her own suffering on herself. In such poems as "In Memory of . . . Grandchild Anne Bradstreet" and "In Memory of Elizabeth Bradstreet," she criticizes herself for embracing such love on this earth as she felt for them instead of looking forward to their reunion in heaven. Her own decrepitude with age probably informed "As WEARY PILGRIM;" the eponymous speaker in that poem almost welcomes his declining physical powers since his body is now less able to tempt him to sin.

Until her death on September 16, 1672, Bradstreet had continued writing poetry, raising her children, and supporting her husband's political ambitions, which culminated, after her death, in his being elected governor in 1679.

The Harvard University Library holds a signed ("A. B.") manuscript of Bradstreet's *Meditations Divine and Moral* dedicated to her son on March 20, 1664, which includes the poem "As Weary Pilgrim" (Dated August 31, 1669). Harvard also has Simon Bradstreet's transcript of her manuscript book "To My Dear Children" with poems and diary entries from 1656 to 1666.

BIBLIOGRAPHY

Bradstreet, Anne. *The Complete Works of Anne Bradstreet,* edited by Joseph R. McElrath, Jr. and Allan P. Robb. Boston: Twayne Publishers, 1981.

———. *A Woman's Inner World: Selected Poetry and Prose of Anne Bradstreet,* edited by Adelaide P. Amore. Lanham, Md.: University Press of America, 1982.

Craig, Raymond A. *A Concordance to the Complete Works of Anne Bradstreet.* Lewiston, N.Y.: Edwin Mellen Press, 2000.

Gordon, Charlotte. *Mistress Bradstreet: The Untold Life of America's First Poet.* New York: Little, Brown, 2005.

White, Elizabeth Wade. *Anne Bradstreet: The Tenth Muse.* New York: Oxford University Press, 1971.

"BRAHMA" RALPH WALDO EMERSON **(1857)** A central figure in Hindu theology, Brahma is honored as the creator of the universe and one of the ruling triad of three gods who create, preserve, or destroy everything. As the speaker in RALPH WALDO EMERSON's short poem, Brahma revels in his indifference to the seemingly momentous choices made by his creation because he knows that whatever happens he eventually will be called on to recreate the universe anew. Hence a murderer (the "red slayer" of the first line) may think he slays and the slain may think he is slain (but they have

little choice but to perform their roles and then retire. When the Brahma has slept through a *kalpa,* a single night's sleep for him, during which the beings he created and their descendants act in accordance with the properties he gave to each, or that they inherited from their, in some cases very distant, ancestors, depending upon where their lives happen to fall within a particular *kalpa.* Then Brahma will awaken, destroy their universe, and create a new one). Brahma has the choice of subtly editing the next cycle, keeping some things and passing on others, before again setting the whole thing in motion (line 4).

It is a fatalistic philosophy insofar as Brahma is concerned. He has command over distance, can see in sunshine and shade, and can even make vanished gods reappear, if he desires, but his indifference to shame and fame (line 8) renders him indifferent to mere human appeals for his aid (indeed, he sleeps through what we would consider the active part of each creation).

He states that those (people and other gods) "reckon ill" (line 9) who leave him out of their plans (his point may be that since everything eventually will be destroyed [or "recycled"], everything created by any god or mortal other than himself is ultimately simply vanity). He takes credit for the novel turns of each creation cycle ("when they fly, I am the wings;" line 10). Like many Hindu gods, his nature contains opposites, thus he can also be the doubter and the doubt. As "the hymn the Brahmin sings" (line 12), he can have a benign influence on human society if one considers those Brahmins who devote themselves to the rituals (and moral prerogatives) of their faith.

Brahma's abode (for which gods pine in line 13) is called the Brahmaloka, representing the highest plain of the heavens. Of the beings Brahma created to help him with creation, the most important to man are the Saptarishi, the sacred seven of line 14 who were the patriarchs of the Vedic religion (based on the Vedas, Hindu sacred texts). Hindu theology has sometimes viewed Brahma, Vishnu or Shiva as separate gods and at other times facets of the one god, Brahma. In the last two lines, Brahma recommends that the internal audience (presumably a lesser god or man) find him (Brahma himself) and turn his back on heaven, but modern Hindus are more likely to worship Vishnu (the god, or aspect of Brahma as the one god, who takes an active role in preservation) or Shiva (the god of destruction [who destroys evil and makes creation possible] or the aspect of Brahma that is devoted to that end).

"THE BRAIN IS WIDER THAN THE SKY" EMILY DICKINSON (1896)

This poem begins with fanciful comparisons and culminates in a metaphysical mystery. The first two stanzas start by asserting that the brain is superior in precisely those aspects by which the largest natural phenomena normally discernable to the human senses (the sky and the ocean) are most notable, their width and depth, respectively. Their first lines also establish either an ecstatic (how grand!) or humorous (since their claims seem rather preposterous) tone.

The second line of each stanza introduces an extranatural element and the seemingly humorous absurdity of an impossible task. The Brain (whose?) cannot be placed side by side with the Sky, the sea cannot be held, and God cannot be lifted or weighed. That is, unless the exercise is performed mentally; the ease with which the mind can perform the suggested tasks adds to the humor as well as the grandeur of EMILY DICKINSON's poem's conceits. Each comparison conveys hilarious or awe-inspiring imagery depending on whether you visualize them physically and literally or symbolically and figuratively.

Each stanza's third and fourth lines present an answer to its metaphysical conundrum with delightful ambiguity. The sky is so vast as to easily contain a human brain (and even the internal audience of the poem, the "You" of line 4 thrown into the balance as an additional humorous element), but the brain can also contain all that is knowable about the sky. The sea could easily absorb a brain and as easily be comprehended by it. In each instance, the answer depends on whether the physical dimensions of the two things are being compared, or the ability to comprehend them. The human intellect may or may not function in the same way as God, a question the speaker leaves open with a conditional phrase: "if they do" (line 11). Even at best, however, the human mind seems capable of emitting only a syllable compared to God's "Sound" (line 12). While a syllable is a sound that seems perfectly discernable and discrete to the human intellect, "sound" contains so many physical and metaphysical dimensions that the best physicists, theologians, and philosophers will never fully comprehend it.

"BROADWAY" WALT WHITMAN (1888)

This poem reads as though the speaker was trying to discover the most appropriate metaphor to describe Broadway, which, as the center of the theater district, is one of New York City's busiest streets, day or night. It is a good poem with which to begin studying WALT WHITMAN's art because his characteristic juxtaposition of opposites is used for more than the creation of lists; with the aid of brilliant transitions, it serves as the unifying principle of the poem.

After establishing the scene with an overview from such a height (or at least intellectual distance) that individuals seem lost in the sea (or at least tides) of humanity, the speaker imagines the passions, gains, and losses that swim in it. He describes its mixtures of evil, bliss, and sorrow as "whirls" (line 3), a term that maintains the aquatic comparison at the same time that it begins focusing on the visual aspects of the street scene as well as its commotion. Note the pleasing ambiguity of his verb usage: the whirls "stem" the street (line 3); in some ways they stop it, but in other ways they feed it just as the various branches of a river serve as its stems.

Whitman calls the questioning glances of the passersby "glints" of love (line 4), a sparkling term that brings to mind the sunlight reflecting off waves and a similar reflection off glass or other polished architectural features. After a short consideration of what the glances imply (another list of contrary items), the poet shifts his focus to some of the architectural aspects of the scene. These serve as both the portal (the entrance to a venue) and the entire arena (line 6).

Prior to the advent of asphalt roads, rocks sometimes were quarried, cut into slabs and placed in the road as "flagstones" (line 7). The reader is invited to follow the speaker's view from these paving stones, over the curb and toward the top of the huge hotels (lines 8 and 9). The weakest part of the poem mentions the inimitable tales these architectural features might tell if they could, a commonplace saying. Mercifully, the speaker's glance returns to the sidewalk, where the feet can be viewed in a variety of gaits. They remind him of the "parti-colored" world (line 10), a description that conveys the variety of its hues as well as its festive nature.

Throughout the poem, Whitman's ambiguous diction shifts through colorful possibilities like a kaleidoscope, effectively capturing the vitality of the street. This is especially evident in the last line. Referring to Broadway as "visored" paradoxically implies that it has a face (which is what a helmet's visor protects), but that it is screened or shielded. It may be "unspeakable" in the sense of being so vast and so constantly changing as to be beyond human powers of description, but the term also designated those things 19th-century America considered so perverse that the very words were banned from polite company. It is both a "show" (whose chief function is entertainment) and a "lesson" (whose chief purpose is education). The nature of that lesson depends on what the reader brings to Broadway. It could be a warning against all the negative things the speaker enumerated throughout the poem, or it could be an invitation to experience its vitality for yourself.

BROOKS, MARIA GOWEN (c. 1795–1845)
Born Mary Abigail Gowen in Medford, Massachusetts, the future poet's search for identity and security can be seen in the many name changes she adopted in her relatively short life and in the confusion surrounding the year of her birth (which might have been 1794). She went by the name of Abigail until her father died when she was 13, leaving her without funds but in the care of a guardian (John Brooks, widowed when Maria Gowen's sister died) to whom she was quickly betrothed despite his advanced age.

The married couple was soon in financial straits, but she began publishing anonymous poems. Perhaps in some way hoping to remain as mysterious as the romantic heroes then in vogue, in lieu of her name her first book (*Judith, Esther and Other Poems*, 1820) identified the author only as "A Lover of Fine Arts." She had changed her name to Maria Abigail Brooks, and eventually shortened this to the name Maria Brooks. After her husband's death in 1823, she lived with her

uncle in Cuba and soon inherited his property. This enabled her to move to Hanover, New Hampshire, and to travel in Europe. Here she met Robert Southey, the famous romantic poet already serving as the poet laureate of Great Britain. In his house she finished her most famous work, ZOPHIEL (1833), which benefited from his editing and his connections with London printers. He also provided her with yet another pseudonym, Maria del Occidente, under which name the poem appeared. In 1843 she wrote *Idomen, or the Vale of Yamuri* (again as Maria del Occidente), and followed this with an "Ode to the Departed" the next year. She had returned to Cuba by this time, where she died of tropical fever in Matanzas on November 11, 1845. Her frequent movements and the frequent financial reversals of her youth meant that her family homes have not been preserved for the sake of their connections with her, and her poetry is barely remembered in the 21st century.

In addition to *Zophiel,* a weirdly visionary fantasy, Brooks is represented in this volume by the "SONG OF EGLA." The latter is a woman's lament that her lover is too slow in returning to her. The New York Public Library holds a small collection of the poet's correspondence and a corrected manuscript of *Zophiel.*

BIBLIOGRAPHY
Granniss, Ruth Shepard. *An American Friend of Southey.* New York: De Vinne Press, 1913.
Low, Dennis. *The Literary Protégées of the Lake Poets.* Burlington, Vt.: Ashgate Publishing, 2006.

"BROWN OF OSSAWATOMIE" JOHN GREENLEAF WHITTIER (1859)
John Brown was a militant abolitionist who advocated, successfully solicited funds for, and tried to lead a slave uprising in Harper's Ferry, Virginia, until his capture on October 18, 1859. He was quickly tried, and his hanging on December 2, 1859, drew immense interest in both the northern and southern states. Unfortunately, JOHN GREENLEAF WHITTIER unwittingly relied on a falsified newspaper account for the central incident of his poem. Although the kissed baby was a fabrication, the sentiments expressed in the poem illustrate the strength of the lingering hope for a peaceful reconciliation between the two regions.

That Whittier was trying to present a balanced view is evident in his title. Referring to the eponymous character by only his last name indicates considerable emotional distance between the speaker and the subject, and calling him "Brown of Ossawatomie" identifies him as the executioner of five men as a reprisal for attacks on antislavery towns in a Kansas uprising in 1856.

The use of the antiquated verb form "spake" instead of "spoke" in the first line hints at admiration for Brown, however. That it is almost biblical captures something of his character, for he thought he had been chosen by God to end slavery in America, and it also tends to raise him to the level of an Old Testament prophet. His refusal to let a priest paid by slaveholders help him prepare for his imminent death (line 2) not only demonstrates his irascibility but also his courage in facing his execution without benefit of clergy. The sensitivity with which our literary Brown conceives of the tender scene of a slave-mother praying for him on the steps of the gallows (line 4) probably belongs to the poet instead of the historical Brown, but his willingness to use even his own death to advance his cause belongs to both.

In the second stanza, Brown is brought through the crowd that has come to witness his execution; they jeer (line 8) because an armed slave rebellion was their greatest collective fear. The slave-mother appears with her little child pressed close to her, and, Christlike, the condemned man forgets his own suffering. An important difference is that it is the adult in this scenario who is redeemed by the contact.

In the 21st century, the image of a white man who crossed the color line to kiss an infant would merit little attention, but in pre–Civil War Virginia, where the entire economy was built on slavery, it would have been incendiary. To the New England poet, it lent the "grisly fighter" (line 12), a martyr for his faith in abolitionism but not for his religious faith, the halo of a saint. The speaker again blurs this distinction in the next stanza, when he admires Brown's "Christian sacrifice" (line 16).

The fourth stanza distinguishes the speaker's admiration for Brown's "generous purpose" (line 14) from his recognition of Brown's folly in pursuing good through evil means. Although he just witnessed a scene of sub-

lime humanity, it does not erase his knowledge of the midnight terror Brown unleashed through his "borderer's pride of daring" (line 16). Although today the term Border States designates the slaveholding states that were adjacent to the free states during the Civil War, the speaker uses the term "borderers" to designate the ruffians on both sides of the slavery debate who conducted raids on both sides of the Kansas/Missouri border. They hoped to influence the outcome of the popular vote that would determine whether Kansas would be raised from territorial status to become either a free or slave state. Kansas was admitted to the Union as a free state in 1861.

The speaker renounces Brown's call for violence in the fifth stanza, expressing his hope that Virginia's Blue Ridge Mountains never hear the northern rifle or "see the light of blazing homes flash on the negro's spear" (line 18; a wonderfully pictorial image calculated to send shivers of terror down the backs of confirmed slaveholders). Instead, he hopes that the angel Truth will teach them that right triumphs might and justice is more than "mail" (line 20; his use of this term for the flexible armor more typical of medieval combat than 19th-century warfare may imply that their attitudes are equally antiquated).

Virginians were already well armed in anticipation of a northern invasion, but the speaker claims it will do them no good. Although they might "strike the pouncing eagle" (a symbol of federal authority; line 23), they cannot stop the dove of Love. This vague closing line probably conveys the fading hope that the South will abandon slavery peacefully after it recognizes the brotherly love that prompts northern well-wishers to discourage the practice.

BRYANT, WILLIAM CULLEN (1794–1878)

The future poet began life most auspiciously on November 3, 1794, in Cummington, Massachusetts, as the son of a physician and grandson of a prominent judge. A precocious although sickly child, Bryant published his first poem at the age of 13 and began studying Greek and Latin even as he suffered through such early 19th-century medical cures as bleeding and ice-cold baths to cure his chronic headaches. He first achieved recognition for "THANATOPSIS," a meditation on death written while he was still a teenager. He attended Williams College in Williamstown, Massachusetts, for a year before undertaking the independent study of law. Admitted to the bar in 1816, he worked as a lawyer in yet another western Massachusetts town for 10 years.

It was his travels to the local forests of the still pristine East Coast mountains that most stoked his imagination, however. Such poems as "A FOREST HYMN" reveal the depth of the spiritual feelings the wilderness experience stirred in his breast. Anticipating HENRY DAVID THOREAU, the speaker feels closest to God when he is communing with nature. "OH FAIREST OF THE RURAL MAIDS" praises the wholesomeness of a product of the virgin forest, while Bryant's "INSCRIPTION FOR THE ENTRANCE TO A WOOD" encourages city dwellers to seek out the tranquility to be found in the wilderness, highly praising the restorative power of nature while minimizing the risks of that unfamiliar environment. Even in the wildest nature, his "The MURDERED TRAVELLER" suggests, a man has more to fear from other men than from the elements.

In "The TWO GRAVES," he hints that even second-growth forests (those that regenerate after the first logging of an area) and meadows might offer a superior form of heaven. All trace of the pioneering couple in the poem has disappeared from the landscape, but he senses that they will be resurrected like the other faithful just as the land has regenerated around him. He found several kindred spirits among the painters of the Hudson River School, penning "TO [Thomas] COLE, THE PAINTER, DEPARTING FOR EUROPE" as a reminder to his friend not to forget the primitive forests he loved to paint on this side of the Atlantic. Bryant eventually also delivered a quite lengthy eulogy for Cole after the painter's death.

Ironically, the great nature lover Bryant's poetry brought him the recognition that led him away from the countryside, and he accepted an editorship at the *New York Review* in 1825. His somewhat satirical "HYMN TO THE CITY" may convey his sense of loss at the change of venue, but such sentiments did not keep him from the *New York Evening Post,* where he became editor in chief in 1829. Under his guidance, the paper advocated the abolition of slavery as early as 1836, a cause that eventually prompted Bryant to support the Republican Party. A decade earlier he had penned "The AFRICAN CHIEF" to counteract an assumption of racial inferiority that was frequently used as a defense of slavery, and Bryant continued to lend his support to the antislavery movement until the end of the Civil War. After the war, his poem, "ABRAHAM LINCOLN" predicted that his freeing of the slaves in the Emancipation Proclamation eventually would be viewed as the assassinated president's proudest monument.

His sensitivy to other cultures is also evident in "An INDIAN AT THE BURIAL-PLACE OF HIS FATHER," but his real message in that poem is that the changes created in the landscape by European settlers, especially their carelessness with the watersheds, will eventually condemn their civilization to the same doom their progress inflicted on their Native American predecessors. The waters get their revenge in "The FLOOD OF YEARS," a view of life rendered as a disaster movie a couple of decades before the technology was available to portray such catastrophes on film. The devastation of civilizations in the poem is the result of time and not flood, however.

Bryant traveled extensively, journeying as far west as the Mississipi River and as far south as Florida. He began such early studies of the local fauna and flora as "ROBERT OF LINCOLN," "TO THE FRINGED GENTIAN" and "The YELLOW VIOLET" with a close description of his subject, an approach he adapted to the much larger canvas of "The PRAIRIES." The first three of his trips to Europe led to a travel book, his *Letters of a Traveler* in 1850. Perhaps his greatest worldly pleasure, however, was the repurchase of his ancestral home in Cummington 30 years after his widowed mother had been forced to sell it in 1835.

He continued writing poetry throughout his lengthy life, and his poem "The POET," founded on his decades of dedicated service to the muse, contains some of the best practical advice that one poet can provide for another. In his seventies he returned to his early interest in ancient Greek and published translation of Homer's epic poems. His wife of 45 years died in 1866, and Bryant died in New York City on June 12, 1878, after nearly 50 years as the editor of the *Evening Post.*

Bryant's boyhood home, repurchased and refurbished by the poet in 1865, has been preserved as the

William Cullen Bryant Homestead. The University of Virginia is home to the William Cullen Bryant Collection, and Williams College also holds some valuable material.

BIBLIOGRAPHY

Brown, Charles H. *William Cullen Bryant.* New York: Scribner's, 1971.

Bryant, William Cullen. *The Letters of William Cullen Bryant,* edited by William Cullen Bryant II & Thomas G. Voss. New York: Fordham University Press, 1993.

Foshay, Ella M. and Barbara Novak. *Intimate Friends: Thomas Cole, Asher B. Durand and William Cullen Bryant.* Hensonville, N.Y.: Black Dome Press, 2001.

McLean, Alfred F., Jr. *William Cullen Bryant.* New York: Twayne, 1989.

"BURNING DRIFT-WOOD" JOHN GREENLEAF WHITTIER (1890)

The speaker in JOHN GREENLEAF WHITTIER's poem is an elderly man who uses the burning wood to prompt memories of the dreams of his youth. Although ostensibly expressing regret that he did not achieve everything he once imagined possible (memorably referred to as "vain desires and hopes that failed" in line 8), he seems more than compensated by the richness of his imaginative life.

His first comments are self-denigrating. Every "waif" (here, piece of driftwood, but the term is also used to designate street urchins or orphans) that he burns releases old dreams, fancies, and "folly's unlaid ghosts" (line 4), his abandoned (or orphaned) projects and dreams. This sets the tone for the first two stanzas of the poem, culminating in his realization that only driftwood (the poor fragments of "vain desires and hopes that failed," line 8) remains of the swift ships that once sailed the enchanted sea ("keels" [line 5] are the single center beams running the length of a ship to which other framing elements are attached like ribs. Whittier's use of the term here is a good example of synecdoche, a trope in which part of a thing [the keel] is understood to represent all of it [an entire ship]).

His imagined ships let him travel the world. He crossed the Atlantic to see "my" towers in Spain as well as the "Fortunate Isles" (in Irish legend, a heavenly paradise across the western sea; line 12). On the Mediterranean Sea, he saw Arcadia (a district in modern Greece noted for the simplicity of its rural life) and grazed the siren's rocks (line 16. In Homer's *Odyssey,* the sirens were beautiful singing maids who lured sailors to their doom on the rocks surrounding them. The implication is that the speaker in this poem got as close to their divine singing as was humanly possible without destroying himself in the attempt).

He also visited Africa (where the legendary "Prester John" once was a powerful king) and Asia (the court of Kubla Khan, a Mongol emperor known for the splendor of his palace). Favorable winds scented with jasmine (a tropical Eurasian genus made up of more than 200 species) blew from the Fountain of Youth; he also enjoyed love from rose-filled bowers and gold from Eldorado (of South American legend). His gallant ships followed blind Adventure but failed to reach Content (line 28). At this point, what had been a physical quest turns into a spiritual one. Only those ventures based on Love succeeded, for they were piloted by a clear-eyed Duty to "a good beyond my own" (line 31).

To later dreamers (mariners on the Sea of Dreams [line 37] who could hope to meet the famously rich caliph of Baghdad as he was described in an eighth-century Persian epic, *The Arabian Nights*), the speaker bequeaths "the fair, fond fancies dear to youth" (line 38). He will turn his personal attention to "the sober grounds of truth" (line 40). No longer young (it is not May, he notes, and the days are growing darker), he will desist from rebuilding castles of passion and desire, contenting himself with warming his age-chilled hands as he feeds the driftwood of their wrecks into the fire.

Instead of dwelling on his losses, however, he considers them to be gains as he sings his praise for what remains (lines 49–52), his wisdom and the miraculous advances in technology that brought more of the world's wonders to his door than he dared to dream. He has also become conscious of "holier signs" (line 61) of Love and divine Power and righteousness. He has seen "the man evolving from the slave" (line 64), a phrase that references the Civil War's end to American slavery but may also refer to his own growth, in the sense that he is no longer driven by his passions. He is willing to wait with folded, overwearied hands for life to take its course because he is confident of the gracious Fatherhood (line 66).

The "waiting time" (line 69) must be good if "Faith and Hope and Charity" sit at his evening's hearth fire. The phrase is biblical (1 Corinthians 13:13), and one senses that the chief thought in this entire poem echoes the same chapter, especially a line in its 11th verse ending with "when I became a man, I put away childish things." He still has the remaining friends with whom he shared love, joy, and tender memories of the dead. The departed have left on the last, long voyage that the speaker and the others will soon join. Death is so close he can hear its solemn monotone and recognize its origin as a whisper of the Eternal Sea. He can see its "mirage-lifted Isles of Peace" (line 88), a vision of heaven very similar to the Fortune Isles mentioned in line 12.

"BURROWING YANKEES" ANONYMOUS (1776)

By the start of the American Revolution, the colonists had been studying the advantages of surprise, concealment, and cover at the hands of their Indian adversaries at intermittent intervals for more than a century and a half. These tactics served them well in attacking the British retreat from Concord on April 19, 1775, but the deciding factor in their ability to inflict unacceptable damage at Bunker Hill on June 17 of the same year was the breastworks that blunted the effectiveness of the redcoats' frontal assaults. The lesson thus observed was put to good use when, after the taking of British Fort Ticonderoga in upstate New York, the rebels were able to bring the captured artillery to the hills close enough to Boston to bring the city and its harbor into range. The guns were protected by entrenched militia, and not wanting to chance another headlong assault on a well-fortified position, the British chose to evacuate the occupied city in March 1776.

Since this poem surfaced in Halifax, the city in Canadian Nova Scotia to which the British transported their Loyalist evacuees, its sentiments predictably rested with the British cause. To downplay the enemy's recent successes in military engineering, the speaker likens their efforts to those of a mole. Despised for its tunneling proclivities, that garden pest suffers from the hereditary blindness that the speaker here compares to the rebels' blindness to their own folly. The second half of the first stanza reveals a serious problem for the Loyalists, however. In contrasting the rebels with the "true Britons" with whom they pretended an alliance (which proved useful in the French and Indian War that ended 15 years earlier), the speaker admits that the colonists must have a separate identity and interests distinct from those of England.

The second stanza contrasts the pure blood of England with the inferior stuff that runs in British-American veins. The latter is but the dregs (the residues left after the more desirable liquors are siphoned off), the lees (the sediments settling out during the fermentation process), or the drains (presumably either those samples drawn off to test a wine's stage of development or those wines determined to be so inferior that they are deliberately drained instead of being bottled or consumed). The build-up in militia strength around Boston had reached the point where there had been talk of attacking the British garrison prior to the evacuation. The speaker goads the rebels to come on, confident that the British would soon see their backs (line 8; British military tactics in that era were frequently based on the rank and file being disciplined enough to withstand an enemy's volley before discharging their own weapons at closer range; undisciplined opponents tended to waver at that point, providing an opportunity for a disastrous rout if they fled before the bayonet charge that immediately followed the British discharge).

True British hearts are not swayed by threats. The lion (the animal most often chosen to represent that country in the iconography of the day) will terrorize the rebels, revealing the error of their presumption. The speaker is confident that the rebels will eventually be driven from the land (line 14; this would have been an especially appealing thought for someone living in exile). He offers a drink (the "health" of line 15) in honor of the great King George III (of Great Britain and Ireland, the titular sovereign of the British-American colonies). The speaker would have him determined to root "all such insolent vermin" (line 12) from the earth (a thought that returns the poem to its opening image of the mole).

"BURY ME IN A FREE LAND" FRANCES ELLEN WATKINS HARPER (1864)

Penned near the close of the Civil War, this poem recapitulates the most graphic images created by a century of abolitionist poets. Its primary purpose was to end slavery by inflaming the passions of the Northerners who shared the poet's hatred of that institution until they were willing to pursue their cause to its inevitable conclusion. For its initial audience, the poem was especially poignant not only because it reminded them of why they were fighting but because the young men who were still being killed were now dying in the invasion armies of Generals Grant and Sherman. The only way to keep them from being buried in a Southern slave-holding state was to win the war.

The speaker of the poem was most likely a Union soldier since few other men besides slaves belonged to a group who would regret possible interment in the Confederacy, and his familiarity with abolitionist literature is broader than one would usually find in a plantation worker. A third possibility is that we are hearing the voice of a confirmed abolitionist who did not recognize the Southern secession from the Union or the legitimacy of their cause, a man or woman for whom all of the United States is answerable for allowing slavery to continue in any part of it.

By 1864, the Civil War was becoming a single-issue conflict, a sentiment revealed in the first stanza of this poem by the speaker's disregard for all other aspects of his life that might have influenced the location of his grave except for his hatred of slavery. The specter of slavery haunted the nation, and the poet drew on the macabre traditions of the ghost story to reveal how deeply the national nightmare had affected the speaker.

The speaker imagines his own unquiet grave, but slavery seems even more terrifying. Notice the creative reversal the poet made here: it is the trembling slave (line 2) who disturbs the dead, and the slave's "shadow" (another ghastly term) that fills the tomb with "fearful gloom" (line 8). Equally disturbing is the thought of the "coffle gang" (a line of prisoners chained together) being led to the "shambles" (line 9; the term denotes a place of destruction, which in this poem is a slave auction).

The power of the next 14 lines derives from FRANCES ELLEN WATKINS HARPER's use of action verbs (for example, "rise," "torn," and "flash"), her rendering of dramatic incident, her appeal to several of the reader's senses, and an occasional strikingly original visual effect. One of the sounds she presents (a slave mother's despairing shriek, line 11) strikes not only the reader's ear, but also the haptic sense; one can almost feel as well as hear "the trembling air" (line 12). One of the few weak spots in the poem is the use of the same adjective in line 16 to compare the weakness of the infants torn from her breast to that of trembling baby doves removed from their nest. The first use is unforgettable, but the second cheapens the impact of the term when a different adjective would have served as well.

In line 14, note how marvelously the poet used what modern cinematographers would describe as an extreme slow-motion close-up in an age before camera technology could produce that effect. The lash is described as "drinking her blood," an image only possible if the reader were somehow brought close enough to see the leather soaking up the liquid. Nearly as vivid is the focus on the very instant when hounds seize their prey (line 18). The next two lines recall all the turmoil and Northern guilt in regard to the Fugitive Slave Act; the pleading of the recaptured slave being placed back in chains would fall on deaf ears at the scene but echo resoundingly in abolitionist circles.

America banned the importation of slaves in 1812, which significantly increased the market value of those already held. Each man, woman, and child suddenly represented a significant store of wealth to the slaveholder, the person who profited most directly from their natural increase. The notion that young girls might be purchased for the purpose of sexual as well as economic exploitation, as suggested in the sixth stanza, more than doubled the moral outrage of those who opposed all the other aspects of slavery.

The poem began with the speaker's consideration of his gravesite, a novel but rather tepid subject compared with the vivid heat generated by his hatred of slavery. Notice how his tone shifts as he returns to the initial question; by this device, the two opening and two closing stanzas frame the poem's core in addition to providing the rationale for recalling its troublesome imagery. The speaker is much more prone to abstraction when he discusses his own circumstances; he resents the "bloated might" (line 25) that oppresses the slaves whom he is now ready to consider his brothers (line 28). He is so self-effacing that he does not want a high monument (such as might be erected for a war hero); ridding the land of slavery is the extent of his desire.

"BY BROAD POTOMAC'S SHORE" WALT WHITMAN (1872)

After experiencing the seasonal changes of 53 years, the rapidly aging WALT WHITMAN could easily apply their lessons to his own life, which seemed doomed by an early winter of poor health. In again visiting the Potomac River, a scene important to his transformation a decade earlier from a self-absorbed sensualist to an important commentator on the state of the nation with the moral authority of his service as a volunteer nurse behind him, he marveled that he could still feel the old emotions.

In this poem the speaker again finds himself on the shore of the Potomac River, which had earlier divided the North from the South in the Civil War. To his surprise and evident irritation, he finds his body responding to the stimulus of spring as it had in his younger days (a Freudian scholar might make much of his uttering, ejaculating, and babbling "old tongue" [lines 1–2], perhaps supposing that the speaker had substituted one body part for another). As if stimulated by the animal magnetism that the poet celebrated in his earlier poems, his old gay (the term had no homosexual connotations for another half century) heart felt "the full flush spring returning" (line 3). He is rejuvenated by Virginia's "pellucid" (clear) and silver summer sky, its odors, freshness, forenoon purple hills, soft and green "deathless" grass (the adjective is central to the meaning of the poem, line 6) and especially its blood-red roses.

He would have the roses perfume his book, and the Potomac subtly wash (the "lave" of line 9) his every line. His appeal to "O spring" (which neatly combines the river, the season, and his own revitalized juices) to contribute to his pages before he closes (that is, before he finishes writing them and before he dies; line 10) seems almost sexual in its phrasing: "Give me of you O spring." When he asks the same of the purple hills and grass, it becomes clear that his writing draws on a blend of internal and external springs that includes at least a subconscious sexual element.

C

CANADIAN POETIC INFLUENCES The earliest works of Canadian poetry were virtually unknown in the United States until well into the 20th century and hence had almost no influence on the poetry of that country prior to 1900. However, Canada's growing prestige both economically and as a producer of first-rate literary and artistic talent since that time have generated increasing interest in those early works which helped provide it with a national identity, and their influence is likely to increase throughout the coming centuries. Here is a quick introduction to the half dozen writers one should read in order to gain even the scantest familiarity with the history of Canadian literature.

English poetry in Canada began with Robert Hayman (1575–1629), the governor of a Newfoundland colony from 1618 to 1628. To his *Quodlibets* (a word of Latin origin roughly translatable as *What You Will* or *Anything at All*) goes the honor of being the first (1628) book of poetry written in Canada.

It was not until the 19th century that Canadian poetry really came of age, however. Robert Goldsmith (1794–1861) is generally credited with being the first important Canadian poet in English, while Octave Cremazie (1827–79) celebrated the French heritage of the bicultural nation with such poems as "Le Drapeau de Carillon" ("The Flag of Fort Carillon." While the English and French were struggling for control of the continent, the latter's Brigadier General Louis-Joseph, Marquis de Montcalm led a hugely outnumbered army to a surprising victory at the fort later known as Ticonderoga on July 8, 1758. Montcalm was fatally wounded on September 13, 1759, in defense of Quebec, which fell to the British. Many Canadian poems commemorate Montcalm and British general James Wolfe, who died in the same battle). Renowned for his historical poems, Louis-Honoré Frechette (1839–1908) enjoyed the highest international reputation of the French-Canadian poets prior to the 20th century.

British-born Susanna Strickland Moodie (1803–85) brought an emigrant's sensitivity to poetry about her adopted nation, as did James McIntyre (1828–1906). McIntyre was a former Scot who seemed most impressed by the cheeses he found in Ontario. His titles such as "Oxford Cheese Ode" and "Ode on the Mammoth Cheese" remind us that poetry can be a popular culture medium.

Another former Scot (although his parents lived in England at the time of his birth), Robert William Service (1874–1958) penned what has become the most famous Canadian poem south of the border, "The Shooting of Dan McGrew."

BIBLIOGRAPHY

Bender, Louis Prosper. *Literary Sheaves, ou la littérature au Canada français: The Drama, History, Romance, Poetry, Lectures, Sketches, Etc.* Montreal: Dawson Brothers, 1881.

Marcotte, Gilles. *Le temps des poètes: description critique de la poésie actuelle au Canada français.* Montreal: Montreal Editions, 1969.

Marshall, Tom. *Harsh and Lovely Land: The Major Canadian Poets and the Making of a Canadian Tradition.* Vancouver: University of British Columbia Press, 1979.

Rand, Theodore Harding, ed. *A Treasury of Canadian Verse.* Toronto: W. Briggs, 1900.

Vincent, Thomas B., ed. *Narrative Verse Satire in Maritime Canada, 1779–1814.* Ottawa: Tecumseh Press, 1978.

CARIBBEAN POETIC INFLUENCES   In

literature, the term "Caribbean" generally refers to those countries of the Greater Caribbean basin with a history of colonization by European powers and African slavery. This includes the island nations extending like the rim of a bowl to separate the Atlantic Ocean from the Caribbean Sea: Cuba and the Bahamas; Belize (formerly British Honduras) in Central America; Guyana, Suriname and French Guiana on the northeast coast of South America; and all the island nations between them.

The literature of those nations colonized by the Dutch, French, and Spanish in the area had very little influence on American poetry prior to the 20th century. Curiosity about the new territories acquired from the opportunistic Spanish-American War of 1898 increased interest in those countries, such as Cuba and Puerto Rico, that gave the United States the prestige of being an empire, and eventually their island neighbors, but the chief influence from those quarters on American poetry occurred after the temporal limits of this volume.

That the story is different for those countries colonized by the British stems in part from the earlier access American colonists had to them, their use of English as an official language, and the developmental benefits of British colonial policy. While the British were no less unprincipled in exploiting their empire for the benefit of the homeland than their European rivals, they tended to work toward that goal by creating administrative units in the colonies that replicated their own. Their enfranchised colonists enjoyed British traditions like representative democracy and relative freedom of the press. Printing began in Jamaica (in the 1720s), Barbados (1730), Antigua (1740s) and Grenada (1765); all were relatively early starts for the region (Tifflin 57). No fewer than 15 newspapers started in Jamaica alone before 1800 (Tifflin 58). This meant that any news happening on these islands would have at least theoretically been accessible to the American colonists. That news was not always good.

While often lucrative, possession of their empires had the potential of embroiling the European nations in wars of conquest or defense with their rivals. Hence the French and English staged a series of increasingly violent conflicts that culminated in Great Britain's victory in the Seven Years' War in the middle of the 18th century. The Caribbean colonies were also at risk in the Napoleonic wars of the early 19th century, and the region saw additional fighting in the Spanish-American War.

The Caribbean also presented the United States with the problem of slavery both as a moral sinkhole and with models of violent revolt, a few of which were successful. There were no fewer than six slave rebellions in Barbados from 1675 to 1816, and a revolt in Guyana led to an ex-slave named Cuffey ruling the country for a year. In 1791, a slave revolt begun by Toussaint Louverture culminated in Jean-Jacques Dessalines's proclamation of Haiti as the first independent black state. In time, more than half a million Africans had been forcibly expatriated into Jamaica alone. In the United States as a whole, approximately one-sixth of the population was of African descent, and in the southern states the ratio was much higher. Eventually a day of reckoning for permitting such an evil as slavery to control regional politics and shape national policy would have to arrive, and each act of repressive violence brought that historical moment inevitably closer.

To a large extent, the Caribbean influence on American poetry prior to the 20th century is incalculable in its scope since those slaves who had been shipped from Africa and ultimately relocated in America after forced servitude in the islands brought with them rhythms that influenced the oral traditions of the southern plantations. Over the course of several centuries, its greatest impact was on American music; it was instrumental in the creation of jazz, the blues, and rock and roll in the 20th century.

More immediately, however, the poetry from the Caribbean which had the greatest impact in the United

States attacked the institution of slavery. Thus *Jamaica, a Poem in Three Parts* by an anonymous 18-year-old, brought the horror of slavery to London in 1776. The British poet William Cowper quickly added his voice of protest, and the American poet PHILIP FRENEAU, in such poems as "TO SIR TOBY," also attacked Jamaican slavery. In the first half of the 19th century, the easiest way for a poet to reach print above the Mason-Dixon line (the result of an early survey that was immortalized for separating North from South in the song "Dixie") was with poems attacking the abomination both in the Caribbean and domestically. This development is discussed in "ANTISLAVERY POETRY," another article in this volume.

The work of the antislavery poets and other crusaders helped sway public sentiment to the point where the British essentially declared war on the international slave trade in 1807 and banished slavery in their Caribbean colonies in 1833. The French revolutionists temporarily banned slavery in 1794, but Napoleon reinstated it six years later. It was not until 1848 that the French ban was reinstated. In the United States, a divided public sentiment on this issue necessitated the Civil War.

In addition to Freneau, MARIA GOWEN BROOKS spent considerable time in the Caribbean (as a Cuban plantation owner), an influence that can be felt in her poetry. In Haiti and elsewhere, the winds of freedom and a new nationalism were fanning a native poetry that was rapidly coming to terms with the implications of its colonial past, but the mainstream American writers prior to 1900 had few opportunities for exposure to their work other than a few antislavery poems. Even STEPHEN CRANE, who served as a war correspondent in Cuba in the 1898 war against Spain, was unaware of the burgeoning Caribbean poetic tradition.

BIBLIOGRAPHY

Arnold, A. James, ed. *A History of Literature in the Caribbean.* 3 vols. Amsterdam and Philadelphia: John Benjamin Publishing, 1994–2001.

James, Louis. *Caribbean Literature in English.* New York: Longman, 1999.

Tifflin, Helen. "The Institution of Literature." In Arnold, vol. 3.

CARY, PHOEBE (1824–1871)

The poet's birth on September 4, 1824, at Mount Healthy, a farm then eight miles north of Cincinnati, Ohio, was preceded by that of her sister Alice, four years earlier. This was significant because Alice helped foster Phoebe's intellect, instilling in her a love of poetry that would probably not have proven so fruitful had she been left to fend for herself with only the Bible, a few novels, and religious journals in their childhood home. Although their father was fond of reciting poetry, their mother's death in 1835 was a terrible setback that saddled the two girls with increased domestic burdens as well as tremendous grief. As girls, Alice provided Phoebe with an appreciative audience and eventually the opportunity to include her poems in her sister's books. They moved to New York City (1851–71) to further their literary careers, and shared an apartment and soon their own home. Neither sister married, and together they formed the nucleus of an important literary salon, hosting an informal group of writers and other intellectuals who met in their home on Sundays. The two sisters continued to write poetry for the last two decades of their lives until Alice became bedridden in 1869. Phoebe devotedly cared for her until Alice's death on February 12, 1871. The grief-stricken Phoebe suffered malarial fevers and died in Newport, Rhode Island, on July 31 of that year. In addition to the poems placed in her sister's books, Phoebe is best remembered for two volumes of poetry published in her lifetime: *Poems and Parodies* (1854) and *Poems of Faith, Hope, and Love* (1868). She also coedited *Hymns for all Christians* (1868).

Much of what is known about the Cary sisters is found in a remembrance by Mary Clemmer Ames, their friend. She portrayed Phoebe as a paragon of piety and parody, a natural wit whose frequent flashes of sometimes pointed humor were, because of her sweet temperament, never painfully barbed. Cary sometimes used equally polished parodies to attack even the best male poet's portrayals of weak women. For example, in *The Vicar of Wakefield,* a well-known 18th-century novel by the British author Oliver Goldsmith, a song suggests that a lovely woman's only way to avoid guilt and public shame is to die. In "WHEN LOVELY WOMAN," Cary countered that a woman's last experiment to try is to cry.

The other Phoebe Cary poem discussed in this volume, "DOROTHY'S DOWER," is poignant as well as humorous, for it deals with the evolution of a couple's attitudes toward money throughout the course of their relationship. Since the poet was actively involved in the struggle for women's rights (even briefly helping edit the famed suffragist Susan B. Anthony's *The Revolution*), it should come as no surprise that the husband is more culpable of the two.

Cary Cottage, the family home from 1832–50, has been preserved in North College Hill, Ohio. The Alice and Phoebe Cary Collection is archived at the University of Virginia.

BIBLIOGRAPHY

Ames, Mary Clemmer. *A Memorial of Alice and Phoebe Cary, with some of their later poems.* Ann Arbor: Scholarly Publishing Office, University of Michigan Library, n.d.

Cary, Alice and Phoebe Cary. *The Poems of Alice and Phoebe Cary.* Ann Arbor: Scholarly Publishing Office, University of Michigan Library, n.d.

"CAVALRY CROSSING A FORD" WALT WHITMAN (1865)

In terms of mobility, the general prestige of their branch of service, and their élan, the cavalry were the jet fighters of their day. WALT WHITMAN may have personally witnessed such a scene as he recreates here when he successfully searched for his brother, who had been listed among the wounded infantry at Fredericksburg, and joined him for a couple of weeks at the army camp.

In one of his most strikingly beautiful poems, Whitman's approach seems almost cinematic. The poem begins with three iambic feet as if to suggest the first three in a line of mounted soldiers ("A line in long array") before the pattern is broken just as the soldiers are forced to adopt a serpentine course through the islands. Although their arms may flash in the sun, the clank is described as musical, and the appreciative speaker draws the reader's attention to the sound. The splashing horses of line 3 appeal both to the eye and the ear, and like a cameraman of the 20th-century western, the speaker focuses on groups, then individuals, and finally their characteristic "negligent rest on the saddles" (line 4). Returning to his focus on their motion, the speaker notes that some leave the water while others are just entering it.

Whitman's use of color is especially striking in this poem. Like the silvery reflection of the water, the glint of the soldiers' arms is set off against the green of the islands. The men's faces are brown from dust and the sun, so the eye is drawn to their guidons as the only other sources of bright primary colors in the scene. Described as "scarlet and blue and white" to suggest that they are pennants and not the national flag, they identify the troops as a specific unit of the Union Army. That they "flutter gaily" in the wind (line 7) reinforces the tranquility of the scene.

"THE CHAMBERED NAUTILUS" OLIVER WENDELL HOLMES (1858)

Combining a snail-shaped shell with a body and mind like that of its cousins the squid and the octopus proved a strategy that enabled this cephalopod now limited to the western Pacific to survive more than 150 million years, according to the fossil record. Like the squid, it propels itself by releasing small jets of water as it comes close to shore at night to hunt shellfish or scavenge.

OLIVER WENDELL HOLMES began the poem by recalling a myth specific to this animal; as "poets feign" (line 1), it could stretch "webs of living gauze" (line 8) across the shell and use that living sail to cross the open ocean. This gives rise to speculation as to the enchanted gulfs it could explore, home to Sirens (line 5; in Greek mythology these were sea-nymphs who called sailors to their doom) and sea-maids (mermaids; line 7) that lie on naked coral reefs "to sun their streaming hair" (line 7).

He cannot know any of that since he has only the empty shell on hand. He accurately describes its discrete chambered cells and their "irised ceiling" (line 14; the inner shell has a mother-of-pearl shine), but returns to speculation in describing its "frail tenant" and with a "dim dreaming life" (lines 11–12). The specimen before him has had its shell "rent" (broken, line 14, or perhaps sawed in half to reveal its exquisite structure) and "its sunless crypt unsealed;" a metaphor inviting comparison with human architecture.

The poet then turns to the animal's natural history, which he apparently likens to that of a snail or other less spectacular animal because he focuses on its years of silent toil devoted to building its lustrous spiraling coil. Modern science agrees that it creates an additional chamber each year (line 18), but its predatory nature probably calls its "soft step" (line 19) into its new home (or at least the new chamber added onto the old) into question.

This brings him to the application (here he calls it a "heavenly message," line 22); following the usual pattern of 19th-century American nature poetry, he announces what he has learned from observing this aspect of nature that will better help him conduct his own life. First, however, he expresses his gratitude to the "Child of the wandering sea, Cast from her lap, forlorn" (lines 24–25) for delivering a clearer note than Triton blew on his conch shell (line 26; Triton ruled the waves in Greek mythology). In an image reminiscent of the nautilus shell he refers to "the deep caves of thought" (line 28) in which a voice sings the message of the last stanza.

The moral is to keep growing spiritually (the soul's building of ever more stately mansions, line 29), leaving the "low-vaulted past" (line 31) for ever loftier temples until finally free from the outgrown shell (the physical body after death) by "life's unresting sea" (line 35).

The image of a progression of temples, each better than the former, may be a political statement. Applied to the poet's family history, it suggests that he may have viewed his father's ministry as an advancement over its more fundamentalistic predecessors and his own even more liberal beliefs as an advance over his father's.

"CHANTING THE SQUARE DEIFIC"
WALT WHITMAN (1881) This poem celebrates four aspects of God by associating them with the four sides of a square, and each aspect assumes the role of first-person speaker on a rotating basis. Four seems a rather arbitrary number, but it has the advantage of being represented by a readily recognizable symbol (the "square" of the title). It also happens to be the number of religious traditions with which WALT WHITMAN was familiar, and which he draws upon for examples in this poem.

The first section of the poem presents the unlimited might of the deity, a feature honored by Jews and Christians with the name Jehovah, by Hindus with the name Brahm, and by the ancient Romans as Saturinus (lines 3–5). He is superior to time in that time (personified as Kronos, his Greek name) is only one part of him. He relentlessly makes laws and punishes those who transgress against them. Remorselessly taking the lives of those who sin, he otherwise remains as distant and immutable as the seasons, gravitation, and "the appointed days" (of birth and death. Thus he may also be considered the God of predestination and fate; lines 10–11).

The second section celebrates the gentler side of God, the Consolator (line 13) who further identifies himself as Christ, Hermes (the ancient Greek god of speed, messenger for the other gods), and Hercules (representative, perhaps, of the many Greek figures born of women but sired by gods). He consoles men by absorbing all sorrow, labor, and suffering (line 17), a service for which he has been and will continue to be rejected, tormented, and crucified. He is the "cheer-bringing God" (line 21) who dispenses hope, charity, and love, gifts that will not perish although he knows he is destined to die young.

Satan appears as the third, perpetually rebellious side of the square. Despised yet proud, he constantly and eternally broods and plots, and vows never to change.

The fourth section is devoted to Santa Spirita, the Holy Spirit. He is life, "lighter than light" (line 36). Beyond both heaven and hell, he includes both Savior and Satan. He contains contradictions and oxymorons (he is at once the most ethereal [line 41] and most solid [line 44] of the sides, and though he completes the square he also contains all the other sides [line 40]). He also breathes through these songs (line 45).

"CHARLESTON" HENRY TIMROD (1862) On December 20, 1860, South Carolina became the first southern state to secede from the Union, and President Abraham Lincoln's refusal to abandon Fort Sumter in strategic Charleston harbor was viewed as an affront to the state's sovereignty. On April 12, 1861, Confederate artillery began a 36-hour barrage that culminated in the surrender of the fort, and the Civil War had begun.

Throughout most of the rest of the war, the Confederate-held fort kept Charleston harbor open even as a

Union blockade tightened around every other southern port. By December of 1862, when HENRY TIMROD'S poem first appeared, the city seemed so calm that the poet compared it to the Indian summer (in many climates, the warm spell that follows the first frost of the fall but precedes the first snowfall) in the first stanza. While the war progressed elsewhere (in "the broad sunlight of heroic deeds," line 3), Charleston awaited the enemy's arrival like a patient god with her stockpiled thunderbolts (line 6). Fort Sumter loomed on the horizon like a cloud with indented parapets (the "battlements" of line 7) visible along the top.

Although the city lacked the great cliffs of Gibraltar (or "Calpe") that dominate the strait between the Atlantic Ocean and Mediterranean Sea, it did have Fort Moultrie, a heavily armed fort on a nearby island with such low walls that effective bombardment from enemy ships would be very difficult. The "dogs of war," although used metaphorically in line 11, actually had a very bloody combat history as early as the ancient Romans and, in the New World, as recently as Hernando de Soto's 16th-century march across the American South.

In the sand dunes of the flood plain and on other nearby islands lay an additional thousand guns on the lookout for blood like the tigers of an Asian jungle (line 15). Within the city, grave men walked who may wield "the patriot's blade as lightly as the pen" (line 20; the line reminds the modern reader that Confederate soldiers frequently considered themselves patriots faithful to the call of their respective states and the region, and not rebels). Their collective inheritance included chivalrous notions of feudal aristocracy, an attitude that, especially in their formal literature, tended to place the southern belle on a pedestal. Here such maidens, who would weep over a bleeding hound (line 21), caught the strength of the warriors "whose sword [they] sadly bound" (line 24), rendering the city "girt without" (surrounded by defensive weapons) and "garrisoned at home" (everyone was mentally on a war footing even though the battle had not yet come to them; line 25).

Although the blockade did not close the port, vessels were being stopped on the open seas by "a hundred foes" (line 29), but ships still delivered badly needed steel (weapons, but the South was so largely

agrarian that it also had to import many of even the most basic industrial commodities) from England and the West Indies (neutral ports where European goods could be sold to Confederate agents and then shipped to Charleston on blockade runners). This brought summer (a season of high energy, industry, and even happiness) to her homes and their courtyards. Yet, the "hostile smoke" from a U. S. Navy steam-powered warship (from the shore resembling a frail, floating oak) could be seen on the horizon.

The speaker wonders if the city's defenses (largely centered on the "palm-crowned islands" of the bay) can keep her unscathed through the spring (lines 37–40). Her faith enables her to remain calm as she awaits either triumph or death (lines 43–44). The latter may seem a foregone conclusion since God has already inscribed her doom "in the temple of the Fates" (line 41), but all that he is really saying is that the future will unfold in accordance with God's will. It is certain that the city will crumble eventually (since all cities do), but that fate could be thousands of years in the distance.

In fact, the spring brought nine ironclads on April 7, 1863, but they were repulsed. Fort Sumter was attacked by sea again on August 17 and September 9, and for two months the following summer, but it was not evacuated until February 17, 1865, when Sherman's army marched north following its destruction of Savannah.

Fort Sumter has been preserved as a national monument, and Charleston's surviving pre–Civil War mansions hint at the architectural elegance that once graced the city.

"CHAUCER" HENRY WADSWORTH LONGFELLOW (1873)

This is a biographical poem celebrating the life and work of Geoffrey Chaucer (1340–1400). Unlike conventional 19th-century prose biographers, HENRY WADSWORTH LONGFELLOW did not begin with a lengthy list of Chaucer's ancestors and their various trades, ponderous material that makes for slow reading. Nor is Longfellow interested in relating colorful anecdotes from the medieval poet's life, whether Chaucer was happily married, or how he managed to put bread on his family's table. What mattered to Longfellow were the critical questions most germane to one writer's appreciation of another: Does his work live, and what lessons could he take from it to better his own poetry?

Like one of Chaucer's *Canterbury Tales,* the sonnet begins by setting the stage simply but effectively with the barest introduction of character and setting: "An old man in a lodge within a park" (line 1). Like Chaucer, Longfellow proceeds with enough concrete sensory details to let the reader develop a keener sense of what the room is like, in this instance by focusing on the paintings that line its walls. His reference to them as 'portraitures' (line 3) brought the line to the 10-syllable meter required of formal 19th-century sonnets, but the term usually is reserved for depictions of humans and not animals; paintings dealing with animals or inanimate objects as their subjects are usually called "still lives." That a hawk, hound or deer could be the subject of portraiture suggests such close attention to the details of their depiction that the rendering could be called photographic; that would have been high praise at the time when this poem was created as it represented the culmination of a desire for art to be so perfectly executed as to be a nearly accurate rendering of real objects or people. Such realism was also becoming fashionable in literature as well as in the plastic arts.

An alternative, equally viable, reading of the "portraiture" of the animals would place them in the same frame as the hunter, in which case they could serve as accoutrements in what photographers call an environmental portrait. In that case, the term would have been used more idiomatically, but the essential point of the present argument is the same: the animals are so realistically depicted that the speaker of the poem must have felt a sympathetic twinge at the sight of the "hurt" deer.

Such considerations are central to the meaning of this poem because they establish the aesthetics by which the speaker will judge Chaucer's work: Is it rendered so artfully that the reader feels as if he is experiencing actual life, rather than an imitation of it? Perhaps to emphasize the difference between life and art, to suggest that Chaucer is the old man in the lodge, and to echo language four centuries removed from his own, Longfellow uses the very antiquated verb form

"listeneth" (line 4) to describe the procedure by which the writer transmutes his sensory perceptions (his means of accessing the reality that surrounds him) into words that will hopefully engender similar feelings in the reader. This unidiomatic term also signals a transition from the visual to the aural; the old man hears a lark and, as we learn at the end of this poem, so successfully captures the experience that the speaker hears it as he reads of the experience.

Writers, the poem suggests, are so tuned in to life that although the old man took the precaution of insulating himself behind two barriers (stained glass and heavy "leaden" lattices strain the natural light and sounds before they intrude in his chamber and on his thoughts), he still heard the lark. In a moment of purposeful ambiguity, Longfellow's use of the term *lark* may refer to a bird outside the chamber, or to the highly amusing quality of some of the Canterbury tales. Hence, the old man may laugh at life's ability to penetrate artificial barriers, or he may already be so attuned to his craft that he "laugheth" as well as "listeneth" (both in line 7) to the tale he is creating. Longfellow may be making a statement about the writing process when he relates that the old man "writeth in a book like any clerk" (line 8). The point may be that the creative process occurs in the head of the writer, and that the actual placement of pen to paper is relatively uninteresting.

Calling Chaucer the poet of the dawn places him near the start of canonical British literature at the same time that it connects him with the lark mentioned in the poem. Next we have two biographical facts: in addition to writing the *Canterbury Tales,* Chaucer also wrote shorter poetry. The final lines affirm that Chaucer's work does indeed live, for as the speaker reads the lines he hears the crowing cock and other birds and sniffs the odors of a plowed field or flowery meadow that the poet left on the page for him to experience.

"CHEROKEE LOVE MAGIC" ANONYMOUS (19th century) As a formula for retaining affection, this poem focuses on the changes wrought in the singer by the object of the charm. His/her redness (line 1) already adds a dimension of physicality to the affair, and it may also signify luck, for he now feels as

beautiful as the rainbow. The color may also be reminiscent of the blood of a successfully hunted prey animal, an invitation to continue feasting on the speaker's flesh now that his heart, blood and flesh have been taken (lines 2–4). There is clearly a sacrificial quality in the speaker's announcement of his love's possession of such vital organs, and even his eyes (line 5). As evidence of what 20th-century forensics would call a sharing of bodily fluids, he notes that she has taken his saliva, and that their saliva has been blended forever. Praising her as a wizard (line 8) elevates her from the more prosaic aspects of life; it also serves as an invitation for her to continue exercising her power over him and again insists on how her love has ennobled and transported him.

Quite apart from the supposedly irresistible magic aspect of the formula, most people would be very much pleased by such attention if they had not heard it before. If delivered within the context of the entire traditional belief system, it could turn out to be quite magical indeed.

"CHICAGO" JOHN GREENLEAF WHITTIER (1872)

On the evening of October 8, 1871, a small fire in a barn escalated into a conflagration that burned for two days, killed at least 200 people and left more than 75,000 homeless. It apparently began shortly after 9 P.M., or after vespers (the evening prayer service for Catholics, Episcopalians, and Unitarians), as the speaker points out in the first line. In one wild night the city's shrines of prayer (60 churches, according to line 5) and grain markets were destroyed by a "fiery hurricane" (a "firestorm" in modern parlance is a fire so huge that it creates its own tornadic winds. Although the Chicago fire was aided by a strong pre-existing wind, the total destruction within the burn zone [firestorms can generate temperatures in excess of 2,000 degrees Fahrenheit] and eyewitness accounts of its extraordinary behavior suggest that it reached firestorm intensity).

Subsequent development west of the Mississippi River has rendered obscure the poem's reference to Chicago as "the City of the West" (line 8), but by the 1870 census it had a population of nearly 300,000. Its thriving stockyards and extensive railroad connec-

tions contributed to its exponential growth, dwarfing such other "western" cities (from the perspective of the densely populated East Coast, where some locales had been occupied for more than two and a half centuries by 1870) as San Francisco (almost 150,000 in 1870) and Denver (fewer than 5,000). By 1880, despite the setback of the fire, Chicago was home to more than half a million people and had even overtaken St. Louis in size, so a distraught citizen's pronouncement that the city was dead (in line 8) was decidedly premature.

The broken chronology of the poem probably reflects the poet's experience of the fire. At the distance of a thousand miles, he would have learned first of the horrendous dimensions of the catastrophe and based his initial reaction on what he knew of the distant city: its churches and grain markets will be destroyed. The second stanza assumes that the fire came under control overnight, although in fact it raged another 36 hours. The arrival of additional telegraphed reports (the "wire" of line 13) informed him that the city was still in flames, and the third stanza conveys the urgency of eyewitness accounts of the disaster. This includes a tribute to the bravery of the citizenry and their firefighters, who grudgingly gave up ground until they had nothing left to fight "the fiends of fire" (line 10). Even then they were able to face "the blinding glare" (line 11) with "the dumb (silent) defiance of despair" (line 12). In this context, *despair* probably means "desperation" [a mental state encouraging reckless behavior] rather than "despondency" [which would more likely mean that they had felt so bad as to resign themselves to their fate without actively resisting it]).

In the fourth stanza the poet commits a pathetic fallacy, the illogical assertion that nature was influenced by or reacted sympathetically to human emotion. Thus the fire died in tears of pity (line 16) as if it read the messages of hope telegrammed into the city. The Chicago Fire was one of the first great American tragedies following the massing of materials and managerial expertise that helped the North win the Civil War. Not only did the telegraph kept everyone informed of the disaster, but the infrastructure (especially a highly developed rail network) was in place to facilitate the delivery of aid. Hence the world reached out "full-handed" (with the necessary material support; line 20) to rebuild an even fairer city in which each cornerstone will be laid with love (line 24).

With so much help on the way, the speaker instructs the stricken city to throw off its woeful "ashen sackcloth" (line 26; among religious penitents, donning such a garment might symbolize their humility. Here the appeal seems not based as much on religious principles as upon pride) and rebuild with the ease of Amphion (line 27; an eventually tragic figure in *Oresteia,* an ancient Greek play by Aeschylus. He was such a moving musician that the stones needed to build a fortress around the city of Thebes apparently danced themselves into place [thus providing another example of the pathetic fallacy]).

As if affected by the fire's heat, the primal sin of selfishness shriveled in every heart, replaced by "the angel" (line 32; such imagery would naturally please a Quaker like Whittier, for that sect put great stock in the inherent goodness of man). The fiery holocaust provided Christ another opportunity to preach "the Gospel of Humanity" (line 36). Thus the speaker would have Chicago's spires again fret the sky as a sign of God's presence and as proof that (disinterested, brotherly) "love is still miraculous" (line 40).

"THE CHILDREN'S HOUR" HENRY WADSWORTH LONGFELLOW (1850)   The surprise of this heartwarming poem is that the father is the chief benefactor of the children's hour. Like most fairy tales, this one begins by blurring time: the first line suggests it is almost morning and the second line indicates it is almost night. Either way, the ambient lighting (or lack thereof) introduces a dark emotional undercurrent that more brilliantly sets off the foreground material (a father's obvious love for his daughters, and vice versa). Among the additional dark elements treated comically are the siege plotted and executed by the three *banditi* (this use of the Italian plural of bandit in line 29 reveals the speaker's willingness to join in the imaginative fun of the game) and, perhaps because their small size brought a siege of mice to mind, the mythical Bishop of Bingen (who, during the Great Famine of 1315–17 [which was real enough], cornered the grain market. Everyone else in the town either perished or fled, leaving him alone with a great tower filled with food until every rodent in the region descended upon what soon became known as the Mouse-Tower [line 28]). In keeping with the European traditions of the fairy tale, after overwhelming his attackers the speaker in the present poem threatens his captives with the horrible living death of permanent imprisonment in his dungeon, a feature usually absent from American architecture.

Less humorous are the poem's hints at the cost of the rigidly structured life led by a mid-19th-century American adult male in his dual role as businessman and father. Although he is a good provider (the study's three doors [line 19] suggest the opulence of the house, for example), the strain of positioning himself between the dark economic consequences of failure in a society with very few social programs and the daylight of continued prosperity may well explain why he evidently spends the bulk of his evenings in his study and has but a single hour reserved for interaction with his daughters. Such anxiety may have adversely affected his health; although he welcomes the diversion and the only dungeon with which he really threatens the interlopers is in the deepest recesses of his heart (lines 35–36), the final image of the poem is that of his own death and decay. Although this fairy tale lacks an explicit moral, it implies that a parent can receive far more in exchange for all the love, care, and expense involved in raising children if their love and antics can divert him (or her) from the cares of the world.

Notwithstanding its use of fairy-tale imagery, the poem is every bit as soft and sweet as the children's voices (line 8) and the onomatopoeic patter of their little feet (line 6). Despite hearing and seeing their advance, the speaker is complicit in their ruse in pretending not to have noticed their advance although he cannot spare himself the delight of studying each of their faces in turn (the kids have the same names as the poet's three youngest children; evidently his sons Charles and Ernest were barred by age and gender from the girls' conspiracy). They charge from three directions, surround and nearly annihilate him with their kisses, seeming to be everywhere (line 24).

The battle turns when the "old mustache" (a synecdochical detail that reveals something of the speaker's appearance even as it stresses his experience, masculinity, and wisdom) captures the three of them in his fortress (probably in his arms) and promises to keep them in his heart forever and a day (another distortion of time such as is common in fairy tales).

"CHRIST'S REPLY" EDWARD TAYLOR (published 1939)

This poem responds to EDWARD TAYLOR's "THE SOUL'S GROAN TO CHRIST FOR SUCCOR." To a nonbeliever, the reply initially seems terribly condescending in tone. The opening stanza sounds like a lullaby to quiet an unruly infant for whom the words have no meaning, instead of a precise response to the spiritual questions raised by a serious adult in the earlier poem. Immediately, however, the internal audience is thrown back on his faith; he must trust Christ as completely as an infant would trust its father. At first glance Christ may seem rather free with His promises, yet He has merely asked a rhetorical question and has not really promised anything. A truly devout believer would not be troubled by this, however; having again merged with the power of God, Christ can do anything. On another level, it is fitting that His response seems patronizing: the rewards of heaven are so great that they may be beyond human understanding and the infantile desires of this world.

In the second stanza, Christ adopts the image suggested by the troubled Soul in the earlier poem and places the "yelper fierce" within the conventional Christian image in which He assumes the role of shepherd over the faithful. The enemy of man is used like a sheepdog to keep the faithful in the flock until they are "taken to the pound" (line 11; the "pound" is merely a livestock enclosure like a sheepfold. They are not being led to slaughter; they are merely being taken home).

The Soul had asked Christ to break the yelper's teeth, thus rendering him less fearsome, and in the third stanza Christ states that they have already been broken. Using another agrarian image, He brings the Christians under his wing like a mother hen does to its chicks. In keeping with His strategy of revealing how childish the fears are, he addresses the Soul as "my pretty heart," "my sweeten," and "my chick" (lines 15, 18, and 21). Since both He and the Soul are spiritual beings and hence genderless in their pure, heavenly state, no homoerotic suggestion was intended.

So far His response has been emotional, but midway through the fourth stanza He engages the Soul's intellect. He uses what was then state-of-the-art geography (the poem was written around 1685) in stating that the earth's poles would kiss each other and that parallel lines would converge before any harm came to the Soul (lines 21–23). Satan would exaggerate the believer's sins until they seemed the highest pinnacle on earth in order to shake the Soul's faith, but such mountains would seem like mites if Satan could prevail only once (the Soul under Satan's influence would commit such outrageous sins as to dwarf those already troubling him).

In the sixth stanza, Christ reminds the Soul that His death provided the means of removing the stain of his sin. In subsequent stanzas he promises to continue his leniency although the sin arose from the Soul's willfulness, to curb the yelping of the beagle (much of the terror should dissipate with the naming of this relatively small and immensely popular breed of dog), and to honor true repentance with a pardon even if his sins multiply (as they have in the past each time the Soul sought a pardon, line 50).

Although Satan had discouraged the Soul by suggesting that he was already lost, Christ tells him to fear not even the fires of hell (another of the fears used to keep the believers in line). Although it may seem as if "cursed vermin sins" crawled over the Soul (line 61), these are Satan's own; Christ recognizes the Soul's "true sanctity" (line 65).

The 12th stanza introduces the interesting question of the unpardonable sin, which might be atheism or apostasy (renouncing one's beliefs), but is less likely to be a garden variety of blasphemy. According to the Bible, the worst offense has to be blasphemy against the Holy Ghost (compare Hebrews 10:26–29, Matthew 12:32, Mark 3:29–30 and Luke 12:9–10), the third dimension of the Holy Spirit.

The Soul had been a stall (a small merchant's booth) for selling Satan's wares, but in the 13th stanza Christ promises to replace it with a tabernacle filled with God's spirit (line 77) if the Soul will repent. Slow to anger, Christ will show that even his wrath is full of grace. In thus pardoning all, He "frowns with a smiling face" (line 84). He will even forgive "outward postures," evidently things like speeches and gestures that could influence other souls, if the Soul repents; His grace is more than 30,000 times greater than that needed for this task (lines 87–90).

To Satan's wicked charge that he (and the threat of eternal hellfire) is responsible for the Soul's apparent generosity, Christ instructs the Soul to denounce Satan as a thief for thus misappropriating another's due. Christ recognizes that the Soul's thoughts sometimes wander during prayer, that he does not always embrace sermons, that his fear of eternal punishment sometimes slackens, and that his "zeal in chilly seasons lags" (his religious fervor may be less intense when he is faced with adverse circumstances, line 101). He attributes all these faults to Satan's powerful temptations, and will "show a pleasant face" (line 108) if the Soul receives His grace.

In the meantime He urges the Soul to remain vigilant while he remains on the earth, and to accept unpleasantness like white frosts and showers (such things as death and illness) as part of His plan for preparing the Soul. Just as gold is sometimes melted to remove its impurities (the "dross" of line 120; baser metals float to the surface because they are lighter than the gold in which they had been mixed), the Soul is being refined like a precious metal and should not bewail its losses.

Like a military officer inspiring his troops, Christ encourages the soul to keep fighting His battles while He will be both vanguard and rear guard, thus securing two of the tactically important points on a battlefield. Jesus will be delighted if the Soul will anchor his heart on Him as a ship would trust a rock into which it had anchored.

"THE CITY IN THE SEA" EDGAR ALLAN POE (1845) The speaker in this poem views the devastation after an entire city was inundated by the sea. Its location "far down within the dim West" (line 3) suggests that he was thinking of Atlantis from the perspective of the Greek philosopher Plato in 360 B.C.; his *Dialogues* described the location of the mythical sunken city as beyond the Strait of Gibraltar in the Atlantic Ocean. The worst, the best, and the rest of the people in EDGAR ALLAN POE's city have gone to their eternal rest (line 5), leaving shrines, palaces, and towers that bear

no resemblance to known architecture (Plato's Atlantis was an advanced civilization that vanished 9,000 years before he imagined it). From the city, only the melancholy waters can be seen.

No sunlight (referring to it as "rays from holy heaven" hints that the city's demise may have involved divine retribution; line 12) penetrates deeply, but light from the "lurid sea" silently streams up the torrents, domes, and pinnacles, lighting up the kingly halls, temples (the "fanes" of line 18), and city walls (reminiscent of those of Babylon [line 18]. The reference is probably not to the city once famed for its hanging gardens, one of the wonders of the ancient world, but a far earlier city destroyed by God for its wickedness [cf. Isaiah 13:19]. The lighting seems too uniform for a modern reader to attribute it to the phosphorescence present in some deep-sea creatures, so a likelier explanation is that Atlantis was so advanced as to create perpetual lighting, a civil engineering feat so well executed that it even survived immersion in the ocean depths). The ancient streets featured gracefully carved ivy and flowers, and shrines featured friezes (an architectural term for a horizontal, frequently sculpted pane near the top of buildings) decorated with carvings of the viol, violet, and vine (perhaps representing music, love or fidelity, and agriculture, or [in reverse order, and since the city might have been destroyed for its hedonism] wine, women and song).

The melancholy waters blend turrets and shadows so that all seem pendulous (swinging) in the air, while a personified Death looks "gigantically" down on the town from a proud tower (lines 28–29).

Open temples and graves "yawn level with the luminous waves" (line 30), but neither such riches as the diamonds in the idols' eyes nor the jewels of the dead tempt the waters away. No ripples curl "along that wilderness of glass" (as they might in the grass of a landscape; line 37). The city is deep enough that surface swellings, the result of pleasant winds on happier seas, cannot be felt; not even the "heavings" (of a hurricane at full force) hint that other seas are less hideously serene.

In the last stanza, a stir in the "air" reveals some movement as if the towers had been thrust aside or lost their tops. The waves grow redder, and "the hours breathe faint and low" (a sure sign that something metaphysical is afoot; line 49). Without sound (even "earthly moans"), the town will settle. Hell, rising from a thousand thrones, will pay it reverence (compare Isaiah 14:9–10, in which the former great kings of earth come forth to ask the newly fallen if they are as powerless as the former kings have become).

An alternative interpretation of the "light from out the lurid sea" (line 14) might connect it with underwater lava flows or midocean vents instead of human engineering, but such phenomena typically do not cast lights so bright as to illuminate towers while leaving the surrounding water motionless. They would explain, however, why the waves in line 48 have a "redder" glow, and the hue and heat of burning lava would blend nicely with the fires of hell with which the poem ends.

"CLEMENTINE" ANONYMOUS (c. 1849)

The charm of this folk song, as much beloved by modern grade school choirs as it was by the miners who flocked to the gold fields in the year following the discovery of gold in California in 1848, lies in its refusal to sentimentalize its subject. Although the essential components of the tale would have made a fine melodrama for the Victorian stage, any pathos surrounding the death of this young woman is undermined by the speaker's focus on seemingly irrelevant things. Attentive listeners feel a surge of pleasure when they connect the most unusual of these details with the images and story elements of the stanzas following the ones in which they appear.

The opening lines state that the title character and her father were so at home with mining that they lived two layers removed from the earth's surface. The chorus reveals that she died, that the speaker had a relationship with her, and that he may be in some way culpable for her death, for which he apologizes ("dreadful sorry," line 4).

Given her subterranean existence, it should come as no surprise if her complexion is described as "light" (line 5), although the statement that she was like a fairy suggests that she may also have been light in weight or in spirit. Because the stanza begins with statements about her appearance, at first a reader is likely to inter-

pret the statement that her shoes are "number nine" as a comment on the size of her feet, which would be larger than average but not unreasonably so. The seeming incongruity of this new information with the prior assertion that she is fairylike is resolved in line 7: her footwear was not sized for her feet. She wears sandals made of herring boxes, an indication that she was as hard-pressed financially as many of the pioneering miners had been.

However irregular her wardrobe might have been, her habits were regular. Precisely at nine every morning she "drove her duckling" to the water, but anyone with a passing familiarity with fowl would question her technique. Ducklings are more inclined to be led than driven, and she could have sped up the process by carrying the poor bird. Unfortunately, she hit her foot against a splinter (from her herring box sandals?) and fell into the ocean. The speaker was close enough to see the soft and fine bubbles (which connected her with the "foaming brine" of the prior stanza) she blew from the ruby lips he would never kiss again (lines 13–14), but as a nonswimmer he could not help her.

It seems fitting that Clementine would be interred in a graveyard with myrtle, roses, and posies, for like them, the clementine is a nonnative cultivated plant. The gallows humor the speaker uses is shocking; the reader has not been sufficiently prepared to think of Clementine as fertilizer (line 20). Perhaps it is merely poetic justice that she returns to haunt his dreams in the penultimate stanza, but the speaker is nonplussed. He deftly turns the horror of "her garments soaked in brine" aside with the most humorous line in the poem: Though he used to hug her, "Now she's dead I draw the line" (lines 22–24).

Although Clementine was gone, she was not forgotten. In the last stanza her father peaked (sickened), pined (became distraught), and thought he ought to join her (line 27). Although it is not a medical diagnosis, most of the people who like this poem would agree that he died of a broken heart.

"THE COLLEGE COLONEL" HERMAN MELVILLE (1866)

Many officers on both sides of the Civil War had been college men, either students or professors, before the conflict began, so the elements of this poem's title would not have struck HERMAN MEL-VILLE's initial audience as an incongruous juxtaposition of ranks from the usually distinctly separate worlds of war and peace. Melville was frequently intrigued by such duality when it could be found in a single human nature, but he probably chose the title only partially in reference to the colonel's prewar background. Although the poem honors a real scholar turned soldier, it is centered on his military service. The point may be that the Colonel has acquired enough experience and knowledge to surpass that of his advanced formal education, and the title may also suggest a wealth of experience so vast and profound as to make its possessor a virtual storehouse of knowledge, almost a college unto himself.

The situation of the poem is a victory parade for returning veterans, and the eponymous colonel is riding at the front of his regiment for perhaps the last time. His wounds are now the most conspicuous aspect of his appearance, but Melville also notes his control over his steed, a term generally reserved for an especially spirited horse. Ever more interested in the inner man, he also detects a certain coldness in the colonel's interaction with the animal (line 4).

The parade continued past the speaker, who briefly contrasts the soldiers' appearance with that of the same men who marched forth just two years earlier. He likens their change to a battle flag; they are now practically a remnant, half-tattered, battered, and worn (line 7). Melville had never been to battle, but in attempting to understand these men, the speaker draws on the author's experience as a sailor. The men seemed utterly exhausted ("spent"), like the surviving shipwrecked sailors who finally made landfall on a beach after a ponderous surf and treacherous undertow carried off their shipmates.

The parade now past, the speaker's interest returns to the colonel: he goes beyond the rigidity of the man's bearing and his pale color to recall the lines in his brow. Earlier in American history, many colonists admired the evident stoicism with which Native Americans faced hardship; now the colonel's demeanor seems as inscrutable. Note the use of *lones* instead of *lines* in reference to his brow (line 14); this not only suggests that his "Indian aloofness" separates the man from the rest

of humanity, but it also touches on the loneliness of his isolation. The term signals a shift from contemplating the outer man to contemplating the inner man; subjectively, it feels as if a thousand years of human experience, encompassing everything from pain to prayer, had been compressed into the (at least four) years of his military experience.

Although he had witnessed the jubilation attending the army's return, heard the adulation of the crowd and perhaps even smelled the flowers of the victory wreaths, such sensations are mixed with his own pain. This does not emanate as much from the physical sensations attendant upon his lost leg, maimed arm, or fever (a list which again turns from the external to the internal), but from his spiritual angst. Long periods of physical distress and personal acquaintance with mortality as well as morbidity long ago taught him to disregard the importance of his physicality. Rather, his pain comes from a deeper, almost philosophical source.

Throughout his work, Melville preferred the voice of raw experience to that of erudition. Although the author generally preferred enlistment in the ranks rather than service at the helm, this officer's extensive, first-hand experience of the war is evident not only in a list of his injuries, but also in the particularly gruesome battlefields on which he served. His incarceration at Libby Prison, a prisoner-of-war camp for officers, could not have been as horrific as the experience of the camp for enlisted men at Andersonville, Georgia, would have been, but the dimness of that experience (line 29) could have resulted from his wounds, illness, or limited diet. The reference to the leanness of his brooding (line 30) not only speaks to a lack of food in the camp but also refers to the most profound yet elemental questions a man with no comforts or distractions is forced to ask himself. The speaker will not presume to know what incredible truth the experience led the colonel to, but his ejaculation ("Ah heaven!" in line 31) suggests that its magnitude must be incredible.

"COME SLOWLY—EDEN!" EMILY DICKINSON (1890) One need not be a Freudian critic to appreciate EMILY DICKINSON's imagery. In this poem, the speaker resorts to the language of flowers and the exotic, nearly intoxicatingly sweet (and in this poem, erotic) scent of a flower native to the Old World to set the mood for the poem and, in the language of the 21st-century personal ad, perhaps more. The tone is less subtle than instructive, however, as the internal audience is informed of the speaker's desire to slow down the pace of their relationship. In exchange, she offers "Eden!" with almost ecstatic pleasure. Perhaps because the name of the biblical garden of paradise brings flowers to mind, she thinks of jasmines, and the fact that the flower is also used to flavor tea provides her with the opportunity to elaborate on her instructions. She would prefer that he sip his jasmines (line 3) as her bashful lips are unused to his attention.

The Bee of line 4 is evidently fainting because of the size of his load, for he reached his flower late on his rounds (line 5). That he would hum round her chamber is probably a pleasant enough sensation, given the circumstances, but she offers her most important advice in line 7. He should observe that the Bee slows himself to "count his nectars" before entering the flower, whereupon his needs will be addressed ("Balms" are soothing or healing ointments).

"COMMEMORATIVE OF A NAVAL VICTORY" HERMAN MELVILLE (1866)

It has often been said that all sailors are brothers of the sea because they share its hazards and hardships. This poem celebrates the hero of a naval victory, described as a type of perfection in the first stanza and possessed of powerful social charm and charisma in the second, but it also touches upon the human cost of achieving such success.

Sailors can come "of gentlest breed" (line 1; in an American context, this could either refer to the Quakers or another sect for whom nonviolence was a central tenet of their religion, or to scions of such wealth and position that they would normally be isolated from acts of physical violence and possessed of a refined elegance of manner polished by the best education that money can buy). Although such backgrounds were not common among the enlisted men of the U.S. Navy of the 19th century, a few of the officers shared them. The opening stanza suggests that military service on the sea makes many more of such gentlemen, building

upon their innate strength of character (as though it were the metal from which a sword could be crafted), refining it by the discipline of arms, and "tempering" it with waves (line 4; in metalworking, tempering consists of hardening a metal such as steel by repeatedly heating, hammering, and then cooling it with water). The resulting damasked blade (damasked swords are made from Damascus steel, a relatively primitive process that adds fine waving lines that can be elegant in the blade) flings its beam and lends "the last grave grace" to the warrior (line 6. The phrase not only refers to the deadly menace the fighting man has become to enemies afloat, but also to his "gravity," his dignified manner and substantial character).

Such distinction brings to the speaker's mind a work by Titian (a 16th-century Italian painter of the Renaissance) in which the "hawk, the hound and sworded nobleman" reveal the king to be "of hunter or warrior race" (lines 7–9; save for the hawk, this description [especially the demeanor of its subject] suggests Titian's 1533 painting of the *Portrait of Charles V*).

Years after the victory the hero will be a social lion, feeling his "festal [festive; line 12] fame" in the instinctive glance a woman throws him. He can rest on his laurels; his deed colors the autumnal wine and makes barren places shine (line 18).

However, the laurel wreath is seldom seen without "pensive pansies dark" (line 20). Here follows one of the most insightful statements HERMAN MELVILLE ever made, a theme not only evident in much of his poetry but in many of his novels as well:

> There's a light and a shadow on every man
> Who at last attains his lifted mark (lines 21–22).

Although he may nurse "the ethereal spark" through the night, it is precisely the nights that are the problem. Then the spirits who had hailed his worth (his crew, and perhaps especially that portion of them who died during his successful battle) "sleep in oblivion" (line 26). His dreams are haunted by a nightmarish shark that "glides white through the phosphorus sea" (line 27).

Such an image inevitably brings to mind Chapter 42, "The Whiteness of the Whale," of the poet's novel

Moby-Dick. The narrator relates that it was the whiteness of the whale that most appalled him. White sharks (and polar bears, he argues) attain the heightened hideousness of unnatural contrast because they combine the celestial innocence and love associated with that color with an irresponsible ferocity.

"CONCORD HYMN" RALPH WALDO EMERSON

See "HYMN SUNG AT THE COMPLETION OF THE CONCORD MONUMENT."

CONNECTICUT WITS

From the mid-17th century onward, there was enough wealth and talent gathered in a few towns near the Massachusetts coast to support a thriving intellectual community. Although their men of letters tended to devote themselves to the ministry, individual poets such as ANNE BRADSTREET and EDWARD TAYLOR found their voices in verse. They were still isolated in that pursuit.

The Connecticut (or Hartford) Wits was the first serious writer's community in America in which the production of poetry (albeit in the service of a political agenda) was a major goal. Three members of this fortunate group (JOEL BARLOW, Timothy Dwight, and John Trumbull) gained lasting fame through their poetic efforts and are still widely anthologized. Three others (David Humphreys, Theodore Dwight, and Richard Alsop) gained some notoriety for their verse, while a trio of future physicians (Elihu Smith, Mason Cogswell and Lemuel Hopkins), two future public servants (congressman Uriah Tracey and judge Zephaniah Smith) and the lexicographer Noah Webster, among others, helped provide an appreciative audience in the poets' crucial formative years.

As a movement, the Connecticut Wits can be dated from 1785 (when David Humphreys finished his diplomatic work in Europe and began work on *The Anarchiad,* a series of collaboratively authored satires against such developments as Shays's Rebellion) to the publication of the last installment of *The Echo,* a similar series, in 1807. The chief political aim of the group was the preservation of the newly formed United States and the strengthening of its federal power. On the local level, the group was also concerned with modernizing the Yale College curriculum.

Unofficial membership in the movement varied as several of the young men pursued their careers beyond Connecticut, but most benefited from their association with the group. Joel Barlow is represented in this volume by "ADVICE TO A RAVEN IN RUSSIA" and "HASTY PUDDING." Timothy Dwight is remembered as the author of "Columbia," a patriotic song written during his service as a chaplain with the Continental Army (1777–78), and "Greenfield Hill" (1794). John Trumbull's "M'Fingal" (1782) attacked the Tory opposition to American independence.

BIBLIOGRAPHY
Howard, Leon. *The Connecticut Wits.* Chicago: University of Chicago Press, 1943.

"CONTEMPLATIONS" ANNE BRADSTREET

(1650) In the golden hour before sunset on a fall afternoon, the speaker is captivated by the picturesque beauty of the leaves and fruit on the trees. Ever the good Puritan, she studies nature for clues of divine favor. The scene before her was so perfect that she wonders at the goodness, power, wisdom, and glory of its creator. Transfixed with pleasure, she feels more in heaven than on earth, as if there were neither winter nor night.

In the third stanza she focuses on a majestic oak. Although the tree is admirable for its strength and stature, the hundred or even thousand years since it sprouted are nothing compared with eternity. Viewing the brilliant sun through its leaves leads her to contemplate the glory of "this universe's eye" (line 26). Fortunately, her knowledge and faith preserve her from thinking of the sun as a deity. Although Galileo began studying the stars with a telescope 40 years before ANNE BRADSTREET's poem was published, neither his invention nor his subsequent knowledge had reached the speaker. More modern science would have replaced the word *universe* with *solar system* without changing the essence of her argument. She is connecting with the earliest human experience of which she is aware, albeit from the safety of her own religious beliefs.

The fifth stanza recalls that the Bible put the sun in its place. Psalm 19 implicitly rejects its divinity by comparing it with two seriocomic human figures: a bridegroom rushing from his chamber and a strong man rejoicing at an opportunity to race. An individual in either role can be ecstatic and even glowing, but remains unworthy of worship. Like poets in more primitive societies, the speaker personifies the morn and earth, providing them with coquettish gestures to complement the sun's masculine role. Like a naturalist, however, she notes the sun's effect on birds, insects, and plants, and the descent from a superior life form to less advanced ones not only replicates the order in which they would probably first come to her attention, but also demonstrates her search for the basic principles of life. The sun's heat revivifies all life, vegetable as well as animal, and in all its masculine potency it can dive into "the darksome womb" of nature (line 35), rendering it fruitful.

She has observed the sun's speed in its straight daily path as well as the seemingly oblique path it follows in the course of a year. Everyone on earth is aware of its pleasing fervor and scorching force. The sun's presence determines day or night as well as the four seasons. She hails it as a creature "full of sweetness, beauty and delight" (line 42) but again stops well short of considering it divine. Although the sun is so strong that human eyes cannot look upon it and no "earthly mould" (man is so insignificant that he can be lumped together with everything else on earth) can approach it, the Creator of the sun ("that bright luster") must truly be so majestic as to merit admiration and adoration forever.

Transported by the beauty surrounding her, she wanders off the path in the wood and, raising her eyes to the skies, wants to sing whatever inspired song (the work of her "amazed Muse," line 54) seemed appropriate. She seeks to magnify the great Creator by adding her art to nature's beauty but quickly discovers her lack of capacity. Nature provides an answer. If the grasshopper and cricket seem to glory in the little music they can make, can she not at least warble (like a bird) in the Maker's praise (line 62)?

The 10th stanza serves as a transition to the Garden of Eden from the present nature in which she is immersed. The personalities and actions of people even as far back as the biblical stories can be brought back to life for the man who recalls them. He could even see glorious Adam and the dangling apple that reduced him from lord of all to a naked slave. Note how Bradstreet, indulging in what later generations might praise as feminist revisionism, leaves the blame for his fall completely on Adam's shoulders regardless of Eve's influence. He is banished like a criminal and, like all men, must labor for his bread from then on. A "backslider" (line 77) is one who believes in his religion but lapses into error or neglect of his faith.

Stanza 12 looks at Eve's plight immediately after the birth of Cain, who seems already to be crying at his misfortune and forlorn fate. Eve regrets trading bliss for wisdom and being misled by Satan. As adults, Cain sees that Abel's animal sacrifice was greeted with fire while his was not. He thinks of the thousand ways he can kill his brother to enhance his own future. The earth soon gets her first taste of blood, and often since, she has had so much of it as to sicken at the taste (this is the meaning of "cloyed" in line 95). Cain is left to fear death from everyone he meets and builds the first city walls for protection. Just as the speaker can think back to all men in history, Adam can imagine his descendents. Unfortunately, because of his original sin of eating the apple of knowledge, he sees them clothed in black in consciousness of his sin and their inevitable guilt and punishment.

Having returned to her own time, the speaker compares the current life expectancy with the advanced old age attained by biblical figures. Methuselah died after 969 years, but in the 17th century it was very rare for people to live even a 10th as long. We shorten even that brief time with vain pursuits and idle pastimes. In contrast with the freshness visible everywhere in nature as it is renewed each year, man dies. Even as he lives, worldly care soon replaces the blissful ignorance of human infancy, and after an individual's death even the names of places fall into oblivion. Unlike natural phenomena, however, man is destined for resurrection and immortality (line 140).

By now the speaker has found herself beside a river, a prospect even more agreeable than the woods. Nothing stops its eventual flow; temporary obstacles only enhance its force and a hundred brooks augment its volume. Taking her clue from this aspect of nature, the speaker wishes that her own rivulets (presumably those who join with or nurture her) might press on together with her to the vast mansion of heaven.

When she notices the fish in the river, she thinks them capable of traveling to far-off coasts and of life in either salt or fresh water, migrations of which only a few anadromous species like salmon are capable. Although the fish follow their natural inclinations, they experience no happiness. Like wanton people enjoying their liberty, the fish frisk in the air but soon drop back to the depths where they devour each other.

In contrast to the speaker's earlier inability to perform, a nightingale (Philomel; line 178) begins to serenade overhead, enrapturing her to the point where she wished she herself had wings. Since, in the speaker's opinion, birds do not toil, hoard, worry, or mourn, their lives seem enviable. This is especially true since their main concerns are teaching their offspring to sing and then migrating to a warmer climate.

Man, on the other hand, is frail, vain, ignorant, weak, sorrowful, sickly, and pain-racked. His troubles never cease and are exacerbated by friends and his nearest relatives as well as by his foes. Yet this frail, sinful, sorrowful "lump of wretchedness" (line 205) is still reluctant to leave this life despite all its torments and the promise of heaven.

Thoughts of the divine transformation ahead may have led the speaker to recall the transatlantic voyage in her own past. Like the mariner who thinks himself master of the seas during fair weather but longs for a quiet port when storms arrive, one who lives without turmoil, with constant, uninterrupted exposure to all the delights of earth (including sweets, friends, honor, and treasure) can easily mistake earth for heaven. Eventually, sad affliction will enable him to see that secure honor, wealth, and safety is possible only in heaven.

The last stanza anticipates the thought and central image of "Ozimandias," the famous 1818 sonnet by the British poet Percy Bysshe Shelley. As the product of the English system in which kings and queens enjoyed life at the apex of social as well as political life, thoughts of royalty easily came to mind when she considers the possibility of a human existence sheltered from life's usual knocks. Even the indulgence afforded kings eventually ends, however, and Bradstreet provides a couple of lists of the order in which individual kings pass from the earth. First they die, then their monuments are destroyed, and finally their names are forgotten. Line 229 repeats and partially elaborates on these items, but Bradstreet's choice of rephrasing them as parts, ports, and pomp, words seemingly chosen because they repeat their initial sounds throughout this short series, diminishes the importance of the things they represent as irreverently as time turns everything to dust. Only those who know that their names have been engraved in white stone (a reference from the second chapter of Revelations) are assured of immortality.

One of the secondary advantages of religion is the ways in which it can add layers of meaning to life. As this poem demonstrates, a Puritan not only saw the beauty of nature around her, she also enjoyed an active intellectual life. Bradstreet had the additional advantage of exposure to classical literature. Although she freely mixes Greek and Roman names for the ancient gods, and uses philomel, an alternative name for the nightingale as though it were a proper noun like Philomela, a victimized damsel eventually turned into a nightingale in a Greek myth (line 178), such references reveal that she was using all her resources (direct experience, religion, and education) to come to an understanding of the meaning of human life.

COOKE, EBENEZER (c. 1667–c. 1733)

To have moved from London to Maryland in the late 17th century meant leaving the theatrical center of the Western world with all its commercial and intellectual enticements to settle in a comparative wilderness. While Ebenezer Cooke is chiefly remembered for his authorship, he was also a lawyer prosperous enough to make at least five trans-Atlantic voyages, a land agent, and a landed gentleman (after receiving his inheritance from his father). His surviving literary work consists of four eulogies, a history of Bacon's Rebellion (a short-lived back-country armed challenge to the established government based on the latter's economic and military nonresponsiveness in 1676), his masterwork on a tobacco buyer's escapades and its less successful sequel, "Sotweed Redivivus, or the Planter's Looking Glass" (1730).

"The SOT-WEED FACTOR" (1708) is remarkable for its early satires on provincial mores, traveling salesmen, and substance abuse (alcohol), three fertile sources of American humor for the next 300 years. It is about as accurate in its portrayal of early colonial life in the middle colonies as the science fiction novels of the 19th century were in depicting life on Mars. Because it is a satire, the title character, a tobacco buyer/English manufacturer's representative, loses all his stock and his clothing but survives for another day instead of starving or becoming a frontiersman in lieu of facing embezzlement charges. As a comedy of manners, its backwoods targets might seem too easy but the poem can be read as a study of a "frontierization" process as it reshapes the character of the urbane speaker.

BIBLIOGRAPHY

Barth, John. *The Sot-Weed Factor* (historical novel). Garden City, N.Y.: Doubleday, 1960.

Cohen, Edward H. *Ebenezer Cooke: The Sot-Weed Canon.* Athens: University of Georgia Press, 1975.

Cooke, Ebenezer. *Early Maryland Poetry: the Works of Ebenezer Cook, Gent. and Laureate of Maryland.* Edited by Bernard C. Steiner. Baltimore: John Murphy, 1900.

"THE CORN GROWS UP" ANONYMOUS **(19th century)** For the Navajo tribe of the American southwest, rain was of vital importance, and this song connects the precipitation with a vital agricultural commodity. Perhaps only those who live in such an extremely arid region would watch the dark clouds with such focus that each drop of water seems to register in this song. Since the rain comes from heaven it follows that the corn also does, becoming almost manna from that source.

Among many Native American tribes, naming things and especially repeatedly chanting the names was thought to increase their abundance. This song not only serves that ritualistic function, it may also capture some of the growth cycle of the plant as well as conveying some primitive instruction for its cultivation. Youthful corn may require actual rainfall, but toward the end of the growing cycle such drops as fall from "a dark mist" (line 8) might sustain the plants.

CRANE, STEPHEN (1871–1900) Stephen Crane lived for his art, willingly going to hell for the sake of a good story (or at least to New York's Bowery and other havens of sin). Born November 1, 1871, the son of a Methodist Episcopal minister and a mother whose family had a history of service to that church, Crane inherited ill health (five of his 13 siblings died in early childhood), weekly sermons on damnation, multiple relocations in accordance with his father's postings, and a love for writing. His father died when the poet was eight years old, and his mother, who had been a locally active speaker against alcoholism and other vices, died in 1891. Crane's college education consisted of rapid failures at Lafayette and Syracuse, but the precocious writer was already working as a newspaperman and rapidly improving his fiction. His serious education took place in New York City's Bowery, a district trading in every conceivable vice, and in free-lancing for the city's newspapers. For a typical assignment, he might dress like a bum and expose himself to the rigors of the city's inadequate charity food and lodging. It was all camp to his bohemian friends, the fledgling visual artists, writers, and men about town with whom he sometimes lodged, but it did bring him true empathy for the sufferings of the poor whom he so closely observed. He may initially have been acting out his rebellion from his staid parent's lives (Cady 28), but he also sought such a devotion to his art as could be found among the impressionist painters. Throughout his adult life, he lived as though constantly aware that death was rapidly approaching, and much of his extravagant experience eventually turned up in his work in one form or another.

Crane finished his first novel by the age of 21. *Maggie: A Girl of the Streets* is as remarkable for its original tropes as for its unsentimental rendering of the title character's plight. Although that self-published project was initially unrewarding financially, Crane chanced upon a few Civil War issues of the magazine *Century.* This led to *The Red Badge of Courage,* which made Crane famous at the age of 23, and he began his best poetry while working on that novel. He became a widely traveled adventurer and a serious artist but remained a very poor businessman.

It did not seem to register with him that, if he needed to consort with street toughs of various persuasions in order to advance both his journalistic and artistic aims, the subjects of his study might also use him to advance their own ends. Thus he succeeded in bringing a series of unfortunates to the attention of an American public intent on denying their existence and unwilling to see any connection between their own attitudes and the conditions that trapped such victims of social prejudice, and several of his disreputable acquaintances succeeded in bringing him to the attention of the police and a phalanx of rival, sometimes jealous, reporters. Consorting with women like Dora Clark (whom he tried to protect from police harassment in 1896) had given him *Maggie,* but outside of New York City a growing infamy for a time kept pace with the spread of his literary fame. Smoking, drinking, late hours, poverty and hard, extended bouts of writing shortened his life even as they enabled him to meet the people he preferred to write about and to put them at ease.

Newspaper assignments sent him west to Nebraska and south to New Orleans, Texas, and Mexico (two very good stories, "The Blue Hotel" and "The Bride Comes to Yellow Sky" eventually came from the adventure). His first book of poetry, *The Black Riders and Other Lines,* appeared in 1895. Further journalism assignments took him south, where he spent a harrowing night at sea after being shipwrecked in 1897 (an experience informing "The Open Boat," another of his great stories). While in Florida he met Cora Taylor, a kindred spirit who, like Crane, had chosen an unconventional life. He became an international war correspondent before the age of 30 when he covered a Greco-Turkish war (with Cora) and stayed for a time with her in England. He may have been aware of having had tuberculosis throughout his life (Davis 273), and after he sailed to cover the Spanish-American War in Cuba, he may have taken unnecessary risks in hopes of sparing himself the indignity of slowly wasting away. He returned from the fighting exhausted and stricken with malaria in addition to his other maladies, but he had conducted himself honorably and usually wrote well, although not always in as timely a fashion as his editors would have liked. He also penned *War Is Kind,* his second book of poetry, and much additional prose work. In the meantime, Cora Taylor had stayed in England where she had enjoyed considerable social success as the wife of the famous American author. Returning to her, Crane enjoyed a final year of productivity and

a generally harmonious domesticity despite financial woes and the slow but inexorable failure of his health. Unfortunately, tuberculosis ended the short hungry life of this extraordinary writer on June 5, 1900, in Badenweiler, Germany, where he had been carried in a last desperate gasp at regaining his health.

Crane's poetry has often been dismissed as bleak naturalism that underscores the futility of human effort in the face of overwhelming social as well as natural pressures. Much of his imagery (and the vital freshness of his imagery remains the most important attraction of Crane's poetry) seems to reinforce this interpretation: an apparent madman runs in pursuit of the horizon in "I Saw a Man Pursuing," and a man relishes the eating of his own heart in "In the Desert." His antiwar poetry is less abstract; in "War Is Kind" he juxtaposed realistic portrayals of battlefield deaths with scenes revealing the inadequacy of the comforting words delivered as the next of kin is notified. The speaker in most of his poems is emotionally detached from the individuals he observes as they attempt to understand their cosmic importance ("A Man Said to the Universe") or reach a separate peace with a mortal enemy ("A Youth in Apparel That Glittered").

One of Crane's childhood homes has been preserved in Asbury Park, New Jersey. Major Crane archives can be found at the following universities: Columbia, Syracuse, and Virginia.

BIBLIOGRAPHY
Cady, Edwin H. *Stephen Crane.* Boston: Twayne Publishers, 1980.
Crane, Stephen. *The Works of Stephen Crane.* Vol. 10: *Poems and Literary Remains.* Charlottesville: University Press of Virginia, 1975.
Davis, Linda H. *Badge of Courage: The Life of Stephen Crane.* Boston: Houghton Mifflin, 1998.
Wertheim, Stanley, and Paul Sorrentino. *The Correspondence of Stephen Crane.* New York: Columbia University Press, 1988.

"CREDO" Edwin Arlington Robinson (1897)
The unconventional line break between the octave and sestet of this Italian sonnet underscores its basic insistence on the difference in the speaker's experience when he is stuck in the world of night without hope

and in the same place but with the knowledge (or at least the feeling) that the light is sure to return. Both parts of this poem are surreal, but the sense of the sestet seems predicated on the speaker's assumption that if darkness exists, so must light. In this regard EDWARD ARLINGTON ROBINSON's poem is a partial answer to the prevailing NATURALISM of the decade in which it appeared, a reaction against a pessimistic worldview such as dominated the poetry of STEPHEN CRANE.

The opening line establishes the situation: the speaker cannot continue because he cannot see the stars (especially the North Star in the Northern Hemisphere) on a night so black he calls it not merely cloudy but "shrouded." The term evokes the shrouds in which cadavers were traditionally wrapped before burial, a connotation that suggests the speaker may have figuratively if not literally died. His hearing almost fails him as completely as his sight. That he finds no whisper in the air implies that no one is close to him, and he hears a living voice so far away it sounds like a bar (a single measure or rhythmic movement in a musical composition) from lost, imperial music (perhaps a fanfare), played "when fair and angel fingers" unconsciously wove dead leaves to garlands "where no roses are" (lines 6–8). Garlands are sometimes created to honor the heroes of earthly acclaim but also are used as funerary wreaths, so the lines may be implying that the speaker died in a heroic (or martyred, to account for the angel's involvement) manner. Alternatively, he may be catching a hint of the trumpet announcing Judgment Day. The reader may feel as mystified by the scarcity of clues and sensory perceptions as the speaker is at this point.

The sestet begins in the same place, but with logic that seems a parody of the 17th-century French philosopher Rene Descartes's famous dictum proving his existence ("I think, therefore I am"), the speaker welcomes what he fears ("the black and awful chaos of the night," line 11) as a sign that he must exist if he can feel something, even fear. This helps him recover other aspects of his personality, including his faith and hope. The "far-sent message of the years" (line 13) might have originated in the distant biblical past (compare God's creation of light in Genesis 1:3) or, at the other end of time, in the Judgment Day when everyone will

be resurrected, or in the speaker's faith in such miracles. With so few clues provided as to the identity (or former identity) of the speaker, and because the symbols associated with "the coming glory of the Light" are nearly universal among the world's major religions, it may not be judicious to think of the speaker in exclusively Judeo-Christian terms.

"CROSSING BROOKLYN FERRY" WALT WHITMAN (1856)

Because it ostensibly presents WALT WHITMAN's strategy for gaining immortality through his art (or at least his hope that he may know somehow when his work is read and appreciated in the coming centuries), this poem provides valuable clues to his aesthetic values and his motivation as an artist.

The first section celebrates the multitudes of people (a "flood-tide;" line 1) that the speaker meets on the ferry and the countless multitudes of people soon to be settling the West (the "clouds of the west" [line 2], although both the tide and the clouds also refer to the features of the landscape). S/he ends by considering those who will cross "from shore to shore" (those who will take the same ride, but also everyone from the Atlantic to the Pacific) in the future. Then he pays his future audience the compliment of stating that they are more in his meditations than they might suppose.

The two major themes of the poem, the speaker's enjoyment of the sights and his desire to share them with his future readers, are delightfully rendered in the ambiguity of the opening line of the second section. As the poem unfolds, nearly equal emphasis will be placed on the speaker's gaining as well as giving "the impalpable sustenance of me" from everything and at all hours. Here he calls attention to his craftsmanship, the "well-joined scheme" (line 7; "joinery" is a technical term revealing the poet's background in carpentry; it refers to the skill of interlacing the ends of two boards together which is so essential to the art of furniture-making). Although he will have disintegrated, he counts on the similarities of past and present and "the glories strung like beads," his recording of the smallest sights and sounds (line 9). He hopes that the currents of interest and emotion that carry him away will be transmitted to the reader like the tidal rush of the river beneath him. Other people will make the crossing and watch the river, the islands, and the ships. He hopes that many centuries later his audience will have a similar experience based on his artistic rendering of the scenes.

In the third section, the speaker emphasizes his place in the scenes. Time and distance do not matter since those who enjoy the view he is describing must also note his presence in the picture. In fact, he is more than a guide; his art aims at getting the reader to consciously see things through his eyes. Lest this seem too much of an imposition, in the second stanza he shifts the focus to his extraordinary powers of observation. None of the other travelers will take note of the way the seagulls oscillate their bodies beneath their motionless wings (line 28) or the ways in which the setting sun turns part of their bodies to glistening yellow but leaves the rest in strong shadow. The reader is clearly in the presence of an artist, if not more: He points out the "fine centrifugal spokes of light round the shape of his head" in the water (line 33; the description is reminiscent of the halos surrounding the heads of saints in medieval paintings). He saw the colors change in the vapor, the white sails of ships and the sailors working in their rigging. He felt the swinging motion of the hulls and describes their "slender serpentine pennants" very effectively (line 40). He saw the flags of all nations, the "scallop-edged" waves, the far-off gray walls of the storehouses, and the smaller boats and barges that service the larger ones (tugboats help larger vessels and barges turn in the limited confines of the harbor; lighters are barges used to load and unload cargo ships). For added dramatic effect, he contrasts the smoke (a "flicker of black") coming from foundry (factory) chimneys with the "wild red and yellow light" over the rooftops.

The fourth part re-establishes the speaker's contact with the future travelers, those who will see all the things mentioned in the prior stanzas and who will love the cities and the river as he does. He anticipates that future passengers will look back on him just because he looked forward to them (line 52) "even though I stop here today" (even if his ride or his life ends today) and tonight (even if he dies or stops writing for that night and perhaps forever).

The next section begins with rhetorical questions about his relationship with his future audience and how many years separate him from that reader. He again argues that the time, distance, and place do not matter. Like them, he also lived in Brooklyn, walked Manhattan streets and bathed in the river, and he also "felt the curious abrupt questionings stir within me" (line 59; although this may refer directly to his discovery of his sexual orientation, it could also apply more generally to everyone). In crowds of people, on his night walks, and in his bed, such feelings were sometimes aroused. He was struck "from the float" like a particle struck from a solution (the simile is based in chemistry: a solution is a blend of substances [salt and water might be taken as an example]. When the conditions that supported the blending are changed [by heating or cooling, for example, or by adding more particles than the liquid can contain], the solution may not be able to hold all the particles in it and will release some. Whitman's point is that he did not fit in with the rest of society; line 62). Taking his cues as well as his identity from his body, he realized what he was and what he should be.

In part six he talks about his "dark patches," the depression that made him doubt his work and the quality of his thought. Like the audience, he has known evil and was even evil himself (line 70), and the litany of his sins includes all the seven traditional deadly sins (pride, envy, gluttony, lust, anger, greed and sloth). He also blabbed, lied, acted cowardly and meanly refused, but the transgression that bothered him the most was hearing young men call his nighest name (by a very familiar nickname or other term of endearment; *nigh* is an antiquated term meaning "near"), feeling their arms around his neck or their flesh leaning against him, and seeing many whom he loved in public places—but never telling them a word (lines 79–81).

His use of the past tense throughout this section is extremely significant, for it suggests that giving up his old role in favor of his true identity made him an honest man. Formerly he recognized the wolf, the snake, and the hog in himself (line 75) as he laughed, gnawed, and slept (line 82), but now he is free to take on the great or small role that is truly his (lines 83–85).

By the seventh section, the speaker is so sure of the connection he has made with the future audience that he assures them that he was thinking of them just as they think of him (line 87). He holds out the possibility that he may yet somehow know of their attention and might even be enjoying it, and that despite the time and distance (and his death), he may be looking at them even now, for all they know.

In the penultimate section he revisits some of the more memorable things mentioned earlier, but now he thinks there are no gods that can exceed those who clasp his hands and call him by his nighest name. He likes the subtlety of those of both genders who look in his face, an act that "fuses me into you" and "pours my meaning into you" (line 97; Freudian critics might profitably ponder such a line, but he is apparently also using procreative metaphors as an illustration of or analogy for the process by which he is recreated by the reader). By this point, both reader and speaker should understand what he promised without naming, what study cannot teach, and what preaching cannot accomplish.

The final part again rejoices in the river, the gorgeous sunset, the tall masts and hills. He calls for the "baffled and curious brain" to throb and throw out questions and answers (line 106), and for the suspension of "the eternal float of solution," and for young men to call him by his nighest name. He wants readers to live, and to perceive that he is perhaps looking upon them (line 112). More details from earlier in the poem follow, but now he wants appearances to indicate what you are, and for his body and yours to be hung with the most divine aromas (line 122).

The last stanza of the ninth section addresses the "dumb (a term perhaps used in the old-fashioned sense of "incapable of hearing [or listening]" instead of "unintelligent"), beautiful ministers" (line 126). We (by now the speaker calculates that his ideal reader is identifying with him) receive them "with free sense" (reason unhampered by doctrine) and from then on are "insatiate" (always open to additional nourishment and never satisfied; line 127). Fully comfortable with our new identities, we will not be foiled or allow the priests to withhold themselves from us (at various times in American and world history,

churches have prevented people it labeled as deviants from joining their customary rituals. This could happen formally, through excommunication in some religions, or informally, through social pressure). We will still use them, even "plant [them] permanently within us," for we love them without understanding them. They also have perfection and "furnish [their] parts" (fulfill their role) toward eternity and toward the soul.

"THE CROSS OF SNOW" HENRY WADSWORTH LONGFELLOW (1886)

In the sleepless nights that can accompany old age, HENRY WADSWORTH LONGFELLOW would have us believe that he sometimes had hallucinations in which the face of his second wife appeared on the wall. In the 19th century, people who believed in the efficacy of such visions and other means of contacting the dead were called spiritualists, a surprisingly widespread movement that remained strong well into the 20th century. Although many people fell prey to the legions of confidence men and women willing to capitalize on their grief-stricken state with contact-the-dead scams, the true believers were often prompted by biblical promises of the immortality of the human soul. They typically did not believe in the haunting by ghosts in the horrifying forms embraced by late-20th-century popular culture in connection with Halloween but in a love so strong that it could transcend death.

Both ghost-lovers and spiritualists would appreciate the appropriateness of the conditions in which Longfellow saw his vision, for he continued to sleep in the very room in which his wife died following very tragic circumstances. Her dress caught fire as she was sealing a locket of her daughter's hair (a far more popular keepsake in the 19th century than later), and Longfellow was severely burned as he put out the flames but failed to save her life. It is probably a testament to his will that her gentle face (line 2) appears as he must have so often seen it during their 19-year marriage instead of in the agonized aftermath of her "martyrdom by fire" (line 6). He admits that his night-lamp was responsible for the halo that surrounded her face, but he insists that her life was as blessed as any preserved by legend.

Although the poet saw only a picture of the Colorado mountain with its cruciform snow-filled crevices, he liked the image so well that he took it as emblematic of his circumstances. As her death occurred in July 1861, internal evidence ("I carried this cross eighteen years," line 13) dates the composition of the poem as 1879. As an image, the cross "upon [his] breast" (line 11) suggests the white welts that can scar a burn victim, but it reminds him not of her death but of her life in much the same way that the Christian cross represents not the death of Christ but his life and the promise of Resurrection. Instead of reminding him of her suffering, the pristine snow brings to mind her purity.

As a testament of his undying love for his late wife, this Italian sonnet, the product of the poet's intellect and lifelong practice of his craft as well as of his heart, stands as an enduring memorial.

"CRUMBLING IS NOT AN INSTANT'S ACT" EMILY DICKINSON (published 1951)

One of the things 21st-century fighter pilots tend to believe is that it is never one mistake that kills you, but a series of errors that undermine the built-in redundancies of their space-age technology. In this poem EMILY DICKINSON's speaker expresses the same belief (and advocates the same close attention to seemingly minor details) in his/her religious faith.

The first line presents her thesis and the second line clarifies what is meant by an instant's Act: "a fundamental pause" (a moment when the major fundamental ethical laws are reversed or are thought irrelevant or unimportant). She argues that this does not happen in nature because dilapidation's processes are smaller and more organized decays (a statement that brings dentistry to mind. Although nothing else in the poem leads in that direction, in dentistry, too, her general rule applies).

Three of the four illustrating analogies making up the second stanza are drawn from housework, and each would be a minor indication of neglect if so much were not riding on the outcome. A cobweb can easily be overlooked, but a "Cobweb on the Soul" (line 5) is a much more serious thing since it proves the presence of spiders and probably much worse. Add a "cuticle" (presumably an amount equal in size to the hardened layer of skin framing a fingernail; line 6) of dust and you have almost a recipe for disaster, a "Borer" (something that bores in the sense of making a hole) in the "Axis" (an alliance, perhaps a reference to the implied contract between a believer and God), or an "Elemental Rust" (line 8) that can eventually erode even the strongest metals.

The third stanza attributes this slow but inevitably corrosive process to the devil's work. The speaker concludes by asserting that no man fails in an instant (no proof is provided), and that "slipping" (a verb close to that used for "backsliding," turning one's back on one's religion) is "Crash's law" (line 12).

The sense of the final lines is that crumbling is a slow process with several steps that can be compared to slipping when slipping is only a step on the way to crashing and failing. As a whole, the poem argues that moral slippage (resulting in a mistake large enough to be visible) is a direct result of crumbling (a series of much smaller and more gradual mistakes) but leads directly to crashing and failing. Although the meaning of these lines can seem unclear in their details, the implication is clear: small sins and compromises begin the process that leads to the destruction of the soul.

D

"THE DALLIANCE OF THE EAGLES"
WALT WHITMAN (1880) One of the mistakes naturalists must avoid is anthropomorphism, the interpretation or description of animal behavior in human terms. WALT WHITMAN was not a trained scientist, but devoting his life to poetry gave him a keen interest in nature and the ability to preserve in verse such astonishing natural phenomena as he was privileged to observe. Once he saw two eagles falling together from the sky.

This was so unusual that he takes pains in the first line of the poem to establish that he was taking his customary stroll along a river when it happened; he wants the reader to know that he is describing a real incident and not an extraordinary flight of his poetic imagination. He was not exaggerating, and modern readers who want to see it for themselves should find a copy of a fascinating Public Broadcasting Service (PBS) documentary based on a season's filming of sea eagles, close cousins of the bald eagles Whitman is probably describing. The highly territorial birds try to intimidate interlopers, and the encounters frequently end with their locking talons and plummeting toward the sea in a raptorial game of "chicken." Eventually one breaks away from the other and either resumes its aerial assaults or flies away from the more aggressive victor.

The most astonishing aspect of this poem is how much Whitman got right; it takes all the scientific advances of 21st century cinematography, especially its high-powered lenses and slow-motion film, to reveal the same details that the poet caught with his naked eye. If stripped of its erroneous interpretation of the event as mating behavior, Whitman's account could provide perfect narration for all the gyrations of their aerial combat as well as their fierce stabbing beaks and hammering wings. At times they fall in rapidly spinning circles with their claws linked in the center and their backs and heads whirling on the outside.

The language of the second and third lines ("the dalliance of the eagles, the rushing amorous contact high in space together") captures an extraordinary moment, but naturalists have established that Whitman was almost certainly viewing a scene of combat and not of love. Eagles, as the PBS film reveals, mate on their nests in the same rather prosaic manner as most birds.

It is tempting to think that Whitman would have withdrawn the poem had he become aware of its scientific inaccuracy. It is even more tempting to think that Whitman, elsewhere in his poetry a celebrator of androgyny and a reveler in homoerotic imagery, might have liked it even more. Its rather conventional assignment of gender roles based on pursuit behavior by presumed males and indifferent or retreating behavior by presumed females is an example of anthropomorphism based on the prevalent social norms of the author's day.

"DANK FENS OF CEDAR, HEMLOCK BRANCHES GRAY" FREDERICK GODDARD TUCKERMAN (1860) At twilight, FREDERICK GOD-

DARD TUCKERMAN's speaker asks why an unpleasantly damp swamp (the "dank fens" of the first line) has such a hold on his heart. A quick survey reveals the dominant foliage in the area, including cedar (a misleading Eurasian name adopted for several North American cypress species), hemlock (possibly the Eastern or Carolina Hemlock) and pitch pine trees. Together they offer a limited palate ranging from the very dark green of their needles to the black of their trunks, with large clumps of Spanish moss adding subdued silvery gray highlights to the scene. Collectively, they project an aura of death, an association the poet reinforces with his diction: remnants of rain and "droppings of decay" litter the ground. The more active life appears to have been bled from the scene like the red autumnal leaves that have wasted away (line 4), and the thick leaves weaken what little daylight remains.

The sestet suggests that, in the bog's isolated tranquil darkness, "the bread of tears becomes the bread of life" (line 10). This is not only botanically accurate (decaying vegetative matter is often highly nutritious for the seedlings that develop in it), it also serves as a transition to the speaker's mental state (which he describes in similarly organic ways). In such an oasis from "the roar of the day (line 11) . . . fresh griefs beat tranquilly" (this oblique reference to the heart as the [metaphorical] seat of emotions connects with the mention of that organ in the 6th line, aiding the poem's coherence). The "loves and vows" which grow in gray shadows (not only with the fuller consciousness of life that includes death and decay, but also deeply rooted in fertile soil and aided by secrecy) become far dearer than "lovely lights and roses" (that are more easily acquired).

"DAREST THOU NOW O SOUL" WALT WHITMAN (1868)

The speaker in WALT WHITMAN's poem faces the problem of death by coaching himself as if his soul was distinct from the rest of his being. This has the advantage of imagining a companion on the journey to "the unknown region" (line 2) where there will be neither ground for the feet nor a path to follow. His chief fears are of being lost (having no map or guide; line 3) and of becoming isolated from the voices, touch, and sight of other people. Neither his intellect (for that seems to be the part of his personality

that is shaping his arguments) nor his soul has any idea of what to expect (lines 8–9).

At some point even the ties between the rest of his identity and his soul will end. When only the eternal ties of Time and Space survive, he expects that darkness, gravitation, "sense" (a word encompassing both the body's capacity for sensory perceptions and the mind's search for reason and order in the universe; line 12) will perish along with any other of the bounds that humans experience.

The novelty of bursting forth to "float in Time and Space" (lines 13–14) is so great that the speaker begins looking forward to it. With the soul somehow prepared for the new adventure, the speaker feels "equal equipt" (equipped with the right tools for the job [thus being equal to the task], but the phrase may also imply that the speaker and the soul are equally prepared for the change; line 15) "at last." Whitman's parenthetical phrase ("O joy! O fruit of them all!") implies that he anticipates a fusion of the two after death, a thorough integration of the intellect and soul that eludes mortal life. He finally arrives at a point where he views death as the fulfillment of life, or at least a portal to the "joy!" and "fruit of all!" (line 15), that he anticipates from being integrated into eternal Time and Space. He is now joyous at the very prospect of uniting his sense of self with his soul and thus fulfilling his earthly destiny.

"DARE YOU SEE A SOUL AT THE WHITE HEAT?" EMILY DICKINSON (1891)

EMILY DICKINSON seems so astoundingly modern in most of her poems that it can be shocking to realize that she lived in the heyday of the village blacksmith, when everything iron from horseshoes to wagon rims had to be custom-made at the local level.

At first the poem reads as though the reader were being invited to see a soul immersed in the torments of hell. The internal audience is cautioned "to crouch within the door" (line 2) as if invited to view an illicit act that may put their own souls in danger, but the initial readership, more acquainted with such scenes, would have soon realized that it was their flesh at risk because of the many physical hazards lurking in such a workplace. In the center of their town blazed a red-hot fire stoked with coal and oxygenated by a huge bellows. When the glowing ore had "vanquished Flame's conditions" (gotten as hot as it could under the circumstances; line 5), it "quivered" from the forge (a sign that the iron was nearly molten and hence malleable). The parts that received the most heat (the end of an iron rod, for example), would be white hot, described here as the color of "unannointed Blaze" (unholy fire; "to anoint" is to sanctify with holy oil during a religious ceremony and but "to be anointed" can also mean being chosen by God).

In even the smallest village a blacksmith could be heard hammering the heated iron into the desired shape on an anvil (line 10). In the hands of a skilled craftsman such work might produce an "even ring," a description that might refer either to sound (unlikely, since "clamorous clangor" would be more apt) or to a perfectly formed iron loop that the speaker offers as a symbol of the "finer forge that soundless tugs within" (the conscience, or the inner workings of God on the soul; lines 11–12). Such divine work refines the soul while the hammer and blaze of life shape "the impatient Ores" (the souls not ready for heaven) until the "Designated Light" (the newly minted "perfect soul") leaves the forge (and all the troubles of this world) behind.

THE DAY OF DOOM MICHAEL WIGGLESWORTH (1662)

The creative challenge of this poem was to make Christ's message more immediate by gathering all the references to Judgment Day in the Bible, arranging them in chronological order, linking them with transitional phrases, illustrating them with specific examples drawn from colonial life, and rendering the whole in a ballad meter with which his intended audience would be very familiar. The poem's straightforward narrative in New England vernacular made the apocalyptic events come alive for its initial audience. The effect was enhanced by the intellectual climate in which it appeared; of the few books that fell into the hands of the average man or woman in early colonial Massachusetts, the most dominant were the family Bible in the home and the Bay Psalm Book in church. The printed word in general, and especially in those texts that dealt with religious matters, was held in far

higher esteem than it would later be. The colony was medieval in the sense that everything revolved around the church, and individual Puritans routinely scrutinized their daily lives for evidence of divine favor.

The Day of Doom was one of the most successful poems ever published in America because it provided an interactive experience for its initial audience. It was anchored in the Bible, which most New Englanders accepted as the word of God, and because MICHAEL WIGGLESWORTH used a common hymn meter, it lent itself to song. Many of the Puritan readers would have recognized all of the author's references, and a century and a half before it started becoming fashionable to document sources, Wigglesworth provided citations to assist those who were less familiar with his source. Some of his readers would consider it a work of faith to compare the poet's use of the material with the original, and the two were close enough for many of them to accept both works as the word of God. Most of them could not only recognize the familiar verses but also aspects of their own lives and those of the people around them that clearly put them at risk of eternal damnation. The initial audience must have found it engrossing to imagine certain of their peers in the assorted groups of the condemned.

As a horror story, the poem's most fearsome aspects are the swiftness with which the end of time overtakes everyday life, the severing of all earthly connections, and the irrevocable judgments meted out en masse by the celestial court. The chief torture of hell mentioned in the poem is eternal burning without any comfort from other souls. Only a 10th of the poem deals with the arrival of Christ in the beginning and the delivery of souls to their fates at the end. The rest of the poem deals with the trial, and part of its charm for readers of a later century is the colorful arguments advanced by the differing groups of the condemned.

The opening stanzas show the world morally as well as physically asleep; "carnal reason" (human reason, which is at least partly based on the desires of the flesh; line 3) thought the night's calm would last forever, but the speaker exposes their various types of hypocrisy. Some people had been drinking the prior evening in slothful expectation that the good times would continue. Similarly thinking themselves secure, vile wretches lay "wallowing in all kind of sin" (like pigs in mud, an agricultural image with which everyone in America at the time was familiar; line 9). Even the best of men scarcely kept their lamps (the guiding light for their souls) spotless. "Unwise virgins" (line 13; presumably those who have abandoned chastity or are eager to do so) are also exposed, even though they had been wise enough to conceal their sins from human society, and even the wise have slumbered.

Whereas the second stanza associated sin with dirt, the third stanza reminds the reader that once before, God cleansed the world by drowning everyone but Noah and his family. Notice how subtly the poet connects the condemneds' drowning of their cares and fears (probably by the consumption of alcohol) with their drowning in the flood. Like contemporary men, the ancient victims had been complacent in their security. Because the majority of 18th-century Americans lived on farms, they would have connected the depiction of sinners caught suddenly in a snare (line 31) with vivid images of animals similarly surprised.

The miracles of the Day of Doom begin at midnight in the fifth stanza, when a light brighter than the noon sun illuminates the land. Jesus and his associates arrive en masse to judge both the living and the dead (line 48), and the noise of the skies being pulled apart is more terrible than thunder. The initial audience would understand that to damp a lamp (line 53) meant to reduce its brilliance by wetting the wick of its candle and perhaps to extinguish it. The stars, personified, frightened and dismayed, quit their usual places.

Christ's arrival has the same chilling effect on the blasphemers as if their hearts had been "thrilled" by swords (line 60). Just as their words obscured His until now, the atheists were unable to perceive Him until confronted with His glorious presence. Even the bravest men ("Stout Courages") tearfully lament that their former strength was their undoing, and even the most powerful rulers are abashed at the dreadful sight.

For 18th-century New Englanders, reference to the "robes" of great men (line 82) called to mind the clergy of either the Anglican or the Catholic Church. True Puritans believed that even the most faithful adherents to other Christian sects would ultimately be damned, and their tearing of their own robes, hair, and flesh

recalls the incidents of self-mortification undertaken by many of the Catholic saints. This reinforced the rightness of the Puritan path for the initial audience. Horror fills the world of the poem, but no one is permitted to die from it on the Day of Doom.

After the initial shock, some try to hide in caves, valleys, or mountains, but others try to escape by leaping into the ocean. Notice the delightful ambiguity of line 93; "senseless blocks" may refer to the rocks to which the desperate men run, or to the men themselves. The terror of the moment is aptly captured in such descriptive phrases as "Judge's ire, more hot than fire" (line 99). Not even the darkest things can be hidden from His flaming eyes.

The Judge arrives surrounded by angels; His majesty terrifies every creature. Quakes shake the earth as if she were trying to cleanse herself or be born (lines 115–116). The sea recedes but wild beasts flee into it. It is beyond earthly or even angelic power to describe the bright glory, and the speaker desists from the attempt for fear of transgression (line 128). The Judge calls forth the dead not just from the land and sea, but also from the fire and air (line 139); this line not only recalls those who were cremated but goes back to antiquity for its four essential elements of earth, air, fire, and water.

The laws of nature are further transcended when the living are "translated" (line 145) to immortality. Both the faithful Puritan and the sinner ("the renate and reprobate") will receive their respective eternal rewards and never die again. Like bailiffs or sheriffs, angels (the "winged hosts" of line 153) gather everyone from all shores, even apprehending the human moles from their holes and using force when necessary. Everyone is sorted into groups according to merit and probable reward.

At Christ's right hand are the Christian martyrs who suffered for their faith and sealed their testimony with their blood (line 174). Next to them were the afflicted who not only accepted their misery without complaint but loved God more because His chastisements kept them from straying. Those who were ready to bear such suffering but who were spared such tests were also added to the sheep. Next came the flock of lambs "whose faith was weak, yet true" (line 194), including an "infant throng" whom Christ sanctified. All of the saved have white robes and faces full of pleasure because they have been "conformed" (line 207); they share in the Lord's divine glory.

At Christ's left hand are the goats, beginning with the hypocrites who formerly thronged among the righteous but with insincere hearts. Next come those who turned away from Christ, and the devil and seven even more evil accomplices already have possession of them, those who ignored His call, and the lewd blasphemers. They are joined by Sabbath-violators, persecutors of saints, those who did not love the true believers, adulterers and the unchaste, the greedy, the unethical, wicked children and the parents who misguided them, liars, murderers, "and men of blood" (line 262), witches and drunks (stanzas 31–33).

The next few stanzas are rarely anthologized in the early 21st century because they brand adherents to all other faiths as heathens and infidels destined for everlasting fire. A fierce and deadly lion, a dragon, and legions of hellish fiends and spirits stand ready to transport the damned. In dismal chains the sinners await Christ's decree.

All are silent, then Christ mildly tells the elect that all their sins are pardoned (stanza 38). He points out that even they have been judged, so no one else can hold a grudge or charge Him with partiality. In stanza 40, He explains that God chose these elect before creating the world and sacrificed Him (Christ) to save them. For their sake, Christ took human form and suffered unjust reproach and scorn (line 320). In stanza 41, Christ recalls the many sorrows He endured as He drank His bitter cup, including the pain of crucifixion, the experience of His Father's anger, and the blood He shed to save the elect from hell.

The elect, Christ explains, were chosen from every nation. They could have been as vile as humanly possible and yet by God's grace are they set free. No one may object because the nature of grace means that God may choose whomever He pleases (stanza 43). Similarly, Christ underwent punishment for those He chose, and the elect from both groups are granted immediate bliss. For their part, Christ's elect lived fruitful, penitent, self-denying, and charitable lives, and bore their crosses well.

The blessed ones are promised they will never again be annoyed by sin and are given thrones to help in judging (stanza 48). The wicked grind their teeth in envy, for the murdered and the humiliated now judge. No wicked are neglected or respected (stanza 51); all face eternal woe and endless misery. New England inherited much of its class consciousness from England, so several stanzas repeat the promise of equality before the celestial court.

The accused must give a straight account of their misdeeds and are confronted with evidence they cannot deny. Everyone must bear witness against himself, so his sins condemn him (stanza 56). The light shines on "all filthy facts and secret acts" (line 466) no matter how trivial or ancient, but no shocking details are provided. In stanzas 60 to 65, the sinners are asked why they did not heed the many warnings and lead better lives. In stanzas 66–67, all who stand on Christ's left are condemned.

No one is able to clear himself, but the following stanzas offer their excuses and the Judge's reply. The hypocritical priests point out the souls they saved and the sacraments they performed, but Christ asks why they could not follow the right path. Like inattentive servants, they had left their master's will undone (stanza 73). In regard to their consumption of holy wafers and wine representing Christ's flesh and blood, Christ asks how they came into His presence with their sins ("vile raiment," line 607). They tainted the spiritual meat, and thus the rituals and communal dining sign and seal their fate.

Next came those who reformed their lives after receiving His Word. Christ angrily reminds them of the abomination in their hearts (line 672) and their hypocrisy. They came to Him not as dutiful Christians but compelled by fear of hell, and took up religion to ease their consciences (stanzas 89–91).

When sober ethical businessmen advanced with accounts of their clean living and good deeds, Christ replied that they owed God true piety as well as honesty. Adopting a business analogy, he asks if they would have accepted 20 pounds where a thousand pounds (an enormous amount of British currency at the time) was due. Their boasting of their straightforward deals also mars their appeal, for God can see iniquity in the heart when men cannot (stanzas 98–99). Since they had neither true love nor faith, their vanity led them to believe they could scale heaven with ladders of their own (lines 806–807). In haughty pride they laid Christ aside and trampled on his blood (lines 815–816). Even the Ninevites and Sodomites (line 821, evil residents of two cities of the Old Testament) did not turn their backs on Christ, but these men took pride in their names among men. Their gold is brass and their silver is dross (the waste products rising to the surface of molten precious metal; line 864) because their righteousness without faith merits shame and damnation.

To the multitudes who died before reforming their behavior, including those who died young, Christ argues that they had the great gift of the Sabbath to seek God's face in their hearts (line 880) and turn from the devil. They should not have had time for "carnal pleasure" (line 885; as used here, the term refers to all pleasant human sensations) and toys when they often were told and saw that death comes at all ages. If earnest, they would have made some effort in the right direction, but their pretenses cover wickedness.

Stanzas 114–115 deal with those who argue that they were led astray by the actions of respected men of learning and arts. Christ asks how they could forsake the rule by following the example of men when they know most men are liars (line 929). To those who point to some among the saved who led them astray, Christ asks how they could follow the defects of those good men (who sincerely repented in their hearts) but not their good parts (stanza 119).

To those who argue that the rules were difficult for even the brightest men to understand, Christ asks why they did not follow the plain truths and study the harder ones. Although God reveals the mystery of piety to babes and conceals it from the world, they ought to have done the good they knew (stanza 123). For those who feared for their lives and property to live piously among evil men, Christ answers that they chose to save their skins instead of their souls (stanza 128).

Others tearfully throw themselves on the well-known mercy of God, asking if a few offensive years merit everlasting pain (stanza 131), but grief is too late at the end of life (line 1072). Christ points to many among the saved as evidence of God's clemency, but those of the "stiff necked race" (line 1085) refused his cords of love. They grew worse instead of better, and mercy refused and grace misused deserve severity (lines 1103–1104). Every crime must be punished, and instead of punishing the sin, it is now time to punish the sinner (stanza 139). Now no one will regard the misery of anyone who did not hear the voice of wisdom. Instead of wondering at their fate, the damned should wonder why they lived in sin despite the danger. God takes no joy in punishing, but it is necessary because he delights in displaying justice and plaguing sin (stanza 143).

A group argues that since they were not among the elect from the beginning they should not be held accountable (stanzas 144–146). Christ rejects this as an attempt to separate the ends and the means, and argues that he condemns none but those who swerved from righteousness. Besides, how did they know they were not of the elect (stanza 151)? Their choices condemned them.

Numberless heathen are brought forward to argue that they never heard the word (stanza 156). Christ answers that they will be punished only for their own transgressions. When they persist, He says that He gave them knowledge, clear sight, and right judgment, all of which they lost (stanza 162). They had not been true according to the light of nature (line 1310) and must perish for not improving themselves.

Next come the dead infants, who complain that Adam's sin was not theirs (stanza 167) and beg for mercy. They ask why Adam, the chief offender, goes free while the innocent are punished. The Judge responds that it was not Adam's fall, but both his and theirs (stanza 171). Christ doubts that they would have protested had Adam not fallen, so they should accept punishment just as they would have accepted reward. Moreover, they would have fallen had they been in Adam's place (stanza 176), and they should realize that His grace would not be grace if He lacked the liberty to bestow or withhold it (stanzas 178–179). Admittedly, their sins are not as great as those of people who actually lived, and he therefore allows them "the easiest room in hell" (line 1444).

Finally all the sinners accept the reasoning behind their fate and stand silenced and ashamed (stanza

182); all rue their births and envy the dogs and other animals that do not face damnation. Their numbers are more than the motes in the air, than their hair, or the sands of a beach (stanza 185). They can neither argue nor flee, and must be cast into the burning lake (line 1619). Their pleasures and treasures have been taken, and privileged birth and education avail them not (stanza 191). Christ fires the earth's foundation, and the flaming sky will drop about their ears like molten lead (lines 1534–1537). Neither the attendant angels nor their fellow sinners will aid them, and the condemned regret bringing down others with them. The saints are unmoved, and their former friends among the elect are now more friend to Christ (stanza 195). Not even saved brothers or wives pity the fallen (stanza 197). Mothers claim only their saved children, and the pious father prefers that his graceless son burn in hell (stanza 199) and rejoices when Christ delivers the sentence.

Christ orders the sinners' departure for the lake (stanza 201), and the damned realize the pain of separation from Him and the terror of eternal pain. Their cries ascend to the skies, but without hope or help (stanza 204). They can only gnash their teeth and gnaw their tongues (line 1636) until chased to hell like chaff or dry dust in the wind. On the edge of hell their hands and feet are chained before they are tossed in (stanza 209). They wail, cry, and howl all day and night, forever suffering death but never actually dying (stanzas 210–211). The speaker cannot describe the 'exquisite torments' (line 1689) and plagues of hell, but the lightest pain there would be intolerable here.

The worst sufferers are those who knew the right but would not live in it; their pains are sevenfold. Even the Amorites and Sodomites are punished less. "Experience and woeful sense" (line 1733) painfully teach those who would not believe or credit their preachers. They torment their hearts with poison darts (line 1739) but still cannot die. Turning back to the saved, the speaker finds saints encouraged and thankful that their foes are punished. They sing a song of endless praise to Christ and proclaim his justice. They have eternal rest and enjoy the divine presence (stanza 220). Grief's watercourse and sorrow's source are turned to joyful streams, while their old distress and heaviness

vanish like dreams (stanza 222). They are eternally pleasured by God's embrace (stanza 223) and need not fear punishment for abusing it. Through Christ's transcendency, they are made kings and priests to God and reign with Him eternally.

"DAYS" RALPH WALDO EMERSON **(1857)** This poem is RALPH WALDO EMERSON's dramatization of the Latin proverb carpe diem (seize the day). The speaker begins with disparaging remarks about the relative unimportance of the Days, mere daughters of time who seem hypocritical in that their promise is frequently unfulfilled. Each seems a barefoot dervish (line 2), an alien image combining the ecstatic mysteries of an eastern religious sect with the commonality of bare feet. They seem at once powerless and endless as they file past, bearing gifts as varied as diadems (royal crowns) or faggots (bundles of sticks which may be cheaply procured for burning), which they offer according to the will of those who would receive them (line 5). There seems no limit to what they may bring; a short list begins with bread, but ascends to kingdoms, stars and the entire sky in a single line.

The speaker watched their progress from his shaded garden, forgetting his "morning wishes" (line 8; he may be referring to the idealistic dreams and goals of one's youth). Too late realizing his missed opportunities, he hastily took a few herbs and apples before the Day silently departed. In a complete reversal of their relationship at the beginning of the poem, it is now the departing Day whose face reveals her scorn for the person who did so little with the opportunity that is forever passing.

"THE DEACON'S MASTERPIECE: OR THE WONDERFUL 'ONE-HOSS-SHAY'" OLIVER WENDELL HOLMES **(1858)** In early 19th-century Protestant sects, a deacon is a preacher's assistant, and a parson (line 6) is a (frequently college-educated) minister. The former is more likely a permanent resident of a town, and the latter was likely hired from elsewhere to assume his post. In the course of time, a deacon may have seen several parsons come and go, and is likely to have developed very entrenched notions of correct ministry. The poem's subtitle, "A

Logical Story," suggests that this deacon's somewhat irrational thinking will be exposed.

A "shay" (a rough transliteration of the French term *chaise,* correctly pronounced in English with a long *a* and a *z* on the end: "shaz") is a two-wheeled carriage pulled by one horse. Although the poem makes fun of the deacon's New England accent, essentially presenting it as symbolic of his limited sectarian views, the fact that he would own such a vehicle devoted to conveying one or two people instead of (probably, in addition to) a more versatile conveyance suggests that this deacon is possessed of more than average wealth. This impression is reinforced by his careful selection of the choicest materials for his masterpiece as well as his pride in its construction.

OLIVER WENDELL HOLMES's opening stanza tells of the first hundred years of the shay's existence but hints that something happened on its very last day that scared the parson "into fits" and frightened people "out of their wits" (lines 6–7).

In 1755, George II (to be replaced in 1760 by George III, the king whose reign saw the American Revolution) still ruled Great Britain and its American colonies. The poem's characterization of him as a "snuffy" (e.g., a user of snuff, but probably also fully possessed of the airs the consumers of such a high-priced product sometimes assume towards the less privileged; line 11) old "drone" (a male bee whose sole purpose is to eventually mate with the queen; as used here, it characterizes the king as someone who lives at others' expense and whose only real contribution was fathering the next king) of "the German hive" (raised in the Hanover court, George III was a duke in that German country as well as king of England. Royal blood was then held in such high regard that it could lead to marriage to the families of foreign royalty, and the laws of succession were so strict as to trump more nationalistic considerations). To make 1755 more real to his contemporaries, the speaker in this poem points to the famously terrible earthquake in Lisbon, Portugal, of November 1 (lines 12–13) and the rout of General Edward Braddock (July 9) near Fort Duquesne (modern Pittsburgh) in the French and Indian War. The reference to the army's being "done so brown" calls to mind the torture by fire of captured foes, an atrocity, like scalping, sometimes committed in that brutal era (lines 14–15). Perhaps to suggest the narrowness of the deacon's interests, the speaker notes that he finished the shay on earthquake day, an association that foreshadows its remarkable end.

In the third stanza, the speaker notes that in the building of chaises (as in all human endeavors) there is always a weakest spot. This might be in the hub (the center part of a wheel), tire (since it was constructed before the advent of rubber tires, this refers to the iron band fitted by a blacksmith around the circumference of the wheel to increase its durability), felloe (the spoke-grabbing outer rim of a wheel), spring (a mechanical coil designed to cushion passengers from the bumps in the road), thill (a shaft attached on either side of a draft animal to connect him with the buggy), panel (perhaps the floor and walls of the chaise, or some substructure intrinsic to their composition), crossbar (wooden props placed for reinforcement under the floor panel), floor, sill (the horizonal, load-bearing base of a frame), screw, bolt or thoroughbraces (leather bands placed beneath the frame of a carriage to support its weight and to serve as springs). All these things are replaceable, so a chaise breaks down but does not wear out (lines 25–26).

The fourth stanza reveals the deacon's pride. His shay was going to beat the town and the surrounding countryside because he would design its weakest point to withstand as much strain as the rest of the vehicle. Because wood was the basic carriage material of choice in the 18th century, the deacon knew which types of wood would best serve a particular purpose. Thus he used oak, lancewood, ash, whitewood, and elm (especially the settler's elm of line 45, by reputation already growing before the first pilgrims arrived in 1620 and so tough that it would chew up the wedges [even "their blunt ends [were] frizzled like celery-tips," a wonderfully visual detail] designed to split a log when they were driven by sledge hammer into the cuts opened by axe or saw). Its metal parts (a linchpin performs the vital role of locking a wheel into place on its shaft) were fashioned from the finest bright and blue steel, its thoroughbraces from bison hide, and its leather trimmings from a pit (where they probably received an extra-long curing since they were found only after the tanner had died; line 55).

Generations lived and passed away, but the shay stayed as fresh as the day it was finished (lines 58–64). It was still considered a handsome carriage in 1810 and continued in service until the fateful year of 1855. However, nothing keeps its youth but a tree and truth (some trees are still remarkably resilient after having lived centuries. The only "truths" normally lasting so long are religious; lines 75–76).

On the day of its 100th anniversary, the shay was beginning to show its age in its overall condition, but not in specific spots such as the whippletree (a cross-bar or singletree in front of the vehicle to facilitate easier attachment to the traces fitted on the horse). The parson took it out behind a scrawny (rat-tailed and "ewe-necked" [its neck was not thicker than that of a female sheep]) horse (line 99; a sign that the family is not as affluent as it once had been, or that it had passed possession of the old cart on to the parsonage).

The parson was probably working over the following Sunday's sermon (November 1, 1855, fell on a Thursday) when the horse stopped beside the meetinghouse. At 9:30 (the same time of day at which the earthquake had struck Lisbon a century earlier), he found himself sitting on a rock surrounded by bits of the shay looking as if they had been ground in a flour mill (line 114). Like a bursting bubble, it had gone to pieces all at once (line 118).

The only interpretation the speaker provides is that "logic is logic" (line 120). By thus linking the carriage to thought, he may be implying that the old deacon's beliefs are as antiquated and useless as his wrecked carriage.

"DEATH OF AN INFANT" LYDIA HUNTLEY SIGOURNEY (1827)

Death is personified in LYDIA HUNTLEY SIGOURNEY's poem as a jealous, ruthless killer bent on spoiling everything humans find attractive, but even he is too moved by the child's beauty to take away everything. In an age of relatively high infant mortality, the initial readership would not have found the poem overbearingly sentimental.

Death dashed out the beauty on the infant's brow and, by touching veins with ice, forced the rose from its cheek and lip. He lowered the curtain on the child's wishful tender eyes by binding their "silken fringes" (the eyelashes) forever. Likewise, he silenced the murmuring sound so dear as to charm the mother to tears. Only the cherub's smile withstood Death's attention; he dared not steal "the signet-ring of Heaven" (line 18).

"DE BLUE-TAIL FLY" ANONYMOUS (19th century)

The youngest and cutest of the slaves would sometimes be chosen to work in the manor house as house servants. Although this could seem like relatively light work to the field hands, it brought the youth into constant contact with his chief oppressor, the man who owned everything and everyone. In this poem the speaker recalls waiting on his master's table, handing him the plates of food, passing the bottle "when he git dry" (an observation that suggests a drinking problem; line 3), and brushing away the blue-tail fly.

The chorus, delivered in the poem's present as opposed to the past tense of its reminiscences, finds Jimmy (who could either be the speaker or someone for whom the speaker felt responsible) cracking corn (perhaps wasting the family's rations or focusing on his own needs instead of attending to his plantation chores. Alternatively, he may only be grinding that poor fodder down to the point where it could be used like a coarse flour, and the speaker's lack of concern may indicate his content with second-class food because of the nourishment provided to his soul by the events he subsequently describes). Either way, the speaker does not care about the corn because the old master has gone away. The fun of this poem resides in its gradual revelation of the connections between all its disparate elements and the dialect in which the story is told.

The master would sleep after dinner and the speaker would have to keep the flies off him, especially the blue-tail fly (such constant identification of the colorful insect is one of the more humorous aspects of the poem).

One day the master rode through a swarm of the flies and was bitten on the thigh. The speaker had enough empathy with him at that moment to wish that the devil would take the offending fly. Although by the speaker's account the master and not the pony had been bitten, the animal bolted, jumping and pitching until he tumbled the master into a ditch. The resulting death was evidently suspicious enough for a jury trial, which attributed the accident to the blue-tail fly.

The master was buried under a persimmon tree, a detail that may have some bearing on our understanding of the poem. When ripe, the fruit of the American persimmon is very sweet, but until then it is acidic. Could a similar observation be made about the speaker's possible plot against the master? The irreverent epitaph on the burial stone, again attributing the death to the fly, suggests some hostility existed towards the man before his death.

The speaker would let the old master rest since, as they say, all things are for the best. He will never forget the master and the blue-tail fly, however, and appears to have been as eager to be free of the master as the master had been to rid himself of the insect pest.

"DERE'S NO HIDIN' PLACE DOWN DERE" Anonymous (19th century)

For Christians who believe in the literal truth of the Bible, heaven and hell are real places. In this poem the first speaker is a sinner who discovers the truth too late and finds himself scrambling among the rocks to find a place to hide. Unfortunately, the rock he chose echoed his cry that there is no hiding place "down here" (heaven has traditionally been located above the earth (see 2 Corinthians 5:1, for example) and hell waited beneath its surface [as in Numbers 16:30–32 and 2 Peter 2:4]).

Lest the reader misconstrue the rock's reply as a mere literal echo, in the second stanza the rock explains that it is also burning (compare Revelation 16:20 for a lake of burning brimstone and Matthew 13:42 for a furnace of fire) and wants to go to heaven as well as the speaker. It then reaffirms that there are no hiding places.

The third stanza provides an omniscient speaker's recap of the situation. The sinner gambled and fell. He wanted heaven but had to go to hell.

DICKINSON, EMILY (1830–1886)

The future poet was born on December 10, 1830, in Amherst, Massachusetts. She had the deepest roots possible in her hometown, where her grandfather helped found the Amherst Academy from which she graduated in 1847. Her grandfather also built the grand house in which she was born and lived for her first 10 years, but he lost it through financial reverses. Her father's triumphant purchase and extensive renovation of the property in 1855 visually established him as a pillar of the community and a seemingly irresistible force within his household. A Yale-educated lawyer, U.S. Congressman, and treasurer of Amherst College, her father was eventually able to provide Emily with the financial security to remain anchored in the family home, which she rarely chose to leave.

Emily Elizabeth Dickinson's advanced education ended in 1848 after a single year at Mt. Holyoke in South Hadley, Massachusetts; a letter to a childhood friend documented the highly regimented routine girls were forced to follow at this female seminary. Although she seems to have found the faculty and most of the 300 students amiable, her letters reveal her acute homesickness, an affliction exacerbated by the college's refusal to let any of the girls absent themselves from the school even on Sundays. She really blossomed as a poet in the select company of an extended family that included her sister, her brother, and his family, in the lasting relationships she formed with her closest friends, and in the flora and fauna of her backyard. She was also blessed with an extraordinary sensitivity to the printed word. In 1870, she told Thomas Wentworth Higginson, an influential critic, that she knew something was poetry if it made her whole body cold beyond the power of any fire to warm her, if it made her feel as if the top of her head had been blown off (*Selected Letters* 208). Although in time she wrote prodigiously, only 11 of her poems reached print before her death. She wrote beautifully observant letters to her friends, including several men whom she admired from a distance, but she appears to have been more content with the sensations aroused by thinking about them than she could have been in their company. Most nights of her adult life were spent in a narrow bed not much wider than a coffin lid.

In her youth, Dickinson enjoyed the social life of rural Amherst, meeting the dear friends and a few of the later correspondents who, along with her brother and sister, would help her develop a sense of the ideal audience for her poetry that facilitated her sustained creativity. Unfortunately, she suffered a panic attack early in 1854 (Longsworth 36), the first incontrovertible symptom of a pathological anxiety beyond the reach of 19th-century medicine. In declining an invitation to visit Abiah Root, a cherished childhood friend, in July of that year, she wrote that "I don't go from home, unless emergency leads me by the hand" (*Selected Letters* 118), a declaration that makes her withdrawal from human contact seem a willful decision instead of a compulsion. In December 1854, she wrote that she went out shopping once every month or two with her younger sister Lavinia (*Selected Letters* 126). She was strong enough for a three-week visit to her father the congressman in Washington, D.C., (with a side excursion to Mt. Vernon to visit George Washington's grave and estate) early the next year and to tarry a couple of weeks in Philadelphia on the return trip, and still attended Sunday sermons for another decade, but she was becoming ever more reclusive to the point where even visitors to the family home were unlikely to see her. The increasing isolation of her mature years meant that few new intimates could be found to replace those whose deaths could turn her porcelain life (beautiful but fragile) into broken crockery (a metaphor the poet used in an 1858 letter [*Selected Letters* 144]). Her losses included the unexpected deaths of many treasured friends throughout her adult life, and the deaths of her father in 1874 and mother in 1882. Isolated by her illness, she evidently channeled her need to communicate with a wider society into the poems which became her "letter to the world," to borrow a phrase from one of her poems. Thus this terribly painful and extremely awkward affliction was a medical mystery but a boon to her poetry.

Her other illnesses included a crippling eye condition that once forced her to give up writing and reading in order to preserve her sight; in 1864 and 1865, she lost a year's productivity to a Boston doctor's care that forced her into a carefully darkened Cambridge, Massachusetts, boardinghouse (Longsworth 48). The torrid pace of her writing cooled after that experience, but she still persisted in her art.

At the age of 32, Dickinson began wearing white clothing as if symbolically wedded to her poetry or devoted like a nun to this peculiar secular habit. When she died (of what was then diagnosed as Bright's disease) on May 15, 1886, her manuscripts were left in the hands of editors who, although well meaning, tended to force the poems into compliance with late-19th-century aesthetics. The poems were still powerful enough to withstand this heavy-handed approach and, four years after her death, her first book (*Poems by Emily Dickinson*) quickly went through six printings. Rivalries between her principal editors prevented her poetry from attracting an even larger audience. It would be more than 70 years after her death before her poems (with their artistic integrity restored by a more sympathetic editing) gained international fame.

The many Dickinson poems discussed below are surprisingly remarkable for their variety. Although they were dismissed for their irregular rhymes and meters when they first reached print (and by modern philistines with their ignorant assertions that all her poetry could be sung to the tune of "The Yellow Rose of Texas"), Dickinson's fans point out that her "sprung" or "slant" rhymes frequently reinforce her meaning. A quick introduction to her work might focus on such nature poems as "A NARROW FELLOW IN THE GRASS" and "BEES ARE BLACK WITH GILT SURCINGLES;" philosophical poems such as "SAFE IN THEIR ALABASTER CHAMBERS;" poems dealing with loss and death such as "AFTER GREAT PAIN A FORMAL FEELING COMES" and "BECAUSE I COULD NOT STOP FOR DEATH" (a "Yellow Rose" poem); and romantic poems like "The SOUL SELECTS HER OWN SOCIETY," "DID THE HAREBELL LOOSE HER GIRDLE" and "WILD NIGHTS." Part of the miracle by which she achieved so much in spite of directly experiencing so little of the outside world can be fathomed in such poems as "TO MAKE A PRAIRIE." "To shut our eyes is Travel," she once informed a friend (*Selected Letters* 211). The poet was also fortunate in being privy to much that befell her parents (she helped tend her mother during the extended illness of her final years) and her siblings, who led less secluded lives.

The orderly family mansion in which she spent most of her life now serves as the Emily Dickinson Museum in Amherst, Massachusetts, where her writing desk (simple, small, and square) and her only surviving white dress have been preserved. Harvard University's holdings include the poet's manuscripts and bedroom furniture, including the bureau in which many of her poems were discovered after her death. The Jones Library in Amherst holds a large collection of Dickinson materials, and the Amherst College library also has a valuable archive. The Emily Dickinson International Society publishes the *Emily Dickinson Journal* and the *Emily Dickinson Bulletin*.

BIBLIOGRAPHY
Dickinson, Emily. *Emily Dickinson's Selected Letters*. Edited by Thomas H. Johnson. Cambridge, Mass.: Harvard University Press, 1971.
———. *Open Me Carefully: Emily Dickinson's Intimate Letters to Susan Huntington Dickinson*. Edited by Ellen Louise Hart and Martha Nell Smith. Ashfield, Mass.: Paris Press, 1998.
———. *The Poems of Emily Dickinson, Including Variant Readings Critically Compared with All Known Manuscripts*. Edited by Thomas H. Johnson. Cambridge, Mass.: Harvard University Press, 1955.
———. *Poems: Variorum Edition*. 3 vols. Edited by R. W. Franklin. Cambridge, Mass.: Harvard University Press, 1998.
Habegger, Alfred. *My Wars Are Laid Away in Books: The Life of Emily Dickinson*. New York: Random House, 2001.
Longsworth, Polly. "The 'Latitude of Home': Life in the Homestead and the Evergreens." In *The Dickinsons of Amherst*. Photographs by Jerome Liebling. Essays by Christopher Benfey, Polly Longsworth, and Barton Levi St. Armand. Hanover and London: University Press of New England, 2001.

"DIDN'T MY LORD DELIVER DANIEL" Anonymous (19th century)

The title, first four lines and refrain of this poem refer to the biblical story of Daniel in the lion's den (Daniel 6:7, 16–22). The prophet was tossed in among the big cats for breaking the king's law against praying to God instead of the sovereign. God sent an angel to shut the feline jaws, and Daniel emerged without a scratch.

The same prophet recorded a similar miracle in the court of Nebuchadnezzar (Daniel 3:15–30). All who refused to pray to the king's golden idol were to be thrown into a fiery furnace, and three Jews (the "Hebrew chillun [children]" of line 6) were immediately put to the test. Although the flames were so hot that their guards were killed, an angel saved the three men.

Jonah was swallowed by a whale (line 5) when he refused God's call to warn the evil city of Nineveh. The ship in which he attempted to flee was battered by a tempest until the sailors reluctantly threw him overboard. A great fish swallowed him whole, and three days and nights later disgorged him on the beach only a day's journey from Nineveh (Jonah 1:17–2:10).

If, the speaker argues, God can perform these miracles for the biblical prophets, why would he not do them for every man (line 7). The second stanza is devoted to the events predicted to precede the Last Judgment (see Matthew 24:27–29 and Luke 21:25–26 for such changes in the moon, sun, and stars as the speaker describes here). Like Michael Wigglesworth's "The Day of Doom," the speaker predicts howling winds and prayers from those who never prayed before when that day comes (lines 16–19). He will not have to worry because he set foot on the Gospel ship, which landed him on Canaan's shore (line 23). That ancient land stretched from the Jordan River to the Mediterranean Sea, and extended much farther still under King David, but the name was probably chosen for this song to represent not only the Holy Land, but all the lands and peoples under the Lord's dominion.

"DID THE HAREBELL LOOSE HER GIRDLE" Emily Dickinson (1951)

Perhaps because her external audience would have been very familiar with this common perennial plant (native to North America as well as popular with gardeners), the speaker dispensed with the description of the unique aspects of its flowers with which similar poems often begin. Instead, she focused exclusively on the application, the ways in which a natural phenomenon can furnish insights into human life. Her thinking was so advanced and the triggering image of the poem was so provocative that it was not published for a full 100 years after Emily Dickinson wrote it.

A century prior to the advent of sex education in schools and women's studies programs in colleges, at a time in American history when many girls were kept ignorant about even the most rudimentary facts of the biology of human reproduction, this poem illustrates one of the ways in which such information could be disseminated. The harebell is a type of bluebell; and the tubular shape of its nearly translucent bell-shaped flowers evidently reminded Dickinson of ladies' undergarments (or a silken skirt or dress), for she begins by asking if the flower "loose her girdle."

The poem is less about sex than about the relationship between the sexes after the flower acquiesces to the "lover bee," however. She questions whether the bee (a stand-in for human males) would still respect the "harebell." The term is rather reductive when used to represent women; part of Dickinson's artistry lies in its implied suggestion that a bee's visit reduces the flower to a mere reproductive recipient in much the same way that she focuses all the reader's attention on this single aspect of the flower.

Talk about intimacy issues! Doubtless, innumerable women have wondered at the sudden change that comes over some males immediately after a relationship is consummated. Up to that point, flighty lovers seem to worship them like religious objects, but who will "hallow" them now? That term suggests that they were being treated like objects even while they were apparently being venerated.

The geography of the "Paradise" mapped out in the second stanza would probably be covered on the first day of a modern sex education classroom, and mass media have removed any obscurity surrounding the "persuading" and "yielding" that can occur in a courtship. Like Adam and Eve, any couple can face complications when biblical sex enters their relationship; this poem cautions women that some of these changes can permanently destroy the happiness of their innocent Edens. The most visible of these changes can occur in the male; a man who early on seemed an earl (an extremely noble man) might behave differently after a certain point in a relationship.

"DIVINA COMMEDIA" HENRY WADSWORTH LONGFELLOW (1867)

The great Italian poet Dante Alighieri (1265–1321) called his most famous work simply *La Commedia,* and two centuries later an admirer added the adjective necessary to make it *The Divine Comedy.* For his translation into English, HENRY WADSWORTH LONGFELLOW chose to maintain the Italian words for the three books into which the body of the work is divided. The speaker, ostensibly Dante himself, is given a tour of the Inferno (Hell) and Purgatorio (Purgatory) by the Latin poet Virgil (70–19 B.C.). Virgil's *Aeneid* featured a visit to Hades, the underworld in which his hero found the woman who killed herself when he left her, and it undoubtedly pleased Dante to imagine the eternal torments suffered by his political enemies in his own version of hell. Enjoying a far happier fate than Virgil's Dido (a suicide) did, Dante's heroine Beatrice guides him through Paradiso (Heaven).

Longfellow published six of his own sonnets as "Divina Commedia" in *Flower-de-Luce* (1867) and added two of these sonnets to the start of each of the books of his translation of Dante's *Commedia.* The first of these likens reading of Dante's work to a religious experience, suggesting that when the speaker enters "here" (line 9), the tumult of the time fades to "inarticulate murmurs" (line 13) just as the noise of the world retreats for a laborer who kneels to pray in a cathedral. Both laborer and poet lay aside their burdens "while the eternal ages watch and wait" (line 14) to determine if the former's life can merit salvation and if the latter's creations can stand the test of time as did Dante's work. The emphasis on doors and gates in the sonnet may indirectly point to the gates of hell in the *Inferno* above which Dante placed the famous line: "Abandon hope, all ye who enter here." However, the reader who embraces Dante's faith will find the *Commedia* as a whole to be extraordinarily optimistic.

Longfellow may have added the second sonnet in hope of reducing the distance between Dante's medieval world and the modern reader. He might have had any of the many great Gothic cathedrals of Europe in mind when, in the second sonnet, he wrote of the strange sculptures adorning their towers. The famous Notre Dame de Paris (chiefly constructed between 1163 and 1250, with another century's work on its adornments) might be taken as the most accessible example, and one does indeed find a "crowd of statues" (line 2) around its portals. These range from the biblical kings, prophets, saints, the Apostles, and the Virgin Mary to a gallery of the early kings of France, and offer innumerable niches suitable for the bird nests (not tolerated in the 21st century) of line 3. A "parvis" is the court in front of a building, and the conglomeration of aforementioned statues might be viewed as the "blooms" located in these areas, especially if the "vast minister" (presumably a sculpture of Christ) seems a cross of flowers (line 5). Many cathedrals of the time featured "fiends and dragons on the gargoyled eaves" (line 6. Gargoyles were the carved figures functioning as waterspouts on the roofs of buildings, and chimeras were similar in appearance but merely ornamental. They typically take the form of hideous monsters perhaps designed to ward off evil spirits, a strange concession to pagan superstition in the presence of all the Christian imagery. The present author prefers to view such beings as being driven out from the building by the assembled cast of holy figures). These figures watch "the dead Christ between the living thieves" (line 7; compare Mark 15:27 in which Christ dies before the two thieves who were crucified at the same time) above a scowling Judas.

At this point the speaker celebrates the spirituality of the medieval world in which belief in Christ, God, and biblical literalism meant that heaven and hell were as physically real (and perhaps not as geographically distant) as China. On one level this made for exciting times as each person presented an opportunity for the forces of good and evil, not personal demons and guardian angels but real agents of God and Satan and sometimes even these principals themselves, to struggle mightily over possession of an individual's soul. Thus the medieval craftsmen poured tremendous energy into their religious art as an outlet for their own "agonies of art and brain" (line 9) even as they portrayed the suffering and resurrection of Christ. With "exultations trampling on despair" (line 9) even though they deeply felt their Savior's "hate of wrong" and "passionate outcry of a soul in pain" (lines 10–11), they built their great churches, sculptures, and divine comedies. At their best, and Longfellow's emphasis on "this poem" in line 13 shows that he counted Dante's masterpiece "of earth and air" among their best efforts, they could achieve "a medieval miracle of song" (line 14), part of the chorus of the great works of faith produced in the era.

Longfellow's third sonnet is the weakest of the six and chiefly serves as a transitional passage (in this sense it might be viewed as a dim reflection of the experience of the inhabitants of the Purgatorio section of *Divine Comedy,* although their transitional phase is far more painful). "I enter" (line 1) is a poor beginning but it does link this sonnet with the prior two and suggests that the speaker is both entering the cathedral and entering the poem. In the gloom he finds Dante, addressed as the "poet saturnine" (the adjective refers to a sullen or melancholy disposition; line 2), and strives "to make my steps keep pace with thine" (to walk at the same speed as Dante leads the tour, but also to attempt writing poetry at Dante's level). Both the landscape of the poem and the cathedral might have unknown perfumes in the air (the latter's coming from incense), but a "congregation of the dead" (line 6) is more likely in the former while the votive candles would be found in the church. The "hovering echoes" (either part of the ambient noise of Purgatory or the cathedral, or perhaps the spirits found in the former) haunt the place like the rooks (a type of crow) that fly about the tombs in Ravenna (Italy), where Dante is buried. He can hear "rehearsals of forgotten tragedies" (accounts of past actions, especially sins; line 10) from the confessionals (of Purgatory, we hope; those on earth are supposed to be nearly soundproof) and lamentations from the crypts (underground tunnels frequently used as human bone yards beneath some European cities). A "voice celestial" encourages the penitents with the "pathetic" (soothing and sensitive, but not sympathetic) verse from Isaiah 1:18 promising that their sins will be cleansed.

Although the speaker is still in Purgatory in the fourth sonnet, his reunion with his beloved Beatrice makes it seem more like heaven. Her veil is snow white as befits someone who has gone through the purification of purgatory, and her garments are "as of flame" (line 1). Now totally pure, she speaks his name "with stern rebuke" as his heart melts. "Sobs of shame" (line 7) gush from his lips as he makes full confession (a necessary ritual if he is to enter heaven). A gleam like dawn in a forest increases on his forehead. He is left with the remembered dream that brings "the perfect pardon which is the perfect peace" (line 14). This is likened to the transformative experience of drinking from the river Eunoe (enabling one to recall all the good in life) and the river Lethe (enabling one to forget the torments of human life on earth and the pain of leaving behind its delights).

The fifth sonnet begins in the cathedral, where the windows blaze with stained-glass representations of saints and holy men and the great rose window depicts Christ's triumph (lines 4–5; the most famous rose windows are those of the cathedrals of Notre Dame de Paris and Chartres. Since they are considered the high point of stained glass art, it seems fitting that they suggest the lighting in heaven). Beatrice is again with Dante, and she "smiles her words of praise" (line 8). Accompanied by an organ, choirs sing Latin hymns of peace, love, and benedictions to the Holy Ghost (lines 9–10. One of the most important mysteries of the Catholic Church is that of the Holy Ghost, who is at once the third "person" [or aspect of the one divinity] who, with God and Jesus Christ, forms the Holy Trinity even though He is identical with and inseparable from ["consubstantial with" is the Church phrase] the other two). The church bells proclaim the "elevation of the Host" (the moment in a Catholic Church mass when a priest raises small pieces of bread, representative of Christ's sacrifice and thought by some to actually become His body in another miracle, heavenward before administering them to the faithful) over the housetops and through heaven.

The last sonnet praises Dante as "the star of morning and of liberty" (line 1). This is high praise but refers more to the poet's rather unfortunate political career than his poetry. Italy at the time was divided into city states, which tended to align themselves with either the papacy (based, of course, in Rome) or the Holy Roman Empire (dominated by German princes). In Italy the Guelfs supported the papacy and the Ghibellines favored their imperial opponents, and Dante's Florence wavered in its allegiances. Dante was first a Ghibelline and then a White Guelf (after they had divided into White and Black factions). In 1300 he was briefly one of the most important political men in Florence, but by 1302 he was forever banished from the city under penalty of death. The good news was that these political developments gave him both the time and the inclination to write.

Dante quickly became the national poet of Italy in the sense that, as Longfellow notes in lines 5–8, he gave voice to city, sea, mountains, and trees, until his lines became the "footpaths for the thought of Italy" (line 8).

His fame is "blown abroad from all the heights" until "a sound is heard like a mighty wind" (lines 9–11). The sense of the final four lines is that those unfamiliar with Roman Catholicism and the new converts to that religion (the "proselytes" of line 12) will hear Dante's "wondrous word" (a phrase that refers not just to the poem, but to the poet's version of heaven and hell) in translation. Many readers will be amazed, and many will doubt (either the traditional religion of their native land, or Dante's version of the afterlife; line 14). Longfellow could have added that few readers will be unaffected by the experience.

"DOROTHY'S DOWER" PHOEBE CARY (1854)

Several of the great psychologist Sigmund Freud's observations about humor are pertinent to this poem. For example, he theorized that if an audience shares a writer's basic set of values, humor can be used to reinforce the group's identity by reinforcing the perceived difference between the in-group and the other. PHOEBE CARY's poem was written from a woman's perspective, with the parsimonious husband clearly intended as the target of its central joke. Freud also implied that humor can come from pain and can be used as the weapon of last resort, just as in this poem the poor wife gets the final word even though she faces an uncertain economic future because of the husband's failure to keep the promises he made while courting. Its humor is timeless because it is based on the misconceptions each gender can bring to courtship and marriage. Enlightened 21st century audiences can laugh and cry at the same time as they ponder not only the husband's foibles but also the cruelty inherent in the 19th-century's desire to keep women ignorant about money.

The point-of-view character is Dorothy; everything happens in her presence, although the speaker is an omniscient third-person narrator who quickly sheds any pretense of objectivity. One of the delights of the poem is that the class backgrounds as well as the personalities of the two central characters are revealed through their language, and their speech suggests a refined gentility that could only come from relatively affluent childhoods in their era.

Before the wedding, John seems to "shed" gold upon her (line 4), with the verb suggesting that the precious metal comes to him naturally, that he has an abundance of it, and that he cares no more for it than a dog cares for the hair it sheds. He promises to grant whatever she wishes or wants (lines 5–6), but although the speaker realized that he "stood metaphorically" (he was not speaking literally; line 3), the naive Dorothy may not have been able to make that distinction.

Recognizing her immaturity, he tells her that she can spend her entire dowry on candy (lines 9–12). Although she apparently has the better financial sense of the two (preferring instead to save the money for an emergency; line 10), he dismisses her concerns as mere teasing and teases her in return, asserting that the more she spends the more it will please him (lines 14–16). There could be a sinister side to his jest, however, for he likes her "sweet, dependent ways" (line 13). If she had no financial resources, she would have to remain sweet because she would be entirely dependent. However, the tone of the poem is as light as a comedy of manners; "enchanted" (line 8), he is as much a victim of that century's blasé attitude towards personal finance as she is.

The poem is divided into three sections to denote the passage of time, and changes in the couple's relationship and in their attitudes about money. They are married in the second section, and their money woes have become a source of irritation. In response to an apparent request from her, he responds that he has not got the money "by him" (line 18), which implies that he may have adequate funds invested somewhere. Fortunately, she has not spent her dowry, and he now encourages her to do so. In fact, he wants to borrow 20 dollars from her, which he promises to pay back the next day.

The third section picks up the argument several years later. Now he pushes rudely past her (line 30) and, without even calling her by name, presumes to inform her that money does not grow on trees. She needed the money for a child's shoes and her doctor, but he tells her to "get up some new disaster" (line 32); his language suggests that she is fabricating the need. She and "her" children would bankrupt John Jacob Astor, a tycoon who made millions in the American fur trade (line 36). John's choice of a man who had died in 1848, six years before the poem appeared, may undercut his pose as an up-to-date, successful businessman.

He asks what became of her dowry and calls himself a fool for courting a woman who would rely on him for her money (lines 37–38). She reminds him that she lent it to him, and he counters that he spent it on the family instead of on sugar candy, as a woman would. She counters that most of it went for cigars and brandy (line 48), two self-indulgent luxuries that helped him maintain his pose as a businessman.

Note how deftly the author chose a title that would encompass all the changes Dorothy undergoes in the course of the poem. At first glance it seems to refer to her dowry, but by the third stanza its possessive noun might be read as a contraction in order to pun on dower/dour. Thus the title raises two interlinked questions: What happens to Dorothy's dowry, and why would she have such a sour countenance?

"DREAM-LAND" Edgar Allan Poe (1844–5)

Edgar Allan Poe's collection of negative imagery purports to be an eyewitness account of a visit to a land of ghosts and ghouls. The speaker took an obscure and lonely route (line 1) to this supernatural realm although the poem's title suggests that the loneliness stemmed from his/her sleep, one of the basic things everyone must do alone. The "ill angels" who haunt the place were probably the minions of Satan when he fell from grace; their origin can be traced to the British poet John Milton's *Paradise Lost* (1667). The speaker must have reached the very heart of their dominion because he found the black throne from which "reigns upright" (which could indicate the ruler's posture or his just rule) an Eidolon (a Greek phantom) named Night (line 3). He was beyond the last Thule (the northernmost inhabited regions of which the ancient Greek geographers were aware; line 6) in a "wild weird clime" outside of space and time (lines 7–8).

The geographical features of the undiscovered country include bottomless valleys, boundless floods, fissures, and caves, and "Titan woods" (named for the Titans, the earliest Greek gods who parented the more famous gods such as Zeus and Apollo, who eventually supplanted them. The name suggests huge forests with gigantic trees of ancient age). No man can discover the "forms" (land formations or spirits?) in the place because "tears drip all over" (tears a mortal might shed when either finding himself in such a terrifying place or when meeting the spirits of old friends, or perhaps it indicates a local weather anomaly or other phenomenon that drenches everything; line 12). Mountains topple "evermore" into seas without a shore (perhaps because the rugged coastline consists of high cliffs). The land may display volcanoes because the seas "relentlessly aspire unto . . . skies of fire" (lines 15–16). The still and chilly waters of its "lone and dead" lakes are endlessly covered with the white "snows" of the "lolling" (drooping or slouching) lily (line 20; since white lilies have traditionally been viewed as symbols of innocence and purity, the fact that they droop may suggest lapses in virtue that counteract the positive associations their presence might otherwise suggest).

The lakes and their lilies so impressed the speaker that he immediately repeats their four-line description with the important substitution of *sad* for *still*. The water must be moving, for he can detect its incessant murmuring by the gray woods and the swamp "where the toad and the newt encamp" (Poe may have chosen these animals to add to the eerie gloom of the place. Compare Shakespeare, where these two amphibians contribute bodily to the witches' brew in *Macbeth* [Act IV, scene I]. They also appear in *King Lear* [Act III, scene iv] and *Timon of Athens* [Act I, scene viii]).

By dismal "tarns" (small, often glacier-fed mountain lakes) and pools (lines 27–28), dwell ghouls (spirits or mortals delighting in unwholesome pastimes) in the most unholy, melancholy nooks. Here the traveler meets "sheeted Memories of the Past" (line 34), the white-robed shrouded forms of friends long before committed to the earth and heaven.

For the deeply grieved, it is a peaceful soothing region (perhaps since it proves the existence of an afterlife and facilitates a reunion with the deceased; line 40). For the "spirit who walks in shadow" (a phrase that could indicate the deceased, a mourner, or an evil spirit), it is an Eldorado (a mythical New-World city of gold). The traveler may not openly view it because its king has forbidden exposing the mysteries beyond the grave to the weak human eye (until the "[black mourning-]fringed lid" [of the coffin] is lifted; lines 43–47). Thus the sad soul who passes must behold the scenes

through darkened glasses (probably such as were used to view the solar eclipses; line 50).

The last stanza repeats the six lines of the opening with the important change that he has now "wandered home but newly," whereas the poem begins with his having but newly reached the land of Night.

"A DREAM WITHIN A DREAM" EDGAR ALLAN POE (1849)

The key to this poem by EDGAR ALLAN POE may lie in the kiss that the speaker has planted on the brow of his internal audience. That it would land not on the lips or neck not only reveals a lack of amorous passion but hints that he considers his audience to be inferior to him in age, status, or wisdom. His use of the imperative mood ("Take this kiss") in the first line reinforces this sense of the distance between them; it is as if he were hoping to impart knowledge with the kiss but even has to instruct the recipient in how to receive that gift ("upon the brow"). A similar clue lies in his parting not with a lover's vow, but with an avowal that he fears may be so far above his auditor's level of consciousness or intelligence (or attention span) that he must beg for his message to be heard ("thus much let me avow," he pleads, with an implied promise that his message will be brief and succinct [line 3]). The kiss might be a way of narrowing the distance between them, a physical manifestation not just of his good will but also of his desire to plant knowledge in the recipient's brain.

The speaker is not insensible of the criticism leveled at him in the past that his "days have been a dream" (line 5). This implies that he has been wasting his life either by doing nothing practical (by devoting himself to an impossible goal) or by doing nothing at all. He counters that if hope (animated to the extent that it can fly) has departed in a night or a day (thus introducing the issue of the brevity of time into the calculation as well as suggesting the difference between an emotional and an intellectual grasp of life; line 7), in a vision (in a vain illusion, but alternatively, in accordance with an established goal or, especially for an artist, a unique perspective that may be vital if s/he is going to create something new in the world) or not, it is irredeemably gone (line 8). Everything and everyone, he insists, is but "a dream within a dream" (line 10. This implies that no matter how one lives, the ultimate meaning of life may be beyond human control or understanding, and thus the man who spends all his time engaged in pursuits deemed constructive by the internal audience or even his entire society may be just as guilty of wasting his life [perhaps even more so] as the person who questions, thinks, and ponders alternatives, and may even live what is usually charitably dismissed as "an alternative lifestyle").

The second stanza brings the audience, at least mentally, to the tumultuous shore of an ocean, a very romantic setting in its isolation and desolation. The roar of the surf might represent the noise of life as it swirls around him, and even the few grains of golden sand he can grasp (line 14) will "creep" through his fingers and be lost to the deep (just as the sands in an hourglass record the passage of time, but time itself is forever lost in the abyss of eternity). Implicit in this metaphor is his criticism of the life spent more commercially; even if he devoted his life to and finally succeeded in seizing fistfuls of real gold, he could not hold onto it. Thus he weeps and weeps (not only for his own seemingly wasted life, but for the human condition; line 17).

If the person without vision or "true" consciousness cries to God, it is more likely an appeal for greater strength in pursuing his own vain ends (lines 18–19). The speaker has transcended the limited perspective of the commercial world, but his lament seems to be based on the impossibility of saving other people from making the same mistake. At the same time, he recognizes the impossibility of saving anything at all "from the pitiless wave" (of time; line 21). This leaves him on uncertain ground; instead of asserting that everything is a dream within a dream as he had earlier (lines 9–10), he can now only ask whether there is anything "real" about even that perspective.

DUNBAR, PAUL LAURENCE (1872–1906)

The child of two former Kentucky slaves, Dunbar was born in Dayton, Ohio, on June 27, 1872. Although by that time the Emancipation Proclamation and the Thirteenth Amendment had eliminated slavery, Dunbar suffered throughout his youth from the economic disadvantages stemming from racial prejudice. His

father had served in the infantry and later the cavalry of two Massachusetts regiments in the Civil War, but his mother (Matilda Murphy Dunbar) behaved even more heroically, raising her four children after separating from her husband when the poet was still a child. The precocious Paul began writing poetry early and continued writing, although forced to labor in a series of menial jobs. His formal education ended when he graduated from Dayton Central High School in the same 1891 class as aviation's Orville Wright. Despite his humble beginnings and the brevity of his life, he managed to write 11 volumes of poetry, four collections of short stories, and five novels. His poetry won him national (he was invited to read at the Chicago World's Fair of 1893) and eventually international recognition (in 1897 he recited his poetry on the London lecture circuit). Praised and encouraged by such influential cultural figures and critics as William Dean Howells, Frederick Douglass, Booker T. Washington and W. E. B. DuBois, he was invited to ride in President William McKinley's inaugural parade (1897). His very short professional career had barely reached half a decade, but he was already the most famous African-American poet and one of the most famous black Americans of his time. President Theodore Roosevelt presented him with a ceremonial sword. It was to his mother's care that the poet returned, however, after his four-year marriage to fellow poet Alice Moore ended in 1902 and his health failed. He died of tuberculosis on February 9, 1906.

The four poems discussed in this book reveal the impact that, first, slavery, and then, the lingering problem of racism had on the black community, the black family, and finally an individual. "An ANTE-BELLUM SERMON" demonstrates how a pre–Civil War preacher had to tailor his message to accommodate two mutually exclusive audiences, the black parishioners who needed to draw strength from a sermon with some relevance to their enslaved condition and the ever-vigilant white masters who hoped to prevent the dissemination of any thoughts of freedom. His chosen text rightfully put the needs of the former ahead of the fears of the latter, and it should be viewed as a profile in courage because of all the legally sanctioned violent means the slaveholding classes had at their disposal to enforce their will.

The most charming aspect of "ACCOUNTABILITY" lies in its portrayal of a lovable rogue who manages to put food on his family's table regardless of the external criticism he anticipates and his internal moral dilemma. He manages to muster entire realms of philosophy in his defense and reveals a thoroughly rich imaginative life and startling command of rhetoric in the process. "The REAL QUESTION' deals with an even more desperate speaker who questions the importance of the ongoing national debate about the gold- or silver-based American dollar. The real question from his perspective is why so little money of any type trickles down to the poor.

These poems were rendered in a phonetically transcribed dialect that passed for southern black patois and was partially responsible for bringing the critical attention to the poet's work that established him as an authentic voice for his race. Although a great deal of humor leavens Dunbar's dialect poems, most of his poems convey the pain that racism inflicted on the African-American community. Such poems as "WE WEAR THE MASK" reveals his command of standard written English and acknowledge the unfortunate role humor sometimes plays in perpetuating harmful stereotypes. Coming from the pen of an acknowledged master of humorous dialect poetry, this poem challenges the complacency of a white America that sought to share in the laughter but refused to see or change the appalling conditions that spawned it. Less frequently anthologized, Dunbar's poem "Sympathy" is in some ways even more disturbing. The speaker identifies with a caged bird that tries to use song as an outlet for its misery, as it is kept by artificial barriers from reaching its potential enjoyment of all that nature would bestow as its birthright. The caged bird's song is a plea to heaven to restore the freedom that is beyond its individual capacity to achieve, and the blood smeared on the bars by its battered wings attests to the earnestness of its prayer.

The most important archives for the poet are the Paul Laurence Dunbar Papers at the Ohio Historical Society in Columbus. The Dayton and Montgomery County Public Library's Paul Laurence Dunbar Collection includes photographs of the poet at several stages in his life, and the New York [City] Public Library and the University of Delaware have several of his letters. The home in which he died was preserved by the State of Ohio and eventually incorporated into the Dayton Aviation Heritage National Historic Park.

BIBLIOGRAPHY

Alexander, Eleanor. *Lyrics of Sunshine and Shadow: The Tragic Courtship and Marriage of PLD and Alice Ruth Moore, A History of Love and Violence among the African American Elite.* New York: New York University Press, 2001.

Dunbar, Paul Laurence. *The Collected Poetry of Paul Laurence Dunbar,* edited by Joanne M. Braxton. Charlottesville: University of Virginia Press, 1993.

———. *In His Own Voice: The Dramatic and Other Uncollected Works of Paul Laurence Dunbar,* edited by Herbert Howard Martin and Ronald Primeau. Athens: Ohio University Press, 2002.

Gentry, Tony. *Paul Laurence Dunbar.* New York: Chelsea House Publishers, 1989.

"EACH AND ALL" Ralph Waldo Emerson
(1839) At first glance the philosophical conundrums
Ralph Waldo Emerson presents in the first half of this
poem may seem absurd, yet they are consistent with
several modern scientific principles. The first of these
is that observation of an event or behavior changes it;
thus the fieldworker in the red cloak gives little thought
to a spectator, but "all are needed by each one" (the
moral presented in line 11). A spectator thinks differently of a scene that lacks a single human element, and
whether or not the fieldworker earned the sobriquet
of "clown" by his behavior (the term "clown" is more
likely only borrowed from European literature, where
its broader meaning was merely "rural laborer"), such
a low-level employee may act very differently when no
one else is around.

Just as modern scientists insist that a tree falling
unheard in a forest makes no sound, it is necessary (and
very important to the animal) that someone or something hears the heifer's call (line 3; a heifer is a young
cow). A sexton is a church employee whose responsibilities include ringing the bell to mark the passing of
a church member; in fulfilling that role he little suspects that Napoleon will stop to enjoy the resonance in
the clear mountain air (lines 5–8). Napoleon is equally
impervious to the bell as a messenger of death, even as
his files (the lines his armies form in passing over the
Alps under his command) sweep onward to their destiny. You are also unaware of the lessons your neighbor
learns from watching you, and vice versa.

The speaker argues that nothing is good alone,
but weights his examples too heavily in favor of that
proposition. Thus he brings home a captive sparrow
(instead of a more expressive bird) and is disappointed
that it cannot produce the same reaction in him that it
had in connection with the river and the sky (lines 13–
18). Similarly, seashells (instead of the pearls or precious gems he might have found) are beautiful when
wet but dull when dried, away from "the wild uproar"
(line 28). A maid seems especially beautiful only in her
virgin trains (in a wedding dress; alternative readings
would place her with the other girls, or in the "snow-
white" [read "unassailably virtuous"] choir) and less
enchanting (this 19th-century speaker argues) upon
becoming a gentle wife (line 35). Since beauty has
proven so deceptive, the speaker decides to covet truth
instead. Beauty steals back into his senses, however,
in a violet's scent, massive trees, eternal sky ("full of
light and deity," line 47), rolling river, and bird songs.
Under their collective influence, he gives himself up to
the beauty of "the perfect whole" (line 51).

"THE EBB AND FLOW" Edward Taylor
(published 1937) Although its title draws on fluid
dynamics and its imagery deals with fire, this poem
considers the problem of sustaining spiritual arousal
at the highest level. Edward Taylor's very personal
relationship with God began when He "wroughtst
[His] sweet print" (touched him. Modern readers tend
to visualize this in connection with fingerprinting, a

19th-century discovery in regard to forensic science, but such an image is far too literal. Taylor's antiquated form of the verb *wrought* [to create or produce] more accurately conveys the metaphysical transformation of Taylor's experience).

The speaker's heart was made God's tinderbox (line 2), a metaphor based on common experience in the centuries before safety matches were invented. In its simplest form, a tinderbox would contain flint and steel, which produce sparks when the former strikes the latter, and perhaps a small amount of easily combustible material such as straw or organic rope fibers to catch the spark and burst into flame. The speaker's affections were the tinder (or kindling material) into which God's sparks fell by drops (an image that combines both the liquid and fire metaphors). The "holy sparks of heavenly fire" always caught and often would flame (in his breast or spirit).

Having devoted himself to God, it seems as though he has become His trim censer (an incense burner) full of the golden altar's fire but chiefly useful to offer up sweet incense unto "God entire" (in all aspects, including the father, son, and Holy Ghost). He no longer feels His sparks as they drop from "holy flint and steel" (line 12). In other words, as a minister he feels almost like a piece of church equipment, serviceable in God's work but missing the all-consuming passion with which he felt God's direct impact on his soul.

This instills doubts that grow in him like the buds on plants (line 13) for fear that he mistook a mocking swamp gas (the "ignis fatuus" [false fire] of line 14, a bioluminescent methane gas produced by rotting vegetative matter also known as will-o'-the-wisp or fox-fire) for God's fire, or that His altar's fire has gone out or become hidden in ashes. In other words, he fears he may have been mistaken about the reality of God's working in his soul and is also fearful that the old fire with which he valued his relationship with God has burned itself out. These doubts are assuaged "when the bellows of [God's] spirit" blows away his ashes, leaving his fire to glow anew (lines 17–18). The reference is to the bellows used in a blacksmith's shop to intensify the heat of the forge by forcing more oxygen into contact with the combustible materials and flames. This means that he becomes reinspired as God wills it.

"EDWARD" ANONYMOUS **(19th century)** This folk song unfolds like a poorly told murder mystery with the first voice belonging to the mother of the murderer and the victim and the second belonging to her son.

Like a forensics expert, the mother asks how the blood got on the point of her son's knife. He responds that it is the blood of his old coon dog that chased the fox. Perhaps unconvinced, she repeats the question, and the second time he claims it is the old horse's blood. The third time she asks, he admits it is the blood of a brother with whom he had an argument about a holly bush.

Subsequent stanzas follow the same question-and-answer format. Before his father gets home, he will sail away in a "bunkum boat" ("bunkum" refers to nonsensical or insincere speech) with his wife, but they will leave their infant with its grandmother, the internal audience of the poem. They will also leave the old gobbler (slang for a turkey) behind.

Since each stanza repeats what the named item has done for the second singer and includes the phrase "me, me, me" (as in line 4), the son might be thought a self-absorbed psychopath without empathy for the animals and brother he claims to have stabbed or for his mother's feelings. He recalls what each thing has done for him but expresses no remorse for his misdeeds. He also gives equal weight to abandoning his gobbler and his infant (tellingly referred to as an "it" when he talks of leaving "it" with his mother).

"ELDORADO" EDGAR ALLAN POE **(1849)** On January 24, 1848, James Marshall, the manager of a lumber mill in the California foothills of the Sierra Nevada mountains, found a few flecks of gold in a stream. Attempts were made at first to keep the news quiet, but by summer echoes of the shout of "Gold!" first heard in San Francisco in the spring would be heard around the world. The following year, which happened to coincide with EDGAR ALLAN POE's death, saw epic migrations from virtually all points of the compass to the gold fields.

The situation of the poem invites comparison with HENRY WADSWORTH LONGFELLOW's "EXCELSIOR," with the important difference that the discovery of gold has given a materialistic spin to the quest. The poem joins a gaily dressed (*bedight* is a term as old-fashioned as the notion of a knightly quest) gallant near the end of his long journey. Having maintained his bravery although he lost his tune (grammatically, the 6th line, "In search of Eldorado," might provide the name of his ditty or identify the subject of his quest), his youth, and any hope of succeeding, he encounters a "pilgrim shadow" (line 15; the reference suggests that the restive spirit that invigorates the American dream had its roots in the pilgrim's emigration and invites comparison between their search for God and his search for gold).

The pilgrim spirit tells him to look over the "Mountains of the Moon" (a literal impossibility at the time; line 19) and down into the "Valley of the Shadow" (line 21. The original audience would have caught the reference to Psalm 23:3: "Yea, though I walk through the valley of the shadow of death, I will fear no evil: for thou art with me. . . ." Thus the knight can be understood to be approaching death). On a metaphorical level, that reference, and the pilgrim's encouragement to "ride, boldly ride" if you seek Eldorado (lines 22–24) may be a warning to the external audience that greed leads to death.

Both *shadow* and *Eldorado* demonstrate the value of the long *O* as the most sonorous sound, and the latter, like the *Nevermore* refrain of the poet's most famous poem, "The RAVEN," illustrates his characteristic use of an *r* as the most producible consonant. That the knight may be emblematic of the soul's quest or ultimately an emblem of greed underscores the complexity of the image. Thus it can be seen that this poem exhibits most of the features Poe enumerated in "The PHILOSOPHY OF COMPOSITION" and may have been constructed in the same way.

It is perhaps characteristic of Poe's poetry that the key terms *shadow* and *Eldorado* are repeated in the same place in each stanza but with a different meaning each time (note the value Poe placed on "the variation of the application of the refrain" in the aforementioned essay). The "shadow" of the third line is the naturally occurring result when an object is placed in front of a light. In the second stanza it represents the sadness of the heart, in the 15th line it is a spirit, and in line 21 it suggests death. In addition to rhyming with shadow,

"Eldorado" might be a song title or just refer to the acquisition of wealth at the end of the first stanza. By line 12 it has acquired specific geographical features, although none of them resemble the present landscape. In the third stanza it is treated as though it were a real place to which one could be given directions, and in the last line it may represent the greed that can lure you to your doom.

"ELYSIUM IS AS FAR AS TO" EMILY DICKINSON (published 1951)

In EMILY DICKINSON's poem the speaker awaits word from the adjacent sickroom as to a friend's fate in this world. She is not chiefly concerned with the two possibilities (heaven or hell, represented here by "Felicity or Doom," line 4) that New England Christian sects have traditionally considered the postmortem outcomes ultimately awaiting the soul, but whether her happiness (represented by "Elysium" in line 1) will continue. The reference is to the Elysian Fields most memorably presented in the *Aeneid* by the first-century B.C. Roman poet Virgil as a place teeming with benign nature and inhabited by the spirits of the good (priests and such) and the great (most notably the title character's [Aeneas's] father), whereas the bad faced torment in a space similar to the Christian hell. That the speaker would use pagan instead of Christian references calls into question her faith in the afterlife, at the same time that it elevates her sick friend by implying that s/he was worthy of Elysium. In Virgil, Aeneas must endure a torturous and lengthy journey before arriving still alive at Elysium; awareness of this precedent probably led to the speaker's reference to Elysium's being "as far" as the next room instead of "as close." The same phrase also alludes to her inability to intervene in her friend's crisis.

"Fortitude" was a common virtue among the heroes of the Elysian Fields, but here the speaker celebrates that trait in the souls of those who must wait while a loved one suffers. In this instance the speaker is so intent on the struggle next door that she focuses not just on hearing the footfalls of the doctor or attendant who will bring news of the patient's condition, but on their accent (line 7). The outcome is so important to her that she listens for the spring or hesitance in that herald's steps as the first indication of the good or bad news. The opening of the door (line 8) separating the two rooms will lead to her learning if her personal Elysian Fields (made happy by the goodness of her friend) will be restored, or if the friend has opened a door leading, for better or worse, to eternity.

EMERSON, RALPH WALDO (1803–1882)

Although his lectures and essays were generally better than his poetry, the Sage of Concord deserves a place near the center of the American pantheon of poetry for his influence on the poets he nurtured and the independence he fostered. The future inspirational speaker was born into the family of the Unitarian minister of Boston's First Church on May 25, 1803, but his father died when Ralph was seven years old. His mother, Ruth Haskins Emerson, continued raising her six remaining children on an annual stipend for seven years from the church (McAleer 45) that she eventually supplemented by taking in boarders, providing her son with a practical example of self-reliance. This would eventually become his most important message to the nation as he preached an American progress based on individual insight and ingenuity from the pulpit of the secular lectern. The buoyant optimism everywhere evident in his public writing argues that he somehow managed to transcend a series of tragedies haunting his private life, including the premature deaths of siblings during his childhood and of his oldest child, and his impoverished youth.

Biographers tend to make much of the future poet's seemingly lackluster performance at Harvard in order to contrast it with his subsequent fame. They rarely give full weight to the emotional and physical challenges he had to overcome, as he was younger than many of his classmates and faced the burden of working his way through college in addition to the demands of his course work. Reducing something as complex as a college education to a single number, whether it represents a grade-point average or a student's rank in his graduating class, cannot account for extenuating circumstances such as those Emerson had to face. It must be admitted that the records reveal a mediocre student (he finished 30th out of 59 in the class of 1821) and his immediate path after college was anything but outstanding: He continued

teaching school, a vocation with which he had some acquaintance even before college and which he had pursued during his academic vacations. At that time it was generally not necessary for a teacher to have attended college, and many schools were privately and not publicly funded. This meant that teachers were frequently poorly paid, but Emerson's brother ran a school for young ladies that provided Ralph with a relatively lucrative position.

After four years of teaching after college, Emerson was ready for a change. Either the flesh was too weak (he had trouble with his eyes and other health problems) or the spirit was too strong (he already had some reservations about accepting all the tenets of the church) to permit an immediately successful return to school. He reluctantly withdrew from the Harvard Divinity School and taught another year. By presenting a sermon for the approval of an Association of Congregational Ministers, he received a license to preach in 1826 (McAleer 86). Health concerns (tuberculosis ran in his family) led him to travel to Charleston, South Carolina, and St. Augustine, Florida, for his health. In 1827, he re-enrolled in the divinity school (perhaps reasoning that although experience led him to doubt, additional education might remove that obstacle) and continued preaching. While serving as a visiting preacher in Concord, New Hampshire, he first met his future wife, a beautiful albeit consumptive teenaged heiress named Ellen Tucker. In that age of outstanding orators, the golden-throated minister must have seemed especially attractive, and the couple married on September 30, 1829. Up to that point (and after her death as well), Emerson can seem something of a cold fish, but his letters, poetry and private journal reveal that their love touched him deeply. Unfortunately, she died on February 8, 1831. A contested will held up the final installment of Ralph's inheritance until 1837, when he began averaging an income of $100 a month from his investments (McAleer 108). Such bald financial facts can make him seem an unscrupulous opportunist, but such an interpretation runs counter to all that is known of his true character. For months after his wife's death, Emerson daily visited her tomb and finally took the exceptional step of opening her coffin (March 29, 1832; McAleer 109). This allowed him to bring closure to the emotional crisis attendant upon her death. Later in 1832, he resigned the ministry of the Boston parish that had paid $1,800 per year (Richardson 91), a princely sum that suggests he was already on his way to substantial wealth even without his wife's dowry. He left for Europe on December 25, 1832, a distancing of himself from the legal squabbles attending his inheritance that further underscores the true nature of his love for his first wife.

The crisis of conscience that led Emerson to resign as the junior pastor of his Boston church was based on his willingness to value personal revelation instead of accepting the primacy of church doctrine. He did not believe, for example, that communion wafers could literally become the real flesh of Christ, and therefore refused to officiate over that sacrament. For more than 200 years, his family had been furnishing New England with Harvard-educated clergy, a fact that helped him attain the prominent Boston post. Unfortunately, he had become an important symbol of faith before he had discovered his true beliefs (Richardson 91).

His sojourn abroad took him to the chief cities of western Europe and such leading English writers as Samuel Taylor Coleridge, William Wordsworth, and Thomas Carlyle. He returned to America in 1834 but would return to Europe in 1847 to lecture and in 1872 for his health. He began making a living through the public lectures that he then developed into books. In 1835, he married the seemingly wealthy Lydia Jackson after generously agreeing to assign her inheritance to her impoverished sister. They would have four children, including a second Ellen Tucker Emerson. Like his first wife, Lydian (the name she adopted after he had fashioned it for her) had seen him for the first time as a substitute minister. His lecture fees and investments provided the resources necessary to purchase their spacious Concord home and to hire servants to tend it. The couple asked his mother and one of his brothers to live with them, but the brother died before he could move in. Emerson created two of his most important essays in the next two years, "Nature" and "The American Scholar."

Surrounding himself with friends and other transcendentalists, he was able to turn Concord into the intellectual center of America from 1840 to the start of the Civil War. He provided a shelter, employment, and encouragement for HENRY DAVID THOREAU, to ease the younger man's penury, and edited (with Margaret Fuller) and largely financed *The Dial,* the journal that publicized the philosophical movement known as TRANSCENDENTALISM. Emerson continued to write essays, lectures, and enough poetry to fill the three volumes published in his lifetime: *Poems* (1846), *May-Day and Other Pieces* (1866), and *Selected Poems* (1876). A generous, highly moral, and principled man, he opposed slavery to the extent that he publicly mourned the execution of the murderous John Brown. In the years following the Civil War, the quality of his literary production gradually tapered off. In his prime, he could mesmerize audiences (he gave approximately 1,500 public lectures in a career spanning nearly half a century) with his powerful voice. Near the end of his life, it faded in strength even as his mental powers began to wane. He died of pneumonia in Concord on April 27, 1882.

Emerson's transcendental philosophy led to the production of poems like "BRAHMA" and "HAMATREYA" that helped introduce mainstream America to Asian philosophy. His love of nature can be seen in "The RIVER," his "Hymn Sung at the completion of the Concord Movement, April 19, 1836" celebrated the start of the Revolutionary War near his home in Concord, and "The POET" is an essay on that important subject that helped WALT WHITMAN find an audience. His most important books are *Nature* (1836), *Essays* (especially the first series, published in 1841), and *Representative Men* (1850).

Emerson's home in Concord from 1835 to 1882 was restored following an 1872 fire and has been preserved, although the furniture from the poet's study is on display at the Concord Museum. The Emerson Society holds annual meetings and publishes the *Emerson Society Papers.* Harvard University holds the largest collection of Emerson material, and additional manuscripts can be found at the Concord Public Library and at UCLA.

BIBLIOGRAPHY
Buell, Lawrence. *Emerson.* Cambridge, Mass.: Harvard University Press, 2003.

Clavel, Stanley. *Emerson's Transcendental Etudes.* Edited by David Justin Hodge. Stanford, Calif.: Stanford University Press, 2003.

McAleer, John. *Ralph Waldo Emerson: Days of Encounter.* Boston: Little, Brown, 1984.

Richardson, Robert D., Jr. *Emerson: The Mind on Fire.* Berkeley: University of California Press, 1995.

Sacks, Kenneth. *Understanding Emerson: "The American Scholar" and His Struggle of Self-Reliance.* Princeton, N.J.: Princeton University Press, 2003.

Smith, Harmon. *My Friend, My Friend: The Story of Thoreau's Relationship with Emerson.* Amherst: University of Massachusetts Press, 1999.

"AN EPITAPH ON MY DEAR AND EVER-HONOURED MOTHER MRS. DOROTHY DUDLEY, WHO DECEASED DECEMBER 27, 1643, AND OF HER AGE, 61" ANNE BRADSTREET (1643)

This poem is chiefly valuable for what its idealized portrait of the society matron reveals about life in early colonial Massachusetts. As the wife of the governor of the colony, ANNE BRADSTREET's mother was indeed worthy, and the speaker's assertion that she lived an unspotted life meant that no public sin was attached to her name. The ideal mother of most eras is loving, but colonial law placed far more emphasis on her being an obedient wife (line 2) than would later be the case. It was not unlawful for a man to beat his wife, and most of the property rights belonged to the husband.

Mrs. Dudley was a friendly neighbor and full of pity for the poor, whom she often fed and clothed from her own supplies. It was considered virtuous for the mistress of a prosperous household to be "wisely awful" (line 5) to her servants; the latter term meant awe-inspiring. Most servants were indentured, which meant that in exchange for a fee, or often just the voyage to America, they gave up most of their rights for a specified number of years. Since this gave them little incentive to work efficiently or even cheerfully, 17th-century management practice provided their masters with the tools needed to instill terror in their hearts, or at the very least, to constantly remind them of their place. Failure to keep the servants productively employed had moral as well as economic implications for anyone in that largely feudal society. Mrs. Dudley was always kind to her servants, but she was also good at maintaining discipline by appropriately rewarding both good and bad behavior.

Although mothers in less prosperous households might be expected to teach their children such skills as reading, even a societal matron was expected to properly inculcate religious and moral values in her children. That her mother did this in accordance with church doctrine becomes evident when Bradstreet calls her "a true instructor" (line 7). She kept an ordered house and family.

Both publicly and privately, religion played a very important role in her life. She frequently attended church services and routinely prayed on her own for lengthy periods. The penultimate couplet of the poem contains high praise for a Massachusetts pilgrim of either gender:

> Religious in all her words and ways,
> Preparing still ("always") for death, till end of
>   days
>
> (lines 11–12)

The "end of days" was Judgment Day, a time when the pilgrims fervently believed that all the souls of everyone who ever lived would be gathered, judged, and dispatched to either eternal salvation or eternal damnation. Every aspect of their private as well as public lives was supposed to be managed with this end in view.

In an era of large families and relatively short life expectancies, it was rare for a mother to live long enough to see each of her children have children of their own. In conducting her life so well, she left blessed memories.

"ESSENTIAL OILS ARE WRUNG" EMILY DICKINSON (published 1951)

This poem points out that the best, or at least the most enduring, scents from the rose do not occur naturally but only as a result of a torturous process. Time and natural processes are perceived as the principal enemies since together they lead to the decay of the "General" rose (line 5; the adjective suggests that the same fate awaits all roses, but its capitalization may also suggest that the speaker has in mind an individual rose of such distinction as to merit a title. It works both ways).

Unlike the unprocessed rose, the manufactured oils still maintain enough of their aroma to "make Summer" (a felicitous phrase that conjures the magic by which scents can, by prior association, return the inhaler to a different emotional place and time; line 5). Many people were fluent in the language of flowers in the 19th century, when the presentation of a particular type of blossom could deliver messages that individual men and women found awkward to deliver verbally. Thus a lady's "drawer" (line 6) could still be emitting signals of summer vitality as well as romantic love (the special meaning attached to red roses) even after her death (one possible interpretation of her "lying in ceaseless rosemary"). An alternative reading might focus on the lady's prevarication: to "lie" in rosemary could mean misrepresenting feelings of constancy, fidelity, or remembrance (the meaning associated with gifts of that flower). Rosemary would have been a good choice for such representations because of its staying power; its aroma is "ceaseless" in comparison to the more transient odors of other plants.

On a Freudian level, the poem could be interpreted as an exposure of female vanity. It would take a registered nurse to explain the ways in which essential oils cannot always be produced naturally, that the "gift of screws" (literally the application of pressure on the flower blossoms to extract the nectar and oils contributing to their scent; line 4) can aid in their production, and that roses are not the only things that can dry out. But perhaps the poet did not intend for the reader to carry the examination of ladies' drawers quite so far.

EUROPEAN POETIC INFLUENCES Most British-American colonists thought of themselves as not only full citizens of the Crown but also heirs to a rich tradition of British literature. Intent on maintaining that identity, they tended to ignore "continental literature," by which they meant anything written in the major languages of Europe beyond their ancestral island home. Prior to the Revolutionary era, wide exposure to even English poetry was typically limited by a shortage of books and the funds to purchase them, but almanacs and newspapers frequently printed poems,

and some of the wealthier colonists kept well-stocked private libraries.

Instruction even in such prestigious schools as Harvard centered on ancient Greek and Latin instead of the modern European languages and literatures. Political luminaries such as BENJAMIN FRANKLIN, John Adams, and Thomas Jefferson were privileged to spend years in the European courts on diplomatic missions, and economic opportunities and vacations lured other Americans onto the Continent. It was not until George Ticknor's 1815–19 studies in Germany, France, Spain, and Portugal that the languages of these countries began to be taught at Harvard. For 18 years, Ticknor exposed the youth of the nation's cultural elite to the literatures of western Europe, a successful experiment that encouraged emulation by other colleges. Hence Bowdoin College hired one of its most promising graduates, HENRY WADSWORTH LONGFELLOW, as chair of its modern languages department, provided that he could acquire the necessary languages by studying for three years in Europe on his own. Longfellow wrote his own French and Spanish texts during the five years he taught at Bowdoin after his return, then Harvard snatched up this rising star. After another year's private study in Europe, he took over the chair made prestigious by Ticknor's labors before that predecessor's retirement, and he taught for an additional 18 years at Harvard. Exposure to European literature (including Swedish and Danish) encouraged him to try his own verse, which, although written in English, often relied on European models. In studying the Finnish epic *Kalevala* soon after its rediscovery in 1849, Longfellow must have been struck by the similarity of its content to the Ojibway tales that had been translated into English by Jane and Henry Rowe Schoolcraft. He soon synthesized these two sources into his SONG OF HIAWATHA, introducing into English the Hiawatha meter (four trochee feet per line) of the *Kalevala* that struck his initial audience as so appropriately alien that it suited his primitive subject.

Although modern Italian literature had very little influence on American letters prior to the 20th century, the sonnet, and other fixed forms (such as terza rima) developed in Renaissance Italy, continued to furnish instructive models for subsequent world literature, including American. French forms such as the rondeau were also adopted by English poets and came to America as part of the nation's British inheritance.

In the 1840s, German philosophers helped inspire American transcendentalism, a new movement popularized by RALPH WALDO EMERSON and others. His "EACH AND ALL" aims not only at the representation of natural phenomena but also at revealing a metaphysical principle with aesthetic implications. Such insights helped open the doors to the cultural relativism implied by Emerson's "BRAHMA" and "HAMATREYA," which went so far beyond even European models as to incorporate religious insights from India. The influence of the movement was also evident in the poetry of HENRY DAVID THOREAU, whose "FOG" and "The FALL OF THE LEAF" infuse their subjects with religious mysticism.

Much later in the 19th century such influential critics as William Dean Howells praised the work of the major Russian writers as well as their continental counterparts, a trend that helped make the work of the most famous Russian poets available in English. Early translations of Mikhail Lermontov's *A Hero of Our Time* and "The Demon" were published in London (in 1853 and 1876, respectively). The composer Modest Petrovich Mussorgsky's famous opera *Boris Gudonov* (1869) brought the Alexander Pushkin story upon which it was based to the attention of America's cultural elite. Pushkin's famous *Eugene Onegin* inspired English translations prior to 1900, and a volume of his translated poems was published in Boston in 1888.

The naturalism that dominated American literature from 1890 to 1920 owed much to the plebeian sympathies of such French writers as Victor Hugo and Émile Zola. Its pessimism and materialistic determinism can be seen throughout much of the poetry of STEPHEN CRANE and the early poetry of EDWIN ARLINGTON ROBINSON.

BIBLIOGRAPHY

Greene, Roland Arthur. *Unrequited Conquests: Love and Empire in the Colonial Americas.* Chicago: University of Chicago Press, 1999.

Taupin, René. *The Influence of French Symbolism on Modern American Poetry.* Translated by William Pratt and Anne Rich Pratt. New York: A.M.S. Press, 1985.

Vines, Lois Davis. *Valéry and Poe: A Literary Legacy.* New York: New York University Press, 1992.

"EVENING SONG" SIDNEY LANIER (1877)

The internal audience for SIDNEY LANIER's simple love poem is a lover with whom the speaker is already on fairly intimate terms since he addresses her as "dear Love" (line 1). Having taken her to the seashore at sunset, he points out the pale yellow sand, the sun, and the sea. When one is in love it is easy to find reflections of love in everything, so the sun seems to be kissing the sea as it sets. He points out how natural it is, how unashamed they are "in sight of all the lands" (line 3), and how long their kiss lasts, three lessons (especially the length) they can apply to their own kissing.

In the second stanza he points out how the blending of sea and sun makes the former seem to dissolve and colors the latter like the rosy wine in which Cleopatra dissolved a pearl. She might be dazzled by his education, by his apparent knowledge of royalty (and the great lovers who have preceded them), and perhaps by the implication that their love is as noble and as worthy of sacrifice as that of Cleopatra. Just as the Egyptian queen drank the pearl-enriched wine, Night is drinking up both the sea and the sun that apparently dissolved in it. There is a slight change in his tone as he tells her to lay her hand in his; probably only an English major or linguist would note such a subtle shift to the imperative mood.

Feeling extraordinarily confident (or playful) at this point, or transported to raptures by their location, their physicality or other manifestations of their love, he orders the sweet stars to come forth "and comfort Heaven's heart" (line 9), perhaps creating their own personal mythology. Sometimes waves can have phosphorescent qualities and their white caps can reflect whatever ambient light strikes them, but the real attraction of line 10 is his rhetorical virtuosity. She is unlikely to have heard a statement like "Glimmer, ye waves, round else unlighted sands" before.

He calls on the Night to divorce sun and sky (he wants it to get darker and even more romantic), but never to separate their lips or their hands.

"AN EVENING THOUGHT: SALVATION BY CHRIST, WITH PENITENTIAL CRIES: COMPOSED BY JUPITER HAMMON, A NEGRO BELONGING TO MR. LLOYD OF QUEEN'S VILLAGE, ON LONG ISLAND, THE 25TH OF DECEMBER, 1760" JUPITER HAMMON (1760)

At a time in American history when the basic humanity of slaves was challenged not by fringe hate groups but by mainstream culture, a 49-year-old slave, clerk, and craftsman, JUPITER HAMMON, took up his pen on Christmas Day to produce this poem celebrating not just the advent of Christ and His promise of salvation, but also the fact that this opportunity applied to all men regardless of color or social standing.

His argument begins with a statement with which even the fiercest oppressors of his race had to agree if they were Christian: only Christ offers salvation (line 1). Almost immediately he also asserts the subversive premise of the poem, that the promised Redemption (explained in the eighth stanza) was available to everyone who loved Christ's holy word (line 4). The basic equality implied by this part of the message was almost as revolutionary, and potentially as dangerous, a development as Christ's teaching was when He personally delivered it. The notion of flight, whether to Jesus (line 5) or elsewhere, was also generally not one that slaveholders would want to be widely disseminated. The double ambiguity of asking for "Salvation from our King" (line 8) lies in the identity of the king (King George III of England, political sovereign of the Americas, or Jesus Christ?) and in the prepositional phrase (does the speaker desire salvation as a gift from the king, or deliverance from the king's authority?). The third stanza seems to clarify the matter in favor of the Lord, but the speaker, perhaps inadvertently, has already raised serious questions about the justice and morality of slavery as well as the equality of men.

The fourth stanza asks Jesus to extend his grace to every nation that lacks (the "han't" of line 15 is a contraction for "has not") the Lord of Salvation. The speaker asks for the preparation necessary to receive grace from the God who gave his only Son (see John 3:16). The world's redemption was purchased by the Precious Blood of Jesus (lines 29–30), who was God's captive slave (at the time of the crucifixion? Line 32). The speaker would hasten "Tribunal Day" (more commonly called "Judgment Day," line 36), but in the meantime Christ hears the cries of the oppressed (line 40; see Psalms 102:20). He would have the Lord impart true motion to "our benighted souls" and let the hearts (of all the world) accept Christ's salvation.

The 13th stanza contains a rather cryptic reference to Revelations (5:11–13), in which not 10,000 (as in line 49) but 10,000 times 10,000 (or 100 million) and an additional thousands of thousands of angels cry along with the beasts of, under and above the earth and those below the sea, that the sacrificed Lamb is worthy of worship. Alternatively, Jude 1:14 quotes Enoch's prophecy in which the Lord will come with 10,000 saints on Judgment Day (with no mention of their being "louder than the Ocean").

Today, the speaker asserts in the next stanza, is the Day of Salvation; he would awaken every nation to the opportunity of finding a safe abode in the word of the Son of God (line 60). Salvation can set the sinner free; thus we fly unto Jesus and to the glory of our king (line 68). The blessed of the Lord have but to accept the word to have their souls "fit for heaven" (line 72). He asserts that we turn to Jesus with hearts and souls ready to magnify His name, and would welcome the heavenly dove that would increase our love since we have already experienced fear. Thus Salvation "high and low" (even the slaves have the opportunity, the phrase reminds the audience in line 82) promises heaven to the soul that relies on Christ. He would have Jesus, the heavenly dove, accept our repentance and let us share the tender love of God with the angels.

"EXCELSIOR" HENRY WADSWORTH LONGFELLOW (1842)

HENRY WADSWORTH LONGFELLOW'S study of self-sacrifice takes the phenomenon to its logical conclusion, self-immolation, in response to a completely abstract ideal. The tension of the poem lies in the contrast between the objectivity of its approach and its sympathetic depiction of the ardent youth in the grip of his passionate devotion.

The story of the poem is familiar to most modern adventure travelers: a poorly prepared and ill-provisioned hiker dies rather than abandon his project in the face of inclement weather. His other mistakes are also obvious; he begins an unassisted final assault at twilight despite physical problems ("from his lips escaped a groan," line 14) and at least three warnings from the local inhabitants. His body is not recovered until the next day. He probably fell victim to hypothermia instead of an avalanche since he was only half-buried in the snow (line 37) and retained the banner in his frozen hand.

Two people who warned the youth pointed out specific hazards on the trail ranging from the gathering storm, a torrential stream, overhanging trees, and an avalanche. The maiden's offer of a resting place for his head might be interpreted as a warning that he would pass up his chance for a meaningful relationship if he persisted in his march. Like many religious seekers, he is willing to forego such temptations as a sacrifice to his ideal.

The speaker muddles the straightforward action of the poem with a pathetic fallacy in the last stanza when a voice from the serene sky echoes the fallen youth's motto. A *pathetic fallacy* occurs when a writer describes some phenomenon of nature as if it were reacting in open sympathy with the human emotions, as in the assertion that tears fell from the sky at the death of a heroine. Is the device used here as a demonstration of the cosmic rightness of his cause, or as a call for additional sacrifice from anyone who might adopt the slogan? It was probably intended to mystify the moment by suggesting a transcendence of some sort. It attempts to restore balance to the poem's central question; without it, a reader might too easily conclude that the youth foolishly died for nothing.

Two mountain passes in Europe bear the name of Bernard because that saint created a hospice at each to care for such hapless travelers as the youth of this poem. At slightly more than 8,100 feet, the Grand Saint Bernard Pass offers passage between Switzerland and Italy, since the surrounding mountains are much higher, and this was the pass more closely associated with the famed rescue dogs such as the "faithful hound" that discovered the hiker's body in this poem. Although the view is not literally one to die for, the use of such a spectacular setting suggests a possible interpretation of the Latin word on the youth's banner. It is usually translated as "higher," and might serve as the inscrutable and yet suitable answer to the perennial question as to why people climb mountains.

Knowledge of the historical significance of the setting broadens the application of the poem. The Saint Bernard Pass was used by conquering armies for more than a thousand years, and the names associated with it are legendary: Hannibal, Julius Caesar, Charlemagne, and Napoleon all crossed it with their armies. Since hikers and mountain climbers usually do not bear banners with them on the trail, the device recalls another venue in which youth willfully sacrifice themselves for an ideal, service in their nations' militaries. By making his protagonist a mountain climber or hiker instead of a soldier, the speaker was able to admire self-sacrifice for an ideal without compromising it with political or military baggage. The horrid last stanza was unnecessary because the youth's insistence on bearing his banner up the mountainside was mystery enough for one poem. His passage attracts not because it leads to death but as a portrait celebrating passionate, youthful exuberance.

"EXPERIENCE IS THE ANGLED ROAD"

EMILY DICKINSON (published 1951) This poem celebrates the philosophical conundrum presented by the rival claims of predestination and free will. The problem is probably unsolvable by the human mind, but the poet opens with an attempted application of Yankee practicality: taken by themselves, the first two lines suggest that experience is better than theory. Ironically, this is itself only a theory, and the next two lines wonder that the Mind would prefer the "angled road" of experience (which might as well be random; certainly the end result of such a choice cannot be seen) to its own path. This mistake is compounded when the Mind tries to lead (control) experience. That approach is belittled by EMILY DICKINSON's use of *presuming* in line 4; the term suggests that attempting to control experience is an arrogant act rashly co-opting the prerogatives of a higher power.

The fun of the second stanza arises from the ambiguity surrounding the phrase "Discipline of Man" (line 6). Grammatically, it is unclear if man is being disciplined by some higher force (a more straightforward interpretation supported by the last two lines) or if his own inner discipline compels his choice. While the speaker can admire how complicated this paradox is, the process inevitably leads to "Preappointed Pain" (line 8), a rather unhappy end result that argues for predestination but takes precious little joy at that conclusion.

F

"FABLE" RALPH WALDO EMERSON (1846)

A fable is typically a moralistic story in which animals act like humans. The delights of the genre in the hands of a master (such as Aesop, the ancient Greek) often include having the animals retain much of the nature peculiar to their species, and an ending that frequently surprises despite its intrinsic connection with the personalities revealed in the tale. RALPH WALDO EMERSON is much too heavy-handed here; the squirrel's sermon on the mount merely belabors the obvious.

The triggering incident of the poem's conflict occurred when the mountain called his opponent a "Little Prig" (line 3), a name with which a member of the propertied class (such as one might find in old England) might dismiss an upstart. A prig might be either a petty thief or a dandy, or (less likely in this case) an arrogant conformist who smugly and stubbornly upholds the proprieties of his privileged class regardless of the circumstances in which he finds himself. Perhaps because, given the nature of squirrels, an accusation of thievery would be too hard to defend against, the squirrel focuses on the issue of size instead of morality in his rebuttal.

First, however, the narrator gratuitously introduces the squirrel as "Bun" (line 4), perhaps to indicate where his sympathies lie. Squirrels were (and are) considered game animals in certain parts of the country, where the bun is the hind parts. Adopting that name for a pet squirrel is rather like choosing Porkchop as the name for a pet pig, but people did.

Bun unleashes the best four lines (6–9) in the poem, mentioning the weather as a hint that the mountain is not as omnipotent as he might seem. If "all sorts of things" are necessary to make a year or a sphere (the earth), then even a squirrel might be as important as a mountain. He is willing to give the mountain his due (as "a very pretty squirrel track," line 16), but carrying a forest on his back may not be as intrinsically valuable as the ability to crack a nut, which the mountain is unable to do.

"FACING WEST FROM CALIFORNIA'S SHORES" WALT WHITMAN (1860)

By the start of the Civil War, the United States had secured possession of all the territory that would eventually form the conterminous 48 states except for a small strip of land that later became part of New Mexico. Large migrations and immigrations had made it evident that the West would soon be thoroughly explored and settled, and many people were already wondering what would happen when the frontier would be closed (when no more land was freely available for homesteading, a milestone reached about 30 years after this poem appeared).

WALT WHITMAN seems to be speaking for the entire nation as the speaker describes himself as "a child, very old" (line 3). In this context, his adjectives of "inquiring, tireless, and seeking" aptly describe the fledgling country as it turns its attention finally back to "the house of maternity" (line 3), the ancestral home of its far-distant Asian ancestors (humanity was thought to have developed in Asia, not Africa, at that time). Thus the "circle [was] almost circled" (line 4) in several senses: the westerly migrations of peoples had almost encompassed the entire planet, thus completing what seemed a cultural (perhaps even a biological) imperative. As a token of the historical moment when Americans were beginning to think globally for the first time, it seems fitting that an elemental circle with its innumerable millennia of mystical associations seems to describe the process.

The speaker traces the migrations from their supposed start in Hindustan (a name variously applied to northern regions of India and sometimes the entire subcontinent) and Kashmere (a sometimes independent region whose fluid boundaries frequently included parts of modern Pakistan. The modern English spelling is 'Kashmir'). He condenses perhaps tens of thousands of years of history into a single phrase when he describes how the migrations moved from the North (his land of "God, the sage, and the hero" [line 6] might aptly describe India, China, and several western European nations). They also moved from the South, perhaps from "flowery peninsulas" (a description bringing the tropical flora of Malaysia to mind) and the spice islands (now part of Indonesia).

Again contemplating the supposed ancient home of western civilization brought pleasure and joy to the speaker, but it leaves him pondering the location of what man was seeking so long ago, and questioning why it has not yet been found.

"FAIRYLAND" EDGAR ALLAN POE (1829) This is EDGAR ALLAN POE's parody of poems by the great Irish poet Thomas Moore (1779–1852), whom he mentions in a humorous footnote to line 33: "plagiarism—see the works of Thomas Moore—passim—Edr." ("Passim" means that the referenced material occurs often in the cited text, and "Edr" is an abbreviation for "Editor" although Poe himself added this footnote.) Moore evidently thought that rustic scenes were more romantic than urban venues, for his typical poem is set in just such a vale as Poe lampoons in his first four lines (see, for example, "At the Mid Hour of Night," which begins

"At the mid hour of night, when stars are
    weeping, I fly
To the lone vale we loved. . . ."

The situation in the Moore poem is that the speaker returned to the scene where earlier his voice and that of his internal audience had commingled, but as the weeping stars hint, his lover has evidently died because he thinks he hears her voice "from the Kingdom of Souls." The point of Poe's jest is that Moore committed a pathetic fallacy, the flawed logic that has nature reacting in sympathy with the human events that unfold in a work of art. Poe may have learned something even more valuable from just such lines as these because, as he observes in "The PHILOSOPHY OF COMPOSITION," the death of a beautiful woman is the most poetic (because it is the most melancholic) subject in the world. Such a tragedy was not coincidentally the surprise lurking in Poe's most famous poem, "The RAVEN."

As Poe points out in his fifth line, moons wax and wane in Moore's work, as two of the latter's titles suggest: "The Young May Moon" and "Oft, in the Stilly Night Air." Moore's characters often "put out the starlight with the breath from their pale faces" (Poe's line 10), and in "At the Mid Hour," the couple's voices "breathed like one on the ear" (Poe seems to be implying that these suggestive passages are weakened by their metaphysical elements). About midnight "by the moon-dial" (a farcical invention since the moon rises more than an hour later from one night to the next), a moon more "filmy" than the rest comes into the perfect position (in a bracketed aside, Poe tells us that trial and error revealed such an effect to be best. The humor lies in the juxtaposition of this editorial commentary at just the moment when Moore was trying his most romantic image; lines 13–14). Like a spotlight resting on a mountain's crown, its "easy drapery" falls over strange woods, the sea, spirits on the wing, and every drowsy thing (the insertion of *over* preceding each item in this list provides an example of the humor of repetition even as it suggests that the speaker has become frustrated by Moore's repetition; lines 22–24). In the morning their "moony covering" (presumably, the fog, mist, and clouds) is soaring in the sky "like—almost any thing . . ." (these last four words constitute the line

33, which Poe identified as plagiarized) "or a yellow albatross" (a whimsical example. Most albatrosses are predominantly white or black and, while the former might appear yellow in the right lighting conditions [one species bears the popular name of "yellow-*nosed* albatross"; still other species have pairs of yellow feet and a streak of yellow feathers on their heads and necks], there is no "yellow albatross" in name or hue, except for an Australian butterfly of which it is doubtful Poe had any knowledge).

Moore's lovers no longer use the moony covering for the same end as before, "videlicet" (a Latin-derived term substituted for *namely* to introduce specific examples; line 35) a tent (what makes this among the funniest lines in the poem is its use of the high-class Latin term to introduce such a prosaic noun, and its ribald element if Poe is implying that such a "tent" was their only covering), which the speaker thinks "extravagant" (a double entendre, since he may be referring to their not taking advantage of an available resource, the moon, in an almost economic sense, or he may be commenting on their "exceptional" behavior). It "atomies" (breaks up into the smallest possible parts) and dissipates in showers, from which butterflies (perhaps the poet was something of a lepidopterist after all) "who seek the skies and come down again" have brought a specimen upon their quivering wings. (Poe's bracketed interjection of "the unbelieving things!" [line 44] implicitly compares the butterflies to human skeptics who either want tangible proof before they will admit the existence of supernatural, or even religious, phenomena, or to weak-willed believers who lack the faith to fully commit themselves to reaching heaven).

This poem is an excellent example of the humor of which the young Poe was master. He so impressed his West Point classmates that they raised the funds to print his first collection of poetry after he was released from that institution without graduating. The joke was ultimately on them, however, as that book was filled with serious poetry and classical allusions.

In his essay on "The POETIC PRINCIPLE," Poe defends Moore as an underappreciated, "true" poet whose fancy was so great that it predominated over all his other faculties. He appears to seriously recommend the lines beginning with "I would I were by that dim lake" as among the most profoundly, weirdly imaginative lines in the English language, although he regretfully cannot remember them on that occasion (Moore does have a poem by that title). Poe took his adoration of Moore to an entirely different level when he composed "The LAKE" using the same locale in Virginia that inspired Moore's "A Ballad: The Lake of the Dismal Swamp" during the Irish poet's visit to America three years before Poe's birth. Moore's poem contains references to the dim shores of the dusky lake, but in "The Poetic Principle," Poe may not have felt it prudent to refer to a title by another poet that so closely mirrored his own. Moore's ballad tells of an Indian who ends up searching for his lover's spirit at the lake, whereas Poe's poem celebrates the emotions the lake itself stirs in the speaker's breast without the added narrative interest of a poignant tale of lost love.

"'FAITH' IS A FINE INVENTION" EMILY DICKINSON (1891)

This epigrammatic poem may attack the hypocrisy of those whose faith is based only on what they can see; such faith is so shallow that deeper answers are necessary when a crisis arises. Part of EMILY DICKINSON's humor lies in the notion of faith being based on physical objects; no faith is necessary if the existence of the things in question can be proven. The unusual rhyme of "Gentlemen can see" with "emergency" is also pleasing, as is the image of the sophisticated men smugly congratulating themselves on their fine invention until they must scurry to rethink their ideas. Humor also arises from the physical scale involved: the crisis of faith setting off this feverish activity is so small that it requires microscopes.

"THE FALL OF THE LEAF" HENRY DAVID THOREAU (1863)

Although the speaker asks the internal audience to thank God (at the same time she does so), the personified deity he describes most resembles the pagan god Apollo, as the ancient Greeks fashioned the sun. The opening stanzas revolve around a culinary conceit, with God seasoning the year as if perfecting it for human consumption. He will touch upon each of the four seasons in turn, beginning with the winter in which, he notes, the sun kindly slants his rays and can be plainest seen (because of the clear winter sky unobstructed by foliage) on the shortest days. Like a good chef, God also regulates his heats (line 5), throwing in his harsher cold to protect man from gluttony with the summer's sweets and tempering the cold to prevent man's pouting about the winter's "crudity" (rawness, but in keeping with the poem's culinary metaphors the term may pun on "crudités," a French term for raw vegetable sticks; line 8).

The third stanza echoes the frequent calls of RALPH WALDO EMERSON, HENRY DAVID THOREAU's mentor, for the independence of the American spirit, which Thoreau here even extends to independence from nature (lines 9–10). Free of control by the current season, he can recall late fall-ripened fruits and the color of that sky even in early July. Then, with summer's garishness gone, some "grains of night tincture the noontide air" (line 20). As if it were chosen to demonstrate the maturing of the mind as well as of the crops, the term *grains* conjures not only the seeds of the various fall-ripened cereal grasses, but also suggests the smallest particles generally encountered. Their presence in the fall sky suggests the dust of harvesting but also the artistic technique designed to add a grainy texture to a painting. A "tincture" is a dye or stain that adds a distinctive tinge of color. The dust and other debris in the fall air might be represented as the "grains of night" in the sense that they represent the end of the year's growth and hint at the onset of winter, when vegetative nature seems dead.

It would not have been lost on Thoreau, distinguished as a naturalist for his close observation of nature, that the fall shadows were longer than those of summer at "noontide." As the poem appeared in the pivotal year of the Civil War, the military metaphor of shadows as "sentries" was close at hand (line 23). Like an experienced nature cinematographer (operating long before the advent of motion pictures), he comes in for a close up on the rich darkness of the pine needle's shadows (line 28).

In their natural setting, and because their call is so associated with the heat and shortening days of autumn, the crickets' songs can be "slumberous [here, sleep-inducing] lays" (line 29). Secure in subterranean tunnels, they can still be heard, adding a "film of autumn" over the summer (in a transcendent moment,

the aural sensation of the cricket's call is thus represented visually; line 36).

In that age, sailing was still an important means of navigating the oceans, so the flocks of birds reminded Thoreau of fleets of ships (line 37). To "beat" is to sail into the wind, a feat that is only possible by tacking (changing the angle at which the wind strikes one's sails by steering so that the bow of the boat is first on one side relative to the wind direction and then on the other. Thus it is necessary to zigzag if one's goal is directly upwind). The birds' distant calls are barely audible as "clicks" from the ground, but they "beguile" (entice) others to join them on their way (line 40).

The late season curling of the leaves (or perhaps the sound of the wind through the trees) reminds him of a pipe organ, bringing a "prelude of the Fall" to mind, with the "Fall" also referencing each leaf's descent to the earth (line 44). Note the gentleness of the lilting alliteration with which each leaf's fall is described in line 46: "It lightly lays itself along." A benign hand (God's or Nature's?) "pillowed" them (an image in keeping with the softness of the stanza; line 47) to sleep on the old year's throng.

Birch trees are brown and "sere" (withered), and leaves float without mourners upon a watery "bier" (a coffin and its stand) in a distant pool. A jay (probably chosen for the contrast of its blue against the yellow leaves of line 54) "screams" (as if terrorized by the fear of death or the coming winter), and Thoreau picks up the edible burrs of the chestnuts as his heirlooms (passed on to him from the dying season; line 56).

He relates not only to the poverty of the "threadbare" trees, but also to their bravery as they rear their boughs to the October sky (line 60). They seem knights awaiting Winter's cavalry, keeping "a simple Roman state" (in which function held place over ornament) since they lost their Persian luxury (their leaves; the wealth of Persia [modern Iran] and other fabled eastern courts fascinated Europe and America).

FEMALE VOICE, FEMALE LANGUAGE

The argument for a new language adequate to express the full weight of the female experience belongs to feminists of the second half of the 20th century. While the female American poets of prior centuries generally stopped short of demanding complete linquistic independence, an awareness of gender inequities helped them find their voice. Even the Puritan governor's daughter ANNE BRADSTREET challenged the male domination of poetry. In "The PROLOGUE," Bradstreet argues that her language (or at least her personal language skills) was inadequate to compete with the great male poets, but she quickly used the shield of her gender to plead for the reader's indulgence. She would be content, she argues, "to let Greeks Be Greeks, and women what they are" (line 37). Perhaps she had taken her cue from the powerful Queen Elizabeth I, the ruler of England until just a few short years before the poet's birth, who disingenuously disarmed her political opponents at an important juncture in her career by claiming they had nothing to fear from a mere woman. Bradstreet's most frequently anthologized poems reveal her evident satisfaction with her roles as wife and mother (for example, "IN REFERENCE TO HER CHILDREN"). Some poems, such as "A LETTER TO HER HUSBAND, ABSENT UPON PUBLIC EMPLOYMENT") hint at a charged sexuality that would not meet their match in the poetry of American women until the 19th century.

No one made a living wage from poetry until a sudden profusion of well-funded literary journals created a market in the early 19th century. Hence PHILLIS WHEATLEY found her poetry as well as her person bound first by her slavery and then by her dependence upon the continued goodwill of her benefactress. The implied censorship resulting from her circumstances probably limited her to a much smaller range of acceptable subjects than most poets could tolerate, but she succeeded in getting her voice heard by adopting the poetic forms demanded of serious art in the 18th century. At the turn of the 19th century, the British romantic movement opened the way for a more private, subjective poetry like that embraced by MARIA GOWEN BROOKS.

The 19th century began with an American society that still turned a deaf ear to women's voices in matters of public consequence and ended with women providing the impetus and, most important, the leadership for social reform. Women figured prominently in the antislavery movement, and female poets contributed significantly to the cause. Their most typical and, perhaps, most effective tactic was to dramatize those incidents involving emotional as well as physical suffering: the breaking up of families was the focus of SARAH LOUISA FORTEN's "The SLAVE GIRL'S FAREWELL" and FRANCES ELLEN WATKINS HARPER's "The SLAVE MOTHER." The antislavery poetry by white poets demonstrated that empathy with others of their gender could cross racial and economic lines, and by the end of the century it was crossing oceans as well. Such sentiments informed FRANCES SARGENT LOCKE OSGOOD's "The INDIAN MAID'S REPLY TO THE MISSIONARY" (which praised the inherent worth of a young Native American woman) and LYDIA HUNTLEY SIGOURNEY's "The SUTTEE," which dramatized a murderous Hindu ritual compelling a widow's suicide.

By the end of the 19th century, women were making their voices felt on a broad spectrum of such diverse issues as the prohibition of alcohol, the 40-hour workweek, the suffering of immigrants (EMMA LAZARUS was especially active for this cause), and international peace (a cause to which JULIA WARD HOWE lent the prestige she had gained as the author of "The BATTLE HYMN OF THE REPUBLIC"). That other women were so meritoriously leading public lives informs the speaker's reaction in SARAH M. B. PIATT's "The PALACE-BURNER."

Discontent with the institution of marriage inspired some of the most interesting poems. In the early 19th century, women had few means other than marriage to advance socially and financially, and marriage usually gave a new husband power over whatever economic resources a wife might bring to their union. Thus the speaker in Osgood's "The LADY'S MISTAKE" was horrified when she found out that her beau had misrepresented his finances. The eponymous character of PHOEBE CARY's "DOROTHY'S DOWER" is not so fortunate; despite her husband's early assurances, his evident respect for her feelings diminishes as quickly as her funds do. Many people found themselves in mutually antagonistic circumstances like those portrayed in SOPHIE JEWETT's "ARMISTICE;" all such a couple can hope for is that a temporary cease-fire in their fighting will allow them to keep up appearances in society.

That even the best marriages involved significant compromises was perhaps more than the greatest American female poet was willing to bear, at least when it came to her own destiny. EMILY DICKIN-

SON's knowledge of sex is evident in "DID THE HARE-BELL LOOSE HER GIRDLE," while such poems as "WILD NIGHTS" and "I STARTED EARLY—TOOK MY DOG" reveal her passion. Her jealousy of the status that marriage can bring to a woman can be seen in "'I'M WIFE!'—I'VE FINISHED THAT" and "REARRANGE A 'WIFE'S' AFFECTION." "SHE ROSE TO HIS REQUIREMENT" argues that marriage can diminish a woman. It would be misleading to suggest that "The SOUL SELECTS HER OWN SOCIETY" (which in some respects conveys one of the most beautiful sentiments of any love poem ever written) announces a preference for her own company over that of others, but even the first line celebrates an individual's right to such a choice. That she was equally independent, challenging, and insightful in her many poems about faith, loss, and death, and tremendously skilled in evoking the essence of the few animals that found their way into her poetry from her garden, ensured that subsequent critics never again could use the phrase "women's poetry" in the derisive, dismissive manner that many had before Dickinson's voice was heard.

"FIFTEENTH AMENDMENT" FRANCES ELLEN WATKINS HARPER (1871)

On January 1, 1863, Abraham Lincoln's Emancipation Proclamation technically freed all the slaves in the rebellious states but preserved slavery in other places. Only with the defeat of the Southern armies would the majority of black Americans no longer be considered property, and those who still found themselves enslaved in "loyal" areas usually had to wait for legislative action on the state level to achieve even this most basic legal recognition of their humanity. It was not until the ratification of the Thirteenth Amendment to the U.S. Constitution in 1865 that slavery was outlawed throughout the nation, and in 1868 the Fourteenth Amendment guaranteed equal legal protection for almost everyone (occupying hostile forces and, sadly, Native Americans were among the groups still excluded) on American soil. The Fifteenth Amendment, ratified on February 3, 1870, extended the right to vote to the male former slaves, providing them and their descendants with important assistance on their long march to total equality.

The first line of this poem ("Beneath the burden of our joy") is among the best that Harper ever wrote. She rejoices as the wires of the transcontinental telegraph (first completed on October 26, 1861) "trembled" (a most apt verb that accurately conveys the pulsing electric currents that carried the message and the speaker's excitement) with their important information. News of the ratification is so good that she animates the telegraph to the level of an oracle ("Fashion with words your tongues of fire," line 3) and musters a rather awkward but new phrase ("the nation's high behest") as if more idiomatic terms were inadequate for the task.

She would have the news outstrip (outrun) the winds (no worries, since electricity travels at the speed of light) as it hastened past the ocean's caves (a probable reference to the transatlantic cable, first completed in 1858, and permanently connected in 1866). On the local level, church bells (that usually "call to praise" God) should add their sweetest chimes to the songs of joyful triumph. The rising race, newly crowned as brothers and men, should "shake off the dust" (of forced political inactivity as well as that of agricultural labor; line 13). A personified Justice asserts her claim, and from their brow fades the ban (on civil rights). Newly baptized in freedom (in the 21st century, most Protestant denominations had abandoned the term *chrism* to designate their baptismal oils; line 17), and with the precious ensign (a banner of freedom, which almost every late-19th-century American would picture as a star-spangled emblem of the nation) in hand, the former slaves should place their formerly despised name among the noblest.

Calling Black America "a ransomed race" (line 21) likens its history to that of the Jews led by Moses out of slavery. God should be praised for letting them through a crimson sea (see Exodus 14:26–29), which in their case was the "storm of fire and blood" of the Civil War. God turned the "war-cloud's light" (line 24) to show them the way to freedom.

"FIRST-DAY THOUGHTS" JOHN GREENLEAF WHITTIER (1853)

The Religious Society of Friends was founded (or at least led) by George Fox in England around the year 1650. The name "Quaker" stems from their reverence for Christ, in whose awesome presence one should tremble and shake (and some of the pioneering Quakers did this literally during their meetings). An important early convert was William Penn, whose father had gained such prominence in the English court that in 1681 he (the son) was given a charter for Pennsylvania. Penn quickly turned the colony into a bastion of religious tolerance and civil liberty as well as a homeland for the Quakers. The sect refers to Sunday as First-Day, so the title refers not only to those thoughts that occurred to a pious man on meeting day, but also JOHN GREENLEAF WHITTIER's thoughts about the meeting as an institution.

This poem presents the thoughts and feelings of a sincere Quaker toward their church services, which for the first half of the poem are described largely in terms that differentiate them from those of other Christian sects. Unlike the bombastic rhetoric designed to frighten the congregations of other denominations, the Quakers met in calm, (emotionally) cool silence (lines 1–3), without a sermon, hymns, organ music, censers (incense-burning vessels) or stained glass windows (reduced here to a "dim light falling through the pictured pane" [line 6]).

Such austerity enables the speaker to hear the same quiet, small voice ("syllabled by silence;" line 7) that the prophets heard, and to read on his heart an even more divine law than Moses saw on his tablets (line 10; a reference to the Ten Commandments, enumerated in Exodus 20:1–17 and Deuteronomy 5:6–21; the "tables of stone" upon which God inscribed the Commandments are in Deuteronomy 5:22).

In silence among his brethren, the speaker would strive against his sins, "wandering fancies" (line 12), and anxieties (the "sore disquiet of a restless brain" of line 13). Once his duty is made plain (by what Quakers refer to as the Inner Light), he will proceed not selfishly or cowardly, but cheerfully ("walking as one to pleasant service led" [line 20]). He will do God's will as if it were his own, trusting only in His strength (lines 21–22).

"THE FLESH AND THE SPIRIT" ANNE BRADSTREET (1650)

Devout Puritans were expected to be on their guard against the seductions of the flesh for fear of losing their chances at immortal life. In this poem, ANNE BRADSTREET imagines two sisters who are in some ways the twin aspects of human existence. Although no one should be surprised as to the eventual winner of the debate, part of the interest of the poem lies in the ways Bradstreet stacks the deck to insure the proper outcome. It also reveals the internal turmoil felt by many Puritans as they came to realize that in their struggle to overcome the temptations of this world their greatest enemy was their own flesh.

The usual problem for such exercises is that the torments of hell, rooted as they are in physical sensations, can be more striking than the pleasures of heaven. In this poem, however, the Spirit speaks from sad personal experience. Note that the encounter occurs on the banks of Lacrim (a variant of the Latin term for *tears*) flood, that the sisters' weapon of choice is reason, and that they will focus on the past and future instead of the present (lines 2–4). These are choices that generally do not play to the strengths of the flesh.

Three voices are heard in the poem, beginning with that of the speaker, who introduces the other two. That she is hardly an impartial moderator is evident in her introduction of Flesh, who "had her eye on worldly wealth and vanity" (lines 5–6). The speaker's dismissal of Flesh's concerns as vanity reduces them to worthless products of earthly pride, whereas Spirit's thoughts are described as the products of a higher sphere.

When Flesh speaks, it is easy to see why the speaker held her in such low regard. She asks if Spirit can live on meditation alone and if speculation alone can satisfy her impulses (the "notion" of line 14). Dismissing Spirit's hope of heaven as an unattainable dream of dwelling beyond the moon, she holds the language of Puritan theology up to scorn when she asks if the treasures stored in heaven really make the wealth of the world seem poor (line 18). Only the insane ("the fancy sick") or the drunken ("sot") believe in such hallucinations ("shadows which are not," line 20). She seems to accept the Puritan work ethic but undercuts that message by immediately focusing on the advantages of variety (line 24). Her most foolish statement is that earthly honors and fame last, and she also points out the many precious stones to be found here. Earth offers so many pleasures that Flesh considers it foolish to give them up for things unknown, or only imagined.

In the first line the speaker refers to the "secret place" where she heard the two debaters, and when Spirit calls Flesh the unregenerate "part" (line 37), it becomes clear that we are listening to an internal debate. Flesh is "unregenerate" in Puritan mythology because it will become mere dust, whereas on Judgment Day the Spirit will be regenerated and relegated to eternal damnation or reward. Spirit has vowed to carry their deadly feud to the grave and argues that Flesh has descended from Adam whereas she has a heavenly Father (lines 46–48). While the tone of Flesh's discourse ranges from satirical to teasing, Spirit's tone is openly combative.

Spirit calls Flesh a hypocrite and recalls having become a woeful slave to the flesh when she trusted her sister's flattery in the past. She hates the pleasures of the flesh and again renounces the treasures of this world. The greatest honor Spirit can achieve here is a triumph over the flesh, which she envisions in purely physical terms: upon winning the battle, she will be crowned with laurel while Flesh will be led away as her captive.

Spirit explains that she has food from heaven and ambition for things high above the capacity of the flesh to perceive (lines 67 to 74). With a woman's eye for fashion, Spirit envisions herself garbed not in relatively trashy gold and silk, but in the glorious royal robes of heaven. She will have a halo instead of mere precious metals on her head. She has learned from the Bible to expect walls of jasper around the heavenly city, pearl gates, streets of transparent gold and angels as porters. A crystal river flows from the throne of Christ (the "Lamb" of line 94), and since glory radiates from God, there is no need for additional illumination. Unlike the flesh, the Spirit will then be free from sickness and aging, and her beauty will remain bright and clear. The Flesh will not qualify for the "city pure" because it belongs with other unclean things, but the Spirit is willing to give up this world and all the pleasures of the flesh for the sustenance she will receive in heaven.

"THE FLOOD OF YEARS" WILLIAM CULLEN BRYANT (1876) From the distance of the age of 82, two years before his death, WILLIAM CULLEN BRYANT looked back on his experience to realize that the life and work of men takes place only in the present.

This could have led to the depressing conclusion that would run counter to the prevailing optimism of the rest of his poetry, so this poem presented philosophical as well as aesthetic challenges.

The first line suggests a deist conception of God as the prime mover (the force that created the universe, in this instance dramatized as the Hand holding the Urn) who takes no subsequent interest in directing his creation. It also introduces the dominant image of the poem, an irresistible flood that while ultimately destroying everything it touches, briefly supports all life on the foremost edge of its waves (lines 4–5). That the flood in question is made up of time instead of water adds an extra metaphysical dimension to the conceit; it also explains why life is only possible on the foremost edge, for that represents the present.

The speaker's perspective is godlike because he is detached from the events he describes physically (the waves do not reach him, and although he is cognizant of the "roar of mingled noises" [lines 6–7] made by all life at once, he is not discomforted by it), temporally (he is able to see the Hand at the beginning of time as well as the distant future) and emotionally (he makes no effort to aid the drowning people and shifts his attention to the next scene as rapidly as the present one passes; only in the last third of the poem does he express any sorrow). His observations lack the randomness of mere chronology, however; for his choice of scenes in the first half of the poem moves in a continuum in at least four orders. His list begins with a country lad and leads to the city. It starts with the most active endeavors directly involved in sustaining life (farming) to those artists professionally more concerned with representing life than with more directly engaging in it. It also moves from the pursuits of peace to those of war, and from life to death.

About the only order he does not admit is that by which humans distinguish between each other; the plumed chief sinks with his followers (lines 26–27), the emperor goes down beside the felon (lines 28–29), and taken together, they warrant less attention than the five lines (15–19) devoted to revelers. Such juxtaposition of opposites underscores the speaker's objectivity and privileged perspective: he can view and understand the roles individuals play in widely diverse cultures, but he exhibits little empathy with their plight. The clash of mighty armies can jar the air with their drums and thunders, but slayer and slain only tint the bloody foam of the wave (lines 19–25).

Those who attend funerals and sickbeds last scarcely longer than the objects of their concerns. Turning his attention to the arts, the speaker begins with an orator skilled enough to move "the living mass as if he were its soul" (line 38). A preacher attracts similar crowds, but everyone is eventually swallowed by the waves. The order with which the speaker addresses the plastic arts appears to have been dictated by their distance away from lifelike representations and toward abstract thought: sculptors and painters (most of whom still had a photographic realism as a major goal) and even poets (line 47) are flung under with their work still unfinished.

In the second third of the poem, the speaker recognizes the relationships between victims beginning with the strongest bond, that of a mother with her infant (line 54). To help his audience visualize the plight of two lovers, the speaker provides them with a moonlight that turns the spray "to glistening pearls" (line 56) until one wave drowns him and another takes her. The white hair of an aged man can briefly be seen in the stream.

The wave dissolves walled cities, palaces, fortresses, and towers (lines 66–67; note how the eye seems to run over a succession of architectural heights in this doomed landscape exactly as a wave would). The wave ends entire civilizations, including their languages.

Looking back over the ocean of the past, the speaker sees only wrecked fleets, battlements overgrown with moss, and roofless, forsaken temples. Eroding memorial stones, broken religious altars, and deserted streets lead to the lost jewels (the list includes sardonyx [milky quartz with alternating brown and white bands of other minerals] and chrysolite [a pale green stone compounded of iron and magnesium] as well as the diamonds and other gemstones that are still considered precious; lines 86–88) that continue to sparkle although the banquet halls have turned to dust.

Bridal wreaths, locks of a lover's hair (a popular keepsake in 19th-century America), and scrolls perhaps bearing a lover's words or a vow of friendship (all such things as might outlast their owners because of the special care they received) briefly float among printed materials, then all sink (line 97). Such a maudlin list brings tears to the speaker's sentimental Victorian eyes as he perceives them not as emblems of affection but as remnants of the dreams and promises inevitably broken by time.

Looking ahead of the deluge, he finds phantoms of dissolving forms resting on flowery banks, and eventually serpents and skeletons until, in the distance so far that darkness seems to bar the way, he can see "where the Life to come touches the Life that is" (lines 119–120). He cannot see beyond that, but relies on the sayings of "the wise and good" (line 123) that all the "sweet lives" overwhelmed (line 127) and all that was good, noble, truly great, and worthy of love, including "infants, ingenuous youths, sages and saintly women who have made their households happy" (lines 127–132; the last item on the list reveals the speaker's Victorian bias as to the proper role of women) will be swept along on the caressing waves past verdant islands and ever-fresh flowers. Old friends will be reunited, and mothers will again embrace their lost children. All the old sorrows are forgotten (line 143) or recalled just to make the present seem sweeter. Wounded hearts are healed forever (line 145), and unlike "the grief-shadowed present," neither grief nor broken ties will mar the new reign. There will still be "eternal Change" (line 150), but it will proceed hand in hand with everlasting Concord (line 152), a happy ending that promises eternal happiness.

"FOG" HENRY DAVID THOREAU (1843) In this short poem HENRY DAVID THOREAU salutes his subject (and the protean abilities of his own mind) by jumping from one way of looking at it to another with the same ease and rapidity that the fog changes shape. He begins prosaically, seemingly ready to dismiss the phenomenon as a "dull water spirit," but as if energized by the multiple meanings of "spirit," he rapidly (so quickly that a dash seems the appropriate punctuation) jumps to thinking of it as a Protean god (in Greek mythology, the god Proteus could predict the future but would only do so for those who could hold him while he assumed a variety of challenging and sometimes threatening shapes).

With a more scientific approach, he can think of the fog as a descended cloud "fast anchored" (securely anchored) to the ground (line 2). Perhaps the notion of an anchor put him in mind of a ship, for his observation that the fog "drawest (a verb form putting him briefly in touch with the language and thought of antiquity) too much air for shallow coasts" (the implied analogy compares the fog to a ship too large and too heavy to float in shallow water). Because it is too heavy for the air (and because it tends to evaporate in direct sunlight), it can be viewed as the branch of the ocean that flows to the sun. Like a determined naturalist, the speaker turns from sight to scent in an attempt to capture the essence of the substance. In calling it the incense of earth (line 5), he again suggests its mystic potential, which he romanticizes by noticing the perfume the flowers have added to it.

The fog is like the ghost of bodies of water of various sizes (a "rill" is a small stream) come to revisit the scene of their birth (lines 6–7). It exists as the night thoughts of a personified earth or as an important feature of a human dream about the earth (the syntax of line 8 supports either reading); either of these might be viewed as "dream drapery." A dew cloth might be either the fine coating of moisture on an object formed when the air temperature drops to the point where it becomes saturated or (less likely under any but the hardest survival conditions) an actual cloth put out to capture that moisture. Fairies, like pixies, are a mythical race of small impish creatures, so a "fairy napkin" is an object (like the dew) suitable for such service by the wee folk. Having thus examined the fog at nearly the smallest level that the unaided eye can manage, the speaker jumps to his final image, an overview of the phenomenon that addresses it as a relatively majestic "wind-blown meadow of the air" (line 10).

Although the poem gains coherence by constantly linking the fog with various types of spirits, such a project probably required a lighter, more playful hand that could render it (or even individual lines from it) memorable.

"FOR DELIVERANCE FROM A FEVER" ANNE BRADSTREET (17th century; published in 1867)   Because the colonists lacked all knowledge of bacteria, they tended to view disease as a manifestation of God's power designed to punish their sins or remind them of the tentative nature of their lives. In this poem, ANNE BRADSTREET recalls a few of her symptoms and gives thanks for her survival and for the chastisement that God sent for her instruction.

Her fever had been marked by intense pain, extensive sweating, headaches, and such weakness that she found it hard to speak (line 8). She was so feverish that she feared the illness as a symbol of God's wrath. The most interesting line of the poem is probably the 11th; she was unable to read her "evidence." She may have been referring to the Bible, but individual Puritans also scrutinized their lives for evidence that they were among the elect, the relatively few people chosen by God for heavenly reward. To lose such assurances would be terrifying for true believers like Bradstreet; note that she is more afraid of losing heaven than she is of dying.

Perhaps delirious, or perhaps in the rapture of true belief, she cried out for her Savior's aid. God is the internal audience for this poem, and she reminds Him that she told Him she cared not for her flesh if its decay leads her to heaven. He heard, removed her torment, and spared her life. She finishes with praise for her God, and to the Lord who redeemed her soul from hell.

"FOR EACH ECSTATIC INSTANT" EMILY DICKINSON (published 1891)   It is tempting to think of EMILY DICKINSON's poem in exclusively sexual terms because of its elegant language, but it can be more broadly applied to the human condition. Notice how, when read aloud, the hard consonant sound of the first syllable of "ecstatic" forces a reader to slow down even though the second syllable takes the accent. Although the first line is rhythmical, the wide variance in its vowel sounds and its shift back and forth from emphasized consonants to emphasized vowels quickly build to an emotional climax like successively higher waves before flattening in the final word. When this effect is coupled with the "keen and quivering" of the third line, words echoing the 'k' sound first heard in ecstasy even as they suggest the highest states of physiological arousal, it is hard to imagine that the speaker had ecstatic moments unrelated to sex in mind.

Assuming for a moment that the ecstasy of the first stanza is exclusively sexual, what then is the nature of the anguish that must be paid in recompense? If a child is produced, then both parents are suddenly and irredeemably vulnerable in ways they had not imagined prior to the conception. Their increased vulnerability exposes them to numerous slings and arrows as their offspring must learn from her own mistakes. Having formed the closest emotional bonds possible, they must suffer with an empathy they had previously not imagined.

Even if no child results, the closeness of the emotional bonds established, reinforced and perhaps exacerbated by the sexual act can lead to recriminations, especially if the partners have chosen their mates unwisely. There are few lines more evocative of an unhappy marriage than the last two of this poem as the couple argues over money (the "bitter contested farthings" of line 7) or other trivial concerns while not facing their real problems, hidden beneath the surface in "Coffers heaped with Tears."

Does this poem have to be about sex? Almost any ecstatic moment in any field of human endeavor, whether it comes from a wedding, the birth of one's child, the successful founding of a business empire, seeing one's words in print for the first time, or even an impressive string of touchdowns or knockouts, must be paid for by years of preparation or subsequent years of care.

The morality behind the poem apparently stemmed from Puritan roots because of its stress on the discrepancy between momentary pleasure and its far more lasting repercussions (extending even to the "sharp pittances of years" in line 6), but it is interesting that Dickinson stripped this poem of any explicit reference to conventional religious thought. Whatever this omission implies about the religious beliefs of the author, it definitely broadened the poem's audience by suggesting a more universal phenomenon, the suffering experienced by those who tremblingly violate their core beliefs. Even without thoughts about the immortality of the soul and the threat of perpetual damnation, however, it seems bad enough for the speaker of this poem to suffer in this life.

Is the thinking behind the poem unequivocally and hopelessly pessimistic? Although it is tempting to dismiss it as an example of the sour grapes penned by a poet who seemingly kept the world at arm's length by choosing to live behind closed doors, it would probably benefit anyone to realize the implications of a moment in intellectual as well as emotional terms. We need not fear for the continued propagation of our species as a consequence of such consideration, however, because the drive for ecstatic, keen, and quivering instants is hardwired in our genes.

"A FOREST HYMN" William Cullen Bryant **(1825)** The general public in William Cullen Bryant's day was far more likely than their 21st-century descendents to criticize those who neglected their church attendance by idly spending time in the wilderness. They would have commented on the absence of Christ in the speaker's reveries and his turning his back on his religious community. This poem is Bryant's answer to such criticism, and he framed his argument in words and images that they could understand.

One of the pleasures of poetry is the creative use of stanza breaks and variations in line length to present a novel pattern to the eye. In this poem, Bryant forgoes that enticement, although he may have chosen solid, even formidable, blocky stanzas of blank verse (unrhymed iambic pentameter) in order to convey the majestic solidity of the big trees. Unfortunately, he inserted stanza breaks where new paragraphs should be started if he were writing in prose, and the end result resembles a broken log with its branches already trimmed. This is, however, one of his most important poems; it celebrates the reverence the poet felt for nature by equating it with a religious experience.

The first line opens with a clever aphorism that seems correct. In the absence of eyewitnesses, no one can dispute its accuracy, although perhaps the oceans, the mountains, or any other geological feature might rival groves of trees as "God's first temples." Poetry is chiefly about emotion and not cultural anthropology, however, and although there is no historical basis for the speaker's assertions in this stanza, there is no doubt about the effectiveness of his imagery. The second line conflates perhaps a million years of human history, from the first cutting of a log (although "hewing the shaft" might also refer to carving a column from stone) to laying the achitrave (the cover, suitable for engraving, of the stone placed upon and connecting the supporting pillars in a Greek temple), and framing the vault (high arched ceilings). Even before any of that, however, he imagines a man spontaneously kneeling as he prayed "to the Mightiest" (line 7) under the "sacred influence" (line 8) of the massive old trees. Why neglect such an ancient sanctuary in favor of those built by the frail hands of man (line 20)? He will offer a hymn that, if God accepts it, will be "thrice happy" (line 22). Since so much of the poem transfers Christian imagery to a forest setting, perhaps the speaker is thinking of the Father, Son, and Holy Ghost. Alternatively, he could have the composer/singer, the reader/audience, and God in mind, or the three components could be the past, present and future of man, each of which is celebrated in this opening.

The second stanza acknowledges that God grew the forest until it was "a fit shrine" for a "humble worshiper" (line 33) "to hold Communion" (the phrasing is that of the established church) with his Maker. The forest's dim "vaults and winding aisles" (language the speaker borrows from church architecture) do not project the human pomp and pride that cathedrals do, and the vanity of "fantastic carvings" (especially the High Gothic sculptures of gargoyles and other flying monsters that have nothing to do with modern religion) is also absent. Instead, God's presence "fill'st" (line 38; the form of the verb recalls those used in popular translations of the Bible and conveys the speaker's reverence for the process) the solitude. God can be heard in the music of the soft winds in the treetops and felt in the coolness of the forest shade as well as in the tree bark and the moisture on the ground. He notes the passing bird, the spring that waters the scene, and a mighty oak. The tree inspires the second weakest phrase in Bryant's poetry: ". . . I stand and seem/Almost annihilated. . . ." (lines 56–57). Perhaps he was thinking of those moments in the Torah when people are literally consumed by fire. The word "overwhelmed," if substituted for this phrase, would have spared the speaker the embarrassment of seeming to be almost something or rather, nothing (if totally annihilated), and set him up for a more interesting active verb rather than having him merely stand there. Here

the trees have "crowns" (which suggests that they *rule*, although the pun is based on the botanist's use of the term to designate the limbs and foliage at the top of a tree) and not vain human princes. A delicate forest flower seems "an emanation of the indwelling Life" and a "visible token of the upholding Love" that are the soul of the universe (lines 66–68).

The third stanza begins with the worst line in all of Bryant's work: "My heart is awed within me when I think. . . ." Although he evidently aimed at a transcendent moment and perhaps a reminder of the profound effect nature has on him, it would have been better to either describe his elation richly enough that the reader can better sense the sincerity of his rapture, or (better yet) to deal with the subject so movingly that the reader's heart is moved in some way. Expressed with a passive voice and further hampered by a fuzzy connection between the head and the heart, the line leaves the reader wondering where else would his heart be other than within him. The poet stumbled, but recovered with "the great miracle" of the perpetual work of creation, "finished, yet renewed forever" (lines 72–73). The resurrection promised by the church can everywhere be seen here as the new trees grow from the wastes of the old. In the renewal of the young trees from the death and decay of the old ones, "Life mocks the idle hate of this arch-enemy Death" (lines 84–85) by setting on his throne (the "sepulcher," a burial vault) and taking nourishment from "the triumphs of his ghastly foe" (line 87).

Holy men have hid in the wilderness and outlived their generations, and other holy men have criticized them for it. The speaker prefers to retire in the solitude to reassure his feeble virtue in a place where the passions are stilled. Men forget their pride when they see God's tempests, thunderbolts, floods (the great deep "uprises" and throws himself upon the continent; lines 106–108), and whirlwinds. He would have God spare him and his family and friends "from these sterner aspects of thy face" (line 112). Instead, he hopes they meditate on His milder majesty and the order of His works and learn to similarly order their lives.

FORTEN, SARAH LOUISA (1814–1883)
The poet is chiefly remembered as a member of a very

prominent black Philadelphia family actively involved in the abolitionist movement. Her father, James Forten, Sr., was born in freedom and made his fortune as an innovative sail manufacturer. He threw his considerable wealth and all his prestige into the antislavery movement, helping to found the Free American Society, the American Moral Reform Society and the Convention of Color. In 1802, he helped present a petition to abolish slavery to the U.S. House of Representatives.

The poet's mother, Charlotte, helped establish the Philadelphia Female Anti-Slavery Society, and Sarah later served on its board for a couple of years. Charlotte's youngest daughter would be largely forgotten today were it not for the handful of poems Sarah wrote under several pseudonyms (including "Ada") before her marriage to Joseph Purvis in 1838. Her archives are relatively bare, but because of her father's prominence, the Pennsylvania Historical and Museum Commission has placed a marker in front of her childhood home in Philadelphia. It served as the birthplace of the American Antislavery Society in 1833. The poet returned to it with her children after her husband's death in 1857. Central Michigan University holds some of her correspondence, and some is available as part of the Black Abolitionist Papers available on microfilm at the University of North Carolina.

The content of the two poems discussed below suggests that the poet depended more upon the conventions of the Victorian stage than on firsthand experience or true empathy with her subjects' experience. The argument of "The SLAVE" (1831) is that those fortunate enough to have attained their freedom in the Revolutionary War (in which the poet's own father participated) owe it to their race to continue the struggle against the slavery they so rightly despised. "The SLAVE GIRL'S FAREWELL" (1832) dramatizes the poignant moment when the eponymous character bids goodbye to her mother shortly before being shipped abroad by the slaveholder.

BIBLIOGRAPHY

Basker, James G. *Amazing Grace: An Anthology of Poems about Slavery, 1660–1810.* New Haven, Conn.: Yale University Press, 2002.

Winch, Julie. *A Gentleman of Color: The Life of James Forten.* New York: Oxford University Press, 2002.

"FOR YOU O DEMOCRACY" WALT WHITMAN (1860)

For WALT WHITMAN, the promise of democracy in America included acceptance and equal rights for all groups. With each step it took away from prejudice, he hoped the country would move toward the biblical ideal of universal brotherhood. This poem celebrates his utopian vision of an indissoluble continent (a concept with special appeal as the battles over slavery had already led to serious talk about secession from the country) that is home to "the most splendid race" ever (line 2).

The speaker of the poem has (or wishes he had) godlike powers so strong that he could make "divine magnetic lands" (line 3; the phrase connects animal magnetism with spirituality, a duality most evident in sex). He will perform his nation-building task with the life-long manly love of comrades (lines 4–5 and 9–10).

The second stanza begins with a botanical metaphor to suggest how the change will take place; he will plant companionship "thick as trees" (line 6) along the rivers, shores, and plains. His cities will be inseparable; like friends they will encircle each other's necks with their arms (line 8).

This will be the speaker's service to Democracy, whom he addresses familiarly as *ma femme* (French for "my woman"), and he sings these songs for her.

"1492" EMMA LAZARUS (1883)

One of the potentially great advantages of American diversity is its theoretical access to the totality of human experience. The nation is enriched to the extent that each successive wave of immigrants is able to maintain contact with the language, customs, and literature of the old country while acquiring the means of communicating with established American culture, and this poem provides ample evidence as to how that process could work. While 19th-century Americans generally celebrated 1492 as the fortunate year in which the voyages of Christopher Columbus began the continuous European colonization of the Americas, for many Jewish Americans like Lazarus the year was also infamous.

The same Ferdinand and Isabella who financed Columbus also succeeded in conquering Granada, the last kingdom in Spain ruled by the religiously tolerant

Moors (Islamic Africans), in 1492. Earlier, the royal couple had decided to unify the nation by establishing their Catholicism as the state religion, and now no place in Spain was safe for Jews, Protestants, or other "heretics." Thousands of people suffered heinous tortures in the state-sanctioned terror campaign known as the Inquisition, the "flaming sword" of line 2. For the speaker of this poem, it seemed almost providential that as one haven closed another opened. A major problem was that the New World was not yet ready to receive them; like Adam and Eve (who were forced from Paradise by an Angel with a "flaming sword" like that mentioned in line 2), they would have been left in a howling wilderness had they somehow managed to emigrate to America at that time. Religiously tolerant Holland presented a more practical immediate option as well as the best eventual access to America. The first Jews arrived in New Amsterdam (the Dutch colony later conquered by the English and renamed New York) in 1654. In the other colonies, only Rhode Island and Pennsylvania were openly tolerant of non-Christian religions, and Jewish immigration continued so slowly that the first North American synagogue (in Newport, Rhode Island) was not built until 1790.

The eponymous year is the internal audience of this poem. In addressing it as "two-faced" (lines 1 and 9), the speaker evokes the image of Janus, the Roman god of gates and doorways who was also associated with beginnings and endings. The craft behind the poem is most apparent in the poet's adherence to the demanding rhyme scheme of the Italian sonnet (the first eight lines of which are rhymed abbaabba) while applying the Roman allusion to a particular point in Jewish history. Like the Roman god (and the capricious heads of the European states), the personified year opened and closed various gates and barriers. The poem celebrates the Jewish people (heralded as "the children of the prophets of the Lord" in line 3) who survived the hounding of hateful zealots. The poem builds to a transcendent sestet (last six lines of an Italian sonnet conventionally rhymed cdecde) in which the problem of the octave (first eight lines) is solved. Like the new land promised to Moses and his followers, America offers freedom from the grim barriers of hatred that keep heart from heart (line 14).

The unacknowledged irony of the poem is that 1492 marked the beginning of the European conquest of the Native Americans of both New World continents. In celebrating the importance of American freedom for one historically marginalized group, it implicitly calls into question the genocidal policies behind the anti-Indian wars still being waged on the western frontier. An important advantage of multiculturalism is the empathy that voices from a group previously terrorized can generate for the oppressed. This has allowed a succession of voices from religious and ethnic minorities to assume their vital role as the conscience of the nation.

FRANKLIN, BENJAMIN (1706–1790)

As a printer, inventor, community activist, scientist, and statesman, the sage of Philadelphia had enough work to last several lifetimes; he became famous as the only man to sign the four most important documents securing American independence. As a poet, however, Franklin's career was remarkable for its brevity. Although he had produced two ballads by the precocious age of 12, the circumstances surrounding their creation, his innovative use of poetry to improve his prose style, and his subsequent abandonment of the muse reveal much about the adverse literary climate in the early 18th-century American colonies.

In his *Autobiography*, Franklin related how he became enamored with poetry and other literature as a child. He chose the subject of his first two poems with an eye on their marketability; they were immediately struck off at his brother's printshop and young Franklin was dispatched to sell copies on the street. The first ballad, on the recent drowning deaths of a local lighthouse keeper and his two daughters, sold well, but the second, on the death of the notorious pirate Blackbeard in far-off Carolina, was of less interest in Boston (398 [page numbers in this entry refer to *The Norton Anthology of American Literature*, 2nd ed.]). That the poems were privately printed was typical of the era, and the dispatching of the poet to peddle his wares among the fishmongers and other tradesmen indicates the absence of a means by which a writer could be paid for his work beyond his immediate sale of the copies at hand. Adequate copyright protection was still a century and a half into the future; pirated editions were perfectly legal and brought the poet nothing to live on. Franklin's father stepped in before the youth had produced anything to attract the attention of other printers, however. His ridicule of the poems and argument that poets were generally beggars effectively ended Franklin's public career as a poet.

Franklin was not altogether done with poetry, however. In an attempt to improve as a prose stylist, he devised a system by which he wrote down the central themes of a published article by a famous author, rendered them into verse, and then put the work aside until he had forgotten the particular expressions of the original. Recasting the verse back into prose taught him much about the art of writing, which Franklin considered a principal means of advancement in his life.

As a young man, Franklin became friends with James Ralph, who decided to devote himself to poetry as a profession (418, 424). Ralph's financial difficulties and imbroglios, in which Franklin was briefly entangled, reinforced the warnings about poetry and poverty that Franklin's father had made clear to him.

Eventually, Franklin took steps to rid himself of his habits of "prattling, punning and joking" (455–456); his desire to speak only when it was profitable effectively silenced the nascent poet in Franklin for good. He continued to read, enjoy and privately profit from poetry throughout his life, however.

"FREE LABOR" FRANCES ELLEN WATKINS HARPER (1857)   This protest poem strikes at the financial props of slavery by focusing on the labor-intensive production of cotton that was at the heart of the old plantation system. It also answered those sectionalists who argued that slavery was a regional problem confined to the southern states by countering that the consumption of goods inextricably linked the northern consumer economically as well as morally to the inhumane conditions in which many slaves were held.

An "easy" garment (line 1), free from the taint of forced labor, does not irritate the conscience of its owner. No "tears of hopeless anguish" (line 3) or bloodstains went into its materials or construction (the "warp" of line 7 designates the vertical, typically longer, threads of a fabric being woven on a standing loom and the "woof" are the threads woven horizontally through them). No untoward sounds echo within the folds of the "free" (or more accurately, "hired") labor garment while "some sad despairing cry" can be heard when a morally compromised garment rustles. The agony of years (of enslavement) will not show in the free garment's texture, and it will not carry the forlorn sigh of a woman's heart whose "only wreath of household love" (her family, including her offspring from whom she easily can be separated; line 19) is rudely torn apart.

Lightly will the free garment press the speaker's form, and no voice will rise to pierce the sky from its seams and folds (to discover the source of one such scream, see "The SLAVE MOTHER" by the same author). That voice shall not bear witness at the throne of God (line 25) that the speaker "nerv'd" ("moved," since to give something nerves is to give it life and movement; line 27) Oppression's hand (to perform the morally corrupt deeds required to force slave labor to create profits).

FRENEAU, PHILIP MORIN (1752–1832)

Few of his contemporary poets were as committed as Philip Freneau to supporting democratic ideals. He actively attacked the king and his minions even when the cause of American independence looked bleakest, and after the war he remained an important voice for a decentralized Jeffersonian democracy. The extreme partisanship and vehemence of his political poems is frequently striking; in "A Political Litany" (1775), he blasted the

"Pirates sent out by command of the king
To murder and plunder, but never to swing."

The "pirates" in question were the officers and crews of Royal Navy vessels. The verb in the second line refers to the common practice of hanging pirates, but before the war was over, Freneau would try his own hand at privateering (state-endorsed attacks on an enemy's shipping that typically encouraged a victorious ship's crew to pocket the proceeds from whatever prizes they captured as compensation for the risks involved).

This son of a wealthy merchant family and wine importer was born in New York City on January 2, 1752. He learned enough Latin, from tutors and a prep course, that he was able to enter Princeton (then the College of New Jersey) at the age of 15. Unfortunately, his father died the autumn before he enrolled, a tragedy that was to broaden the poet's horizons by forcing him to earn his living after college. He became the roommate of a future president (James Madison) and graduated in the class of 1771. His mother's remarriage in that same year largely negated any dreams he may have had about leading the life of a landed gentleman (his father had purchased 1,000 acres in New Jersey in the year of Philip's birth) in the grand old English style. He seems to have drifted for a few year but was suddenly made aware of his familial obligations when his stepfather died in 1773.

By this time, however, he had already discovered his life's work and had published his first volume of poetry in 1772. As in much of the poetry written in that era, the influence of the British poet Alexander Pope (1688–1744) was readily apparent. That Freneau was also already stressing native materials can be seen from the title poem of the collection, "The American Village." Determined to make a name for himself, he proceeded to hone his craft throughout his life, although he lacked the independent means necessary to devote himself entirely to the practice. His frustrations at having to support himself by teaching and a succession of other low-paying ventures is evident in "To A New England Poet" (1823); the country was not yet able to support even its best poets because it lacked magazines that could pay high prices for their work and copyright protections that could preserve what in later centuries would be known as intellectual property. Unable to immediately devote himself to the muse, in 1776 Freneau sailed off to the West Indies on a merchant ship, an excursion that led to his learning enough seamanship to soon become the ship's mate (second in command) and eventually to captain other vessels. He saw enough of the Caribbean to pen "The Hurricane," a landsman's reaction to a monster storm that dwarfs the human science and engineering of the vessel upon which he is forced to weather the storm, and "To Sir Toby" (1784), his indictment of Jamaican slavery.

Prior to his departure to the sea, Freneau had expressed a growing sympathy with the colonial struggle against Great Britain in his increasingly partisan poetry. It was not until 1778, however, when he saw the damage inflicted by the British army upon his adopted state, that he joined the New Jersey militia. His education and experience led to his being given a sergeant's rank and sent to scout the shore, but his nautical background made him too valuable for his assignment. After three months he was named captain of the *Indian Delaware,* a Caribbean merchantman, and until his capture, he alternated between short naval and infantry assignments. He briefly returned to the sea as master of the *John Couster* in 1778, but his greatest success at sea came as an infantryman when his militia company captured the icebound *Britannia* on December 30, 1779 (Axelrod 97). Although he left the militia after his tour of duty expired in 1780, he was subsequently captured as third mate on the *Aurora* following a short but deadly exchange of fire with a larger ship. Six weeks of confinement followed on a derelict vessel, a misadventure that prompted him to write "The British Prison Ship" (1781). At some point he received a bullet wound in the knee, a fact that helped him apply for a meager government pension nearly 50 years after the conclusion of the war.

Freneau returned to the sea as captain of commercial vessels from 1786 to 1790, and again from 1802 to 1804, but at first there seemed to be more captains available than ships, and later he lacked the shore connections that could keep his vessels loaded and sailing, and cargoes capable of returning the necessary profits. On April 15, 1790, he married Eleanor Forman, and in the coming decade they would be blessed with four daughters.

Freneau contributed to Hugh Henry Brackenridge's short-lived *United States Magazine* (1779) and served as editor as well as contributor for several newspapers, most notably Philadelphia's *The Freeman's Journal* (1781–84) and *The National Gazette* (1791–93), which he owned. As a journalist and newspaper editor, he favored independence from Britain (and celebrated the colonial army in such poems as "To the Memory of the Brave Americans" [1781]). Throughout his postwar journalism career, he continued to be highly partisan, casting aspersions on those who opposed Thomas Jefferson's arguments against the formation of an exceptionally strong federal government.

Although best remembered for his Revolutionary War poems, Freneau was a poet of broad interests. His many nature poems include "ON A HONEY BEE" (1797), a humorous treatment of the evils of excessive drink. In a late (1822) poem "ON OBSERVING A LARGE RED-STREAK APPLE," the speaker grudgingly admires the perseverance of the year's last apple, which hung on its denuded stem well into winter.

Although the people of his day were less likely to see its subject as in any way controversial, "ON THE EMIGRATION TO AMERICA AND PEOPLING THE WESTERN COUNTRY" predicts the coming greatness of the country in the arts, agriculture, and political power without recognizing the suffering this advance would continue to visit upon the displaced Native Americans. "The INDIAN BURYING GROUND" (1787) contrasts the burial positions found in two cultures. The speaker argues that the sitting position of a cadaver found in a burial mound surrounded by provisions and weapons implies a greater faith in a physical resurrection than the prone position favored by European tradition.

Despite his lack of independent means, Freneau continued writing books throughout his lifetime: *The Poems of Philip Freneau, Written Chiefly During the Late War* (1786); *The Miscellaneous Works by Mr. Philip Freneau, Containing his Essays and Additional Poems* (1788); *Poems Written between the Years 1768–1794* (1795); *Letters on Various Interesting and Important Subjects* (1799); *Poems Written and Published During the American Revolutionary War* (1809); and *Collection of Poems on American Affairs and a Variety of Other Subjects Chiefly Moral and Political* (1815). Such bland titles little invite readers of subsequent centuries, but Philip Freneau was by no means as unimaginative as they make him seem.

Late in life he took up farming, but largely survived by selling parcels from the family estate when not losing them to lawsuits by bill collectors. On October 18, 1818, fire destroyed Mount Pleasant, his ancestral home and current residence. Unlike Benjamin Franklin, with whom he shared a remarkably varied professional career, he never had a knack for accumulating wealth despite taking at least a few preliminary steps in almost every field (law, the ministry, and even the post office) that he considered appropriate to a gentleman of his class and education. He died of hypothermia near Freehold, New Jersey, after becoming disoriented (and perhaps slightly drunk) during a snowstorm on December 19, 1832. Despite his many adventures, he had nearly doubled the average life expectancy of his generation.

The Philip Freneau Papers are housed at Rutgers University. The Monmouth Historical Association of Freehold, New Jersey, the New Jersey Historical Society, and Princeton University are also important repositories of Freneau's work.

BIBLIOGRAPHY

Axelrod, Jacob. *Philip Freneau: Champion of Democracy*. Austin: University of Texas Press, 1967.

Bowden, Mary Weatherspoon. *Philip Freneau*. Boston: Twayne, 1976.

Leary, Lewis Gaston. *That Rascal Freneau: A Study in Literary Failure*. New Brunswick, N.J.: Rutgers University Press, 1941.

Marsh, Philip Merrill. *The Works of Philip Freneau, A Critical Study*. Metuchen, N.J.: Scarecrow Press, 1968.

Vitzthum, Richard C. *Land and Sea: The Lyric Poetry of Philip Freneau*. Minneapolis: University of Minnesota Press, 1978.

"FROM PENT-UP ACHING RIVERS" WALT WHITMAN (1860)

One of Whitman's immeasurable contributions to subsequent American literature was his frank discussion of sexuality, and in this poem he has created a speaker who is so entirely wrapped up in his sexual identity that he feels he would be nothing without it (line 2). Like an insecure exhibitionist, he exaggerates the masculine potency (hence the title) that, he insists, compels him to sing about the phallus (line 4) even if it totally alienates him from society (forcing him to "stand sole among men" [line 3]). Like a tedious bore, he belabors the obvious: "superb" (21st-century commentators would more likely say "normal") children and adults need a "song of procreation" as an outlet for their primal muscular urges and desired "blending." They are willing to sing "the bedfellow's song" (imaginatively embrace a willing if fictive partner [although a Freudian critic could have great fun with the concept of "the bedfellow" by itself]), delighting in that "correlative body" (lines 5–9). The "hungry gnaw that eats me night and day" (line 10) springs up spontaneously ("from native moments," line 11), but only renders him desirous of a more fulfilling relationship.

He sings that "true song of the soul" at random intervals until it is reborn "with the grossest nature or among animals" (he might have been inspired by the naturalness with which animals coupled, although the phrasing might be read as a confession of bestiality, or of his own bestial nature; line 15). They informed his poems, as did an entire spectrum of sensory delights such as the smell of apples and lemons, the sight of birds "pairing" (either forming couple bonds or coupling), the feel of wet woods and lapping waves, and the (insatiable) mad pushes of waves upon the land, which anticipated the "strain" (in perhaps both a musical and sexual sense; line 20).

Finally he enjoyed the "welcome nearness" of another person and the sight of a perfect body (line 21), perhaps that of a swimmer naked in the bath or floating on his back (line 22), or of an approaching female form. Such things set his "love-flesh" (line 23) aching, and led to a "divine list" of desirable attributes from face to foot.

Finally he has achieved the "mystic deliria, the madness amorous, the utter abandonment" (of sexual union; line 25). He whispers "I love you" to an unidentified audience by whom he wants to be entirely possessed. Together they will escape "the rest" (which might indicate other people, social expectations, or everything else; line 28), going off as free and lawless (subject to no restraint but also without regard for any laws regulating intimate behavior) as flying hawks or fish in the sea. Passionately trembling at the furious storm careering through him, he takes "the oath of the inseparableness" with the woman who loves him: that the two of them become so united that they do not care for anyone else, but only to enjoy and exhaust each other (lines 30–35). Fully trusting in the committed relationship, he yields control of his body like the master (or captain) yields control of a vessel to a pilot (a specialist with the knowledge required to navigate a particularly treacherous stretch of water) or as a sol-

dier defers to a general's commands (line 38). At that point "the program hastening" (line 39); he seems to regret the time spent alone with his "repinings," with many people but not the right one, and all the foreplay ranging from fingers through his hair, the long-sustained kiss, and the close pressure that makes any man "drunk, fainting with excess" (line 45). His loitering is keeping him from what the "divine husband" knows (presumably, the knowledge resulting from "the work of fatherhood;" line 46). He exalts victoriously in the embrace of the right bedfellow in the night, in the "act-poems" (a term recalling an important definition of poetry that stresses not the words on a page but the reception it generates in a reader's mind; line 48) of eyes, hands, hips, bosoms, the trembling arm, bending curve and the clinch (the thought is that the items in this list might be considered poetry since they are equally capable of generating the same feeling in a viewer that poetry is in a listener or reader. The list is ordered by increasing levels of intimacy).

Also enjoyable, if slightly less climactic, are the throwing off of bedclothes, the unwillingness to leave and a rejuvenated joy in shining stars and dropping dews (Freudians, take note). Thus he celebrates the "act divine," its role in procreation and (his own and/or his lover's) stalwart loins (line 57).

"FURTHER IN SUMMER THAN THE BIRDS" EMILY DICKINSON (published 1968) The "minor nation" celebrated in EMILY DICKINSON's poem probably consists of a variety of insect (such as ants) that swarm in unobtrusive masses (or at least their winged queens and drones do). This seasonal phenomenon may occur after the birds arrive in the spring, after the birds mate, or after their fledglings take to the air (Dickinson does not state exactly what it is that the birds have done to attract the speaker's attention at this point in the poem). The insects might be considered more "pathetic" in the sense of being individually weaker than more advanced animals (or pitiable since the overwhelming majority of them will die before establishing a new colony), yet their social nature permits the speaker to think of them as a nation. The central emphasis of the poem lies in a comparison of their behavior with the choreography of religious ceremonies.

The speaker appropriates the word "Mass" (line 4) from the Catholic or Anglican churches, diction that signals the transition to an emphasis on the comparison and away from direct observation.

The most conspicuous difference between the two is the insects' lack of "Ordinance," not just ordained clergy but all the customs or rites that provide order for the human rituals. Instead, there is a gradual Grace (an invigorating if less than holy spirit that slowly spreads among the insect throng; line 6. It becomes a meditative Custom (line 7; the word "pensive" can be used for either wistful daydreams or deep thought) that gradually becomes "Enlarging Loneliness," a term that may imply that the ants (or whatever) do not gain a sense of community like the human celebrants at the same time that it may suggest the clusters of insects are growing in number and size.

A quest typically involves the intellect as well as an emotional investment in a particular goal, but an "Antiquest" (line 9)? Dickinson may have intended to deepen the mystery of the phenomenon by coining a word that suggests its purely instinctual aspect. Whatever is the nature of this animating force at noon late in August this "spectral Canticle" (literally a ghostly song [that of the locust or other sound-producing insect instead of the ant?]) arises as a perfect emblem of tranquility (to typify "Repose," line 12). The term *spectral* may also suggest an image, in which case the song might be figurative and not literal. In that case, their swarming may be interpreted as a visual manifestation of the glory of God, or a celebration thereof.

Nature may still be as nourishing (since no Grace yet "Remit" [abate or diminish], line 13), and the horde is still at full strength (as Furrows have yet to appear on the "Glow," a word that may capture some of the effect of the late fall light on the swarming insects at the same time that it suggests a transcendent or nearly religious experience). There is, however, a discernable "Druidic Difference" (line 15) in Nature. The Druids, adherents of the earliest, nature-worshipping religion to appear in England, are best remembered for their construction of Stonehenge. The symmetrical arrays of huge stones at that site accurately predicted such celestial events as solar solstices and lunar cycles, so the poet may be emphasizing the insects' awareness (on some nonintellectual level) of the changing seasons.

G

"GIVE ALL TO LOVE" RALPH WALDO EMERSON **(1847)** For this poem, the middle-aged (43-year-old) RALPH WALDO EMERSON with a great deal to lose created a speaker who counsels giving everything to love. Even if obeying the heart meant surrendering friends, family, time, wealth and credit, your good name, plans, and the muse, you should not refuse (lines 1–6). It is an interesting philosophy, but the ease with which the speaker advocates giving up everything generally held valuable (especially by mature people) suggests that the advice is insincere.

Calling love a brave master, the speaker advises giving it scope and following it utterly, but to "hope beyond hope" (line 10) suggests that the enterprise may have very little chance of succeeding. In a transcendent moment, love dives (a term usually designating a downward movement) high and higher "with wing unspent" (which may suggest that even more thrills are possible). A god, it knows its own path (another warning that the potential lover will be relinquishing control over his own life).

Love was never meant for average people (the "mean" of line 18) but requires courage and completely confident souls. It rewards lovers by making them more than they were, and with the promise of permanently ascending flight.

Before the internal audience leaves all for love, however, the speaker warns him to keep forever "free as an Arab" of his beloved (Emerson was probably thinking of the romantic image of a nomadic tribesman whose survival in a harsh desert depended on his free travel from one oasis to another; line 32). He should cling to the maid as to life itself, but when "the vague shadow of surmise" of a separate joy (when she realizes the limits of her connection with the lover; lines 36–38) flits across her young bosom, she should be fancy-free. The internal audience should not detain her by the hem of her dress (or other "vesture" [clothing]), nor keep the palest rose she flung from her summer (read "youthful") diadem (a tiara or other crown).

He may have loved her as he loved himself, albeit a self of purer clay (a substance probably chosen not only for its biblical connection with the creation of Eve, but as a reminder that she is, after all, only human; line 44), and her parting may dim the day and steal grace from life. He should know that "when half-gods go, the gods arrive" (lines 48–49), an ambiguous phrase that may do more than simply demote the stature of love. It may imply that the maid will replace him (a half-god) with a more ideal mate, or that real love will follow this ill-advised adventure, or that he may go all the way mad (since mere mortals are traditionally mere playthings for the gods in most classical literature, and unable to bear the magnificence of their presence).

"GIVE ME THE SPLENDID SILENT SUN" WALT WHITMAN **(1881)** This poem may show WALT WHITMAN at his most humorous, for the speaker of the opening stanza of this poem sounds like the antithesis of the celebrated singer of the Brooklyn and Manhattan scene. The most fun can be found when he requests a field of uncut grass (line 3) in which to enjoy his solitude and the primal sanities of nature (line 11). In addition to indulging in all the freshest, ripest fruits and grains, he could learn contentment from the "serene-moving animals" (line 5). At night he would have unimpeded views of the stars, and dawn could provide walks among beautiful garden flowers. He would share this Eden with a "sweet-breathed woman" of whom he would never tire (line 8) and who would bear him a perfect child. Instead of public expression, he would "warble spontaneous songs" for his own ears only (line 10).

The second stanza partially explains this change of heart: the speaker is tired of ceaseless excitement and has been racked by war-strife (line 12; an earlier version of the poem appeared in 1865, the last year of the Civil War). At the same time that his heart incessantly cries for the benefits of rural solitude, he still adheres to his city. Although feeling enchained and glutted (lines 16–17), he feels enriched of soul by the "forever faces" he meets. He sees what he sought to escape, but his own soul tramples that which it asked for.

In the second division (the poem is divided into two numbered sections), he repudiates all that he had asked for, including the splendid silent sun. Instead of buckwheat fields in which the bees hum in August, he would have faces, streets, sidewalks, "interminable eyes," women, comrades and lovers "by the thousand" (line 25), a new one every day. He prefers such shows as the green soldiers marching down Broadway, flushed and reckless, and the march of the returning veterans (old and worn, noticing nothing). He prefers the shores and "the wharves heavy-fringed with black ships" (an extraordinarily brilliant description, most apt if the vessels were viewed from great height; line 31).

He really prefers an intense life within the city's public rooms and torchlight processions, the dense brigades on their way to war, and people with strong voices and passions (line 36). Even despite seeing the wounded (line 39), he forever prefers the powerful throbs, faces and eyes of the Manhattan streets (lines 38 and 41) with their "turbulent musical chorus" (line 40).

"GOD IS A DISTANT—STATELY LOVER"

EMILY DICKINSON (published 1891) Every religious faith has mysteries that can seem absurd to the uninspired. In this poem, EMILY DICKINSON humorously misinterprets the love of God by confusing it with the human emotion and questions the divinity of Christ by suggesting that God could be viewed as a lover so distant that he sends forth His Son (Christ) to act as his matchmaker or envoy. This in turn reminds her of a similar affair which turned out badly for a different distant lover. Miles Standish, a powerful leader among the Massachusetts Puritans, supposedly sent John Alden to ask Priscilla Mullen to marry him. She chose to marry the envoy instead of her earnest but distant suitor.

Since God is omniscient, however, He avoids a similarly unpleasant outcome by announcing that in His case, the divinities cast in the Miles and Alden roles were "Synonyme" (or "synonymous," line 9). They (God and Jesus, in the roles of distant lover and envoy, respectively) are the same divine being.

"GO DOWN, MOSES" ANONYMOUS (19th century) The story of Israel's bondage in Egypt (recorded in Exodus 6:26–14:31) was a great inspiration for the American slave community because of its happy ending. That biblical precedent made it seem as though only a new Moses were needed to drive the scourge of slavery from the land.

The opening stanza recalls the harshness of the slavery of the children of Israel ("oppressed so hard they could not stand," line 3) and intersperses it with their own message: "let my people go." The chorus echoes the voice of the Lord (Exodus 8:20) when he commanded Moses to tell the pharoah to release his people. Perhaps for the sake of brevity, the song dispenses with God's hardening the heart of the oppressor to the point where a succession of plagues (everything from frogs to fleas) failed to obtain his consent, and cuts to the most effective measure: the death of every first-born child (line 9) not in a house with a lamb's blood mark over the lintel and side posts (Exodus 12:22–23).

Thus were the children of Israel set free, and with "Egypt's spoil" (line 13; in Exodus 12:35–36 this includes jewels of silver and gold, raiment [clothing] and whatever else they required). Moses led them to the water's edge and according to God's will, stretched out his "rod" (his staff, the emblem of authority with which he had earlier performed miracles in the pharoah's court; line 25. In the Bible, Moses uses his hand to orchestrate this change). The water divided (Exodus 14:21), and the children of Israel escaped to the other side.

Like a Calvinist sermon, the song turns from the biblical example to the application: like Israel, you will not get lost in the wilderness if you have "a lighted candle in your breast" (line 37). We can all flee from bondage and in Christ be free (lines 39 and 41). We need not weep in our chains without hope; a beautiful morning will dawn "when time breaks up in eternity" (that is, come Judgment Day; line 49).

"GODS" WALT WHITMAN (1881)   This poem is the literary and theological equivalent of a high-wire act as WALT WHITMAN delicately balances between sacrilege and reverence. In the opening stanza, for example, the speaker asks his/her "Lover divine and perfect Comrade" to be his God, but the same readers who would consider this blasphemy if the perceived internal audience were merely human would have to admit that the same line could pertain to their feelings about Christ. The speaker reinforces this reading by referring to the Lover's contented waiting and adds "invisible" and "certain" to his traits, but the same adjectives could be applied to an earthly lover if the relationship must not yet be disclosed. Addressing the lover as "Comrade" (a term Whitman frequently used in the *Calamus* sections of *Leaves of Grass* for those who share his delight in "manly love") offers one possible reason why the relationship might have to remain a closely guarded secret.

Christ is often thought "the Ideal Man" (line 4), perfect in all the ways the speaker enumerates including "dilate in spirit" (line 6, a phrase implying the enlarging or enriching of the spirit, but it might also imply a dilution, a weakening by virtue of becoming less concentrated). Either way, he asks this Ideal Man to be his God.

The speaker next applies the same formula to Death, asking it to be his God because it is the "usher to the heavenly mansion" (line 9). This seems to result in a "stagnant" tie, from which he asks "aught" (anything) of the mightiest and the best that he can "see, conceive or know" (line 11; this short list could include all that comes to him from his senses, his intuition and imagination, and his understanding and intellect. In the most humorous turn of the poem he asks whoever or whatever can thus free his soul to be his God (lines 12–13).

The penultimate stanza provides a list ordered from the most abstract (ideas and the [human] race's aspirations) to the more concrete: the heroisms (which might not have accomplished anything tangible) and deeds (which have produced a result) of rapt enthusiasts. He would have all of them be his gods.

The final stanza (again arranged from the least tangible to the most) lists the things which have been worshiped as gods at earlier points in human history, from Time and Space, the Earth, "some fair shape I viewing, worship" (line 19; a reference that could allude to the Lover celebrated in the opening stanza or any physical object), the sun and a star. He would ask all of them to be his gods.

"GOOD-BYE MY FANCY!" WALT WHITMAN (1891)   Near the end of his biological life WALT WHITMAN took the opportunity to bid farewell to his imaginative life. Personified as his Fancy, it was evidently as cherished by him ("dear mate, dear love!") as any human connection could have been. Knowing that he was "going away," perhaps the most pleasant euphemism for dying because it sounds like a vacation (line 3), he lists the mysteries that await: he does not know where he is going, what awaits him there, or whether he again will see his fancy (whether he will retain his consciousness).

On the verge of issuing his last words (line 6), he decides to take another look back at this life. Like an old-fashioned pendulum clock, his heart has run down to the point where it is ticking more slowly and faintly (line 7). The result is inevitable, and the three euphemisms he produces for death each present different interpretations of life. He might "exit" like an actor leaving the stage, a conceit already proverbial when Shakespeare lent it to Antonio in the opening scene of *The Merchant of Venice* (lines 77–79). Conceiving of death as "nightfall" emphasizes its naturalness, and at the same time that it comments on the brevity of life (the speaker's entire existence can seem but a single day), it offers the hope of resurrection or rebirth, just as a new dawn eventually follows each nightfall. Conceiving of death as a purely biological function (it occurs when the heart stops) may hold the least promise, and he unflinchingly faces this prospect with characteristic panache. The ambiguity of "soon the heart thud stopping" (line 8) resides in whether the "heart thud" is the normal heartbeat that merely ceases, or whether "thud stopping" conveys the pain of an almost violent attack. Cleverly, Whitman has admitted that either outcome is possible.

Looking back, the speaker relishes the long life in which he and his Fancy delightfully lived, "joyed" (line 10; "enjoyed" would have been more idiomatic but Whitman's word may also imply a sexual connotation) and caressed together. The pleasurably recollected sex acts ended with a physical "separation," and that term is used in a transitional way since it reminds the speaker to again bid farewell.

Like an operatic actor whose stage death can extend to three or more arias, the speaker does not want to be too hasty, however. The addition of a few more verbs ("slept," "filtered," and "blended"; line 12) helps substantiate his claim of long life with his Fancy. They have "really blended into one" (line 11; the language is that used in some marriage ceremonies), and if they die—if no vestige of his consciousness remains after his death—then his Fancy and he will die together. Thus their relationship has, in a way, transcended death, raising it to the pantheon of great loves.

Since his Fancy makes up so much of who he is, the speaker is confident that if any sense of his identity survives his death, it must include his Fancy. That still leaves many mysteries, but the speaker optimistically anticipates the possibilities. They may be "better off and blither" (line 15; the second term means "more light-hearted") and learn something (a possibility that suggests that death can be a growth experience). Or perhaps now the Fancy is ushering him to "the true songs," or Death, reduced to a mere mechanical "mortal knob," is simply performing its "undoing, turning" functions (line 17). For the last time, the speaker

bids farewell, but his last words (". . . hail, my Fancy") salute and celebrate that aspect of his life that meant the most to him.

"GRACE" RALPH WALDO EMERSON (1842) Although this poem is ostensibly addressed to God, it seems the god of social convention rather than a more serious divinity. The poem's meaning resonates from the word "preventing" in the first line, one of the most unconventional descriptors ever applied to a divine being unless it refers to a lesser deity such as the god of social mores. The poem is less an insincere prayer than an indictment of the speaker's own timidity, and its tone is closer to sarcasm than reverence.

The third line lists the means by which society controlled individuals: by publicizing both good and bad examples of behavior, by upholding its customs until they had the force of social laws, by instilling fear of exposure and even ostracism, and by slowing everything down until inertia overcame impulse. The items in this list of defenses clearly come not from God, but from society. The central image of the poem is its *parapets,* a term calling to mind the high walls of medieval fortifications, but this connotation not only underscores their artificiality, it may also imply that the barriers the speaker faces are obsolete. He castigates the defenses by referring to them as "scorned bondmen" (slaves) but does not dare to look beyond them.

The surprise of the poem is that the metaphorical barriers supposedly serving as protection against external threats have been internalized and now defend the speaker against his own urges. The colorful language used to describe "the roaring gulf" and "depths of sin" to which he might otherwise have descended (lines 6–7) reveals just how attractive an unbridled ego could be. The speaker has apparently felt so fenced in by his life of social conformity that he does not feel as if he fully realizes who he is or what he is capable of.

On the other hand, this poem is entitled "Grace," conventionally considered a gift from God but also an attractive virtue and a desirable human trait. Part of the self-knowledge for which the speaker longs is the knowledge of one's limits. Despite his plaintive tone, the speaker seems to realize that without Grace, and without boundaries, he would not just have looked at sin but committed himself to a life of it.

GRAINGER, JAMES (c. 1722–1766)

Although James Grainger was born in Scotland and committed the worst sins of his adult life in the British colony of St. Christopher (modern St. Kitts) in the West Indies, several major publishers have included excerpts from his most famous and controversial poem, *The Sugar Cane*, in their anthologies of American literature. Although *Cane* was apparently intended as an anatomy (in the 18th-century literary sense) detailing everything necessary for the production of that crop, its most horrifying aspect for a modern reader lies in the banality of its evil. The author's urbane tone and obvious educational advantages easily place him near the apex of the British society of his day, but the discrepancy between his enlightened language and his advocacy of the slavery that helped him realize his nightmare of frivolous luxury would be laughable were it not so tragic. His voice emanates from the very center of a hurricane, a moral vacuum that uprooted entire nations from their African homes, streaked the shores of every Caribbean island paradise with their innocent blood, and converted the wages from the worst imaginable sins into the cold currency that continued to fund such enormities in London and other major European capitals.

After completing his education in medicine in Edinburgh, Grainger briefly served as a regimental surgeon before quitting the army and befriending Samuel Johnson and several of the other leading British intellectuals of his day in London. He next turned his opportunistic eye to the colonies and managed to marry into wealth and social prominence with no less than the daughter of a former governor. Unfortunately, his death of a tropical fever on Christmas Eve a few years later spoiled the family's holiday festivities for the season, and a new overseer had to be found to serve in his place. This was not before he managed, in *Cane*, to pen his instructions on how to choose the best slaves based on their age, health, geographic origin in Africa and the specific uses the buyer has in mind. For those without the patience for "poetry," he produced a prose version of his practical advice on the subject as filler for his 1764 tome on West Indian diseases.

His wife's fashionable home in St. Kitts lasted until the 20th century, a hundred years after the curse of slavery had been lifted from the island. England's Oxford University has some of his letters to Lord Kinnard and Bishop Percy.

BIBLIOGRAPHY
Bolland, O. Nigel. *Struggles for Freedom: Essays on Slavery, Colonialism, and Culture in the Caribbean and Central America.* Belize City, Belize: The Angelus Press, and Kingston, Jamaica: Ian Randle Publishers, 1997.
Gilmore, John. *The Poetics of Empire: A Study of James Grainger's* The Sugar Cane. London and New Brunswick, N.J.: Athlone Press, 2000.

"GREEK ARCHITECTURE" Herman Melville (1891)

Herman Melville praises the sensitivity of the ancient Greek architectural tradition in this very short poem. He is especially impressed by its emphasis on displaying taste rather than attempting to overwhelm visitors by the mere enormousness of its buildings, by the integrity of its ornamentation, which remains central to the composition of its structures (thus avoiding the decorative excesses, the "lavishness" for its own sake, that tended to dominate earlier and later buildings), its emphasis on "form" (its focus on the building as an artistic unit expressive of the individual designer's appreciation of its overall aesthetic appeal), and its consideration of the site upon which a new building would be placed.

Changes were not made in its traditional designs for the mere sake of novelty or an architect's self-aggrandizement (the "innovating willfulness" of line 3). Instead, the entire design process was conducted with due reverence for the "Archetype," the most perfect building already in existence.

In this poem, Melville endorses a conservative philosophy of architecture that would not have appreciated the building of a glass pyramid in the center of the classical architecture of the Louvre in Paris, for example.

H

"HAMATREYA" RALPH WALDO EMERSON (1846)

The transcendental thinking behind RALPH WALDO EMERSON's poem is simple enough: men pride themselves in their possession of land, but time will find them in their graves, delivered by death into the land's possession. Their offspring, toiling under the same delusion of ownership, will look beyond their property lines with greedy eyes. The family's growing affluence, evidently tied directly to the prosperity of the farm, eventually provides them with such luxuries as European visits ("crossing the seas and back," line 23). Despite all their pride, however, they also will become mere mold.

This leads to "Earth-Song," a response from the earth itself. Noting its own age, and that of the stars, the sea, and the shores, it asks where the similarly old men are. Although their property titles, ensured by force of law and backed by the entire kingdom, seem permanent, every link in that chain will eventually be washed away. Perhaps the most poignant point in the poem is ". . . every one wished to stay, and is gone" (lines 55–56). Ultimately, they cannot hold the earth, but it will hold them.

Upon hearing the Earth-Song, the original speaker was no longer brave (lines 60–61). His greed cooled "like lust in the chill of the grave."

HAMMON, JUPITER (1711–c. 1806)

Born on October 17, 1711, in Oyster Bay on Long Island into the slavery from which he never escaped, Jupiter Hammon at least had the good fortune to work for a slaveholder in New York instead of on a southern plantation. He was given enough training to serve the family as a valuable clerk, and later in life he was able to view the formal gardens on their estate. He also was exposed to the fine things with which his labor and that of others like him furnished the manor house, which was completed by 1767.

Hammon took up his pen on Christmas Day in 1760. The Christian message of his first poem led to its being published immediately and to his being generally recognized as the first African-American poet to reach print. Of the two widely anthologized poems by Hammon, "AN EVENING THOUGHT: SALVATION BY CHRIST, WITH PENITENTIAL CRIES" (1760) is the more typical work as it reveals the depths of his religious beliefs. It can be viewed as a declaration of spiritual equality for its assertion that the promised salvation extends to all believers regardless of their race, and it hints that religion may hold the key to the slaves' salvation in this world as well as in the next. "An ADDRESS TO MISS PHILLIS WHEATLY" (1778) is remarkable as a communication between the two published black American poets of the early Revolutionary War era. He characteristically advised her to shape herself in accordance with Christian doctrine, but she evidently made no public answer (or recorded private response) to him. Although his poetry is frequently marred by lapses in diction and unnecessary breaks in meter (damning shortcomings given the aesthetic preferences of the day), its chief merit is its fervor. Hammon escaped with the Lloyd family when the British army occupied the estate during the Revolutionary War, and he returned to help them restore the manor after the enemy left.

Hammon is chiefly remembered for his few poems and an important "Address to the Negroes of New York," his speech from 1787 which advocated the adoption of Christianity as a means of achieving social progress. The Society for the Preservation of Long Island Antiquities has restored the Joseph Lloyd Manor House, the estate upon which Hammon served, to its appearance of 1793, but the Hammon archives hold very little beyond his published texts.

BIBLIOGRAPHY
Hammon, Jupiter. *America's First Negro Poet; the Complete Works of Jupiter Hammon of Long Island.* Edited by Stanley Austin Ransom, Jr. Port Washington, N.Y.: Kennikat Press, 1970.
James, Elisabeth Sheryl. *All Black Voices Count.* Jackson, Miss.: Town Square Books, 1998.
O'Neale, Sondra Ann. *Jupiter Hammon and the Biblical Beginnings of African-American Literature.* Metuchen, N.J.: Scarecrow Press, 1993.

"A HAND-MIRROR" WALT WHITMAN (1860)

Something untoward has happened to the speaker of this poem (or to his internal audience, a possibility that will be considered later) to create what modern readers would refer to as an identity crisis.

The tone of WALT WHITMAN's poem (and its theme) become clear in the speaker's admonition to hold the mirror "sternly." He becomes so hypercritical that he instructs himself to see "this" instead of "yourself" in the mirror, and his self-loathing is so severe that at first he cannot recognize himself ("is it you?" he asks in line 1). In a marvelous conceit anticipating the central image of Oscar Wilde's *Picture of Dorian Gray* (1890), he contrasts the "fair costume" of his external appearance with his inner "ashes and filth" (line 2). He has changed, and a quick inventory contrasts his formerly "flashing" eye, deep voice, and springy step with those of a slave (line 4). His comparison is based on the latter's degraded condition and contains no racial element; like a slave to love, he has apparently placed himself at another person's disposal.

The result is not a pretty picture, and most of the afflictions he lists result from overindulgence in one or more vices. After noting the effects of alcoholism, gluttony, and venery on the breath and skin (line 4), he adds the symptoms of tuberculosis ("lungs rotting away piecemeal") and chronic indigestion so bad it seems cancerous, or at least ulcerous (the "sour and cankerous" stomach of line 6). Proceeding from the outermost to the innermost symptoms, he finds rheumatism and "bowels clogged with abomination" (line 7, and the euphemistic description may also suggest a moral indictment). At the worst, the "dark and poisonous streams" circulating in the blood may have included diseases such as syphilis, an almost incurable disease at the time.

The worst effects are less apparent, however. For a poet to lose control of his voice and vocabulary (his "words babble" in line 9) is a singular disaster, and for a confirmed sensualist like Whitman, diminished capacities for hearing and touching are nearly as bad. He seems to have lost his brain, heart, and the "magnetism of sex" (line 10).

If any vestige of the poet's customary optimism remains, it resides in the hope that all the debilitating symptoms he described were projections based on a single (exceedingly self-absorbed) look in the mirror (line 11) and the possibility that such an awareness of these potentially disastrous outcomes may encourage him to control his self-destructive tendencies. The delightful ambiguities of the concluding line center on two words. The "beginning" in question may have been his innocent glance in the mirror, or it may go all the way back to the speaker's once having been an innocent infant or refer to the relatively joyful start of the relationship (or lifestyle) that precipitated the present crisis. The "result" may have been a full-blown identity crisis, the speaker's irredeemably fallen or disease-ridden condition, or the unwholesome, entirely unsatisfactory current state of affairs.

Thus far this commentary has dealt with the speaker's use of the second-person pronoun as though he were addressing himself. While this most powerful reading tends to interpret the poem as an expression of the poet's self-loathing, it also has a much broader application. Perhaps the speaker is holding the mirror up for those he meets in the streets, an act of discourtesy compounded by his running commentary on their afflictions. Like the ancient Greek philosopher Diogenes, who reportedly thrust a torch into the faces of strangers before asking if they were honest, the speaker may be in search of the perfectly healthy person, or at least someone who did not betray the innocence of his infancy. In other poems, Whitman's speakers imaginatively embrace the experience of virtually everyone they encounter, but this poem admits that there may also be an unsavory side to that approach. Like the outtakes of a documentary film that do not fit the program for which they were shot, the people (or single person) encountered here shake(s) the wholesome optimism at the center of almost all of the poet's other poems. Collectively, their afflictions constitute a warning against overindulging one's passions or too frequently satiating one's desires.

"THE HANGSMAN'S TREE" ANONYMOUS (19th century)   This very dramatic mid-century folk song probably cautioned the younger members of a family against being too prodigal in their spending. Although the reason for the debt is not given, it is clear that the initial speaker lacked the foresight to save enough money to pay "a fee" (line 6) or at least the foresight to avoid situations where the penalty might be capital punishment. The song opens with his pleading with the "hangsaman" to slack the rope because a possible savior is approaching in the form of his father. Unfortunately, that worthy has not brought the gold or receipt necessary to set him free, but has come to see him hanging from the gallows tree. The high-stakes bondage game resumes until interrupted by another rider, this time the condemned man's mother. She has also neglected to bring the necessary instruments of delivery, and like the speaker's father, has come to see him hang.

Subsequent stanzas reenact the same scenario as various other relatives arrive to witness the spectacle. Their poor sense of timing may suggest to the attentive listener that the condemned man's inability to make his own timely payment(s) may have deep roots in the family genes.

Finally help arrives in the form of his true love, who has brought both a receipt and more gold and has not come to see him hanging on the gallows tree. Hopefully the two of them will live happily ever after, but her tardiness nearly cost him his life.

HARPER, FRANCES ELLEN WATKINS (1825–1911)   Born on September 24, 1825, to a mother who was destined to leave her an orphan at the age of three, the future poet had the great fortune of being raised in a family of educators. Her uncle, Rev. William Watkins, ran an academy for the children of free African Americans in a state where slavery was still legal, and she attended his school until finding work as a domestic servant at the age of 13. Again fortune smiled on her, for her employers granted her access to their library and encouraged her to write. She published her first book of poetry, *Forest Leaves,* at the age of 20 and briefly taught school in Columbus, Ohio, and in Little York, Pennsylvania. Hired as a traveling lecturer for the Anti-Slavery Society of Maine, she delivered her first speech at New Bedford, Massachusetts, in 1854. *Poems on Miscellaneous Subjects,* her second book, was also published in that year.

In 1860 Frances Harper married an Ohio farmer, and the union was blessed with a daughter. After her husband's death in 1863, she moved to Philadelphia and resumed lecturing (her specialties included abolition, women's rights, and temperance) and writing. From 1867 to 1892 she produced four novels, of which the most successful was *Iola Leroy* (1892). Her other poetry collections include *Sketches of Southern Life* (1870) and *The Martyr of Alabama and Other Poems* (1894). She died of heart failure on February 22, 1911.

Harper's "An APPEAL TO THE AMERICAN PEOPLE" asks its target audience to keep the promises of freedom made to the black soldiers of the American Army in the Revolutionary War and implicit in the language of that era. In such poems as "BURY ME IN A FREE LAND" and "The SLAVE MOTHER," she attempted to present scenes so horrific that her target audience would not rest until the cause of such violent injustice was rooted out. "FREE LABOR" examines the moral cost of using slave-produced goods. The most joyous of her most frequently anthologized poems is "FIFTEENTH AMENDMENT," celebrating the potential benefit of the law extending voting rights (and eventually, full civil rights) to black Americans.

The house in Philadelphia where Frances Harper lived from 1870 to 1911 has gained the status of a National Historic Landmark but is not open to the public. Her name is also kept alive by the Frances E. W. Harper Literary Society at the Newark (New Jersey), Public Library.

BIBLIOGRAPHY

Boyd, Melba Joyce. *Discarded Legacy: Politics and Poetics in the Life of Frances E. W. Harper, 1825–1911.* Detroit, Mich.: Wayne State University Press, 1994.

Foster, Frances Smith. *A Brighter Coming Day: A Frances Ellen Watkins Reader.* New York: Feminist Press at the City University of New York. Distributed by the Talman Co., 1989.

Harper, Frances E. W. *Minnie's Sacrifice, Sowing and Reaping, Trial and Triumph: Three Rediscovered Novels.* Edited by Frances Smith Foster. Boston: Beacon Press, 1994.

"HASTY PUDDING" JOEL BARLOW (1796)

The chief attraction of a mock epic is the virtuosity with which the poet can focus attention for an inordinate length of time on a subject so ordinary that the reader has probably given it little prior thought. In this poem JOEL BARLOW has the audacity to set a cornmeal porridge before his audience, a dish that sounds exotic to modern readers only because the more nutritious oatmeal has replaced it as the blandest commodity on the nation's breakfast tables.

The poem begins with the speaker's survey of the surrounding countryside (audacious Alps hide the skies and shorten the days because the sun clears them so late in the morning and sets behind them so early) and the political climate (French flags—here called Gallic because of the Latin name [Gaul] for what later became France—only recently had been raised over conquered Savoy). For the speaker, the flags represented the spread of freedom and democracy because it meant the death of kings (Louis XVI of France had been guillotined on January 21, 1793), but for this poem he chooses a virgin theme well suited for "the purest frenzy of poetic fire" (line 8).

He challenges other poets, including those who prefer hurling their "thunders round the epic field" (those

who write about the fate of nations being decided on a battlefield and those who undertake the arduous task of writing an epic poem [a book-length study typically devoted to such ponderous affairs]; line 10), those who seek inspiration through alcohol abuse, and those who sing the praises of a distant woman (in the tradition of the Renaissance troubadours, whose protestations of courtly love were largely for show). His own poem is based on "the sweets I know, the charms I feel" (line 15), his morning incense (since he can smell it) and his evening meal. He appropriates the troubadour's language in enticing his "dear bowl" (line 17) to "glide over my palate" (note his smooth language) and "inspire my soul." Milk so fresh that it still retained the cow's body temperature (milk pasteurization would not be developed until almost a century later, but at that time, warm milk delivered straight from a healthy cow was considered safe as well as wholesome) cooled the porridge to the point where it could be eaten without the precaution of blowing on each bite.

Part of the fun of a mock epic is the twist the poet gives to the conventions of the genre. Here, in language worthy of the finest court poet, Barlow implies his objective: to gain universal admiration for his subject, which could easily be achieved if "those mild morsels [could] in my numbers chime" (if his metered poetry could match the smoothness of the pudding; line 25). Instead of calling on Calliope, the Greek muse of epic poetry traditionally invoked for assistance when writing in that genre, Barlow takes the pudding for his muse. He recalls the origins of maize and dedicates the poem to the Native American woman who first ground the corn, used a sieve to obtain uniform grains, added yeast to aid in its rising and stirred it in boiling water until the "dry knobs" could be dissolved with a ladle (lines 38–46). Notice how his references to this benefactress change as he comes to appreciate her largess: the "lovely squaw" (a term used disrespectfully when adopted by white culture to designate Native American women; line 33) becomes a "tawny Ceres" (the adjective still dwells on her race, but likening her to Ceres, the Roman goddess of agriculture, suggests she is divine; line 37). Although her name has been lost to the ages, he offers that of Oella (the fabled Incan princess whom he had mentioned in his "Vision of Columbus") in its stead. He would have her fame extend as far as the rays of her father ("Sol," the Latin name of the sun god, line 54).

During his lengthy travels, the speaker experienced a soothing joy upon greeting a "long-lost, unforgotten friend" (line 62). He had been unable to find the pudding in corrupted Paris, where drunks usurp breakfast (the "morning board" of line 66), or in London, where lisping its name with a Yankee drawl would merit a proclamation from the Crown (the loss of his American colonies and the recent beheading of the deposed French king had put George III on guard against the spread of America's radical revolutionary ideas, and anyone who might harbor them, in his realm). Countries further north lacked the short gentle showers and "ethereal fires" (line 75) of powerful sunlight required to grow corn. Only in Savoy was he gleefully reunited with the yellow face, the strong complexion "of the true Indian race," line 78).

In other lands it bears different names: Palanta (Italy), Palante (France), Mush (Pennsylvania), and suppawn (the Dutch in New York adopted the Algonquian term). The speaker is certain of its proper name, however, since he has known it from his youth. "Hasty pudding" underscores the ease and speed of its preparation and the rapidity with which it can be consumed.

Other people ("gaudy prigs") may condemn the meal because pigs eat similar fodder, but the speaker scorns the jest and asks if he should be called a calf just because he drinks milk, or if the pigs should be called human because they eat human food. He trusts his sweet song will drown out the notes they raise (line 122).

The health benefits of the dish may extend to increased sexual potency, for the speaker's father ate it and sired 10 sturdy freemen (lines 125–128)! Like a constellation (thought by astrologers to shape one's personality and future), the pudding "ruled" his birthday (he was born during a season of its prominence), and all his bones are made of Indian corn (line 130). He likes the grain roasted, boiled, smothered or baked, but finds the pudding best.

He even prefers it to succotash (a dish from the southern United States), for which he thoughtfully provides a truncated recipe: drench mixed beans and corn with butter and served with a slice of bacon. He has also tried Virginia's hoe-cake, Johnny cake, and New England's addition of pumpkin to sweeten the hasty pudding. He prefers the simplest blend, and would choose it over dumplings, sweet suet puddings, corn bread and apple pastries.

The second canto (the Italian word for "song," adopted as one of the traditional names for part of a longer poem) focuses on the health benefits of the simple fodder developed before "the vicious rules of art" (line 158) began mixing food that could kill the stomach and sink the heart. Under the new system, cooks had to sweat and children gave up their antics and soon died. From this the Yankees were spared; numerous offspring attend the abundant feast furnished with "simples" (line 167; the reference is to simple fodder, but Barlow puns on the use of the same term for medicinal plants). For hasty pudding, the milkmaid brings one ingredient, and the mother boils the other. The ease of its preparation provides the latter with the time to comb the kids' hair before school.

He cautions, however, that even hasty pudding can be made badly. Its rules begin with correct cultivation of the grain, including reverence for "thy mother earth" who loves the "sons of toil" who court her yielding soil (lines 193–195). With spring tillage, the ox repays its winter fodder. Soon the tender "germ" (young plants) emerge from the ground (or "shoots"). Three times in the spring the field should be plowed or hoed to control the weeds (modern farmers tend to use herbicides engineered to spare the crops while killing the weeds that would otherwise compete with them for nutrients). By the start of summer, when Cancer rules the astrological skies, the temperatures should be high enough to support the corn's rapid growth. When a plant gets large enough that its branches reach those of its neighbors (personified, they entwine their arms and kiss; line 221), they should be able to flourish without further attention.

His description of the plant's natural history compares its stalks with a ship's mast, or at least its "top gallants," the highest rigged sails and masts on the biggest ships of the day. It reaches for the sky like a state-of-the-art vessel that "bears the standards high" (that proudly flies its national emblems, often the official flag; line 226). Other implied comparisons further stress its height: it is as high as a hop-field (hops resemble vines and are commercially valuable for their use in beer production. Individual hop plants can reach almost 50 feet [15 meters] if they can attach themselves to something offering support to that height; line 230) and the speaker calls the cornfield a "grove," a description usually used for trees.

The plant's sex life also interested him. The ears of corn swell as if pregnant (line 29) or grow like "suckling" pigs after their silk (the hairlike strands extending from the top of each ear) have captured enough pollen to fertilize the grains. This leads him to the reproductive proclivities of his own species, in evidence here because a fully grown cornfield can offer more privacy than other areas on a crowded farm. Here the maid can meet her swain for "little thefts of love," the green ears of corn he puts in her basket in exchange for the promised wedding and a present kiss (lines 233–239).

The more serious thieves are raccoons by night and squirrels by day, but the speaker does not begrudge their intrusions because they are denied the true delight of hasty pudding. In October, carts loaded with grain fill the corn-house (line 256), where it is ground into the powdered gold of cornmeal. This new crop exterminates the old (unprocessed kernels of grain; line 261).

The third canto begins after the corn has been carried from the field still in its husks, which presents an occasion for the neighbors to gather. Alternative seats are given to males and females, so much merriment ensues as they remove the husks. A red ear gains kisses as a reward, whereas a fungus-blackened ear permits its finder to use it to smear his friends (line 281). The time passes merrily, and whoever grabs the last unhusked ear wins. Then the housewife prepares the pudding, adding salt and the corn flour to the boiling cauldron.

This brings the speaker to the rules for eating the pudding. Some like it with molasses, which blends the useful with the sweet (line 311). That is especially good in winter (when the north wind drives the shivering cow). He can relate to cows since he often milked and fed them and mourned the slaughter of their children. He recommends a good barn for the winter and

including potatoes, pumpkins, corn, and mashes (a by-product of beer production) in its fodder to increase a cow's cheer. In spring she should produce enough milk to nurse human infants as well as her own.

He prefers adding the pudding to his milk until a small island rises above the brink, and likes to attack it with a relatively shallow-bowled spoon, having found that pudding sticks to deeper spoons (lines 345–352). Ideally these would have the volume of a small section of goose egg shell that encompasses half the distance from center to side. One can either wear a napkin like the French or (his favorite method) lean over the bowl placed on the knee. This inelegant posture (proper dining typically takes place at a table and rarely involves moving the body toward the spoon) belies the formal language of the poem but is in keeping with the speaker's preference for simple pleasures.

"THE HEART ASKS PLEASURE—FIRST"
EMILY DICKINSON (1862)   Perhaps as a reflection of her exposure to the heavily Calvinist strains that permeated earlier New England culture, EMILY DICKINSON believed that any pleasure would be balanced by pain. The various stages of pain enumerated in this poem seem disproportionate to the Pleasure so innocently and even charmingly sought, until one considers the initial attractiveness of sin and the extraordinary punishments Judeo-Christian tradition typically meted out for such lapses.

Much of the effectiveness of the poem lies in the resonance between its accurate account of the successive psychological stages leading to despair and the simultaneous descent of the soul until it appears to be trapped in hell. At the same time, the poem says a great deal about love and the suffering it can entail.

As a love poem, the first line exquisitely captures the initial attractiveness of a new romance. Almost immediately, as the pangs of love become evident, the afflicted person may wish to withdraw from the source of such pain, and then requires little Anodynes (painkillers; line 3) to deaden the suffering. No trip to the drugstore is required; any number of rationalizations, assurances, explanations, and other postures can suitably dull the pain without improving the underlying condition.

As the poem is devoted to the sensations of love, the break between stanzas can suggest a leap to a postcoital experience. At this point, the poet's intimacy issues come to the fore. To sleep (line 5) not only means to lose consciousness, it can also suggest such an indifference to morality as to place the lover's soul in mortal peril. By having granted such unlimited access to the soul, the lover in this poem has also surrendered so completely to another that even the will to live has been compromised. That Dickinson, having so thoroughly thought the process through, was unwilling to grant such authority to anyone else is evident in her calling the interloper an 'Inquisitor" (line 7), a term connected with the torturers of the dreaded Spanish Inquisition. The poet valued her personhood (and her poetry) too much to risk it.

Of course the poem can also be viewed as a descent into hell, with the first line establishing the connection between desire and sin, and the rest of the first stanza dealing with the compromises necessary to continue living in a fallen state. Death comes as sleep in the fifth line, and the torments of Hell will probably be eternal as only the Inquisitor, a very sinister figure, can grant an end to the suffering.

"'HEAVENLY FATHER'—TAKE TO THEE"

EMILY DICKINSON (1914)   This poem offers ironic commentary on the notion of original sin based on the Creation story in Genesis. In Puritan theology, for example, man is considered innately depraved because of the failure of Adam and Eve to obey God's commandment against eating the fruit of the Tree of Knowledge in Eden. To say that "We are Dust" echoes the language of Genesis 3:19, and all subsequent human mortality and morbidity supposedly came as an inheritance from the earliest couple.

Instead of pleading for a chance at Redemption through God's grace (a prayer essentially asking Him to "take us to thee"), the speaker tells Him to take ownership of the "supreme iniquity" (the original sin; line 2), since he set up Adam and Eve to fail. After writing so much poetry that relies on sprung rhyme and sometimes idiosyncratic rhythms, perhaps EMILY DICKINSON enjoyed the variety of creating two trochee lines (marked by the repetition of a stressed syllable

followed by an unstressed one) of equal length with perfect end-rhymes:

"Fashioned by thy candid Hand
In a moment contraband-"

                                        (lines 3–4)

The Hand (God; this is an example of synecdoche, a trope in which a part of something is used to represent the whole thing) was "candid" in the sense of being open and honest about the significance of the tree. The second line not only refers to His warning (He instantly forbids access to the tree), it may also indict His action during what might be considered "a contraband moment."

Although we (the speaker has begun speaking for "us," presumably all of humankind) appreciate the respect shown by God's evident trust in us, on one level we feel as though we are apologizing for his duplicity. Since he is omniscient as well as omnipotent, Adam and Eve had no real free will when it came to their decision-making about the forbidden fruit. He must have known that their sin was inevitable, and yet he took inadequate steps to shield them from it.

"HE FUMBLES AT YOUR SOUL" EMILY DICKINSON (1896)   On the most appropriate level, EMILY DICKINSON'S poem studies the process by which God informs an individual of His existence and the transcendent bliss awaiting the believer at each stage of this awakening. Because pleasures this intense can often seem like pain, He carefully prepares the soul by degrees (line 4); sometimes musicians do something like this with preludes or preliminary rhythms that prepare their audience for the full musical experience that awaits them (line 3).

Human nature is brittle (line 5) compared with the power of God. Many Christians believe that the chief goal in life is to live in such a way that one becomes worthy of spending eternity in His presence, an outcome they frequently refer to as a reward. The thinking behind this poem is that an unrefined soul would not only be objectionable to Him, but that such a poor soul could be instantly shattered by the experience (perhaps like a fine crystal wineglass will shatter if a singer can maintain a certain pitch long enough for it to resonate at the frequency required for this trick). The oxymoronic phrase "Ethereal Blow" (line 6) perfectly conveys the supernatural aspect of the far more awesome forces to which such a fragile soul will be subjected. Some mystery surrounds the process by which either the sound of far-off hammers (since the line signals a transition to internal phenomena, perhaps the speaker is hearing her own heartbeat) or their actual impact (they only sound "fainter" [line 6] in comparison with the Ethereal Blow) thus steels the soul.

All of this is rather scary, as the physiological responses (implied in lines 7 through 9) indicate. These include irregular breathing, almost feverish brain activity and perhaps distortions in perception so that time seems sped up, and these things happen so automatically that one may not be aware of them until they start returning to normal. Note how deftly the poet's use of unidiomatic diction reinforces the reader's sense of magic in the process: the breath "straightens" and the brain "bubbles Cool."

Even for one so laboriously prepared, what happens next is so far beyond human imagination that it brings only the imperial thunderbolt (line 11) originally associated with the Norse god Thor to mind. Note how the dashes in this line slow down the reading to match the pace of action being described. In a moment of transcendent pleasure or pain, He "scalps your naked Soul" (line 12), an action accomplished in a flash compared with the timing of the preceding line. The image was more provocative during the 19th century when scalping, in some ways the ultimate violation of another person, was still being practiced by warriors of both races on a succession of western frontiers eventually extending to the Pacific Ocean. Its use may also suggest some reticence on the part of the speaker toward any relationship with any god or man who would seek to possess so much of her soul, thereby altering and perhaps even negating at least part of her identity.

The end result may be so far beyond human understanding that the language used to describe it must encompass several contradictory possibilities. It is clear that the prepared and newly refined soul has forgotten about its self and the bodily sensations of which it had been so recently and intensely aware.

It seems to soar so far above the earth that it can observe "Winds taking Forests," a rather apocalyptic vision were it not for the qualifying phrase "in their Paws" that follows (line 13). While "taking" suggests destruction, the use of "Paws" may suggest a protective embrace. The soul is now positioned to observe the universe, which can only be described as "still," a word that in the context of this line offers meanings as diverse as still enduring; quiet (and this may imply that all life and energy have ended); or free from commotion (which would emphasize the soul's tranquility, as if it had been granted a perspective like that of a god). Similarly, the final dash of the poem might imply the end of the soul's consciousness or the beginning of a new stage in its existence so engrossing that there is no time to continue communicating via such limited means as language. The one thing that is clear is that for a fervid believer, even the most profound sensations a human can experience in this life are magnified by religious ecstasy.

Once in a great while this poem will produce snickers in the back of a university poetry class, and some benighted soul (usually misled by the opening line) will charge that the poem is really about an encounter with a lover who is unskilled at foreplay but who nevertheless manages to get the job done. Such impertinence deserves the traditional fate administered to heretics but usually only receives a strict admonishment to read the entire poem closely before trying to understand it. The second and third lines implicitly reject this interpretation when they compare him to musicians capable of dropping "the full Music on." He is clearly not unskilled.

"THE HEIGHT OF THE RIDICULOUS"
OLIVER WENDELL HOLMES (1830)   The speaker in OLIVER WENDELL HOLMES's poem discovers that the practice of humor can be a deadly serious undertaking. He sets the tone in the opening stanza by slightly varying the traditional opening phrase of the fairy tale: "Once upon a time." By announcing his "wondrous merry mood" (line 2) and his expectation that men would "as usual" (line 3) praise his lines as "exceedingly good," he demonstrates a pride that begs a comeuppance in the best tradition of comedy.

In the second stanza the speaker commits the unpardonable sins (for the humorist) of talking about how funny something is and then laughing at his own joke instead of simply telling it. His diction is just a shade different from the utterly conventional (he "laughed as I would die" instead of the tired old formula of "laughing until I thought I would die;" line 5), a change that not only suggests that there may be something to his implied claim of being a good writer but also foreshadows the tragic end of his story. To call something "queer" (line 5) conveyed no suggestion of sexual orientation in the 19th century; it meant "astonishingly odd and hence unexpectedly funny," so he is again singing his own praises. By the eighth line he has sobered up from the intoxicating humor to the point where he can return to business.

The third stanza includes two measures of self-deprecating humor since the poet was only 5 feet 2 inches tall on his best day. Such an emphasis on the speaker's lack of size (his slender physique stands in marked contrast to the servant's "mighty limb" [line 12], thus creating humor through the juxtaposition of opposites) recalls the title's reference to height. The speaker also implies that he is so unworldly as to believe that the servant waits on him out of kindness (lines 9–10). Thus he has removed himself from an economic plateau above most readers' level (he has a servant after all) to an intellectual level far below it (since most readers would have a more practical view of why one performs his job), a virtual pratfall.

Because the poem revolves around the personalities of the two people it presents, the external audience can appreciate the speaker's manipulation of the servant in the next stanza, but here again the language foreshadows the poem's denouement. The speaker hands the servant a message for the printer with the irresistible aside that "there'll be the devil to pay." As predicted, the luckless man takes the bait and "peeps" (line 18; the verb conveys the furtiveness with which the servant acts but is comical enough in itself to soften the implied violation of the speaker's trust) at the note.

This leads to a scene that would be gratifying for any writer, and the sixth and seventh stanzas follow the poor man's reactions as closely as a doctor watches a cherished patient's symptoms. Note the movement from one sense to another (from sight to sound to physical convulsions) and the increased intensity conveyed by each pair in the succession of verbs and adjectives that follows ("grew" becomes "shot," "chuckling" leads to a roar, and "split" leads to "burst," lines 21–27). Like the victim of an epileptic seizure or other uncontrollable "fit," the poor victim collapses.

The speaker's penance consists of watching the "wretched man" (a description that may indicate both the poor servant's condition and the speaker's weariness with him) for 10 sleepless days and nights, and the poem ends with the lesson the speaker takes from the adventure.

"HE PREACHED UPON 'BREADTH' TILL IT ARGUED HIM NARROW" EMILY DICKINSON (1891)

Perhaps the principal beneficiaries of EMILY DICKINSON's decision to avoid publication of her work were the clergy of Amherst who were thus spared the angst of realizing that a major poet would be auditing their sermons. The subject of this poem might have lectured on the unlimited love of Jesus, the unlimited power of God, the length of eternity or a myriad of similarly limitless topics including (Heaven help him!) the use of the term "breadth" in the Bible, where it repeatedly appears in connection with the dimensions of the cross and of the churches. On the occasion in question, the reach of the luckless minister evidently exceeded his grasp, at least as far as the speaker in this poem was concerned.

The preacher's turning his attention to "Truth" was no better; he may have tried to answer Pontius Pilate's taunt to Christ as recorded in John 18:38: "What is truth?" For most Christians, Jesus had already provided the answer in John 14:6: "I am the way, and the truth, and the life; no one comes to the Father but through me." The minister may have set about listing the innumerable signs by which we know the Truth, an approach the speaker rejects because "Truth never flaunted a Sign" (line 4). In other words, the Truth should be sufficient unto itself without the support of signs such as logicians depend upon when they use theorems to support their theses. The minister's flawed search for Signs that support the Truth must inevitably fail because of its reliance on his intellect instead of his faith. To conclude that the Truth proclaimed the preacher a Liar (line 3) seems an especially harsh judgment, but it also indicates the extent of the speaker's dissatisfaction with such an uninspiring spiritual guide.

Simplicity (not stupidity but a philosophical simplicity that seeks to communicate great ideas in simple terms in hopes of being better understood) fled from "his counterfeit presence" (line 5) in the same way that a personified God would shun Fool's Gold (iron pyrite) in the speaker's opinion. Such an "enabled" man (line 8; note how the speaker uses the term as do many 21st-century behaviorists: an "enabler" is someone who, with the best intentions, helps another individual persist in dangerous or damaging behavior) would confuse even the "innocent Jesus."

"HER BREAST IS FIT FOR PEARLS" EMILY DICKINSON (1894)

This charming poem finds EMILY DICKINSON's speaker marveling at his good fortune. His love's body is first rate (although to a more modern audience such a cold appraisal of her breast may suggest that he is a successful [and disappointingly boastful] suitor, for Dickinson's Victorian contemporaries the term usually meant little more than the décolletage, the French term for the neckline upon which a necklace would be displayed). The speaker lacked the means of acquiring the wealth to adorn her with the pearls that would complement her beauty ("I was not a 'Diver'" he explains; line 2). Her face was so beautiful it could have belonged to a queen, but he lacks even such a crest (a feature of a coat of arms) as a run-of-the-mill nobleman might possess. In short, she was so far above him that he considered himself a sparrow in contrast with her attractiveness. The fact that "Her heart is fit for home" (line 5), however, suggests that she has an ingrained penchant for domesticity that is all the opening such a sparrow as the speaker needs to make himself a home. Although the "twigs and twine" with which he builds (line 7) are remarkably inferior to the jewels and social prominence that would seem her more natural accoutrements, they are "Sweet" enough for both of them that he perennially nests in her heart.

"HERE FOLLOWS SOME VERSES UPON THE BURNING OF OUR HOUSE JULY 10, 1666" ANNE BRADSTREET (published 1867)

Fires were very common in the 17th century because most homes were wooden, lit by candles and heated by an open hearth. This poem is valuable for its insights into the ways ANNE BRADSTREET's religion could bolster a good Puritan in the face of such a calamity and its portrait of the richness of a prominent colonial woman's daily life.

The speaker was awakened in the night by thunderous noise and piteous shrieks of "Fire" (lines 1–5). The understatement of the sixth line ("Let no man know is my desire") is almost humorous under the circumstances, and the coolness of its tone underscores the fact that the poem was written long after the incident. Despite this flaw, notice how Bradstreet uses a succession of sensory impressions to bring her experience to life. After the sounds woke her, she saw the light (a term that always held a double meaning for a Puritan), and immediately asked God to strengthen her heart. She escaped and watched the flames consume the dwelling. When she had to turn away, she drew on the Bible for support. In the spirit of Job, she blessed God's name, rationalizing that all her goods really belonged to him (line 16) and realizing that she should be grateful for all she still had.

Often as she passed the ruins she would remember where she sat or slept, and the specific place of a trunk and a chest that once held her most prized possessions. Her pleasant things are in ashes, so she can no longer entertain guests, eat at her own table, or hear the pleasant tales and recollections that once amused and enlightened her. In an age so long before the advent of mass media entertainment, a major source of "things recounted done of old" (line 32) was not just the Bible, but the personal narratives of the family and its guests or stories adapted from their reading.

Gone are the homely light of the candle and the welcome voices of the family, which began with the bridegroom's. Note how she implicitly contrasts the light and noise of the fire with the silence of the ashes that has replaced them. She bids her fond memories good-bye by dismissing them as vanity, in the sense that her losses were based on the impermanent things of the material world. Still sad, she chides her heart for valuing earthly wealth instead of her immortal soul and refers to the house and her memories as "dunghill mists" (line 42). In an era when draft animals provided most of the nonhuman labor on a farm and other animals provided all the meat, their manure would commonly be shoveled into heaps until it could be scattered on the fields. "Mists" is perhaps too elegant a word for the vapors emitted from the decomposing pile, but in the right light at certain ambient temperatures its heat waves would be visible. Rationalizing that everything she lost was mere manure helps her turn her attention toward the magnificently furnished house awaiting her in heaven.

Note how the language of commerce informs the next few lines; Christ purchased and paid for the permanent dwelling (line 47). Money was relatively scarce in the colonies, and it was important for the speaker to distinguish the permanence of complete ownership (the bill was paid) from mere possession (it could have been purchased with borrowed funds). The speaker is not only contemplating the heavy financial losses attendant upon the fire, but also adding coherence to the poem by again implying that no one really owns anything on earth.

Secure in her vision of an abundant afterlife, she bids farewell to her earthly possessions and thanks God for the gift of his sacrifice and this loss, which focuses her attention on heaven. Some of the tension involved in the renunciation of the world is still evident in her penultimate line, a prayer for Christ's continuing help with this painful process.

"HERE THE FRAILEST LEAVES OF ME"

WALT WHITMAN (1860)   In this uncharacteristically short work WALT WHITMAN marvels that his poems, appearing on the frail leaves of his books, will last longer than the other things. These include the buildings he worked on as a carpenter and all the newspapers and other work he printed.

A third meaning of the leaves (beyond the pages of his books and other remnants of his labor) appears in the second line, where they shade his thoughts, like shade-producing trees. Like the leaves with which Adam and Eve covered their nakedness but exposed

their sin (they would not have minded their nakedness had they not eaten of the forbidden tree of knowledge), they also expose his thoughts.

Since the poem appears in the homoerotic *Calamus* section of *Leaves of Grass,* Whitman may be suggesting that these longest lasting "leaves of me" may be closer to his heart than other of his *Leaves.* This is reinforced by the final line's declaration that they expose more of him than all his other poems. Since he lived in a homophobic society, he was probably judicious in not exposing his thoughts (line 2) even more assertively.

"HE SCANNED IT—STAGGERED"   EMILY

DICKINSON (1951)   This poem provides the reader with a poet's conception of the final thoughts of a suicide. As if the speaker were somehow swept up in that subjective world, only partial information is provided in the first stanza. The antecedent of the pronoun "it" in the opening line is unclear; could it have been a poor financial statement, a Dear John letter from the lover who was leaving him, some other bit of bad news, or even his own suicide note? Perhaps the poet decided to keep the triggering incident a mystery in order to broaden the application of the poem. If readers are kept uninformed as to the nature of the calamity, they are told of its effect on the subject: he staggered. Within the context of the poem, to "drop the Loop" could suggest a noose, a misdirection that nevertheless foreshadows the final outcome. The third line explains—partially—that he lost touch with his past and, perhaps his present; time is as disjointed as everything else in his life. Like a trapped animal, he "caught helpless" (line 4) at a "sense" (an empirical sensation, with which, unfortunately, he cannot connect. The same word also suggests his reasoning ability in general, as well as a single reason to abandon his design or to continue it). He acts "as if His Mind were going blind," a brilliant description that again suggests asphyxiation.

Completely out of touch with reality, he "groped up" (a phrase conveying the awkwardness of his motion) "to see if God was there" (line 6; this was perhaps his last shot at securing aid from an outside agency). Groping backward "at Himself" suggests that he was trying to keep in touch with his own physical reality. His absent-minded caress of the trigger suggests that his death was, on some level at the very end, an accident, but the verb ("caress") also suggests that he may have, characteristically, put his love into the wrong things. In the end, he merely "wandered out of Life."

Modern practitioners of suicide intervention have found that unsuccessful suicides often recover their equilibrium and most go on to live out their natural lives. The tragedy presented in this poem probably followed from the short period of time between the devastating blow and the final one.

"HIS MOTHER'S WAY" Sarah M. B. Piatt

(1880) The real subject of Sarah M. B. Piatt's rather maudlin (from a modern reader's perspective) poem is the difference between male and female sensitivity. It was produced at a period in American history when women were beginning to make their voices heard on a national level, and much of the strength behind these formerly suppressed voices came from their empathy for the downtrodden and oppressed.

The initial speaker in this poem is a boy young enough to openly confide in the second speaker but old enough that nothing is lost on him. A more modern audience might think his family dysfunctional because of the mother's depression ("she just knows how to cry," according to her son; line 1). To a Victorian audience, however, her temperament would seem exemplary; her tears are precipitated by an old glove, ring or passing stranger. The first two items were probably family heirlooms, but the third turns out to have been a passing tramp. The title character could cry both her eyes red over him (line 5), but her husband dismissed him as a tramp, beggar, or some other word that the second speaker was unwilling to repeat (line 7). Evidently surprised by the second speaker's reaction to the word, the boy explained that "we have to call them that" (thus revealing his socialization against identifying with people from the less privileged classes.

Although his mother could afford lace curtains (line 23), she cried because "the shabbiest shawl" (line 9) was priced beyond the reach of the poor. His father, because he is a man (line 11), never cried at all, even if his coat was not "right new" (a regional expression conveying the meaning of "brand new" or "in the very

latest fashion," line 13). He would not cry over the death of a canary, his son's new white kitten or (in a humorous twist that emphasizes the first speaker's youth) even his (the father's) own death. He tries to disarm his wife's sorrow with the humor of exaggeration: he announces that he would sleep with both pistols near his head that night because the ragged fellow might return (lines 17–20).

The mother will not be so easily distracted, however, and continues to peep out and to weep over the unfortunate, very cold man with "no pleasant place to stay" (line 26). Because his eyes are still blue and not gray (which might have indicated the cataracts that sometimes afflict the eyes of the elderly), she thinks he is still young enough to work and asks why he cannot (lines 27–28). By looking into his eyes she has recognized his humanity; she places the blame for his condition not on his own shortcomings but implicitly criticizes society for its neglect of the elderly as well as the poor).

The second speaker willingly (perhaps eagerly, because of the lad's gender) dismisses the boy's report as babbling (thus demonstrating that her intentions are more serious than idle gossip; line 29) and confronts the "sweet sirs" in their offices who would laugh at the mother's grief. Such women may not be foolish; even the businessmen's "white hands" (a sign not only of personal hygiene but also a hint that they are free from blame [or consider themselves to be]; line 35) may have stains as "sad as wayside dust" that woman's tears cannot wash away (lines 33–36).

Although babies possess "more love than you can measure" (line 38), the pursuit of wealth darkens their perspective until their fellow men are left to wander, tormented by wind and cold. Anticipating the rejoinder that prisons can hold the vagrants, she counters that inmates are served unwholesome bread (line 44; if her knowledge was not gained from her own volunteering work, it could have been learned from the prison reform movement, another social cause embraced by Victorian progressives).

The most successful men enjoy books, leisure, lamps (as opposed to candles or no light at all), jests (typically at the expense of those less fortunate or otherwise different from themselves) and wine, but "fierce outside whispers" [from those marginalized by the white, male-dominated, affluent society] moan that those comforts (and the sense of self-worth and human dignity that they bestow) should belong to everyone. Thus the poem reflects the historical moment when sadness over social injustice turned to anger and action.

"THE HIVE AT GETTYSBURG" JOHN GREENLEAF WHITTIER (1869)

A three-day battle that began on July 1, 1863, is considered the highwater mark of the Confederacy. Its greatest general (Robert E. Lee) had gambled that its largest and best army could deliver such a decisive blow to the Union Army that it would bring a victorious end to the Civil War. The two massive armies had ground each other to a halt in Gettysburg, Pennsylvania, when, on the third day, Lee sent more than 12,000 men charging about a mile across an open field into the very center of the opposing forces. A majority of the attackers were shot and shelled to pieces, and the survivors and the rest of the Southern army limped home, where they would be forced to continue fighting on their own soil for almost two more years.

One might expect a poem with JOHN GREENLEAF WHITTIER's title to portray the hyperactivity of swarms of desperate men as the battle reached its zenith. A Quaker, however, might imagine a more productive hive dedicated to peaceful productivity. For members of his sect an individual's inner light was more important than the Bible, and this explains why he seems to dismiss the Samson legend (Judges 14: 6–9) as an "old Hebrew myth" (line 1) instead of referring to its source as a sacred text. Whittier found (or imagined) the bees had returned to the former Civil War battlefield and, like the bees that inhabited the carcass of a lion Samson killed with his bare hands, they were inhabiting part of something that had formerly been ferocious.

Gettysburg was the spot where the "ravening" (voraciously predatory, line 11) Treason (the speaker's Northern bias is revealed here) received the injuries with which it crept back to die in its lair like a mortally wounded lion. Left in its wake was a blood-stained and shattered drum, an instrument that had played a vital role in regulating camp life, conveying orders to massive groups of men, and coordinating troop movements, but which now supported a beehive. No ghostly sentinel challenges the bees, but their in-flight humming noise suggests the low rumble with which drums once sounded reveille (only later did bugles replace them).

In a crisis that prefigured his later betrayal by Delilah, Samson's first sweetheart betrayed the secret of the riddle with which he had perplexed the Philistines: they were to tell him how meat came from the eater and sweetness came from the strong (a reference to the bees which had taken residence in the carcass of his slain lion). In Whittier's Civil War analogy, "union, peace and freedom" were plucked from the broken "jaws of wrong" (lines 27–28). Just like that "old-time athlete" whose memory of the battle with the lion made the honey seem even sweeter, "we draw a purer life" (one unmarred by treason and the slavery which the Quakers opposed) from the bitter strife of the late war.

HOLMES, OLIVER WENDELL (1809–1894)

The house of a minister in Cambridge, Massachusetts, welcomed the birth of the future poet, doctor, professor, novelist, and humorist on August 29, 1809. He graduated from Harvard in 1829 and, in 1830, saved a battleship, the USS *Constitution,* with his poem "OLD IRONSIDES." After becoming a physician by studying in Paris and at Harvard (M.D. 1836), in 1838 he became a professor of anatomy at Dartmouth and practiced medicine in Boston. In 1840 he married the daughter of a Massachusetts Supreme Court Judge, and their union eventually produced the famous U.S. Supreme Court Justice who shares the poet's name. From 1847 to 1882 he taught at the Harvard Medical School (where he also served as dean from 1847 to 1853). To the Civil War effort he added poems such as "Is the Old Flag Flying Still." As a humor columnist he wrote "The Autocrat of the Breakfast-Table," for the *Atlantic Monthly,* a magazine he cofounded and named. He also penned three award-winning scientific/medical papers, a biography of Ralph Waldo Emerson, three novels including *Elsie Venner* (1861) and a travel narrative (*Our Hundred Days in Europe,* 1888). He died in Boston on October 7, 1894.

Holmes published five books of poetry from 1836 (*Poems*) to 1880 (*The Iron Gate, and Other Poems*). Of the commonly anthologized poems, the humor of "My Aunt" appears the most dated while "The Height of the Ridiculous" better stands the test of time. "The Deacon's Masterpiece" attacks the lingering religious conservatism of the Calvinists, and "The Chambered Nautilus" demonstrates the poet/doctor's interest in science.

The remaining Holmes homes are privately owned residences not open to the public. The Library of Congress, Harvard University, Johns Hopkins University, and the Concord (Massachusetts) Free Public Library house the Holmes archives.

BIBLIOGRAPHY

Gibian, Peter. *Oliver Wendell Holmes and the Culture of Conversation.* New York: Cambridge University Press, 2001.

Holt, Edwin P. *The Improper Bostonian: Dr. Oliver Wendell Holmes.* New York: Morrow, 1979.

Tilden, Eleanor Marguerite. *Amiable Autocrat: A Biography of Dr. Oliver Wendell Holmes.* New York: Henry Schuman, 1947.

"'HOPE' IS THE THING WITH FEATHERS" Emily Dickinson (1951)

At first glance, this seems less like a poem written by a great poet and more like the sentimental verse favored by the less gifted writers of Emily Dickinson's era. As an image, a little bird seems too precious, being more at home in a pantry (though a captive there) than in the soul of an Arctic explorer or storm-tossed sailor. The poem seeks to defamiliarize the bird by casting it in the role of indomitable hero, granting it the scope of action and the means of communication (in this case, an image of endurance) that demonstrate its fitness for that incredible role.

Dickinson was a keen birdwatcher who was less interested in amassing a large checklist of the different species than in observing the individual birds and their contributions to the ecosystem of her garden. As such she was probably eyewitness to the tenacity with which small birds held fast to their swinging branches in the sharpest gales, even when pelted with hail or shivering in the falling snow. They may not literally sing at such times, but they are indeed poetic if not outright heroic because they never stop being what they are.

On perilous seas, recollections of the little birds and memories of their songs could make endangered sailors flush with memories of their homes and the feelings of security they inspired, and above all the desire to do whatever it takes to see them again. If a tiny bird on a wire-thin twig can withstand forces stronger than any gale on the open seas, then a human being should be able to do and survive much more.

The third stanza might seem unconvincing because Dickinson famously never cared to expose herself to "the chilliest land" or "strangest Sea" (lines 9–10), but the speaker in this poem personally claims first-hand knowledge gained from a perilously active life. The speaker relates having heard a bird sing in very adverse winter conditions on ice- and snow-covered hills. Even in such times of dire emergency (the "Extremity" of line 11), it never asked for a crumb "from me" (line 12; the phrase leaves open the possibility that it may desire other assistance from a higher source), but remained a model of self-sufficiency.

"THE HOUSE ON THE HILL" Edwin Arlington Robinson (1893)

This poem is haunting because the speaker is so taciturn. The situation finds him (or her) rather unwillingly accompanying the internal audience to the ruins of an old house. Note how capitalizing the word "House" (line 2) and the phrase "House on the Hill" in the last stanza raises these words to the status of a proper noun; this is not a random building but one of special significance to the speaker for some reason. In spite of the speaker's reluctance to continue, each stanza brings him closer to the ruins and perhaps to the memories he may be trying to repress, or to the realization that everything he owns and his very life will someday rot and expire. Edward Arlington Robinson's poem maintains its light tone at the speaker's expense; the poet seems to revel in the speaker's obvious discomfort (since he keeps repeating not only the same phrases but even the simple sentence patterns) as if the speaker may believe in ghosts but is unwilling to admit it. On another level, the poem celebrates the staying power of the word. Instead of there being nothing else to say, a poet can grant limited immortality, or at least a lengthier human interest in the inhabitants of a house than their decaying artifacts can. Art tends to endure longer than other manufactured things.

The alternating refrains of the poem are paradoxical; in one, although the speaker insists there is nothing more to say, he still finds something to add in each stanza. In the other, he repeats that "they are all gone away" as though he hopes to convince his companion (and perhaps even himself) that this is indeed true. In the same vein, notice how another paradox unites the first two stanzas. In the first, we are told that the house is shut and still, but in the second, we are informed that the winds "blow bleak and shrill" (line five) through its broken walls. Similarly, although the speaker asserts that there is no one today to speak of the departed inhabitants, he forgets himself and his companion. The latter seems intent on "fancy-play" (line 13), a phrase that might refer to conjectures about the lives of the former residents, ghost stories, or even poems such as the one produced here. Although the speaker keeps reassuring himself that they have all gone away, the sixth stanza hints they might somehow be an unappreciative audience upon whom the present company's skillful talk is wasted.

The building of a house on a hill suggests an inclination towards aesthetic appreciation of the landscape, a certain level of affluence (since the building materials must be hauled up to the site and its water must either be found there or pumped to it), or both. Part of our fascination with such a place is the visual discrepancy between whatever elegance and charm refined taste once brought to it and the tattered remnants that now greet the eye. Similarly, the window supported by the "sunken sill" (line 11) formerly brought light and perhaps a charming landscape filled with life into the home, but now it seems to offer a window into ruin and decay and hints at the grave. Perhaps the speaker is not troubled by the possibility that the house is haunted but by the visual reminders that his own home and even his own life are similarly destined to decay.

"THE HOUSE-TOP: A NIGHT PIECE"
HERMAN MELVILLE (1863)   The New York City riot of July 13–16, 1863, exposed the very worst elements of American society. What began as a protest against drafting soldiers for the Civil War soon escalated into a race riot in which more than 1,000 people were brutally murdered, perhaps revealing the ugliest face white racism had ever shown north of the Mason-Dixon line up to that point. HERMAN MELVILLE, a city resident at the time, here reveals his disappointment.

The poem begins with the heat of a sleepless, steamy night that "binds the brain," a metaphor that points towards the rioters' senseless acts of violence (line 2). It also brings to mind the tropics, and the speaker implicitly compares the oppression felt in woods infested by tigers "vexing their blood and making apt for revenge" (line 4) with that rising from the riots.

Nearby the "roofy desert" (line 5) appears as vacant as Libya (a North African country mostly situated in the Sahara. Melville never seems to want us to forget that he began his adult career as a traveler, but some readers may find his Asian tigers and African deserts a distraction from the nearby riots). From afar the "Atheist roar of riot" sounds like a muffled surf (line 8). To the west, "red" (murderous as well as colorful) Arson can be seen at two different locations. The ship and wharf rats have taken the town, and both "civil charms" (the benefits, such as freedom from fear, that ordinarily accrue from civilization) and the influence of the various churches ("priestly charms" that normally terrify hearts into unselfish behavior) dissolve like a dream (line 15). As the night progresses, Draco (a constellation shaped like a dragon, but also the name of the author of a very severe seventh century B.C. Athens law code) comes to restore order with artillery (and Union soldiers, fresh from the Battle of Gettysburg), "corroborating Calvin's creed" (transgressors receive very strict penalties like those facing sinners in Calvinism; line 21) and with measures like the "cynic tyrannies of honest kings" (who recognize the need to impose their sometimes seemingly cruel will in order to maintain peace).

The lawgiver came, delivered, and received the devout thanks of the town, but a "grimy slur" remains on the republic's faith in the natural goodness of the common man, who up to this point enjoyed the status of "Nature's Roman, never to be scourged" (line 27; ancient Roman law prevented the use of whips on its uncondemned, fully enfranchised citizens [for a biblical reference, see Acts 22:25]).

HOWE, JULIA WARD (1819–1910)   Julia
Ward was born into a world of wealth and privilege in

New York City on May 27, 1819, but dedicated a large portion of her life to social reform. The daughter of a banker, she received her education at the hands of private tutors and, in 1843, married Dr. Samuel Gridley Howe, the superintendent of an institute for the blind. The couple successfully parented their three daughters and a son and edited *The Commonwealth,* a Boston antislavery newspaper, for a short time in the early 1850s. Mrs. Howe's two unsuccessful dramas, *The World's Own* (1857) and *Hippolytus* (1858), followed. Throughout her life, she lectured and wrote extensively on progressive causes ranging from immigration and prison reform to women's suffrage and race relations. Her travel writings include *A Trip to Cuba* (1860) and *From the Oak to the Olive* (1868), her account of a pleasant trip to Europe. Her interest in gender issues led her to write *Sex and Education: A Reply to Dr. E. H. Clarke's "Sex in Education"* (1874) and *The Hermaphrodite,* a novel not published until 2004.

Although she published five books of poetry (*Passion Flowers* [1854], *Words for the Hour* [1856], *Later Lyrics* [1866], *From Sunset Ridge* [1898], and *At Sunset* [1910]), she is chiefly remembered by later generations for "The BATTLE HYMN OF THE REPUBLIC" (1862), her improvement on a pre-existing melody that subsequently came to represent all the Union's war aims in that conflict and, along with the Southern anthem of "Dixie," the entire Civil War. A deeply religious person, she tried to turn the notoriety she gained from that tune to good use in founding a peace group and attempting to create a Mother's Day (which was not celebrated at the time) devoted to antiwar sentiments.

After her husband died in 1876, Mrs. Howe published a memorial tribute and then continued with her active public life. She wrote a biography of the women's rights activist Margaret Fuller (1883) and, in 1884, served as director of the Women's Department at the World's Industrial and Cotton Centennial Exposition in New Orleans. Her interest in social reform led to her writing *Modern Society* in 1881. She died on October 17, 1910, in South Portsmouth, Rhode Island.

The most complete archive of her manuscripts and correspondence is stored as The Julia Ward Howe Papers at the Library of Congress. The Concord (Massachusetts) Free Public Library also holds a few Howe letters and pictures. The house she shared with her husband on Chestnut Street in Boston has gained National Historic Landmark status but is not open to the public.

BIBLIOGRAPHY

Grant, Mary Hetherington. *Private Person: An Account of the Life of Julia Ward Howe from 1819–1868.* Brooklyn, N.Y.: Carlson Publishing, 1994.

Hall, Florence Howe. *Julia Ward Howe and the Women Suffrage Movement.* Boston: D. Estes, 1913; New York: Arno Press, 1969.

Howe, Julia Ward. *Reminiscences.* Boston and New York: Houghton, Mifflin, 1900.

Williams, Gary. *Hungry Heart: The Literary Emergence of Julia Ward Howe.* Amherst: University of Massachusetts Press, 1999.

"HOW MANY TIMES THESE LOW FEET STAGGERED" EMILY DICKINSON (1890)

Human bodies tend to become extremely rigid with rigor mortis a few hours after death and even more so after morticians have embalmed them. In this poem the speaker examines the body of a housewife; her sympathetic touch and her desire to hear the woman's voice again indicate that they had been fairly close.

In an age with few labor-saving devices available in the household, the speaker's first memory is how hard the woman worked. Not only did she sometimes stagger under the load (line 1), but her forehead was often hot from the exertion (line 5). EMILY DICKINSON was wonderfully prescient; since the poem was written before the Civil War, she could not have drawn on the science fiction of the 20th century or the robotics of the 21st century for her striking, original conception of a body of steel in the first stanza. Without life, the cadaver seems as metallic and lifeless as so much steel, a manufactured material much valued for its tensile strength and just on the verge of revolutionizing American transportation and architecture when the poem was written.

Since the poet takes such an unflinching look at death, the present author can do no less. The cadaver's lips might seem "soldered," a term suggesting a metal seal, because with age one's lips can shrivel, but in modern mortuary practice they are more commonly sewn together. Joining two strips of metal together with a "rivet" (line 3) would enable them to open at the other end like a humanoid robot's jaws, but the speaker was more likely thinking of death as a rivet. Like industrial rivets strong enough to hold bridges together, death has permanently sealed her lips. To a furniture maker, "hasps of steel" (line 4) refers to a simple plate with a slot in it that could join two parts of a chest by fitting over a staple or U-clamp through which a lock or simple latch rod could then be secured. The poet probably chose "hasps" because its structure forces a speaker to almost whisper its final three consonants, and may have punned on "steel" as "still" to further emphasize the quiet of the dead.

In the second stanza the speaker describes the body more tenderly, suggesting that the internal audience should stroke the forehead and lift the hair of the deceased "if you care" for them (line 6). If you permit yourself to hold her hand one last time, you will find her fingers have become like adamant, a stone so hard it was long thought impenetrable. The speaker was apparently on such intimate terms with her that she would often sew or undertake some other domestic task in her presence; it strikes her as unusual to see no thimble on her sewing fingers (line 8).

Will the dead housewife be missed? Already the flies buzz at the window, when formerly they would have been chased from the house. The sun now shines in bravely, whereas before it would have probably been curtained off, and the "freckled pane" of the window (line 10) would have been cleaned. Now a cobweb swings from the ceiling fearlessly because she is no longer on her guard against them. Like a domestic goddess, in life she maintained her house like a fortress against such unpleasantness. Now only death has made her "indolent" (line 12) to the point where she does not address such intrusions. That she now lies in daisies, a flower commonly associated with innocence, suggests that she as strictly maintained her morality as she had her spotless household.

"THE HUMBLE-BEE" RALPH WALDO EMERSON (1847)   This poem presented the challenge of taking a subject (now more commonly known as the bumblebee) with which the external audience was exceedingly familiar and upon which RALPH WALDO

EMERSON had little new information to share with his contemporaries. Dispensing with the usual 19th-century approach of closely describing the insect in the opening stanza, the poet began by almost immediately emphasizing its significance to him. Note how the easy rhyme and hopscotch (as in a rhythm suitable for a game of hopscotch or jump rope) trochee establish the light tone of the verse in the opening couplet:

> "Burly, dozing humble-bee,
> Where thou art is clime for me."

Similarly easy is the poet's license in substituting "Porto Rique" for Puerto Rico for the sake of rhyming it with "seek" (lines 3–4). Had the poem appeared anonymously, the reader might suspect these lines to be the product of an untrained or folk artist, or a child, and Emerson's point may be that the blocky bees have the ability to instill a childlike wonder even in sophisticated adults. He maintains that mood throughout the first five lines by pledging to follow "thee alone" (thus personifying the insect to the extent that he wants to develop a personal relationship with it); the line conveys the reverie that prompts small children to focus their complete attention on such a novel insect because of its large size (the most common American species reaches nearly an inch, or 25.4 cm., in length).

In the sixth line he begins a more adult description of the animal; his conception of the "animated torrid zone" implies knowledge beyond that of a small child. "Zigzag" and "waving lines" (lines 7–8) might refer to either its bands of colorful hairs or its erratic flight. He would have the bee keep nearer this hearer (a pleasing internal rhyme) for its "singing over shrubs and vines" (a phrase that may convey a sense of its departing speed as well as suggesting its happiness in its habitat).

He salutes the "Epicurean (an adherent to the philosophy that pleasure is the highest good, or more simply, a pleasure-seeker; line 16) of June" as a sailor of the atmosphere and swimmer through the air. He would have it wait until he comes close enough to hear its hum, since everything seems painful ("a martyrdom") without (that exquisite pleasure; line 19). That "breezy bass" (line 30) is especially noticeable when it displaces the green silence of May.

By the fourth stanza, the year has progressed to midsummer, and instead of being an important harbinger of spring, the bee now seems a "petted crone" (a figure rather more tolerated than necessary, which seems to have outlived its usefulness; line 32). Now it drowsily enlivens banks of flowers and tells of "gulfs of sweetness" that could be found (among the wildflowers) in "the Indian wildernesses" (the speaker's nostalgia for really wild nature [which had to be actively sought in the eastern Massachusetts of 1847] probably informed his interpretation of the bee's message). The bee's hum also conveyed immortal leisure, cheer, birdlike pleasure, and Syrian peace (a reference to the 1840 intervention of the great European powers to prevent further war [and by their calculations, the solidification of power in the hands of a militant Egyptian, Muhammed Ali] in the Middle East. For an optimist like Emerson, such cooperation among nations represented a hopeful sign for lasting world peace).

The bee, with his attention focused on flowers (the poet thoughtfully provides a list of them in the fifth stanza), had never seen anything unsavory or unclean. This "yellow-breeched philosopher" (line 52) feasts only on the fair and sweet, mocks at fate and care, leaves the chaff and takes the wheat (eats only the most nutritious part of a plant, a sign that it is a good judge of worth; line 57).

When fierce winter hits, the bee hibernates ("slumbers deep"). By sleeping through the want (of food) and woe that may torture humans, the bee's hibernation makes such suffering ridiculous (as far as it is concerned).

"THE HURRICANE" PHILIP FRENEAU (1785)

PHILIP FRENEAU's poem suggests the train of thought that might occur to a passenger on a sailing vessel in a hurricane. Unfortunately, the speaker's state of mind does not permit him to imaginatively embrace the storm or create vivid images of the barque's plight in the reader's mind. Instead, he contrasts his own predicament with that of the happy man safe at home. Notice how the verb "trims" (line 2) bridges the gap between the two worlds; it is unusual when applied to a landsman's stirring of a fire but perfectly idiomatic aboard a ship, where sails are routinely trimmed (partially rolled up

and secured with ropes or lines) to optimize their sailing advantage or to prevent damage should the winds prove too forceful. Both men might hear the tempest's roar, which leads the speaker to think of the wind losing its strength in groves of trees. Unfortunately, the storm reminds him that there are no trees to soften the wind where he is, and he is again aware of the precariousness of his situation.

As if it were too painful to again consider the man safe ashore, he thinks of birds, a squirrel, and even wolves, all of which would be safely ensconced in appropriate shelters. All are blessed except for the wretched company in which the speaker finds himself, who are destined to remain strangers to repose because the unsettled ocean allows no rest (lines 11–12).

As darkness overtakes them, the speaker has the morbid thought that he may have seen the sun for the last time. Instead of returning to their homes, his shipmates will sleep on coral beds beneath the waves, "unpitied" (line 18) since no one will witness their drowning. They will go where no charts, compass, or pilot can guide them. What new Columbus could lead that voyage?

He notices that as death and darkness surround them in the raging tempest, he hears no friendly voice or words of comfort. He realizes that there can be no friendship or comfort on such a raging sea. The pilots have become too frightened to steer the vessel, so she gropes along "as mountains burst on either side" (line 34). He is convinced that all will be lost since the crew is no longer applying its skill. The science that led to the precise construction of the vessel and charted its course must also fall before the fury of the storm.

"HUSWIFERY" EDWARD TAYLOR (c. 1683?)

While "husbandry," the management of animals for agricultural profit, was chiefly a masculine pursuit in early colonial America, the "huswifery" of the title refers to the predominately female measures of domestic economy by which a woman could keep her family fed and clothed.

Few objects have so thoroughly come to represent colonial America in the modern mind as the spinning wheel, the labor-intensive means by which homegrown fibers from flax or sheep's wool were spun into the threads and yarns that could be fashioned into clothing. The chief challenge of this widely anthologized poem results from the speaker's dual roles as an individual Christian soul and as a minister engrossed in God's service. His request for the Lord to "make me . . . Thy spinning wheel complete" (line 1) is purposely ambiguous. He could either be asking for a complete spinning wheel or to be made into one; it all depends on whether the "me" in the opening phrase is read as a direct or indirect object. The second line appears to clarify the matter by asking Him to make the Holy Word into the speaker's distaff, usage that makes the speaker the recipient and not the object of the Lord's making/remaking, but lines 3–6 feature aspects of the speaker (his "affections" [or religious sentiment], soul, and conversation) as the things to be used. The sixth line indicates that when the process has been completed, the speaker will be as ready for service as a finished spinning wheel.

The second stanza follows the completed threads from the spinning wheel through the loom on which the fabric will be fashioned in accordance with God's will. It will be softened and cleansed before being dyed "with heavenly colors" and adorned with sparkling "flowers of paradise" (lines 11–12). If this seems out of keeping with the stereotypical Puritan preference for drab clothing, remember that the poem refers to God's handiwork and not man's. In one sense, the redeemed man can be viewed as one of the sparkling flowers of paradise since he descended from Adam and Eve and has been restored to purity by divine choice.

The third stanza asks God to clothe all aspects of the speaker's personality with the divinely rendered cloth so that his ways will be glorious and will glorify God. At the same time, God will see from such garments that he is clothed "in holy robes for glory" (line 18).

In addition to its insights into the Puritan worldview, the poem is valuable for preserving the terminology of the spinning wheel and weaving processes of colonial America. It also lists the components of the human personality as they were viewed at the time: "understanding" (or intelligence), will, affections, judgment, conscience, and memory" (lines 13–14), all of which could be shaped by God if a Puritan were as completely open to that possibility as the speaker is in

this poem. As a minister, EDWARD TAYLOR was anxious to serve God's will in shaping the souls of other people (serving like a spinning wheel and loom through which God could shape the fabric of their lives according to His will). The speaker also hopes that by such good service he was acting in accordance with God's design and therefore would be welcome in His sight.

"HYMN OF THE CITY" WILLIAM CULLEN BRYANT (1830)

How can you tell when you are reading a satire instead of a straightforward poem? One clue in the present case is that throughout the rest of his work, WILLIAM CULLEN BRYANT sings of the virtues of the wilderness. He was more likely to commune with God during one of his frequent forays into wild nature than to discover His word in an urban environment, but at first glance the opening lines of this poem show that he was at least able to admit the possibility that God could also reach someone there. This attempt to make that statement in verse seems rather half-hearted, however. The syntax of the opening stanza is so convoluted that its meaning (solitude, natural landscapes, and open water are not necessary to commune with heaven, to see God, or to hear His voice) can be lost.

In the second stanza the speaker finds himself in a crowded city and, despite noise and congestion so bad that it chokes the streets, he can discover evidence ("His steps," line 8) of the Almighty. Notice his dismissal of tall buildings as "proud piles" (line 12) built by man, pejorative language that Bryant would never use for a natural structure of similar height elsewhere in his poetry.

In the third stanza the speaker elaborates on the impediments that keep city dwellers from realizing the majesty of God that manifests itself so freely in nature. Despite his assurances, very little of the golden sunshine will be able to "light their inner homes" (line 15), nor will the inhabitants be able to see the unbounded skies, the ocean's plenty, or the intriguing objects found on the shores. Although they will not be able to hear the sea or the rain, the next stanza assures them that the Holy Spirit can also be heard in the incessant voices and footsteps of the restless mass of humanity.

Only when the "hour of rest" comes (line 25; since the speaker describes the street noise as incessant throughout the poem, the phrase could easily be taken as a euphemism for either sleep or death) does the city denizen enjoy the same quiet moment that his more adventurous brethren might experience in a mid-ocean calm. The speaker asserts that such a moment "breathes of Him" (line 29) who takes care of the city while it sleeps, but when he calls the city "vast and helpless" (line 30) he implies that it will offer no help to one seeking God.

"HYMN SUNG AT THE COMPLETION OF THE CONCORD MONUMENT, APRIL 19, 1836" RALPH WALDO EMERSON (1836) RALPH WALDO EMERSON intended this poem for the 60th anniversary of the battles of Lexington and Concord, which marked the beginning of continuous hostilities in the Revolutionary War. In 1775, units of the British Army had marched all night from Boston in hopes of capturing military supplies and the most vocal leaders of the growing American independence movement. After a short chaotic skirmish at Lexington in which several colonists were killed, they marched on to Concord and began searching for contraband. Alarmed by the growing numbers of hostile militia forming up around them, a small detachment of soldiers began tearing up the bridge to cut the militiamen off from the town. The "shot heard round the world" (line 4) was fired to stop them.

In the second stanza, the speaker claims that time had already silenced the participants on both sides and swept the old bridge down the stream. The term "conqueror" in line 5 refers to the colonial militias, which decimated and nearly cut off the retreating army until a relief column saved it much closer to Boston.

The third stanza notes that even the present generation will perish, but on that day they placed a "votive" (line 10; this religious term suggests a wish or request delivered in a prayer) stone. Their wish is that memory will "redeem" (restore the reputation of) the participants in the battle even after their own sons are dead.

The fourth stanza appeals to the spirit that emboldened the heroes who faced death in order to "leave their children free" (line 14). The spirit should "bid" (command) time and nature to spare the monument

("the shaft" of line 16) raised in honor of the combatants and the spirit of independence.

Today this poem is inscribed on a monument overlooking the restored bridge in a beautifully maintained park that seems a fitting birthplace for American liberty.

"AN HYMN TO THE EVENING" PHILLIS WHEATLEY (1773) This less interesting companion piece to "An HYMN TO THE MORNING" reaffirms PHYLLIS WHEATLEY's Christian beliefs. As soon as the sun left the shore of the Atlantic Ocean (the "eastern main" for a New Englander like Wheatley), a thunderstorm shook the heavens. While she admires the majestic grandeur of the spectacle, she studiously avoids references to the pagan myths with which the ancients once sought to explain them. When the west wind (pointedly called a zephyr instead of Zephyrus, the Roman god from whose name the common noun is derived) brings the odors of spring, she preempts any personification by stating that this incense was exhaled from its wing (lines 3–4). Similarly, she chose the word *purl* to convey the sound of the streams (line five) instead of a word like *babble,* which is also used to describe human noises. Although the birds resume their music, she provides no hint of any supernatural force in the evening woods.

The sunset brings to mind the beauteous dyes used to color fabrics, and she especially admires the deepest red in the west. Instead of recalling equally colorful myths, however, she calls for living in such a way that virtue glows in each man's breast so that each becomes a temple of God on earth (lines 9–10).

If she were writing in prose, Wheatley would not have left the modifier dangling in line 11. She apparently meant that the good Christian should retire for the evening filled with praise of God, personified as both the giver of light and the one who lowers the sable curtains of night. Lines 13–14 read best as a prayer for placid slumbers for weary minds and for their being made more heavenly and refined (and therefore less objectionable to God), benefits extended to those who follow the advice advanced in the first two lines of the stanza.

Lines 15 and 16 are remarkable for their emphasis upon work. Following the program outlined in this stanza lets "the labors of the day" begin more purely. Note that the speaker seems more concerned about labors than about laborers; she would have the former more guarded from sinful snares even though the latter would seem at greatest risk. In defense of the poet, it could be argued that the contorted syntax of these lines is in keeping with the transcendent mysteries they are meant to convey.

Having thus re-emphasized her Christian beliefs, the speaker can indulge in personification and mythology: like a king, night seals her eyes with its scepter, and like the birds mentioned in the first stanza, she will stop singing until Aurora (the Roman name for the goddess of the dawn) rises.

"AN HYMN TO THE MORNING" PHILLIS WHEATLEY (1773)

This atypical poem provides a rare glimpse at the humor of PHYLLIS WHEATLEY, a poet whose aims were generally profoundly serious. The fun begins with an invocation of the muses that was hardly calculated to win their favor. Instead of the lengthy praise for the most appropriate of the nine, followed by a plea for her aid that one often finds in more conventional poems, the mood of this light verse is imperative. The muses are commanded to attend, assist, and refine her work, and the poet's more specific instruction reduces them to the manual labor of pouring the notes along (line 3) as if they were mere water bearers at a bath. When she finally does get around to calling on a specific muse, it is Calliope (in line 13), the muse of book-length epic poetry, who probably would have been bewildered if not angered at being summoned for such relatively frivolous day work. The less famous Polyhymnia (muse of songs for deities) or Euterpe (for lyric poetry) would have been more appropriate choices. Wheatley even inserts a pun in the second line; pairing "strains" so closely with "labors" insists on a physical definition of the term, while the general context of the stanza favors an aesthetic reading (strains are musical or poetic passages).

The reason for haste evident in the speaker's curt commands is given in the fourth line: the arrival of dawn (here identified as Aurora, the Roman goddess of that phenomenon) demands a song. In the second stanza the speaker changes her tune, respectfully hailing Aurora while admiring "all the thousand dyes" (line 5) that color the sunrise. Her salutary effects are immediately evident; first a gentle breeze brings motion to the leaves, and then the birds begin singing their "harmonious lays" (line 9), looking around and shaking their plumage.

As if to demonstrate how little stock the poet places in the deities of classical myth, she all but forgets Aurora in the third stanza in order to seek shelter from the heat in the "groves" (line 11; note how the poet's elevated diction maintains contact with the ancient myths even as she takes unrelated actions). She directs Calliope to her sacred lyre, not to inspire the poet's work but evidently more for her personal pleasure. Similarly, the other muses are to be employed at fanning the pleasing fire; what is important is the effect the bowers, gales, and colorful skies are having in the poet's bosom (a term used by both genders in the 18th century in the same way that a modern speaker would say "in my heart").

The arrival of the "illustrious king of day" (Apollo, the sun god) signals the end of the dawn in line 17. Wheatley drops in another pun, but to good purpose: The "shades" driven away by the sun of the present day are both the dark shadows so prevalent at dawn and the inconsequential ghosts of all the supernatural beings of the pagan myths she was so recently entertaining for the reader's amusement. Although the sun is personified in the last stanza, it is clearly the plain heat of day that forces the poet to conclude. She dismisses her efforts as "abortive" (line 20) not only in reference to the sudden and complete termination of the song, but perhaps also as a further indication of her knowledge that such paeans hold no supernatural power.

I

"ICHABOD" JOHN GREENLEAF WHITTIER (1850)

Daniel Webster was renowned as one of the best orators in the United States. As a five-term congressman, four-term senator, and secretary of state for four years, he was a consistent voice for increasing federal power. By 1850, antislavery sentiment in the North had reached the point where many people preferred even secession from the union to the expansion of slavery into additional states and territories. Great statesman that he was, Webster used his talent and immense influence to gain political support for a series of compromises that preserved the union. Unfortunately, these included the Fugitive Slave Law of 1850, which forced northern law enforcement officials to assist in the apprehension and return of runaway slaves. This poem demonstrates the level of disgust felt by many New Englanders for the man who had for almost 40 years so powerfully represented their interests on the national stage.

The central image of JOHN GREENLEAF WHITTIER's poem is the drumming out of an individual from amid the ranks of angels. He has lately grown so repugnant that the speaker will not even mention his proper name but calls him *Ichabod* ("Inglorious" in Hebrew) in recognition of his fallen state. Unlike the saints and angels depicted in early Christian iconography, Ichabod has lost the radiant aura that once suggested his glory.

The speaker of the poem ostensibly defends Ichabod from those who would torment him by reminding them that the devil (the "Tempter" of line 5) has a snare for each of them. Instead of their scorn, Ichabod deserves their pity. The speaker would prefer silence (the word "dumb" in line 9 refers to an inability to speak) to the outbursts of "passion's stormy rage," which seems the more natural reaction when one who "might have lighted up and led his age" (lines 10–11) instead falls into benighted darkness. Would-be scorners should instead take their cue from the angels, who would weep over a peer's "fiend-goaded" descent "from hope and heaven" (lines 13–16), and not brand his "dim, dishonored brow" with deeper shame (line 19).

In advocating for a long lament "from sea to lake" in line 22, the speaker lags behind the time if he meant Lake Superior, the westernmost of the Great Lakes, because no fewer than four states were further west. In fact, California's admission to the Union in 1850 as a free state was one of the progressive results of the Compromise of 1850, which included the Fugitive Slave Law. The line may refer to Lake Ontario, however; as the easternmost of the Great Lakes, it would more closely represent the end of the region in greatest agreement with the New England views of the speaker.

Probably taking his cue from *Paradise Lost,* the famous epic by the British poet John Milton, Whittier pictures Ichabod as a fallen angel in chains. Since love and honor have been lost, only power remains, and Satanic pride. Ichabod, the speaker claims, has lost his soul (line 30). He counsels reverence for the old days, when Ichabod's fame still lived, and advocates walking backward to avoid having one's eye see this fallen leader and his current shame.

"I DIED FOR BEAUTY—BUT WAS SCARCE" EMILY DICKINSON (1862)

The speaker of this poem, newly deceased at the time of the encounter she is recalling, may be having a bit of fun with "Ode to a Grecian Urn." The 1819 poem, penned by the British poet John Keats, describes an exquisitely carved ancient vase and concludes, famously if rather cryptically, that

> "Beauty is truth, truth beauty,—that is all
> Ye know on earth, and all ye need to know."

How might one die for beauty? At the time EMILY DICKINSON's poem appeared, eating disorders were not the problem they would become a century later, and plastic surgeries were unknown. The speaker provides no clue, but the new occupant of the adjacent grave recalls the Keats equation (line 7) and recognizes their kinship. They evidently talked for a long time, not just until the moss covered their lips but until it also covered up the names on their tombstones. They made strange bedfellows; his rustic, ungrammatical, and perhaps biblical speech seems especially awkward surrounded by the language of one who may have lived for beauty as well as died for it.

Perhaps the Keats equation provides a clue to the poem's meaning. In 1862, many soldiers were dying in the Civil War for what each side thought was the truth. Dickinson, largely silent about the war in her other poems, refused to be swept up by either cause, and she provides no suggestion that the young man's reason for dying was more noble than the speaker's. The humor of this poem and its ultimate meaning may lie in the application of a lighthearted tone to its macabre subject.

Since Dickinson believed in the immortality of the soul, this poem supplies further evidence that the corruption of the flesh held little terror for her. It may also dramatize her hope that her dedication to poetry will count as much toward her salvation as if it had been devotion to a religious faith—the "truth" in the eyes of a true believer—and that part of her reward will be the opportunity for lengthy discourse with a wide range of people whom she was unable to meet during her life.

"I DREADED THAT FIRST ROBIN, SO" EMILY DICKINSON (published 1891)

Those things which previously brought cheer to one's life can be freighted with an entirely new set of associations for someone in mourning. While EMILY DICKINSON's poem is remarkable for its perversion of the traditionally celebrated harbingers of spring into objects of dread and for its multiple layers of meaning, the poet's art is equally evident in her buildup of the suspense regarding the speaker's situation.

The first stanza introduces the speaker's morbid subjectivity; she views a robin not only as an object of dread (line 1) but even as an agent of actual injury (since he brings pain; line 4). Of more importance than the bird is her changing relationship with her pain; although the robin could be "mastered" (line 2), she could not claim such a victory over her pain or even directly approach it. Instead, she has had to look into the future (to the day of the first robin's return) for a time when she could very tentatively risk feeling anything again. She constantly has to monitor her progress and dares not name her loss for fear of being overwhelmed by her grief.

Having passed the first tests (survival until spring and reconnection with her emotions), she finds that she can become accustomed to the robin although "he still hurts a little bit" (line 4). She may have been dreading his return because the departed had a special affinity for that season or simply because it singled the passage of time into that portion of her life marked by the absence of the loved one.

The second stanza is the most challenging of the poem because it deals so abstractly with her coping strategy. Her main hope was to last until the "first Shout got by" (line 6); the complex phrasing pleasingly combines the robin's role as herald of spring (since heralds used to deliver public notices at full voice before the advent of more effective means of communication) with the more general expression of elation a New Englander might use to announce the arrival of spring after a typically arduous winter. Less specifically, the line may indicate an emotional state so fragile that she thought the first shout (an unexpected shock to her system) might completely shatter her.

It is perhaps a sign of how detached from life the speaker had become that she speaks of "all the pianos in the woods" (line 7). The phrase evokes all the bird songs and other sounds of life that have returned with spring, but it also suggests how alien the sounds of normal gaiety have been in the deep woods of her despondency. As a further indication of her alienation, note her use of "mangle" in the next line. The image is from the industrial revolution that swept many Americans into completely artificial environments; a few lost limbs to the powerful new machines. That she would think of a piano in this connection demonstrates the extraordinary imagination of the poet and an additional incongruity in the speaker's perceptions. The latter's fears are unreasonable on the physical level, but emotionally, the image makes perfect sense.

Daffodils are among the first of the popularly cultivated flowers to bloom each year, and it is a sign of the speaker's return to normalcy that she is beginning to think in terms of fashion. Although her emotional state is still shaky (she worries about being "pierced" by the flower's yellow gown in line 11), that fact that she is cognizant of the contrast between the bright colors and the black mourning clothes worn as tokens of bereavement in her century suggests that she is continuing to respond to external stimuli.

In the fourth stanza the speaker remembers having wished for the grass (perhaps over the grave?) to have hurried so that he (the tall grass or the deceased?) would be too tall to look at her. The distorted sense of her person, miniaturized almost to oblivion in this image, reveals how vulnerable she felt at that time.

The birds and the bees have a special figurative role in a poem about how life reasserts itself following a great loss. The speaker wished the bees would stay in their own "dim countries" (line 19) and wondered what word they could have for her. Perhaps they represent a need to live an active fruitful life, a message she was incapable of understanding at the time.

By the sixth stanza, she perceives that all the flora and fauna have returned and that her mourning has reached the point where it almost seems a ridiculous pose. Whereas she formerly may have felt as bad as the

"Queen of Calvary" (line 24), the saddest of women on that saddest of Christian days when the Savior was crucified, flirting with such a pompous title provides her with the (nearly comic) perspective needed to look beyond her recent misery.

The last stanza may contain a topical as well as a timeless reference. The thought carried over from the previous stanza is that each creature and flower salutes her "as he goes," a phrase that suggests the passage of still more time and additional seasons. By then her mourning plumes seem childish (line 26), and she lifts them in acknowledgment of their "unthinking drums." Figuratively, she is again acting in accordance with nature's rhythms.

Because this poem was probably written in 1862, the second year of the Civil War, the last stanza may refer to the volunteer soldiers (conscripts were added later) of the Union Army who marched through Amherst and other northern towns on their way to war. That so many young men were sacrificing themselves provided the mourner with yet another perspective; she can only ineffectually lift what now seem the childish plumes of bereavement to acknowledge "their unthinking drums" (line 28), but she understands better than most people the suffering that the deaths of so many of them will entail. The progress of the war through its various seasons and landscapes will provide still more ways that the speaker will be distanced from what had been a staggering bereavement.

"I DWELL IN POSSIBILITY" EMILY DICKINSON (published 1929)

In its spirit and imagery, this poem reads more like the nature-worshipping WILLIAM CULLEN BRYANT than the supposedly closeted EMILY DICKINSON. Perhaps in answer to Bryant's celebration of the freedom and inspiration he found in the primitive forests of his day, Dickinson substituted "Possibility" as the focal point of her existence. Since this rather nondescript term is described as a fairer house than prose (line 2), it is tempting to think that she was referring to poetry.

With its occasionally uneven line lengths, judicious use of white space between stanzas and wide margins, poetry certainly looks more airy (an advantage like having more windows; line 3) than prose. The claim of superior doors (line 4) might be based on the opportunity poets have of presenting their ideas in the most striking manner. Individual poems can be set off like precious jewels, and their relative brevity generally allows for more numerous entries per volume than prose works of the same overall length.

In the second stanza, however, it becomes clear that "Possibility" is closer to the promise of heaven than it is to even "poetry." The comparison of the dwelling's rooms to Cedars "impregnable of Eye," suggests a miracle of biblical proportions. The trees are repeatedly praised in the Bible not only for their great height and strength (Psalms 29:5, for example, uses the breaking of the great cedars as a test of the Lord's strength) but even for having been planted by God (Psalms 104:16–17). The sky forms a "gambrel" roof (line 8) probably because overhead it can hardly be said to slope at all, but the natural obstacles closer to the horizon line can seem like the steeper lower section of such an "Everlasting" roof. The superior architectural features of her dwelling as pointed out in the first stanza are a result of the divine planning that went into them.

Her anticipation of the "fairest" visitors (line 9) probably implies the worthiest souls as well as the most attractive. Her occupation would be spreading her "narrow hands" (limited like everything else on this earth) to gather Paradise.

Everyone probably has a unique vision of her personal heaven, and the opportunity to safely embrace the open spaces celebrated in this poem probably were tremendously exciting to someone like Dickinson, who by all accounts led a rather sequestered, domestic life.

"I FELT A FUNERAL, IN MY BRAIN"

EMILY DICKINSON (1862)   Her many poems about death reveal how deeply EMILY DICKINSON would feel the loss of each of the very few loved ones in her life. In this poem the speaker so values such a connection that a funeral service, real or imagined, is almost unbearable. Dickinson's use of onomatopoeia (words that mimic the sounds they represent) plays a key role in making the experience as nearly painful for the reader as it would be for her, and her masterful laying of ambiguity atop ambiguity can be as discombobulating for the reader as it is for the speaker.

The opening line introduces the subject of the poem, the speaker's depression. The funeral may actually have occurred (in which case s/he is sharing her feelings on that occasion), or she may be using a funeral as a metaphor to help the reader share her feelings; the phrase "in my brain" makes either situation plausible. The repetition of the onomatopoeic word "treading" (line 3) hits the ear like a heavy step on a hardwood floor just as the repeated "beating" (line 7) conveys the sound of a drum (or a heartbeat; all subsequent American poets owe a tremendous debt to EDGAR ALLAN POE not only for his pioneering use of the same devices but also for his explorations of subjective, often crazed, mental states). Such sounds intrude on the speaker's consciousness until "it seemed" (everything is kept highly conditional and subjective in this poem) that "sense was breaking through" (line 4). The likely meanings of that last phrase include (a) that an external stimulus (a sound) was registering in her brain; (b) that she was becoming rational again (things were beginning to make sense); or (c) that her hold on reality was disintegrating (like the plank in line 17).

The second stanza finds everyone seated, and the service may or may not have been beneficial for the speaker. It is described as dull and repetitious (like a drum beating), but the numbing it brings to her mind (line 8) might be better than her anguish. From the moment she heard them lift a box (presumably a coffin; line 9), the line separating external stimuli from the inner workings of her mind is hopelessly blurred. They "creak" across her soul in their boots of lead (line 11; that element was probably chosen to stress the weight of their steps, but it may also hint at the relative insensitivity of the people who wear them, since pure lead is a relatively stable, inert element), and then space (and not the church bells) begins to toll.

By the fourth stanza her syntax is as shaky as her reasoning, but the sense of it seems to be that the bells were so loud that the heavens seemed a bell (line 13), and that everything else (summed up as "Being") seemed an ear except for the speaker and Silence, a strange race finding itself (or "themselves," if the speaker means to group herself with Silence) wrecked and solitary.

At that point a "Plank in Reason" broke from the strain (line 17). The speaker fell (like a coffin into a grave) and continued falling, hitting "a World at every plunge" (line 19); if she has descended into madness the various Worlds might refer to her attempts to fashion a complete personality from various parts of her fragmented psyche, or perhaps her succession of altered mental states makes the world seem continually alien. The last line indicates a total breakdown in which she has "finished knowing."

Alternatively, if one assumes that the funeral really happened and that the poem represents the altered sensations experienced by someone in the deepest throes of bereavement, the poem may reveal a speaker so emotionally involved with the deceased that she continued identifying with him/her to the point where all the sensory input from this world seems an unwanted intrusion. Mentally she remains with him even into the grave, then imagines the various alternative worlds he might inhabit until (a) she realized that she could travel no further with him, or (b) she realized that everything ended at the grave. Either way, she has effectively bid good-bye to ("finished knowing") her former friend.

Yet a third interpretation would have her mentally staging a funeral for someone she loved who was no longer available. She is scarcely sensible of the people still around her until she realizes that she has only been rationalizing her dream of reuniting with him. With this "Plank of Reason" broken, she can then purge herself of the hopes and memories they shared (the "different worlds") and finally pronounce herself finished with him.

"I HEARD A FLY BUZZ—WHEN I DIED"

EMILY DICKINSON (published 1896) The startling premise of EMILY DICKINSON's opening line will not trouble those who believe that one's personality makes up a large part of the soul or is determined by it; thus the immortality promised the soul by church authority and tradition would extend to the personality and perhaps the memory as well. Nor will it bother those readers who believe that the major aim of poetry (and the other arts) is not to depict reality with photographic precision but to engage the reader's intellect and/or emotion. The tools at a poet's disposal to achieve this goal include an omniscient point of view that can extend, even as it does here, to the last instant of consciousness before death and to contact with a departed soul.

The speaker recalls hearing a fly buzz at the precise moment of her death. The room had become still, like a sudden lull in a storm (a metaphor that suggests a brief respite from the physical pain of dying as well as a view of death as a lull between two periods of activity, the life and the afterlife). That she is surrounded by friends and/or close family is apparent because of their having no moisture left for their tears and by her ability to make eye contact with them. Their empathy with the speaker is such that they gathered firm breaths for the "last Onset" (line 7; the term can refer to the beginning of the final throes of her suffering, or the last time ever that she will change, by becoming an immortal soul unfettered by the human body) "When the King be witnessed" (lines 7–8). This is an interesting clause because it may be either a minor oath (that reveals the speaker's exasperation when she recollects what happened next even as it serves as a promise that she will tell the truth) or a euphemism for dying (perhaps a derivative of the more common euphemism of "going to meet one's maker").

The speaker had, as they say, put her affairs in order (finally giving away her keepsakes [tangible reminders of her love of this life and the memories she treasured] and signing away the rest of her possessions) save for a small oversight, a glitch that permitted a fly not only to come into the house but to make its way to that very room ("interposed" [line 12] is a polite way of saying "butted in").

The last stanza turns Dickinson's powers of nature observation onto a fly, reduced to its essence as a "blue, uncertain, stumbling buzz" (line 13). Then "the Windows failed" (the speaker lost her sight, but since the phrase recalls the proverb that "the eyes are the windows to the soul," the poet delivers a euphemism for death that stresses the speaker's inability to communicate with the living, who may also have held out the faint hope of receiving some intelligence information about the afterlife based on what they saw or heard at the moment ["when the King be witnessed"] of the speaker's passing).

The speaker's final comment, "I could not see to see" (line 16) would seem to suggest that there is no afterlife, a rather hopeless final realization that she will never see (or live) again. However, since we have it on the speaker's authority that she is talking to us from beyond the grave, the entire poem argues for an afterlife.

Of course the fly is a troublesome image, as it suggests that the speaker may not have kept her house in the perfect order that her mourners probably thought. Could it symbolize some small sin that nevertheless keeps her from seeing "the King"? Probably not; the calmness of her conversational tone is not what one would expect from a speaker in the grips of eternal punishment. The obvious discomfort of the family and/ or friends gathered around her deathbed suggests that she lived very well, and her focus on the fly suggests that she was not the sort of person who would tolerate such disorder (or sin, if you will) as it represents. She seems more amused by it than otherwise; her faith had long since instructed her on the corruptibility of our flesh and the transience of this bodily existence. Some readers may squirm at the prominence of the fly and his apparent proximity to the dying speaker's eye, but the soul may have no concern for the body once it passes.

"I HEAR IT WAS CHARGED AGAINST ME" WALT WHITMAN (1891)

This poem answers those who were too threatened by WALT WHITMAN to explain exactly how his ideas represented a challenge to such institutions as organized religion (he preferred long solitary walks that allowed him to commune with nature) and the family (as if even the greatest poetry in the world could influence an individual's sexual orientation or dissuade many people from entering the marital relationships upon which American society was based). Instead of defending his "choices," however, this poem attacks the imprecision of the attackers' language by asking what Whitman has in common with institutions.

Instead of destroying existing institutions, Whitman asserts that he will establish a new institution "in the Manhatta" (wherever his message is accepted) in every city, fields, and woods, and in every "keel that dents the water" (a colorful description of the impact made by the bottom of a boat; line 5): the "dear love of comrades" (Whitman's code words for the fullest possible relationships of same-sex partners; line 7). Unlike other institutions, his institution will lack edifices, rules, and trustees (line 6).

"I KNOW THAT HE EXISTS" EMILY DICKINSON (1891)

EMILY DICKINSON's poem begins with a profession of the speaker's faith in God despite her inability to see Him. Although she has no doubt as to His existence, she is angry because this lack of tangible proof seems a mean trick on the human race that has horrendous repercussions.

This reminds her of the child's game of hide-and-seek; somewhere, waiting in silence so as not to betray His position, God has hidden His "rare" life from "gross" (disgusting, but also "unrefined," a term applied to those who have not been made ready for His presence) human eyes.

Although this may seem harmless fun, requiring only an instant's preparation and lasting only that long, the speaker calls this a "fond" (meaning "affectionate" but also "foolish") Ambush (a trap for the unwary, and in this case, the unwilling). Ideally this will lead to Bliss ("ecstasy," but the term is also often used as a synonym for "heaven") "earning her own surprise" (line 8).

What if, however, the seeker is unable to find the Hidden? Does not the game prove "piercing earnest" (deadly serious) if the glee "glaze" (like the eyes of the dying and the dead; line 11) in "Death's—stiff—stare—" (line 12; note how the dashes slow the pace of the phrase as if the speaker were fathoming the full horror of what has happened). It looks as if the fun is too expensive and the jest "crawled too far" (line 16; how wonderfully the phrase conveys the speaker's repulsion) if it leads to people losing their chances at heaven as a consequence of their not finding the hidden God.

"I LIKE A LOOK OF AGONY" EMILY DICKINSON (1890)

Part of the challenge an intensely introspective artist such as EMILY DICKINSON must face is the realization that some of her impulses stem from very dark sources. In this poem, which in its own way is more frightening than anything penned by EDGAR ALLAN POE, the speaker sounds like a serial killer attempting to justify her crimes by blaming her victims.

Most people begin studying nonverbal communication long before they learn to speak and continue the practice throughout their lives. Miscommunication is still common when words are added, however, even if the speaker is not deliberately trying to mislead his audience. Here the speaker (hopefully only imaginatively) exacts painful restitution for the apparent discrepancy between a man's facial expressions and his actions.

Perversely, she likes the look of agony on a man's face because she can then be certain of his true feelings. Mere agony does not satisfy her, however; convulsions are even more preferred because they are involuntary and hence cannot be faked. A throe of pain cannot be simulated (line 4) only if its source is readily apparent, so that the entire first stanza suggests deliberate physical torture.

Torture can lead to death, a circumstance with which the speaker is familiar enough to accept glazed eyes as incontrovertible truth. Now, at last, the lying eyes will deceive her no more. She then has time to note the sweat beads on the victim's forehead, which she knows are not feigned because they are by "homely Anguish strung" (line 8). They are evidently to her liking, since she figuratively identifies them as jewelry. Since she finally admits that Anguish is ugly, some remorse at the crime may already be creeping into her consciousness. The secondary meaning of "homely" would have her still displacing the blame for her actions since it may suggest that the crime arose from her own ("home") anguish.

"I LIKE TO SEE IT LAP THE MILES"
EMILY DICKINSON (1891)   The first steam locomotive to be used in America predated EMILY DICKINSON's birth in 1830 by a single year. By 1853 a train ran from her hometown of Amherst, Massachusetts, to New London, Connecticut. Six years before 1862, when she wrote this poem, trains crossed the Mississippi River for the first time. On May 10, 1869, the last of an unbroken line of rails stretched all the way from the East Coast to California. The new railroad technology changed American society to its very roots, and

this poem provides some clues as to how the reclusive poet felt about the transformation. Unfortunately, it is not one of the poet's best; the playfulness of its opening stanza, her jumping from one simile to another between stanzas instead of following one until it led somewhere important, and her somewhat gratuitous insertion of a strained biblical comparison in the last stanza disappoint readers who value the poet for her thinking.

She begins as if she were describing one of the living beings whose essences she frequently captured in her verse. It seems to "lap" up the miles (line 1) and "lick" up the valleys (line 2); the verbs suggest the ease of a cat lapping its milk and cleaning its saucer. This is where her close observation ends, however. She thinks it feeds (instead of drinks) at tanks, and makes no mention of the wood or coal on which a steam engine's fires were fed at the time. These lapses may have been conscious choices to preserve the mystery of this riddle poem for as long as possible.

Of more concern to her is the impact the railroads are having on the private lives of the people who live by them. Note how her creative use of a stanza break after the fourth line leaves a modicum of ambiguity as to whether she is calling the train's ability to circle a pile of mountains a "prodigious step" (line 4) or if that phrase describes the train's ability to spy into the shanties by the sides of the roads (lines 5–6; a deeply private person, Dickinson would have strenuously objected to such intrusions into her own life). She also decries the changes the lines are making in the environment, focusing on the quarries mined for their rocks, their noise pollution (the "horrid, hooting stanza" she mentions in line 12 probably refers to their whistles), and their evident disregard for safety (a train will "chase itself down hill," line 12).

Dickinson evidently aimed for a transcendent ending by comparing its sounds (line 14; she uses the word "neighs," a reminder that the trains were widely known as iron horses) to those of the apostles John and James, whom Christ called "Boanerges," or Sons of thunder (Mark 3:17). Since the biblical brothers delivered sermons about their Savior, perhaps Dickinson implies that the steam engines announce the arrival of an advanced technology with its godlike powers.

She also reaches back into ancient history when she compares its promptness to that of a star; certain stars were long thought fixed in their unchanging positions in the heavens. Returning to the equine simile with which she began the last stanza, she appreciates its "docile and omnipotent" (line 16) stop at its stable door. The second adjective is such an exaggeration that it might be perceived as a warning, perhaps anticipating a future time in which technology, no longer "docile" (note how even the steam engine "complains" as it goes about its work, line 11) will have the capacity to destroy us.

"I MARK THE SUMMER'S SWIFT DECLINE" HENRY DAVID THOREAU (1842)

The uneven line length of HENRY DAVID THOREAU's short poem (more suggestive of a sketch than a finished poem) may reinforce its pathos, for the speaker admits the triple failure of being unable to catch remote sounds (line 5), to communicate their music to other people, and to engender their emotions in a reader/listener (the last two failures were introduced in the ambiguity of the word "strains," a term with both musical and emotional significance, in the seventh line).

The first stanza presents an observation (summer is dying) supported by three pieces of evidence: the grass is becoming matted and dull, gales are already rustling through the woods, and the leaves have fallen (or are beginning to fall). A "sward" (line 2) is a grassy meadow or other open space, and its "springing" may have resulted from the resiliency of the stems of mature weeds and grasses. These may seem "grave" (line 2) in shades of dark brown and black instead of their high-season colors, and that term also helps maintain the funerary tone of the poem. In the best line, the "aged year" turns on its couch of leaves, a phrase that generates either an image of a personified prostrate year with its energy at low ebb, or a still active year just beginning to "turn on" the process that results in the piles of leaves.

The most striking feature of the second stanza is the urgency detectable in the speaker's voice as he realizes the inadequacy of his tools. Like a frustrated visual artist, he can only "mark" ("note") the season's passing but cannot "catch" the sounds or reproduce them in

his art. He feels moved to "sing the requiem for the dying year" but has perhaps missed the summer of his life when his powers might have been equal to the task. It is perhaps emblematic of his declining state that he could see an inviting couch in the pile of leaves.

"I MEASURE EVERY GRIEF I MEET" EMILY DICKINSON (published 1951)

Although at first glance the "narrow, probing, Eyes" (line 2) with which the speaker in EMILY DICKINSON's poem measures Grief when s/he meets it seem so horribly intrusive that her enquiry borders on sadism, her interest stems not from idle curiosity but from a search for understanding of her own suffering. Her own grief hurts so deeply that she feels someone else's pain only can equal her own, or be "Easier" (line 4).

Time plays an important role in what modern psychology refers to as the recovery process, and upon meeting someone in the grieving process, the speaker asks herself how long the afflicted have suffered, even though her own pain is so monumental that it seems to have always been a part of her. She also wonders if it hurts them to live, as it does her, and if given the choice, they might die rather than continue suffering (lines 11–12). At length some will resume smiling, but for her their seeming return to normalcy is not even like a lamp with very little oil; it is only an imitation of such an inadequate light (lines 15–16). In the fifth stanza she wonders whether even thousands of years might give them (or her) any relief from the pain. In contrast with the relatively short-lived experience of Love, their pain might continue aching "Through centuries of Nerve" (line 22; notice how the phrase maintains her stress not on the passage of time, but on the persistent [and seemingly increasingly acute] suffering).

In the seventh stanza, she introduces the possibility of an afterlife. Just as among the living, the Grieved are many, and Death is only one cause of such suffering. It comes but once, however, "and only nails the eyes" (line 28; this subjective description might deliver an empathetic shock to the reader's nerves, but the qualifying adverb "only" suggests that her own suffering must, incredibly, be even more painful than that horrendous act would be). The other causes of Grief include "Want" (presumably reflecting a need like that for food, so basic that, unmet, it causes pain), "Cold" (which she identifies as "Despair"), and "Banishment" (not just from one's country but from such meaningful people that you miss seeing their Eyes, lines 29–31. As an additional torment, the sufferer is allowed to see the "Native Air" but not the Native Land, in other words, although s/he may remain in the same geographical locale, the loss has rendered it beyond recognition).

Although she cannot always determine the cause of another sufferer's grief, she can take a "piercing Comfort" (line 35) from "passing Calvary" (from contemplating the life and meaning of Christ, including his suffering and the promise of Redemption). Although "piercing Comfort" would seem an oxymoron in normal usage, here the speaker's grief is so pervasive and defining that it seems to require a violent act to reach her. The entire line may also present the argument advanced by many theologians that the searing pain of loss serves as a reminder that this life is short, so one needs to focus on the afterlife. Thus the sight of a newly acquired wound can arouse some hope (or "comfort") within the speaker even as it sparks an emphatic response to the victim's suffering. The phrase "passing Calvary" may not only refer to the wounded people she encounters, but it also may convey the notion that pain and suffering are a natural part of mortal life, another phase that must be passed as part of the growth process.

Although she notes that crosses are sometimes worn fashionably and thoughtlessly, she is "fascinated to presume" (line 38; such elevated diction signals her escape from the morbid dungeons of despair) that some of those people who wear them share the same deeply personal relationship with Christ that has alleviated her own suffering.

"I'M NOBODY! WHO ARE YOU?" Emily Dickinson (1891)

The challenge of Emily Dickinson's poem is to figure out its situation based on the scant information provided in its eight short lines. The voice we hear is conspiratorial, yet the speaker has apparently never met the internal audience before (or pretends not to have). She introduces herself as "Nobody," but capitalizes the word and puts an exclamation point after it as though it were a proper noun or at least a point of honor. Although she asks her audience's name, she resumes talking before the reply is given. Her offer to share the name (or title) of Nobody immediately connects the two of them, especially after her auditor (perhaps nonverbally) accepts the designation. Pleased at finding a kindred spirit, the speaker begins solidifying her bonds with her new acquaintance by identifying the two of them as a pair and pleading for secrecy upon pain of banishment for their apparent violation of a social norm of some kind. Notice that although they just met, the speaker's referral to the two of them as "us" (line 4) establishes a group identity in opposition to the "they" who apparently form the other, dominant group. The speaker's assertion that "you know!" assumes that her new friend shares the same background or at least the same attitude.

Feeling that she is with a friend, the speaker is comfortable enough to begin sharing her confidences. While she assumes that the two of them seem content with their successful avoidance of celebrity status, she cannot resist poking fun at the Somebody who achieves it. She reduces the glamour of societal acclaim by focusing on the work it requires ("How dreary," she exclaims in line 5) and then compares the exalted personage to a Frog. One of the humiliations of actively pursuing a public life is the necessity of constantly trying to keep your name in the spotlight, a process that the speaker compares to a frog's incessant croaking "all the livelong June" (line 7). She further deprecates the "other," the in-group against whom she has so recently found an ally, by comparing them to an admiring bog. If one thinks of a bog as full of potential traps for the unwary, her analogy also suggests how dangerous it can be to assume a leadership or celebrity role. Even the most basic popularity might come at a high price.

"I'M 'WIFE'—I'VE FINISHED THAT" Emily Dickinson (published 1955)

In this poem, Emily Dickinson's unorthodox punctuation enables her to perfectly convey her ambiguous attitude toward marriage. If one imagines that the speaker had some reservations about the lack of autonomy that wedded bliss could bring in an era when the "obey" clause of the bride's wedding vows was often viewed as a sacred oath, then the poem should be read as if an ellipsis followed "that" in line 1, a colon followed "state," and a period followed "Czar." Thus an unmarried woman would be seen as the absolute ruler of her own life (just as the czars, or [more accurately transliterated, the tsars] ruled imperial Russia until the communists gained control in the Bolshevik Revolution of 1917). Becoming a married woman could theoretically mean at least some freedom from the responsibilities attendant upon autonomy. It could seem a "safer" (line 4) state not only because one's husband could act as a buffer against the outside world (women were often "protected" from learning about their husband's finances, for example), but also because many mid-nineteenth-century American girls had been schooled to consider themselves physically weak and mentally inferior to their future husbands.

Warming to her subject, the speaker now considers a girl's life to be odd when viewed from the "soft Eclipse" (line 6); such language reflects the fact that in becoming a Mrs. she was given a new name as well as a new identity as someone's wife. People in heaven must look at their former lives with similar wonder. Heaven (like marriage) is completely comfortable, but life on earth (her girlhood) was painful. Such comparisons finally seem frivolous; she stops with the assertion that "I'm Wife!"

An alternative interpretation would have her gloating throughout the poem. A period would follow "state," and exclamation points would follow "Czar," "now," and "so." In this reading the speaker considers her former state so beneath her that she struggles to find the right words for it. Formerly dominated (perhaps) by her own parents, she now rejoices at the prospect of ruling her own household. A major reason why it seemed safer to be married is that the Miss label exposed one to irresponsible gossip and awkward social situations; although she apparently has been only newly admitted into the sorority of married women, she relishes the fact of her promotion. While acknowledging by the term "soft Eclipse" that marriage may in some ways seem to diminish the value of her personhood, the change was definitely worth it. Now that she can meet other married women on terms of equality, she has freed herself from the pain of social inferiority and uninvited pronouncements on her personal life. It was enough to say "I'm Wife" because propriety demanded that, barring some public outrage, a woman's personal life inside the sacred institution of marriage was not open to public speculation.

Which reading is closer to Dickinson's own thoughts about marriage? Because she never married and because she was an acute observer of the people around her, she probably encountered many newlyweds as smug as the speaker in this poem seems to be. Dickinson was probably less sanguine than the speaker about the softness of the marital Eclipse, the wife's dream of total power in the household, and the possibility that matrimonial bliss could last nearly as long as the eternity that heaven promises, but this poem provides ample evidence that she well understood the advantages as well as the costs of marriage. In penning the speaker's exuberant proclamation of "I'm Woman now!" (an ejaculation that infers that someone like the poet was less of a woman for never marrying; line 3), she admits that a person might maintain her identity and even grow in confidence as a result of marriage.

"AN INDIAN AT THE BURIAL-PLACE OF HIS FATHERS" WILLIAM CULLEN BRYANT (1824) WILLIAM CULLEN BRYANT was fortunate enough to travel extensively in the woods and mountains of New England before they were cleared, mined, and dammed, and like the romantic poets everywhere else, he preferred the ragged crags and waterfalls of untamed nature. Although he was a more direct beneficiary of the displacement of the Native Americans than his European counterparts, he was also more aware of their plight and understood that their passing from the land had important implications for his own culture. The ecological warning that ends this poem was remarkably prescient; 200 years later, the aquifers and watersheds of the American heartland are gravely imperiled.

Largely ignorant of Native American cultures and probably cognizant of the fact that many of his immediate readers would have little interest in the subject, Bryant wisely chose the veneration of the dead as the starting point to bridge the gap. The speaker is a Native American man who has returned to his father's grave, as many of the newer New Englanders were wont to do. The warrior elite evidently had been at the apex of his culture, for he expresses his shame that their weakness forced their withdrawal from the landscape that had played such a prominent role in their legends. This had been his childhood home, and he can as easily remember its features as a settler's child could recall the details of the old homestead. As another point of connection with his white audience, he refers to the mountains as the fences of his former property (line 11).

He has had enough contact with white Americans to know their fondness for lawns, but he would prefer the unchanged woods to their cultivated land. He understands their sheep, cattle, and laborers, but his cultural background encourages him to think of the buggy as a war chariot instead of a pleasure vehicle. He would prefer herds of deer bounding over fallen trees, with a noble Indian warrior, armed with arrows (carried in the "quiver") and ornamented with feathers (the "plumes" of line 33) and the scars of previous battles, challenging the wolf and wrestling with the bear as lord of the woods.

He recalls the rites the Indians performed at a burial mound, including the placement of wreaths, and a chief's communion with the god of thunders. Now a wheat field covers the ground, and the plow has turned up not only the objects buried for the use of the dead in the next life, but even the skeletal remains of people as varied as an infant and a powerful chief. The initial American readership could probably relate to a young mother's grief as she buried her first-born more than the audience of later centuries who have been privileged to live in times of much lower infant mortality rates.

The speaker's people melt like spring snow before the noon sun and will likely be driven into the Pacific as the whites fill the land, but because he is so attuned to nature, he predicts that the settlers' irresponsible stewardship will also doom their own civilization, ultimately leaving just their tombstones behind. Because they divert rivers and disturb springs at their sources, they will turn the land into an uninhabitable desert.

"THE INDIAN BURYING GROUND"

PHILIP FRENEAU (1787) As a product of the "Age of Enlightenment" and a fire-eating member of the Revolutionary generation, PHILIP FRENEAU questioned many Christian beliefs. In the first stanza of this poem, he reduces the authority of the church (and implicitly challenges the divinity of Jesus Christ, who promised the kingdom of heaven for his followers) by referring to those who base their belief in eternal life on the teachings of the Bible as only "the learned" (line 1). He finds their arguments unconvincing, and his own "old opinion" (line 2) is that the supine position in which Europeans traditionally have buried their dead indicates "the soul's eternal sleep" (line 4).

Anecdotal evidence based on the excavation (or desecration) of a Native American burial mound reveals that a dead man was placed in the seemingly more hopeful sitting position of a participant at a joyous feast (line 8). Representations of game animals (the "imagined birds" of line 9), a bowl and venison jerky (or deer meat "for a journey dressed") were buried with him, all of which suggests that his active soul knows no rest. The placement of his bow (with the bowstring already bending it for immediate action) and stone-tipped arrows in the mound further indicate that, although his life had been spent, his soul was thought to remain active.

In the fourth stanza the speaker addresses the internal audience as "stranger." He is humorously cautioned against saying that the dead lie in the mound, for they sit. Notice that the language of the warning is very sinister, however: To say the wrong thing is to commit a fraud upon the dead (line 18), and we have just been told that the spirits know no rest (line 12).

Further evidence suggests that the grave was not as recent as one might think. Petroglyphs are still half visible on an exposed rock (line 24). The "children of the forest" (line 28; a slightly pejorative euphemism frequently used to denote native people of all ages since they are schooled only in natural law and remain innocent of civilization) once played beneath the same tree that now shelters a shepherd.

Since a few North American tribes were known to be matriarchal, the speaker imagines an Indian queen and the "barbarous forms" (line 31) of warriors who chide those who loiter on their sacred ground. Calling the woman a "pale Shebah" (line 30) associates her with the power of the captivatingly beautiful biblical queen but also moves towards individualizing her portrait by suggesting that her skin pigmentation was lighter than that of the African queen of biblical renown.

At midnight a ghastly hunt ensues, but both hunter and deer are only spirits (the "shades" of line 36). Fearful people with vivid imaginations (the "timorous fancy" of line 37) will see the painted chief with his pointed spear, and reason shall bow before "shadows and delusions" (line 40) in the area.

"THE INDIAN MAID'S REPLY TO THE MISSIONARY" FRANCES SARGENT LOCKE OSGOOD (1850) This poem celebrates the self-sufficiency of women by studying a girl whose circumstances the dominant American culture generally would have deemed inferior on the bases of race, gender, religion, and culture. She is also presumably younger and far less educated than the Christian missionary who attempts to convert her, yet she has so enthralled the speaker that he is unable to take her eyes off her.

The greater part of the maiden's attractiveness resides not in her physical beauty, but in her elasticity, which is the essence of youth. She contains a multitude of possibilities that the poem presents as a list of contraries, a pattern established in the description of her attitude ("half earnest, half sportive") in the opening line. Her posture ("listening, she stood") indicates a willingness to consider new ideas that is balanced by an impulse to stand her own ground. Thus she can seem both "queenly" and a "child of the wood" (line 2), and her body language conveys the sensuality of a healthy animal (witness her parted lips and quickened heart rate) held in check by a natural reserve (downcast eyes and locked hands; lines 3–4).

Perhaps taking her cues from the plastic arts, FRANCES SARGENT LOCKE OSGOOD completes the visual aspects of this poem with sufficient background material to create an environmental portrait without overburdening it with an overabundance of concrete sensory details that could have distracted from the central focus of her portrait. The elevated diction of the fifth and sixth lines (which describes the pure sunset burning like fire through the shade of the "forest's majestic arcade") appropriately introduces the image central to the poem's meaning: either the girl's intellect and spirit already are winning the struggle with her natural impulses, or she is at that moment receiving the message that will lead to the same result.

In marked contrast to the attention she lavished on the Indian's appearance, Osgood provides so few details about the Missionary's looks that he seems almost physically absent from the scene. His speech about the goodness, glory, and power of God instantly filled the Indian maiden with impassioned rapture and praise for her maker, however, and his lesson about the life and death of the Savior (Jesus Christ) brought tears down her cheeks. In his fond zeal (line 15), he sought to "wile her within the pale of the church" (to convert her to his religion, but the verb "wile" means to trick. While "the pale" refers to an enclosed area wherein her soul would be safe, life within such boundaries might seem too narrow an existence given her people's embrace of the whole of nature). Given her background, the missionary has as little chance of winning over a cloud, a forest fawn, or a ray of starlight to his religion as he has of converting her.

The "wild child of freedom" (such an appealing moniker that it almost seems criminal to rob her of that identity), "all impulse and grace" (completely natural and charming, although in a religious context, *grace* may imply that she is living in accordance with God's will; line 20), listens in "sad, unbelieving surprise" at this part of his message (presumably, the missionary has reached the point where he asserts that only through Christ can she be saved, and that everyone who does not accept Him is doomed). As a partial refutation of this argument, she points to the skies. Perhaps irritated by such recalcitrance, he threatens God's wrath if she strays from the truth he has just given her.

Her response was "wild, sweet and incredulous" laughter (lines 26–27) that rang through the woods (switching verb tenses [from past to present tense, initially] in the middle of a work is generally considered bad form because it disrupts the external audience's sense of when the events are happening. Here it might have been excusable if everything up to that point could be considered part of the back story, and everything that followed was rendered in present tense. Alas, it was not to be: in line 26 the poet reverted to the past tense and even incongruously has the innocent child of the forest speak with a blend of biblical verb forms and standard written English).

Anyway, she proudly stood up to his criticism (revealing the pride in her heritage that 21st century Americans can celebrate; line 27) but lowly and reverently answered it (thus demonstrating the personal modesty that a mid-19th-century audience would find very endearing; line 30). Her response is to quote God as stating that the woodland is the true church of his "child" [by which term she either may be indicating herself, or Jesus Christ as the Son of God, a possibility that might indicate how closely she has listened to the missionary].

Although seriously flawed as a work of art (which is tremendously disappointing as its basic materials were so promising), the poem can be viewed as an important historical document because it reveals the impact that WILLIAM CULLEN BRYANT had on later poets (see his "A FOREST HYMN" for the origin of the maid's response in this poem). Its cultural relativism (note that the maid's natural religion is as valued as the missionary's Christianity) also demonstrates the impact that TRANSCENDENTALIST POETRY had on later poetry. Its nearly complete focus on the maid can be viewed as a reflection of the growing importance of women in the era; in this connection, note how the author's celebration of the heroine trumped all the other artificial barriers society tends to place between people, including distinctions based on class, race, and religion.

"INDIAN NAMES" LYDIA HUNTLEY SIGOURNEY (1827) LYDIA HUNTLEY SIGOURNEY's poem offers specific examples as proof of the assertion given in its prose epigram that the Native Americans cannot be forgotten because many of our states and geological features bear their names. This hardly seems a challenging task, but its redeeming grace is that the names provide the background for occasionally vibrant glimpses of tribal life that serve as the foreground of the poem.

The speaker begins by quoting the internal audience to the effect that the races have all died who once could be seen in their lightweight canoes on the crested waves (a feature often found in the waters of the Atlantic Ocean and the Great Lakes, and occasionally on other inland waterways). No longer can the hunter's shout be heard in the forests (lines 5–6; such noise would probably have been a relatively rare phenomenon even in the heyday of the vanished hunter/gatherer culture as it would tend to scare off whatever additional game was present in the area. Only an exceptionally large kill or the successful culmination of an extremely difficult pursuit would seem to warrant such an outburst). The speaker counters by pointing out that the internal audience cannot wash the Indian names out of the waters (lines 7–8; perhaps the contrast between the extreme virility evident in a hunter's exultant shout and the domesticity implied by the metaphor of washing were designed to highlight the relative nobility and bravery of the former).

The second stanza presents the billows of Lake Ontario and the thunder of Niagara Falls. At the time when the poem appeared, the "red" Missouri River (line 13; such coloring probably stems from the author's conception of the poor soils of the distant west, or a reference to the fact that the lands in question were held by "red" Indians) was still bringing in rich tribute in the form of beaver pelts. The Rappahannock River flows through a rich valley in northern Virginia.

Views of Native American culture in the 20th century were largely shaped by the cinemagraphic appeal of the migratory tribes of the High Plains with their teepees and mounted warriors. The speaker's reference to the Indians' "cone-like cabins" (line 17) underscores the fallacy of thinking that all tribes from coast to coast lived in the same way. It may specifically reference the Algonquian wigwam, a conical structure for which saplings formed the support and bark or animal hides covered the top and sides, or even far more substantial structures. These, too, have "fled away like withered leaves" (line 19), but, as the fourth stanza reveals, the states of Massachusetts, Ohio, Connecticut and Kentucky derived their names from Indian languages.

The most famous of the three mountain names provided in the last stanza belongs to the Alleghenies, a range running from Pennsylvania to Virginia and forming part of the Appalachian Mountains. Mt. Monadnock stands by itself in southwestern New Hampshire, and Mt. Wachusett (or "Great Hill" in Algonquian) is in Maine.

"THE INDIAN'S WELCOME TO THE PILGRIM FATHERS" Lydia Huntley Sigourney (1835)

Is it possible for a modern audience to overlook the historical inaccuracies of a poem in order to appreciate its sentiment? To begin with, the poet furnished a headnote providing the historical background of the poem but got the date wrong; Samoset arrived in the Pilgrim settlement on (approximately) March 16, 1621. The pilgrims themselves had only arrived on November 11, 1620, and it was not until December 15 that they found a place with a suitable harbor and began building Plymouth Plantation. This was not "on the sterile plain" (line 2), but in a largely wooded terrain except where the natives had already cleared the land for their own crops. According to William Bradford, the first elected governor of that place, half of the company died in the three months that followed and only six or seven of the remainder were fully fit at any time. Thus Samoset's arrival was far more crucial to the survival of the enterprise than it would have been a year later. His intervention led to a treaty of mutual defense with his tribe and the colonists' acquisition of Squanto, an interpreter who chose to stay with them and taught them to hunt, fish, and cultivate corn.

The "red-browed" (line 17; Lydia Huntley Sigourney may imagine him in a war paint that Bradford does not mention and thus perpetuates the incorrect racial characterization of the native people as red Indians) "chieftan" who subsequently came upon them was Massasoit, a Sachem of the Abnaki tribe whose welcome was probably predicated on his own need of a strong alliance in the face of pressure from the Narragansetts, a far more powerful tribe. Since the Native Americans identified themselves in terms of their tribal membership, the future of his "race" (line 26) was an alien concept.

The poem begins with the Pilgrim Fathers surveying the wintry landscape still close to the "Wrathful main" (the Atlantic Ocean; line 4). As they imagine the future crops, a church, and a school, they stoically hid any regrets about leaving England's "velvet green." The natives they encountered earlier had at first fled and then assaulted them with arrows, so Samoset's friendly overtures were indeed a surprise.

In sharp contrast to the benevolent kindness Samoset and his tribe extended (the New World's welcome of lines 23–24), that welcome became a "blast" (line 25; the term may reference crop blights as well as the explosive impact of the colonists' gunpowder) and a "ban" (a reference to their exile from the land) for the Native Americans. Unlike the farsighted Pilgrim Fathers whose progeny eventually built mansions on their new land (line 37), the Indian's descendents were swept from their native land.

The speaker's empathy for their plight extends to their sorrow at the loss of their fathers' graves, important sites for many North American tribes. S/he can be certain that few of the descendents of the white European settlers will aid "outcasts from the forests wild" (line 39) because one of the chief controversies of the decade centered on the forcible removal of the Cherokees on a 1,000-mile march from their ancestral lands in Georgia to the Oklahoma plains. In accordance with the Indian Removal Act of 1830 and the Treaty of New Echota signed by representatives of the tribal minority in favor of relocation, by 1839 the entire tribe had been dispossessed. Including the losses to exposure after their arrival in the middle of winter, about four people died for every mile of this "Trail of Tears." Similar atrocities were forced on the western Indian tribes until the last decade of the century.

"I NEVER LOST AS MUCH BUT TWICE" Emily Dickinson (1890)

Among the gravest challenges facing the devotees of any religion is the reconciliation of their faith with the pain attendant upon the death of a loved one. Faced with a new personal loss, the speaker in Emily Dickinson's poem compares her most recent despair with the depths of her own suffering when two other people close to her died (were "lost to the sod," line 2). Subjectively, it felt as if everything had been taken from her until she seemed a virtual beggar at God's door without spiritual resources of her own (lines 3–4). Her rhyming of "sod" with "God" suggests that accepting those deaths and her own pain was not an easy struggle; such a close linking of these words is almost like darkening God's name with soil.

Her earlier losses were recompensed by the descent of angels (line 5), which suggests the birth of additional family members to fill the void left in her heart, or at least the addition of new people or interests in her life. Once again facing a crisis, she returns to the guise of the beggar at God's door in the last two lines. Her initial response is anger; she calls God a burglar (line 6) as if the death was nothing less than a theft from her family. Then she appeals to His bounty; the trifle a successful businessman might give could seem inconsequential to a banker but represent significant aid to a beggar. Finally moving toward reconciliation, she recalls her personal relationship with God the Father and throws herself on His mercy as a poor supplicant.

"I NEVER SAW A MOOR" Emily Dickinson (1890)

The speaker of EMILY DICKINSON's poem asserts that just as she is quite sure of the existence of Scotland and the ocean even though she has never been to either place, she can be as confident in her belief in God and Heaven.

Moors (line 1) are the Scottish wetlands that feature peat bogs and the heather of line 3. Billows (line 4) are the large waves or ocean swells that can be found on the sea of the second line. The fun of the poem lies in the speaker's evident belief that Heaven is as much a physical place (a "spot" as she calls it in line 9) as the other two locales, and she could not be more confident if she had a ticket or other tangible evidence of its existence.

The poem may have grown out of the pun in the first line. The systems of ropes and anchors that secure vessels are also called "moors;" metaphorically, they may be the tenets by which one's faith is tethered. Since the speaker acknowledges that she has not seen even one of them or the sea, which tests the strength of a ship's mooring just as the billows and buffets of life can test one's faith, her faith can be viewed as touchingly childlike or dismissed as facile tautology.

"IN MEMORY OF MY DEAR GRANDCHILD ANNE BRADSTREET WHO DECEASED JUNE 20, 1669, BEING THREE YEARS AND SEVEN MONTHS OLD" Anne Bradstreet (1678)

Poetry can have a therapeutic effect on those who practice it in times of the deepest sorrow, and this poem illustrates how that process can work. ANNE BRADSTREET picked up her pen while still in the throes of misery over the death of her namesake grandchild, an event so recent that her grief has the physical manifestations described in the first line.

As a Puritan, the author could not blame God for her loss. Instead, she broadly attributes her sorrow to the amorphous heavens, and the sky is the first of a list of ephemeral things that gradually lead her to acceptance of her plight and reliance on her faith to overcome even this sorrow. To gain perspective, the speaker focuses on her own disappointment and achieves a degree of emotional distance by thinking of the child as one of many "fading things" (line 4). At first glance this seems an oddly cold phrase; it seems to imply that the speaker blames herself for wasting her hopes on such a sickly child. Actually, the phrase signals the poem's shift away from the speaker's grief to her abstract thought about the foolishness of assigning great value to anything on earth since everything is temporary. Thus, she is no longer thinking of her dead granddaughter when she introduces the concept of price in connection with her loss (line 6).

It was customary for practicing Puritans to closely examine natural phenomena in hopes of finding manifestations of God's will or hints of divine pleasure. This speaker's list of temporary things declines in beauty as it progresses. She begins with a withering flower, but finally grants it but a single hour (line 10). Next comes a bubble, then the frustration of brittle glass, and finally a shadow, the most insubstantial thing she can think of. With so many reminders surrounding her, the speaker thinks herself a fool for imagining that she really owns anything (or anyone) on earth.

Finally addressing herself to the deceased, the speaker looks forward to going to heaven where she will again meet the child. In the meantime, she comforts herself with a vision of the child's being united with the Savior in endless bliss.

"IN MEMORY OF MY DEAR GRANDCHILD ELIZABETH BRADSTREET, WHO DECEASED AUGUST, 1665, BEING A YEAR AND A HALF OLD" Anne Bradstreet (1678)

The first half of this requiem is addressed to the deceased. It reveals how fond ANNE

BRADSTREET was of the beautiful child but also reminds her not to overly mourn since she can take comfort in her belief in the child's immortality.

In the second stanza, the speaker tries to understand the meaning of the infant's death. The event seems perverse because, taking her cues from the vegetative world in August, she is used to things dying only after they mature. This death seemed both so unnatural and untimely (line 11) that, like any good Puritan, the author can only affirm that it represents the will of God without arriving at any simpler explanation.

"IN PATHS UNTRODDEN" WALT WHITMAN (1860)

This poem might be considered WALT WHITMAN's "coming out," a public announcement of his renunciation of closeted desires in favor of admitting his "need of comrades" (line 18). This is a step that the speaker in this poem is not yet ready for; he declares his independence only in seclusion by an isolated pond (line 2) whereas the poet inserted the poem in the book upon which he staked his public reputation. In mainstream mid-19th-century America (represented here as "the life that exhibits itself," line 3) there were no openly homosexual role models of any prominence whose precedent he could follow. At first he tried to accept the standards of straight society by internalizing the "pleasure, profits, conformities" (line 5), but the unpublished standards by which the soul of a man can rejoice in comrades (a key term for Whitman) are clear to him now. To avoid being misinterpreted, he has the speaker announce that "the soul of the man I speak for" (the author, presumably; line 7) is the one doing the rejoicing.

The speaker's attitude toward his former life might be summoned up in a single onomatopoeic word: away from the "clank" (line 8; it is the sound of chains) of the world, he can "tally" (reckon on, or count) the "tongues aromatic" (perhaps the scented leaves of the Calamus grass [from which he borrowed the name for this section of *Leaves of Grass*] or the remembered tongues of lovers; line 9) in the secluded spot. No longer humiliated by the desires of his hidden life "which contains all the rest" (line 11), he resolved to sing only songs of "manly attachment" (line 12). Projecting them, he bequeaths "athletic love" (line 14) and his

celebration of the need "of" comrades (the preposition considers their needs and not just his own and renders the phrase more explicitly sexual than "for" would do), the secret of his "nights and days" (line 17; by reversing their idiomatic order, he emphasizes the former), to all young men.

All of this occurred on a "delicious" (line 15) ninth-month afternoon in his 41st year. Use of the Quaker practice of numbering the months (to avoid honoring the pagan gods [Thursday and Wednesday, originally Thor's day and Woden's day], and Roman emperors [July and August were named in honor of Julius and Augustus Caesar] whom many divisions of time were named after) not only reveals the poet's own background, it suggests that the occasion may have constituted a rebirth.

Although "trodden" is the past participle of "tread," "untrodden" is an archaic term for "retraced." Thus Whitman's title implies that the poem is an autobiographical retracing of his paths in life. The title is not primarily an ungrammatical description of the isolated landscape, although that setting is an important component of the poem.

"IN REFERENCE TO HER CHILDREN, 23 JUNE 1659" ANNE BRADSTREET (1678)

That she survived eight deliveries and that all eight of her children (Samuel, Dorothy, Sarah, Simon, Hannah, Mercy, Dudley and John) survived to adulthood is a testament to ANNE BRADSTREET's good health, parenting skills, and affluence. Although eight would not have been considered an exceptionally large number of children in her era, it was ample enough that she could humorously compare them to a brood and herself to a mother bird. This poem is remarkable for taking that comparison through to their adult lives as it chronicles the older children's departures. In keeping with the worldview of a mother bird, Bradstreet provided fewer details about what the children were doing than about the distance of their flights and their distance from her.

The nest in which the eight birds (four cocks and four hens; line 2) were hatched was the same one commemorated in "UPON THE BURNING OF OUR HOUSE JULY 10, 1666." Although the opening of this poem makes it seem as if the children required only time and nutrition before they instinctively took flight and began singing, their mother knew well the pain, care, cost, and labor each required (lines 3–4).

To the oldest, already in London, she will continue sending mournful chirps until he returns or she dies. Her sentiment is beautifully conveyed:

Leave not this nest, thy dam and sire,
Fly back and sing amidst this choir.

(lines 10–11)

Here she fudges a bit; "dam" and "sire" usually refer to the female and male parents, respectively, of domestic mammals instead of birds.

Her eldest daughter had already married and moved first south and then north, and her mother singles her out for her beauty. The second daughter has flown to the east, also married, and her mother praises her complexion (her notably white complexion, while perhaps signaling poor circulation to a physician, would have been especially valued prior to the 20th century's fixation on tanning. At the time, it could signal that a young woman was affluent enough not to have to labor in the sun; line 21).

The ambitious fourth child went to Harvard "to chat among that learned crew" (line 28) that he might "chant" above the rest (the college chiefly produced ministers at that time; line 30). He might even surpass the nightingales.

Evidently staying in character, she numbers the other children not by their birth order but by their apparent readiness to leave the nest. The fifth is therefore her seventh child because he has evidently gone to school or taken other steps toward independence, having flown to the shrubs and bushes (an apprenticeship or boarding school seem likely possibilities). The other three will stay at home until, as ordained (as God wills), they will fly to their destinies.

Although birds cannot cry, she fears that some of the brood might get caught for want of watch while pecking corn and void of care (line 45; that is, she is afraid that they might become too worldly and thus neglect the state of their souls). This is followed by a list of the ingenious ways by which the colonists were able to catch birds for food.

Nets (the "fowler's snare") could be cast over them as they feed or after they are lured in by bells or mirrors (lines 46 and 49); they might be picked off a branch by an "untoward" (unseemly or annoying) boy; or they might find themselves stuck on a limb smeared with gooey bird-lime (line 51). Greedy hawks might take the others.

Although she long kept off all harm with her wings, as her children depart she has more cares and fears than ever for they are ignorant of many perils. She urges them to remain cautious, and she will continue to sing (produce poetry) until her weak "lays" (verses, but within the avian frame of reference the term may pun on the production of eggs and/or the lives of her offspring; line 68) end with her life.

Then from the top bough she will take flight "into a country beyond sight" (line 75) where she will sing with the angels in eternal spring. She asks to be remembered to her grandchildren for the care she has provided her children, including introductions to joy, misery, good, evil, life-saving means, and deadly threats (lines 88–90). Although dead, she will in that way continue to live among and advise them. She bids them farewell, but will be happy if all goes well with them.

"INSCRIPTION FOR THE ENTRANCE TO A WOOD" WILLIAM CULLEN BRYANT (1817)

By 1817, Massachusetts had been under the plow for almost 200 years. Although most of the rest of America had not yet become so domesticated, WILLIAM CULLEN BRYANT knew the value of the wilderness experience and already realized that something was lost as its native forests were irretrievably converted. This poem is not primarily about preservation, however. It focuses on the meaning of the forest and, by extension, the frontier, on the American psyche. Rather than being limited to a specific wood, it serves as a reintroduction to nature for an audience that was increasingly settling for an entirely artificial existence. Like a skillful guide, Bryant was aware that some of his readers had no wilderness experience and that many people associated wilderness with fierce animals and other dangers. Note that his title promises "a wood" and not the unlimited and potentially terrifying "woods"; he will go out of his way to make this trip as pleasant as possible.

The very first word of the poem underscores one of the major differences between the city and the frontier. In the former locale you are advised to look upon strangers with fear, but the proper frontier spirit encourages you to reach out to them just as the poet does with the undeniably friendly greeting of "Stranger." Thus the very first thing you notice in the wilderness is the way it changes how you view other people. The rest of the poem deals with the way it changes how you view yourself.

By "the world" (line 2), Bryant evidently meant just the human portion of it. The deep well of depravity and misery he describes was fed by two founts: the religious tradition of original sin and his practice of law. In this poem he shares the palliative measure he adopted, exposure to the uncorrupted nature of the wilderness. Just the calm shade, sweet breeze and green leaves will begin the restorative process, although at first you still remember your life among men with loathing. The theologians of his day argued that nature also fell (the animals began eating each other, for one thing) when man fell from grace in Eden. Bryant argues that most of God's wrath was directed at man, and he draws upon an agrarian image to describe how misery and guilt were linked together. Before fossil fuels were available, two large farm animals (when available, powerful oxen or draft horses) were placed side by side in wooden yokes in order to harness their power for plowing or other laborious tasks. Since his imagery has so closely linked misery to the guilt of original sin, Bryant implies that by avoiding massed humanity, it is possible to visit places that are less disturbed and less disturbing.

The northern woods were once so heavily wooded that a squirrel could theoretically travel from the shores of the Atlantic to the Mississippi River without touching the ground. Since these were old-growth forests, the trees tended to spread their foliage high above the ground, forming a canopy that Bryant describes as a "thick roof of green" (lines 15–16). The phrase marks his turn from the cares of mankind to complete immersion in nature. First you notice the birds singing with wild abandon, then a squirrel in its characteristic, seemingly playful, pose. Insects fly in the sunbeams, but instead of being pests, in Bryant's woods they entertain with their dance (line 21). Bry-

ant personifies the trees and the sky; the former share the speaker's contentment and the latter blesses the scene like a priest (line 25). A wildflower seems to enjoy its tenuous existence on a canyon wall almost as much as the hummingbird or insect that sucks its nectar. Even the mossy rocks and fallen trees "breathe fixed tranquility" (lines 28–33); the phrase is a celebration of their contributions to the ambiance of the scene rather than a personification, since their breaths are "fixed" and not kinetic. The rivulet, on the other hand, is more animated, even laughing as it rejoices (line 36).

The poem is framed in the sense that it returns through several of the images with which it began. The audience is again made aware of its own existence as you are cautioned not to disturb the wren as it drinks from the stream. The cool wind again stirs the leaves, and the final image of the poem illustrates the change that wilderness can bring to a person. Whereas in the beginning, you found humanity repugnant, by now the wind comes like a playful, embracing lover (lines 39–42). This transcendent moment signals that you are again ready to embrace humanity.

"IN THE DESERT" STEPHEN CRANE (1895)

The shockingly stark imagery of STEPHEN CRANE's poem is appropriately set in the desert, for the tormented man's bitterness has isolated him from his fellow man and almost all the other pleasures of life. Although the speaker addresses him as "friend," he describes him as a scarcely human creature. The fact that he is naked, bestial, and squatting (lines 2–3) may universalize his predicament. He is more than a symbol of human depravity; he is unquestionably evocative of our shared primal ancestry.

The phrase "holding one's heart in one's hands" suggests a willingness to meet strangers as though they may become friends, and to treat friends as though they might become family. Such an impulse leads the speaker to ask whether the beast's food is good even though it is holding its heart in its hands in order to eat it. The surprisingly civil, even urbane character of the beast's response suggests that only a seemingly civilized man is capable of such depravity. He likes his heart and all its bitterness because they are his; even terribly debilitating and ultimately deadly emotions can make one feel alive.

"I READ MY SENTENCE STEADILY" EM-ILY DICKINSON (published 1951) Most people become aware of the death of others very early in their lives, but only gradually do they figure out that this phenomenon also applies to them. EMILY DICKINSON'S poem presents a truncated grieving process as the speaker's reaction to this "news."

In the first stanza the speaker applies the resources of his/her intellect and her knowledge of contractual and criminal law in an attempt to bargain her way out of the business. The steadiness with which she claims to have read and reviewed her sentence suggests that on an emotional level she has already accepted its finality, but her grammatical slip in referring to the "extremest clause" (line 4; instead of "most extreme") may signal that she was not quite as much in control of her emotions as she would have us believe, and/or that she (like the rest of us) lacked the knowledge and ability to beat this rap on a technicality.

Some ambiguity surrounds "the shame" of the fifth line; it could conceivably refer to the indiscretions of Adam and Eve (in Calvinist theology, their eating of a forbidden fruit constituted the Original Sin, which destined all their descendents to suffering and death), her commission of an individual sin or crime, or her future execution. With all the cards thus stacked against her, she naturally regards "May God have mercy on your soul" (line 7), the traditional (and in some states, mandated) end of a death-sentence pronouncement, as a "Pious" (but essentially empty) form (line 6). The jury's vote of "Him" (line 8) reveals their decision to leave the possibility of mercy to God; they offered none.

As if acting as her own spiritual counselor, the speaker made her soul familiar with "her extremity" (a euphemism for her execution calculated to minimize stress) so that it would not be "a novel Agony" (line 10). Just as she did when she adopted the stance of a defense attorney in the first stanza, the speaker adopts the tone of an emotionally distant, perhaps even patronizing, public servant. Thus the speaker, in evident denial about her own fate, made her soul acquainted with and even friendly with Death (line

11), an accomplishment that minimized any potentially disruptive "Hint" (line 13) that she questioned the possible injustice of the sentence. Like an efficient official, she announces the end of the matter as if she could return unto her usual duties.

"I RECKON—WHEN I COUNT AT ALL" EMILY DICKINSON (published 1929) Any list poem immediately presents two problems: What do the items have in common, and what do they reveal about the speaker and/or the situation. EMILY DICKINSON'S poem may represent the speaker's response to what has generally become an empty phrase, the admonition to "count your blessings."

The opening line conveys the speaker's initial reluctance to perform this task even as it provides two clues as to his/her philosophical nature. The distinction he implies between "reckoning" and "counting" calls into question the validity of the exercise, since he evidently prefers just to enjoy things and not categorize or count them. To "reckon" seems a far less formal activity than to "think;" it signals that his response will probably be focused on the process of compiling a list instead of representing his carefully considered opinion. He further implies that his opinion may be of little consequence since he does not always "count" (he himself may have no intrinsic value and sometimes not even practical [or situational] value). This self-negating approach may also account for the remarkable brevity of his list as well as its general emphasis on intangible as opposed to material things.

It seems self-serving when a poet has her speaker begin a list of the most important things with "poets," and the rest of the poem attempts to justify this choice. The speaker's second choice (and his entire response) may have been inspired by a literary anecdote concerning a famous Greek named Diogenes. Upon being asked what he would like by a solicitous Alexander the Great, the ancient philosopher requested that the conqueror move aside since he was blocking his sun. "Summer" might contain much, and "the Heaven of God" reveals something about the speaker's religious background since its diction comes from the Judeo-Christian tradition. One of the problems with listing as a literary strategy is that the end product could consist of an infinite number of items, a difficulty from which the speaker escapes by arbitrarily announcing the end of his list in line 4.

Having completed his list, the speaker reexamines it in the second stanza and concludes that he needs only the first item since poets comprehend "the Whole" (line 6; the term may refer not just to the entire list, but to everything in the universe). He concludes that Poets are "All" (line 8), and he can dismiss the rest as "a needless Show." Their art can make "Summer" (with all its teeming luxuriance) last "a Solid Year" (line 9; the finite limit of that period of time would seem to suggest the limits of this philosophy, even if the year is understood to represent an entire lifetime).

The Poets can "afford" (a verb that connects with the notions of "value" in a material sense introduced in the opening stanza even though its principal meaning here is "offer" or "provide") a "Sun" (and by extension everything that it shines upon) the East "would deem extravagant" (line 11; this refers not only to the astounding opulence of some of the famed royal courts of Asia, but also to the conception of the sun as a god as it was honored in ancient Egypt and elsewhere). Poets seem capable of producing a heaven on earth, a comparison fostered by the speaker's reference to the "Further Heaven" (the reward promised by many religions) in line 12.

The last five lines are syntactically convoluted but they may mean that it would be an egregious sin to dream of a heaven as beautiful for those who worship God as the one the poets create for those who worship them. The plural pronoun ("Them" in line 13) may refer to the Trinity, the three manifestations of the one God. "Grace" (line 15) refers to the mercy God freely extends to those He chooses. To "justify"(line 16) means to absolve from guilt, but within early New England theology, the term also referred to the preparation of the soul for its divine reward. This interpretation reinforces the notion that poets can be "all," as stated in line 8.

Alternative interpretations of the last five lines could note their connection with the question of economics introduced by such terms as "value" and "afford" earlier in the poem. They could be interpreted as implying that (a) the returns God could expect in exchange for making the reality of heaven equal to or exceeding the poet's or theologian's dreams would not justify the undue expenditure of His Grace, or (b) it would be asking too much of God's Grace that he would inspire poets to adequately convey all the promises of heaven. The former possibility has the advantage of connecting with the sense of personal unworthiness that the speaker conveys in the opening line.

"I SAW A MAN PURSUING" Stephen Crane (1899) Crane learned much about obsessions, compulsions, and depravity in his short, artistically productive life. In this poem, the speaker wants to sound like the voice of reason and sanity when he intervenes to prevent a man from wasting time in what he views as an obviously futile pursuit of the horizon.

The speaker may not be as suitable for his role as he imagines, however. By his own admission he is "disturbed" by the pursuer's actions (line 3), and he provides no justification for the self-righteous, aggressively intrusive way that he "accosted" the man (line 4). Note the arrogance with which he begins lecturing not only on the limits of the other man's chosen pursuit but even on his personal limits.

His comeuppance is swift, if not fully realized. The pursuer "cried" (a word that may convey his exasperation at the uninvited interruption as much as it indicates his loud voice) that the speaker is a liar and ran on (line 8).

A late 19th-century man would be more likely than his 21st-century counterpart to interpret a man's running as a futile pursuit of the horizon, but the second line suggests that even the speaker is impressed by the runner's speed. Even for those who share the speaker's assumption that running is a frivolous pursuit, however, the poem has value in its caution against being so presumptuous as to criticize another person's métier.

The arts, sciences, and every other human endeavor are limited by the current state of knowledge in the chosen field. This poem should encourage those who would extend the horizons of their specialties to persevere in their quest despite the negative feedback they receive from their more conservative critics.

"I SAW IN LOUISIANA A LIVE-OAK GROWING" WALT WHITMAN (1860)

In 1848, the poet was employed in Louisiana as the editor of the New Orleans *Crescent*. His experience might have been as lonely as that of the speaker in this poem; within six months he returned to his beloved New York. Like the speaker, he probably realized it was time to leave when a tree started "uttering joyous leaves" (line 3) and looking lusty (line 4).

The moss he describes in the second line is Spanish moss, a bromeliad so prominent that it became one of the most easily recognizable symbols of the old South. Hanging from the trees but taking no nourishment from them, its gray tendrils twist into a mat somewhat resembling a human beard. A Freudian scholar would probably make much of the speaker's admission that an oak's "rude, unbending, lusty" look made him think of himself (line 4), suggestions that were probably not far from the poet's mind when he considered the image. Instead of developing such parallels between moss-draped limbs and human anatomy, however, the speaker focuses on the tree's isolation. Realizing that he could not live (or at least write; the "leaves" he cannot create may be the pages of his book) without his friend, he brought away a twig with some moss on it. A Freudian interpretation of the image is unnecessary because the speaker recognizes that it reminds him of "manly love" in line 10. Acknowledging the deep roots of his own desires, he recognizes that unlike the oak he cannot flourish "all [his] life" (line 12; the phrase can mean "in every aspect of his life" as well as "for his entire lifetime") without a friend or lover near.

"I STARTED EARLY—TOOK MY DOG" EMILY DICKINSON (1891)

Magical things can happen at the beach if you are properly receptive to them. An invigorating mixture of salt air, exercise, unfiltered sunlight, open water, and isolation combine with the tactile novelties of stepping on continually shifting sand and feeling the splash of cold water fill your shoes. The speaker in EMILY DICKINSON's poem tried to maximize her experience by choosing a companion (her dog) whose senses would in some ways complement her own without burdening her with the necessity of talking. The early start was necessary if she wanted to avoid other people and have any chance of seeing such wonders as the mermaids (line 3) in the early morning shadows and haze. Everything seems to have a life of its own and, like a good host receiving a visitor, takes just as active an interest in her as she does in it.

It is evidently a very warm day (or at least a very magical one) for she sees frigates (large seabirds most at home in the skies over tropical oceans) "in the Upper Floor" (line 5). From their perspective high in the sky she would resemble a mouse run aground on the sand. Nature seemed so benign that day that she imagines the birds trying to help her. Evidently she associates the bird's name with the swift medium-sized naval vessels that were named after them, for the "Hempen Hands" that would be extended from a ship would probably be ropes spun from hemp, the fiber commonly processed from hemp plants to fill such important shipboard needs. The phrase signals a turning from natural to human phenomena (sailors are often called a ship's "hands") and from an external to an internal emphasis. No man moved her (line 9) until a sudden tide of passion swept up her body; the third stanza finds her not physically awash up to the neck in surging seawater (a chilling and possibly life-threatening misfortune) but focused on the pleasant sensations associated with some of her erogenous zones, represented by the clothes that cover her from her "simple shoe" (line 10) to her bodice.

By now she has forgotten the dog she brought with her; his short-lived presence probably signaled that she was not obsessed with sex and did not come to the beach for that purpose. Her lack of concern for the animal after the single line in which he appeared is another indication of the unreality of the seascape; the real focus of the poem is the speaker's experience of a sexual fantasy.

Her passion is so intense that its tide (personified as "He" in line 13) may consume her, although her less than fortuitous phrasing ("He would eat me up") suggests that she may have some intimacy issues. These would have been of no small concern to the thinking women of her mid-19th century (the poem was thought to have been written in 1862). Although many of the laws placing all of a wife's property at her husband's disposal had been changed and the attitudes sanctioning a man's physical correction of his wife (a euphemism permitting an entire spectrum of abuse) were being challenged, there was still tremendous societal pressure on a woman to defer to her mate's demands. It would be safer and less jarring to deal with images, like the sparkling dew on a dandelion's sleeve (line 15). Exactly what she "started" (line 16) at that point can only be inferred from the dashes used in the same rather suggestive manner adopted by the steamier romance novelists of the middle of the 20th century. The tide of her passions (and probably her dream lover, perfectly in tune with her sensations) follows close behind her. It starts again at her heel, but by now her shoes are overflowing with Pearl (line 20). This suggestive substance signals another shift in sensibility, another turning outward.

Perhaps basking in the afterglow of such a delightful morning, she seems immersed in her own little world until meeting the Solid Town (line 21), or at least a few inhabitants of it so stolid that they seem incapable of ever knowing such a passion. His services no longer required, the tide bows (like a perfect gentleman, but the gesture may also acknowledge her mastery over her passion; line 23). He leaves her "with a Mighty look" (line 23), his last attempt to dominate her (at present). Notice how many of her unstated concerns are conveyed in the simple phrase "at me" (line 24), a tacit admission that she feels objectified by even her dream lover's possessive male gaze. As if realizing that she is unwilling at that time to make all the compromises necessary to more openly accommodate her sexuality, her vast sea of passions "withdrew."

"I SPEAK YOUR NAME" Sophie Jewett (published 1910) Although the situation is frequently very painful in life, a forced separation often leads to the best love stories and poems. In Sophie Jewett's poem the speaker, perhaps because their love is forbidden by familial or societal interference, must speak the name of his or her love "in alien ways" (line 1). The phrase suggests an unconventional relationship, although it might also mean that they were formerly so close that the speaker never used her proper name, or that s/he is enjoying the pleasant self-torture of saying Margaret's name (and its diminutives) with

different inflections as a way of feeling still close to her. It is a rainy, probably miserable November in the poem, a month rendered warmer by the feminization of its "lashes" (line 2) and by the speaker's imagining the absent Margaret in its light. Appropriately, the speaker recalls Margaret's love of such seemingly inhospitable landscapes, but at the same time s/he may be using the months in a more conventional manner. Poetic tradition often figured the whole of human life as a single year, a comparison fancifully maintained in the references in popular culture to a May/December relationship in reference to a marriage in which one partner is very much older than the other. In such a scheme, November is so late in life that a body can seem as fading and withered as the land. In that time of peace and looming death, the speaker has no regrets about spending so much of the past life with Margaret.

The second stanza recalls Margaret in the fullness of her June glow; it transcends time to remember her always on her best day. The speaker calls her name across the months, however, an indication that s/he values all the time they spent together. While the opening of the third stanza continues hinting at a forbidden love, the 10th line also conveys the urgency of a love for Margaret's golden hair so great that God separated them and not some human agency. Notice the poignancy of the image of the sea placed "between our eyes" (line 11); one senses that they spent much time gazing into each other's eyes before this separation. "Fret" (line 11) is a descriptor not common in male descriptions of their own behavior in the late 19th century; such diction and the subsequent mention of "my soul's demand" suggest that the speaker is female. In any case, the truth of Margaret's soul responds in a way that seems closer than if their hands were joined. If for some reason the speaker cannot publicly proclaim Margaret's name (and their relationship), she will nevertheless speak of it in a low voice to God, "who listens" (line 14). As they both evidently believe in the power of prayer, that approach seems to hold the speaker's best hope of a reunion at present.

"ISRAFEL" Edgar Allan Poe (1831) This is Edgar Allan Poe's reworking of the Orpheus myth. Although he substituted a lute for the Greek's lyre,

both musicians had the ability to control animals and inanimate matter with their songs. It is interesting that Israfel appears only in an introduction to the Koran by an English translator and not in the Koran, and that the Houri, the pure beings of surpassing beauty who populate paradise, are the poem's only other connection with the Muslim religion. Poe's real theme is the power of the best musician to cast a spell on his audience, and he may have varied his rhythms, line lengths and even the number of lines per stanza to illustrate the insufficiency of the speaker (or the poet or any other mortal, for that matter) to reach such sustained heights of ecstasy in his art.

A lute resembles a guitar on steroids, with popular variations sporting 13 to 15 strings, broad necks, and swollen soundboards. Note that the two opening lines do not specifically identify Israfel as the spirit "whose heart-strings are a lute" but only state that such a spirit (which might be shared by all or permeate the place in some unspecified metaphysical way) dwells in heaven. None sing "so wildly well" as the angel Israfel, whose voice could silence the giddy stars (this thought has metaphysical implications. In early religions, stars were often thought to influence human destiny even on an individual basis. From the ancient Greek mathematician/philosopher Pythagoras to the advent of a science-based astronomy, many western Europeans believed that the planets in our solar system were held in place by heavenly spheres, and that their movement created harmonious sounds called the "Music of the Spheres." Under either system, silencing the stars meant stopping their movement, thus bringing time to a halt for the duration of a song).

The second stanza suggests other wonders, such as a personified moon who blushes with love at her zenith, while lightning (the "red levin" of line 12) and the seven Pleiads (a constellation whose appearance and disappearance is associated with the coming of spring and fall) stop to listen to Israfel.

The stars (or "starry choir," a term that could refer to singing angels [line 16]) attribute Israfel's "fire" (the source of his power) to the "trembling live wire" (line 21) of the unusual strings of his lyre (a stringed instrument of even greater antiquity than the lute. This reveals flawed thinking on the choir's part, for if Israfel

could achieve miraculous results with either instrument, then the magic more likely resides in the musician and not in the instrument).

The third stanza provides a glimpse of heaven where Israfel trod (walked) and "deep thoughts are a duty" (line 24). Love is there "a grown-up God" (the hyphenated adjective may refer to the more sensual pleasures afforded the blessed who will spend eternity there, in Poe's conception of the place). Even the glances of the Houri (splendid, dark-eyed female spirits) contain "all the beauty we worship in a star" (line 28).

The speaker praises Israfeli (an alternative spelling that Poe used twice in the poem) for despising uninspired songs, arguing that he deserves laurels and a merry long life because he is the wisest of bards. The "burning measures" of the primary emotions (grief, joy, hate, and love are enumerated in line 37) he evokes on the lute serve the ecstasies of heaven so well that the stars (a source of divine harmony) may as well be mute.

Heaven belongs to Israfel, but in this world of sweets and sours our flowers are merely flowers (and not expressions of divinity). The contrast is so great that the sunshine of our happiness is equivalent to the shadow of his perfect bliss. If the speaker could trade places with the angel, the latter might not sing a mortal melody so wildly, and a bolder note might swell from the speaker's lyre in the sky.

"I TASTE A LIQUOR NEVER BREWED"

Emily Dickinson (1890) A popular antidrug message of the late 20th century encouraged people to "get high on life," and this poem suggests what that euphoria could be like if religious ecstasy took the place of alcoholic spirits. The poem begins with a metaphysical enigma; since liquors are produced by distillation, it is normally impossible to "taste a liquor never brewed" (line 1). Knowledgeable social drinkers would also be puzzled by her choice of drinking liquor from tankards. Since liquors frequently have a very high alcohol content, they are generally consumed from small glasses. Tankards are generally reserved for less potent beers and ales; to be drinking liquors from them (line 2) would soon result in an advanced stage of intoxication. The tankards of the poem are especially exquisite since they are "scooped in pearls," and the preciousness of those jewels, their iridescent qualities, and prominence in the Bible (Matthew 13 and I Timothy 2, for example), provide further clues as to the source of the speaker's good spirits. Even the popular European wines cannot touch its quality.

Drunk on air and debauched by dew, the speaker reels through summer days (and the second stanza) from "inns of molten blue," by which she means the heavenly summer skies. Like a confirmed alcoholic who has learned to hold her liquor, she keeps drinking when such lightweights as the drunken bee are shown the door. In addition to being a snazzy name for an inn, a "Foxglove" (line 10) is a bell-shaped crimson wildflower. Even after the butterflies have finished their drinks (since a dram is about 1/16 of an ounce, it would not take too many drams to fill a butterfly's stomach), the speaker keeps drinking.

The last stanza takes the drinking experience to its limit, conflating the hallucinations (a common symptom of delirium tremens, an advanced, sometimes fatal stage of alcoholism) of the confirmed alcoholic with the visions of heaven the speaker experiences in her rapture. Angels and saints run to their windows to see her come from Manzanilla (the name of a dry sherry. Dickinson may also have been thinking of Manzanillo, a Cuban port from which a fine rum would be shipped).

One of the problems of alcohol use that leads to its abuse is that it can seem so attractive from the outside.

American society tends to wink at the problem until it cannot be denied; notice that the speaker's conception of herself as a "little tippler" (line 15) appropriates one of the hundreds of quaint euphemisms used for drunkenness by which the disease of alcoholism seems acceptable. It seems appropriate that the angels and saints would run to see the rare spectacle of a drunk in heaven since alcohol generally leads one in other directions.

"I'VE SEEN A DYING EYE" Emily Dickinson (1862)

In Emily Dickinson's day, the death experience was more typically acted out in private homes than in hospitals or doctors' offices, and the attendants were often family members. This made it a far more intimate experience for all concerned, and in this poem the speaker relates how one terminal patient's eye traveled about the room, perhaps finding something in the next world to focus on, before becoming inanimate. The author may have described the eye as "soldering" to reveal its merely mechanical or mineral properties once the human spirit had left the body. To solder is to heat an alloy to its relatively low melting point and then to pour or drop it onto two metal surfaces; when it cools, it will bond the two surfaces together. The speaker may be using this physical phenomenon as a metaphor to suggest that dying could be the spiritual uniting of two distinct stages of existence, life and the afterlife.

J

"JESSE JAMES" ANONYMOUS **(19th century)**
This eulogy for the infamous outlaw emphasizes those
qualities (physical courage and strong family ties) that
he had in common with many good men everywhere,
while focusing on the unsavory aspects of his assassination at the hands of a gang member, as if his own
"martyred" blood could atone for the murders he committed. Much of the bandit's notoriety can be attributed to his longevity; as a teenager he was active in the
savage guerrilla fighting in the border states of Kansas
and Missouri in the declining years of the Civil War,
and he chanced to outlive most of his criminal cohorts
until 1882.

The opening line of this poem attributes the murders
of many men to the killer's youth, implying that he
should not be held responsible for the crimes he committed while still a lad. The song chiefly deals with the
last three years of his life, beginning with a train robbery at Glendale, Missouri (line 2; the date was October 8, 1879, when the outlaw was 32 years old). While
his gifts to the poor (line 3) are largely apocryphal, his
well-documented thefts from the rich were typically
high-profile, high-risk jobs including train and bank
robberies. He had "a hand," which is to say that he
was good at the technical aspects of his chosen trade,
a brain (which enabled him to plan heists and elude
capture) and a "heart" (which explains the mourning
of his wife and "three" children in the song's chorus
[the poet may have arrived at an average: Two of his
offspring survived to adulthood, but a set of twins died

in infancy]). The chorus carries the narrative to April
3, 1882, when a "dirty little coward" shot (Thomas)
Howard (the alias Jesse James used; line 7).

Robert Ford is named as the assassin in line 9, and
the speaker questions how it must feel to kill someone after eating his bread and sleeping in his bed (line
11). Moreover, James is portrayed as "a friend to the
poor" who would "never see a man suffer pain" (lines
13–14), a man who might rob a Chicago bank (which
James did not) and rob a train (and its relatively affluent passengers) and thus spare the poorer communities of the rural states (which, in fact, bore the brunt of
the gang's sprees).

The fourth stanza (excluding the chorus) correctly
states that the Glendale robbery occurred on a Wednesday, but the fifth stanza incorrectly implies that James
was shot on the following Saturday night, a dramatic
condensation of time with two advantages: It skips two
years of additional robberies, and it demonstrates how
thoroughly reformed and domesticated the outlaw had
become. Instead of indulging in weekend revelries,
James is shown talking to his family on that traditional
party night. The actual slaying took place on April 3,
1882, a Monday. The stanza also implies that it is more
honorable to be a robber (like Jesse James, who used
violence or the threat of it against victims) than a thief
in the night (who less frequently physically harms a
victim; line 23), a suggestion of dubious merit.

Although a few of "the people" (line 25) might
hold their breaths (in sympathy) upon hearing of the

gangster's demise, the overwhelming majority probably were glad to be rid of the menace. The outlaw may have been killed "on the sly" (line 28) and laid to rest in the traditional pose of hand on breast (as if in testament to the Lord), but even the speaker admits that the devil will be "upon his knee" (eager to take possession of his soul; line 30). As in a formal eulogy, an attempt is made at presenting the bland details of the deceased's birth (actually in Clay County, Missouri, and not the Shea County of line 31) and genealogy ("of a solitary race," a phrase attempting to elevate the deceased above other men, but the designation also hints at the erroneous notions of racial purity that were of some importance to a family of prewar slaveholders, as the James family had been).

In the penultimate stanza the poet identifies himself as Billy Gashade, about whom little is known aside from his admiration for a bank robber who could not be taken by a lawman. The final stanza returns the attention to the dead man, his mourning widow and children, and the coward who shot him.

JEWETT, SOPHIE (1861–1909) Relatively little is known about Sophie Jewett. Born in Moravia, New York, she was one of four siblings soon orphaned and raised by relatives in Buffalo, New York. She never married, and from 1886 to 1888, she traveled in Europe with her older sister, the artist and Mount Holyoke College professor Louise Jewett. For 20 years beginning in 1889, Sophie Jewett taught English literature at Wellesley College. As Ellen Burroughs, she published *The Pilgrim and Other Poems* (1896). Under her own name she published a modern English version (practically a translation of a manuscript she found at the British Museum) of *The Pearl* (1908) by the anonymous 14th-century poet who she believed also penned the more famous *Sir Gawayne and the Green Knight*. Her religious beliefs prompted her to write the children's biography of *God's Troubadour: the Story of Saint Francis of Assisi* (1910). Her poems were collected for a memorial edition (1910), and her *Folk Ballads of Southern Europe* (1913) and *Italian Sketches* (1917) were also posthumously published.

Jewett is represented here by two poems about relationships. "ARMISTICE" deals with a temporary truce between two lovers who enjoy their boating party despite the prior day's quarrels and their certain knowledge that tomorrow the fight will resume. The distance between the lovers in "I SPEAK YOUR NAME" is more geographical (and perhaps social, for it hints at a forbidden love) than emotional.

The chief archival records of Jewett include her sister's account of their Paris trip in the Louise Jewett papers at Mount Holyoke College and the text of a colleague's testimonial at the memorial services held for her at Wellesley. The University of Texas has one of her letters in its Robert Haven Schauffler Correspondence collection.

BIBLIOGRAPHY
Jewett, Sophie. *The Poems of Sophie Jewett*. New York: T.Y. Crowell, 1910.

"THE JEWISH CEMETERY AT NEWPORT" HENRY WADSWORTH LONGFELLOW (1852)
Rhode Island was founded in 1636 by Roger Williams as a haven against the religious intolerance of the Puritans who ruled the Massachusetts Bay Colony. In 1658 a few Jewish families availed themselves of the new colony's religious tolerance, a rarity in most parts of the world at the time, to organize as the Yeshuat Israel Congregation in Newport. In 1677 they created the Hebrew Cemetery, the oldest Jewish cemetery still existent in North America, which HENRY WADSWORTH LONGFELLOW visited in 1852.

The poem begins with the contrast between the nearby sea and the stillness (in both sound and motion) of the Hebrews in their graves. Their small community had contributed immeasurably to the success of the "fair seaport town" (line 2), but their heritage prompts the poet to find connections with their biblical origins. Hence the trees are white with the dust (line 5) one would expect to find in the deserts of ancient Egypt; their motion reminds him of curtains and their canopy reminds him of the tents that sheltered the chosen people as they escaped from the pharaoh's tyranny, a flight that brings an exodus of death to mind.

The shape and disrepair of their fallen old brown sepulchral stones reminds the poet of the tablets containing the Ten Commandments "written with the finger of God" (Exodus 31:18) that Moses brought to his people from Mount Sinai then shattered in disgust at their stiff-necked backsliding (Exodus 32:19). The last names of the dead resonate with foreign accents and climes, but Longfellow was familiar with their first names, such as Abraham and Jacob, from his reading of the Bible (lines 15–16).

The fifth stanza presents a divine solution to the thorny theological problem of death, promising that the faithful will enjoy eternal life (line 29). Most of God's promises in the Torah are based on earthly prosperity (although Deuteronomy 6:24 promises preservation "alive," for example, this is followed with the important qualifying clause "as at this day." More typical is Deuteronomy 5:33, offering the prolongation of one's days in one's own land as a reward for following the Lord's ways. There is, however, a strong rabbinical tradition supporting the fundamental Jewish belief in the afterlife).

Longfellow found the nearby synagogue closed (line 21), and long acquaintance with Europe sensitized him to the romantic potential of vanished civilizations. Much of his work at this time might be construed as a search for a usable past; he was eager to discover and immortalize such ruins as the American landscape could offer. Gone (temporarily) were the Psalms of David and the rabbis reading the Decalogue (the text of the Ten Commandments that were inscribed on the tablets mentioned in the third stanza of the poem) in the ancient Hebrew tongue of the prophets (line 24).

Although the congregation was not in evidence during the poet's visit ("Gone are the living," he announces in line 25), his technique is to present as much of the alien (for him) culture as he can. Thus "a hand unseen" (like the hand of God) keeps "green" (fresh in the memory; line 28) the graves and the remembrance of the dead. He wonders what "burst of Christian hate" (line 29) drove these "Ishmaels and Hagars" across the desert ocean (in Genesis 16:1–12, Hagar is a servant to Sarah, the barren wife of Abraham. Sarah sent her to Abraham to bear him a child, and an angel informed Hagar that her child would be called Ishmael and that everyone would be against him. By Genesis 21:12, Sarah had her own son by Abraham and banished Hagar and Ishmael as rival claimants to her son's inheritance, but Ishmael flourishes anyway).

In Europe, Jews were often forced to stay in restricted areas such as the German ghetto and "Judenstrass" (Jew's Street) mentioned in line 33 and taught to endure anguish and "the death of fire" (a reference to the Spanish Inquisition during which many Jews were burned alive as heretics; line 36). They lived on unleavened bread and the bitter herbs of their exile, washing it down with bitter tears (lines 37–40). In the Catholic Church they were denounced as Anathema Maranatha (or nonbelievers in Jesus Christ [1 Corinthians 16:22]; line 41), and Mordecai (the archetypal Jew who in Esther 3:4 refused to pay homage to a king for religious reasons. He would have been killed had not Queen Esther herself intervened and had his chief persecutor hung in his place; Esther 7:10) was humiliated in the streets.

Pride and humiliation accompanied Jews everywhere, but they bore physical beatings as unshakably as a continent (lines 45–48) because their historical patriarchs and prophets prepared them for the coming time. Unlike English, Hebrew is written from right to left, which Longfellow uses as an analogy for the way in which their life, lived in accordance with biblical law, became a "Legend of the Dead" (line 56).

At this point Longfellow declared "dead nations never rise again" (line 60), an extrapolation based upon his interpretation of the empty synagogue and its old cemetery that was happily premature when applied to even those Jews of Newport. In 1763, the Newport congregation dedicated what has become the oldest synagogue in the United States. Although it closed by the end of that century, it reopened in 1883 and continues to serve as an active synagogue. It also has been honored as a National Historic Site.

"JOHN BROWN'S BODY" ANONYMOUS (1862)

The armies of the Confederate States of America began the Civil War with a string of victories that thoroughly shocked the North. The words to this song could not have been better calculated to infuriate the Southerners, since John Brown represented everything they hated and feared. Although admitting that his body was "a-moldering" (being consumed by mold) in his grave (where it had been placed following his hanging on December 2, 1859), it asserted that his soul continued marching and that it was engaged in the Lord's work just as the militant abolitionist had been. The chorus celebrates this possibility as though it were evidence of God's will.

Most Southerners argued that the war was about states' rights, and many Northerners felt that it was about preserving the Union. The second stanza of this song correctly stated that the abolition of slavery was John Brown's goal and implies that he willingly sacrificed his life for that cause. The third stanza suggests that he is continuing to do the Lord's work and implies that taking up arms in a righteous cause will be favorably viewed in heaven. The last stanza not only personifies the stars but has them "looking kindly down" on Brown's grave. As they hear the line sung, an audience may be excused for interpreting the "stars of heaven" as God, Jesus, the saints, and/or whatever gods they believe in.

For additional poems on John Brown by other poets, see John Greenleaf Whittier's "Brown of Ossawatomie," Julia Ward Howe's "The Battle Hymn of the Republic" and Herman Melville's "The Portent."

"JOHN MARR" Herman Melville (1888) Much

of the poignancy of this poem is lost without the poet's lengthy headnote, and it is generally a bad sign if a work of art cannot stand on its own merits without such an explanation. Herman Melville identifies the speaker as an old mariner who retired to the Midwest but subsequently lost his wife and child (perhaps a complement necessary to avoid insinuation about his sexual orientation as he longs for the company of the friends of his youth). In his dotage, he has now begun addressing his former shipmates during the daytime because his dreams of their former service together are the most vital things in his life.

Once the shipmates faced the dangers of the sea together with songs on their lips and an attitude of philosophical resignation to their fate: "life is a storm— let storm" (line 8). Such men seem to fly through life like birds, petrels (an order of birds that includes the albatross family so at home on the open ocean that they return to land only to reproduce) afloat, and larks (a variety of songbirds with songs so jubilant that they lent their name to any thoughtless endeavor pursued for its own sake and the happiness it brings) ashore (line 14).

At night they surround Marr, ever young, not like half-remembered tunes or half-forgotten faces, but like the tides (line 20) that return to the same river each day, always rendering it new and vivid. Formerly their lives were entwined like the gulfweed, the brown tropical Sargasso seaweed of the tropical Atlantic, ever driven "to new embracements" (line 38). Now, however, he feels as if he were flung ashore by the surging waves to languish alone on land.

Every night (and, metaphorically, in the late evening of his life), he regains their shadowy fellowship. Their tattoos, earrings, and curled lovelocks (line 35; a lock of hair separated by a ribbon or band, like a pony tail) float around him. He calls them "unworldly" (an adjective with three possible meanings, each of which works here: (*a*) spirit- or ghostlike, since they exist only in his dreams; (*b*) naïve, in the sense of being simple in spirit or childlike in their innocent attachments; and (*c*) unable or unwilling to function within normal, land-locked society) "servers of the world" (since their service makes international commerce possible; line 37). They are all present and dear to him, whether their ghosts visit his home or whether he has joined them on China's seas in his dreams (China and the Far East were sources of silks, spices, and other extremely valuable trading commodities in the 19th century).

Like Melville himself, the old mariner evidently served on a merchant vessel, a whaler, and a warship, for he asks where all his shipmates from these adventures have gone (lines 40–44). Unlike the poet, he can recall a battle "on the wilds of midnight waters" (line 46). He also witnessed a burial at sea, recalling how they vainly tried to see into the depths as a brother sailor slid from the slant plank into the darkness (lines 50–51).

He wishes them well, hoping that these gunmates "lashed in shotted canvas" (prepared for burial by being sewn into sailcloth and loaded with weights [the iron "shot" more typically fired from weapons] so that they would not float; line 52) never again have their rest bothered by "All hands up hammocks" (the command that all sailors leave their sleeping hammocks and report for emergency duty immediately; line 53), the sound of battle trumpets and the boom of naval gunnery. In war, as in the many shipboard chores in which teamwork was essential, they were so in sync that their hearts seemed to beat in unison. The old man yearns to clasp (and to relive) such memories as their pulling together on the main halyard (the rope attached to the heavy mainsail, which could be raised by the brute force of a team of men working as a single unit) and to hear again their chorus (a sea chantey employed by working sailors to help synchronize their movements [and probably lighten their spirits]; line 62).

"JOY, SHIPMATE, JOY!" WALT WHITMAN (1871) This short poem provides the reader with an excellent opportunity to see the poet's growth over time, because "GOOD-BYE MY FANCY," WALT WHITMAN's poem of 20 years later, deals with similar materials in a more sophisticated way. Although his psyche seems fragmented in both poems, this is the more optimistic poem because of the speaker's hope that his soul as well as other parts of his identity will survive death or at least maintain enough consciousness to enjoy the voyage. He not only anticipates the upcoming change, he encourages everyone else to view death with similar joy. Any reader can be viewed as his shipmate since all mortal life has, in one sense, the same destination.

Alternatively, his first and last lines ("Joy, Shipmate, Joy!") seek to share his joy with the shipmate who may be identified as his soul (thus becoming the internal audience) in the second line. References to "our" life and departure identify the soul as at least a fellow traveler in both the former existence and that to come. If the speaker shared the poet's years, the "long, long anchorage" (line 4) would have consisted of a little more than half a century of relative drudgery when compared to the leaping, swift course of the ship of death and the anticipated adventures of the afterlife.

The second line consists of a parenthetic statement ("Pleased to my soul at death I cry") that is crucial to this understanding of the poem, since it can be interpreted as identifying the internal audience (his soul) and situation of the poem. An alternative reading would interpret the line as merely an emphatic statement expressing the heights of the speaker's joy as he sailed through his life, and as he looks forward to the unknown adventures at and perhaps after death. His life has been so exciting that he remembers it with pleasure on his deathbed. This reading has the advantage of dispensing with the metaphysical questions associated with the soul/identity dichotomy and the possibility of the speaker's consciousness on the ship of death.

A third possibility (albeit a less likely one given the poem's date and its appearance in the "Songs of Parting" section of *Leaves of Grass*) would interpret it as an expression of the speaker's jubilance in leaving the "long, long anchorage" of social restraint. Thinking of the voyage as a metaphor for a new relationship of some kind would explain how the shipmates' prior lives have ended and their new life has begun. Of course it is also possible that the speaker is so ecstatic because a real ship is again underway. Few people are so happy in their career choice as this sailor appears to be, but many can relate to the joy of leaving a "long, long anchorage" behind. In this connection, it should not be forgotten that America was increasingly becoming a highly mobile society when this poem appeared. New lives were often started once an immigrant ship left its foreign port, or when similar vessels left the eastern seaboard with settlers for the American West Coast or other destinations. Thus the central metaphor of the poem would have been very familiar to the poet's contemporaries.

K

**"KEATS" HENRY WADSWORTH LONGFELLOW
(1875)** The extraordinary career of the British poet
John Keats (1795–1821) ended far too early with his
death in Rome from tuberculosis. This Italian sonnet
celebrates the young romantic by comparing him to
the eponymous hero of his lengthy (more than 4,000
lines divided into four books) poem of 1817, *Endymion.* Unfortunately, the comparison is too facile, and
HENRY WADSWORTH LONGFELLOW's poem offers no new
insight into the Keats poem or into the lives of shepherds or poets. Nor does it offer anything close to the
achievement of even the first line of its predecessor: "A
thing of beauty is a joy for ever."

Generally speaking, those mortals who succeed in
becoming lovers of a god in Greek or Roman mythology rarely lead happy or productive lives. Such was
Endymion's fate; he fell in love with the moon goddess Selene and gained eternal sleep (not death, but
perpetual unconsciousness) for his trouble. Although
50 daughters came from their union, Endymion was
oblivious to all that.

To think Keats a shepherd like his hero is to sell
the medical student/poet short. He had the power to
bring nightingales (a European bird famed for its nocturnal songs; line 5) to life for his readers. The speaker's search for the shepherd/poet takes him into the
cold realm of night, wherein he finds only a broken
shepherd's pipe (line 8) and a white marble tombstone
bearing the epitaph provided in lines 10–11 (unfortunately, a friend of Keats added his own preface to the

poet's tombstone which identifies the fallen as a very
bitter young English poet whose deathbed thoughts
centered on the malicious power of his enemies).

Longfellow (or at least his speaker in this poem)
thought that the anonymity of the original epitaph was
too small a reward (the "meed" of line 11) for Keats's
poetry, and would rework Isaiah 42:3 in its place. In
the biblical original, God used the bruised reed and
smoldering flax as examples of the things that would
not distract his servant from the more important task
of bringing His truth to the earth. Longfellow com-
mandeers the imagery to suggest that Keats was broken
like the bruised reed and not allowed to burst into the
flame of poetic maturity because of his untimely death.
It is an interpretation that tends to denigrate instead of
celebrate all that Keats was able to accomplish.

**"KILLED AT THE FORD" HENRY WADS-
WORTH LONGFELLOW (1867)** The Civil War called
off the best and brightest of the nation's youth, and an
estimated 620,000 died of wounds or disease out of
the approximately 4 million men who served on the
two sides. Many died ugly deaths in the trenches, but
in this poem HENRY WADSWORTH LONGFELLOW sanitized
that experience for a postwar audience that had read
chilling newspaper accounts of the fighting for more
than four years.

In this poem the speaker witnessed the death of a
good-humored, handsome, honorable soldier, "the
light and life of us all" (line 3). The dead man had

remarkable leadership abilities including a voice that the speaker compares to a bugle call, a charisma that forced everyone to watch him, and a laugh and pleasantness that hushed discontent.

The prior night the speaker and he had been riding down to the picket-guard (soldiers stationed on the perimeter of an army's position to provide notice of an advancing enemy) at a ford (a point on a river where the water was shallow and the banks were low enough to permit crossing by infantry, cavalry, artillery, and/or supply wagons). To assuage any guilt over the victim's role in the war, he is not shown in the midst of battle or even thinking of the conflict at all. He is humming an old song about roses when a "whistling ball" (more than a thousand different types of bullets were used in the Civil War including the old roundball used in muskets long before the Revolutionary War. The minnie ball, a conical bullet with ridges at its base that fit the grooves of a rifled barrel, had a distinctively sharp whistle that was markedly different from the usual shriek of shot and shell in the period. It traveled much faster than its predecessors and hence typically shattered any bone it struck; line 15) "stilled his voice" (a bloodless euphemism for his death). The speaker heard something fall and whispered as one would out of respect for the dead in a room where a body could be visited prior to its burial (lines 19–20), but received no answer.

His immediate external audience, especially those who lost someone in the war, would have appreciated the speed of the death, which involved little suffering. The combat veterans among them might have won-dered if it were not the unnecessary noise of his humming that gave his position away since the darkness of the rainy night and the density of the woods made it impossible for the speaker to see that the rider next to him had fallen. The enemy (or "friendly") sniper or picket who fired the shot must have been similarly handicapped. The scenario in which the unlucky man died was not an unfamiliar one, however. Although he lingered for a week after the incident, in 1863 the famed Confederate, Lt. General (a "three-star" general second in command only to Robert E. Lee) Stonewall Jackson, met his doom when struck by three bullets fired by his own pickets as he rode in the dark to check on his lines near Chancellorsville, Virginia.

In the poem the luckless soldier is carried back to the silent camp. By the surgeon's lamp the speaker saw two white roses (his pallor probably stemmed from blood loss, but the flower it brought to mind is typically associated with innocence and purity) on the victim's cheeks and a blood-red rose (symbolic of passion, courage, and unself-conscious beauty) over his heart (line 28).

In the last stanza the speaker envisions the same bullet speeding north until it hit a heart that ceased to beat without a cry or murmur (line 34). The church bell tolled for the passage ("from cross to crown," or from the trials of this life to the heavenly rewards of the next; line 36) of a woman (probably a lover, given all the roses scattered about the poem) whose death (probably from the shock of learning of the soldier's death) left her neighbors wondering.

L

"THE LADY'S MISTAKE" Frances Sargent Locke Osgood **(1839)** Although the Revolutionary War did away with the British class system in America under which a relatively few hereditary nobles received power and prestige as their birthright, it also deprived the new men (those who had achieved wealth and power from the opportunities suddenly available to them) of the privilege of official recognition of their new status. Marriage had represented one of the few venues available for upward mobility in the pre-Revolutionary days, a fact that could boost the attractiveness of even aged members of the titled nobility in the very informal marriage markets of the day. By 1839, however, only those most insecure in the social position to which their new money seemed to entitle them would seek a link with the old-world nobility by marrying their children into their ranks. The surprise of Frances Sargent Locke Osgood's poem is how much the speaker reveals about her own unattractiveness in the course of heaping scorn on her former beau. Readers (and presumably, the internal audience as well) can laugh down at both of them from the security of their assumed moral and intellectual superiority.

Notice how the speaker chooses a variety of expressions in the first stanza to convey essentially the same information about her beau's features: His eyebrows, hair, mustache, and teeth were all false. All of them would have passed muster, however, if only his heart had been true (line 5), a statement that titillates the reader with the expectation that some scandal will be revealed shortly.

The second stanza reveals that the beau's rosy complexion, normally an indication of good circulation and hence, good health, youth and vitality, resulted from his use of makeup. Similarly, his shapely calves, normally suggestive of masculine fitness and power, are illusions created by his tailor. Even this would have been acceptable, if his love had been sincere. The indictment that "his love was but show" (line 10) further whets the reader's appetite.

In the third stanza, the speaker turns from attacking his appearance, which could fool others but not her, to revealing her surprise that his "flattering tongue" was deceitful (line 14). One might expect that she had discovered a broken promise or a luckier rival for his affections, but in fact her disappointment is more elemental: He has no fortune.

A modern comedic writer might have stopped at this point. The actual ending is in some ways more interesting, however, because it introduces an element of complexity in the speaker's personality. Her discovery that her beau is not a count (and hence not a member of Europe's hereditary nobility) is the deal breaker. Was she really so naive as to place such emphasis on her beau's ancestry, which carries few perks in America, or was she sophisticated enough to throw up this dodge when her real disappointment was his lack of money? In the 19th century, ladies were ideally not supposed to be interested in such base material concerns. In the

184

21st century, such a speaker might be hesitant to reveal herself as a stereotypical gold digger interested only in a prospective mate's money.

"THE LAKE- TO-" EDGAR ALLAN POE (1827; 1845)

This poem exists in two versions; the 1845 version is discussed here. Lake Drummond, still surrounded by bogs and the pine trees mentioned in the sixth line and one of only two freshwater lakes in Virginia, is thought to be the lake that inspired this poem. EDGAR ALLAN POE was so enamored of the isolated loneliness of the lake that, in the third line, his speaker lapses into labored syntax as a means of revealing the uniqueness of his love for the spot and the hold it has over him. The main thought behind "the which I could not love the less" would normally be phrased "for which my love could not have been greater." He began establishing the mood of the poem by referring to his "haunting" of the "wild lake" and a possible pun on "the which/the witch." Similarly, the "pall" of line 7 refers to the darkness of night, but it is also the term used for the mourning cloth covering a coffin or tomb, and even for the coffin itself (pallbearers are the people who carry a coffin to the gravesite).

When night came and the mystic wind began murmuring, he would awake to the terror of the lake (lines 7–12). He was not frightened, but felt "tremulous delight" (line 14; a mixed feeling that may hold an important clue to understanding why his most frightening work [typically in short story form] is so pleasurable for a reader). He would not be taught or bribed to define that feeling (perhaps a pleasurable melancholy) for all the wealth of a gem mine nor for love, even though that love came from his internal audience (or possibly, the reader).

The waves of the lake are poisonous (a superstition probably stemming from the darkened tinge from the tannin produced by the surrounding trees), and its gulf (which can designate an abyss as well as a bay or inlet) would be a fitting grave for him who would take such solace (a suicide is probably implied) to his "lone imagining" (line 21). This would appeal to a solitary soul (like the speaker) who could think that dim lake a paradise.

LANIER, SIDNEY (1842–1881)

The southern poet who led the most interesting (and in many ways, the most typical) life of his generation was Sidney Lanier. On February 3, 1842, he was born into the comfortable family of a Macon, Georgia, lawyer. He was given the early musical training and private education that enabled him to enter Oglethorpe College as a sophomore at the age of 14. He graduated with honors in 1860, but the Civil War quickly put an end to what might have been an even more promising academic career. His four years in uniform included participation in the Seven Days Battles near Richmond, Virginia, from June 25 to July 1, 1862, and terrifying service as a mounted scout, but he was finally captured as the signal officer on a blockade-runner. He had to endure four months of privation as a prisoner of war.

Upon his release in 1865, he finished *Tiger Lilies*, his only novel, married the propitiously named Mary Day, and tried teaching and assisting with his father's legal practice. In 1872 he traveled alone to Texas and, in March of the next year, to Baltimore, Maryland, in search of a more advantageous economy. He became first flutist in the latter city's Peabody Orchestra, and his poetry brought him a lectureship at Johns Hopkins University in 1879. Unfortunately, he died in Lynn, North Carolina, on September 7, 1881, of the tuberculosis he contracted while a federal prisoner.

In "The SHIP OF EARTH," penned shortly after the close of the Civil War, Lanier voiced his concern that everything had changed. It seems as if God had abandoned the world, leaving men to fight it out under the most barbarous conditions. Faced with a scene reminiscent of a bloody battlefield (or battleship deck), the speaker recognizes that man is unable to cope with such overwhelming misery without divine guidance. The second poem, "EVENING SONG," chronicles a lover's campaign of seduction. As they walk along the seashore at sunset, he points out a few of the lessons they could learn from nature and implies that their love could be as grand as those of antiquity. Caught up in the moment, he seems to command the sea and the stars.

Lanier's fashionable birthplace has been preserved as the Sidney Lanier Cottage in Macon. Because of his celebrations of southern gentility, statues and busts of the poet may occasionally be encountered from Baltimore to New Orleans, and schools, lakes, and bridges have been named in his honor. The Sidney Lanier Papers at Johns Hopkins University represents his most extensive archive. The Middle Georgia Archives at the Washington Memorial Library of Macon also holds a few Lanier items, and Harvard University has a copy of the letter he sent to WALT WHITMAN to purchase a copy of *Leaves of Grass.* The 10-volume centennial edition of his collected works was published by Johns Hopkins Press in 1945, but all of his poems are contained in the first volume. The second volume contains his scholarly book on *The Science of English Verse* and essays on music.

BIBLIOGRAPHY

Gabin, Jane S. *A Living Minstrelsy: The Poetry and Music of Sidney Lanier.* Macon, Ga.: Macon University Press, 1985.

Mims, Edwin. *Sidney Lanier.* Port Washington, N.Y.: Kennikat Press, 1968.

Starke, Aubrey Harrison. *Sidney Lanier: A Biographical and Critical Study.* New York: Russell & Russell, 1964.

"THE LAST LEAF" OLIVER WENDELL HOLMES **(1831)**   There are many ways of marking the passage of time in poetry, and this poem offers several of them. First of all, its situation depends on the reader's understanding that most people led less hectic, more geographically restricted lives at the time of its composition. An unfamiliar face can generate some interest in those who rarely see them, and the speaker was so curious when an old man passed by his door that he had to find out who he was. The town was so quiet that he heard the old man's cane on the pavement stones, which prompts him to tell the internal audience (the person within a poem to whom it is implied that the speaker is relating his tale, as opposed to the readers of the poem) what he found out about him.

To his surprise, the speaker discovered that in his prime, "not a better man was found" (line 10). Although this might seem to refer to the man's high moral character, his wealth, or some other attribute, usually the phrase refers to a robust physicality. This introduces the problem of the poem: the speaker, evidently around the same age as OLIVER WENDELL HOLMES (22), is taken aback to learn that the decrepit stranger once had been remarkable for his vitality. This

interpretation is reinforced by his explanation that the "pruning knife of Time" (line 8) had cut him down. At first glance this may seem a very bleak lesson for the speaker since it implies that he will undergo the same process, but within the rustic metaphor lies a mitigating circumstance. Just as trees are pruned—a year's new growth is trimmed back so that their energy is diverted to fruit production instead of additional growth—so might a declining physical prowess enhance a person's potential for growth in other aspects of his being. That point is evidently lost, however, as the speaker focuses on the old man's loneliness since all his contemporaries have died.

The speaker's first thought turns to the man's lost loves; the "mossy marbles" of the sepulcher now press down on the lips he had once kissed, and the names of his friends are found on tombstones. Recalling that his grandmother had once praised the man's beauty in rather conventional terms, comparing his complexion to a rose, makes the lesson of his own morbidity even more personal for the speaker, forcing him to take ever closer looks at the physical manifestations of advancing age.

The speaker's growth as a consequence of encountering the old man leads him to identify with him. Initially he found it humorous that his clothing was so old-fashioned; three-cornered hats and breeches were fashionable men's wear during the American Revolution, which ended 50 years before the poem was published. By the last stanza, his empathy with the old man is so complete that he looks far into his own future, where he might also outlive the other people of his generation. Younger people may then smile at the speaker's diminished stature and old-fashioned demeanor, but the last stanza implies that with the aging process come important lessons in the conduct of life. These include the humility of accepting the inevitable and of serving as a physical reminder that the health, as well as the clothes, of youth is transitory. The vision of himself clinging, as the last leaf on an old forsaken bough (lines 47–48), not only unites the central images of the poem, it also suggests that one of the keys of longevity is to draw strength from your identity even if your clothes (and your core beliefs) seem outmoded.

"THE LAST NIGHT THAT SHE LIVED"

EMILY DICKINSON (published 1951) This poem is unlike the others that EMILY DICKINSON wrote in that it lacks her characteristic ambivalence about religion and her evident joy in language. That does not mean it is less poignant or less accomplished; it reads like a carefully trained observer's eyewitness account of the passing of someone she loved.

The night was common enough except that the Dying made Nature seem different to those on the deathwatch (stanza one). That "great light" gave special emphasis to (or "italicized," line 8) small things normally overlooked. The closest sympathizers went between the final room and other rooms that contained "those to be alive tomorrow" (line 12), irrationally blaming them for continuing to exist while she must end. A "jealousy for [the dying woman] arose" (line 15; this startlingly frank admission may refer to a jealousy based on (*a*) her being the center of attention; (*b*) her advancement to her reward before the others; or (*c*) jealousy of place around the deathbed or for the esteem in which the various parties were held by her or the closeness of their relationships with her).

They waited, the time seeming "narrow" (offering little of interest, line 18) because their souls were "too jostled" to speak (line 19; this brilliant image may refer back to their jealousy of place, if that were indeed intended in the fourth stanza). Notice came of her final crisis.

That "she mentioned, then forgot" (line 17) disappoints those hoping for memorable final words but demonstrates her diminishing mental faculties. As "lightly as a reed bent to water" (lines 22–23) she barely struggled, gave up the fight, and died.

The survivors smoothed her hair and positioned her head, then waited for "Belief" (line 28) to regulate their "awful leisure." This may indicate their reliance on the minister and church custom to provide order to their mourning, but its deeper meaning is that their faith in God and His mercy had to "regulate" their disappointment (temper their reactions and soften their sense of loss) at losing her and their helplessness after there was nothing else they could do.

"LAUS DEO" JOHN GREENLEAF WHITTIER

(1865) The title, "Praise God" in Latin, conveys the poet's rejoicing at the news that Congress had passed the Thirteenth Amendment to the U.S. Constitution (January 31, 1865). The Civil War (and the continuous effort of such staunch abolitionists as JOHN GREENLEAF WHITTIER) had galvanized antislavery sentiment in Amesbury, Massachusetts, to the point where the abolishment of slavery was celebrated nearly as joyously as the nation's independence. Relishing the sounds of this success, Whittier used onomatopoeia to convey the clang and roar of bells and guns (line 2), and subjective description to show his personal elation (the belfries [the place, often in the steeples of churches, where the church bells hang] "rock and reel" and the cannons "peal on peal, fling the joy" from one town to another; lines 4–6).

Church bells were often tolled (sometimes one stroke for every year of the deceased's life) to commemorate the passing of a member of their congregations, a tradition to which the speaker alludes in the second stanza, when every stroke announces the burial hour of the crime (of slavery; line 9). It also seems the voice of God, and like Moses, whose initial response was a feeling of inadequacy (Exodus 3:11), the speaker asks who they (the townspeople and members of his congregation as well as himself) are to warrant seeing this glory and hearing this sound (lines 15–18).

In the Bible, the speaker reminds us in the fourth stanza, the Lord has used the whirlwind, the earthquake, and the thunder to execute his will (see Job 37:9, 38:13, and 37:5, respectively), breaking iron walls and gates of brass (He breaks brass gates and iron bars in Isaiah 45:2, Psalms 107:16, and elsewhere). Like Miriam, the sister of Aaron and Moses, the speaker would have everyone sing of the Lord's casting the mighty down and drowning the horse and rider who previously enforced the bondage of His chosen people (lines 27–30; Exodus 15:20–21).

The sixth stanza references Christ's "agony of prayer" (line 32 and Luke 22:44), that moment prior to his arrest on the Mount of Olives when, fully comprehending His faith, He asked God to spare him from the torture and crucifixion that awaited Him. The implied comparison is that the nation, and those who prayed for the abolition of slavery, suffered mightily as long as that institution survived. Now, however, His will is evident.

The Civil War, the speaker argues, combined the cruel rod of war with that of righteous law, creating a situation in which the wrath of (antislavery) man is praiseworthy (lines 40–42). For biblical parallels, compare Moses' use of the rod as an instrument of God's vengeance (Exodus 7:10–12, 17–21, and elsewhere) with Numbers 17:8–9, in which one rod among 12 blossoms as a sign of God's favor.

With the sin and heavy curse of slavery dead and buried (which would not legally become the case until December 6, 1865, when the 28th state fulfilled the quota mandated by the Constitution [three-quarters of the states, plus one; or 28 states out of the 36 then existent]), a fresher national life was about to begin (lines 45–48). Even the sad will rejoice and those incapable of speech will be given a voice (line 53 echoes Isaiah 35:6). The sound of broken chains (which formerly bound the slaves; line 58) tells the world that God reigns.

"LAY DIS BODY DOWN" Anonymous (19th century)

The speaker in this poem has taken the plunge, risking his/her life in a desperate gamble to reach free soil across the Ohio River before being chased down and captured. His strategy is simple: walk north by night, keep to the back roads, and hide in or near graveyards to sleep during the day. He feels most at risk when resuming his trek each evening, "laying [his] body down" as his half of the wager. Fugitive slaves usually had to leave their families behind and give up hope of being reunited, a tragedy the speaker acknowledges when he looks forward to heaven where his soul and his loved one's soul (the poem's internal audience) can meet when he lays his body down (dies). Their situation may not be as entirely hopeless as that, however, since he feels their closeness when he lays his body down (sleeps) "in de day" (line 11).

"LAY THIS LAUREL ON THE ONE" Emily Dickinson (published 1951)

This is a very difficult poem to decipher. The first two lines suggest that the Laurel, associated with honor, immortality, and victory (since winners of the Olympic Games were given laurel wreaths to wear on their heads), should be given to "the One too intrinsic for Renown" (lines 1–2). The speaker seems to indicate that s/he has a better idea as to who should be celebrated instead of the one who achieved celebrity status. The entire poem seems to turn on the meaning of "too intrinsic" (line 2); it could conceivably refer to someone too genuine or centered in the sense of being sufficient unto herself to care about fame.

Another important but equally puzzling clue ("Laurel-") begins the third line. The speaker may be questioning the entire notion of fame, which the laurel wreath has come to symbolize, but that would render the remainder of the line problematic: "veil your deathless tree." This is most likely a reference to Greek mythology: the major god Apollo began chasing a beautiful nymph named Daphne until her father, a relatively minor god, saved her from this rape by changing her into a laurel tree. Defeated, but still smug, Apollo made a wreath from the tree, thereby providing the laurel's connection with "greatness." He thus becomes "Him you chasten" (line 4) in the double sense of (a) render chaste by eluding his grasp, and (b) castigate and reprimand. The phrase that provides the last words of the poem ("that is He!") sums up her feelings about the true nature of the god, outing Apollo as an unsuccessful rapist. Thus the poem celebrates Daphne, hailed as "Laurel" in line 3.

This would explain how the laurel can convey two meanings for the modern florist: worldly success, but also a treacherous ambition that would win at any cost. The poem also may help explain how Emily Dickinson felt about the intrusive nature of fame, and why she so deliberately avoided it by keeping all but 10 of her poems unpublished during her lifetime.

LAZARUS, EMMA (1849–1887)

Today this poet is chiefly remembered for a poem written to raise money for a pedestal for a statue she never got the opportunity to see. She was born into a prosperous New York City merchant family on July 22, 1849. Home-schooling (first by tutors and then by her father) adequately prepared her to produce *Poems and Translations* at the age of 18, two other volumes of poetry (including *Songs of a Semite*), the novel *Alide,* a couple of plays and an influential collection of essays. Despite ill health, she became an active voice against the discrimination faced by successive waves of eastern European immigrants, especially the impoverished Russian Jews who had fled for their lives from the pogroms of their native land. By 1883, she was famous enough to be invited to donate a poem for the fund-raising efforts associated with the Statue of Liberty, a gift from the French by their sculptor Frederic-Auguste Bartholdi, which lacked funds for an appropriate base.

She frequently summered at the family's second home in Newport, Rhode Island, and made two trips to Europe, the first for half a year in 1883 and the second from 1885–87. It was during the second trip that *Liberty Enlightening the World* was unveiled in the New York harbor (on October 28, 1886) and that the poet's cancer was accurately diagnosed. Because her steamer arrived back in New York after dark, Emma Lazarus never got to see the statue.

"The NEW COLOSSUS" celebrates not only the Statue of Liberty but also the emerging power of the United States and the influx of new immigrants who contributed immeasurably to its success. A second poem discussed in this volume, "1492," illustrates the enriched meanings possible when a poet combines knowledge of her cultural heritage (her ancestors were among the Jews exiled from Spain in that year) with information from the dominant culture of her society.

Emma Lazarus died of Hodgkin's disease on November 19, 1887, in the city of her birth. The American Jewish Historical Society owns many of what remain of her personal papers, including the handwritten copy of "The New Colossus" sold in the Statue of Liberty pedestal auction. Columbia University also has some of her correspondence in their archives.

BIBLIOGRAPHY
Lazarus, Emma. *Selected Poems.* Edited by John Hollander. New York: Library of America, 2005.
———. *Selected Poems and Other Writings.* Edited by Gregory Eiselein. Orchard Park, N.Y.: Broadview Press, 2002.
Young, Bette Roth. *Emma Lazarus in Her World: Life and Letters.* Philadelphia: Jewish Publication Society, 1995.

"LEAVES OF GRASS'S PURPORT" WALT WHITMAN (1891)

In continuously adding poems, transplanting others to different places in the volume, and weeding a very few, WALT WHITMAN tended his *Leaves of Grass* with the skill and devotion a professional gardener lavishes on the chief estate of his care, the one upon which he knows his reputation will rest. At the same time, as lord of the manor, at the end of his life the poet could look over the vast expanse of his property with a great deal of satisfaction.

Purport is an interesting word in that it promises insight into the author's intention but also an appraisal of the work's importance. Whitman begins by denying that he wrote with a conventional moral purpose, listing four ways that he could have dealt with evil: exclusion, demarcation (establishing clear boundaries between good and evil), destruction ("picking out evils from their formidable masses," line 1), and identification (exposing them). Instead, he wishes to "add, fuse, complete, [and] extend" (line 2). In other words, he will acknowledge (and even celebrate) some of those impulses and desires that most religions condemn by connecting them with the divine ("the immortal and the good").

In describing his song (as well as its word and scope) as "haughty" (line 3), Whitman acknowledges that his pride sometimes borders on arrogance, but he also suggests that the superiority of his work merits such conceit. It was his aim (and frequently his method) to "span vast realms of space and time" (line 4), thus remaining relevant by a process akin to evolution to the various "growths and generations" of his audience by virtue of his continual, "cumulative" (line 5) additions to his work.

The third stanza introduces the process by which Whitman strove to obtain the lofty goals he set for himself. At age 36, he was a bit more than a "ripened youth" (line 6) when his first edition of *Leaves of Grass* appeared in 1855. His short list of the action verbs describing how he pursued his work ("wandering, peering, dallying;" line 7) also pertain to an active life in general, but his most important verb, "absorbing," suggests how he took the events of "war, peace, day, and night" (line 7) and made them serve his genius. Although steadfastly attending his task throughout his life, he finds it ending in sickness (his lengthy medical history includes a paralyzing stroke in 1873), poverty (although *Leaves of Grass* increasingly garnered critical attention, it was not a best seller in the poet's lifetime), and old age (line 9).

The last stanza finds the poet so close to the end of his life that for years Death has dogged his steps (and more recently, his "seated shape" [he is losing the use of his legs, but the same phrase may also contain a hope that while his body is the seat of much of his identity, his soul might survive the destruction of that part of his existence so pejoratively dismissed by this euphemistic term]; line 11). Although he continues to sing of life, yet he devotes much attention ("mind me well;" line 10) to his impending doom. Personified, Death sometimes comes face to face with him.

"LETTER FROM A MISSIONARY OF THE METHODIST EPISCOPAL CHURCH SOUTH, IN KANSAS, TO A DISTINGUISHED POLITICIAN" JOHN GREENLEAF WHITTIER (1854)

This poem challenges a reader's definition of what constitutes a poem. Such a thing was easier to determine when this appeared; since it lacked rhyme, meter and even uniform or predictable line lengths, many people would question its merit. Subsequent developments have, of course, reduced the importance of those standards. The division of the work into stanzas, the placement of the lines on the page and the initial capitalization of each line are more than enough to earn the classification as poetry in the 21st century should its content prove meaningful and memorable. This poem remains, however, unmitigated propaganda, and the chief motivation for JOHN GREENLEAF WHITTIER's following some of the conventions of poetry was probably to shield him from the accusations of fabrication that would so hurt his cause among those unsophisticated readers who would mistake a prose version of the same material for a real letter.

The poem satirizes the hypocrisy of a man who uses the church as a cover for his real mission, the extension of slavery to the Kansas territory. Its dateline identifies the letter's origin as the Douglas Mission in August 1854. The "Mission" probably took its name from Senator Stephen A. Douglas of Illinois, the

author of the Kansas-Nebraska Act that became law on May 30, 1854. The new legislation left the important question of the expansion of slavery to a popular vote by the residents of a proposed new territory, and an unforeseen consequence was the violence that erupted as large groups of proslavery and antislavery settlers and interlopers tried to influence the election.

The speaker arrived via Westport (present-day Kansas City, Missouri), where he helped organize a Vigilance Committee to whip, tar, and feather those Yankees "who despise the prize of the high calling" of those saints who would plant "pure gospel institutions" in the heathen wilderness (lines 9–10). He "groaned and strove and wrestled" (from the pulpit; such exertions would have seemed ludicrous for a staunch Quaker like Whittier, whose sect ordained no ministers and sometimes sat in complete silence for an entire meeting) for half an hour like Jacob at Penuel (a reference to Genesis 32:24–30 in which the biblical patriarch wrestled all night with an angel). Even rough riverboat hands wiped away tears (line 19), cried out their support, and hurled racist epithets in response to his exhortations. An impromptu assembly formed a committee to keep out Yankees who failed "the Shibboleth of the Nebraska bill" (in Judges 12:4–6, the Gileadites used a pronunciation test [the word *Shibboleth*] to determine which of the refugees from a war were enemy Ephraimites. Some 42,000 of those with incorrect pronunciations were killed on the spot. In this poem [line 30], the Shibboleth is the word *Nebraska,* which will presumably reveal New Englanders because they stereotypically drop their *r* [that is, *Harvard* becomes "Hahvaahd;" presumably *Nebraska* would be pronounced "Nebahska"]).

The locals also appreciated the speaker's account of his visit to Washington, D.C., and the news that the president and his cabinet regularly hear Sunday sermons. He ends this section with "Selah!" (a Hebrew word used in many of the biblical songs with a meaning like "Reflect" or "Contemplate what has been said" [see Psalms 3:8 and 4:2]).

Things are also going well at the Kansas Mission. The brother who acted as overseer during the speaker's absence assures good crops, although one slave ran away until the Indian converts found and shot him (line 46; the northern audience would be outraged at the conversion of Indians to a Christianity that included racism and sanctioned homicide). The surrounding heathens are already feeling the influence of the speaker's message of love, as their purchase of slaves indicates. He wishes the distinguished politician success in visiting Chicago to fight "the wild beasts of Ephesus" (possibly a reference to St. Paul's mission to establish the church at Ephesus in what is now Turkey), "Long John" (presumably a reference to John Parker Hale, the Free Soil Party's U.S. senator from New Hampshire from 1847 to 1853 and its candidate for president in 1852) and the "Dutch Free-Soilers" (the Pennsylvania "Dutch," a corruption of their word *Deutsch,* which more accurately reflects their German heritage. As in New England, antislavery sentiment was strong in Pennsylvania).

In his postscript the speaker claims that all is lost because the Yankees (stalwart men with "faces set like a flint of Plymouth Rock" (line 62) are flooding into Kansas; their as yet small numbers arrive like the rain patter before the big thunderhead drowns the prairies (lines 67–68). He would prefer to be a quiet naval chaplain, a clerk, or even the doorkeeper at the White House rather than to live among Yankee tents so numerous that their canvas tents on the prairie resemble a becalmed fleet of ships (lines 74–75). He thinks he hears a voice from the bayous (the swampy areas drained by slow-running streams in the Mississippi Delta region) where alligators guard against filibusters (a tactic by which a minority can delay legislative action by invoking procedural rules and monopolizing debate until the measure is shelved so that other business can proceed). Cuba seems to beckon like a ripe golden orange; the speaker's gospel could carry there on Quitman's bowie knife and Colt revolvers (John Anthony Quitman, promoted to major general for his leadership in the Mexican War, was an avid secessionist as early as 1849 and, while governor of Mississippi, an advocate for Cuban liberation from Spain). Beneath a Cuban fig tree, the Distinguished Politician could watch his sugarcane and slaves increase "like a patriarch in his eastern tent" (line 89).

Although the poem ends at that point, the subsequent history of Kansas frustrated the speaker's hopes.

Radical abolitionists who shared the poet's sentiments soon began raising funds for the settlement of Kansas. On May 21, 1856, proslavery forces raided Lawrence, Kansas (the county seat of Douglas County and perhaps therefore the site of the Douglas Mission from which the letter supposedly originated), an incident that prompted John Brown's retaliatory raids. Widespread election fraud invalidated a proslavery victory at the polls, and an antislavery legislature eventually passed an antislavery constitution that permitted Kansas to join the Union on January 29, 1861.

"A LETTER TO HER HUSBAND ABSENT UPON PUBLIC EMPLOYMENT" ANNE BRADSTREET (1678)

This is one of the most widely anthologized ANNE BRADSTREET poems because it deals lovingly with a sensuality that was frequently disparaged in Puritan texts, yet it seems less than elegant because it begins with a list. Instead of merely stating that she misses her husband, Bradstreet starts by considering the ways in which he completes her. This poem attempts to show how they are united into one being, and the ambiguous syntax of her first two lines reinforces this central image. The lack of a verb in the first two lines leaves this an open question; the items serve as the greeting of the letter. Does the poet's use of possessive pronouns signify that he owns these parts of her, or does it mean that she owns him? The list suggests not only how important he is to her, but also her pledge of these things to him.

It might be interesting to consider which items in her list might have special significance to a mid-17th-century Puritan wife. To tell her husband that he is her head may reflect a widely held cultural bias. A Puritan husband was more than a figurehead; he frequently exercised complete authority over the rest of the family. Not only did property rights favor the male as head of household, but because of his supposedly greater intellectual capacity, a man could be expected to better understand the Bible and the (always male) religious and legal authorities of the church and the community. Anne Bradstreet, a woman of superior education and training, might have hesitated before calling her husband her head if her mental capacity had been more appreciated. Her purpose here, however, is not to write a feminist tract but to tell her husband precisely how much she misses him and to get him to miss her. Calling him her head not only plays into his male vanity by reminding him of her supposed weakness, it may also hint that by his absence he is not fulfilling the responsibilities inherent in his role as head of the family. A dutiful Puritan would take pains to rectify this shortcoming if he were not fully engaged in the colony's business.

The "heart" and the "life" need no elaboration, but he is her eyes in the sense that she was restricted by custom and perhaps personal preference to the far more limited domestic sphere. Drawing his attention to this aspect of their relationship would undercut her desire to get him to come home as soon as possible, however. Since he serves as her eyes on the larger world because of his broader engagement with it, he might feel that she would directly benefit if his exposure were more intense and longer.

The items of the second line are even more reciprocal in the sense that both parties share in the "joy" and their worldly possessions. At the time, a "magazine" signified a larder or storehouse, but for a Puritan poet to mention her "magazine of earthly store" refers not just to material possessions, but to all the aspects of her life on earth she treasured. She is saying that he means the world to her.

The situation of the poem is stated in lines 3–4; since they are one being, how is it possible that he has gone off while she remains at the family home in Ipswich. The verb "lie" was frequently used geographically (New York lies south of Boston, for example), but for a homesick husband it would also convey an image of his wife's recumbent posture. Similarly, a "neck" could not only be a body part, but also either a narrow strip of land or a local vicinity, as in "this neck of the woods." The point is that he has gone far away, but the term is not just geographical, it is also anatomical. The "many steps" separating heart from head might have held a deeply personal meaning for the couple.

To understand the middle of the poem it is necessary to divorce the constellations she mentions from their use in the popular culture pastime of astrology in the 21st century. Bradstreet was relying on astronomy.

During the summer solstice, the point at which the sun appears highest over the Massachusetts horizon, it reaches the area occupied by the constellation Capricorn during the night. During the autumnal solstice, it reaches the area occupied by Cancer. In mid-winter, earth seems to "mourn in black" (line 7) because it is cold and the nights are longer. Like the sun, Bradstreet's husband exudes heat, which the poem rather explicitly identifies as sex. While she "joyed" him (whatever that means), she felt neither storms nor frost, and he melted her frigid cold (lines 11–12). Without him, her limbs are chilled and numbed. She desires the summer of his return, and her present contentment lies in viewing those fruits (of the womb; Luke I:42) which "through his heat" she bore (line 14). Seeing his face in each of theirs may bring remembrances of their conceptions to mind, for she exclaims "O strange effect!" (line 16) and marks how tedious the days grow.

When he returns, she hopes the sun may stay burning within the summer of her glowing breast (this last item of the list with which the poem began may tie the whole thing together). The breast (especially the heart beneath it) is the welcome house of her dearest guest, who she hopes will not leave again until he dies. Again she recalls the biblical formula (flesh of my flesh; Chronicles I:11; Samuel II:5; and elsewhere) and asserts their "oneness" even though they are temporarily apart.

"LIFE IS A TOIL" ANONYMOUS (19th century)

The traditional role of wife and mother represented a trap for those 19th-century women who would have preferred more active roles in the larger world. The initial speaker in this poem was a passerby who happened to see an unhappy old woman ("the picture of doom," line 2) sweeping her doorstep in the rain. S/he listened to her song then watched as she lay down, died and was buried (line 28).

The old woman's discontent appears to have its origin in the discrepancies between her youthful condition and her present state. In the chorus she defines life as a toil and then notes the changes that occurred in the things that were formerly dear to her: love has become trouble, beauty fades, riches flee, pleasures dwindle, and prices double. Nothing is as she would wish it (line 8), and she is too busy working to really live.

The third stanza provides her morning schedule. In an era before the advent of even the most rudimentary labor-saving devices, she sweeps, dusts, cooks, and washes dishes, finishing just in time for "potting and panning" (presumably either washing pots and pans or filling them with food for the noon meal; line 11) from 10 to 11. Soon after breakfast she must plan the dinner. Two stanzas later she notes that each season brings only a change in the type of work one must do, but not in its quantity or the drudgery it entails.

Line 13 contains about the only ambiguity in this poem: the "worriment" that goes in a bonnet might be contained within the troubled head that wears it, or refer to the care it takes to craft such apparel. There's too much ironing and nothing pays for the time "wasted" on it. Only trouble and dirt last.

On the night before she died, she dreamed of an island. She found no rest even there, but had to sweep away the waves before they swept her away (line 24). Convinced that this was her fate, she folded her apron, died, and was buried in the dirt that she had spent her life combating.

"A LIGHT EXISTS IN SPRING" EMILY DICKINSON (1896)

On the surface, EMILY DICKINSON's poem seems only a meteorological report. The quality of light in early March (perhaps enhanced by the reflections off whatever snow still lingers, although the poet does not consider that possibility in this poem), colors the fields in a unique way. Prior to the emergence of grass (or at least the coalescence of that plant into lawns, line 9), the clear air, and lack of leaves permit a view of the furthest tree. As the season advances, however, the special quality of that air is lost, leaving us with the same feeling as if trade had "encroached upon a sacrament" (lines 19–20. To fully comprehend this phrase, imagine paying a baker for a holy wafer and a vintner for a sip of wine [and hearing someone haggle over their prices] at the altar just before these commodities are administered as part of the holiest rites of a religious sect).

If, however, the year in question is meant to represent an entire human life of 70 years, then "March" would roughly cover the years from 12 to 17½ and early March (when the month is "scarcely here," line 3) might last from about age 12 to age 14, which roughly indicates the period when most people undergo puberty. Science cannot adequately explain or recreate all that "Human Nature feels" during that period (line 8). It presents things in such a new light that "it almost seems to speak to you" (line 12). Then, "as Horizons step" (line 13; this phrase may refer to the boundaries of which one suddenly becomes aware at that age, or perhaps the goals that one creates as part of becoming an active, more forceful individual, that inevitably dim one's perception of other horizons) or "Noons report away" (a phrase that not only indicates the passage of time, but may also connect with the notion of "trade" as that term is used pejoratively in the penultimate line: most people immersed in the workaday world cannot comprehend that phrase, with its implied devotion of the best part of one's days to official duties, without a twinge of regret). The precise meaning of "the Formula of sound" (line 15) is unclear, but the gist of lines 14 to 16 may be that the time (of glorious Spring) passes without fanfare. We "stay" (continue to live), but the memory of that time of unlimited horizons makes our mercantile and industrious lives seem mundane by comparison.

Because Spring is the breeding season for many animals, and because our own species is not unaffected by its charms, the increasing sunlight of March may stimulate us in a physiological way, coloring all our perceptions with the glow of good health and increasing vitality. Perhaps the interpretation of the landscape (especially the "lawn," "furthest Tree," and "furthest Slope" of lines 9–11) and their possible connections with human anatomy is best left to the Freudian critics, but for many people, the sexual urges felt in the springtime of their lives can speak to them in a language only a God could understand. For their purposes, perhaps the inexactitude of the meaning of the images of the fourth stanza might represent the transcendent ecstasies of love. For most people, the sudden onset of sexual awareness and reproductive urges can color everything, a phenomenon outlived by some and, perhaps, remembered with regret for its passing. They may never be so content again, and their subsequent lives may seem tarnished for the tradeoffs that may in some way be held responsible for that loss.

"A LITTLE MADNESS IN THE SPRING"

EMILY DICKINSON (published 1951) The iconic symbol of Spring Madness has traditionally been the spring hare. Normally reclusive masters of camouflage and retreat, during their spring mating season they leap into the air with wild abandon and chase each other with what seems an absolute disregard for whatever monsters (from their perspective) may be lurking in their path. However, this poem is not chiefly concerned with advocating venery in general or with the sex lives of royalty in particular. No less a figure than Shakespeare devoted much of two earlier dramas (the two plays devoted to the reign of Henry IV) to the development of the man who became Henry V, in many respects a great king of England whose military exploits were celebrated in the play bearing his name as its title. Although the future king's wayward behavior was a source of concern for his father, it could be argued that young Harry's peccadilloes prepared him for his future success by making him intimately acquainted with the nature of the common people he would eventually lead. Experience with irrational behavior in his youth (the spring of his life) may also have helped him settle into the harness of state by settling the curiosity he might otherwise have had about life beyond the majesty and decorum of the court.

The most delightful ambiguity in the poem surrounds the "Clown" of the third line. The poem warns the king against taking himself too seriously; only the most foolish clown, enthralled by his own seemingly limitless political power, would also think himself the true master of nature. On the other hand, the phrase "God be with the Clown" may not only ask God to protect the fool the king becomes in such circumstances, it also may celebrate his indulgence (he is "with God" in such pursuits). By thus acknowledging all aspects of his human nature, the king (and by extension, the rest of us) can come closer to fulfilling God's grand design (or, in a more secular age, his human potential). Modern psychology also celebrates the vital role that occasionally "letting one's hair down" or "letting off steam" (to use the lay phrases associated with the phenomenon) plays in maintaining mental (and even physical) health. Developmental psychologists also would be thrilled at the implications of "ownership" of the "whole Experiment of Green" (line 5); in other words, in permitting yourself to make mistakes in your youth so as to gain the self-knowledge that leads to becoming a fully developed adult.

A sense of "Ownership" encourages wide-ranging explorations of the self at the same time that it implies responsibility; although the notion of a "Clown who ponders" might seem an oxymoron, God (or at least our modern sympathies) is with the person who admits the errors of his/her youth (at least to himself) and has learned from them.

"LONE FOUNTS" HERMAN MELVILLE (1891)

HERMAN MELVILLE once tried earning money by lecturing not on his South Sea adventures but on Greek art and architecture. He was not a success, and this poem helps us understand why. The message is that artists (and perhaps others) should study classical (meaning ancient Greek and Roman) models in order to acquire the taste necessary to avoid youthful errors in judgment. It is a very conservative philosophy, not calculated to rapidly advance society, science, or the arts.

The first two lines advise that although "youth's glorious fable" (in the context of the poem this probably refers to the illusion that the present generation's artists and musicians are the best ever) "flies fast" (offers dramatic excitement), one should not view the world with "worldling's eyes" (that is, with the jaded perspective of a sensualist). Nor should one swing with the popular trends like a weather vane in the wind (line 3), but "foreclose" (usually a legal term for the seizure of property as a penalty for nonpayment; here its meaning is closer to "preempt") surprise by taking a longer view of the issue (by "standing where Posterity shall stand," line 5).

To achieve this difficult perspective, the poem suggests standing where the ancients stood (developing classical standards for art) and, drinking from lone "founts" (line 7; the term means "fountains" but metaphorically it also means "sources"), imbibing and embodying the wisdom that never ages. In prescribing "lone" founts and the very personal use of the hand for dipping, the speaker may be suggesting that you should develop your art according to your own insights while remaining mindful of the timeless traditions of your métier.

LONGFELLOW, HENRY WADSWORTH

(1807–1882) Born on February 27, 1807, the son of a successful lawyer and future U.S. congressman, Longfellow had the deepest possible roots in the Portland, Maine, community. His ancestors crossed on the *Mayflower,* and his maternal grandfather, who built the brick mansion in which the poet was raised, was a Revolutionary War general. The poet graduated from nearby Bowdoin College in 1825. His undergraduate translation of Horace caught the college administration's eye, and he was offered what many people would consider the dream assignment of a lifetime: a chair in the modern languages department if he would consent to study in Europe (at his father's expense) to acquire the skills he needed.

Prior to the 19th century, American colleges favored the ancient Greek and Latin languages and literatures, since exposure to the classics provided all their students with a philosophical as well as linguistic base, and those students preparing for the pulpit ideally developed the ability to access many of the earliest religious documents. Since students were then mainly able to communicate in their newly acquired languages only with their professors, their peers, and such recent college graduates as they might chance to encounter, the need for people more skilled in modern languages quickly became apparent.

A quick study, Longfellow learned French, Spanish, Italian, and rudimentary German among the native speakers of these languages in three years (1826–29). Upon his return to America, he taught at Bowdoin for five years in a field so new he was forced to write his own French and Spanish texts. In 1831, the professor married a Portland teenager named Mary Potter, and she joined him on his next trip to Europe in 1835. He immersed himself in Dutch and the Scandinavian languages, having first secured a professorship at Harvard which would be waiting for him upon his return. Unfortunately, his wife died following a miscarriage during the trip.

In 1837 Longfellow began 18 years of teaching at Harvard, taking over from George Ticknor, the first and, at that time, the foremost professor of modern languages in America. Longfellow's success as an academic may have slowed his production as a poet; although he had published his first verse at the age of 13, he did not publish his first collection of poetry (*Voices of the Night*) until 1839. That he then managed to continually write and publish books of poetry despite the demands of continually developing lectures for his students could serve as an inspirational model for the poets of later centuries who face similar pressures.

Longfellow returned to England and Germany in 1842, a sojourn permitting him to write *Poems on Slavery* (represented in this volume by "The SLAVE'S DREAM"). The next year he married Fanny Appleton after a seven-year courtship. Income from his books helped him to quit teaching in 1854 (he felt the demands of instructing other people in elemental grammar kept him from his true vocation and strained his eyes and nerves), and that was even before the success of *The SONG OF HIAWATHA,* a best seller. In fact, most of his books sold exceedingly well. He and his wife, scions of wealthy families, were able to entertain lavishly with the aid of their servants. Longfellow was a gregarious and extremely likeable man who developed many friendships that lasted for decades.

His personal life was repeatedly marred by tragedy, however. In addition to his first wife's miscarriage and death, he had to bury a year-old daughter in 1848, and in 1861 his beloved second wife died horribly. Her dress caught fire while she was sealing packages of her daughter's curls (in an effort to create a very personal and very popular 19th-century memento), and the poet was severely burned in an attempt to extinguish the flames. He was eventually able to soldier on, however, continuing to write and maintaining his incredible fame. He traveled again to Europe in 1867 and kept writing until his death on March 24, 1882.

Longfellow may have conceived of his art as an exclusively public medium; he rarely writes of his own pain or even the suffering his literary characters should probably have experienced in the situations in which he places them. Characteristically, he could write about the death of a village blacksmith's mother, but not about the death of his own mother. Although that character's thoughts of his loss could bring a tear to the strong man's eye, they did not interfere with his daily production at the forge; similarly, Longfellow seems not to have wanted his personal feelings to mar his poetry or his public image. It is significant that the two most personal Longfellow poems discussed in this volume were not published until after his death: "Mezzo Cammin," penned in 1842, reveals a midlife crisis and the restless ambition that drove his success, and "The Cross of Snow," honoring his second wife, was not written until 18 years after her death.

Isolated by wealth, class, and the ivory towers of the Harvard campus, Longfellow's poetry suggests that he was little touched by the major events of the dynamic period of history in which he lived. Although his antislavery poems gave service to that cause, "The Warning" suggests that the southern slaveholder had more to fear from a general slave uprising in his own section of the country than from New England. Although it may also have reminded southerners of northern industrial (and hence, military) might, his poem "The Arsenal at Springfield" deals abstractly with the stockpiled weapons of war and makes pleas for peace based on economic and religious arguments. His chief contribution to Civil War poetry, "Killed at the Ford," depends heavily on the sentimentality that provided him with a large Victorian audience. That he was more comfortable dealing with less passionate times is evident in the care he lavished on "The Jewish Cemetery at Newport." Mistaken in his impression that the Jewish community no longer existed in that part of Rhode Island, he tried to understand its seemingly vanished culture with a sensitivity not evident in his disregard of the political and social movements of his own time and place.

As a way of protecting himself, Longfellow may have turned personal challenges into abstract poetry. His academic background schooled Longfellow to look at both sides of such an issue, and his exposure to the varied cultures of Europe further discouraged him from partisanship. Thus "A Psalm of Life" can be read as a youthful declaration of independence from a pessimistic determinism supported by the full weight of biblical authority, while "Excelsior" presents the alternative

view that youthful exuberance can lead to disaster. In keeping with Victorian ideals, "The Children's Hour" presents an idyllic family relationship centered on a father's interaction with his children as well as his ability to surround them with the security of material blessings. At the same time, however, its darker undertones suggest an awareness of their very real need for his protection. "Nature" likens aging to the process by which mothers prepare their children for bed; in Longfellow's conceit, Mother Nature leads an aged man into a dotage that helps him realize the futility of lingering over the passing illusions of this life. "Aftermath" provides further evidence of his concern for his declining powers.

Such poems as "Keats," "Chaucer," "Milton," and the six sonnets of his "Divina Commedia" reveal that Longfellow also could be inspired by his reading, although they do not represent his best work. More rarely anthologized for college-level audiences are his famous "The Courtship of Miles Standish" and "The Midnight Ride of Paul Revere," lengthy historical poems frequently committed to memory for 19th-century recitations. In addition to his own poetry, Longfellow edited *The Poets and Poetry of Europe* (1844) and *Poems and Places,* a 31-volume anthology that he began in 1874 and completed in 1879. He also translated many continental European poems into English, including Dante's *Divine Comedy.*

The house in which the poet was raised has been preserved as the Wadsworth-Longfellow House by the Maine Historical Society. The Longfellow National Historic Site in Cambridge, Massachusetts, preserves the mansion (a gift from his father-in-law to Fanny [the former Frances Appleton, his second wife] upon their marriage) where the poet lived from 1837 to 1882, and the family's furnishings. Bowdoin College, Harvard University, and the University of Virginia hold the largest Longfellow archives. The Longfellow Site in Cambridge also holds extensive correspondence by the Longfellow circle in addition to the letters of the poet. His name is also kept alive by the Longfellow Society, a creative writing enterprise that publishes its members' work in *The Longfellow Journal.*

BIBLIOGRAPHY

Calhoun, Charles C. *Longfellow: A Rediscovered Life.* Boston: Beacon Press, 2004.

Gale, Robert L. *A Henry Wadsworth Longfellow Companion.*
  Westport, Conn.: Greenwood Press, 2003.
Wagenknecht, Edward. *Henry Wadsworth Longfellow: His
  Poetry and Prose.* New York: Ungar, 1986.

"LONG, TOO LONG AMERICA" Walt Whitman (1865)

At first glance, this poem sounds
like a jeremiad conveying a prophecy of doom as the
just retribution for a nation that has overindulged its
children by not teaching them about pain and loss. The
opening line sets the tone: The speaker begins by chas-
tising America's lack of discipline. Apparently judging
the country from the long perspective of history, he
further boosts his authority by suggesting that he has
observed how the entire generation had been trained
and asserting that he can see them "en masse (lines 4
and 5)," a French term meaning "as a group." He saw
them grappling (wrestling) with the direst fate and
"recoiling not" (not trying to avoid the challenge). He
ends by claiming special authority as the only one who
has figured out what those "children en masse" really
are (Walt Whitman also used the word "En-Masse" in
a much more optimistic and celebratory way in "One's-
Self I Sing." Here his tone seems much more darker).

Most students of American history would question the assertion that the country had been traveling
"roads all even and peaceful" (line 2) before the Civil
War. The nation's collective colonial heritage includes
Indian wars, genocide, witch trials, the martyrdom of
Quakers by religious zealots, and French and English
wars over control of the continent. In the Revolutionary War, battles occurred from Canada to Georgia. A
punitive war against the Barbary pirates represented
the first overseas action by the U.S. military. A second
war with England in which the nation's capital was
occupied and the White House burned followed that,
and active American involvement in the Texan rebellion against Mexico was followed by a full-scale war.
Economic historians (and the bankers and businessmen of the fledgling nation) could also point out the
various economic panics and busts that blighted the
general prosperity of the country.

If the speaker's statements about history are somewhat shaky, his predictions for the future seem much
more accurate because (like most prophets who with-

stand the test of time) he hedged his bets. He is correct
in his inference that the Civil War changed the entire
fabric of American society, providing the survivors and
their children with the means to build what would
become the economic and military powerhouse of the
20th century. The war taught the American capitalists
how to harness the energy of large armies of men and
seemingly unlimited wealth to complete such national
projects as the transcontinental railroad, and the more
that free men found they could accomplish, the larger
their dreams became.

The tone of this poem suggests a much darker interpretation, however; it seems to warn that if the children
en-masse obtain unprecedented power, they may turn
out to be monstrous. Although the speaker is vague as
to how this experiment will turn out, the emphasis he
places on the children's learning to overcome "crises of
anguish" (line 3) suggests a loss of empathy that could
deaden the moral fiber of the nation, a development
with potentially disastrous consequences when it is
combined with nearly unlimited power. If read within
the context of his other poetry, however, one finds little to support the notion that Whitman ever feared the
ends to which the American people would put their
growing power.

"LOOK DOWN FAIR MOON" Walt Whitman (1867)

In the American Civil War,
some battles continued for several days as the casualties mounted into the tens of thousands, and the dead
and dying sometimes had to be left where they fell. In
Walt Whitman's poem the speaker does not discriminate in favor of one side or the other, but asks for the
entire battlefield to be cleansed by the night rain.

Much of this short poem's power resides in the discrepancy between the speaker's prayer to the moon
and his realistic description of the wounds of the dead.
The former is a rite of such antiquity that it was probably undertaken as a mere formality or even as a protest: the speaker may have become so disgusted by the
death and destruction he witnessed as to have given up
whatever more traditional faith he had previously held.
The moon, rain-producing nimbus clouds, and the
fallen men seem the only things he can now believe in.
The only vestiges of Christianity still in evidence reside

in the speaker's implied faith in the purifying power of the rain, a natural form of absolution sacred only in its association with the moon, and in the cruciform positions of the (thus nearly sainted) dead who lie on their backs with their arms outspread (line 3).

Introducing the ancient formulas onto a Civil War battlefield elevates the latter by implying that it is a struggle of the same magnitude as such epic conflicts as the Trojan War. At the same time, however, the poem's focus on the ghastly, swollen, purple faces of the fallen (line 2) might be viewed as criticism of those arts and cultures that have celebrated warfare throughout recorded history. Note how the order of these adjectives in the second line suggests that the speaker is almost forcing himself to take increasingly closer looks at the faces of the dead, as does their placement after the noun ("faces") that they modify.

LOWELL, JAMES RUSSELL (1819–1891)

Born into the family of a Unitarian minister on February 22, 1819, Lowell received his bachelor's (a fourth-generation graduate; class of 1838) and master's degrees from Harvard and became a lawyer. Soon his family's wealth enabled him to devote himself to poetry and other interests. In 1851 he traveled to Europe, an adventure he repeated four years later after being named to the Smith Professorship of Modern Languages at Harvard, and again in 1872 after he retired from teaching. In 1857 he became the first editor of *The Atlantic Monthly*. In 1877 he became the American minister to Spain, and from 1880 to 1885 he served as the ambassador to England. He died at his childhood home in Cambridge on August 12, 1891, having outlived his two wives and three of his four children.

Today he is chiefly remembered for *The Biglow Papers* (1848, with a second series in 1867) and "A Fable for Critics." (1848). The former is a collection of witty letters in verse cast in the New England dialect of Ezekiel Biglow. The latter satirizes contemporary American writers by subjecting them to the judgment of Apollo. Each work was topical in the sense that it relied on the readership's familiarity with and interest in the politics and literature of the year in which they appeared; as centuries pass this may not prove to be the best strategy for attaining literary immortality.

Lowell's humor is also evident in "SHE CAME AND WENT," a poem to an alluring vision of a girl or angel that graced his tent on a camping trip. "TO THE DANDELION" teaches us to admire and value even the gold of a roadside weed as a reminder of spring and childhood innocence.

Elmwood, Lowell's birthplace and the site of his death, now serves as the official residence of Harvard University's presidents. It has been granted National Historic Landmark status but is not open to the public. Harvard University and the New York Public Library hold extensive Lowell archives.

BIBLIOGRAPHY
Duberman, Martin B. *James Russell Lowell.* Boston: Houghton Mifflin, 1966.
McGlinchee, Claire. *James Russell Lowell.* New York: Twayne Publishers, 1967.
Wagenknecht, Edward. *James Russell Lowell: Portrait of a Many-Sided Man.* New York: Oxford University Press, 1971.

"LUKE HAVERGAL" EDWIN ARLINGTON ROBINSON (1897)

The most disquieting aspect of this poem is the voice of the speaker, the filter through which the horrific details of the situation in the poem are slowly revealed. At first the speaker seems helpful enough in directing Luke to a particular gate, but the formality of the tone as evidenced in the use of both his first and surnames suggests a coldness out of keeping with the situation as it is presented in the first stanza.

The surprise of the poem stems from a reader's early expectation of a lover's tryst aided by a speaker who at first appears to be relaying the time and place of the assignation. Foremost among the romantic conventions sprinkled throughout the first stanza is the time; the setting sun not only beautifies the sky but also adds crimson highlights to the vegetation, drenching it in red, the traditional color of romantic love. It also presents the prospect of a deepening darkness that promises to shield the lovers' private moments. The vines suggest that the chosen site will offer the seclusion and immersion in nature much preferred by poetic lovers, and the western gate holds not just the promise of a reunion but also the route by which an elopement could progress, should it come to that. The speaker's repetition of the most critical direction in the message suggests that Luke's best interests are at heart; if he goes the wrong way, it will not be as a consequence of the speaker's negligence. As though sensitive to the transforming potential of love, the speaker intimates that the leaves will whisper about the girl, a detail conveying awareness of the altered state of consciousness that love engenders to the lover: All nature seems complicit or at least empathetic.

Some of the leaves will strike Luke like "flying words" (line 5); the descriptive participle at once suggests a sympathetic understanding of the subjective reality of the lover, for words aimed at conveying love can also hasten it. If an elopement were intended, the phrase also might convey an eager assent to that plan. Up to this point in the poem, things scarcely could be going better.

In the second stanza the reader gains a truer understanding of the situation, however. Gone is the objective tone that permitted optimism to prevail in the first stanza. The very first word is shockingly negative, but even at that late moment hope remains that the "fiery night" in Luke's eyes refers to the ardency of his passion, which to the speaker seems so intense that even dawn's light cannot penetrate it.

A shift in the speaker's diction appears to signal a change from a merely informative messenger to a messianic harbinger from a much darker place. The poem's thrust has shifted from an external to an internal emphasis, and the speaker suddenly seems to be predicting only unrelenting despair for Luke. The "western glooms" are gathering in his eyes, and only "the dark" (perhaps unfathomable despair, the oblivion attendant upon death, or a suicidal impulse) can end his torment. As though the aim were to systematically remove such philosophical or religious props as might sustain Luke in this hour of his greatest need, the speaker raises doubts about the benevolence of a God who slays himself with every flying leaf. Note how deftly Robinson has not merely returned to the most striking image of the first stanza but has imbued it with an entirely new message: Each falling leaf represents the death of God. Even more startling is the speaker's laconic insistence that "hell is more than half of paradise" (line 14); to the extent that her message offers

Luke any relief from his torment, it insists on his following the darkest path imaginable.

The third stanza adds a macabre twist with the annoucement that the speaker came from the grave with the message and with the aim of quenching (as one would a thirst) the kiss on Luke's forehead that blinds him to his designated path. There is but one bitter way to rejoin his lost love, and the speaker implies that Luke knows the way to it.

By the last stanza, Luke has gone so far down the designated path that he may already be at the western gate. Here, as promised, are the crimson leaves laden with, it is now clear, their message of death. Luke is advised not to heed them (to solve the "riddle" they present) but to place his faith in the girl's call.

If that were all, the poem could be viewed as having hammered home the last nail in the coffin of romantic optimism, for it implies that life ends with the grave. Yet the speaker's background belies this essential point, for the speaker's very presence implies that resurrection is possible and that the grave is not the end.

As is frequently the case when supernatural elements enter literature, it remains an open question as to whether the messenger is demonic or angelic in origin and intent. On one level, the speaker in this poem seems to counsel Luke to embrace his despair and, possibly, suicide. On another level, however, the speaker clearly points out where such despair is likely to end and introduces not an indifferent God but a benign deity who willingly sacrifices himself (the painful slaying of line 13) to get his message to the troubled man. In this reading, the repetition of the title character's surname plays a crucial role because of its Dickensian pun.

In *Great Expectations* (1861), the great British novelist Charles Dickens created the name Havisham for a hideously vengeful woman. Robinson appears to have borrowed the trope in naming Luke, for his Havergal sounds like "have her gall" in the same way the Dickensian precedent sounds like "Have a sham." Since "gall" (as the rhyme scheme would have us pronounce the last syllable of his name) suggests a bravery carried all the way to impudence, the speaker may be viewed as interceding on Luke's behalf to prevent his throwing his life away, literally or figuratively, in his pursuit of the impudent girl (or demon) whose path he seems intent to follow. The faint Dickensian echo in his name would be appropriate if, like Miss Havisham, the mysterious creature is (or was) intent upon wishing him harm.

A feminist critic might argue that this poem is mistaken in its implied fear of the missing girl's power, and that the real problem is not that she has enthralled him (notice how intent he is upon heeding her call) but that he wants more out of the relationship than she is willing or able to give. Note the rather dismissive kiss he received on the forehead (instead of the lips, as lovers are wont to deliver) and his unwillingness to accept the circumstances. Such a reading is even more terrifying than that of the forlorn lover willing to confront a ghost if it will bring him closer to his love, for it presents the mindset of a male admirer whose sense of entitlement encourages him to stop at nothing in his quest to possess the girl. Such a reader would probably conceive of the speaker as male and unquestionably demonic.

M

"THE MALDIVE SHARK" Herman Melville **(1888)** In the 21st century, at a time when shark numbers were threatened because of their relatively slow reproductive rates and overfishing, the Republic of Maldives (located southwest of Sri Lanka) began protecting the 37 species found around the seven atolls devoted to the tourism industry. None of them bear the name of Maldive shark, but even in Herman Melville's poem the shark is upstaged. This poem celebrates the brave little pilot fish that, azure and slim, swim about the sluggish (the "phlegmatical" of line 1) shark's teeth. The slick little fish alertly attend the shark despite the latter's moral turpitude (a "sot" [line 2] is a drunkard).

The shark is mostly described in merely mechanical terms; its mouth is a saw-pit feeding its insatiable stomach on the dead (the "charnel" of line 5), when it is not serving as a port with its triple rows of serrated teeth (many families of sharks continually grow replacement teeth and many species' teeth have serrated edges, so this information offers no definitive clue as to the identity of the shark in question) providing a preview of the glittering gates of this hell. The subjective description of the shark's head as Gorgonian (the Gorgons, the most famous of which was the Medusa slain by Perseus, were mythical Greek monsters so hideous that any man who saw them would die instantly) is undercut by the haven ("an asylum in the jaws of the Fates," line 12) it offers to the pilot fish.

Because pilot fish, like the dolphins that surf in a ship's bow wake, can use the fluid dynamics of a larger fish's movement through the water, they often appear in advance of such "friends" (line 13). They took their name from the mistaken belief that they led sharks (here characterized as lethargic dotards; line 15) to their prey and never joined their host in the feast that ensued. Melville describes them as the eyes and brains of the shark, neither of which is true. Reducing such a marvelous creature as the shark to a "ravener [a greedy devourer] of horrible meat" (line 16) reveals the bias of the 19th century; it has justified the wanton slaughter of the animals to the point where some species are nearing extinction. It may be accurate to describe their forage as "horrible meat" since most species are scavengers as well as predators, but the speaker is probably referring to their exceedingly rare attacks on a luckless sailor or swimmer.

"MALVERN HILL" Herman Melville **(1866)** In March of the second year of the Civil War, Union general George McClellan invaded the Virginia Peninsula with more than 100,000 men. Richmond, the southern capital, lay only 80 miles away. The drive stalled just six miles from that goal, and a Confederate counterattack devised by Robert E. Lee convinced McClellan to withdraw. On July 1, 1862, Malvern Hill was the last major battle in a series of six collectively known as the Seven Days Battles.

In HERMAN MELVILLE's poem the speaker is a Union soldier who returns to Malvern Hill in May (line 2) to address the trees as witnesses to the attack. He reminds them that McClellan stood "at bay" (line 4; the term describes a hunted animal that, cornered, must turn and fight) within sight of the forests where his dead comrades lay. That they died fighting is evident in that some lay "with the cartridge in their mouth" (in the process of reloading by biting open a paper cartridge containing black powder and a ball [the iron missile fired from the weapon] before ramming them down the rifle barrel) or with "fixed arms" (with their bayonets attached to their weapons in anticipation of hand-to-hand fighting; line 8) facing south. The final positions of the dead bring cypress glades to mind (a famed swamp in southeastern Virginia still boasts large stands of the majestic bald cypress). The tangled forests had already presented the invading army with enough logistical nightmares to enable the numerically weaker Southerners to keep them at bay, and nearly three more years of fighting in the same general area after Malvern Hill would prove them true "wilds of woe" (line 10).

The second and third stanzas relate the Union experience of the entire Seven Days Battles, a gradual retreat in such good order that although they were forced from their initially close proximity to Richmond they were never thoroughly routed. For the first six days it was "march and fast [starve], retreat and fight" (line 17), sometimes so hard pressed that the speaker asks the elms if they remember the "haggard beards of blood" worn by the soldiers (line 20).

They followed their battle-smoked flag and it never fell (line 22. Because of the smoke and noise, troops advancing across a battlefield were often told to follow the flag. This insured that they would arrive at a targeted point with enough concentrated firepower to make a difference. To have gone through the campaign without losing the flag through a succession of such perilous circumstances is a testament to the fighting acumen of the unit). They husbanded (preserved and nurtured) their strength and "received their yell" (line 24. By reputation, the famed rebel yell, sounded during a charge as an instrument of unit cohesiveness and psychological warfare, could

be heard for miles away even above the sound of artillery and small arms fire). At Malvern Hill the Union Army stood their ground, inflicting heavy losses on the desperately attacking foe (although McClellan continued their retreat the next day). The speaker asks if Malvern Wood muses and broods over the thousands of casualties.

In the rather surprising ending the elms on the battlefield answer that they remember everything but have their own cares (filling twigs with sap and greening their leaves in spring) no matter how the world wags (line 34).

"THE MAN-OF-WAR HAWK" HERMAN MELVILLE (1888)

The Man-of-War Hawk or Frigate Bird is unique in that it can stay aloft for days on end, sometimes effortlessly gliding above tropical waters and forcing slower marine birds to drop or disgorge their catches, which it can then recover in midair. HERMAN MELVILLE's highly pictorial poem celebrates a sighting of such a bird so high above a ship that an arrow cannot reach him (line 4). In the foreground is the black ship, in the middle ground the ship's skysail (the highest square sail on a fully-rigged three-masted ship) resembles a sunlit cloud, and higher still is the black bird. As the adult wingspan can reach seven feet or more, such a bird could be visible very high above a ship's deck.

The speaker relates to the bird in a metaphysical way, asking whether such a low flier as man can ascend to such heights (not physical heights, of course). Its seemingly effortless existence keeps it out of range of earthly misdeeds, temptations and subterfuges (represented by the arrow); no amount of human reasoning can attain its "placid supreme in the sweep of his reign" (its tranquility and comfort as a consequence of being such a master of what it is and where it lives).

"A MAN SAID TO THE UNIVERSE" STEPHEN CRANE (1899)

This poem challenges the Christian notion of a benevolent God by having an apparent believer proclaim his existence to the universe. Note that he addresses his exclamation to "Sir" in keeping with the Western tradition of conferring male gender upon the deity. His assertion also faintly echoes that of Rene Descartes, a 17th-century French-man whose rationalistic theory famously began with the premise that "I think, therefore I am" and extended to a proof of the existence of God.

There is apparently no God in this speaker's universe, however. Instead, an indifferent universe acknowledges the unnamed man's existence but adds that it feels no obligation towards him. The similarity between the man's utterance and that of Descartes may imply that the French philosopher's optimistic faith in the power of human understanding is unrealistic, or at least ineffectual.

"MANY THOUSAND GO" ANONYMOUS (18th century)

The speaker in this early protest song has so recently escaped (or been released) from slavery that he is still thinking of freedom in terms of the negative things it will enable him to avoid. Chief among these is the monotony of the slave's diet; an American "peck" is equivalent to eight quarts in volume, or almost 538 cubic inches. Thus all he remembers of his meager rations are two gallons of corn and a pint of salt (the subject of the third stanza).

All slaves were theoretically subject to whippings typically administered by the slaveholder or, on larger estates, by his overseer. This could be a brutal business, inflicting excruciating pain and sometimes incapacitating injuries upon the victims; a severe beating could leave them with broad scars across their backs for the rest of their lives. The speaker differentiates between the "driver's lash" of the second stanza and the "hundred lash" of the fourth. The former could be a more indiscriminate blow delivered with little forethought as a means of hurrying one's work, while the latter would be a severe punishment on a more formal basis (with someone actually counting the lashes) designed as an object lesson in terror for every slave on the plantation.

To offset such horror, the song ends with the realization that the mistress would not call for him any more. This may seem like comic relief, but it would be no laughing matter for a slave who had labored in the fields all day to have to assist with food preparation, water fetching, and furniture rearrangement in the evening.

"A MARCH IN RANKS HARD-PREST, AND THE ROAD UNKNOWN" WALT WHITMAN (1865)

This poem presents a common soldier's view of the aftermath of a losing battle during what was for him only a lull in the fighting. Hard-pressed by the victorious enemy, the army proceeds "with muffled steps" (line 2) to avoid giving away their position in the woods in the darkness, conditions in which an ambush might be sprung at any moment. After midnight they come upon a rural church that had been turned into a field hospital. Entering, the speaker finds a sight "beyond all pictures and poems" (line 7) illuminated only by the dim candles and lamps carried from one casualty to another. A single torch (a blazing knot from a pitch pine branch would typically burn slowly enough and brightly enough for this purpose although its color would vary depending upon the intensity of the flame) gave off a "wild red flame" and much smoke (line 9; such lighting would have suggested the fires of hell to most of WALT WHITMAN's contemporaries). Groups of soldiers lie in the shadows on the floors and in the pews, but the speaker finds a young soldier for whose abdomen gunshot wound he is momentarily able to stop the bleeding.

The speaker is eager to absorb it all, from the contorted faces and bodies to the odors of ether and blood, as a crowd of additional wounded fills the yard. Occasional screams, shouted orders and the "glisten" of surgical tools (a term that suggests they are blood-covered; line 18) as they catch the torch's glint return to the speaker as he "resumes the chant" (returns to remembering and writing these reminiscences. Calling them a chant suggests that he has undertaken the exercise almost religiously, as if bearing witness to the scene was a sacred obligation; line 20).

The order to "Fall in, my men, fall in" (line 21) forces him back into his line (it also puns on "fallen, my men," a suitable lament under the circumstances). First, however, he tends the dying lad, who returns a half-smile at the kindness before calmly closing his eyes. Powerless to render further assistance, and perhaps overcome at last by the horror, he speeds forth into the darkness. Resuming the march "ever in darkness marching" (line 24. The phrase suggests a depressed mental state, a resignation to commit to whatever evil is necessary to avenge the casualties, an inability to admit the moral consequences of his participation in the war, and a reflection on the fact that common soldiers were typically not informed as to the reasons or ultimate goals of their campaigns as well as the physical darkness of the night), he again finds himself on "the unknown road," which can serve as a euphemism for life in general (and the death waiting at the end of it) as well as a reference to his unfamiliarity with the local terrain.

"THE MARCH INTO VIRGINIA" HERMAN MELVILLE (1866)

As strange as it may seem to readers of later centuries, this poem accurately portrays the jubilance with which an all-volunteer Union army entered Virginia on July 16, 1861, during the fourth month of the Civil War. Thirty miles later, on July 21, 1861, they attacked a hastily assembled Confederate army at Manassas (or Bull Run to the Southerners, who named battles after geographical features like the Bull Run River instead of the closest town), in the first major battle of the Civil War. The two armies were about equal in size (estimates of their combined strength range from about 60,000 to 67,000 participants) and both were as green as the high summer grass that sweltered beneath their feet. After a single day's fighting, about 3,000 of the invaders were casualties or missing, as were about 2,000 of their Southern peers. A Union assault that almost succeeded turned into a debacle when Stonewall Jackson's Virginians finally held the Southern line, and all that kept it from turning into a truly deadly rout was the inexperience and exhaustion of the Southern defensive line. The alacrity with which the Northerners returned to the safety of their capital was by all reports hampered by their being joined on the road by equally panicked civilian spectators, whose number included a very few overly optimistic U.S. congressmen who had followed the army in anticipation of a picnic but who ended by making a spectacle of themselves.

Perhaps because his initial audience was very familiar with the battle and its aftermath, HERMAN MELVILLE opened his poem with an interpretation of its meaning instead of a dramatization of its events. Thus his speaker comments on the sentiments of the day instead of more actively sharing them, an approach that leaves him sounding like a rather cold fish. The "lets and

bars" of the opening line refer to the obstacles and barriers that, overcome, justify the trust and cheer (line 3) that result when a larger and/or more just cause (such as ending slavery) is served.

Not very smoothly, the poem takes a different tack in the fourth line by noting the things brought to war by youth and age. The former is disparaged for its misplaced enthusiasm (the "ignorant impulse" of line 4), "turbid ardors" (murky romantic attitudes), and vain joys (line 8), but all wars "are fought by boys" (line 6) who become the "champions and enthusiasts of the state" (line 7). The more aged wait in the rear until stimulated by the possibilities of additional power (line 10), when they launch their plans and schemes (the "preparatives of fate," line 11).

In line 6 the speaker proclaimed that "all wars are boyish," a theme that he illustrated in the second stanza. No one predicted the disaster; hearts ardent for war spurned the precedents of prior wars and the warnings of the wise, the "contemned foreclosures" (despised thwarters) of surprise (line 15). Banners "play" (dance in the wind, but their slogans also act upon the emotions), bugles call, and "the air is blue" (loaded with jingoistic patriotism; line 17) and "prodigal" (that is, "reckless"). Thus the Union soldiers marched off as eagerly as to a picnic party, with almost drunken glee filing toward their fate as "Moloch's uninitiated" (a biblical reference to the children sacrificed by fire in honor of a pagan god; see 1 Kings 6:7, 2 Kings 12:17, Ezekiel 23:37, and elsewhere).

Their intellectual experience is largely expectancy and happy conjecture (the "surmise" of line 26) about the mysteries of battle. The speaker describes their emotional condition in traditional religious terms. Saints are said to experience rapture in the presence or apprehension of divine glory; here the soldiers are similarly and somewhat painfully ecstatic about their own enterprise, although the glory of war is admittedly transitory (line 28). Both saints and soldiers have a chance for immortality, although the latter's best hope is a role in a laudatory ("belaureled") story. Cheerfully they progress toward the battle, "chatting left and laughing right" (line 30).

Some of these happy soldiers will perish within three days, "enlightened" (another quasi-religious term; line

32) by "the vollied glare" (literally the muzzle flashes of a volley from the enemy's weapons). Others will survive the shame of the disorderly retreat and resolutely (or "like to adamant" [a very hard stone]. The phrase also implicitly contrasts their more sober, battle-hardened resolve to the attitudes described here; line 35) return to share the pain of Second Manassas (line 36).

The Second Manassas (or Second Battle of Bull Run) lasted from August 28 to 30, 1862, and pitted about 63,000 Union soldiers against about 54,000 Confederates. An estimated 14,000 of the former and 9,500 of the latter were dead, injured, or missing after that engagement, and the energetic Southern general Robert E. Lee came close to cutting off the entire Northern army. Although the battle delivered a serious blow to Northern morale outside the army, a year of bitter fighting between the two Bull Runs meant that the second battle did not completely shock the nation like the first despite its far greater engagement and casualty figures.

"THE MARTYR" HERMAN MELVILLE (1866)

The subtitle of this poem promises to reveal the immediate reaction of the American people to the death of Abraham Lincoln. The poem begins with the assassination on April 14, 1865. As HERMAN MELVILLE notes, the president was shot on Good Friday (the day traditionally honoring the crucifixion of Christ). Calling Lincoln's death a "prodigy" (line 2) not only emphasized the shocking impact of the news, it also interprets the event as an omen (the direction of which will be made clear in the second half of the poem).

Five days earlier, Robert E. Lee had surrendered his Army of Northern Virginia, the principal Confederate Army and the only one with even an outside chance of winning the war in the field. All that remained was to convince the other Southern armies of the futility of continuing the effort, and the last battle of the war was fought in distant Texas less than a month later. The president had already laid out his plans for reuniting the nation, an approach marked by "pity, clemency and calm" (lines 3–5). Like Christ, he was ready "to redeem the evil-willed" (line 7), and Melville portrays him in the same paradoxical role of the kind conqueror (line 8). They (John Wilkes Booth and his co-conspira-

tors, in the context of emotions so inflamed that all the inhabitants of the rebellious states would be touched by the Union's vengeance to some degree) killed him in his kindness and in their blindness (lines 9–10). In an era when extraordinary courage was frequently exhibited by the warring armies, the fact that Lincoln was "killed from behind" (shot in the back of the head with a derringer while watching a theatrical performance; line 11) seemed especially cowardly.

The refrain starts with the "sobbing of the strong" (line 12) and the nation's mourning (the "pall upon the land") but warns of the iron hand of the weeping people.

The next stanza continues drawing implicit parallels between Lincoln and Christ, suggesting that despite their bloody deaths each revealed the "father" in his face (God, but in Lincoln's case the term also recalls his paternal attitude toward the offending states; line 18). Each might have been called "the Forgiver" (line 20) replaced by the "Avenger" (line 21). Thus Melville connects one of the deepest and earliest currents of American Christianity, the promise that Christ will return to earth as a "wisely stern" (line 22) judge at the end of time, with the righteousness of those who will exact their revenge against the "parricides" (those who murder their parents or other close relatives; line 25). Their vengeance seems divinely inspired since the Avenger will do "what the heavens call him to" (line 24). Lincoln's kindness and the blind madness of the conspirators is again recalled, but this time Melville focuses on the blood on the assassin's hand (line 28).

Booth was hunted down and shot by federal troops near Bowling Green, Virginia, on April 26, 1865. Nine other conspirators were convicted, with their fates being decided to a large extent on how soon after the assassination they were tried. Four were hanged on July 7, 1865, and three were given life sentences. The other two served years in prison. With Lincoln out of the way, sentiments like those expressed in this poem moved his successors to impose harsh political penalties on those states that lost the war.

"MASSACHUSETTS TO VIRGINIA" JOHN GREENLEAF WHITTIER (1843) The poet's introduction to this poem referenced the seizure of George

Latimer on the streets of Boston on October 18, 1842 for being a runaway slave from Virginia. As JOHN GREENLEAF WHITTIER noted, Latimer was freed after a negotiated payment of $400 to his former owner, but the case so infuriated New Englanders that more than 50,000 Massachusetts residents petitioned Congress to prevent their state authorities from having to assist in any subsequent recoveries. The Virginians, proud of their heritage but dependent upon slavery to maintain their agricultural economy, interpreted the petition as an affront to their state and its institutions. Their politicians thought this an encroachment on states' rights, a principle that they would take up arms to defend.

As if he were trying to cool down the heated debate, Whittier (ever the good Quaker observant of the pacifist sentiments of that sect) uses the northern winter as a metaphor to convey his message. They might not have liked "the blast from Freedom's Northern hills" (line 1), but he calls it a greeting without haughty challenging, the "battle bugle's peal" or "clang of horsemen's steel" (a message unaccompanied by war, although the lines also serve as a reminder that Massachusetts has these things). The snow still lies undisturbed around silent arsenals, and a thousand merchant sails (a probable reference to the thousand ships launched to recover Helen of Troy at the start of the Trojan War) fill the ports, although none are being used for war. Although they hear Virginia's threats, no one suspends his honest labor in fear. Their hardy fishermen strain at their lines while wrestling with the storms (line 18). "Rough as the waves they roam" (line 19), they laugh at "the slaver's threat against their rocky home."

He reminds Virginia of the Massachusetts men who fought in Virginia against the hated British Brigade Major of Cavalry Banastre Tarleton and Major General Charles Cornwallis. Boston's Faneuil Hall (a meeting house in which revolutionary leaders like Samuel Adams and James Otis spoke) echoed Patrick Henry's call for liberty or death (delivered in Virginia on March 23, 1775). Virginia's sons must prove false to such memories if she scoffs at freedom and spurns the Declaration of Independence. Must Massachusetts also turn from truth and duty? Must she hunt the slaves flying from their hateful hell (line 33), taking up the

bloodhound's yell above the graves of the fathers and tearing wretched slaves from their sanctuary (comparable to the horns of the biblical altar, which spared a man in I Kings 1:50 but could not protect him in I Kings 2:28).

Do not think that because "her Pilgrim's blood moves slow, calm and cool" (line 39), Massachusetts will consent to being a sister state's slave and tool. She will offer her heart, hand, and purse as before, but with the loathsome burden of slavery and its bitter harvest Virginia must stagger alone. The southern state may burden God's free air with a woman's shriek beneath the lash (line 46), but only at the peril of bringing the Almighty's wrath upon themselves. They shame the ancient cavaliers (some southerners prided themselves on the aristocratic backgrounds of their ancestors in England) with slaughterhouses (the "shambles" of line 50) where human flesh is sold and calculations of a newborn's market value are heard despite "the maddened mother's cry of woe" (line 52). Virginia's name will sink, but Massachusetts washes her hands forever of slavery's sin, shame, and curse.

The voice of freedom still echoes in the Berkshires and against the man-thiefs (slave catchers) working beneath the Bunker Hill monument (completed in 1842 to commemorate the June 17, 1775 battle that demonstrated the colonists' commitment to fight for independence; line 62). A hundred thousand right arms and voices have been raised in protest from Essex to Middlesex and other towns, and join in crying "God Save Latimer" (line 76). From the backcountry to the ocean shore, free sons and daughters call "No fetters [iron shackles] in the Bay State (Massachusetts)!"

Massachusetts has calmly accepted Virginia's insults and scorn while the latter hunted "our lives" and shook manacles (primitive handcuffs) and gyves (leg shackles) around the former's hearths. She has neither waged war nor flung torches in the "firedamps" (explosive gases such as methane and suspended coal dust often found in mines) beneath Virginia's sinful soil, but leave it to her to wrestle with the "strong upward tendencies and godlike soul of man" (in the slaves she seeks to suppress; line 92).

For Massachusetts and her children, the vow has been registered in heaven not to permit slave hunting or pirates. "No fetters in the Bay State," he repeats for emphasis, and "no slave upon our land!"

"MASSA'S IN THE COLD, COLD GROUND" Anonymous (1852)

Human nature being what it is, even a slaveholder who treated his slaves like the human beings they were was unlikely to engender fondness in every single heart. Because of his dialect as well as his attitude, the speaker in this poem may be a disaffected slave.

The poem opens with two singers: An African-American's mournful dirge powerfully rings around the meadow while a mockingbird sings happily. The speaker is so content with the circumstances that he already looks forward to the ivy's covering the master's grave and smugly imagines that gentleman's sleep in "de cold, cold ground" (line 8). The chorus records that the slaves are weeping in the cornfield, actually bemoaning the fact that the master is in the ground.

The second stanza relates that when the autumn leaves were falling and the weather turned cold (lines 13–14), the old massa (dialect for "master") could not make himself heard because of his frailty (as though he were entering the winter of his years). Now, however, the orange trees are blooming (a sure sign of spring; line 17), and old massa calls no more.

He made the slaves love him for his kindness, and they continue to mourn him although summer is coming (line 19). The speaker cannot work that day because of the flowing tears, so he will try to drive away his sorrow with his banjo (his mocking of the slaves' sincerity brings to mind the mockingbird of line 3, which was also untouched by the death).

An alternative reading would focus on the emotional distance the speaker establishes between himself and "de darkeys" (a pejorative reference to the slaves' race; lines 2 and 11) who mourn their master's passing. It would suggest the more sinister possibility that the speaker could be a white overseer or even the new master. Whereas the old master was content with an unpretentious grassy mound for his grave, the new boss wants ivy to cover it, and probably a good deal more ornamentation and luxury all around. The slaves could be viewed as mourning the added cost (of which they must ultimately bear a large portion) of the new regime, not to mention the speaker's obvious lack of sentiment for the beloved old master and the speaker's inability to connect with their suffering.

"MAUD MULLER" John Greenleaf Whittier (1854)

By 1854 parts of the country had become so urban that the conventional tale of a successful urban bachelor's meeting and courting a beautiful farm girl held some of the same novelty of improbability in America that it had in Europe. As if to suggest that the eventual coupling of this human pair was inevitable, John Greenleaf Whittier sweetly chose to separate every pair of lines into rhymed couplets. Note how the poet's choice of a third-person, omniscient but thoroughly objective speaker helps keep the passion, which could have overwhelmed either of the principal characters, within the bounds of Victorian propriety.

In European poetry, the nubile but naive girl was often portrayed as a shepherdess, an agrarian specialty that not only emphasized her isolation but also suggested a temperament as tractable as that of the sheep she tended. In this poem, however, there is nothing so delicate about Maud. Like the peasant girl in other tales, she is filled with a "nameless longing" that "tilled" her breast (line 10), a metaphor that still seems fresh as well as perfectly suited to the situation in the poem. Modern urban readers may not realize that farmers must prepare the soil for planting by breaking up the relatively hard crust formed over last year's fields with a plow or other machine. The metaphor does not necessarily imply that Maud has been in love before, since virgin (previously uncultivated) soil in farming must also be plowed before planting, but it does suggest that, unlike the merry glee that comes to her as naturally as a song to a bird (lines 5–6), there is an artificial (in the sense of man-made) element in her longing. Instead of being utterly fascinated by a sophisticated stranger like the traditional literary maid, Maud is focused on the distant town, which promises more durable goods as well as the novelty of its myriad charms. As if she were intended as an emblem of the young America in which she lived, Maud is acquisitively and unabashedly materialistic to the core of her being. Well aware that her "simple beauty and rustic health" (line 4) constitute her wealth, she blushes not at the sensuality that the presence of a wealthy young lord seems to awaken in the traditional literary maid, but at her bare feet, tattered gown, and torn hat (lines 3 and 22). These accoutrements render it obvious that she would be an unsuitable match for a man like the judge who is just as greedy as she is.

After an initial exchange of pleasantries, the couple engages in a desultory chat that apparently reveals how little they have in common besides the weather, and he rides off. Note that her fantasies are mainly centered on the silk dresses and other economic benefits the advantageous match could bring to her and her family, and that they have little to do with the judge or his needs. Instead of being poor, she would be in a position to help clothe the poor (43), and she seems to think of the baby that would come from the union (line 42) as another means for shifting the wealth from the husband to the wife.

The judge's desires are just as humorous; he does not fantasize about sharing his fortune and the rest of his life but of abandoning it to share hers as a simple harvester amid the simple joys of nature. Thoughts of the mortification such a disadvantageous match would bring to his proud sisters and vain mother lead him to close his heart, however (lines 36–40).

Thus far they have been at cross-purposes, but the omniscient speaker lets the reader know that their attraction had been mutual and that each had been so moved by it that something more durable could have come from their meeting. Ironically, each makes marital choices that provide them with lives not unlike that which the other dreamed about. Just as she dreamed of marrying for money, he did so, and his wife lived for fashion just as the farmer's daughter fantasized doing.

The farmer's daughter married a farmer, but there is some indication that the rural life was not as fulfilling as the judge once imagined, for her spouse is portrayed as "dozing and grumbling" (line 96) over a mug that probably contained an inexpensive alcoholic beverage in contrast to the red wine consumed by the judge (line 71). Each is seemingly trapped in a loveless marriage in which their prior meeting, for all its brevity, continues to loom large in their imaginations as the best chance they ever had of escaping what they had become. Lines 105–106, containing the saddest words

possible ("It might have been"), are the most memorable in the poem, but the last two couplets suggest that there is no hope for lasting human happiness on this side of heaven.

Note that the maid apparently had the unhappier life because she missed what seems her chief opportunity for an advantageous marriage, usually the only chance available for women of that era to materially advance their lives. While his home life evidently left much to be desired, the judge had all the diversions of a successful career to keep him happy.

"MEDITATION 150 (SECOND SERIES)"
EDWARD TAYLOR (published 1960) For many readers, certain passages of the Bible can seem somewhat risqué. This poem reads as if Taylor were struggling to accept the comparison of two breasts to two young roe (delicate Old-World deer) in Canticles 7:3 (or Song of Solomon 7:3 in the King James version) by providing acceptable contexts in which they could be viewed. The most immediate context is that of matrimony, but EDWARD TAYLOR probably conceives of "the beauteous spouse" of the Lord not as a woman, but as the nurturing aspect of the divine spirit that brings believers to an acceptable beatific state. Although he can admire "the little roes . . . in their shining dress" (lines 3–4), he prefers to think of them as pails full of the "spiritual milk" needed to make spiritual infants grow (lines 5–6).

In the second stanza he compares the celestial nectar they produce to wine. Not yet done with the titillating aspects of his original comparison, he imagines the vessels "trussed up fine" (line 9), but reduces their salacious appeal by placing them back on a roe that suckles its offspring.

In the third stanza, he prays for the Lord to place those nipples in his mouth (line 13) that he might grow worthy to administer the similarly miraculous fodder of the communion wafer.

MELVILLE, HERMAN (1819–1891) Born
on Pearl Street in New York City on August 1, 1819, Herman Melville was the son of a successful wholesaler and importer whose business unexpectedly failed in 1830. The family moved upstate to Albany as an

economy measure, but his father died two years later. The future writer was forced into a series of low-level jobs ranging from farmhand to store clerk. He received only seven years of general education, enough of a start to eventually enable him to educate himself as a writer (and to teach school in those preaccreditation days), but it failed to impress the officials who kept him from obtaining the security of a government job. Learning of an opening aboard a three-master, he sailed to Liverpool as an apprentice seaman. Discouraged by that experience, he would not have continued as a sailor had the family finances permitted a different choice. Within two years, however, he was driven back to the sea by economic necessity.

The future writer's paid sailing experience (as gleaned from Tyrus Hillway's *Herman Melville*) consisted of service on five different ships, beginning in 1839 with about four months (including port time) on the *St. Lawrence,* a merchant vessel that took him from New York to Liverpool and back. His novel *Redburn* (1849) was based on that experience. His whaling career began in 1841 with approximately six months' sailing on the *Acushnet* from Massachusetts to the Marquesas Islands (used in *Typee* [1846]). He saw brief service on the *Lucy Ann,* a whaler that took him from the Marquesas Islands to Tahiti in 1842 (see *Omoo* [1847]), and the *Charles and Henry* took him from Tahiti to Hawaii on a six-month whaling cruise in the same year (see *Mardi* [1849]). All of his whaling service, supplemented by extensive reading, informed *Moby-Dick* (1851). He concluded his professional sailing experience with nine months on the navy frigate *United States,* which took him from Honolulu to Boston in 1843 and led to the novel *White Jacket* (1850).

Melville was something of a rotter as a professional sailor, abandoning the *Acushnet,* countenancing mutiny on the *Lucy Ann,* and making mental notes on the harshness of the navy's overreliance on the corporal punishment he exposed as excessive in *White Jacket.* His years as a seaman or whaling crewman served him better than he served them, providing him with the material for six books listed above and background information for *Billy Budd,* written much later in his life and not published until 1924.

It would be a mistake to attribute all of his subsequent development as a writer to Melville's early experience on the sea, however. One cannot say of Melville that, as his Ishmael claims in *Moby-Dick,* a commercial whaler was his Harvard and his Yale. Melville made up for the deficiencies in his education by undertaking a lengthy apprenticeship based on close study of the books of other writers, and by following his reading with an extended period of experimentation. The early popular success of *Typee* and *Omoo* encouraged his devotion to his true craft, but it left him bewildered when, despite his obvious growth as a writer, his subsequent books did not sell as well. Like the untrained visual artist inspired by his initial success to undertake the serious study of his art only to later learn that it was precisely his irrecoverable primitive quality that prompted the early sales, Melville discovered that the novelty of their subject matter contributed greatly to the success of his first books. He improved as a writer, but his sales remained constantly low.

Although his initial audience tended to relate to *Typee* and *Omoo* as travel narratives, the books so romanticized Melville's experience as to warrant the hybrid label of creative nonfiction. He tried to be even more imaginative in his later books, but they never attained the initial popularity of the first two. Today, his sea books are usually referred to as novels.

Melville married Elizabeth Shaw on August 4, 1847. They moved near Pittsfield, Massachusetts, in 1849, and he continued writing in a variety of genres (including a historical novel of the Revolutionary War, *Israel Potter,* and such psychological studies as *Pierre* and *The Confidence Man*) without finding a mass audience during his lifetime. In 1856, a publisher's warehouse fire consumed all their unsold inventory of his works, a tremendous blow that helped convince him that writing was too insecure a craft with which to support his growing (two sons and two daughters, finally) and extended family.

First, however, he turned to lecturing. He developed three lectures—on Roman statues, the South Seas, and traveling—but each received fewer bookings than its predecessor (Hillway 57). His wife's inheritance from the death of his father-in-law, a Massachusetts Supreme Court judge, helped them move back to New

York City in the middle of the Civil War. In 1866, he began a 19-year career as a customs inspector that only ended when additional inheritances provided financial freedom. His eldest son died by suicide in 1867, and his other son died in distant San Francisco in 1886. Herman Melville died on September 28, 1891, at home on East 26th Street in Manhattan.

He had begun writing poetry before the start of the Civil War and eventually produced five volumes that were self-published but, like their author, deserved a better fate. His *Battle-Pieces, and Aspects of the War* (1866) conveyed his impressions as a noncombatant during the war.

Earlier in his career, Melville had dropped in light verse to leaven the narrative of *Mardi,* but he was much more serious in the two volumes of *Clarel: A Poem and Pilgrimage in the Holy Land* (1876). This was a transitional work in that Melville attempted a new approach (verse) with material he had used successfully in the past (an account of one of his travels). In 1856, he had crossed the Atlantic for the second time as a passenger instead of as crew (the first such trip was in 1849, when he traveled to London to meet with his British publisher). He had visited several important European cities as well as Alexandria, Egypt, and Jerusalem on a seven-month sojourn but still could not fashion it into memorable art two decades later. *John Marr and Other Sailors* (1888) contained his sea-poems, and *Timeleon* (1891) was another assortment of short poems, at least one of which had been written as early as 1864.

The Melville poems discussed in this volume include such flotsam from his sailing days as "The Tuft of Kelp" and "Old Counsel," several of his Civil War poems (including "The Portent," "A Utilitarian View of the Monitor's Fight," and "The College Colonel"), and two poems presenting his views on art: "Lone Founts" and "Art."

Arrowhead, Melville's home in Pittsfield, Massachusetts, from 1850 to 1863, has been preserved as a public museum by the Berkshire County Historical Society. The Melville Society meets twice a year and publishes two periodicals: *Leviathan: A Journal of Melville Studies* and *Melville Society Extracts*. The Berkshire Athenaeum, Harvard University, New York Public Library and the University of Virginia hold the Melville collections most relevant to his poetry.

BIBLIOGRAPHY

Hillway, Tyrus. *Herman Melville.* Boston: Twayne Publishers, 1979.

Kelley, Wyn. *Melville's City: Literary and Urban Form in Nineteenth-Century New York.* Cambridge, and New York: Cambridge University Press, 1996.

Parker, Hershel. *Herman Melville: A Biography.* 2 vols. Baltimore, Md.: Johns Hopkins University Press, 2002.

Robertson-Lorant, Laurie. *Melville: A Biography.* New York: Clarkson Potter, 1993.

"MEMENTO, FOR MY INFANT WHO LIVED BUT EIGHTEEN HOURS" Sarah Wentworth Morton (published in 1823)

The birthing process remained a deadly risk for both mother and child until such advances in medicine as the discovery in the mid-19th century that washing one's hands before assisting in a delivery dramatically improved the survival rates of both patients. Sarah Wentworth Morton's poem relates a grieving mother's attempt to comfort herself following the tragic death of her newborn son.

She began by trying to place his early death within the natural order of things. It happened on a wet day in April with near-freezing temperatures, a background in which she searched for a natural phenomenon of similar brevity. She chose the "snow-drop" rose for its early and short-lived blossoms. The trembling demise of the rose is described in terms that anticipate the infant's death later in the poem, a juxtaposition that suggests both blossom and infant were pure, short-lived, and beautiful.

Her lost boy, "just born to mourn" (a rhyme so facile as to distract from the doleful mood one expects in such a poem), stretched his prematurely decaying arms to the "cold tyrant," a euphemism representing a personified death, and "sighed his little life away" (line 8). Despite its brevity, the rose brings a valley "wasted" by winter an "ethereal balm," the hope of summer.

She takes comfort from the notion that he is in a better place and contrasts the "ruffian world" he has left with the "bright sphere" (perhaps a dramatic burst of sunlight through the clouds) wherein he has joined the cherub train (presumably a choir of infant angels in heaven). With an injured mother's subjectivity and sensitivity, she hears the music of his sweet breath on her ear. His fairy phantom brings kind dreams and (religious) ecstasy, which for all its power is as soft as when seraphs (more mature angels) charm unsettled hearts with their heavenly strings (presumably harps or similar instruments).

"MERLIN" RALPH WALDO EMERSON (1847)

RALPH WALDO EMERSON's poem celebrates not the magician surrounded by the knights of the Round Table in Arthurian legend, but a Beethoven of bards, a man whose original approach to his art strikes the auditor as the unbridled expression of the creator's elemental passion. The speaker does not enjoy a "trivial harp," a jingling serenader, or tinkling piano strings that fail to startle the wild blood in its mystic springs (lines 7–8). Instead, his "kingly bard" (line 9) rudely smites chords as with a hammer or mace (a heavy, spiked club used for smashing armor in medieval combat), which renders "artful thunder." The speaker clearly prefers percussion instruments over strings, but his larger point is that an artist should reach higher (striving to convey "secrets of the solar track and sparks of the super solar blaze" [lines 14–15]) than achieving mere technical perfection.

Like the iconic bard Merlin (and with perhaps a little of the old magical Merlin), an artist should deliver "strokes of fate" that combine the wildest expressions of forest-ripping winds and floods. With "manly hearts" (line 21), such bards would skillfully add human interest and human dimensions to their work by conveying the voice of orators, the din of city arts, the cannonades of wars, the marches of the brave, and "prayers of might" from martyr's cave (line 26).

The bard's manners must be on the same scale as his art. He should not encumber his brain with "the coil of rhythm and number . . . and pale forethought" (with formal rules of poetry or extensive plans for his verse; lines 30–31). Instead, he should "climb for his rhyme" (lines 32–33), entering the upper levels of artistic expression (a paradise complete with angels pointing the way) via "the stairway of surprise" (line 38). (Thus he will prove a benefactor of man), daily dispensing joy "hid in song's sweet influence" (line 42). By adopting natural rhythms, he can subtly create an art that is more alive and to which hearts and feet will march.

Beguiled by sybarites (sensualists wholly devoted to pleasure; line 49. The choice of this very unusual target audience may imply that a bard should attempt to maximize the pleasure that his verse provides), he will decline no task (he will consider no subject too high or low for his study). Merlin's lines reconciled opposite extremes of nature and subdued willful tyrants and lions. His Songs quiet storm winds, bringing forth prosperity and "poetic peace" (line 58).

The bard will not try to create rhymes to fit weak, unhappy times (when he is too weak to strive for greater expression) but should husband his strength until he can soar like a bird from the floor to the "zenith's top" (the redundancy of the phrase reveals the poet's transcendental enthusiasm; line 64). He will not profane his talent by settling for less than his highest expression (lines 66–69), but will focus on those moments (the "open hours" of line 70) when "God's will sallies free" (when he is inspired to create works worthy of a thousand years' admiration). Such inspiration (and dedication to his own insight) will unexpectedly lead him to the doors (of heaven, or at least of the highest artistic accomplishment).

The first half of the poem dismissed formal patterns of rhythm as an artificial encumbrance to true artistic expression, but in the second half, the speaker seems more kind to "rhyme." Acknowledging its modulation of the king's affairs (lines 78–79), he thinks rhyme seems natural because nature made all things in pairs: colors have their "counters" (presumably those that complement or best highlight them by their contrast) and every tone has its answering tone (this might refer to the production of harmony; line 84). Flavors blend with flavors, and "leaf answers leaf" (many plants grow leaves in symmetrical or mathematically predictable patterns, which help maximize their exposure to light and balance the weight of the leaves along the length of their stems). The first emergent (or "cotyledon;" line 88) leaf also frequently has a partner. Human hands, feet, and newlyweds are also coupled, and every mortal man is the product of two married sides (line 91). With rather risqué imagery, the speaker elaborates on how "light's far furnace" smelts balls and bars, "forging double stars," twins and triplets until the animals, "sick with love" and "lovesick with rhyme" (lines 97–98), are woven into the rhythmic (or timely) chorus.

Like (ballroom) dancers, powerful thoughts also arrive in equal couples or, like bachelors or single women, they will lack the posterity needed "to make the lie afraid" (line 111) by preserving truth. Like paired eagle's wings, "Justice is the rhyme of things" (line 115), and Nemesis (the Greek goddess of vengeance) matches the punishment to the crime (or at least finishes the song).

The last stanza associates ruin-filled subtle rhymes with the singing of the Fates, a trio of sewing goddesses who selected the fabric of each human life and manipulated it before cutting it off. In "perfect time and measure" (not in accordance with metrical rules, however; line 127) they build and disassemble "our echoing clay" (a euphemism for man, referring to the material from which God shaped Adam in Genesis, and combining it with a conception of the poet as a divinely inspired singer). The "two twilights of the day" (perhaps those of art and nature, or the twilights of a single day and of an entire life) similarly fold us (the "music-drunken") in.

"MEZZO CAMMIN" HENRY WADSWORTH LONGFELLOW **(published 1886)** The Bible designated 70 years as a typical life span (Psalms 90:10), thus ensuring a midlife crisis for any devout Christian or Jew fortunate enough to reach 35 years of age. HENRY WADSWORTH LONGFELLOW, a college professor lucky and accomplished enough to be traveling abroad at the time, penned this poem in Boppard (Germany) on the Rhine in 1842. Like most good artists, he is his own worst critic in recognizing his failure to produce "some tower of song with lofty parapet," a masterpiece. The sorrow that he blames for his lack of success (line 6) is probably related to the death of his first wife in 1835, but it may also have sprung from any of the innumerable losses that plague human existence. His list of the other causes inhibiting accomplishment center on personality traits instead of external factors such as a lack of funding, an inability to find a publisher, or an indifferent public reception. The love of leisure or

of pleasure (line 4) has its roots in the terrible choice between living and writing about life that confronts most writers, but the third potential dead end evokes the romantic heroes of such then-popular writers as Lord Byron, characters whose uncontrollable passions keep them from consistently productive lives.

Perhaps because the landscape suggested it, he likens his life to the climbing of a hill low enough to see the roofs and smoke from a city's chimneys but high enough that its bells sound soft (line 12). Above he can hear a waterfall (the "cataract" of line 14), which reminds him of his own impending death despite the fact that, at 35, he had only just begun the third, "autumnal" quarter of his life. Metaphorically, he realizes that the time and place are at hand to begin seriously working on his dream if he is going to realize it in his remaining years.

"MILTON" HENRY WADSWORTH LONGFELLOW **(1875)** This Italian sonnet suggests that the verse of the great English poet John Milton (1608–74) was as predictably good and as powerful as ocean waves. The first half of the octave is devoted to capturing the sights and sounds of the seacoast. A "sounding" beach (line 1) resonates with the sound of the heavy waves (the "voluminous billows" of the second line). While the "roll and run" may describe the wave action as it proceeds up the beach away from a viewer, those waves breaking directly off the shore from the observer can seem more "upheaving and subsiding" (lines 2–3). Close observation enabled the poet to note the emerald color of the sheet of water beneath the breaking waves.

In line 5 the ninth wave is personified as a goddess who has the power to draw up "its" loose-flowing garments before plunging upon the shore. As if by magic, flooding the dull brown ("dun") sands changes them to gold. The sestet compares the majestic cadences of the waves with the "mighty undulations" (line 9) of Milton's song. Likening Milton to Homer (the ancient Greek poet credited with composing the famous *Iliad* and *Odyssey* and dubbed the Maeonides because he may have been born in Maeonia; line 11) seems somewhat natural because Milton became blind in his forties and Homer is thought to have also suffered from that affliction. Each also towered over his contemporaries like the ninth (and highest) wave of a set (line 13) and "floods all the soul" of his external audience.

"MISGIVINGS" HERMAN MELVILLE (1866)
HERMAN MELVILLE'S poem deals with the political climate of 1860. When enormous thunderheads (the "ocean-clouds" of line 1) form over the inland hills, darkening the skies to a late autumn brown (line 2), they fill the already sodden valley with horror as the spire crashes down (as the top point of a church or governmental building, its destruction symbolizes the demise of the religious or civil authority that normally protects a town). This leads the speaker to ponder the state of the nation. A storm of similar strength is bursting from its failure to achieve a timely separation of "the world's fairest hope" (democracy, but also America's vibrant economy and the opportunity it presented for a new beginning; line 7) from the crime of legal slavery.

Human nature's dark side is now so evident that a child could read the signs from the mountaintop all by himself. The storms of passion that led to the Civil War have built up until the torrents shout down the gorges, and additional storms have built up behind them. The hemlock (a good solid construction material unrelated to the poison administered to Socrates in antiquity) rafters are shaking, as is the oak in the "driving keel" (the strongest wood chosen for the crucial centerboard of the bottom of the boat. In other words, the ship of state is receiving such blows as to severely threaten its survival).

"MONODY" HERMAN MELVILLE (1891) The
speaker in HERMAN MELVILLE'S poem laments the passing of a former neighbor. The deceased had been one of the few men in whom he felt a kindred spirit, for their friendship interrupted his "loneless long" (long loneliness, but the phrase may also convey longing of some sort; line 2) until an argument (with "neither in the wrong," line 4) led to their drifting apart (or "estrangement"). Death prevents reconciliation, so the speaker writes (or like a Native American, sings) this song as a form of mourning from which he hopes to take solace.

He also makes a pilgrimage or at least looks over to where he used to see the dead man, referring to it as "his hermit-mound" (line 7). Almost as a sign of the man's restless spirit, a houseless snowbird (perhaps a junco or other year-round avian resident) flits. Winter, as if in perfect sympathy, has draped the scene with snowdrifts as though it were mourning crape. Whether or not a house once stood there, the site of the former hermitage (referring to it as a "cloistral vine" in line 11 suggests that its former inhabitant led the monastic life of a spiritual seeker) is now glazed over with ice. Remembering his former friend as "the shyest grape" (line 12) not only refers again to his reclusive nature (grapes have such huge leaves that it is easy to overlook their fruit even though it hangs in clusters) but also suggests the nourishment that the speaker drew from the relationship.

This poem is interesting for its unusual use of the pathetic fallacy, a suggestion that nature was somehow so moved by the human actions described in the poem that it acted in accordance with them. This was a common device in that sentimental age, but Melville's connection of the snowdrifts, among the whitest images possible, with the hanging of black funeral crape, recalls his ruminations on the whiteness of the whale in Chapter 42 of *Moby Dick*. In noting that their absence of color adds an extra element of spectral terror to such animals as the polar bear, the great white shark, and a vengeful white whale, the novelist suggested a viable alternative to the traditional connection of blackness or darkness with death or evil. Here, the poet suggests that the whiteness of the lifeless snow is a better symbol for the irredeemable death of a friend than the traditional black crape hung in a Victorian household to indicate its loss. Mourning families in the 19th century frequently hung black fabric around their doors and windows not only as a tribute to the newly departed, but perhaps also to signal the world that the household is consumed with the grieving process and is not to be bothered.

More troubling, perhaps, for the early 21st-century audience is the speaker's open avowal of love for his former friend. It was common throughout most of the 19th century for male correspondents to write of their impassioned love for each other without, generally speaking, any awareness of or reference to homosexuality. If one were looking for homoerotic imagery in this poem, it would be hard to pass up the reference to his former friend as "the shyest grape" on the "cloistral vine" in lines 11 and 12. A "monody" is a funeral dirge sung by one person for the loss of another.

MORTON, SARAH WENTWORTH APTHORP (1759–1846)

A life centered in Boston mansions cannot shield a poet from the great sorrows of life nor preclude her from sympathizing with those who are less fortunate. Born Sarah Apthorp, a merchant's daughter, on August 29, 1759, the poet was educated in local schools and began her career by composing topical poems for magazines. She married Perez Morton, son of the owner of Boston's famous White Horse Tavern, in the city's fashionable Trinity Church in 1781 and stayed married while he pursued a successful public career as lawyer turned politician. Her husband died in 1837, and she lived until May 14, 1846.

Morton's "Memento, for My Infant Who Lived But Eighteen Hours" can be viewed as an early example of the sentimental poetry favored by the general magazines and their large numbers of female readers in the second quarter of the 19th century. It was based on her personal experience. Her empathy for people of other cultures informed "The African Chief," her most famous antislavery poem, and *Ouabi: or the Virtues of Nature,* a chapbook verse romance that portrayed Native American culture in a sympathetic light. A fashionable Boston neighborhood provided the title for *Beacon Hill: A Local Poem, Historic and Descriptive,* a celebration of the city's important role in the early years of the American Revolution.

Morton sat for three portraits by Gilbert Stuart that have been preserved; the most famous hangs in the Worcester (Massachusetts) Art Museum. The mansion built for the Mortons did not survive the 19th century. Brown University holds a copy of her "Reanimation: A Hymn for the Humane Society" (Boston: no publisher information, c. 1791) bearing a most unusual headnote: "The last stanza is to be sung by those who have been restored to life from apparent death." Apparently Boston was going to start a movement to spread the news that drowning victims can sometimes be resuscitated, a first aid organization apparently modeled on England's Royal Humane Society that was founded (c. 1774) to teach the technique, and her production of this song indicates that at the height of her fame Morton was willing to use her prestige in support of a good social cause. Elsewhere, few libraries hold her manuscripts. The University of Virginia's Sarah Wentworth Apthorp Collection consists of a single item, a receipt for payment for a Gilbert Stuart painting of an Irish parliament member from 1828.

BIBLIOGRAPHY

Morton, Sarah Wentworth. *My Mind and Its Thoughts, in Sketches, Fragments and Essays.* Boston: Wells and Lilly, 1823. Reprint, Delmar, N.Y.: Scholars' Facsimiles and Reprints, 1975.

Pendleton, Emily, and Milton Ellis. *Philenia: The Life and Works of Sarah Wentworth Morton.* Orono, Me.: The University of Maine Press, 1931.

"MUCH MADNESS IS DIVINEST SENSE" Emily Dickinson (1890)

To properly understand this poem it is necessary to divide it into sentencelike units. Although individual lines can seem nonsensical, in the early Civil War year of 1862 (when this poem is thought to have been written), they conveyed sound advice for political survival. The senator from either North or South who loudest argued for war (thus demonstrating "much madness") would have been seen as assuming a leadership role, while those who advocated what would be considered a more sensible approach in normal times, such as a negotiated settlement of the conflict, could be denounced as treasonous. The first would receive majority approval, whereas the second might be "handled with a chain" (line 8) as a dangerous, perhaps criminally insane, person.

However, the thinking expressed in this poem also holds up in the realm of art. To make a breakthrough in art it is necessary to think, feel, and/or express yourself in a way that no one has ever done before. Novel challenges to artistic convention can seem like madness unless they lead to a discovery, but anyone who repeats a process without striving for something new is merely practicing a craft and not producing art. Since majorities are by nature conservative, deviation can be seen as dangerous if the artist becomes so avant-garde that he lacks an audience. In that case, he's likely to be led away in chains to a pauper's prison or at least roughly criticized (figuratively beaten with a chain).

Note Dickinson's use of the verb "demur" in line 7, which could easily be mistaken for the adjective "demure." The latter is most frequently used to describe a shy person, but the former refers to the forceful voicing of one's objections. This distinction is crucial if the poem is to be viewed as an indictment of the coercive tyranny of the majority when it comes to marginalizing minority voices.

"THE MURDERED TRAVELLER" WILLIAM CULLEN BRYANT (1824)

Like any other good mystery, WILLIAM CULLEN BRYANT's poem is effective because it withholds information. It opens after that best of clues, skeletal human remains, was found at the bottom of a narrow valley (the "glen" of line 4). Ironically, the recovery of the corpse occurred just as spring was restoring life, "bloom and joy" to the landscape (line 2). The central concern of the first half of the poem lies in the contrast between new life and irredeemable death, a conceit introduced by a pun on "wastes" in the first line. The term can refer to those areas such as swamps, steep mountainsides, or narrow canyons that will probably never be suitably cultivated, in contrast to the woods, which could be cleared for agriculture. Applying the term to human remains introduces an additional contrast in the poem; the cold detachment of the strangers who deal with the corpse will eventually be juxtaposed with the mourning of those who knew the traveler best.

Although the poem insists on an indifferent nature, the poet may have chosen certain plants and animals to suggest the state of the decomposing flesh. Not only is birch fragrant when it blooms, but its white bark peels off in uneven, sometimes flesh-toned layers. Its buds resemble tassels (line 6), a term that may connect with the ostentation of a funeral parlor or a hearse, and again underscores the carelessness with which the traveler's body was cast aside, and the lack of ceremony with which it is handled after its recovery. Although floral tributes were not yet the multibillion-dollar boon to the flower industry that they would become in later centuries, instead of the few tasteful blooms a thoughtful friend might have brought as a tribute to the departed, the speaker in this poem observes the many spring blossoms that have no connection with the body.

Although dental records had been used to identify corpses in the Revolutionary War, forensic science was still in its infancy when Bryant produced this macabre poem. However, even a rudimentary examination of the site could indicate murder, a conclusion evident in the poem's title. The redbird of line 9 may have attracted the speaker's eye as a reminder of the victim's blood; it suggests an approach to the incident like that of a modern investigator who looks at the clues in evidence and attempts to imaginatively reconstruct the scene at the time when the violence occurred. The victim probably encountered the perpetrators as innocently and naively as the young partridge family currently approaching the crime scene.

The omniscient speaker of the poem relates how for days the deceased's family, oblivious to the fate of the murder victim, anxiously and increasingly sorrowfully awaited his arrival. Returning his attention to the crime scene, the speaker determined that, though unarmed, the victim struggled and probably yelled as he was overwhelmed by the killer's violence. He establishes the time of death as winter, for snow covered the ground when the death occurred, but the sun would have begun becoming visible at the North Pole only at the end of winter, when a wolf and, probably still later, a wildcat began to feed on the corpse (lines 23–24). By the time the speaker arrived on the scene, the body had already been buried, but his empathy with the victim's family leads the speaker to again contrast the nameless, unmourned interment with the wide spectrum of hope and fear the speaker's absence occasioned at his home. Their vigilance remained unrewarded, however; they remained ignorant of his violent death in the narrow glen.

Although it appeared long before the first motion pictures, the poem was cinematic in its scope and probably in its reception by its original audience, unaccustomed as they were to the visual representations of violence that would permeate popular culture in the coming centuries. It also appeared at a time in the nation's history when innumerable individuals, swept up in massive western migrations, were never heard from again. The fear of an unmarked, unmourned grave so haunted Bryant that he returned to the image in poem after poem throughout his career.

"MY AUNT" OLIVER WENDELL HOLMES (1831)

One of the difficult things about humor is its dependence upon a shared set of beliefs between its perpetrator and its intended audience. Fortunately, our society is evolving to the point where OLIVER WENDELL HOLMES's poem has become laughable for its antiquated assumptions about women.

The situation of the poem is that the speaker's aunt had been unsuccessful in her hunt for a mate early in her life and now has made herself ridiculous in trying to remain a marketable commodity for marriage in a social environment valuing youth above virtually everything else. The aunt has gained weight until she strains the clasp on her virgin girdle. The first stanza ends with a bad pun: if life is no more than a span (approximately nine inches), then her waist is more ample than life.

His aunt makes the fashion mistakes of fixing her hair in a way that is too young for her age and refuses to admit she needs her glasses although they are certainly very strong. Her father sent her to a stylish school at age 13, but its limited rules (bring two towels and a spoon) should have warned them both that it would turn out to be little more than a joke.

The third stanza is still moderately humorous for its inventory of the procedures she underwent at the school. She was bound to a board and then (note the juxtaposition of opposites) laced up, starved down, pinched at one end and singed at the other. In other words, the school attempted to correct her posture by mechanical means, demonstrated the correct application of a corset, instilled in her the dread of food and normal human growth that still wounds so many in modern society, forced her into smaller shoes than she really needed to approach their ideal of attractively small feet, and tortured her hair with heat until it acquired the curls then considered most fashionable. The speaker suggests that these torments might be viewed as penance for her sins, foremost among which was evidently vanity.

Her father was so expectant of success following this makeover that he armed himself with a firearm and brought her back by day instead of night lest her charms lead men to desperate acts. He need not have worried; no one pursued her. Now the speaker is inconvenienced by having to see this sad, ungathered rose.

A modern feminist might point out that the aunt's unhappiness stemmed from the expectation that she needed to become someone's wife before she could be anything but a sad, incomplete person. Such a reader also might bristle at the possessiveness implicit in viewing a woman as something that might be gathered, like a rose.

The ending may succeed to a limited extent with some readers because of its paradoxical humor. The entire poem criticizes feminine vanity, but the last three lines reveal the speaker to be far more egotistical than his aunt.

"MY LIFE CLOSED TWICE BEFORE ITS CLOSE" EMILY DICKINSON (1896)

This is EMILY DICKINSON's most pessimistic poem. In the first line the speaker reveals that s/he twice suffered blows of such magnitude that she uses the same euphemism for them ("closing") that she uses for death. She may or may not have been a devout person before those bad things happened to her, but now she has clearly adopted a "wait-and-see" attitude toward her faith. She is so far from being confident in the existence of a benign god, or just so angry at him, that she refuses to mention his name, admitting only that an impersonal "immortality" (line 3) may or may not bring additional suffering (the "third event" of line 4) to her.

The second stanza reveals the extent of her dread of the third event, which will probably be as "huge" and as "hopeless to conceive" (line 5) as the first two. The key word *parting* in the seventh line unifies the poem by connecting with the words *close* and *unveil* (lines 1 and 3); together they suggest events of such enormity that they should have been presented with an artistic flourish (new paintings are "unveiled" when a painter removes a protective cloth to show off his work to a studio or museum guest). Curtains are also "closed" and "parted" at a theater. If such events are taken as a revelation of God's will (therefore providing us with "all we know of heaven," line 7), his theatrical flair indicates such an indifference to human sentiment that spending eternity in his presence would be dreadful.

What were the two events so drastic that the speaker considers them to be "all we need of hell" (line 8)? By withholding such information, the poet gained universality, since readers are free to supply examples from their own experience. A short list of possibilities would include the deaths of one's child, parent, sibling, or spouse (and death merits language very similar to that used here in another Dickinson poem, "I NEVER LOST AS MUCH BUT TWICE"), some permanently crippling and/or excruciatingly painful injury or debilitating illness, or separation from a loved one.

Dickinson scholarship tends to interpret "parting" as separation from a lover. A minor cottage industry has sprung up based on conjecture as to the identities of the mysterious lovers whose departure from this earth (or at least to a point beyond the reach of the poet's arms) led her to compare their absence with hell. Suspects include a particularly eloquent but happily married minister, Charles Wadsworth, whose departure for California in 1862 coincided with the advent of Dickinson's "wonder year," in which she wrote more than one-fifth of all the poems she composed in her life. Such bursts of creativity are rather common, however, once a poet or other artist discovers her voice. Alternatively (or additionally), the pervasive sense of loss that permeates many of her poems from that era may have been influenced by the Civil War; news of the tens of thousands of young men who became casualties at such important battles as Shiloh, Bull Run, Antietam, and Fredericksburg filled the newspapers in that year.

"MY LIFE HAD STOOD—A LOADED GUN" EMILY DICKINSON (published 1951)

The announced speaker of this poem is a gun. It stood loaded in a corner until the owner finally noticed it, thus providing a precedent for the acquisition of superfluous sporting goods that, by the late 20th century, had become a highly cumbersome by-product of American affluence.

Now carried into the woods, he "speaks" for his master and the mountains echo his report. The sparks accompanying a shot make the valley glow, from the gun's perspective, and he prides himself on standing guard all night. In fact, he even prefers it to sharing the pillow stuffed with eider-duck feathers that his owner enjoys. A deadly foe to any enemy of his master's, he stands ready to deliver a flash (the "yellow eye" of line 19) to add emphasis to the triggering gesture of his master's thumb (line 20; as a safety device, in EMILY DICKINSON's day it was necessary to use a thumb to pull back the hammer on some shotguns to cock the weapon; the actual firing could then have been done with the index finger, also appropriately called the trigger finger. An obvious if troubling exception to this general rule would be if the gun were used in a suicide attempt, when the thumb would be the handier digit. Reinforcing this sinister detail is the emphasis placed on the proximity of the gun to the master's head, the fact that "our good day [is] done" [line 13], and the emphasis on the master's death in the last stanza).

So content is the gun in his role that he regrets that their relationship must end with his master's death. The human half of their deadly combination must inevitably precede him in death because an inanimate object even with the power to kill lacks the power to die.

On the level of imagery, there is probably no other poem in American literature that so clearly begs for a Freudian interpretation. Most of the elements are here for a veiled revelation of the sexual history of a heterosexual male (note the preferential hunting for a doe, a female deer, in line 6). The speaker, if not literally a gun, might be interpreted as some other phallic symbol capable of standing (line 1) and bearing a load. The first stanza relates how the owner discovered his sexuality and carried away the newly discovered proof of his virility.

There must be some portion of the human anatomy corresponding with the "Sovereign" (probably meaning autonomous, as if owned or ruled by someone else; line 5) Woods, Mountains and Valley, that respond so glowingly to the speaker's attentions. Like the molten lava spewing from Mt. Vesuvius, an active volcano in Italy (line 11), pleasure flows into the valley.

Having thus far teetered on the brink of impropriety, the speaker backs off in the fourth stanza, contrasting his accommodations with the pillow cushioning his master's head. The suddenness of his transition to sleep can seem a physiological response to the action described thus far.

The word "foe" (line 17) can refer to a rival as well as an enemy, and testosterone-driven combativeness can lead to deadly force. The "Yellow Eye" of line 19 can be jaundiced (so to speak) or jealous, and the "emphatic Thumb" may be in sync with the feelings of another body part. Throughout it all, the speaker is also enormously proud of his potency, claiming that "none stir the second time" (line 18) after he deals with them.

The last stanza reads like something from the poet's riddle poems; it may have been intended to misdirect those readers who would otherwise insist on the poem's sexual innuendos. It may contain bad puns on the importance of length (and length of years) or vague references to the declining male potency that frequently accompanies age.

N

"A NARROW FELLOW IN THE GRASS"

EMILY DICKINSON (1865) One of the great things a poet can do is to enrich our lives by revealing the splendor inherent in everyday life. The voice and tone of EMILY DICKINSON's poem are conversational and its subject, the experience of suddenly and unexpectedly encountering a snake, is nearly universal. The speaker of the poem recalls such a meeting and at the same time provides valuable clues as to the nature of poetic sensibility. The movement of the poem repeatedly unwinds and recoils, transporting the reader from the calm remembrance of the event in the first stanza to the very moment of discovery in the second, and like a serpent sliding through grass and weeds, the poem oscillates between objective and subjective experience. All of the poet's arts are brought to bear on this seemingly unpromising topic.

The snake is viewed from a variety of perspectives, with its movement in the grass first alerting the speaker to its presence. Notice that the diction and voice of the first two stanzas are what you would expect, given the barest introduction to the poet's background. A churchgoing New England lady would tend to recall the serpent's biblical role; a faint waft of sulfur lingers in her calling him a narrow fellow and in the capitalization of the pronoun in the third line. The assumption of a shared disregard for such beings is conveyed by the words, "did you not," a phrase as flinty as one is likely to encounter anywhere in Vermont. Like some satanic spirit, the snake is imbued with almost mystical powers, including the ability to ride in the grass and to make sudden appearances. The exquisitely ungrammatical fourth line ("His notice sudden is—") carries a full measure of poetic ambiguity, at the same time that it accurately relays the impression the encounter makes in the speaker. It may also suggest that the snake is equally surprised. The poet's description of the grass being parted with comb (line 5) is also perfectly in keeping within the world of the sheltered, domestic life of the presumed speaker, and returns her back indoors.

We are, however, in the presence of genius. The perspective of the second stanza is extraordinary; the reader is placed in the tall Grass (with a capital G), from which an unknown thing is about to miraculously appear. The use of the comb places us almost at eye level with the snake, a cinematic effect rather like a closeup. The shock is such that the speaker is at first unable to process the sensory information she is receiving; she becomes aware only of a spotted shaft, until its rapid retreat facilitates a return to her normal perspective. Before that moment, however, is the breathlessness and the intimate intrusiveness of an animal's attack as it "closes at your feet." The focus on the feet also signals yet another shift in perspective; the creature was obviously so small as to constitute no rational threat, and the reader comes to understand that the somewhat ambiguous "it" in line 7 referred not to the striking snake but to the Grass of line 5. Dickinson has succeeded in capturing in words the rapid succession of impressions sometimes attendant upon an unexpected encounter with a snake or other possible danger.

The third stanza presents another shift in perspective; the speaker will now guide us to the monster's lair. She steels herself for the encounter by becoming, at least imaginatively, a small barefoot boy. Gone now is the domestic comb; the image the serpent brings to this mind is of a whiplash unbraiding in the sun. By her diction, especially the word "wrinkled" in line 16, the speaker may signal yet another change in perspective, a return to the naturally domestic metaphors of the person who began the poem. In the fourth stanza, she attempts to compartmentalize the experience, placing it within the context of her other, more benign encounters with nature. She is not entirely successful in this enterprise, however, as the last stanza indicates. Her body naturally reacts to sudden surprise of an unexpected snake with constricted breathing and, in perhaps the most felicitous line the poet ever wrote, a "Zero at the Bone." On a subjective level, just the shock of the experience is almost as disheartening as if the animal had successfully closed at her feet with a dangerous bite.

NATIVE AMERICAN POETRY

All the tribes that inhabited the territory of what became the continental United States were illiterate, save for the very few individuals who learned to write in one of the European languages, until 1821, when a Georgia Cherokee silversmith named Sequoyah created a written alphabet for his tribe. Beyond a shared illiteracy, however, the tribes were far more varied in their separate cultures than the people who inhabited Europe at the time. Any study of their poetry during the time frame covered in this volume must acknowledge that in the 400 years since Columbus came to America, few decades passed that were not marred by warfare, largely predicated on profit and prosecuted with a zeal that frequently resulted in genocide. Significantly absent from the poetry translated from the American Indian languages prior to the 20th century, and published in the anthologies since that time, are accounts depicting the savagery evident in the atrocities perpetrated by both sides and expressions of the grief they occasioned. This is in part due to the multiple layers of censorship through which the poems had to pass, beginning with the self-censorship by the Indians themselves, who were understandably hesitant to voice their true feelings before the representatives of the race that still threatened to obliterate them.

Perhaps the truest perception of American Indian life that does commonly reach the 20th-century reader of poetry is the multiplicity of voices one hears from across the American landscape. Note that the eight poems discussed here span the continent, from the Seneca tribe of the northeastern states to the Nez Perce, a Pacific coastal tribe. Southern tribes are represented by the Cherokee of the Atlantic region and the Navajo of New Mexico and surrounding states. Their published poems are remarkably uniform in focusing on the spiritual aspects of tribal life, while providing very few facts about their daily activities. This deficit reinforces the stereotype of a monolithic Native American culture, when in fact many of the southeastern tribes had settled farmlands, in some cases resembling estates, and both they and the dominant northeastern tribes often accommodated themselves in wooden structures even before the Europeans/white Americans arrived on the scene. Elsewhere, the Plains Indians were practicing the migratory lifestyle romanticized by Hollywood to the point where most Americans think the teepee and (the predominantly northwestern tribal) totem pole were part of the cultural heritage of all tribes everywhere.

The names of most Native American poets have been lost to posterity, a lack of ownership in keeping with the communal nature of many tribes. A notable exception is Handsome Lake, whose poem "A VISION OF HANDSOME LAKE" provided the Seneca with a myth glorifying corn as a divine gift to man and thus raising the prestige of agriculture to the point where his people were content to pursue that lifestyle and abandon their rapidly shrinking forests.

In the absence of writing, all that one generation can pass to another relies on the spoken word. The rhythms, rhymes, and other repetitions of oral poetry can further that end by encapsulating their message within a more easily remembered framework, thus ensuring that the simple agricultural instructions in

"The CORN GROWS UP" are handed down to the cultivators even as the same poem can be viewed as a prayer intended for an entirely different audience. No two such dissimilar intended audiences can be inferred in the poem identified here as "OSAGE RITUAL," for the Chief Messenger whose role it is to recite the poem is thought to have already met a deity and conveys the blessing of her flesh as a talisman against the disruptive influences of other forces. When it came to daily survival, it could be more crucial for the resident of some of the nation's more inhospitable climates to be able to read the weather and the landscape than to peruse any book, and many Native American poems suggest a preoccupation with the surrounding environment and its resident animals. "THREE SONGS OF MAD COYOTE" attributes supernatural abilities to a god or demon in canine form, accessorized with bloody body parts.

The extremes of love and war are represented here by "CHEROKEE LOVE MAGIC" and the Crow Indian "WAR SONG." Each hints at the psychological states a poem may engender when it serves as an incantation predicated on a tribe's religious beliefs. Unfortunately, the limitations of the power of prayer (or at least of one Native American song in particular) became apparent in the tragic events at Wounded Knee, South Dakota. The "SIOUX GHOST DANCE" and its accompanying dances represented the last best hope of the Plains Indians to turn back the flood of encroaching settlers from their land. Embedded within its lyrics were prophecies from such power symbols as the eagle and the crow, but their faith in its efficacy placed hundreds of men, women, and children at risk, with horrific consequences.

The most beautiful of the poems discussed in this volume is "AT THE TIME OF THE WHITE DAWN," a Pima Indian description of a successful Arizona hunt from the point of view of the prey animal.

BIBLIOGRAPHY

Austin, Mary Hunter. *Medicine Songs*. Charlottesville: University of Virginia Library, 1996.

Chichetto, James William. *Reckoning Genocide: Poems on Native Americans*. Morristown, Tenn.: Indian Heritage Council, 2002.

Clymer, Theodore, comp. *Four Corners of the Sky: Poems, Chants and Oratory*. Boston: Little, Brown, 1975.

Hodge, Gene Meany, comp. *Four Winds: Poems from Indian Rituals*. Sante Fe, N.M.: Sunstone Press, 1972.

Sharpe, J. Ed, ed. *American Indian Prayers and Poetry*. Cherokee, N.C.: Cherokee Publications, 1985.

Spinden, Herbert Joseph, trans. *Songs of the Tewa*. Sante Fe, N.M.: Sunstone Press, 1976.

NATURALISM IN POETRY

NATURALISM IN POETRY   American realism generally aimed at faithfully representing the world as the writer or artist perceived it but generally stayed within fairly genteel standards of propriety. By the last decade of the 19th century, the old standards of decency, as their proponents among the New England theocrats and southern aristocrats had fashioned them, were under siege by the rampant materialism of the Gilded Age, the scientific discoveries of Charles Darwin (whose evolutionary models challenged church authority on the important question of the nature of man), and more explicit European avant-garde literature. A few daring young men and women began treating of subjects that their predecessors felt were beneath the high calling of art, and the first victim of their implied criticism of America was the optimism that permeated much of the nation's culture (but not its poetry, where such depressing subjects as the passage of time, loss, and death always maintained their prominence among the handful of what are considered its great themes). For the naturalists, human behavior was determined by heredity and (exceptionally adverse) social circumstances when it was not dictated by mere chance.

In American poetry, the chief practitioner of this new aesthetic was STEPHEN CRANE, but one can find similar approaches in the early poetry of the American novelist Edith Wharton (1862–1937). Although Wharton is better remembered for her subsequent fiction, in some of her early poetry one can discover such artistic flourishes as later came to be taken as representative of naturalism. In "Aeropagus" (1880), she wrote of the fiery sparks whirling at the beginning of a world and the atoms that weave "both world and soul for utmost joy;" it seems a cosmic injustice that sinners must suffer because "the law that quickens must destroy." In "Phaedra" (1898), she gives voice to the Greek mother whose desire (a subject not discussed under the old rules of staid romanticism) for her stepson leads to tragedy for all involved.

For "The Blue Hotel" (a short story), Stephen Crane imagined a Nebraska landscape so remote that man seemed but "lice . . . caused to cling to a whirling, fire-smote, ice-locked, disease-stricken, space-lost bulb." In the poem "IN THE DESERT," the most recognizable aspect of his representative man is the perverse pleasure that creature takes in consuming his heart. In such poems as "A MAN SAID TO THE UNIVERSE," Crane's poetry projects a godless universe so utterly indifferent to humanity that even when personified and forced to acknowledge the existence of man, it still denies any obligation. Much of Crane's best poetry consists of laconic assertions of his disillusioned cynicism.

Of the less frequently anthologized poets, Edwin Markham (1825–1940) is unique for illuminating the bleak prospects facing many farmers in "The Man with the Hoe" (1899). In his poems written at the turn of the century, the future playwright William Vaughn Moody (1869–1910) condemned American imperialism and the country's moral degeneracy, but the preferred landscape in naturalism is the squalid urban slum from which its denizens are powerless to escape.

BIBLIOGRAPHY

Dudley, John. *A Man's Game: Masculinity and the Anti-Aesthetics of American Literary Naturalism.* Tuscaloosa: University of Alabama Press, 2004.

Fleissner, Jennifer L. *Women, Compulsion, Modernity: The Moment of American Naturalism.* Chicago: University of Chicago Press, 2004.

Link, Eric. *The Vast and Terrible Drama: American Literary Naturalism in the Late 19th Century.* Tuscaloosa: University of Alabama Press, 2004.

"NATURE" HENRY WADSWORTH LONGFELLOW **(1874)** This poem takes the concept of the second childhood, the supposed drifting of the elderly into a carefree existence as their mental and physical energies decline, to its logical conclusion. An indulgent and generally benign Nature takes those who survive that long to their deathbeds the way a mother leads a little child to bed. The poem is very charming in depicting the child's half-willingness, half-reluctance to be led

(line 3), and rather chilling in reference to the things the dying man leaves behind—presumably his family, business, and all other concerns, a list that could also include most of his sensory perceptions and intellect. There are inevitably "broken playthings" since man is ultimately incapable of perfection, but the poem emphasizes the decrepitude attendant upon aging to the point where the afflicted man is reduced to impotency. He can gaze upon the things he is leaving behind through the open door of his memory, but he cannot act upon them.

Although he is not entirely convinced that the splendid joys of heaven will be as pleasing as those of this world, his innocence is almost childlike in that he has apparently no doubt that they exist and that he is bound for them. Nature takes away our powers the way a mother takes away toys at naptime, and eventually we lack the energy to resist. Since we are but children when it comes to the profound mystery of death, we lack the understanding to realize how far the unknown transcends the known.

The thinking behind HENRY WADSWORTH LONGFELLOW's poem may be problematic if it leads to patronizing attitudes toward the aged. Few of the elderly so predictably lose all their powers, and thinking of them as children may lead to treating them like children.

"NEVER SAID A MUMBALIN' WORD" ANONYMOUS **(19th century)** This spiritual song recounts the passion of Christ with an emphasis upon His silent courage in the face of His torture. It begins with the spectacle with which some plantation slaves were all too familiar, a whipping (the "scourging" recorded in John 19:1 and elsewhere). The severity of the attack may be conveyed in the word "whupped" (line 1), a term that has come to connote the pummeling administered in a one-sided fight. Repetition of the words "up de hill" suggests the regularity with which the lashes were applied. "Mumbalin'" (a dialect rendering of *mumbling*) also suggests the expletives that usually would have been appropriate under such circumstances but which Christ refused to utter. Instead, He just hung down his head and cried (line 4; the first gesture probably conveyed His shame for the humanity that could perpetrate such deeds in the same way that His crying was probably for the sake of all sinners and not just a result of His own suffering).

Because His former sermons and His defense during His legal trials included talk of "my kingdom (see John 18:36)," His tormentors forced a crown of thorns onto His head (line 5; see John 19:2) to ridicule Him as the king of the Jews, a people subject to the imperial power of Rome and therefore denied a legitimate king. Then they crucified Him (John 19:18), an act described here as nailing Him to the cross in order to emphasize the excruciating pain He suffered.

Finally they pierced Him in the side and He died (line 16). This represents a departure from the biblical account, in which He died after being given a drink of vinegar (John 19:30). The wound to His side was delivered post mortem by a soldier to determine if He was dead, and the fact that water as well as blood came from the wound (John 19:34) can be taken as incontrovertible evidence of His death.

That no less a man than Jesus suffered in precisely the same way (whipping) as so many of them sanctified the slaves' own suffering and rendered them more comfortable in His promise of a place for them in His kingdom.

"THE NEW COLOSSUS" EMMA LAZARUS (1883)

One of the techniques the best writers use is to focus on the character who benefits the most or is most affected by a scene. It happened that among the famous writers asked to contribute something in honor of the new Statue of Liberty, *Liberty Enlightening the World*, EMMA LAZARUS was the most in touch with the group of people for whom it meant everything. Increasingly involved with the reform efforts aimed at ameliorating the suffering of newly arrived refugees from eastern Europe, the poet imagined not only how the statue would look on its permanent pedestal but also what it would symbolize to the world.

Technically, it is not a perfectly executed poem if judged by the most conservative critical standards of its day, because the second line of the sonnet has an extra syllable. The innovative CDCDCD rhyme scheme of the concluding sestet is within acceptable limits, as is the use of run-on lines (as opposed to end-stopped lines, which finish with a punctuation mark) to achieve the rhyme

scheme of the octave. Instead of invoking the muses or celebrating classical myths as her 18th-century peers would have done, Lazarus chose to contrast one of the ancient monuments with the new one. The physical dimensions of the Colossus of Rhodes led to its being considered one of the Seven Wonders of the Ancient World. That predecessor was "brazen" (line 1) in both senses of the word; it was made of bronze and, if its limbs were not exactly "conquering" (line 2), it audaciously forced visiting vessels to sail under it since, as Lazarus notes, its legs spanned the opening of the harbor.

By 1883, the image of "a mighty woman" (line 4) appealed to most progressive Americans. Lazarus imagines the harbor at sunset when not only the statue but the land behind it would appear golden. Liberty's torch not only promises light through the coming darkness, it has the power of "imprisoned lightning" (line 5), and with poetic license Lazarus rechristens her the "Mother of Exiles" (line 6). The statue's look is mild and, in a further point of contrast with the ancient statue, only the air bridges the harbor (line 8) over which she stands. At a time when restrictive immigration laws were beginning to close the nation's borders to people considered undesirable for racial or economic reasons, the poet imagines quite a different message coming from the statue's lips. Instead of welcoming those with ancient titles and the pomp attending them, from the rest of the world she requests "your tired, your poor, your huddled masses yearning to breathe free" (lines 10–11). Since Europe was thought to be overpopulated at the time (hence the "teeming" shore of line 12), she invited the downtrodden people of all nations who would be considered "wretched refuse" (almost garbage) in their native lands to establish new homes in America. Many of the new arrivals had been "tempest-tossed" (line 11) not only during the ocean voyage but also by political whirlwinds, and Lady Liberty showed them the door to their new lives. Like the famous statue they commemorate, the most famous lines of this poem can stir the hearts of freedom-loving people everywhere.

"NOBODY KNOWS THE TROUBLE I'VE HAD" ANONYMOUS (19th century)

This poem is as simple as the message of Christ. Before he confided in Jesus, the speaker's life had been troublesome. In the chorus, s/he may be thanking God that nobody knows about it.

One morning he saw some berries and found the juice as sweet as natural honey (a "honeycomb," line 12, consists of the wax cells constructed by honeybees to hold their honey [and their offspring] within their hive). While this may seem an inconsequential pleasure, it may demonstrate the speaker's spiritual growth because he harmed no one and coveted nothing. It may loosely reference that verse of the Sermon on the Mount when Christ directs his followers to behold the fowls of the air that neither sow nor reap, yet the heavenly Father feeds them (Matthew 6:26).

Life still has its emotional highs and lows, and sometimes he feels so low that he is figuratively almost on the ground (line 16). He attributes this to Satan's hatred, exacerbated because Satan once had him and let him go (when he found Christ).

"NO! COVER NOT THE FAULT. THE WISE REVERE" Frederick Goddard Tuckerman (1860)   Frederick Goddard Tuckerman's sonnet reads as if it were a response to an insult. In the first line, the mysterious speaker's tone is almost imperial (and delightfully ambiguous) as he responds to a critic. The "fault" in question probably refers to a mistake the speaker made or the internal audience's gaffe in having mentioned it (which he may have tried to "cover" with an apology). The entire first quatrain only appears to clarify the situation since the most damning term appears at the end of its most hostile statement ("The wise revere the judgment of the simple"), which might be construed as praise for his adversary's straightforward approach (or philosophical simplicity) or as a questioning of his intelligence. Similarly, the harsh "words of counsel" of such great potential benefit to the unwilling ear might either have been those that earlier criticized the speaker, or the advice the speaker is now offering (lines 2–4).

The second quatrain begins with a non sequitur comparing perfect grief to love: both cast out fear and should moan like an overbrimmed (overflowing) river. The speaker quickly states his true feelings, however. Criticism typically consists of "senseless chaff [teasing

or mocking] and chat" (line 7) from those who insolently bestow ignorant praise or from those who "stoop and peer" (an unglamorous, awkward pose) while picking for a flaw without touching the "quick" (the living parts of a work or the creator's pain) or rubbing the raw (without adding additional injury or alleviating the pain since, the metaphor implies, their probes are too shallow to be effectual).

Instead of such ineffectual remedies, the speaker would prefer one sharp blow like that used to remove the "wild" (infected or misaligned) tooth from a horse's jaw. It is an assertion that suggests the speaker is in touch with the primal forces of creative energy, whereas the poem as a whole may be questioning whether the internal audience is even capable of appreciating what the speaker has done.

"A NOISELESS PATIENT SPIDER" Walt Whitman (1868)   This poem follows a common pattern for nature poetry: Observation of a natural phenomenon is followed by application of a lesson to human life in general or to the speaker's life in particular. It represents a departure from Walt Whitman's usual practice in that he is typically more concerned with the human landscape than the natural. This bias is evident in two aspects of this poem: he provides virtually no information about the spider beyond its isolation on a small promontory and its web production, and he inserts the speaker as an active participant in the first part of the poem.

At his best, as in the 33rd section of "Song of Myself," Whitman was capable of exquisite single-line animal descriptions with a precision reminiscent of Japanese haiku: "the fin of the shark cuts like a black chip out of the water" (line 35). Here, however, his description is remarkable for its focus on an absence: He observes the silence of the spider (but one suspects that the spider is only "noiseless" like the writer whose books have not yet generated critical interest or found a wide audience). By the second line Whitman had already shifted his attention to the speaker, who "marked" (the verb used in the second line and repeated in the third for emphasis; he is evidently so intent on taking a lesson directly from nature that he is taking notes as closely as a college student at an important lecture) the spider's isolated stance and its use of new-spun webbing to explore the "vacant vast surrounding" (line 3). Young spiders of some species can use a loose strand of their silk to catch and ride a breeze to a new location, but this one keeps launching, unreeling, and speeding its filament (a word repeated three times to mimic the repeated action).

The second stanza draws out the parallels between the spider and the speaker's soul. Of course the scale (the soul is surrounded by "measureless oceans of space;" line seven) and the verbs (musing, venturing, throwing, and seeking) are different, but each performer hopes his "gossamer thread" will catch somewhere. Each acts in accordance with its nature, but the speaker almost seems to be praying (he uses the phrase "O my soul" in lines 6 and 20) for his soul to be as persistent as the spider.

O

"ODE" Henry Timrod (1866) As its subtitle indicates, this ode was produced to commemorate the graves of the Confederate dead in the Magnolia Cemetery of Charleston, South Carolina. Prior to the Civil War, Charleston was arguably the richest, most cultured city in America although much of its wealth was produced by slaves barred from sharing in it. Since the first shots of the war were fired at Fort Sumter in Charleston harbor (on April 12, 1861), the city could expect a terrible vengeance such as was visited upon Columbia, the state capitol, when Sherman's Union army occupied it on February 17, 1865. Although Confederate forces held Fort Sumter until that very day, however, Charleston was not burned to the extent that Columbia had been because the bulk of Sherman's army had marched northwest after sacking Savannah instead of northeast.

Although relatively unscathed by fire, Charleston's finances had been so desperately depleted by the war that even the funds necessary to build a monument in the cemetery where so many of its sons were buried were not immediately available in 1866. Hence Henry Timrod's poem begins with a sincere reference to the humble graves of the "martyrs of a fallen cause" (line 2; to call the cause "lost" might reflect ingloriously on the efforts of the soldiers. For those readers convinced that the soldiers died to protect slavery, however, the term "fallen" might suggest that the cause was less-than-righteous or even downright devilish. Fortunately, few of those present during the dedica-

tion services would have interpreted this wonderfully sentimental line in that way, and perhaps many more felt that if the South had merely fallen, it might rise again). In keeping with the religious tone invoked by categorizing the fallen as saintly martyrs, the speaker anticipates the day when pilgrims will visit the site's marble columns as though honoring a holy shrine (line 4).

Although the "blossom of [their] fame is blown" (has reached its full-flowering majesty), the seeds of laurel (the plant traditionally used for victory wreaths) are still in the earth (this is perhaps the most universally beautiful sentiment in the poem) just as the shaft of their future commemorative column is still in the stone (line 8).

In the meantime, on behalf of the tardy years that have not yet honored the dead in marble, behold the tears of "your" (the dead soldiers are the internal audience at this point in the poem) sisters and the flowers they brought in your memory. These may be small tributes, but your spirits will smile more proudly on them than on a future monument molded from cannonballs (line 16). In the last stanza, the speaker calls down angels from the skies, arguing that no ground is holier than where defeated valor lies when it is crowned by mourning beauty.

Eventually the Confederate soldiers did get their massive monuments, and the Magnolia Cemetery is still open and receiving their descendents as well as the general public.

"ODE INSCRIBED TO W. H. CHANNING"

RALPH WALDO EMERSON (1847) Like RALPH WALDO EMERSON, William Henry Channing (1810–84) attended Harvard Divinity School (class of 1829), and became a Unitarian minister. Both men were members of the Transcendental Club (an informal think tank in Boston focused on social and Harvard reform). Channing preached at Brook Farm (a Utopian experiment in idealistic collective farming in West Roxbury, Massachusetts) in 1846. In 1847 he was finishing an influential six-volume biography of his uncle, William Ellery Channing (also a Unitarian minister and an important source of ideas for the transcendentalists). Both Emerson and W. H. Channing were active spokesmen against social and political injustice, as the references in this poem against slavery and American and Russian imperialism indicate. It was potentially embarrassing to dedicate a poem to someone still so young, because his idealism might eventually have led him into associations with which the poet disagreed, but Channing, who eventually served as the chaplain of the U.S. Congress during the Civil War in addition to volunteering in Washington hospitals during that conflict, did little in his subsequent life that would have merited Emerson's censure.

The poem begins with an apology to Channing (the "evil time's sole patriot" of the second line) for the speaker's inability to leave his "honied thought" (probably devoted to his famous essays and public lectures as well as his poetry; line 4) to take a more public role against the priest's cant (insincere expressions of piety or insistence on church authority concerning an issue with which Emerson disagreed) or stateman's rant (lines 5–6). When he even attempts to address politics, the angry Muse confuses him (his frustrated poetic ambitions confound his thought on such issues). Despite this objection, the speaker characterizes those who prate of the culture of mankind and better arts and life (lines 12–14) as blindworms (probably a perjorative reference to worms in general and not to the blind burrowing lizard of Europe that bears that name; line 15) if they support the American War against Mexico (1846–48) or praise the New England spirit of independence while tolerating the hunters (characterized as jackals in line 23) of escaped slaves in New Hampshire.

The speaker contrasts the towering landscape of the Granite State with the little men who inhabit it, comparing the scale to the small bat or wren and the massive oak tree in which it nests (line 27). If a volcano (the "earth-fire" of line 29) consumed the people of New Hampshire, the southern crocodile (those who base their lives on slavery; the implied comparison suggests that both are reptilian [notably lacking in human warmth] man-eaters) would grieve (at the loss of this important political ally; line 31). Freedom is praised, but hidden, and (hypocritical) funeral eloquence "rattles the coffin-lid" (is such an outrage as to disturb the dead).

Channing was evidently among those who suggested northern secession from the United States as a means of removing their connection with slavery (lines 38–39). The speaker counters that it would make no difference, since Boston Bay and Bunker Hill would still serve things (that the fashionable people in Massachusetts would continue to use the products of the southern plantation system, and that both north and south would continue to claim the legacy of freedom and independence won at great cost in such Revolutionary War battles as Bunker Hill [June 17, 1775]). Both north and south are inextricably part of the same snake (a metaphor recalling Benjamin Franklin's early [1754] political cartoon, which depicted a snake chopped into pieces with each segment bearing the name of a British North American colony. The caption was "Join or Die").

The speaker considers the present state of political and moral affairs so backward as to resemble a rider serving the horse, instead of vice versa. Similarly, the cowherder serves the cow ("neat" refers to domesticated bovines, a subclass that includes oxen as well as cattle; line 45), the merchant his purse, and the eater his meat. In that day of the chattel (a term referring to property in general, but then most often seen in connection with the phrase "chattel slavery"), webs weave, corn grinds, and "things are in the saddle and ride mankind" (lines 49–50).

There should be separate laws for men and for things, but the latter runs wild and unkings the former. Although the speaker won't quarrel with progress, calling it fitting that forests be felled for development and the land engineered for human ends, he stops short of thinking that man should be similarly owned and exploited. Man should live for friendship and love, and the state should follow as Olympus (in this context, the Greek gods who were thought to inhabit the mountain) follows Zeus (whom the Romans called "Jove" or "Jupiter;" line 70).

Yet he would not ask the shopman to work in his woods, or an unwilling senator to seek the votes of wild birds. Everyone has his chosen work, and foolish hands (which get involved in work beyond their expertise, as the speaker infers he would be doing if he became a political activist) mix and mar (line 76). The issues are straightforward and the argument over them will continue until dark is light, man has but one gender, and even numbers become odd. Eventually the overgod who marries Right to Might, peoples and unpeoples, exterminates races with stronger races and replaces black by white faces (rarely did phrases so dated and stupid escape from Emerson's pen, a lapse probably attributable to the flawed science of the early 19th century but very much out of keeping with the philosopher's abolitionist sentiments as they were expressed even in this very poem), knows how to bring honey out of a lion (see Samson's riddle of Judges 14:8. He killed a lion and later found bees making their home in the carcass) and graft the gentlest offspring (a "scion" is a heir or descendent) on a pirate or Turk (a nationality probably chosen for their traditional ferocity in battle).

The Cossacks (Russian mounted warriors drawn from its fierce border tribes. Here the term alludes to Imperial Russia and its allies, Prussia [a German nation] and Austria) can partition and absorb Poland (a short-lived accomplishment attempted three times in the late 18th century). They can ruin the disputed country's last noble and render its last poet mute, but straightaway the victors divide. Half take a stand for freedom, and thousands are inspired by and defend the Muse (the point here may be that the speaker is so confident in the eventual triumph of justice that his potential contributions to that cause will not be missed).

ODELL, JONATHAN (1737–1818) Had the Revolutionary War but turned out differently—had

Washington been killed in the fighting on Long Island or betrayed into capture by Benedict Arnold's treachery, to name just two incidents where the fate of the nation was held in the balance—Jonathan Odell might have been celebrated as the leading poet, albeit still a minor one, of his generation of Colonial Americans. Fortunately for America, today he is chiefly remembered south of the Canadian border only as the leading publicist for the Loyalist cause.

Born the son of a joiner (a combination cabinet-maker and carpenter) in Newark, New Jersey, on September 25, 1737, he graduated from the College of New Jersey (renamed as Princeton University in 1896) in 1754 and briefly served as an army doctor in the West Indies. He became a priest in 1767 and assumed responsibility for the church in Burlington, New Jersey, where he thought his chief battles would be against the Methodist missionaries who were active in the area. His prewar publications included the translation from the French of a pamphlet on raising silkworms, which he thought might be of some use to agriculture. As the colonies became more politicized, however, he was publicly criticized after two of his letters were stolen in which his Loyalist leanings were apparent. A lover of liberty, he responded with "A BIRTHDAY SONG FOR KING'S BIRTHDAY," a veritable declaration of loyalty that eventually necessitated his fleeing to New York City. Perhaps his best work in the propaganda war was "The Times, a satirical poem, written during the American Revolution." Forced to flee to Canada when the war was lost, he helped settle Fredericton. It became the provincial capital of New Brunswick, and he became a substantial pillar of that community, at first largely consisting of fellow refugees, although he remained a continual critic of the new United States.

Odell died on November 25, 1818, in Fredericton, New Brunswick. His memory is preserved in Odell Park in that city, and many of his letters, poems, and business records have been preserved in the New Brunswick Museum.

BIBLIOGRAPHY

Edelberg, Cynthia Dubin. *Jonathan Odell: Loyalist Poet of the American Revolution.* Durham, N.C.: Duke University Press, 1987.

Odell, Jonathan. *The New Brunswick Poems of Jonathan Odell.* Kingston, Ont: Loyal Colonies Press, 1982.

Vincent, Thomas Brewer. *Jonathan Odell: An Annotated Chronology of the Poems, 1759–1818.* Kingston, Ont: Loyal Colonies Press, 1980.

"OF ALL THE SOULS THAT STAND CREATE—" EMILY DICKINSON (1951)

The speaker in this poem appropriates the language of the Calvinists and, in some respects, the perspective of their God. Since the human soul is thought to be immortal, it stands to reason that "all the Souls that stand create" (line 1) refers to everyone who ever lived. The "One" that God "elected" (line 2) could only be Jesus Christ to the Calvinists.

The speaker looks forward to the day when "Sense" (line 3; the term may encompass not only the body and its senses, but also that which humans may think of as their reason) "flies away" from Spirit (a reversal of the common perception of death as the soul's leaving the body. Here, the spirit connects with a divine majesty so far beyond our comprehension that our human intelligence has no value. Its departure should not be mourned, at that point). Subterfuge (all manner of artifice and deceptive traps) will be finished. Things (and probably souls) separated by time (the past and present, represented here as "that which is" and "that which was"; line 5) will stand at the same time. The "brief Drama in the flesh" (human life in all its manifestations) will shift like sand (a pleasing if somewhat disconcerting reference to the transience of life as we know it). Figures will show their "royal Front" (their true character; line nine) and everything else will be carved away as easily as a mist. Then all will see the Atom (the single intrinsic coherent perfect elemental Being) God preferred to all the "lists" of clay (line 12). The term "lists" may contain a reference to the medieval knights, the only men considered exceptionally "noble" in their day; "entering the lists" meant signing up for and entering a jousting or other physical competition. Referring to "lists of clay" would not only put down human pretensions of merit and our artificial distinctions between men, it would also include all people since God created Adam from clay (the "dust of the ground" [Genesis 2:7]) and Eve from

his rib (Genesis 2:21–2), and everyone else descended from them.

Such a lesson in divine Constancy may have inspired a similar poem by EMILY DICKINSON on human fidelity, "The SOUL SELECTS HER OWN SOCIETY."

"OF BRONZE AND BLAZE" EMILY DICKINSON (published 1951)

The aurora borealis is a naturally occurring atmospheric light show varying in color and shape and caused by the collision of electrons from the solar winds with atoms of oxygen, nitrogen, and other gases. It is most vivid over the earth's magnetic poles but can frequently be seen as far south as New England, and is known as the aurora australis south of the equator. It can extend over half the sky.

On the night EMILY DICKINSON describes in this poem these northern lights shone "bronze and blaze" although the most common hues are greens and reds. It can appear as curtains of shimmering light so perfect that the poet marvels at the accuracy of their designs, which she believes must have been "preconcerted" (line 4). They are also self-contained, performing their spectacles regardless of the alarms they may cause or whatever happens to the rest of the universe or the poet. They inspire the artist in her, but their scope also humbles her (she is "infected" with "Taints of Majesty," lines 8–9; diction that suggests disease and poisoning). Although she may "strut upon [her] stem" (line 11), the analogy suggests that pride in human accomplishment is misplaced because anything we can do ultimately stems from the facts of our existence. Just as a plant is rooted in the soil and should take no credit for its blossom because the flower occurs in accordance with a natural or divine plan, so should humans not be too proud of their accomplishments (which in any event will pale in comparison with the beauty and extent of the universe). She disdains Men and Oxygen (the limits defined by the human and natural worlds) because of their arrogance (or because of her own arrogance stemming from the "vaster attitudes" the northern lights inspire. The text supports either reading).

Her Splendors, she comes to realize, are Menagerie (mere caged specimens with short life expectancies instead of larger, elemental forces; line 14). The northern lights will continue entertaining for centuries after she is an "island in dishonored grass" (dead, buried and forgotten) of whom only subterranean beetles are aware.

"OH FAIREST OF THE RURAL MAIDS"

WILLIAM CULLEN BRYANT (1832) One of the features of romantic poetry as it flourished in Europe and early 19th-century America was its celebration of chance encounters on rural roads between a propertied, well-educated young man and an unsophisticated but exceptionally vivacious shepherdess. Although such poems were frequently narrative, WILLIAM CULLEN BRYANT's delightful lyrics let the reader imagine the lengths to which her beauty could transport a young man's fancy.

Although he might seem to directly address the maid in the opening line, the young man who serves as the speaker in this poem talks about the girl instead of to her. He wisely limits himself to images from the surrounding countryside, but the qualification he places in his praise of her beauty (she is "the fairest *of all the rural maids*") might have rankled if she were at all nervous about her humble roots. He exacerbates the potential communication problem by speculating that she was born in a forest and never saw the inside of a house until she had passed her infancy (lines 2–4), an exaggeration that tends to maximize the differences in their backgrounds instead of bridging the social gaps between them. He as much as admits the falseness of this vision when he describes her childhood romps in the "sylvan" wilds (line 6); if she were educated enough to understand that this term related to the forests, then her childhood was probably not as wild as he makes it out to be. Before she can object, however, he transitions with consummate skill from praise of her background (which in his hands seems to have been nearly as mystical as that of any ancient goddess) to praise of her inner and outer beauty. Lines 7 and 8 express the conceit upon which the rest of the poem is based: all of the beauty of the woods can be seen in her features.

In the third stanza he praises her extremities, especially the way her fair hair (the "locks" of line 10) catch the (presumably golden) twilight and the leaf-stirring wind generated by her step. He really finds his stride in the next stanza, however, in his comparison of her eyes

with the springs in whose silent waters heaven can be seen. Her lashes are like the medicinal (and perhaps a little hallucinogenic) herbs that line a brook. Just gazing at her eyes and their lashes almost transports him to heaven.

In the last stanza he compares her pristine character (represented by the "sinless breast" of line 18) with forest depths "by foot unpressed," one of Bryant's more delightful near rhymes. In the last two lines he praises her simplicity; she has experienced nothing to disturb the "holy peace" (line 19) that resides in her heart as it does in the inner reaches of a virgin forest.

"THE OLD CHISHOLM TRAIL" ANONYMOUS (19th century) In 1867, a new railroad yard turned Abilene, Kansas, still not much larger than when it was founded as a stagecoach stop 10 years earlier, into the premier destination for the Texas cattle drives. By Abilene's count, some 3 million cattle were shipped east from its pens from 1867 to 1872. At the other end, numerous feeder trails siphoned the Longhorn cattle from southern and central Texas, joining the Old Chisholm Trail proper at Salt Creek, later renamed Red River Crossing, on the Oklahoma border, and following it straight north about 220 miles to the market.

This folk song celebrates the cowboy experience by relating some of the hardships and hazards of the trail. Horses were often the property of the ranchers in much of the West, and the smartest of these entrepreneurs would not expose their best stock to the hazards of the trail. This could easily lead to a situation in which the speaker would price the horse at 10 dollars and the saddle (which he probably owned) at 40 dollars (line 3). The violence implicit in the language of "punching" cattle (line 4) is accurate; many of the famous Texas longhorns were essentially wild animals allowed free grazing until rounded up for branding and much later being *driven* (forced to walk) all the way to market. Pain (or the fear of it) and their natural herding instinct kept them bunched and moving in the right direction.

If the trip was hard on cattle (the best managers learned to pace the drive more leisurely so that the cattle, comfortably fed and watered along the way, would reach the buyers in prime condition), it could be very hard on the trail hands. Successive stanzas in this song point out the very long daily hours, sometimes including night watches over the herd; line 8) and exposure to the elements. Without weather forecasts based on anything other than the shape of the clouds then on the horizon, it would have been very possible to have been caught out without picking up a raincoat (the "slicker" of line 8) or chaps (leather leggings worn over the jeans to ward off brush and, in line 9, rain).

Even in the best weather, the job entailed prolonged sitting in an uncomfortable position ("feet in the stirrups and seat in the saddle," line 11). A sudden lightning storm could stampede the herd, perhaps (but not very likely) resulting in their entire loss (line 14). By that time the speaker has become so inured to the hardships that he claims not to care if they never stop, and he jokes about riding as if it were an eight-day clock (the large mechanical clocks of that day were powered by the energy stored in their pendulums. The clock in line 16 would have a system of levers and wheels so refined that it would only have to have the weight driving its pendulum returned to the top of its height once in eight days).

A certain sadness must have settled in the trail hand's heart at the rather anticlimatic end of the drive. The whole process from ranch to market might be summarized in line 17: "we rounded [them] up and put [them] in [railroad] cars." That this meant the last of "old Two Bars" (line 18) refers to the simple cattle brand identifying every animal's membership in the herd, but on another level it acknowledges the cattles' ultimate fate.

Hands had to be fed food that did not require refrigeration, so the "bacon and beans" of the next line were pretty standard fare, along with a hardtack biscuit and boiled coffee. The next stanza alludes to the poor pay hands sometimes received; the luckless speaker somehow finds himself owing the boss $9 despite having little opportunity to buy anything good along the route. He must return to Abilene, apparently, to draw his share of the cattle sale, then ride at least another 220 miles back to Texas to see his "honey." Perhaps saddle sores or boils suggest the posture of the last stanza (knees in saddle, seat in the sky), or perhaps it is only an expression of the relief he feels at no longer

being responsible for the cattle and the exhilaration of completing the adventure. The chorus ("Come a ti yi yippee," etc.) conveys some of the unique challenges and indescribable pleasures of the trail drive, a combination so attractive that the speaker will not quit the business immediately, but "in the sweet by and by" (perhaps never; line 26).

"OLD COUNSEL OF THE YOUNG MASTER OF A WRECKED CALIFORNIA CLIPPER" HERMAN MELVILLE (1888) The

speaker of HERMAN MELVILLE's poem was once in command of a very fast clipper ship designed to transport passengers from the East Coast and around South America to the riches of California with the greatest speed. On the return voyage he passed through the Golden Gate, where the waters of San Francisco Bay enter those of the Pacific Ocean. He reached Cape Horn, on the southern tip of Chile, with such ease and speed that he put out gay streamers and every inch of sail; *royals* were small sails rigged above the others. The ship was passing over some of the most treacherous waters in the world, where full-blown storms can arrive with little fanfare, but the elated young captain was oblivious to the danger until he heard the fatal call to save the ship. By then, it was evidently too late.

The internal audience of the poem was probably a fellow captain, or at least a seafarer in some capacity, for the Young Master calls him "brother" and does not need to provide him with background information.

Note how the tone changes as the crisis begins. Although the speaker maintains the imperative mood throughout the poem, the voice of cold command used before the danger changes to the voice of experience.

"OLD IRONSIDES" OLIVER WENDELL HOLMES

(1830) It is usually a sad moment for all who sailed on her when a ship is scrapped, a process usually conducted with little fanfare. It was the U.S.S. *Constitution*'s good fortune to be resting in the Boston Navy Yard, where its strikingly beautiful hardwood exterior caught the fancy of the nascent poet, OLIVER WENDELL HOLMES. Other navy ships of the time had longer and more distinguished careers in active service, but largely thanks to this poem, the *Constitution* has been preserved for two centuries after it had been judged obsolete. It remains the oldest commissioned vessel in the U.S. Navy and even today can be viewed at its berth in a suburb of Boston.

The first successful ironclad vessels were not invented until the Civil War, still over three decades away, but the *Constitution* won the moniker "Old Ironsides" because the cannonballs of its heyday tended to bounce off its hardwoods with little effect. Use of the name for the title of this poem not only served as a reminder of the ship's service but also invested the ship with a personality.

With its first word, the poem strikes a responsive chord in the breasts of even today's navy veterans. *Ay,* or *Aye* is still used as an affirmative in that service, and coupled with a second "Aye," the phrase indicates that an order has been understood and that it will be obeyed. Along with the shock of the familiar, the term would have been a virtual call-to-arms to the former and current navy men of its day, the most obvious group of potential supporters for the poet's cause. The first line's appeal is far broader than that, however, since it seems to advocate an attack on that most venerated of all the country's symbols, its flag. The violence of tearing the ensign down is exacerbated by the fact that it is tattered; a merely worn-out flag would have long since been replaced, but in this context the adjective implies that it had been rent by enemy fire. Many patriotic people would think it profane for any hand to be raised against a banner, and by extension, an entire ship, so consecrated in the nation's defense. By 1830, most Americans were so proud of their juvenescent country that they could readily relate to "an eye (dancing) to see that banner in the sky" (lines 3–4).

The poem carries the attention of the reader down from the mast, but it is the sounds that first alert us to the fact that the poet has chosen to render the deck as it appeared in a raging battle. Note that the battle is treated rather antiseptically; we hear a battle shout but no agonized screams from the wounded, and although there is a cannon burst, it is only the roar resulting from the ship's own armament being fired and not an incoming projectile. The reader is even treated to the potent sight of the cannonball's flight, compared to a meteor that sweeps the clouds.

The second stanza reveals the ship in the aftermath of battle, awash in heroes' blood but still hurrying over the waved-tossed sea as its vanquished foes kneel in submission on the deck. The speaker personifies the ship at this point, instilling her with a capacity to feel the victor's tread or a conquered knee, and contrasting these images with that of the harpies, originally repugnant mythological creatures but in this context merely human predators, who would pluck this "eagle of the sea" (line 16; note that the poet has linked the identity of the ship with that of another important national symbol and that the majestic national bird is being treated like a barnyard fowl).

The third stanza suggests a more fitting end for the heroic ship. Holmes envisions the appropriate military honors; the "holy" flag (his intended audience shared his reverence for the symbol) would be nailed to her mast and she would be given under full sail "to the god of storms, the lightning and the gale" (lines 23–24). Essentially, he is suggesting a burial at sea such as was accorded to sailors, an image of such poignancy to military veterans as to further stir them to action.

"ON A HONEY BEE" PHILIP FRENEAU (1809)

The full title of the poem makes the situation quite clear: a honeybee drank from a glass of wine and drowned in it. This mock requiem for the insect reveals much about the traditional American attitudes towards alcohol abuse. That the reader is to view the inebriated state as humorous is clear from the poet's verbs: noting that the bee was born to sip (as one would a fine wine) from lake or spring or "quaff" (to gulp down, as an inexperienced or addicted drinker might drink a cheap beer) stream water, he asks why he came to him on "vagrant" (wandering or wayward, and certainly uninvited) wing. Did Bacchus (the Greek god of wine) tempt the bee by preparing the speaker's glass, and will the speaker "admit [him] to a share" (such gentlemanly diction distinguishes the speaker as an aristocrat who, by virtue of his education and breeding [such were the prejudices of his time], would know not just how to hold his liquor but also how to relish its social implications).

The speaker ponders his guest's troubled background and attributes his plight to exposure to such natural hazards as storms and predatory wasps and insects. The bee might be suffering from what 21st-century psychology would diagnose as posttraumatic stress disorder following his involvement in wars, or be driven to drink to cope with a stressful job, or merely have lost his way. Personifying the insect closes the gap between speaker and insect, and the latter is invited to drink with language suitable for addressing an honored guest: "a better seat you could not take" (line 11). The speaker's empathy leads him to view the wine from the bee's perspective, where it must seem like a lake.

Fully accepting his new companion as a fellow tipster, the speaker encourages him to "let the cloud of trouble pass" (line 15) by partaking of the "fluid that never fails to please and drown the griefs of men or bees." Although "we" (the speaker may be using the plural pronoun to indicate himself alone [in the manner of royalty, since he is the sovereign of his cup] or himself and his comrades) cannot know what forced the bee there and the bee will not tell, we would have the guest go cheerily after bidding a glad farewell. It will fly on lighter wings with a dart that will defy its foes (it will be as lightheaded as a human drunk and its aerial equivalent of a stagger will confuse predators by its random movement, although "the dart" also references the bee's stinger).

But the speaker cautions against too deep a drink, for even bees six feet high (the size of human alcoholics) can die in that ocean (note how the poet keeps enlarging the size of the liquid as if to convey a sense of the bee's increasing intoxication). Like the pharaoh (who unwisely chased Moses and his people into a freakishly emptied Red Sea only to be drowned when God closed the waters upon him; see Exodus 14:28), he would have perished in a sea of red (the color of the wine).

The bee evidently disregards the warning, so the speaker encourages him to enjoy it without fear. His grave will be the glass of wine and his epitaph a tear (lines 33–34). He will take his seat in Charon's boat (who ferried the dead to the underworld, the kingdom of the dead in Roman mythology). We will tell the hive that the bee died "afloat" (they will give the impression that it died at sea in an era when wooden ships, cloth sails and hempen ropes made that a more common misfortune than it would later become. The term may also pun on the bee's being debt-free instead of drowning in debt, a possibility that ties in the earlier references to its vagrancy).

"ON BEING BROUGHT FROM AFRICA TO AMERICA" Phillis Wheatley (1773)

This poem has been condemned because it appears to argue that exposure to Christianity made up for the speaker's enslavement. Phillis Wheatley has been severely criticized and unfairly censored by later generations as a consequence; how could a person of color so thoroughly betray her people as to provide slavers with an argument and an example with which to defend their practices?

If one considers the poem's internal audience, however, an entirely different picture emerges. In the poem's last two lines, the speaker makes it clear that her message was intended for those Christians who discriminate on the basis of color. The entire poem, if read with this situation in mind, should correctly be viewed as an indictment of racism.

The opening line does not equate mercy with slavery; clearly it was slavery and not mercy that captured, shackled, transported and sold the author as a child, forever severing her ties with her natural parents. Both the title and the first line inform the internal audience of the circumstances that brought her to America, reminding them that she is a suitable object for their mercy, and the first two lines establish common ground with the poem's internal audience by asserting that the speaker is, like them, a Christian. The lines commend the mercy that she experienced as a model her auditors might well emulate, especially the mercy shown her that facilitated her Christian education. Mentioning her acceptance of the Christian God and Jesus Christ as her savior argues for her acceptance by her auditors as well. Instead of turning her back on her people, the speaker embraces them by including herself as part of "our" sable race, which some people view with scorn (line 5). She discredits the slaver's biblical rationalizations of slavery by reminding them that all Christians are eligible for heaven. Her last line can be confusing; the speaker is not advocating a whitening process by which even the blackest skin can be refined like flour until it presents no barrier to heaven. The refinement she advocates is really the education of the slave to the tenets of Christianity and the exposure to salvation that she was so mercifully shown, refinements that all Christians regardless of race must undergo if they are to "join the angelic train." The poem reveals the pain the author felt as a result of the racism she experienced, and the poem is her attempt to use her God-given talent and her common bonds with other Christians to fight it.

"ONCE I PASS'D THROUGH A POPULOUS CITY" WALT WHITMAN (1860)

This is a remarkable poem about disengagement. The speaker's detachment becomes evident in the imprecise language of the very first line: his object was "imprinting my brain for future use" instead of enjoying the experience. Of course, as a writer, part of WALT WHITMAN's job was to gather impressions that might be used later for his literary work, and his list of the things he came to study, "shows, architecture, customs, traditions" (line 1) reveals that he did not want to miss anything public and external.

His plans for this literary business trip were all upset when he met a woman who, evidently imagining that she had met the love of her life, stayed with him day and night. At last she held him by the hand, passionately insisting that he not leave. He still sees her beside him "with silent lips sad and tremulous" (line 7). The grammatical ambiguity of the last line leaves it unclear whether the speaker's lips or the woman's are being described. Perhaps the speaker shared the sexual proclivities of the author, and the relationship had been doomed from the start.

"ONE NEED NOT BE A CHAMBER—TO BE HAUNTED" EMILY DICKINSON (published 1951)

It is unlikely that a born skeptic such as EMILY DICKINSON who could not be pressured into admitting faith in God even as a teenager in seminary school would believe in a haunted house as an adult. She realized, however, that the human mind has corridors "surpassing Material Place" (lines 3–4). In other words, the individual mind contains horrors beyond the reach of even the most colorful local storyteller.

Even if ghosts did exist, the speaker reasons it would be safer to meet them at Midnight (traditionally the most frightening hour) than to meet the "Cooler Host" (line 8). This is a moniker of terrible portent not only because it carries the discomfort of lower temperatures (itself often the first clue of a supernatural presence), but also because to "cool" someone can mean to kill them.

It seems safer to run through an Abbey (a monastery or convent). These are rather rare in America, and their use as the setting for a ghost story probably owes much to the anti-Catholic sentiments prevalent among the earliest New England settlers who feared reprisals for Henry VIII's formation of the Anglican Church in 1534. For nearly a century before the pilgrims arrived in 1620 and for more than a century and a half afterward, their peers in England feared that another switch in the official state religion could lead to civil war, or that foreign enemies in nearby Catholic Ireland, France, and Spain would invade their country.

In any haunted house worthy of the name the normal laws of physics are suspended, hence the fear of being chased by stones (line 8) through the abbey. The speaker would prefer that to encountering oneself in a "lonesome place" (a phrase that may refer to the sometimes deadly mental state of depression; line 12). Described as "ourself" hidden behind ourself, abhorrent aspects of one's own personality have the potential to frighten us more than finding an assassin in our apartment.

The Body (line 17; notice that the psyche has fragmented to the point where the body seems a separate entity) borrows a revolver (an item foreshadowed by the poet's use of "chamber" in the first line and her stress on being "unarmed" in the 11th) and bolts the door (an image suggesting a suicide is about to happen). The speaker may be "overlooking" ("facing;" line 19) a specter superior to those any haunted house could muster. With her usual flair, the poet has imbued the line with a rich alternative meaning; the "superior specter" may be God, Who might be overlooked in the sense of being disregarded. The "More" with which the poem ends may refer to more horrors in the afflicted man's brain, or more reasons why he should not end his life.

"ONE'S-SELF I SING" Walt Whitman (1867)

These eight lines might be taken for Walt Whitman's poetic credo. Note the important distinction that his diction implies between singing of "one's-self" instead of "myself." Instead of dealing exclusively with his own experience and private feelings, he is going to celebrate the individuality of a simple separate person as that entity is found and allowed to flourish in a democracy, and the greatness such beings collectively embody (the "en-masse" of line 2). The verb "singing" implies full-voice; indeed, there are few other poets whose work is developed so boisterously or with such unshakable confidence in their own virility and virtuosity. For example, the voice in the rest of this poem reveals the exuberance of a carnival barker.

In sharp contrast to the Victorian reticence popular among many of his peers, Whitman promises to sing of the entire physiology, which means that he will cover (and uncover) all the functions of the human body from head to toe (line 3). He will study both those facial features that reveal the character of the person and the brain, for only when united into "the Form complete" are they worthy for the Muse (line 4; the implication is that he will not merely deliver surface details, but the entire man). He also promises equal coverage of the female as well as the male, thus introducing the important strains of androgyny and homoeroticism that echo throughout his work.

In promising to sing of "Life immense in passion, pulse, and power," he implies that he will not only cover individual lives of exceptional public interest, but also private lives in which these things are manifest. The line also promises a study of the entire nation, and ultimately of Life itself. All life is terminal, and most human lives are marked at some point by toil and pain. Church (as well as societal) tradition condemns some aspects of human existence and expression, but the speaker promises to remain cheerful (line 7) and nonjudgmental, for even apparent aberrations can result from "freest action form'd under laws divine."

What does the term "Modern Man" (line 8) encompass for Whitman? It includes an almost scientific approach to human biology, including sexuality, and an awareness of his growth potential unfettered by any but divine law. Since innumerable ways of ascertaining divine law have been developed, many of which are mutually exclusive, the definition would have to include a certain awareness of cultural and moral relativism that tends toward an ultimate acceptance of only natural law, especially as it manifests itself in what are called scientific laws. To reach his full potential, such an individual would most likely be the product of a Western-style democracy where freedom of action and expression flourish.

"ON MR. PAINE'S RIGHTS OF MAN" Philip Freneau (1795)

It would be impossible to calculate the extent to which an earlier Thomas Paine pamphlet, *Common Sense,* galvanized opposition to British rule in America. In this poem, Philip Freneau supports Paine's subsequent justification of the French Revolution on the grounds that all monarchies are inherently corrupt. Freneau's calling the rights of man "sacred" (line 1) demonstrates the nearly religious regard he held for democratic ideals. In place of Satan and his devils, he attacks kings as the "source of discord, patrons of all wrong" (line 15). His predictions for the new republic make it seem like heaven, or at least a paradise that will endure to the end of time (line 50).

Whereas kings gain their power from the willingness of the multitude to serve their majesty, Freneau suggests a new perspective from which they can look down on the crown as a childish bauble (line 6). He implies that kings were created to solve social problems, but like quack doctors (line 10), they kill instead of curing. He also repeatedly asserts that a king's subjects are little more than a master's slaves (in lines 4, 8 and 21).

Kings are sequestered and their base desires are privately nurtured until they feed on blood and murder (lines 16–17). They build their thrones on "systems formed by knaves" (line 21) and turn the entire earth into a residence for slaves. He yearns for a time in which all kings will be crushed.

From a historical perspective, he argues that they reversed nature's laws by ranking men with beasts and willing them away (line 29); often men were forced to obey fools or madmen. Kings force men into wars, oppress them, or send them clear to India for plunder "to glad the strumpet, or to glut the king" (lines 31–34).

In the late 18th century, the name "Columbia" (line 35) was used to signify the United States in much the same way that "America" continues to be. American commerce is conducted around the world "through each degree" of latitude and longitude (line 38), and the fact that we lack a king teaches others that they can also do without the inconvenience, for kings subsist by wasteful wars (line 46). This republic will be famed around the world and to the end of time for guarding the rights of man.

"ON OBSERVING A LARGE RED-STREAK APPLE" Philip Freneau (1822) The speaker in this poem addresses an apple that remained on the tree in spite of all the hazards of winter. Instead of celebrating its longevity, he questions why it would choose to linger in this "system of decay" (line 7). Whatever quirk of fancy or fate is responsible, it left the apple hanging there alone. Like some kind of inquisitor, the speaker asks if it were not better to fall and rot or end in a cider mill than to suffer in the storm without a leaf for protection. Its suffering would have been over, and it would not have had the humiliation of such a late fall (line 16). If he hangs on long enough, another generation will call him senile and order him away (line 22).

Eventually the speaker grudgingly comes to admire the apple, likening him to an old hermit who only faces suffering and the humiliation of being "a sad memento of the past" (line 28). He would offer a prayer to fate or nature to return the apple to its blossom state, but he knows the apple must perish.

He decides to start a vigil to last until the apple's parting hour. He will then dig a grave in which the apple will rest until three or four shoots sprout from his core. These offspring will attain red-streak perfection, and represent the old apple's only chance to live again.

One of the points of the poem is that death is an inevitable part of life and should at some point be welcomed and not feared. Because the speaker began a death-watch vigil like those normally reserved for dying family members or close friends, he may be implying that there is probably no more hope for human afterlife than there is for this apple. This would be consistent

with the views expressed by Philip Freneau in an earlier poem, "On the Religion of Nature."

"ON THE BEACH AT NIGHT ALONE" Walt Whitman (1856) After the 17th century, when Galileo Galilei turned his telescope to the stars and Anton von Leeuwenhoek made equally startling discoveries with his microscope, it became apparent to many people that entire physical worlds exist beyond the one dominated by humans. It was comfortable to think that they all are subject to the same immutable laws, and any evidence to the contrary could be attributed to our poor understanding of a particular physical law, whereas the basic general principle still held. Walt Whitman's poem demonstrates that this primitive philosophy (upon which all the modern sciences are based) can suffuse even a simple walk on the beach with another layer of meaning.

Alone with his thoughts, the speaker personifies the sea (called the "old mother" in the second line, since all life on this planet was thought to have begun there) because of her swaying to and fro and her husky voice (rendered audible by the waves breaking on the shore). The stars quickly draw him away from this human perception of nature, however, and into the more abstract realm of philosophy. This transition is regrettably signaled by the execrable phrase "I think a thought" (line 3), but it leads to a consideration of the almost musical (hence the word "clef," a single note in relation to which others may be placed on a score) connections between mass (all the physical substance "of the universes") and time, a half a century before Einstein began developing a formula to scientifically express their relationship. The speaker's emphasis on "the future" represents an interesting conflation of the ancient notion that human destiny can be augured by examining the placement of the stars (astrology) and more modern scientific conceptions of the nature of time.

There is, the speaker asserts, "a vast similitude" interlocking all. He conceives of a unified field theory that encompasses all possible combinations of everything. It would be interesting to see his proof of this theory, but scientific proofs frequently make poor poetry. Instead, we are treated to a list of 10 long lines in which opposites are frequently juxtaposed. Among the most interesting sights on this whirlwind tour of the cosmos are the "ungrown spheres" (line 5), the "souls" (line 8), the "identities" that may exist "on any globe" (line 11) and his three artificial divisions of time (past, present and future). The "vast similitude," he reasserts, has always and will always "compactly" hold and enclose them (line 14).

"ON THE EMIGRATION TO AMERICA AND PEOPLING THE WESTERN COUNTRY" PHILIP FRENEAU (1785)

At the time this poem was written, it would have been difficult for anyone to imagine that within 18 years the Western Country of the title would extend all the way to the Pacific Ocean. The new nation's "western woods and lonely plains" (line 1) began on the eastern slopes of the Alleghenies and extended all the way to the Mississippi River, a territory that already seemed immense compared to the kingdoms of Europe.

PHILIP FRENEAU probably borrowed the name Palemon (line 2) for his representative immigrant because in the knight's tale of the English poet Geoffrey Chaucer's *The Canterbury Tales,* Palamon, a prisoner of war, escapes after years of imprisonment to hide in the countryside until an opportunity presents itself to change his fortune. Thus the name had the advantage of recognizably European literary roots without specific ties to any modern country. It also sets up an implied comparison of the more prevalent political oppression of the Old World with the complete freedom of the American wilderness.

In the first stanza, Freneau predicts American success in agriculture, the arts, and political power. In the second, he contrasts the oppression found in Europe with the "happier soil" where no proud despot enslaves the stranger. In contrast to the richer cultural history on the other side of the Atlantic, Freneau applauds the charming landscapes to be found in the untamed Ohio River valley. Untrammeled nature, he argues, is better (or at least bolder) than art (lines 15–16).

The Eurocentric bias of the poet becomes obvious in the language of the fourth stanza. When Freneau states that the Ohio region was only recently "known," he means known to Europeans, and his statement that

the "unsocial" Indian retreats before the immigrant suggests that their traumatic displacement was really almost a matter of personal choice (lines 20–21). The poet's ignorance of American geography beyond the Mississippi is evident in his assertion that the Native Americans can retreat to "darker forests," although he admits that they may find the new streams to be less pleasing than those of their home (lines 21–24).

Freneau indicates that the Mississippi River flowed through countries (line 26); at the time, the United States held the land east of the river (except for Spanish Florida) and the Spanish owned the rest. The French did not regain possession of the land that became the Louisiana Purchase until 1800. Freneau accurately predicted that the Mississippi River would turn into a commercial highway (line 36) with settlement along its entire length (no longer would the "princely flood" of line 31 advance unnoticed to the ocean).

In the seventh stanza, Freneau argues that the spirit of freedom and other virtues will help prevent war and lead to reasonable laws and public order. In the eighth stanza, he contrasts American freedom with the East, where half the population is physically enslaved and "kings and priests enslave the mind" (line 48).

He looks forward to the time when reason will hold sway over the entire land and African slavery will no longer be an embarrassment (lines 52–54). American genius will engage the world and her deeds will outlive death. Perhaps thinking of Plato's Republic or other utopias, he predicts "happier systems" (line 59) than those of the eastern sages.

"ON THE RELIGION OF NATURE" PHILIP FRENEAU (1815)

This straightforward attack on organized religion argues that nature provides all that man needs to know of goodness. Like the Quakers, who believed an individual's inner light could lead him/her to make moral choices that would enhance that life and the lives of their communities, the speaker in PHILIP FRENEAU's poem argues that nature bestows on every tender mind the power of discerning the correct path to virtue and happiness (lines 9–10). There is nothing mysterious about this process (line 12), and if everyone agreed, there would be no more specious arguments from the Sophists (in the context of this poem, a Sophist argues for the sake of argument and thus distorts the truth. The term originally applied to a fifth-century B.C. Greek philosophy that emphasized logic and rhetoric, but sophistry quickly came to signify a deliberately misleading argument). Adherence to the speaker's natural philosophy would provide nations with the knowledge needed to make heaven on earth.

Unlike the belief in original sin spread by Christianity, the religion of nature does not curse mankind or doom it to perpetual torment (lines 19–20). If they reject it, "Creatress nature" (line 24) does not damn them for atheism but deals with man on a more exalted plain. The speaker looks forward to the day when all can agree to such grand systems. Free from fraud, design, and error, this will lead them to truth and goodness. Persecution will retreat, and "man's religion will be complete" (line 30).

"ON THE UNIVERSALITY AND OTHER ATTRIBUTES OF THE GOD OF NATURE"

PHILIP FRENEAU (1815) The rather conventional theology promoted in this poem comes as something of a surprise given PHILIP FRENEAU's revolutionary thinking in the political sphere. While the leading intellectuals of his age embraced deism (the belief that God was beyond human understanding and took no direct interest in human affairs), the speaker in this poem views God as a benign although impartial ruler (line 10) who continues to provide for his creation.

One of the great services poetry provides is sensitizing the external audience to the intrinsic beauty of the things that surround them. The didactic tone of this poem prevents such a discovery, however; the speaker is more intent on telling the audience about the nature of God than in revealing Him in specific phenomena. Thus, in the opening stanza, the speaker argues that God can be discovered in the more common (or "meaner," line 3) phenomena of earth as well as in the stars. Everything that exists must lean on him (line 6), and He never strayed from His works (line 8). In the third stanza, the speaker celebrates God's wisdom in creating a system of fixed general laws that enable him to rule everything on earth.

The rest of the poem contemplates the nature of God. Unbounded by space or time, He is constant in his being as well as in his purpose. His "unlimited perfectings" (line 17) shine through all His attributes, and He is at the center where all virtues meet (line 20). His power transcends all other power in the universe, so it follows that He is a friend to all intelligence (line 22. The logic here seems to be that a measure of intelligence is the extent to which an individual comprehends the seemingly immutable laws of the physical environment [and the moral universe] and applies them to his advantage. From such an assumption, it should follow that an intellectual pursuit of such knowledge is a way of fathoming God's will).

The speaker's optimism nearly reaches its apex in the penultimate stanza; he asserts that the purpose of God's power is to make all worlds blest (line 24). He tops this in the final stanza, however; not only was everything created in accordance with God's approval, but love was the means by which he brought all things into existence (line 26). God still presides over all He created, and provides for them in life or death (line 28).

"ON VIRTUE"

PHILLIS WHEATLEY (1766) This poem establishes PHILLIS WHEATLEY's claim to the mantle of poet by demonstrating her knowledge of classical (ancient Greek and Roman) literature, a necessary qualification if her work was to be accepted by the intellectual elite of her era. That influence was entirely pagan in its religious orientation, which may explain the absence of Christian references in this poem.

The challenge of this poem is that it deals abstractly with an abstract subject. The speaker begins by acknowledging that she cannot comprehend virtue, a "bright jewel" that it may be beyond human wisdom to understand. Her eloquent but self-deprecating phrasing suggests that the fault is hers alone since "Wisdom is higher than a fool can reach" (line 3). Frustrated in the attempt to use her intelligence to solve the problem, she decides to give up exploring its heights and fathoming the depths of its profundity. Lest she sink into despair, she imagines a personified Virtue that would embrace her soul as it hovers over her head. Eagerly (the "fain" of line 9) would the "heaven born soul" converse with Virtue and (in a reversal or sublimation of earthly desire) "court [Virtue] for her promised bliss" (line 10).

By dedicating her life to Virtue (accepting her as an auspicious queen [line 11] not only promised good fortune, it meant pledging complete trust and devotion in that pre-revolutionary age of absolute monarchs), the speaker gains an angelic guardian (complete with "pinions," or wings) to guide "celestial Chastity" (to keep her thoughts pure. This is not to be confused with earthly chastity, although that would likely follow from the speaker's fervent embrace of virtue as a guiding light).

In the first stanza reason failed, but the second stanza glories in the triumph (a term signifying not just "victory," but also a celebratory parade) of faith. Virtue's sacred retinue includes everything that follows from Chastity (purity) of thought, dressed in divine glory. She asks that Virtue attend her throughout her youthful years and not abandon her to the false joys "of time" (that is "of this world;" line 16) instead of leading her to eternal life and bliss.

She has only approximate definitions of Virtue as "Greatness" or "Goodness" (line 18), but hopes that dedication to Virtue will teach her "a better strain" and "a nobler lay" (better songs in celebration and homage). At present, she can come up with an inspiring image of Virtue enthroned with Cherubs (traditionally depicted as baby angels) "in the realms of day" (basking in eternal glory, but the lines may also convey her gratitude because Virtue keeps her from dwelling on such realms of the night as religious doubt and questioning).

"OSAGE RITUAL" ANONYMOUS (19th century)

If words have magical properties, then the naming of children has great potential importance. For the Osage, a once-flourishing tribe centered in what is now the state of Missouri, this poem suggested that naming a child in honor of a god either directly or in association with some definitive aspect of his/her sphere confers something of that divinity's power on the child.

As the poem begins, the chief messenger from the tribe has returned with the goddess of the Evening Star and has asked her to confer her blessings on the children. Unlike other religions in which it is more common for the gods to provide for (or at least influence) the spirits of the children, at least linguistically, in this poem the Osage ask the gods to provide their flesh.

Like a protective grandmother, the goddess tells the little ones to construct their bodies from her body as a way of confusing those interlopers who might see the path of their life (lines 18–22; the danger in that lies in the opportunity for such outside agents to take steps to disrupt the children's destiny). Just as not even the other gods can prevent the Evening Star from going where she will, so will those who make their bodies from her body be unstoppable. Since she is not the only god, she advises them to heed her words and continue the search (lines 37–38).

"OSCEOLA" WALT WHITMAN (1892)

As WALT WHITMAN's headnote explains, this poem was based on the poet's chance meeting with one of the U.S. Marines who guarded the eponymous Seminole warrior after he had been captured. Evidently recognizing that it was time for him to die, he stood up, put on his war clothes and fixed his waist belt. With the aid of a mirror, he painted half his face and neck, wrists, and backs of his hands vermilion (a bright reddish-orange). Despite being a prisoner, he had access to his scalp knife, which he put in his belt. Again lying down, he rested, sat up, smiled and shook hands with all present, then sank to the floor tightly gripping his tomahawk. After fixing his eye on his wife and children . . . here the poem ends, or nearly so. Whitman evidently wanted to add a line in memory of the chief and his death, but only announced that intention in parentheses.

It is tempting to take this poem as evidence of the vital connections the poet made between his life, his reading (or listening), and his art. As Whitman realized that his own time was nearly at an end, he remembered the anecdote related here as a possible model of an exemplary death with dignity.

OSGOOD, FRANCES SARGENT LOCKE (1811–1850)

Born in Boston into a Massachusetts merchant's family from Hingham on June 18, 1811, Frances Locke began writing early and never stopped until felled by tuberculosis in Hingham, Massachusetts, on May 12, 1850. She married the painter Samuel Osgood in 1835 and traveled to London, where she began publishing her books of poetry: *A Wreath of Wild Flowers from New England* (1838), *Poetry of Flowers* (1841), *Poems* (1846), *The Floral Offering* (1847), and others. She also produced three daughters, the youngest of whom was born just four years before her death.

At one point, her increasing popularity made it seem as though she had a chance to forever enter the pantheon of America's most famous writers. Perhaps because of the scandal arising from her fondness for EDGAR ALLAN POE, or merely because literary fashions can change so capriciously, she has been largely overlooked since her death. By the start of the 21st century, even Hingham, Massachusetts, was not boisterously proud of the writer who should be recognized as their most famous daughter.

Her relative obscurity is unfortunate in that her themes seem surprisingly modern. For example, "The LADY'S MISTAKE" can be viewed as a cautionary tale against marrying for money instead of love, a natural concern in an era when women frequently were denied access to careers outside of the home and were sometimes even denied basic property rights in favor of their husbands. "The INDIAN MAID'S REPLY TO THE MISSIONARY" (1850) reveals a nascent feminism that could recognize and value the self-possessed personhood of a girl with whom the speaker can identify even across the barriers of race and religion.

The connection with Poe was based on mutual admiration of their work and, although they publicly revealed their fondness for each other in their verse and in the New York salons where they frequently met (Poe typically with wife in tow), no evidence exists to suggest that their relationship reached biblical proportions. Their situation has been the subject of several scholarly inquiries including *Plumes in the Dust: The Love Affair of Edgar Allan Poe and Fanny Osgood* and, more soberly, in *Gender and the Poetics of Reception in Poe's Circle*. It even inspired a novel, but there is enough to Osgood's poetry that it should be appreciated without regard for a real or imaginary affair. While few modern readers will be as rapturous over her work as Poe was in the August 1849 issue of *The Southern Literary Messenger,* many will be able to relate to the sensitivity she brings to the timeless issue of gender conflict, her humor, and her passion.

Harvard University's Houghton Library holds the Frances Sargent Locke Osgood Papers, including some of her correspondence and manuscript copies of many poems.

BIBLIOGRAPHY

May, John. *Poe and Fanny: A Novel.* Chapel Hill, N.C.: Algonquin Books of Chapel Hill, 2004.
Richards, Eliza. *Gender and the Poetics of Reception in Poe's Circle.* New York: Cambridge University Press, 2004.
Walsh, John Evangelist. *Plumes in the Dust: The Love Affair of Edgar Allan Poe and Fanny Osgood.* Chicago: Nelson Hall, 1980.

"OUT OF THE CRADLE ENDLESSLY ROCKING" WALT WHITMAN (1859)

The title of this poem (and its first line) is delightfully ambiguous since the adjectival phrase "endlessly rocking" might apply to either the cradle or the person who was in it (or both). The mystery is largely preserved until the 20th line, when the first-person speaker reveals that it is he who has been the recipient of all the aural and visual influences enumerated up to that point. He was shaped by the mockingbird's throat, and his reference to it as "the musical shuttle" may be construed as pejorative except that a shuttle is also part of a loom capable of weaving beautiful fabrics. He comes out of the September midnight (although calling it "ninth-month" [Quaker style, for that sect disliked the pagan gods and Roman emperors honored by such names as January and July] also suggests his birth [mimicking the human gestation period of nine months] as either a person or as an artist). "Midnight" conveys a sense of the mystery surrounding birth and also suggests that his life was dark or uninteresting up to that point (when he discovered his interest in "singing").

He first portrays himself as a vulnerable child who, having left his bed, wandered alone exposed to the elements ("bareheaded" and "barefoot;" line 4). He then became aware of visual beauty, becoming inspired by the "showered halo" (presumably a rainbow or related phenomenon) and "the mystic play of shadows" which intertwine (or "twin," becoming double; his use of "twining" would seem to support either possibility) and twist as though alive. His memories include briars, blackberries (introductions to pain and mixed blessings [since blackberries have thorns as well as fruit]), and the bird that "chanted to me." This is not only an unmixed blessing but the first animate being in his life mentioned in this poem that appears to take an interest in him; he quickly adopts this "sad brother" (line 9) with his fitful rising and falling song. Overhead the yellow half-moon "swollen as if with tears" looked on as the beginning notes of yearning and love in the mist generated a thousand ceaseless responses in his heart. From that moment his countless words were aroused, including "the word stronger and more delicious than any" (a Freudian critic could read the dawn of sexual awareness into this phrase while a biblical scholar might recall the moment at the start of Genesis [1:3] when God said "Let there be light"). As he mentally revisits the scene either his feelings or his words start like a flock of birds ("twittering, rising of overhead passing;" line 16) before everything eludes him. He is a man but, by his tears, again a little boy on the sand, confronting the waves (the endlessly rocking ocean, popularly perceived as the cradle of life, might add another possible point of connection with the title. Whitman provides an answer to the riddle of his mysterious title in the penultimate line of the poem).

The poem is chiefly concerned with the discovery of his identity, and at this point he provides a picture of his fully formed self: a "chanter of pains and joys [and] uniter [more properly "unifier"] of here and hereafter" (line 20). He uses all such hints from his memory but swiftly leaps beyond them as he sings this reminiscence.

Addressing "Paumanok" (Whitman frequently used the Algonquian name for Long Island when imagining those parts of it that were largely unchanged from when the Native Americans lived there; line 23), the speaker recalls a lilac-scented May when he observed two feathered guests from Alabama in the briars. The he-bird was always near at hand as the she-bird incubated their four light-green eggs spotted with brown (although not definitive, their coloration pattern suggests that the eggs may belong to Northern Mockingbirds). As a curious boy he would maintain some distance while "peering, absorbing [and] translating" (line 31).

For the rest of the poem the speaker shares his role with the bird, whose song he translates and presents in italicized font. The bird's first song consists of simple rejoicing that he and his mate are together and that the sun is warm. Days are white and nights black, and they will sing and disregard time and their surroundings as long as they are together.

One day the she-bird disappeared. For the rest of the summer the speaker saw the solitary he-bird and heard it calling to the wind in calmer weather: "I wait and I wait till you blow my mate to me" (line 54).

The speaker heard the lone singer all night long "from the prong of a moss-scalloped stake" nearly amid the slapping waves (an example of the use of concrete sensory details to provide the reader with a vicarious sense of the reality of the place being described). He brought tears to the empathetic speaker, who understood him as a brother. Often he listened in the moonbeams, a barefoot child blending himself with the shadows and surrounded by odd shapes, echoes, and "the white arms out in the breakers" (the top of waves often appear white at night as they reflect the moonlight; line 66).

The bird takes over for 49 lines about love. It admires the way each wave is soothed by the wave behind it, but his love does not soothe him. The moon seems to rise late, lagging because it is heavy with love. The sea pushes onto the land with love. It thinks it sees its love fluttering out among the breakers, a little black thing in the night to which he calls loudly. He shoots his voice over the waves and thinks his love surely must know who he is.

Becoming increasing delusional (and/or desperate), he sees his love in the dark spot of the moon and whichever way he looks on land. He hopes she will rise with the stars. He implores his own throat to sound clear enough to pierce the woods. He will shake out reckless despairing carols (lines 99–104) of lonesome love and death as the moon nears the horizon. He pleads with the moon to sink softly and with the sea to hesitate, because he believes he heard his mate responding to his calls. He must listen, but also must make some noise or she may not come immediately. This strategy is reflected in short lines like "Hither my love" (line 111), which could be uttered quickly so that he could resume listening for her. He worries she may be decoyed away by the wind, the fluttering of the spray, or the shadows of leaves.

As the moon sets, with throbbing heart he realizes his singing all night has been in vain. He remembers his past happy life, songs of joy and the feeling of being in love everywhere he went, but his mate is no more with him.

The human speaks for the rest of the poem. The bird's aria sinks, but the stars, winds, and echoes of its song continue. The "fierce old mother" (the sea; line 133) incessantly moans and rustles on the sands, and the boy is ecstatic as the moon drops. The love long pent up in his heart now at last tumultuously bursts [like water from a broken dam]. His ears and soul swiftly deposit the aria's meaning, and strange tears course down his cheeks (line 139). Bird, boy, and sea form a trio, with the sea answering the questions of the boy's soul by hissing some drowned secret "to the outsetting bard" (as the boy begins his career in poetry; line 143).

"Demon or bird!" the boy's soul exclaimed (in homage to EDGAR ALLAN POE's "The RAVEN." Both poems employ a first-person human translator who interprets a bird's call, and both poems deal with the loss of a mate. Both birds also drop the line "Never more," which comes to haunt the human auditor. Whitman's point may have been that he was inspired by the work of other poets as well as by nature.). He asks if the bird sings to his mate or really to him, for its singing has awakened him to his purpose in life (line 147). A thousand singers and a thousand songs with their thousand warbling echoes have begun within him, never to die.

The speaker thanks the solitary singer for projecting him, and pledges to never more stop perpetuating the bird. The honor of this awakening begins to sound like a curse, for he will never escape the reverberations of these cries of unsatisfied love. He will never again be the peaceful child by the moonlit sea, for the messenger aroused the fire of the unknown want, the "sweet hell" within him (line 156). He begs for the clue to his destiny (just as Poe's speaker had), for if he is to have so much, he would have more. He seeks the final word, superior to all, and wonders if he hears it in the waves. In answer the sea lisped "the low and delicious

word death" (line 168) repeatedly. Hissing melodiously, it edged near as if it bore that private message for him alone, rustling at his feet and "creeping steadily up to my ears and laving me softly all over" (line 172). (This suggests a third source of inspiration for the poet: along with nature and the work of other men, he is prompted by an heightened awareness of the human condition, especially its ultimately insatiable desires and knowledge of death).

He does not forget but fuses the song of his "dusky demon and brother" (line 175) with "the thousand responsive songs at random." The key to them is the word up from the waves, "the word of the sweetest song and all songs." The sea, like some old crone [a disparaging term for an elderly lady] rocking the cradle (a gesture that is generally viewed as nurturing, but may also be viewed here as unsettling), delivered that "strong and delicious word" when it "whispered me" (line 182). (Note that the last phrase is not "to me," but "me." The phrase suggests that the sea may not only have whispered its message to him, but also created him [as a poet, but perhaps also as a fully conscious person, aware of the limitations that death places upon the human experience]. Hence forth, the speaker will become the solitary singer, and his message will not only be of death, but also its inextricably linked partner, "life.")

"OUT OF THE ROLLING OCEAN THE CROWD" WALT WHITMAN (1867) In such poems as WALT WHITMAN's "WHOEVER YOU ARE," one finds a speaker who uses the immense language capacities of the poet for the purposes of seduction. Here, a speaker uses the same power to discourage further contact with a lover, and in the process reveals much about the entire history of the affair.

From the very first line of the poem, the speaker makes his feelings clear by comparing his internal audience not just to a drop in the ocean, but a drop in the "rolling" ocean. The sexually suggestive participle characterizes the former lover as a person on the make, and by reminding him/her of this background, the speaker avoids possible criticism for the dumping by pointing out the original terms under which they met. He softens the blow by noting the gentleness of the lover's approach, and follows this with flattery by repeating the things the lover had said. This shows that the lover may have meant something to him after all, but like testimony in a court of law, it also establishes that the lover initiated the contact (the lover is quoted as saying "I have traveled a long way" to meet you; line 3), that s/he merely asked to look at and touch the speaker as a venerated object ("I could not die till I once looked on you," line 4), and that the lover knew the relationship was probably doomed to fail from the beginning ("I feared I might afterward lose you," line 5).

The lover got what s/he wanted (e.g., they met and looked), but when the speaker states that "we are safe" (line 6), he not only implies that he will keep the affair secret, but also that neither of them (or just him; like royalty, a writer can use the third person plural to establish an impersonal tone) views the relationship as a life-changing event. Then he urges the lover to return in peace to the ocean, or the great pool of unattached lovers, but he softens the blow by repeatedly addressing him/her as "my love" and assuring the lover that he (the speaker) is also part of that ocean. In a sense, this means that they are still connected (line 8).

Next the speaker tries to divert the lover's attention by providing him/her with some perspective: "Behold the great rondure" (the curvature of the world) and its cohesion and perfection (line 9), or with more flattery (the "great rondure" may be a reference to the graceful roundness of a body part). Nevertheless, the speaker argues, the irresistible sea must separate them (note how carefully this defuses the issue of responsibility for the breakup).

The last three lines may extend some obscure hope for reconciliation since an hour "carrying us diverse, yet cannot carry us diverse forever" (line 11). The speaker urges patience on the lover, and requests "a little space" (how utterly modern that phrase is!). Instead of offering a prayer at their parting, the speaker wants the lover to know that he salutes the air, ocean, and land every day at sundown for the dear sake of his love. Although at first the last two lines seem to offer some hope, especially in connection with the traditionally romantic hour of sundown, they include no pledge of commitment or even the vaguest promise of the speaker's taking any action at all to get them together again.

P

"PAIN HAS AN ELEMENT OF BLANK"
EMILY DICKINSON (1951)   Thankfully, most people
are spared the severe chronic pain described here. In
fact, since this pain seems infinite (line 6), it seems
likely that only those condemned to hell suffer such
torment. Only there would the pain so thoroughly
transcend the earthbound frames of reference for time
and so abstractly divorce the sensations from any
notion of causality and from specific parts or regions
of the body. Thus the "Element of Blank" expands to
fill all the afflicted soul's time and consciousness. The
pain is so pervasive that it defines the tortured person's existence; the afflicted has no recollection of its
beginning or of a period of time when it did not exist
(lines 2–3).

The second stanza considers what the Future means
to those who face such an eternity. It contains only
pain, and its infinite nature means that its accessible
past holds only more of the same (lines 6–7). The only
change of which it is cognizant ("enlightened to perceive") is the passage of time, but each new period contains only more pain.

There may be on this earth ailments or injuries so
painful that the torture blocks out any consciousness
of anything but itself, but the poor sufferer would be
in no condition to think of it in such abstract terms as
Dickinson has done in this poem. It is a vision of hell
for which the theatrics of burning brimstone and sadistic devils are not necessary.

"THE PALACE-BURNER" SARAH MORGAN
BRYAN PIATT (1872)   The subtitle of this poem, "A
Picture in a Newspaper," relates to a lurid newspaper
illustration of the execution of a female arsonist/revolu-
tionary as retribution for her role in defending the Paris
Commune of 1871. The chief political issue behind the
civil unrest was the question of self-rule for Paris (at
a time when most French cities directly elected their
officials), but the national government's humiliating
defeat in the Franco-Prussian War, broad economic
disparities, and a rich revolutionary tradition (Paris
figured prominently in the successful French Revolution of 1789 and the less deadly upheavals of 1848)
also mattered. The Communards, as the Parisian rebels
called themselves in 1871, gained control of the city
for more than two months, during which they abol-
ished capital punishment using the guillotine, released
workers' tools from the state-run pawnshops, and proposed broad reforms that they did not have time to
enact. The French national army was eventually able
to retake the city, and the noble dream died as tens of
thousands of the Communards were executed, imprisoned, or exiled.

The speaker in SARAH MORGAN BRYAN PIATT's poem
had been looking at the pictures in old newspapers
with her young son when they came upon the illustration of a bound woman standing before a firing squad.
This sparked the boy's interest, and his mother drew
upon the print surrounding the image for an explana-

tion that he could understand: the condemned woman has been burning palaces (line 1). The son's suggestion that the victim might have wanted to see the pretty sparks (line 2) reveals his empathy for her, a sentiment that his mother begins to share. Forced by her son's interest to find a more likely explanation for the condemned woman's behavior, she tries to keep the experience positive by pointing out her obvious courage. In keeping within the Victorian bounds of feminine modesty, the mother quickly adds that she personally lacks such bravery.

Seeking to divert her son's attention, she explains that the story is two years old and that everything about it (including the woman and her dreams of social justice) is now ashes (line 6) and asks him to find newer pictures. To his remark that he would like to have been a French palace burner, she points out the guns that Christian men then used against "wicked little Communists" like him (lines 11–12; in the 19th century, communism was nearly synonymous with socialism, a theory that collective effort and shared profits would lead to social harmony and a just society).

As if relishing his contrariness, the boy asserts that he would have burned the palace. She attributes this response to jealousy (he would burn it because he could not live in it; line 14) and chastises him for not respecting laws and property. He persists in his fantasy, however, and asks if his mother would also have burned the palace (line 16; in addition to her initial conflict between wanting to share the photographic adventure with her son and wanting to instill proper capitalistic ideals in him, she now has to balance the siren call of maternal loyalty against her bourgeois class interests).

Although she can easily dismiss the boy (line 17), she has much greater difficulty dismissing her thoughts. Her son should know that she is languid and "worldly" (in this context, the meaning is "much given to the pleasures of this life;" line 19). Despite her "dainty" need for "light" (perhaps not just lighthearted acceptance of life, but also mental or spiritual enlightenment and maybe even life itself [in contrast to the revolutionary's death]) and music.

Thinking that her son may have seen something in her soul of which she was unaware, she more actively

considers the sweetness of the revolutionary's role and the dead woman's maternal instincts ("lips to kiss away a baby's cry"), femininity ("hands fit for flowers") and idealism ("eyes for tears and dreams;" lines 23–24). She marvels that her dying face seemed so alive and "unappealing" (resigned to her faith and/or still defiant; line 27) and her despair so beautiful. That she could wear even the execution garments (soon to be her shroud) "with grace" (line 28) hints at divine approval for her martyrdom.

The speaker also admired the "calm charm" (passionate reserves) that a woman like the revolutionary (and, perhaps, like herself) could harbor until in a "frightened hour" (line 30) she would strike with stinging poison like a "fair" ("beautiful" but also "just") snake "with a shadowy power" (in addition to arising from an unexpected "shadowy" place, that force must contain an evil element since it led to arson. On another level, at the same time that reflection about the picture has, to a degree, poisoned the speaker's contentment with her bourgeois values, such thoughts are also somehow inspiring and thus, empowering, for the speaker; line 32).

Although she could not imagine personally burning palaces like "the fierce creature of the Commune" (line 24), so "bright with bitterness" and yet so serene, her exploration of that possibility suggests that she, too, might have such passionate reserves.

"PASSAGE TO INDIA" WALT WHITMAN (1871)

WALT WHITMAN's poetry generally celebrates the great achievements of his own time and country, but here he ventures across the Atlantic, through the Suez Canal, and all the way to India, which he views as a cradle of Old World mysticism and civilization's past.

In the first division, he contrasts the miracle of modern engineering (that has only just begun to realize the advantages of steel and concrete construction, a revolution in building materials that led to the creation of "strong light works" [line 3], including massive bridges extending over formerly impossible lengths. Construction on the Brooklyn Bridge was begun in January 1870, for example, and 13 years later it set a record as the world's longest suspension bridge). The speaker finds such modern wonders superior to the "antique ponderous" Seven Wonders of the Ancient World (line 14; these were the Colossus of Rhodes, Great Pyramid of Giza, Hanging Gardens of Babylon, Lighthouse of Alexandria, Mausoleum of Maussollos, Statue of Zeus at Olympia and Temple of Artemis at Ephesus). Other modern wonders include the Suez Canal, opened in 1869 to enable ships to go directly from the Mediterranean Sea to the Indian Ocean without sailing around Africa. The Transcontinental Railroad (completed in the same year) connected America's East Coast with California, and the Transatlantic Cable stretched "elegant gentle [telegraph] wires" (line 7) across the Atlantic Ocean (temporarily in 1858 and permanently in 1866).

Yet the soul cries for the Past, the "dark unfathomed retrospect" of the dead and their ghosts ("the sleepers and the shadows" of line 11). The speaker views the present as an outgrowth of the past, which propelled the present on its course like a projectile (lines 14–15; he probably has a shell fired from one of the rifled artillery pieces of the Civil War era in mind).

In the second section, he exhorts his soul to go to India to clarify Asiatic myths and primitive fables (perhaps because the proud truths of modern science [lines 19–20] alone cannot explain the entire human experience). Asia's and Africa's fables are "far-darting beams of the spirit," containing dreams of "deep diving bibles" (lines 21–23) set in a landscape with temples fairer than morning-sun-drenched lilies and pinnacled red towers burnished with gold (lines 24–25).

It seems God's purpose to have humans span and connect the earth, for races to intermarry, and lands to be welded together (line 35). He sings of a new worship of the explorers, engineers, and workers who labor in God's name and for the sake of the Soul.

The third section returns to the marvels of 19th-century engineering, beginning with the Suez Canal (constructed by the French from 1859 to 1869; the French empress Eugenie [line 44] represented the French court at the opening ceremonies). Perhaps aided by contemporary daguerreotypes or albumen prints (early photographic representations) of the canal, the speaker imaginatively views the strange landscape of sky, sand, picturesque groups, and gigantic dredging machines (lines 45–47) from the deck of a steamship.

Similarly, he sees the Pacific railroad passing along the Platte (a river crossing the state of Nebraska from west to east) and hears its shrill whistle (line 51). It passes the "grandest scenery in the world" (line 52) including the Laramie (Wyoming) plains and their flora, the Wind River (of Wyoming) and the Wasatch Mountains (Utah), Monument Mountain, Eagle's Nest, Promontory (Summit, Utah, where the Union Pacific met the Central Pacific to complete the transcontinental railroad on May 10, 1869), the Nevada mountain range, Elk Mountain, the Humboldt range and Lake Tahoe. Thus the American section of the world has been bridged by rail; eastern and western seas have been connected, and a western road links Europe and Asia.

The dream (of a western route from Europe to Asia) of Christopher Columbus (hailed as "the Genoese" in line 65 because of his birth in Genoa, Italy) is thus fulfilled centuries after his burial.

The fourth part pays homage to the brave sailors whose voyages and expeditions led to the discovery of America and the sea route around Africa that connected Europe with India. Vasco da Gama pioneered the latter (from 1497 to 1499; line 76). Such work fulfilled "man's long probation" (line 79) by accomplishing the "rondure" (graceful circling; line 80) of the world (before his death on the voyage [1519–22], the Spaniard Ferdinand Magellan commanded the first circumnavigation of the earth).

In the fifth division Whitman celebrates the earth as the "vast Rondure" (line 81), using the 19th-century indescribability trope (it is "unspeakable" line 4) to forestall the disappointment readers might experience because of their unavoidable familiarity with the topic. He finds some "inscrutable purpose, some hidden prophetic intention" (line 86) as he begins to span the whole earth with his thought.

The speaker places Adam and Eve in the gardens of Asia, from which "feverish, with never-happy hearts" their descendents incessantly ask why the soul is unsatisfied and where mocking life is taking them (lines 91–92). Numerous questions arise about the human condition, with its "separate nature" (line 96), including the need for a religious or philosophical justification of its existence and its links with the impassive earth that the speaker reduces to "the place of graves" (line 98). S/he assures the soul that the "first intent" remains, and perhaps even now the time has arrived for it to be carried out (lines 99–100).

After the adventurers, scientists, and inventors have done their work, the "poet worthy [of] that name" will come, "the true son of God" (line 105). Then all questions will be answered, all hearts soothed, and the whole earth will be justified. The sun of God will pass all straits and conquer the mountains, finally fusing Nature and Man (lines 114–115).

In part six the speaker sings of the "year of the purpose accomplished" (line 117), when continents marry, as do oceans and climates. The phenomenon will be worldwide, dwarfing the wedding of the Adriatic Sea and the doge of Venice (from the eighth to the 18th centuries, a doge [pronounced "doj"] was the chief executive elected by the Venetian aristocracy. One of his traditional duties was the annual tossing of a ring into the water to symbolize the city-state's marriage with the sea; line 119).

The passage to India would be cooled by air from the far Caucasus Mountains (the geographic feature separating Europe from Asia). It passes the Euphrates River valley (in modern Iraq, where a Sumerian civilization flourished 4,000 years before the birth of Christ). The singer continues to bring forth the past as he travels eastward, eventually beholding the Indus and Ganges (rivers in modern India and their affluents [the rivers which flow into them]), the most populous and wealthiest lands on earth (lines 127–129). He recalls that Alexander the Great's sudden death halted his march to conquer the world between China, the Arabian Peninsula, and Persia (modern Iran occupies only a portion of the former Persian Empire) in 323 B.C. Here he met the teachings of the ancient occult Brahma (of the Hindu religion) and the more recent Buddhist religion (line 135). He lists the conquerors Tamerlane (14th-century fighter who, from his capital of Samarkand in modern Uzbekistan, conquered from India to Russia and from Turkey to Central Asia) and Aurungzebe (Aurangzeb, or Alamgir I, 17th-century ruler of a Mogul empire covering most of modern India, Pakistan, and Bangladesh; line 137), and famous travelers (Marco Polo, whose 13th-century travel to

China and service in the court of Kublai Khan opened up the overland trade route from Europe, and Batouta the Moor [Ibn Batuta, the Moroccan whose 14th-century travels extended from Spain to China, modern Russia, and Mali]), all of whom helped consolidate knowledge of the earth's more distant lands.

In 1492 something in humanity swelled "like the sap of the earth in spring" (lines 145–146). The speaker encounters the sad "shade" (or ghost) of Christopher Columbus, a gigantic visionary who saw a golden world that he colored with gorgeous hues (line 151). Like the chief actor (probably dubbed the "historion," a Latin term for *actor,* as a pun on *historian,* although in the context of this poem, the term implies a history-making figure), Columbus, the "type" (or representative model perfectly embodying certain attributes) of courage, action, and faith, sailed from Palos (in Spain) to fame but subsequent misfortune, brief imprisonment, and (relative) poverty (since he did not receive everything that he had been promised for his discoveries). The speaker notes that the fame attendant upon the efforts of heroes can be deferred for centuries, but when it suits God, it will sprout, bloom, and fill the earth with beauty.

Part seven serves as a transitional passage celebrating the return to primal thought (line 165), the "young maturity" (an oxymoron perhaps chosen to reflect the yin/yang union of opposites that is often a component of eastern religions) that produced "realms of budding bibles" (the start of the world's great faiths). The speaker's mental circumnavigation of the world has returned him to "reason's early paradise" (line 172), a time of wisdom's birth, innocent intuitions, and "fair" (beautiful) creation.

Inspired, in the eighth division the speaker fearlessly sails for unknown shores on "waves of ecstasy" (line 178). He undertakes the task with a laugh and a kiss, letting others "weep for sin, remorse, humiliation" (a dig at conventional Christianity's emphasis on sin and redemption; line 183). His soul and he believe in God more than any priest (line 185), but dare not dally with His mystery.

His soul and he please each other. They enjoy silent thoughts together that "lave him all over" (line 191). With nearly masturbatory imagery, he describes how his moral, spiritual fountain does not wait in the reservoir for "the perfect comrade" (line 200), but launches "superior universes" out of himself. Although he "shrivels" (a verb begging a Freudian or physiological interpretation; line 206) at the thought of God, Nature, Time, Space, and Death, his soul can deal with these immensities. The love he shares with his soul is greater than the sun or stars, but he is cheerfully willing "to give up all" and suffer for others' sake (lines 212–218). He anticipates a time when, with everything attained, the Elder Brother will be filled with complete friendship and love, and the Younger will melt "in fondness in his arms" (line 223).

The last section encourages a flight into the future, to more than India and to deeper waters (to "sound" is to determine the depth of the water over which one sails; line 228) than "the Sanscrit and the Vedas" (Sanskrit is the ancient language of the Hindus in which the Vedas, sacred religious texts, were written; line 228). He will attempt the fierce enigmas and strangling problems despite the "wrecks of skeletons" (the phrase recalls the timbers sticking out of derelict wooden ships like ribs as well as indirectly referencing the human costs; line 232) that failed in the attempt. He will seek the secret of the earth, the sky, and all the natural phenomena between them, then the sun, moon and stars (Sirius is the brightest star in the sky after the sun; line 240).

The blood burns in his veins. He will raise anchor, cut the hawsers (the ropes securing a vessel to shore), and sail to spiritual awareness, having tired of groveling, eating, and drinking like a mere brute. He is through with being darkened and dazed by books. He urges his soul to sail for deep, undiscovered waters only, risking everything but safe in the conviction that all seas belong to God.

"PERCEPTION OF AN OBJECT COSTS"

EMILY DICKINSON (published 1951) Although this is one of EMILY DICKINSON's more abstract poems, the sense of the first two lines could be expressed as: one never knows the value of something (one is basically unaware of that thing) until one contemplates losing it. The rest of the first stanza implies that until that happens, one takes things for granted.

Because the first stanza asserts that value is only added through perception, it follows that there is no absolute value for any object. This leads the speaker to a philosophical leap: there can be no "Object Absolute" (line 5). Like the physicist or philosopher who claims that there is no sound unless it is perceived (because the very definition of the word *sound* includes the requirement that it must be heard; thus sound occurs only when an external stimulus is perceived by the ear), this poem argues that things have no existence until they are perceived, and at that point their desirability is determined ("Perception sets it fair" [line 6] means that recognition of an object makes it desirable). Like spoiled infants, at that point humans tend to quarrel with God ("a Perfectness," line 7) for placing the newly desired object, rendered valuable by its sudden absence, so far from them. The poem criticizes the very human tendency to prefer instant gratification and to criticize God because this world is not set up to cater to one's whims.

"THE PHILOSOPHY OF COMPOSITION"

EDGAR ALLAN POE (1846) Modern critics tend to scoff at the composition process that EDGAR ALLAN POE claims to have used for his most famous poem because it seems too self-serving and mechanical, but at least some of their objections can be answered by the fact that Poe was a major contributor in three major genres: poetry, short stories, and essays. In this essay, some of his language and the principles he advocates blend the boundaries between these usually separate disciplines, but we owe it to the author as an effective creative artist to try to get as much from this effort as we possibly can.

The essay begins by establishing the author's authority; he is so well regarded in literary circles that no less a personage than Charles Dickens, the famous British novelist, would consult with him on matters of literary technique. Notice how carefully Poe has phrased his first sentence to maximize the impression that the two of them were intimate friends: the correspondence consists of "a note now lying before me" (page 1431) as opposed to a far more formal note appearing in a book or article. He then moves on to the extraordinary promise of revealing the precise procedure he used in developing "The RAVEN."

He begins by arguing that the denouement of a story must be developed first if the plot is to consist of a chain of logical events inevitably leading directly to the one that follows (this is "causation"). He then introduces two key concepts, tone and intention, upon which he will elaborate later in the essay, but considerations of "plot" are highly unusual starting points for discussing a poem. This suggests that he originally intended "The Raven" to be a narrative poem, a format for which description, dialogue and (for most early 19th-century American writers) authorial comment were as essential as the facts and actions of the plot. Poe argues that stories are often based on historical or topical events, or a thesis that one may extrapolate from them (1432).

Poe begins, however, with considerations of "effect," which probably explains why "The Raven" strikes most readers as a lyrical instead of narrative poem. Even though his expressed aim is to clarify the composition process, he tries to access "the heart, the intellect or . . . the soul" to come up with a novel (like any other serious artist, Poe places great emphasis on originality) and vivid effect (1432). This process retains much of its mystery despite Poe's evident goodwill; his description includes the mildly schizophrenic act of talking to himself, or to the three components of the self he enumerates, in expectation of a credible answer. He takes pains to differentiate this state of mind at the very beginning of the process from the "fine frenzy" or "ecstatic intuition" in which most poets claim to do all the work on a poem. He implicitly dismisses their obfuscations as mere showmanship and stagecraft, equating them with "the tackle for scene-shifting," trap doors, and other props employed by early Victorian theaters (1432). He argues that his poem was produced with the precision of a mathematical problem with an unlimited audience in mind. It not only had to suit both the popular and the critical taste (1433), but also had to be universally appreciable (1434).

Poe's emphasis on arousing a specific response in a reader comes close to anticipating some of the insights of the reader-response criticism of the late 20th century. The short story has frequently been defined as a narrative piece of fiction short enough to be read at one setting, and Poe apparently draws on this definition when he argues that a poem must be read in a similar length of time if it is to continuously excite the reader and elevate the soul. Like a visual artist intent on placing nothing on his canvas that distracts from a painting's meaning, Poe advocates "unity of impression" and "unity of effect" as conscious goals for poetry (1433).

Perhaps through trial and error (since he provides no other explanation), Poe deduced that his target audience could stand the exhilaration of about one hundred lines of continuous poetical excitement (1834). It took all the skill of a master craftsman to extend this effect for all 108 lines of "The Raven."

Although he consulted his intellect (with truth as its highest object) and heart (with passion as its highest expression) when he searched for a starting point, Poe considers beauty "the sole legitimate province of the poem" because in its contemplation lies "the most intense, the most elevating, and the most pure" pleasure for the soul (1434). This led him to the illogical conclusion that sadness, especially melancholy, furnishes the most legitimate poetical tone.

With a firm grasp of his intended effect in mind, he decided that a monotone embodied within a refrain would provide pleasure because of its repetition. Although the key word of his refrain would remain unvaried, for novelty of effect he decided to place it in a different context in each stanza so that its meaning would constantly but subtly evolve. Since the letter "o" seems the most sonorous (or resonant), especially when teamed with the consonant "r," he had only to find a suitable word to embody that sound. "Nevermore" was the very first word he found that suited his criteria (1435). Only an idiot, a jester, or a talking bird would repeat the same word without trying the patience of the audience, and he chose a raven over a parrot because it was more suited to a melancholic tone. It may seem odd that thoughts of melancholy would lead him to consider the sounds of two letters and a raven before he considered death, but he got there eventually. Remembering beauty as an important goal led him to consider the death of a beautiful woman to be "the most poetical topic in the world" (1436), and for dramatic effect, he chose her bereaved lover as his point-of-view character.

Great short story writers often begin with two imaginary but unique characters (for example, distraught lover and raven) whom they place in a setting from which they cannot escape and listen as they interact within this "close circumscription of space" (1438). Although the unfortunate lover is racked with grief, one of Poe's psychological insights is that deep emotion, even melancholy, contains a modicum of pleasure. Thus his lover will delight in a self-torture leading to "a phrenzied pleasure" (1436; the modern spelling is *frenzied*) in phrasing a succession of questions to which the stock reply will prove increasingly painful. He then found the most painful question and built the last stanza around it, purposely crippling any of the stanzas that were to precede it if they rivaled its rhythmical excellence so as not to interfere with its "climacteric effect" (1437).

There was nothing original in his use of trochaic feet (a two-syllable unit in which the first syllable is usually accented and the second is not) except in his placing them in lines alternating octameter acatelectic (eight of his trochaic feet) and heptameter catalectic (seven and a half of the same feet) meters, followed by a fifth and concluding line of tetrameter catalectic (three and a half feet) (1437–8). Modern poets often seek to blend form and function to convey their meaning, and for them it would have been more enlightening if Poe had talked about the aesthetic values of these choices apart from the novelty of their combination.

The rest of his advice is very valuable; he encourages writers to prolong the suspense and draws attention to the various contrasts he developed, including the poem's movement from the fantastic and ludicrous description of the bird's arrival to the "profound seriousness" of its denouement (1439). He hopes that the reader will so closely identify with the lover as to vicariously experience the same combination of pleasure and pain. He is confident of producing this effect because the "human thirst for self-torture" (1440) is universal.

In contrast with the metaphorical poets, he was careful to realistically present all the elements until the two concluding stanzas of the poem, for he did not want the reader to consider the raven a mere emblem or symbol. By dropping in a metaphorical expression at the end he hoped the reader would begin seeking a moral to the poem, thus providing some of the complexity and suggestiveness that appeals to the artistic eye.

BIBLIOGRAPHY

Baym, Nina, et al. *The Norton Anthology of American Literature,* 2nd ed. Vol. 1. New York: W. W. Norton, 1979. All page numbers in this essay refer to this volume.

PIATT, SARAH MORGAN BRYAN (1836–1919)

Born into a slaveholding family near Lexington, Kentucky, on August 11, 1836, Sarah Bryan lost her mother at the age of eight. After living with several different relatives throughout her childhood, she completed her education at the Henry (as in Henry County) Female College in New Castle, Kentucky. She began publishing poetry in local newspapers, including the *Louisville Courier,* and quickly gained regional and even national notice. In 1861 she married John James Piatt, a fellow poet employed in positions of increasing responsibility with the federal government, when he was not working as a journalist. He began his public service as a low-level government clerk and later served as a librarian for the U.S. House of Representatives. After his appointment as a U.S. consul in Ireland (1882–93), Sarah produced *A Voyage to the Fortunate Isles.* Together they had seven children, of which four survived infancy. Their principal residence was in North Bend, Ohio, until his death in 1917. Sarah Piatt died in Caldwell, New Jersey, on December 22, 1919.

Of the four Sarah Piatt poems discussed in this book, the beginning of "HIS MOTHER'S WAY" comes closest to evoking the unchecked sentimentality that was popular in Victorian America. Fortunately it goes on to reveal how deeply the poet felt about the schisms separating men and women as well as rich and poor. "The PALACE-BURNER" begins with a similar situation: A son's observations about his mother cause the speaker to contemplate gender differences and ultimately to question her genteel role. "WE TWO" examines the speaker's painful relationship with God, a tortured compliance with His will that ultimately leads to reconciliation entirely on His terms. The poet's humor is most evident in "The WITCH IN THE GLASS," which revolves around a mother's teasing her daughter about her beauty and playfully exciting her curiosity.

Although the poet's work has recently enjoyed a popular revival, none of her former residences have achieved museum status. Her letters have also been widely scattered.

BIBLIOGRAPHY

Bennett, Paula Bernat. *Poets in the Public Sphere: The Emancipatory Project of American Women's Poetry, 1800–1900.* Princeton, N.J.: Princeton University Press, 2003.

Michaels, Larry. *That New World: The Selected Poems of Sarah Piatt 1861–1911.* West Liberty, Ohio: Mac-A-Cheek Foundation for the Humanities; Toledo, Ohio: Bihl House Publishing, 1999.

Piatt, Sarah Morgan Bryan. *Palace Burner: The Selected Poetry of Sarah Piatt.* Edited by Paula Bernat Bennett. Urbana: University of Illinois Press, 2001.

POE, EDGAR ALLAN (1809–1849)

Born on January 19, 1809, in Boston to an actress who was soon abandoned by her actor husband and died of tuberculosis (in Richmond, Virginia) before the poet's third birthday, Poe struggled throughout his adult life against poverty and alcoholism. The majority of his childhood was spent in the affluent family of a generally prosperous Richmond tobacco merchant, who took the young lad with them to England for five years of business for his guardian and excellent schooling at Stoke Newington for the lad. His education continued in two of Richmond's better private schools and, for a single year, at the University of Virginia (Charlottesville). He had been a precocious poet, thriving on his early exposure to French and Latin literature, and an even more promising scholar, winning the highest honors in ancient and modern languages at the university (Meyers 23). He was far less adept at gambling, however, a misfortune since there is some truth to his claim that his foster father sent him off to college with only half the money he needed; he may have engaged in that vice in a misguided attempt to meet his expenses. He quickly accumulated a large debt that John Allan, who pulled him from the university, refused to pay. In a theatrical gesture worthy of his natural parents, he joined the army as a private. In less than two years, he became a sergeant major (the highest enlisted rank possible in his day) and was admitted to West Point on the recommendation of his officers. He lasted into the second year, when having convinced himself that he lacked the funding necessary for advancement in the military, he purposely washed out. By the age of 22, he had managed to publish three books of poetry: *Tamberlane and Other Poems* (1827), *Al Aaraaf, Tamberlane and Minor Poems* (1829) and *Poems* (1831). Had he been born a decade later, a growing number of American magazines would have had the circulation numbers and financial backing to offer a sustainable income to such an obvious talent if their editors could have recognized it amid the popular clamor for a sentimentalized domestic poetry. In 1831, however, it may have seemed evident to Poe that poetry did not pay. For two years he labored in obscurity, until a story, "MS. [manuscript] Found in a Bottle" won a $50 prize in a Baltimore *Saturday Visitor* contest. This windfall helped turn him towards editing magazines as a potentially lucrative profession and encouraged him to continue producing the short stories that first brought him the notoriety and lasting reputation he craved. His poetry seems to have dropped in importance behind the editing, critical reviewing, and fiction writing that could bring in more money, but his most famous poem was still more than a decade in the future.

One of the *Sunday Visitor* contest judges recommended him to the owner of Richmond's *Southern Literary Messenger.* Hired as a low-level assistant in 1835, within six months Poe was performing many editorial functions. The job afforded the family-starved Poe an opportunity to maintain close relations with his young cousin Virginia and her mother (his natural father's sister), and the next year he married the 13-year-old girl with (perhaps) the understanding that he would provide her with an education and protection until she reached the more mature age of 16, an age at which many girls married at that time. Although their circumstances were often precarious because of their limited finances, the love that circulated in that tight domestic circle is evident in "TO MY MOTHER," a title the poet bestowed on Virginia's mother as emblematic of his devotion after the death of his wife.

Alcohol led to Poe's undoing at the *Messenger.* He moved to Philadelphia in 1837, where he eventually edited *Burton's Gentleman's Magazine* and *Graham's Magazine* for a year each. As an editor he showed signs of genius, and a journal's circulation tended to multiply with him at (or near) the helm. Perhaps his relationships with the owners too painfully reminded Poe of his childhood dependency on his emotionally distant foster father—the critical issue of finances lay at the center of each conflict—and he eventually left each post without having had the foresight to first line up another one, thus replicating the boom-and-bust cycle that continually plagued him. His success tended to enrich the publishers but not Poe, a discrepancy that gave him the idea of publishing his own journal. He spent several years trying to make this happen.

At the same time that he was breaking new ground in detective and horror fiction and battling his young wife's ill health (she died of tuberculosis in 1847), he published *The Raven and Other Poems* (1845). The title poem, a serious reworking of a similar poem by a contemporary, Thomas Holley Chivers (Wilson 498), brought him considerably more fame than any other work, and for a time his dramatic readings of the poem were a drawing room sensation. His ambitious ownership of the underfunded and short-lived *Broadway Journal* kept him in poverty, however. His use of alcohol predictably increased as a consequence, but after a couple of years he sobered and seemed on the verge of another comeback. Unfortunately, he died during a brief stopover in Baltimore on October 7, 1849, after five days (probably) lost to yet another drinking binge left him vulnerable to hypothermia, pneumonia, and other ailments. In a twist as macabre as anything he ever wrote, his death has been attributed to everything from rabies to tuberculosis.

"The RAVEN" remains Poe's most popular poem and the subject of his essay on its creation, "The PHILOSOPHY OF COMPOSITION." "ANNABEL LEE" conveys the sense of personal loss that pervades much of Poe's writing, and "The CITY IN THE SEA" should interest fans of lost civilizations and science fiction. Fans of his macabre short stories would enjoy his poems presenting subjective, often supernatural dreamscapes (in the idyllic "TO ONE IN PARADISE" as well as in the nightmarish "DREAM-LAND" and "The VALLEY OF UNREST") or his explorations of aberrant psychology (such as inform "ALONE" and "The SLEEPER"). "A DREAM WITHIN A DREAM" examines the fate of the Byronic hero or artist doomed to isolation because his intellectual superiority prevents true intimacy with those around him, while "EL DORADO" links a romantic quest with the pilgrim spirit, a connection implying that American materialism had its deepest roots in its earliest New England theology.

In "FAIRYLAND," Poe criticizes one of his most important precursors (Thomas Moore) for the latter's sentimentalized view of nature, although "The LAKE" represents his true homage to that poet. Much later, in "ROMANCE," he rejected as too easy the rhymes of romantic poetry that first prompted him to write, and in "SONNET—TO SCIENCE," he criticizes the aesthetic principles that burdened much of his poetry with mythological references instead of encouraging him to draw more directly on nature. "TO HELEN," an early poem, celebrates the ability of a beautiful woman to inspire greatness in an observer, while "ISRAFEL" celebrates the power of music to elevate the spirit.

Because of the mystery surrounding Poe's final days, Baltimore has the greatest claim on the poet's memory in the public imagination. The Baltimore Poe House and Museum preserves the former home rented by his aunt and inhabited by Poe for approximately two years ending in August of 1835, and the city's professional football team has been named the Ravens in honor of his most famous poem. The house in Philadelphia that Poe rented from 1843 to 1844 is also a museum, as is the Edgar Allan Poe Cottage in the Bronx, his rented home from 1846 to his death in 1849.

Perhaps Richmond should be viewed as the city with the best Poe connection, however. His mother is buried there, and he lived with his foster parents in Richmond. His work as an editor on the *Southern Literary Messenger* brought him back to the city, and he was married in Richmond. The Poe Museum in Richmond, Virginia, preserves many of his manuscripts, letters, and memorabilia.

Poe's memory is also kept alive by the Edgar Allan Poe Society of Baltimore, which hosts an annual public lecture on his work, and by the Poe Studies Association, which publishes *The Edgar Allan Poe Review*. The University of Virginia, The Free Library of Philadelphia, Indiana University, the Bronx County Research Library and Brown University hold important Poe archives.

BIBLIOGRAPHY

Hutchisson, James M. *Poe*. Jackson: University Press of Mississippi, 2005.

Kennedy, J. Gerald. *A Historical Guide to Edgar Allan Poe*. New York: Oxford University Press, 2001.

Meyers, Jeffrey. *Edgar Allan Poe: His Life and Legacy*. New York: Charles Scribner's Sons, 1992.

Poe, Edgar Allan. *The Letters of Edgar Allan Poe*. 2 vols. New York: Gordian Press, 1966.

———. *The Collected Works of Edgar Allan Poe*. Vol. 1, *Poems*. Edited by Thomas Ollive Mabbott et al. Cambridge, Mass.: Harvard University Press, 1969.

Wilson, Edmund. *Patriotic Gore: Studies in the Literature of the American Civil War*. London: The Hogarth Press, 1987.

"THE POET" WILLIAM CULLEN BRYANT (1864)

Few people have provided those who would follow in their footsteps better advice than WILLIAM CULLEN BRYANT does here. In the first stanza he identifies his ideal audience as not just those who wish to be known as poets, but those with a passion for words capable of creating universally recognized living thoughts. His exquisite definition of poetry is as useful as it is beautiful: thoughts clothed in words of flame. The first thing a poet who aspires to such heights must do is recognize the hard work that goes into immortal verse; such success is not to be won by a dilettante's ballad leisurely framed on a single summer day.

The second stanza begins with seemingly contradictory advice. The verb "wreak" suggests physical vengeance that is usually directed against an offending person. Bryant instructs you to gather all your powers for this effort, but then he directs the application of these terrible forces to your verse, the creation of which he then compares with weaving. He is not mixing metaphors here; he is describing successive stages of the creative process, as he will explain later in the poem.

Unlike the drowsy summer afternoon that a less serious person might wile away by playing at verse, Bryant recommends writing during the lonely hours of silent morning or evening. "Wakeful," the qualifying adjective attached to the latter time in line 9, implies that the poet should work after others have gone to bed. This prospect of the long hours and the fairly complete solitude required for poetry should dissuade aspirants who are afraid to work.

Throughout the poem, Bryant alternates between hot and cold images and diction. Having chilled his audience with a suggestion of how hard the work is, he warms them with the intense physicality of the blood's tingling in the veins, then as deftly shifts between inward and outward states of being. The setting forth of burning words into fluent strains (line 11) suggests a pouring of molten steel into a desired form, a powerful yet familiar image for the increasingly heavily industrialized nation.

The third stanza cautions against passionless efforts. If the goal is to create such strong emotional reactions in a reader that they result in physical sensations, the poet is advised to write with some heat. Mere perfection in a form will not have the desired effect. In the next stanza, he advocates rapid writing unfiltered by any thought of its eventual form so that one's words are directly connected with the passionate thrill of real emotion.

Having by now generated some text, the next step for the poet is to examine it coldly to determine where its meter is broken or its expression is inelegant. To preserve a poem's emotion, however, poets should not attempt to fix these errors without again firing up their passion to the same temperature with which the original emotions were experienced.

The sixth stanza cautions against completely unbridled or inappropriate passion, however, for like a gust of wind that can set the streets to howling but soon dies away (lines 33–34), it will not touch the deepest feelings in either writer or reader. Rather, the poet is to internalize the beauty and write from the love, wonder, and delight of the natural phenomena to which the poem is a response.

The eighth stanza encourages poets to make themselves part of the great tumult (line 45). If they want to write of battles or shipwrecks (common subjects for ballads, or "lays" in Bryant's time), they should place themselves in the thickest fighting or feel the shrouds or stays in their hands and the terror in their hearts. Bryant may seem purposely vague as to whether he means for the nascent poets to actually place themselves in harm's way, but the general tenor of the poem would have them imaginatively embrace such experience in the act of writing whether or not they had personally participated in such scenes.

If the lay succeeds, it might by accident ("haply") endure, prompting later readers to wonder about that mystery (or "witchery") by which merely reading the words can so sway a reader's emotions. Note that the desired effect is always dependent upon "the willing mind" of the reader (line 54).

"THE POET" RALPH WALDO EMERSON (1844)

Throughout his widely influential literary life, RALPH WALDO EMERSON continually lobbied for American self-reliance in a variety of venues. Here he calls for a new approach that would free poetry from the more restrictive aspects of the European tradition. For this to happen, a new generation of poets would have to emerge and the attitudes of the reading public who constitute their audience would have to change. In this essay Emerson sought to accelerate that process by undermining the prestige of the established cultural elite who represented the most conservative resistance to the new aesthetic.

Emerson begins with an ad hominem attack on the personalities of the most popular critics, instead of their ideas: They are "selfish and sensuous" despite their appreciation of beauty within their selected disciplines. Although they are knowledgeable about the technical aspects of their specialties, they tend to divorce art from living. The true poet is superior to these critics because he not only immerses himself in life but he also sensitizes the reader to the spiritual nature of his existence. Poets are complete men because they not only experience nature more deeply than other men but they are also able to express it in such a way that others can learn from them. They feel the complete spectrum of experience and can impart their sensations to others.

Emerson promises to examine both the methods of the true poet as the "man of beauty" and the state of the art in 1844, but first he indulges in a bit of philosophizing that has not worn well over the decades. He postulates that most belief systems are based on a trilogy of love for truth, goodness, and beauty, and in his system these have the most influence on the

Knower, the Doer, and the Sayer, respectively. Because the poet (the "Sayer") draws on the primal energy of the universe, he is as powerful as the man of action (the "Doer"), although Emerson proceeds to diminish the stature of the poet to that of an amanuensis (a transcriber who merely writes down what is being said) for Beauty, "the creator of the universe."

Returning to practical criticism, Emerson argues that the true poet (as opposed to a craftsman skilled in such things as rhyme and meter) announces new things. For Emerson, it is not meter but "meter-making argument" that makes a poem. Those poets capable of creating the songs of nations are not mere lyricists but passionate conveyors of a meter-making argument.

Emerson once marveled when a young poet announced that everything had changed. He argues that while many poems can carry a reader aloft, only a true poem can reveal something new, or a new aspect of the Beauty that is the essence of everything. Emerson is most interested in using poetry as a tool to uncover philosophical insights because he feels that art has the opportunity to come closer to universal truths than the natural sciences. He considers these to be more superficial because they are rooted in the senses.

Emerson is more interested in metaphysics than physics and observes that the poet's symbols and emblems can be as moving as patriotic symbols, although they are more universal. Since any fact of nature carries the whole sense of nature, Emerson argues that no word or image can be offensive when a poet uses it symbolically. This suggests that a true poem cannot be pornographic (note just how far Emerson is willing to travel beyond the conservative aesthetics of the conventional critics), and that any object in a factory town (a locale with which New Englanders were becoming increasingly familiar) can be as worthy of poetry as a spider web or other natural phenomenon. This is Emerson's answer to the 18th-century critics who believed that the elevated language of poetry was best suited to a limited range of worthy subjects. He also seems to be directing the new poet away from wild nature and toward the changes that his aggressively acquisitive compatriots were making in the fabric of human life.

Poets sense the connections between words (and images) more than other men, and the new connections they discover can be very valuable. Their ripe words can call the souls of men to higher forms of existence. Legitimate criticism consists of detecting which aspects of poetry deviate from natural forms. The poet's imagination enables him to see the essential qualities of things, and his best discoveries come not from his concentrated intellect and will, but by opening himself up to nature.

Emerson cautions that those who would use artificial aids such as drugs, coffee, or tobacco to heighten their ability to discover new metaphysical connections will be punished by dissipation and deterioration, and that "the sublime vision comes to the pure and simple soul in a clean and chaste body." He argues that inspiration is more likely to come to those who drink water rather than wine and to those who can enjoy the pine stumps of a forest more than fashions of New York.

Like liberating gods, poets can surprise other men by showing them the connections between man and nature. For Emerson, the value of an imaginative book lies more in the novelty of its tropes than in the poet's intention; such a work can hold a reader like an insanity. Without exposure to these new connections, man may never arrive at new ways of thinking.

After celebrating the poet as symbolist, Emerson takes pains to separate him from a mystic who believes that his chosen symbol could convey the same meaning to all men. He argues that "all religious error consisted in making the symbol too stark and solid" until it became a mere excess of the organ of language. For Emerson, the philosopher Swedenborg comes closest to being the ideal "translator of nature into thought," and Emerson delighted in his depiction of his benighted critics and miraculous angels. Swedenborg knew that men could appear one way to themselves and their peers, and quite differently to those of higher intellect. Everyone has similarly mistaken one thing for another and can appreciate Swedenborg as the poet who brought that phenomenon to our attention.

America seemed to lack a poet who could appreciate the value of its abundant materials and the unique aspects of its national life, someone who can see in it such a carnival of the gods as inspired Homer. There have been true poets before, but Emerson calls Milton too literary and Homer too literal. He counsels the new American poet to proceed symmetrically and abundantly, advice that seems appropriate given the immensity and diversity of the nation.

The typical artist desires to express himself and, after discovering his ideal medium, produces much that is conventional. Eventually he discovers something original and beautiful, which pleasantly surprises him. He would say everything at that level if he could, and Emerson encourages him to "draw out that dream power" through which his unlimited creative energy (Emerson calls it "electricity") can flow. Thus the great poets and artists have no limit but their lifetime and seem ready to render an image of everything. Lest this seem too easy, Emerson cautions that success will be delayed for the radically new poet, and only his intimate circle will believe in him. Eventually, however, "the ideal will become real," and America and all its separate parts will belong to him. Nothing will seem inopportune or ignoble to him.

"A POETICAL EPISTLE, ADDRESSED BY A LADY OF NEW JERSEY, TO HER NIECE, UPON HER MARRIAGE" ANNIS BOUDINOT STOCKTON (1786)

This poem presents the content of a letter (the "epistle" of the title) conveying marital advice from an older woman to her niece only days after the latter's wedding. Its joy lies in a knowledge of human nature so thorough that the anticipated reactions of the bride, for example, seem utterly natural more than two centuries after the poem's initial appearance, and in such an artful rendering of rhymed verse that it rarely sounds forced.

The wisdom of ANNIS BOUDINOT STOCKTON is apparent in her timing. Instead of offering her advice before the nuptials, when her voice would more likely be lost among the bustle, cake, obligatory visits, and gay buzzing of that joyous time, she waited until later. Although her portrayal of the married state ("you with the other grave ones grace the fire's side," line 4) seems like a great fall from the blissful freedom that precedes it, the statement sobers the discussion and probably helped focus the attention of her internal audience (her niece, as opposed to the external audience, the reader).

The language of the next four lines flirts with a more complex picture of the niece than her "usual sweetness" might suggest. That it asks her to "deign" to listen recognizes the still lingering authority that attached itself to her as the bride upon whom so much attention was so recently focused. To lend authority to her own voice, the speaker demonstrates her keen understanding of a young woman's temperament by anticipating the supercilious (or disdainful) smile and gay contempt that often greets unsolicited advice from one's elders at precisely that point in her life. The observation preempts precisely that reaction, but rather than proceeding with an air of presumed superiority, the aunt raises her audience to her level by crediting the niece with similar sense and judgment, attributing her own remarkable insight to long experience instead of intellectual superiority or greater emotional intelligence.

She seems to be putting women down by calling them "capricious things" (line 12), a reading reinforced by her overt attack on the overbearing aunts who would debate matrimonial themes "in every age" (the phrase attacks overbearing older women on the very sensitive issue of aging although it also refers to every historical era; line 14) whether they actually have any experience or not. A 21st-century audience might argue that the line is grammatically ambiguous since its punctuation supports a reading that calls men as well as women capricious things, thus providing a delightful example of outwitting them even in an apparent act of deference. While that point must be granted (and enjoyed for its insight, since men are at least equally guilty of capriciousness at the niece's probable age [mid- to late-teenaged brides were common in the era] as their spouses), the entire epistle seems determined to rein in precisely this characteristic in the niece.

She will not counsel meekness of spirit and prudence, however, since the niece has ample sense (both intelligence and practicality are implied), good nature and a knowledge of economics (which in that era meant understanding less about where the money was coming from and understanding more about how to turn the available commodities into the food capable of nurturing a family). Instead, she focuses on the lurking evils that seem like trifles but which can prove fatal to love.

She should show reverence for her "chosen patron" (a euphemism for *husband* that emphasizes his role as the sole financial support of his wife and family in that

era) by showing him the utmost respect, for neglecting that responsibility also robs (the "rifling" of line 32) her of respect. She should also refrain from public displays of affection because they invite public censure, and avoid demanding protestations of his love in order to maintain the power in the relationship that "fondness" (affection, but in that era it also conveyed the important secondary meaning of naive foolishness) cannot attain. Such public restraint will sweeten their private moments. She should also avoid being rude to him because men (and women!) have long memories (and "microscopic eyes") when it comes to such things.

If her husband chooses to stay at home (note how urban the lives of Stockton's social set have already become; husbands engaged in agriculture worked close to home all the time and more rarely left it), she should cancel whatever plans she has in order to heighten his joy or share his grief (line 60). Thus begin the most dated bits of advice in the poem, and yet the line reveals an expectation that she will have an active life beyond the home. Essentially, she should put the husband's and family's needs ahead of the more superficial aspects of her own life—probably sound advice if his decision to remain at home is such a rare occurrence as she makes it sound. She should not let him know of her sacrifice but rely on him to find out. When he does (modern cynicism would say "if by some miracle he ever does," for we tend to favor open communication), he will prize her endeavors to bring him ease and her willingness to make his pleasure the study of her life (ouch! A feminist might ask why he should be so privileged when they are supposed to be equal partners in the relationship, and a modern therapist might question whether such complete subordination of her own needs to his is entirely healthy for either of them).

She should also refrain from recrimination by not repeating later what, when, or how he said something in an argument (the "jars" of line 68; this could be good advice if both parties adhered to it). If he should prove tenacious in an argument, she should give way even if he is clearly wrong. Let his ignorance pass with a smile, and "let it be your pleasure to forget" (line 78).

She should always cheerfully entertain such friends as he invites even when unexpected and unannounced (especially if she has a house full of servants and a pantry full of food. A modern husband would be well advised to keep such intrusions to a minimum since it intrudes on his wife's home as well as his). At such times she should not use the inconvenience to leverage new fixtures from him, for often have wives drawn their husbands into financial difficulty and the embarrassment of too rich a service given their station in life. Instead, she should treat his friends as her own, defer to his ownership of the house (!), and welcome each guest.

Such rules are designed "to reach the summit of domestic bliss" (line 103) and bring "ever smiling peace." If even one of the aunt's cautions has helped the niece toward that goal, she has not labored in vain. The aunt remains hers (with the implication that further advice is available as needed).

"THE POETIC PRINCIPLE" EDGAR ALLAN POE (1848)   The easiest way to appreciate this essay is to begin with the author's first definition: A poem elevates the reader's soul. Since, in Poe's opinion, a reader's psyche is repelled by exposure to a sustained exhilaration lasting longer than 30 minutes, even the best epic poems, such as the English poet John Milton's *Paradise Lost* and Homer's ancient Greek *Iliad*, can seem like a series of mediocre lyrics because their length forces them to violate the first Unity, the totality of effect or impression produced in a reader. In other words, their length precludes their being appreciated as a single work of art. This is Poe's response to a quarterly review's praise for the sustained effort behind JOEL BARLOW's *The Columbiad* without any regard for the pleasure that more accomplished art can engender in a reader. Poe insists on distinguishing between genius and perseverance. A poem can also be so "improperly brief" (Carlson 453) that it fails to sustain the public's attention. Such a fate befell the British author Percy Bysshe Shelley's "Serenade," which Poe presents in its entirety. A poem ("The shadows lay along Broadway") by the American author Nathaniel Parker Willis met the same fate.

Even more corrupting than a critical focus on length without concern for quality is "the heresy of the Didactic" (456), the insistence that a poem must be judged by the moral truth it reveals. Instead, Poe celebrates a poem for its own sake (especially its elevating effect). The mind's three most obvious divisions are Pure Intellect (concerned with truth), Taste (used for appreciating beauty) and Moral Sense (focused on duty). Taste is connected with morality only insofar as it despises vice because it harms beauty (457).

Beauty can move us to tears because it provides glimpses of divine joy but cannot provide us with permanent access to that high plane. This Poetic Sentiment (which aims at the pleasurable elevation of the soul) can find expression in the sister arts as well as poetry; music may even come closer to actually realizing supernal beauty. He defines the poetry of words as The Rhythmical Creation of Beauty (458).

Poe praises the Proem to HENRY WADSWORTH LONGFELLOW's "Waif" for "the graceful insouciance" (naturalness) of its meter (460) and WILLIAM CULLEN BRYANT's "June" for the intensity of the melancholy it arouses in the reader's soul (462). He argues that the tone of a poem should be "that which the mass of mankind would adopt" in a similar situation (461) but that the highest manifestations of beauty always include a taint of sadness. He considers Edward Coate Pinckney's "Health" especially beautiful, but bemoans the fact that Pinckney (like Poe) was born too far south to benefit from the promotional advantages of *The North American Review* enjoyed by the cabal of New England poets. Critics, however, should not have to point out all the excellence of a work, which should be largely self-evident.

Poe also has high praise for the Irish poet Thomas Moore's "Come rest in his bosom" and "I would I were by that dim lake," which have been unfairly dismissed as fanciful according to the important British poet and critic Samuel Taylor Coleridge's division of poets into fanciful and imaginative categories. Similarly, he finds Thomas Hood's "Fair Ines" fanciful but inexpressibly charming (465) and has high praise for Hood's "The Haunted House" and "Bridge of Sighs." He also liked the versification of Byron's "Though the day of my destiny's over" and Tennyson's "The Princess."

In his conclusion, Poe defines the Poetic Principle as "the Human Aspiration for Supernal Beauty" (471) and reasserts his preference for poetry that elevates the soul independent of the passions stirred in the heart or its fidelity to the truth. While passion tends to degrade the soul, love is "unquestionably the purest and truest of all poetical themes" (472).

Poets experience the true poetical effect in such things as the stars, flowers, grain fields and the twinkling of half-hidden brooks. He ends his somewhat lengthy list of things that induce the poetical effect with the beauty of a woman and the divine majesty of her love. He ends with "The Song of the Cavalier" by Motherwell, which calls on soldiers to take up their swords without a sigh for even the fairest of the land.

BIBLIOGRAPHY
Carlson, Eric W. *Introduction to Poe: A Thematic Reader.* Glenview, Ill.: Scott, Foresman, 1967.

POETRY ANTHOLOGIES

The 19 anthologies of American poetry published before 1900 and identified as such in the Library of Congress catalog reveal much about the marketing strategies of 19th-century publishing. The only one to appear before 1800 was *American Poems,* edited by Elihu Hubbard Smith in 1793 and likely created to capitalize on the patriotism stirring in the new republic. That the principal motive behind two subsequent anthologies was to take advantage of the nationalism rampant at the start of any American war becomes evident in their extended titles: *The National Songster; or a Collection of the Most Admired Patriotic Songs, on the Brilliant Victories achieved by the Naval and Military Heroes of the United States of America, Over Equal and Superior Forces of the British* [in the War of 1812]) and *War-Time Echoes; Patriotic Poems, Heroic and Pathetic, Humorous and Dialectic, of the Spanish-American War.*

The first quarter of the 19th century saw rival volumes of *Specimens of American Poets* published in London (1822) and Boston (1829). The readership of a literary journal were the most likely purchasers of the *Miscellaneous Poems Selected from the United States Literary Gazette* in 1826.

An anonymous compiler in 1837 put together a book of poetry marketed toward women, *Ladies Wreath: A Selection from the Female Poetic Writers of England and America,* that was published in both Boston (Marsh, Capen and Lyon) and New York (D. Appleton and Company). In 1847 a monthly journal appropriated the title *Ladies' Wealth,* and the poems were reissued yearly as *Ladies' Wreath and Parlor Annual,* the 16th volume appearing in 1861. In 1848 Rufus Griswold edited *Female Poets of America,* and the enterprise was rewarded with a second editon a decade later. Pamela Atkins Colman attempted to reach the same audience in 1850 with *The Lady's Vase of Wild Flowers: A Collection of Gems from the Best Authors.*

The first compilation by the first editor with considerable personal influence on public taste, Rufus Wilmot Griswold's *The Poets and Poetry of America,* appeared in 1842. It was so successful as to require 10 editions by 1850.

In 1861 Benjamin Todd tried to generate interest in his own poems by combining them with those of more established poets for *The Bouquet: A Choice Collection of Flowers Culled from the Garden of Humanity.* Prior to the Civil War, the technology of publishing had reached the point where engraved pictures could be placed throughout a text, an innovation that led to the Rev. Robert Aris Willmott's *The Poets of the 19th Century* appearing with 132 engravings; a later edition (1872) expanded that to 141 engravings in its 674 pages. An anonymous 1882 compilation gave equal billing to *Poets and Etchers,* placing poems by T. B. Aldrich, WILLIAM CULLEN BRYANT, RALPH WALDO EMERSON, JAMES RUSSELL LOWELL, HENRY WADSWORTH LONGFELLOW, and JOHN GREENLEAF WHITTIER beside the engravings they inspired. Obediah Craig Maxwell gave this approach a twist by furnishing details about the poets' homes in addition to their poetry. In 1890, Thomas Wentworth Higginson edited a collection of *American Sonnets* that was published in Boston and New York by Houghton Mifflin.

Niche marketers hoped to score with *A Cluster of Poets, Scottish and English* (1897) and in 1894 a collection of poems that had served as song lyrics (*American Song: A Collection of Representative Poems*). Lucy Larcom's *Landscape in American Poetry* collected poems because of their scenic backdrops. Perhaps it was representative of their gilded age that anthologies in 1887 and 1889 were titled *Seven Dozen Gems* and *Gems from an Old Drummer's Grip,* respectively. In this context, drummers were the precursors of traveling salesmen. In 1900 Clarence Edmund Stedman, a poet of modest fame in his own right, edited *An American Anthology* (Boston: Houghton Mifflin).

BIBLIOGRAPHY

Brownlee, James Henry, ed. *War-Time Echoes*. New York: Werner, c. 1898.

Golding, Alan. *From Outlaw to Classic: Canons in American Poetry*. Madison: University of Wisconsin Press, 1995.

Kettell, Samuel, comp. *Specimens of American Poets*. 3 vols. Boston: S. G. Goodrich, 1829.

Maxwell, Obediah Craig. *Our Favorites: Our Favorite Poets and Poems, Old and New, Their Homes Fully Described*. Jersey City, N.J.: Star Publishing, 1891.

Rasula, Jed. *The American Poetry Wax Museum*. Urbana, Ill.: National Council of Teachers of English, 1995.

Smith, Elihu Hubbard. *American Poems*. c. 1793. Reprint, Gainesville, Fla.: Scholars' Facsimiles & Reprints, 1966.

Streeter, N. R., comp. *Gems from an Old Drummer's Grip*. Grotten, N.Y.: N.R. Streeter, 1889.

POETRY IN PERFORMANCE

In terms of its initial audience reception, the most effective public reading of a poem in American (perhaps even world) history would have occured in 1662, had MICHAEL WIGGLESWORTH, the preacher in the frontier pulpit of Malden, Massachusetts, unleashed *The DAY OF DOOM* on an unsuspecting congregation gathered for their regular Sunday services. Wigglesworth was unable to personally deliver his poem to his church, but other ministers delivered it to theirs. To fully appreciate its impact, it is necessary to imagine production values unequaled even in 21st-century cinema. Because their sect had banished much of the regalia of the priesthood and reduced the interior of the church to its barest essentials, their hard wooden pews probably elicited much squirming even before the minister's sermon. The more strict among their number would have had even the singing of hymns banished from the church as a distracting intrusion. They had the right to expect nothing but the unvarnished truth from the pulpit, grounded in a fundamentalist acceptance of the Bible as God's word to man, and Wigglesworth did them the favor not merely of reciting the biblical passages related to the end of the world, but of showing how such events would work themselves out in a small community like their own. Some of the shrieks arising from among the parishioners matched those emitted among the damned in the poem, as Wigglesworth's auditors must have realized that they, and probably almost everyone around them, would be found wanting in the celestial court that awaited them.

Far less appreciative, but bound to their chairs by familial and community ties, were the audiences at the various children's recitals serving as an outlet, as well as the raison d'etre for rote memorization, of long poems in the grade school curriculum of most 19th-century American schools. Many skilled and not-so-skilled future congressmen probably fell in love with their own voices for the first time under such adverse circumstances, and the practice taught patience and perseverence as well as elocution. "Casabianca," by Felicia Dorothea Browne Hemans, was a popular choice, and other poets may also have crafted their most bombastic works with such an audience in mind.

Such formal recitations when they involved a writer's own work could be very useful in helping poets find their voices. With Hugh Henry Brackenridge, PHILIP FRENEAU produced "The Rising Glory of America" for their Princeton commencement in 1771. Several members of the CONNECTICUT WITS also began delivering successful poems in college. A later poet, HENRY WADSWORTH LONGFELLOW, delivered a commencement oration at Bowdoin College in 1825. OLIVER WENDELL HOLMES was named the Harvard class poet in 1829 and continued to deliver topical pieces for that limited audience throughout most of his successful career, and RALPH WALDO EMERSON was given the same post for the Harvard class of 1834. Sometimes established poets could also use such a venue: JAMES RUSSELL LOWELL composed an ode for the Harvard Commencement of 1865, and WALT WHITMAN delivered the commencement poem at Dartmouth College in 1872.

The northern antislavery movement prior to the Civil War provided attentive audiences for those orators who appreciated the relative density and potentially greater emotional impact of their topical poetry. SARAH LOUISA FORTEN was among those who availed themselves of this opportunity. While such major American poets as RALPH WALDO EMERSON and HERMAN MELVILLE saw in the lucrative lecture circuits of their day an opportunity to increase their incomes, they evidently anticipated little demand for their poetry in such a venue. Emerson was successful with his lectures on ethics, self-reliance, and religion, but was not booked for his poetry. An exception was his contribution of the "HYMN SUNG AT THE DEDICATION OF THE CONCORD MONUMENT, JULY 4, 1837," his celebration of the Minutemen who fought the British regulars on the fateful day in 1775 that marked the beginning of continued fighting in the Revolutionary War. Melville was predictably far less successful in his lectures on Greek architecture, and Walt Whitman's proposed lectures or poetry readings never attracted a promoter.

Perhaps the most successful poet after the Civil War in terms of public performance was James Whitcomb Riley, widely known as the Hoosier poet. From about 1875 until after the turn of the century, he sometimes combined readings of his poetry with presentations by lecturers and other performers as well known as Mark Twain. Less spectacularly, Celia Thaxter, a popular poet of the same era, wrote most of her poems for oral performance (Vallier 133) but was largely limited to summer salon readings at vacation hotels and such secondary venues as a Massachusetts State Women's Reformatory.

Near the end of the 19th century, performance poetry (or at least a formal public reading) proved an important milestone for PAUL LAURENCE DUNBAR, who as a high-school-educated 24-year-old was invited to read from his work at the Chicago World's Fair in 1896. Such performances (he had also read for the Western Association of Writers in 1892 in his native Dayton, Ohio) brought him to the attention of William Dean Howells and other influential critics, who were instrumental in winning a national audience for the undeniably talented young man.

In retrospect, it would appear that only gradually were American poets afforded the opportunity to read, recite, or otherwise publicly perform their work as a means of reaching a wider audience and increasing their sales. Only in the 20th century would such endeavors help a few of them become media stars on a national level.

BIBLIOGRAPHY

Callow, Philip. *From Noon to Starry Night: A Life of Walt Whitman.* Chicago: Ivan R. Dee, 1992.

Crowder, Richard. *No Featherbed to Heaven: A Biography of Michael Wigglesworth, 1631–1705.* East Lansing: Michigan State University Press, 1962.

Gentry, Tony. *Paul Laurence Dunbar.* New York: Chelsea House Publishers, 1989.

Howard, Leon. *The Connecticut Wits.* Chicago: University of Chicago Press, 1943.

Loving, Jerome. *Walt Whitman: The Song of Himself.* Berkeley: University of California Press, 1999.

Vallier, Jane E. *Poet on Demand: The Life, Letters and Works of Celia Thaxter.* Camden, Maine: Down East Books, 1982.

POETRY JOURNALS Prior to the American Revolution, colonial newspapers haphazardly published poetry as fillers (Mott, *American Journalism,* 55), but they either reprinted poems from British periodicals or a few native products that were virtually indistinguishable from them (Tebbel, *The American Magazine,* 7). Even 40 years after independence, when the new nation's elite thirsted for an American poetry that, while it could not hope to surpass that of England, could at least avoid comparison by striking off in a new direction, very little of lasting merit was published, even in the typical "poet's corner" of many newspapers (the most remarkable exception was "The Star Spangled Banner," printed in the *Baltimore American* just a few hours after Francis Scott Key observed the bombardment that inspired the poem; ibid 201). Only during the Civil War was newspaper poetry especially important (ibid 391–392), and only at the very end of the century did "the most famous of newspaper poems," Edwin Markham's "The Man with the Hoe," appear in the *San Francisco Examiner* (ibid 585).

Monthly magazines could offer a better venue, but the best efforts of the 45 different printers who attempted to create them between 1741 and 1794 (Tebbel and Zuckerman, 4) did not last long or bring enduring fame or prosperity to their contributors. Publication in 18th-century journals such as the *United States Magazine* and the *American Magazine and Monthly Chronicle* (the most original literary magazine produced before the American Revolution; Tebbel, *American Magazine,* 10) offered some exposure, and critical reviews in such organs as the *Monthly Anthology, North American, Portico,* and *Port Folio* attempted to influence public taste in the early 19th century (Mott, v.1, 182). Until the second quarter of the 19th century, however, even such accomplished poets as PHYLLIS WHEATLEY, PHILIP FRENEAU, and EDGAR ALLAN POE found it impossible to survive on the earnings from their creative work alone. One of the chief advantages enjoyed by the mid-century poets was an abundance of magazines with the financial power to allow writers like Alice and PHOEBE CARY to support themselves; 1825 marked the beginning of the general magazine (ibid 8) with sufficient circulation and financial backing to make poetry pay.

Two of the most prestigious and enduring venues for poetry were created as general-interest magazines near mid-century: *Harper's* (1850) and *The Atlantic Monthly* (1857). Although both drew heavily on the literary hotbeds from which they sprang (New York and Boston, respectively), *The Atlantic Monthly*, founded by JAMES RUSSELL LOWELL, was especially fortunate in attracting high-caliber literary minds to its editorship throughout the 19th century. Unfortunately, even they were hampered by the unprecedented onslaught of sentimental poetry (perhaps the worst were infant-obituary poems, which could read much into a postmortem grin) in the decades both preceding and following the Civil War (Mott, *History*, v.2, 174 and v.3, 230), much of which a 21st-century audience would likely deem unreadable.

Topical poems could find a receptive audience in journals devoted to social improvement including the independence-minded *Pennsylvania Magazine* of the Revolutionary War era, and the *Anti-Slavery Standard* and the similarly abolitionist *National Era* (Mott, v.1, 89 and v.2, 175). In the last quarter of the 19th century, *The Woman's Journal* (1870–1912), simultaneously published in Boston, Chicago and, eventually, St. Louis, was edited by names that still resonate for their cultural significance a century and a half later: Mary A. Livermore, JULIA WARD HOWE, Lucy Stone, William Lloyd Garrison and Thomas Wentworth Higginson.

A similar phenomenon led to the 20th-century creation of "little magazines," a designation indicative of their small circulation numbers and limited staff, but not of their ambition, which was typically to publicize the unique perspectives of a small group of people often united by their interest in an avant-garde artistic or cultural movement. In American literature, the prototype for all such endeavors is *The Dial,* a tran-scendentalist magazine founded and edited by Margaret Fuller and RALPH WALDO EMERSON. Its four-year lifespan (1840–44) is somewhat remarkable for its longevity; without Emerson's assumption of its costs, however, it would have probably folded within the two years more typical of little magazines. Although a few poems appeared within its pages, including Emerson's "The PROBLEM," most issues were filled with essays by such important transcendentalists as Bronson Alcott, William Ellery Channing and HENRY DAVID THOREAU.

Other 19th-century precursors of the 20th-century's little-magazine phenomenon include the *Saturday Press* (1858–66; Tebbel, *The American Magazine*, 215). Similar venues of the 1890s included *M'lle New York* (which tended to promote the French Symbolists when it did publish poetry [Hoffman, et al., 236]), *Lark,* and Chicago's bimonthly *Chap-Book* (a promoter of American literature of many genres).

Journals specializing in poetry continued to have limited success in the 19th century. Noteworthy attempts include the short-lived *The Garland; or, New General Repository of Fugitive Poetry* of Auburn, New York, in 1825, and the far more fortunate *Poet Lore* of Bethesda, Maryland, founded in 1889 and priding itself on being the oldest continually publishing literary magazine in the 21st century.

BIBLIOGRAPHY

Hoffman, Frederick J., Charles Allen, and Carolyn F. Ulrich. *The Little Magazine: A History and Bibliography*. Princeton, N.J.: Princeton University Press, 1946.

Mott, Frank Luther. *American Journalism,* 3rd ed. New York: Macmillan, 1962. Republished, London: Routledge/ Thoemmes Press, 2000.

———. *A History of American Magazines*. 5 vols. Cambridge, Mass.: Harvard University Press, 1938–68.

Tebbel, John. *The American Magazine: A Compact History*. New York: Hawthorn Books, 1969.

Tebbel, John, and Mary Ellen Zuckerman. *The Magazine in America, 1741–1990*. New York: Oxford University Press, 1991.

Thompson, Slason, comp. *The Humbler Poets: A Collection of Newspaper and Periodical Verse, 1870–1885*. Chicago: A. C. McClurg, 1890.

POETRY IN TRANSLATION

Hardscrabble poverty, and remoteness from Europe with its frequent warfare between the continental colonial powers, hampered any natural curiosity about the poetry of foreign lands that might have arisen in early British America. Books were frequently priced beyond the means of the average colonist, and public libraries were not available until Benjamin Franklin and a few friends organized the Library Company of Philadelphia, a subscription library, in 1732. The average citizen was unlikely to learn a foreign language, and most colleges, such as Harvard and Yale, offered training in ancient Greek and Latin rather than the modern languages, as the classics were thought to be of greater advantage to the future ministers and teachers they trained. Toward this end, the two colleges eventually added Hebrew to their required languages to facilitate closer study of the Torah and other religious writings collectively known to them as the Old Testament.

Among the Revolutionary War generation, a few polyglots such as Alexander Hamilton were able to perfect their skills in the linguistically diverse trading of the West Indies, and a prosperous Virginia landowner's son like Thomas Jefferson could find himself in a primary school where French was taught, in addition to Greek and Latin. Unless their parents had emigrated from a European state other than the United Kingdom, however, the very few Americans who were interested enough to attempt such studies had either to learn their languages from books (as did BENJAMIN FRANKLIN, a future ambassador to France) or find a private tutor. After the war, the bombastic pride and continued isolation of the new country did not lend itself to widespread curiosity about other cultures.

That changed in the early 19th century, when Napoleon captured the world's attention, and when a second war with England in 1812 broadened American interest in other countries. If America were to achieve its dreams of becoming a world political as well as economic power, it had to have some knowledge of the people and cultures with whom it would come into contact and sometimes conflict. The task of propagating the newly desired languages fell to the colleges, and in 1816 Harvard created the Smith Chair for the study of modern languages. In 1817 George Ticknor was named to that post after studying in Germany and acquiring additional skills in France, Spain, and Portugal. Although Ticknor did not translate a volume of poetry during his tenure, afterward his *History of Spanish Literature* (1849) continued his life's work of disseminating knowledge about the European classics in America. He also bequeathed his large collection of Spanish and Portuguese books to the Boston Public Library, as a further enticement for others to follow in his footsteps.

By 1825 at least one other college had followed Harvard's lead by creating its own professorship in modern languages. Bowdoin College in Maine began its own program by inviting a recent graduate, HENRY WADSWORTH LONGFELLOW, to teach the major continental languages if he would study in Europe to bring himself up to speed in them. He spent three years acquiring the western European languages he would need and then taught them at Bowdoin from 1829 to 1835. His first elementary grammar texts in French and Italian date from this era, but he was too busy teaching and creating his own poetry to devote much energy to translation. After two more years in Europe, Longfellow began teaching at Harvard, taking up the Smith Chair after Ticknor retired. His greatest contribution to the popularization of international poetry in America was *The Poets and Poetry of Europe*, printed in Philadelphia in 1845. He taught until 1854, when he began concentrating on his own poetry.

By mid-century, knowledge of foreign languages had spread to the point where men like Bayard Taylor were willing to labor over the course of 20 years to translate a major German text like Goethe's *Faust*, published in translation in 1870 with its original meter. There was also a minor informal tradition in which poets turned to translation as they aged; WILLIAM CULLEN BRYANT's blank verse translation of the ancient Greek poet Homer's *Odyssey* appeared in 1872, and his version of Homer's *Iliad* was published in 1916. Over a decade after changing the direction of his career away from teaching, Longfellow found time for translating the work of Dante, including the Italian poet's masterpiece (*The Divine Comedy*) and a much shorter poem on the life of St. Francis of Assisi.

Another poet of note, JAMES RUSSELL LOWELL, taught at Harvard from 1855 until 1876. By then, French and Spanish had become an elective major, additional professors were hired for each language, and soon Italian and German were offered as well. Other universities saw similar growth in their modern foreign language departments throughout the 19th century. This trend continued well into the early years of the 21st century, when more than 50 foreign languages were being offered each year at Yale.

Such avid interest in foreign languages and literatures spawned an even more rapid growth in the market for translations. This trend got a big boost when transcendentalists such as RALPH WALDO EMERSON began arguing for a cultural relativism in the 1840s and sprinkled references to texts as remote from daily American life as the Bhagavad-Gita in their essays and lectures. By 1855 a Boston publisher was printing a translation of the ancient Sanskrit text. A translation of work by the greatest Russian poet, Alexander Pushkin, found a New York publisher in 1846, and as early as 1875 another Boston publisher printed work by a second major Russian poet, Michael Lermontov. Cultural mavens such as William Dean Howells, an eminent editor as well as a leading American novelist for several decades late in the 19th century, helped spread an awareness of the major continental writers, including poets, in their magazine columns.

In the last half of the 19th century, many of the major poets of the western European nations found it possible to attract American translators and publishers, especially if they produced volumes of prose in addition to their verse. A survey of the holdings of the Library of Congress reveals rival translations of the French poetry of Victor Hugo (1802–85) published in New York (1883 and 1887) and Boston (1893) along with numerous London versions. In 1895, the work of another Frenchman was published in Chicago as the *Poems of Paul Verlaine.* The German poet Henrich Heine (1797–1856) fared even better, with various translations of his songs and ballads appearing in Philadelphia (1864), New York (1881, 1884, 1888 and 1892), and Boston (1884 and 1890). Four translations (mostly prose) by the Italian poet Gabriele D'Annunzio were printed in New York between 1896 and 1898. Even a Spanish poet as famous as Rosalia de Castro (1837–85) had to wait until the 20th century to find an American publisher, however.

"POETS TO COME" WALT WHITMAN (1860)

This poem begins with a list of public performers arranged in descending order according to the extent to which their arts are dependent upon words to convey their message: poets, orators, singers, and musicians. Recognizing that his generation was not ready to "justify" (line 2) or understand him, the speaker calls on future artists (whose favor he courts by referring to them as "a new brood, athletic, continental, greater than before known," line 3) to "Arouse!" (an imperative verb form bearing much more of a sexual connotation as well as a suggestion of a much less conscious state than the more common "Arise!" The verb may be reflexive as well as direct; he may be calling for the artists to get excited and to excite their audiences). They are the ones who must justify him.

He writes but one or two "indicative words for the future" (line 5) and advances only a moment before deciding to "wheel" (a dance or military term meaning to quickly change direction in an orderly tactical fashion) and "hurry back in the darkness" (a phrase suggesting that the darkness completely surrounds him, while "into the darkness" would have suggested that the speaker is the one coming from a dark, benighted place. In this respect it represents a reversal of the imagery of the closeted individual who hides aspects of himself from the public).

In the stanza the speaker identifies himself as a man who, slowly walking past, turns a casual look upon you before averting his face (line 7), leaving it for you to "prove and define it, expecting the main things from you" (lines 8–9). This description of what modern behaviorists call the copulative glance (and which is probably an important component of what the gay community calls *gaydar,* a subtle means of identifying the other gays in crowd) suggests that the hidden meaning of "justify me" relates to the speaker's willingness to hint at his sexual orientation in his poetry in an era when it was unacceptable and even dangerous to make such a public admission. The call for future artists "to justify me" is therefore a call for them to celebrate their sexuality in ways that a pre–Civil War person felt unable to do, a plea that had the most resonance for gay poets such as Allen Ginsberg.

The above interpretation owes much to the revelations made in the poems presented in the *Calamus* section of *Leaves of Grass*. Alternative interpretations might focus on WALT WHITMAN's aesthetic choices, especially his use of free verse (an approach enjoying such overwhelming popularity in the subsequent century that it tended to curtail expression in more traditional forms), the frankness with which he dealt with such issues as sex in general (the major realm in which 20th-century writers, largely because of their directness, put those of the 19th century to shame), or his faith in the importance of his work (he remains the most widely represented author in the anthologies of pre-20th-century literature published in the 21st century, frequently accounting for more than 5 percent of the total pages even in those volumes covering fiction and nonfiction as well as poetry). In each of these major areas, the artists (and critics) of later centuries also justified Whitman's work.

"THE PORTENT" HERMAN MELVILLE (1866)

John Brown not only believed that violence was the only way to remove the abomination of slavery from American soil, but that he was chosen by God to lead an army to that goal. In 1856, he first garnered national attention, and much negative publicity for his cause, by having five people executed in retaliation for a pro-slavery raid on Lawrence, Kansas. In 1858, he led a raid that liberated 11 Missouri slaves whom he personally escorted to permanent freedom in Canada. By 1859, he had stockpiled enough weapons to outfit a small army and led 21 men to Harper's Ferry, Virginia, where they seized the federal armory in order to start a violent slave revolt. At dawn on October 18, 1859, federal troops under the direct command of Colonel Robert E. Lee stormed the building that Brown and his followers had turned into their stronghold. On December 2 of the same year, Brown, having been convicted of conspiring with slaves to commit murder and treason, was hanged. He achieved the personal martyrdom for which he seemed destined, and his actions convinced many people that only violence could settle the slave question.

HERMAN MELVILLE's poem begins with Brown's body still swinging from the beam; note how his precise description of the body's movement (it is "slowly swaying") and its gaunt shadow (lines 3–4) vividly render the scene. Directly addressing the region ("on your green, Shenandoah") attaches responsibility for the execution in the valley where it occurred, in a very personal way.

The poem continues with a brief examination of the body. The speaker's sentiments become clear when he not only recognizes John Brown, but greets him ("Lo, John Brown"). Brown had received a sword wound on his head as he resisted the marines who captured him, hence the description of the cut "on the crown" in line 5. Since he is dead, his wounds will not heal any more (line 8).

To make hangings slightly less bothersome to the spectators, condemned men's heads have traditionally been covered with black hoods shortly before the fatal order is given. Thus Shenandoah was spared the picture of anguish that would prefigure its own future in the war. With his long white hair and flowing beard, Brown's appearance had sometimes been compared to that of an Old-Testament prophet. Only his streaming beard showed beneath the executioner's hood, but that was enough to recall his strange demeanor. Eulogizing this "Weird John Brown" as "the meteor of the war" (lines 13–14) not only referred to the brevity and intensity of his prominence on the national scene, it raised him to the level of a natural phenomenon. It also suggested that the nation could have seen in him a portent of its own anguish in the coming Civil War.

"THE PRAIRIES" WILLIAM CULLEN BRYANT (1833)

Until the American Revolution, the West began for the British colonists on the eastern slopes of the Alleghenies. Having experienced the heavily forested eastern wilderness and never before having encountered an ecosystem like the Great Plains, they mistakenly attributed the lack of trees to a lack of water. Their notion of the entire hinterland as the Great American Desert persisted until the 19th century, when federally sponsored scientific expeditions like those of Lewis and Clark and the Long Expedition of 1819 began filling the gaps in their knowledge. Even by 1833, however, WILLIAM CULLEN BRYANT could think of more than a million square miles of some of the most naturally productive land in the world as a mere garden of the American Desert (line 1) despite the fact that the grasses were tall enough to sweep the sides of his horse (line 36) and extended to the horizon in all directions. Frequent wildfires, which consumed the saplings but provided nutrients and open space for the regenerative grasses, were largely responsible for restricting the trees to "island groves" (line 27). Some of the "golden and flame-like" flowers (line 16) that Bryant describes as rivaling the stars in glory and multitude (lines 30–31) had even evolved to the point where their seeds are dependent upon exposure to fire before they can sprout.

Bryant's reactions to the "boundless and beautiful" (line 1) Illinois prairie were as visceral as those he described in INSCRIPTION FOR THE ENTRANCE TO A WOOD." His heart "swells" and his pupils dilate (line 5; the second response indicates a profound emotional connection to the land). Suddenly attuned to his senses, he becomes aware of the pounding of his horse's hooves (line 37) as if for the first time. He used the same approach to convey his impression of the prairie that he brought to his study of individual plants, beginning with a description of its appearance. The rolling hills remind him of ocean billows (line 10), but only the shadows of clouds and wind-driven waves of grass give it movement. Their "encircling vastness" (line 6) necessitated a shift of scale; instead of applying the implications of the natural phenomena to his own life, he applies it to entire races of men: in the natural history of each, "dark hollows" chase "sunny ridges" (lines 14–15). He inquires whether the "Breezes of the South" (line 15) could have fanned a nobler or lovelier scene all the way from Mexico and the Pacific Ocean.

Characteristically, the natural splendor reminds him of its Creator, and he thinks of the uninterrupted expanse of the sky as a temple (line 29). In that case, the hollow hoofbeats of his mount seem like sacrilege (lines 37–38), and he questions whether he is stepping on graves. Only the Mound Builders, some of whose characteristic effigy and burial mounds were erected as early as five centuries before the birth of Christ, left enduring structures on the plains; Bryant accurately considered them contemporaneous with the building of the Parthenon in Greece (line 50). Lacking any

knowledge of what happened to their prosperous civilization, he relies on European precedents to create a mythology for them. The single word "haply" ("perhaps;" line 52) signals his flight into fancy; the primitive people of his imagination harnessed the bison like European oxen, expressed their love in a dead language and played their music on instruments of forgotten form (lines 52–58). In Bryant's time, only the prairie wolf and the gopher dug where the roaming hunter tribes once sacked the former cities of the Great Plains; leaving the vultures (line 72) to feed where today only the prairie hawk (line 16) hunts. Eventually the sole survivor of this imagined holocaust, driven by despair, surrendered from the woods. The triumphant warriors welcomed this romantic loner into their tribe, allowing him to take a new wife from among their maidens, although he could not forget his butchered wife and children.

By Bryant's day, "the red man" had also left the blooming wilds in favor of the Rocky Mountain area, where the beaver still built "his little Venice" (line 97; the Italian city, built in a marsh district, features a network of canals). The bison still roamed out there in numbers that shake the earth when they run (line 101), but in Illinois all Bryant found were their ancient footprints.

Although the plain temporarily lacks human inhabitants, it teems with gaudy insects, four-legged animals, birds, and "startlingly beautiful" snakes (108). The honeybee, imported by Europeans, spreads in advance of them. In its hum he seems to hear the future children, maidens, and worshippers who will fill up the land. Then a fresher wind breaks this reverie, and he finds himself again alone in the wilderness (line 124).

"PRAYER OF COLUMBUS" WALT WHITMAN (1874)

In the sixth section of his "PASSAGE TO INDIA," WALT WHITMAN celebrated Christopher Columbus (1451–1506) as a courageous man as well as an important link in the chain of exploration and communication that was slowly uniting everyone in the world. Perhaps because a temporarily debilitating stroke impaired his own health, in this dramatic monologue Whitman more closely identifies with the Spanish admiral at the lowest point in the latter's career. Having lost the four vessels entrusted to his command to ship-worm and storm on his fourth and last voyage to the Americas, Columbus (who is given the role of first-person speaker in this poem) found himself and his crew marooned in Jamaica for the "twelve dreary months" (line 3) that did not end until June of 1504.

The first stanza describes the situation in which Columbus finds himself: old (53 years of adventurous living represented remarkable longevity in the early 16th century), ill, and confined to a savage (non-Spanish, non-Christian) shore by the sea and dark rebellious brows (not only those expressing the discontent of his sailors, but also those of the Spanish authorities at Hispaniola [the island supporting the modern nations of Haiti and the Dominican Republic]. There the admiral had founded the first New World Spanish colony in 1493, but dissatisfaction with his leadership led to a disgraceful end to his third voyage in 1500. By 1503, he was still so out of favor with the local authorities that the governor of that colony refused to rescue him). As the inveterate walker Whitman would have done, Columbus made his way along the shore to vent his heavy heart (in isolation, presumably, so as not to weaken the morale of his men).

Thinking that perhaps he would not live another day (line 8), he feels that he cannot eat, drink, or sleep until he again communes with God, who becomes the internal audience for the rest of the poem. In Whitman's rendering, the admiral had led a pious life in which the prayers and vigils of his youth were ratified by the active work and reveries of his manhood. He never lost faith even when imprisoned (line 20; this is another reference to his arrest in October 1500. Although he was hauled back to Spain in shackles, he was quickly released and within two years given command of four more ships for his last voyage by his royal patrons). All his "emprises" (chivalrous adventures; line 22) were inspired by God and carried out in accordance with His will.

With all his God-given talent, Columbus was able to reinvigorate the surfeited (the "cloyed" of line 32) elder hemisphere (Europe) by tying it to the new (this is an anachronism since Columbus went to his grave believing that he had found not new continents, but a shorter route to Asia). Similarly anachronistic is the

speaker's attack on the "brutish measureless human undergrowth" (line 36) Columbus experienced in Europe and his hope that, transplanted across the sea, it could rise in stature, perhaps turning swords to reaping tools (an echo of Isaiah 2:4 and Micah 4:3 in which swords are beaten into plowshares and spears into pruning hooks. In Joel 3:10, the process is reversed). He even hopes that Europe's dead cross (representing its moribund Christian sects) may come to life in the new land (line 39).

He thanks God for providing the light of his life, and yields his ships to Him (line 50). Although the admiral had no ships remaining, this should not be viewed as a sign of the poor man's declining mental acuity because the following lines make it clear he was speaking metaphorically. He will cling to God even when the timbers of his life break up like those of a derelict ship.

The prayer seems to end at that point, and the speaker finds himself wondering if he has become either a prophet or a madman (line 56). Even his own work seems strange, and the mighty birth (the "parturition" of line 60) of new worlds mocks and perplexes him. Then, as if blessed with a vision of the future by some divine hand, he sees vast shapes in the sky and countless ships on the waves. He hears anthems in his honor saluting him in new tongues (line 66).

"PREFACE TO THE 1855 EDITION OF *LEAVES OF GRASS*" WALT WHITMAN (1855)

Perhaps the easiest way to approach this essay is to acknowledge its debts to RALPH WALDO EMERSON. WALT WHITMAN heard the Sage of Concord on the lecture circuit and read his essay collections based on them, and he seems to have patterned the prose of this preface on that of his mentor. The connection may explain his overreliance on ellipses throughout the essay, frequently serving as visible pauses on the page as if he were a speaker pausing for dramatic effect from the lecture platform, providing space for the reader to fully appreciate the weight of his words, or disingenuously suggesting the originality of his thought by revealing his struggle to develop the precise language to express it clearly. In the opening paragraph, the ellipses are used to avoid repetition of the word *America;* this rhetorical device reinforces his message of Emersonian optimism and nationalism as the reader/audience is forced to remember or repeat that word to complete a series of aphorisms that have only a tentative connection with each other. The gist is that America is not ungrateful for the contributions of other nations, political systems, or religions, which were fine for their day, but is ready to accept its role as their heir.

He declares that Americans "probably have the fullest poetical nature" and their country is the greatest poem. Their country's plentitude stems from diverse immigrants freed from their traditional bonds who become an audacious crowd and disdain the trivial. Its hospitality will continue as long as its agriculture and fisheries, or as long as men beget children upon women. The country's genius lies in its common people, whose traits include a "deathless attachment to freedom," a fierceness when aroused, and the self-esteem of people who never have stood in the presence of their acknowledged superiors. Their elections have terrible significance, and their president doffs his hat to the people. All these things are unrhymed poetry and await the gigantic treatment worthy of them.

A nation can cut a deep mark if it acts in accordance with its soul, identified as the sum of the profitable uses of individuals or states, present action, and grandeur, and the subjects of poets (an awkward definition at best). It is not necessary to consult the eastern records (Asia was then thought to have been the original cradle of civilization) or consider the modern continents the products of the sleepwalking Middle Ages (the medieval period in Europe lasted for about the 1,000 years preceding A.D. 1500). The pride of the United States lies not in its cities or agriculture, but in its full-sized, unconquerable simple men.

The bard for the new America must respond to the country's spirit and measure the breadth and depth of the land and its waters. He must include the plants, birds, climates, histories, and industries. He must show the friendliness and enterprise of the people, the perfect equality of male and female (progressive thinking for his pre–Civil War era), the defense of slavery and the stern opposition to it that will never cease. His expression will be transcendent and new, resulting in

a great psalm of the republic in which there will be no solid (poetic) forms.

This poet will consider nothing in its place to be bad. In peace he will celebrate all the industry, art, and commerce of the people, but in war he will be the most deadly force, with every word drawing blood. He has the ultimate brain and judgment, sees the furthest, and has the most faith although he is silent about God. He sees that everyone is as sacred and perfect as the greatest artist. He lacks misanthropy and, although he uses the power to destroy and remold, he never uses the power of attack. He accepts man without prejudice as to nativity, color, or belief in hell, and would have no man degraded for ignorance, weakness, or sin. He hardly knows triviality, but enlarges anything into grandeur and the life of the universe just by seeing it and enabling others to see.

Folks expect a poet to indicate the path between reality and their souls. Outdoor people, including hunters, gardeners, and healthy young women who love the manly form (another example of Whitman's progressive thought, since feminine desire was generally dismissed during his era) already unfailingly perceive beauty. The poetic quality is not linked to rhyme, uniformity, or any particular formula, but is the life of these and the soul. Rhyme leads to even sweeter and more luxuriant rhyme, and uniformity helps hide its own roots. The rhyme and uniformity of perfect poems show the free growth of metrical laws just as all beauty comes from beautiful blood and a beautiful brain, while he who troubles about ornaments or fluency is lost. The real poet loves the earth, stands up for the stupid and crazy, re-examines all he has been told, and does not spend his time in unnecessary work.

The greatest poet is the one complete lover of the known universe. Suffering, darkness, death, and fear cannot jar him, and he is sure of the fruition of his love and of perfection and beauty. The pleasure of poems lies not in those with the handsomest tropes, but in those who bring passion to your individual character as you hear it. The greatest poet connects the past, present, and future; he does not moralize but knows the soul.

Simplicity is the art of art, the sunshine of the light of letters. The flawless triumph of art captures with perfect rectitude the movement of animals and the sentiment of plants. The greatest poet is the nondistorting channel of thoughts, things, and himself. Unrestraint proves the old red blood and stainless gentility of the great poets; nothing is finer than their "silent defiance advancing out of new forms." They engage a reader on equal terms. American bards will be generous, affectionate and encouraging of competitors, not regionalists, but lovers of the entire country.

The perfect poem will reflect the structures discovered by scientists, and the beauty of poems is the final applause of science. Any supernatural elements will depart like a dream, for there is nothing more divine than men and women. The master knows that everyone is unspeakably great and that to be is just as great as to perceive and tell.

Political liberty is indispensable to the great masters. They are full of hazard for the despot and full of hope for the slave. Liberty knows no discouragement and is always the last to go; it exists even after helpless innocent people are put back into the grip of the grippers (a reference to the Fugitive Slave Act of 1850 that forced northern authorities to assist in the capture of escaped slaves). Only when life and the souls of men and women end will the instinct of liberty disappear from that part of the earth.

Poets of the cosmos with an emphasis on the real body and soul are superior to the writers of fiction and romance. The real owners of libraries are those who read, and artists who observe natural proportions are superior to those who do not. Clean and vigorous children are conceived only in the presence of models of natural forms, and there is no need of romances as soon as history is properly told. Great poets are known by their perfect personal candor, and there never grew "a being whose instinct hated the truth."

Like HENRY DAVID THOREAU, he bemoans the years men spend moneymaking and the underhanded dodges that lead to surplus while others starve. All that is thought or done affects one throughout life; every depravity or indulgence is returned with interest, while every vigorous, benevolent, and clean action is profitable. All good causes, such as aiding fugitive slaves, continue to benefit those who undertake them. Truth is whatever satisfies the soul. The young man who risks

everything and loses his life has done exceedingly well, while the old man who hoards his riches but risked nothing never achieved anything worth mentioning.

The direct trial for the greatest poet of today is if he does not flood himself with the immediate age as with tides, but instead focuses on the merits and demerits of his own body and soul. Then he might be able to withstand the test of time.

A great poem is a beginning for a man or a woman, and a great poet takes them into regions previously unattained. The work of the priests is done, and a superior breed of prophets en masse will take their place, with every man being his own priest (Whitman's Quaker background may be responsible for this remark).

The English language is brawny and limber enough to satisfy the aspirations of Americans. Everything else must answer to American standards, especially toward the goal of producing "goodshaped and wellhung men" and their perfect mates.

Only the demeanor of the vital and great can satisfy the expectation for the vital and the great; the polite and timid leave no mark. An individual is as superb as a nation if he possesses the qualities that make a superb nation. "The proof of a poet is that his country absorbs him as affectionately as he has absorbed it."

"PRESENTIMENT—IS THAT LONG SHADOW—ON THE LAWN—" EMILY DICKINSON (published 1951)

In the 19th century, many people still believed that it was possible to communicate with the dead (spiritualism) and in other forms of supernatural phenomena. In EMILY DICKINSON's short poem the speaker uses a natural phenomenon (the formation of long shadows on the lawn as the sun sets) to illustrate how a premonition could work.

Because the subject borders on the occult, the speaker suspends the usual laws of the physical universe. Hence there is talk of suns (line 2) even though our planet has only one, and the grass has an emotional life (it becomes "startled" in line 3). The word "Notice" requires an even larger leap of faith, however, since as it is used here, it denotes a formal announcement by an authority of some kind. This suggests an entire system of extrasensory sensations that operates beyond the reach of our tangible sciences and our five universally recognized senses.

Premonitions typically forecast bad outcomes like a serious accident or death just as the long shadows of late afternoon point toward the setting sun; each event represents a type of darkness. Since the phrase "to pass" (line 4) is a common euphemism for death, few lines are as ominous as "Darkness is about to pass," especially with a dash after "Darkness" to indicate a dramatic pause.

"THE PROBLEM" RALPH WALDO EMERSON (1839) The problem was that RALPH WALDO EMERSON, a former Unitarian minister who resigned from a prestigious Boston congregation in 1832 when he could no longer administer the communion rites he had begun to doubt, still felt drawn by the trappings of his former office. He liked a church (a term which may refer to the institution as well as the architecture of individual churches), a cowl (a monk's garment with a hood) and "a prophet of the soul" (line 2). Monastic aisles (probably not just the physical corridors of a monastery, but also the prescribed paths of behavior to which monks are devoted) strike his heart like music, or thoughtful smiles. However, he would not trade places with a monk even "for all his faith can see" (the promise of heaven; line 5). He personally could not endure the vestments and wonders why he finds the garments alluring when others wear them.

The third stanza praises acts of simple piety whether they resulted in the Statue of Zeus at Olympia created by Phidias (in the fifth century before Christ; after 800 years it was carted to Constantinople and probably lost in a fire) or the pronouncements of the Oracle at Delphi (which for more than a thousand years ending in the third century A.D. dispensed cryptic advice from the lips of supposedly divinely inspired women when consulted). The speaker ascribes the teachings of the Bible (dubbed "burdens" in line 14 because of the obligations they placed on the faithful) to the heart of nature, and the litanies of nations to the "burning core below" (the passions of the common people that create the canticles [songs] of love and woe; lines 17–18). When Michelangelo created the dome of St. Peter's Basilica and the groins (curved lines where vaults [ceil-

ing features] intersect; line 20) of Rome's churches, he was under God's influence and "builded [built] better than he knew" (line 24).

Similarly the speaker asks what wove the bird's nest and drove the building of a fish's shell (possibly a reference to cuttlefish or nautilus [free-swimming marine species which, although cephalopods and technically not fish, do grow shells] or simply shellfish, which includes such mollusks as oysters and clams; line 27). Nature grew these holy piles, a force which he implicitly contrasts with the "love and terror" that "laid the tiles" (of most human construction). A personified Earth wears the Parthenon, the Pyramids and England's abbeys like gems (perhaps because) the vast soul (line 48) caused the human master (artist, architect, and builder) to shape them as naturally as the grass grows. This is the same power that uses chanting choirs to entrance a congregation's heart and that inspires sermons. The willing mind can detect whispers from the Holy Ghost in artificial as well as natural designs. The speaker appreciates the beautiful expression of St. John of Antioch (the "Chrysostom of line 65), St. Augustine, and Jeremy Taylor (who blended the thought of those two predecessors). He/she also admires the eloquence of the Anglican bishop Taylor and keeps his cowled (wearing the hooded garment mandated by his order) portrait near, but would not be him "for all his faith can see."

"THE PROLOGUE" ANNE BRADSTREET (1650) At first, ANNE BRADSTREET's prologue reads like an apology for her limitations as a poet, but it should also be read as a declaration of independence, a remarkable proto-feminist document several centuries ahead of its time. The prestige of British poetry was still rising in the mid-17th century; it had not yet reached the point where refined taste insisted on elevated language, noble subjects such as the death of kings, and homage to its Greek or Roman precedents, but as her prologue attests, Bradstreet already felt such pressures. Moreover, the age was so deeply biased against women that it was generally considered wasteful to formally educate them. Bradstreet responded in a variety of ways; first, she disingenuously pleads that since she could not hope to compete in such a celebrated arena, she was forced to shift her focus elsewhere. Then she proceeds to phrase her argument with such precision and such strict adherence to form that even the staunchest advocate of male supremacy would have to grudgingly admit that she was writing poetry, albeit of an inferior sort due to its low subject matter. To avoid being dismissed as uneducated, Bradstreet not only demonstrates her familiarity with Greek mythology but deftly applies it to her own situation. Lest she be thought too proud for having produced a book, initially she so thoroughly and humbly downplays the accomplishment as to prompt male defense of the project.

The initial problem of this poem was that Bradstreet had to create an environment in which her work would be judged on its intrinsic merit and not summarily dismissed as women's work, a pejorative term at that time. This task was complicated because the bulk of her poems focus on what would later be celebrated as women's issues. In the first stanza, Bradstreet establishes her modesty and begins defending her subject matter; she must not focus on great events or royalty or war because her "mean pen" (mediocre talent) is not up to the task. In line 5, she will not even claim the title of poet, for like the historians of her day, real poets focused on those putatively higher subjects. She has no expectation beyond obscurity for her work, and the fact that she chose to write in traditional forms with careful rhymes and strict adherence to meter will not diminish the effectiveness of these choices when abler hands use them more properly.

On the subject of history, most Puritans favored the translated work of Guillaume du Bartas, a Frenchman, because of his focus on Christian history, and Bradstreet devotes the second stanza to contrasting his sugared lines with her own relatively lackluster efforts. She argues that her humbler choice of subject matter was forced on her because she is so simple (line 12), but what to make of her "wondering eyes and envious heart" of line 7? Could that line perk up the reader's interest because of the femininity of the author? This stanza also mentions the Muses for the first time in the poem, but the speaker regrets that they favored Bartas so much and herself so little.

The third stanza begs a Freudian interpretation. The poem shifts from the Greek Muses of the prior stanza to the speaker's personal Muse, and the mood has become far more intimate and subjective. In contrast with the virility of the real poets, the speaker feels no more masculine than a schoolboy. What is the defect that so discombobulates her "foolish, broken, (and) blemished Muse" (line 17)? Although it would take about two and a half more centuries until Sigmund Freud would state it more pointedly, the imagery of this stanza suggests a profound envy for the more obvious parts of the male anatomy, without which the poet, like her Muse, feels inadequate for the task at hand, and the speaker asserts that no art can make up for this irreparable fact of nature (line 18). In light of Bradstreet's substantial achievement in poetry, the stanza seems a remarkably sarcastic, implicit indictment of the phallocentric society into which the poet was born.

In the next stanza, the speaker differentiates her defect from that of Demosthenes, who overcame a childhood lisp to become a great orator. Art proved his salvation, but there is no relief for a member of her gender as her "weak or wounded brain admits no cure" (line 24) despite the fact that she was well enough read in the classics to illustrate her argument with the appropriate reference.

Far from pandering to the gender that not only constituted the overwhelming majority of the poetry-reading public but maintained the patriarchy governing church and state and jealously guarded its power, Bradstreet is openly confrontational. Rendering herself "obnoxious to each carping tongue" (line 25), she anticipates malicious attacks on her lack of domesticity and on her poetry, which will probably be dismissed as either stolen or accidental. She may be so angry on this point that her poem becomes ungrammatical and her diction so contorted that the exact meaning of line 27, "A poet's pen all scorn I should thus wrong" is obscure; everywhere else her work is remarkable for its clarity.

Since classical allusions bore such weight among the educated elite of her day, she tries to bolster support for her feminism by pointing out the exalted stature of the Muses in Greek mythology. She is well enough read, however, to realize that in antiquity, most Greek men did not share her sympathies. The contrast between these Greeks, who did nothing but "play the fools and lie" (line 36), and the reverence for poets and historians expressed in the first stanza of this poem, is profound. The implication is that the subjects explored in women's poetry, especially this woman's poetry, are as valid as the more worldly themes covered in more conventional poetry. The theme of the second half of the poem is expressed in line 37, "(Let) women (be) what they are."

The classical allusions apparently calmed the speaker down to the point where she accepts male dominance as seemingly natural, although she cannot avoid the parting shot of line 39, "It is but vain unjustly to wage war." She claims that all she wants is "some small acknowledgement of ours" (line 42); the possessive final pronoun refers more generally to "our accomplishments as women" as well as "our poetry."

Although her male readership was the implied audience of the entire poem, the last stanza is addressed to the male authors with whom in her day lay the determining voice in evaluating poetic merit. At last she defends the value of her own work; although her own lack of polish will set off the glistering gold of their work, note that since hers is "mean and unrefined ore" (line 47), it is still precious. She is perhaps less sanguine in praising their work than it would appear at first glance; they are not eagles or some other majestic image, but merely high-flown quills who, with their prey, always catch praise (lines 43–44) almost like a feather duster. In insisting on the difference between men's and women's poetry, she requests not the laurel wreaths of the celebrated poets and other predominantly male heroes of antiquity, but a more domestic thyme or parsley wreath from the kitchen. She is confident that if even her most powerful male peers read her lowly lines, they would deem them worthy of an award.

"PROLOGUE" (FROM *PREPARATORY MEDITATIONS*) Edward Taylor (published 1939)

Because love is the greatest gift a human being can tender, Edward Taylor chose to cast this poem and all his meditations in *Venus and Adonis* stanzas (traditionally consisting of six 10-syllable lines rhymed ababcc). Although the Shakespeare poem that lent its name to the form dealt with a pagan god's love for a mortal, Taylor adopted it as a suitable vehicle to convey his love for his Christian God.

In place of the traditional evocation of the muse, Taylor appealed directly to God for guidance in perfecting himself as an instrument whose songs would not be unpleasant to Him. Since the Bible revealed that God created man out of dust and asserted that he would return to dust, in the first stanza the speaker realizes that his efforts are doomed to inconsequence unless God furnishes an appropriate pen, ink, and design.

Most writers enjoy the physicality of pen and paper, and in the second stanza, the speaker puts us in touch with the tools available in the 17th century. Quills were fashioned from bird feathers, but for this audience the speaker would have no less than a quill made of a feather from an angel's wing (line 7). Instead of ink, he would write in liquid gold on crystal instead of paper. Even with such superior equipment, he could only blot (a consequence of too much ink on the pen), blur (which frequently happened with inferior, too-absorbent paper), jag, and jot (signs of inferior handwriting by an unsteady hand) unless God made the scribe (the "scrivener" of line 12; a clerk who typically only copies documents) as well as the pen.

The speaker would gladly sharpen his pen "on Zion's precious stone" (line 16), a phrase that suggests he would gladly study the Bible as a means of proceeding appropriately. Properly inspired, he would persevere until God's glory will flame forth from his song. He only asks that the effort not destroy him (line 19) and that God not laugh at his results; He should overlook the failings in the work of His "crumb of dust" (line 24).

With divine guidance, Taylor will use his pen to prove the existence of God and His supremacy. If God chooses to work through him, His works will shine like flower blossoms or gemstones (lines 29–30). For a good Puritan like Taylor, the process of transformation from dust to gemstone depended not only upon his constant devotion and religious practice, but ultimately upon God's grace.

"A PROMPT—EXECUTIVE BIRD IS THE JAY" Emily Dickinson (published 1951)

Readers familiar with the blue jays of the eastern United States may appreciate this tribute to the raucous bird, and EMILY DICKINSON's contemporaries might have laughed as she compared it to some of the stereotypically pompous officials of her day.

The male bird might bring a business executive (line 1) to mind because of his alert challenge to foot traffic and other intruders into his area; his territorial challenges can sound like the incessant carping criticism of a micromanaging boss. Bailiffs are the officers charged with maintaining order while a judicial court is in session. Their "hymns" (line 2) consist of the official announcements they must make to the entire room. While the calls of the jays might be considered more "brittle" than those heard in the court, the latter tend to be equally brief and authoritative (a consideration expressed by the phrase "warrant in every line."

A brigadier is a one-star general; such powerful men might be seen astride a horse or sitting on a reviewing stand as "confident and straight" (line 6) as the proud bird (blue jays are crested and striped, attributes which, along with their alert martial bearing, probably brought a military uniform to mind). In March (the bird's nesting and breeding season), his "mien" (his appearance) can also bring to mind a magistrate (a minor judge).

PROSODY AND FREE VERSE America lacked a strong tradition of stylistically innovative verse prior to the mid-19th century. ANNE BRADSTREET was the first American poet of note, but the versification in her poems consists of sometimes strained iambic pentameter lines. She did vary the length of her stanzas ("The PROLOGUE" consists of six-line stanzas rhymed *ababcc*. "Contemplations," another early poem, featured seven-line stanzas rhymed *ababccc,* and still other poems were not separated into stanzas at all, and typically consist of successive lines of rhymed couplets. She could also shorten the lines by a foot (turning them into tetrameters) to describe her feelings when her house burned down and in other poems (such as "The FLESH AND THE SPIRIT"), but the metrical simplicity of her forms stands in sharp contrast to the richness of her imagery and the depth of her thought. She found the same basic pattern suitable for her love poems to her husband and her elegies for her infant grandchildren. Placed in the best possible light, her simple versification might be viewed

as analogous to the relationship between her rich personal life and her rather staid Puritanical beliefs: The content of the poems celebrates the freedom of private thoughts that can flourish in accordance with, and less frequently in spite of, the doctrine.

MICHAEL WIGGLESWORTH's *The DAY OF DOOM* was similarly lacking in ostentation when it comes to metrical sophistication, but it made up for its bland presentation with stunning depictions of the horrific catastrophe that Christ's return to earth in the role of judge represents for the bulk of mankind. The use of an unchallenging ballad meter (broken into stanzas of alternating eight and six syllables, the lines sometimes rhyme *ababcdcd,* but more frequently only the six-syllable lines rhyme: *abcbdefe*) may suggest the ease with which the final judgments could be handed down. It had the added advantage, however, that it was also used in *The Bay Psalm Book,* an early American attempt to accommodate church choirs by adapting parts of the King James Bible to serve as the lyrics in their songs. When pressed into church service, the ballad meter became known as the common meter since so many of the religious songs fit this pattern. A third Puritan writer, EDWARD TAYLOR, was far more versatile in his versification, but he intended his poems to facilitate his private communion with God and may not have wanted them to survive him. A glance at his versification reveals much of the history of his development as a poet; early on, rendering the psalms of the Bible into common meter enabled him to develop an understanding of rhythm and pace. From there his experiments with 10-syllable lines can be seen in early works such as "The SOUL'S GROAN TO CHRIST FOR SUCCOR." and "HUSWIFERY" (his most frequently anthologized work), and in such a late poem as "MEDITATION 150." The tetrameter lines that begin "CHRIST'S REPLY" bring to mind a nursery rhyme, an appropriate metrical response indicative of the vast divides separating the human audience from the divine speaker, but the enjambment of the tetrameter lines of "UPON A WASP CHILLED WITH COLD" permit that poem to read as if it were an accurate presentation of a natural speaking voice.

Religion dominated the poetry scene in Massachusetts, and the popular anthologies of American literature in the 21st century generally leave the impression that little was stirring elsewhere in the colonies. The most important exception is EBENEZER COOK's "The SOT-WEED FACTOR," a satire which takes its dominant pattern (successive rhyming tetrameter lines) from the English poet Samuel Butler's *Hudibras* (a satire of the British Puritans completed in 1680).

For an extended period of time, American verse fell under the spell of Alexander Pope (1688–1744), a British poet who regularized verse forms and perfected the heroic couplet (rhymed pairs of the familiar iambic pentameter lines) originally popularized by Geoffrey Chaucer in the 14th century. To have their poems seriously considered from then until the middle of the 19th century, American poets often felt they had to use a traditional verse form to express themselves. The rules were unofficial but well known, and they reinforced the conservative class system of the British homeland. Thus the best 18th-century American poets tended to exhibit their mastery of a relatively few poetic forms, which originally had been borrowed from ancient Greek and Roman texts during the Renaissance, an intellectual and cultural rediscovery that added Italian and other continental models to the realm of "acceptable" verse forms. Instead of searching for an original form more closely linked with their subject and their message, they were likely to rely on their training. Those who came from the ranks of the best-educated people were privileged to have had extensive exposure to the ancient classics as well as the rich history of native British verse at their private schools and expensive universities.

In 18th-century American literature, divides had once existed between the conventional poets who benefited from English educations (or the best American colleges or private tutoring that replicated their exposure to the Greek and Roman classics); those who wrote anonymously with an eye toward rendering scripture into a form more accessible to the masses; and those who sought a public venue for their political views. By the middle of the century, the conventional poets might entertain the faint hope of seeing their work printed on both sides of the Atlantic, while the less educated were more likely to turn their attention to creating the doggerel that sometimes helped fill newspaper space. Neither party could hope to earn a

living by creating poetry, but it was PHILLIS WHEATLEY, by her mastery of traditional form, knowledge of classical myths as well as biblical examples, and the topicality of certain of her subjects ("TO HIS EXCELLENCY, GENERAL WASHINGTON" springs to mind) who was able to convince her peers of her worth.

In PHILIP FRENEAU, who came to be regarded as *the* poet of the American Revolution, we find the first American poet with a wider repertoire of poetic options and a fuller career of creative work. Although his early work continued the practice of tetrameters and heroic couplets, he also wrote three poems in blank verse (lines of unrhymed iambic pentameter), becoming the first poet in America to popularize that pattern (Allen 2). His more popular poems (such as "TO SIR TOBY") make use of the rhymed 10-syllable or eight-syllable lines (in poems as diverse as "The WILD HONEY SUCKLE" and "ON THE UNIVERSALITY AND OTHER ATTRIBUTES OF THE GOD OF NATURE") with which we are already familiar.

The honor of being the first American sonneteer of note, however, goes to David Humphreys, who wrote a dozen of them prior to 1800, and the first major poet to really succeed with the form was HENRY WADSWORTH LONGFELLOW, who used the form to honor his predecessors (see "CHAUCER" and "DIVINA COMMEDIA"). WILLIAM CULLEN BRYANT also experimented with the sonnet (in "TO COLE, THE PAINTER, DEPARTING FOR EUROPE," and a handful of other poems). FREDERICK GODDARD TUCKERMAN (author of "An UPPER CHAMBER IN A DARKENED HOUSE" and other very good sonnets) was the American who most dedicated himself to mastering the form, which EDWIN ARLINGTON ROBINSON also used with success. Among the less frequently anthologized poets, Edna St. Vincent Millay was perhaps the most accomplished sonneteer prior to the 21st century.

William Cullen Bryant's early mastery of blank verse is evident in "THANATOPSIS" and "INSCRIPTION FOR THE ENTRANCE TO A WOOD," but he was also the first American poet to effectively experiment with variations in form that would complement the meaning of a poem instead of shaping his argument to fit a traditional meter (Allen 52). In "HYMN OF THE CITY," for example, Bryant may have intended his eye rhymes ("comes" and "homes" in lines 13 and 15), absent rhymes ("solitude" and "wood" in lines 1 and 3), and irregular line lengths to suggest the incompleteness of the urban experience in comparison to the greater opportunities available in nature to commune with God.

In his essay on "The PHILOSOPHY OF COMPOSITION," EDGAR ALLAN POE tried to demonstrate how he arrived at the metrical pattern for "The RAVEN," his most famous poem. His major points related to prosody include the selection of the particular vowel sound that he thought would strike a responsive chord in an auditor, the adoption of a formal pattern of versification that allowed him to repeat key elements in the poem while continually changing their context so as to constantly alter their meaning, and his choice of a novel combination of metrical lines to underscore the originality of his poem. In a seldom-anthologized essay on "The Rationale of Verse," he less successfully attempted to state the precise principles by which prosody performed its magic, but his constant repolishing of his published poems ("The Raven" appeared in 15 different forms, for example [Allen 62]) indicates that as an artist, he was never able to reduce prosody to the science he thought it might become. Although he used a rhymed tetrameter in most of his poems, he experimented with a variety of other patterns and frequently abandoned what he had chosen in favor of other aesthetic values.

At the very moment when America began producing masters of the conventional forms (a struggle that in some ways culminated in the work of the 20th-century poet Robert Frost, whose mastery was so complete that his poems usually seem the natural expressions of their speakers and many readers are unaware of how precisely his poems conform to and benefit from their traditional patterns), RALPH WALDO EMERSON called for a uniquely American form of expression that fit the seemingly unlimited potential of the nation. Although his public lectures and the essays based on them represent his most natural modes of expression (and in this regard it is significant that his most memorable poem, "The HYMN SUNG AT THE COMPLETION OF THE CONCORD MONUMENT," was also designed with a podium in mind) and Emerson did not discover a strikingly new approach in his own poetry that adequately served his ends, WALT WHITMAN heard his lecture on "The POET"

and was encouraged to continue his experiments with what became known as free verse. Emerson began with blank verse and progressed ever closer to freer forms, but like Moses he was never able to inhabit the realm to which he directed his followers. JOHN GREENLEAF WHITTIER, HENRY WADSWORTH LONGFELLOW, and OLIVER WENDELL HOLMES all found ways of making the traditional forms—tetrameters, pentameters, ballads, odes, and couplets—work for them, but Whitman proved to be the shining beacon by which the vast majority of 20th-century poets were able to find their voices.

Emerson's influence on the younger poet is evident in Whitman's "PREFACE TO THE 1855 EDITION OF LEAVES OF GRASS." Instead of sounding like the professional newspaperman he was, Whitman apparently aped the rhetorical style of his mentor and delivered what would be a stirring speech from a platform but a befuddled essay, with little to tell us of the rationale behind the rhythms of his poetry. The truth is that he may not have cared to reveal his true methods, and may not even have known them. An introduction prepared for his London edition of Leaves (but not printed until 1999 in Selected Poems, page 309) argued that his verse lacked rhyme, the customary verbal melody, and regularity but focused the readers' attention on his earnestness and honesty, which they may find to be of more value than "the usual orderly entertainment given by authors" (310). In an early (1855) unsigned review of the same book, Whitman stated that his new style concealed rhythm and uniformity in the roots of his poems; only the luxuriant fruit they produce reveals their presence (ibid. 116).

An early form of free verse came to America with the Anglican faithful. Although the Puritans and other sects had their preferred forms of the Bible, the official church of England adopted the King James version completed in 1611. Several sections, including the Psalms, were translated by the king's men into perfect specimens of free verse, a fact that probably encouraged Whitman's early experiments in the form. A few topical, political poems from 1850 such as "The House of Friends" and "Blood Money" show Whitman's rapid transition from traditional verse to the new form, and another poem from the same year ("Resurgemus," later renamed "Europe and the 72d and 73d Years of These

States") found its way into the first edition of *Leaves of Grass* (Shucard 158).

Numerous critics have attempted to fathom the principles by which Whitman's free verse operates, and the work of most sounds more like a collection of rules for constructing good prose paragraphs instead of a concise theory of versification. In *American Prosody,* Gay Wilson Allen proposed that Whitman's line is his basic unit, and that subsequent lines form "parallelisms" based on their reinforcement through repetition, denial, or completion of its central thought (222) or repetition of its key words. Allen groups Whitman's lines into couplets, triplets, and quatrains based on their adherence to one of these four parallelisms (224), and devotes the rest of his chapter to his discovery of conventional poetic devices amid Whitman's foliage.

The sea change that swept away the 19th-century's resistance to free verse and dominated most of the 20th century's versification was not entirely of Whitman's (or Emerson's) making. Although the poems of EMILY DICKINSON did not appear in print in sizable quantities until the last decade of the 19th century, she also began deviating from the standard, acceptable metrical forms in the 1850s. It was Whitman's dogged perseverance with free verse that eventually made it acceptable, however, and it also created a popular audience for the verse experiments of Dickinson and STEPHEN CRANE in the 1890s. Dickinson began by taking the rhythms of hymns and subtly distorting their meter and distorting their anticipated rhymes with a variety of near rhymes, eye rhymes and other poetic devices as if to suggest the inadequacy of the thought presented by more conventional lyrics. Eventually she developed more original forms, but the willful deviations in her poetry's regularity continued. Just as the slightest variation in hand-spun pottery is necessary to prove its origin, her best work bears the unmistakable impress of her hand.

As the 19th century drew to a close, the vast majority of poets were still producing poems in traditional forms, including French-inspired triolets, villanelles, rondels, and rondeaus, but the most commonly anthologized poet from the period, Stephen Crane, rejected them in favor of rebelliously bare statements of ironic existentialism and bleak imagery.

BIBLIOGRAPHY

Allen, Gay Wilson. *American Prosody.* New York: Octagon Books, 1966.

Cushman, Stephen. *Fictions of Form in American Poetry.* Princeton, N.J.: Princeton University Press, 1993.

Hoffman, Daniel G. *The Poetry of Stephen Crane.* New York: Columbia University Press, 1957.

Johnson, Greg. *Emily Dickinson: Perception and the Poet's Quest.* University: University of Alabama Press, 1985.

Kirby-Smith, Henry Tompkins. *The Origins of Free Verse.* Ann Arbor: University of Michigan Press, 1996.

Porter, David T. *The Art of Emily Dickinson's Early Poetry.* Cambridge, Mass.: Harvard University Press, 1966.

Shucard, Alan. *American Poetry: The Puritans Through Walt Whitman.* Boston: Twayne Publishers, 1988.

Whitman, Walt. *Selected Poems 1855–1892.* Edited by Gary Schmidgall. New York: St. Martin's Press, 1999.

"A PSALM OF LIFE" HENRY WADSWORTH LONGFELLOW (1838)

The "psalmist" indicated as the internal audience by the subtitle may be a poet (as a maker of songs, or "psalms"), but given the nature of the speaker's complaints, he is more likely a reciter of biblical verses.

A problem is that his theology leaves little room for an ambitious young man or woman to make a significant difference in the world. Referring to him as a "psalmist" suggests that his biblical quotations are mere mechanical recitations whose negative comments about the speaker's future hold no more weight than the auguries of a palmist, a practitioner of the discredited art of fortune telling by examining the lines on a subject's hands. This leads to the situation of the poem as it is revealed in its first two lines: The speaker is reacting to the psalmist's characterization as empty dreams of his big plans for his life.

Notice the care with which the speaker alludes to the Bible without providing his audience with a platform to launch a counterattack. The names of two of the books of what New Englanders would refer to as the Old Testament, Numbers and Psalms, are invoked as ordinary words in the subtitle and first line, although the latter is scarcely recognizable in "psalmist." The most limiting of the "mournful numbers" in the Bible is 70, the number of years Psalms 90:10 provides as the length of human days, but perhaps the implications of

Numbers 13:1–14:45 are more germane to the situation of the poem. Like wayward children, the entire nation of Israel is punished for its lack of faith in its patriarch (Moses) and his conveyance of the word of God. To the pessimistic psalmist, ambition such as the speaker exudes is almost blasphemous in that it aspires to personal greatness instead of relying on faith in God's will. Moreover, if one considers the work of the generations of men who have passed since the time of Moses, it becomes apparent that the ambitions of almost all individual men have had little effect.

To oppose the conservative, pessimistic views of his internal audience, the speaker relies on a Protestant optimism that offers salvation based on good works and faith; his plans are not empty dreams because, as the products of his soul, they offer proof that his soul is not dead. He is careful to use the religious language ("the soul is dead that slumbers," line 3) that will carry the most weight with the psalmist. Similarly, when the speaker quotes the King James version of the Bible ("Dust thou art, to dust returneth" from Genesis 3:19) in line 7, which seems to offer more support for the psalmist's argument than his own, he explains that the verse does not refer to the soul.

The third stanza contains perhaps the best poetic expression of the New England Protestant work ethic. A sense of predetermination, of being chosen by God for salvation before time began, was a major tenet of the old Calvinism of the Puritans. Good work and moral growth signified that the devotee was worthy of divine favor; adherents to that faith would examine themselves and their behavior on a daily basis for signs that they were among the elect as well as for contrary indications that they would be damned to the torments of hell for eternity.

The climatic challenges of the wilderness made the first generation of Puritans (and therefore, their intellectual descendants) constantly aware of their own mortality as if their hearts were beating "funeral marches to the grave" (line 16). The emphasis placed on individual salvation made their theology less pessimistic because there was always an opportunity for personal heroism in the present moment (stanza 6).

The seventh and eighth stanzas introduce a secular reason for living heroically. If you achieve greatness, you may inspire other people. Even if you fall short, a single lost soul, like a "forlorn and shipwrecked brother" (line 31) may come across your more ephemeral "footprints in the sand" and regain hope.

The final stanza calls for action and the courage to accept and challenge whatever fate awaits you by doing what you can ("achieving") and striving to be better ("pursuing"). At first glance, his final admonishment to work ("learn to labor," line 36) and wait may seem inherently contradictory, but within the framework of the oldest strains of New England Protestantism, it makes perfect sense.

"PSALM TWO (FIRST VERSION)" EDWARD TAYLOR (published 1981)

Although the King James authorized translation of the Bible is beautiful, its rendering of the Psalms (or "songs") lacked the rhythm and meter that would have made it easy to sing them. Although EDWARD TAYLOR's versions are markedly inferior in expression to those from which he started, they are interesting because they illustrate one of the paths a poet may follow to develop his skill.

His goal was to alter the texts so that they could fit the common meter used in a majority of the church songs. He did not have to worry about the content of the poems since he was dealing with what he believed were the words of God; indeed, he had to take great pains to insure that he did not distort their meaning in the process of adding, subtracting, or rearranging works to fit each line's syllabic count (each stanza except the last contains eight lines that alternate between eight and six syllables). The second psalm is interesting because it deals with God's response to those who resist him. Although the entire Bible was thought to have been divinely inspired and directed, in this psalm God empowers his earthly king to speak on His behalf to such rebels.

The God of the Hebrew Bible, many of the books of which were retained as sacred texts by the Christians and incorporated into their own Bible as part of the Old (that is, pre-Christ) Testament, had many more human characteristics than He manifests in the New Testament. His mercurial temperament becomes evident in the second stanza as he "laughs deridingly" (line 10), but He has empowered the king of Zion to voice his decree that his chosen people could have all the lands of the earth for the asking. With God on their side, they could break their enemies into pieces with a rod of iron, shattering them like a weak clay pot (stanza four). Even kings should fear God, rejoice in His power, and embrace the king of Zion lest His anger bring down God's wrath.

"PUBLICATION IS THE AUCTION" EMILY DICKINSON (published 1951)

The affluence of EMILY DICKINSON's family provided her with the opportunity to refrain from publishing her poems during her lifetime and freed her from the necessity of supporting herself financially through a serious of mind-numbing jobs so injurious to the creative spirit, or from the distractions brought by a husband and children. Thus she had the freedom to condemn publication as the auction of the mind (instead of the auction of products of the mind). It is true, however, that to find a willing publisher she would have had to create commercially viable verse, an intrusion into the artistic process that made her uncomfortable. Poverty might justify avoidance of "so foul a thing" (line 4), but the real crux of her argument lies in that troublesome term "justifying" (line 3), which in the Calvinist tradition meant the process (usually painful) by which souls were prepared for heaven. Thus if poverty resulted from her abstinence from publication, she could look at it not just as ennobling but as a soul-purifying penance.

She would rather go "White" (with a spotless soul; line 7) from her Garret (a small second-story and [thus presumably second-rate] room) to the "White Creator" (her equally sin-free God) than to "invest" (line 8; she uses the term almost as pejoratively as "infest;" it recalls the central problem of the commercialization of poetry) her Snow (the purity of her vision; line 8).

Like Snow, thought belongs to God ("Him who gave it," line 9) and to Jesus ("Him who bear Its Corporeal illustration," lines 10–11). She would rather sell the air she breathes (referred to as "Royal Air" [line 12]; she puns on the notion of "the royal we," an author's referral to herself with the plural pronoun as a means of maintaining emotional distance from an unpleasant subject. Notice her use of this device throughout the second stanza).

She counsels being "the Merchant of the Heavenly Grace" (the provider of parcels from God; line 13), but would not have her Human Spirit reduced to the "Disgrace of Price" (line 16).

PURITAN POETRY

That colonies as small as those of 17th-century Massachusetts could produce two poets whose work still rewards readers four centuries later might seem miraculous until one recalls that Shakespeare and several of the other glorious Elizabethan poets still lived in the country of their births at the start of their century, that ANNE BRADSTREET was born during the reign of King James I, whose authorized version of the Bible is still perceived as so extraordinarily poetic that many people believe it presents the true voice of God, and that both Bradstreet and EDWARD TAYLOR were products of the same religious movement that produced John Milton, the leading poet of his generation. The first flowering of Massachusetts literati sprang not from the castoff dregs of English society; in some ways, they can be viewed as a late vintage of its finest stock.

The strictest Puritans who settled in Massachusetts were medieval in their longing to have God make his presence felt in every aspect of their lives. The greatest challenge facing the true believers and, especially, their ministers, was reconciling the terrible adversities that, in time, come to every human life, with their faith in a benevolent deity. Thus Bradstreet thanks God not only "FOR DELIVERANCE FROM A FEVER" but also for this chastisement that brings her closer to her faith. A loss of property, as she explains in "HERE FOLLOWS SOME VERSES UPON THE BURNING OF OUR HOUSE," can be equally beneficial, but even she cannot so readily come to terms with the deaths of her grandchildren. Taken as a whole, however, Bradstreet's poetry expresses her satisfaction with her roles as wife, mother, dutiful daughter, and good Puritan.

A major challenge for any religion is to explain the existence of evident evil, death, and loss. The minister Edward Taylor's response can be discovered in the two poems "The SOUL'S GROAN TO CHRIST FOR SUCCOR" and "CHRIST'S REPLY." Perhaps the greater challenge for him personally was trying to maintain his faith at the sublime level of his first experience, a struggle evident in

"The EBB AND FLOW." Much of his poetry examined the fixtures of his world and such specimens of nature as crossed his path for hints at the nature of the divinity that each embodied.

MICHAEL WIGGLESWORTH's *The Day of Doom* placed the apocalyptic terrors of the Bible in the popular church song meter of his day. The result still conveys its primal fears, even though Puritanism continued to wane throughout the 18th century, a victim of the rationalism of the Enlightenment and competition from other sects. Today the term Puritan is used derisively, but the work of its three enduring poets helps later centuries realize how extraordinary it felt for them to live in a world in which God battled the forces of evil for the eternal possession of their souls.

Q

QUAKER POETRY Although the Society of Friends was extremely influential in shaping popular opinion towards such core principles of American democracy as religious tolerance and political independence, its impact on poetry is largely felt through the influence of JOHN GREENLEAF WHITTIER, renowned as the primary Quaker poet. Vestiges of a Quaker childhood can also be found in the numerology and spiritual independence of WALT WHITMAN's poetry.

The Quakers were formed in England by George Fox and a tight circle of like-minded men in 1648 as a reaction against what they perceived as the doctrinal excesses of the Church of England. Their prestige in America was advanced enormously by the extensive land grants awarded to William Penn in 1681 in repayment for a loan to the king by Penn's father. Along with Rhode Island, Pennsylvania became an early haven against religious persecution at a time when the Puritan theocrats of New England were banishing dissidents and, in a few cases, condemning them to death. Rejecting the concept of original sin advanced by other faiths, the Quakers believed in the innate goodness of man and God's communication with an individual through the Inner Light, the small still voice inside one that can serve as a moral compass. Unlike the services led by the ministers of other denominations, in their meetings Quakers often waited for the divine spirit to move one of their number to speak and sometimes adjourned by mutual consent after a period of silence. The society embraced the name Quaker after their

detractors used the term pejoratively in reference to the paroxysms sometimes manifest among a small number of adherents as a literal response to Fox's injunction to tremble at the word of the Lord. In addition to other good works, the Quakers early advocated the abolition of slavery and opposed war and other violence.

Of the Whittier poems discussed in this volume, "LAUS DEO" and "ABRAHAM DAVENPORT" best reveal the poet's religious beliefs. The former celebrates the congressional passage of the Thirteenth Amendment to the U.S. Constitution that banned slavery and interprets that law as proof that God reigns. "Abraham Davenport" recalls the calming influence of a self-possessed man who, convinced that the Lord wanted them to focus on the business at hand, steadied the legislature in the face of a wicked storm. In "SNOW-BOUND," the speaker's mother drew on her Quaker books for inspiring tales when the evening's forced inactivity rendered the family dependent upon their own resources for entertainment. The fact that an uncle, an unrelated schoolteacher and an older woman shared the family's warmth reveals much about the Quakers' hospitality and their sense of community.

Quakers rejected the conventional names of the weeks and months because they honored pagan gods ("Wednesday" is derived from "Woden's Day," for example) or Roman emperors ("August" memorializes Augustus Caesar). They preferred numbers in accordance with biblical precedent (see Deuteronomy 1:3 and II Chronicles 29:17, for example), a tradition that served Walt Whitman well whenever the resulting numerology enhanced the content of a poem. Hence the "ninth-month" is mentioned in "OUT OF THE CRADLE ENDLESSLY ROCKING" as a clue that the speaker is really dealing with his birth as a poet. Whitman's sense of the rightness of professing one's beliefs in accordance with one's personal insights can also be viewed within the Quaker tradition, and the association makes his pronouncements appear far less egotistical (Hintz 67–69).

BIBLIOGRAPHY

Hintz, Howard W. *The Quaker Influence in American Literature.* Port Washington, N.Y.: Kennikat Press, 1965.

Oliver, Charles M. *Critical Companion to Walt Whitman: A Literary Reference to His Life and Work.* New York: Facts On File, 2006.

Vining, Elizabeth Gray. *Mr. Whittier.* New York: The Viking Press, 1974.

R

"THE RAVAGED VILLA" HERMAN MELVILLE (1891)

HERMAN MELVILLE's poem bemoans the lack of appreciation for artistic tradition (symbolized by the broken pottery of line 1), nature (something has clogged up the fountain of the sun; line 4), noble achievement (a spider infests the laurel), beauty (weeds drive out the flowers) and art (a bust of Apollo is burned to make lime; lines 7–8). The culprit is identified in the last line: the aesthetics of the age are being dictated by (and consumed by) "Mammon's tower" (line 8; Mammon is identified with the accumulation of riches in Matthew 6:24 and Luke 16:9–13). In other words, an emphasis on acquiring wealth has become the top priority in American society, displacing the acquisition of taste.

"THE RAVEN" EDGAR ALLAN POE (1845)

This is arguably the single most famous poem in all of American literature, and rightly so. The reasons for its tremendous popularity begin with its accessibility; even younger readers can respond to the talking bird and its rhythmic repetitions whereas a more mature audience will find their patience rewarded with, first, a love story and then a revelation of the narrator's grief, which may be driving him to the point of madness. Poe's older contemporaries could appreciate classical references in the poem, but the implications of having the bird perched upon a bust would not have been lost on those his own age and younger. Class-conscious Americans could appreciate the elegance of the chamber and the correctness of the highly educated narrator's diction, and everyone can appreciate the skill with which Poe turns humor into horror. Ever the master of suspense, Poe slowly reveals the information that lets the reader gradually realize the situation for himself. Although the surface story deals with the occult, the poem rejects the spiritualism popular at the time in favor of a psychological study.

In his essay on "The PHILOSOPHY OF COMPOSITION," Poe points out the originality of its alternating lines of octameter acatalectic with lines of tetrameter catalectic. Few poets since have adopted this measure, but the tightly closed form with its insistence on repetition is a perfect blend of form and function for a mystery. Some of the other novel effects achieved by his application of the principles of rhyme and alliteration contribute more greatly to its success. He suggests that its length is perfect for preserving an audience's emotion for the maximum length of time, but it probably did not hurt the poem's enduring popularity that it also turns out to be a perfect length for inclusion in literary anthologies.

The poem commences with the language of the fairy tale, with the important twist that the time in "once upon a time" is specified as dreary midnight. The situation is rather mysterious since the speaker describes himself as pondering "weak and weary" over many "quaint" (so old-fashioned as to strike even him as weird) volumes of "forgotten lore" (line 2). Such a characterization of his books suggests that he was skeptical of their content, but the fact that he was pondering them implies that he must have been taking them seriously on some level. Judging from the events that then unfold, he had probably been reading fables in which animals talk and act more or less as humans.

The speaker had almost fallen asleep when he heard a gentle tapping on his chamber door; his reaction suggests that the reading material ran to the occult since he quickly offered a rational explanation for the disturbance. He muttered (a verb conveying his irritation with the interruption despite his desultory reading) that it was "*only* this and nothing more" (line 6). Such a self-calming response suggests that his reading, his half-dream, or some other aspect of his life must have frightened him.

The second stanza reveals more information about the speaker and his situation. It was so late on a December night that the fire had nearly burned out. This natural phenomenon paralleled the speaker's dimming consciousness, and the light from each dying ember created a ghost on the floor. He tries to hide his fear by only admitting that he eagerly wished for morning (line 9) but reveals the purpose of his reading: to borrow "surcease" (an end) to his sorrow for the lost Lenore. The angels may use the name of the "rare and radiant maiden" but she will remain nameless on earth for evermore (a euphemism for her death).

At this point something inexplicable happens: each purple curtain (its darkness reinforcing the gloom of the chamber even as its regal coloring points to the wealth of the speaker) emits a "silken, sad, uncertain rustling" (line 13). The speaker is not just scared, he is thrilled, filled with "fantastic terrors never felt before." To still his beating heart, he goes back to the formula that helped him earlier, repeating that it was only a late night visitor at the chamber door. Nineteenth-century readers would be familiar with the raps and moving curtains from accounts of the séances with which spiritualists supported their claims of having contacted the dead.

Suddenly craving human contact probably helped his "soul grow stronger" (line 19). Addressing himself to the unseen visitor, he implored his or her forgiveness with the excuse that his napping made him uncertain of the reality of the faint tapping. The ele-

gance of his language and the precision with which he expresses the correct social phrases indicate his good manners and advanced education, which would have struck Poe's original audience as additional signs of the speaker's wealth. He threw the door wide open, but found only darkness.

He stood, wondering and fearing, and peered into the darkness "doubting" his senses but also perhaps his religious convictions. Above all else, he doubted that it was possible for the spirit of his dead Lenore to return to him even though that was his most fervent wish, leading him to "dreaming dreams no mortal ever dared to dream before" (line 26). The silence was unbroken and the stillness gave no "token" (a term spiritualists could use to designate a noise indicative of the presence of a spirit). His desire soon overcoming doubt, he whispered "Lenore," which an echo murmured back.

Turning back into the chamber, he felt "all my soul within me burning" (with desire, but those of his readers with fundamentalist religious beliefs might take this as a sign of his damnation for wishing to contact the dead; line 31). Soon the tapping began anew, which he decided to explore even though he thought it was caused by the wind against the window "lattice" (strips of wood dividing a window into smaller panes of glass typically found in the more elegant homes; line 33).

Language is as tremendously important in this poem as it must have been to the speaker if his generally formal speech is an indication. Note how his wavering syntax at the beginning of the seventh stanza (one usually would not say "open here I flung" in English but would put *open* at the end of the verbal phrase "flung open") suggests that he is frightened by the situation. Up to this point he has entertained the half-frightening and half-joyous notion that the rapping he heard might have come from Lenore's spirit, a possibility still maintained in his initial description of his guest's entrance "with many a flirt and flutter" (line 37). These hopes and fears are dashed, however, by the appearance of the title character, a "stately" Raven who walks in (like royalty) instead of flying. This is such unexpected behavior that it seems out of "the saintly days of yore" (line 38), a reminder that the speaker's night began with a "volume of forgotten lore" (line 2).

The speaker is one of the chief attractions of the poem. Truly multidimensional, his description of the bird's initial behavior reveals that even upon its arrival he was not unaware of the humor of the situation. He expected at least a semblance of obeisance (an outward sign of respect) from the bird as would befit his role as host and because he belonged to a more advanced, highly dangerous species, but the raven stepped in (his not flying connects with the birds of the speaker's reading; line 38) without hesitation; indeed, it possessed the mien (the bearing or manner) of a lord or lady (line 40). As if elevated by magic (since the narrator does not mention its flight), it perched on a bust of Pallas (or Athena, the Greek goddess of wisdom) above his chamber door. Symbolically, this would suggest the ascendance of the occult over learning and perhaps death over life, but the sculpture also points to the speaker's wealth, his education in classical Greek literature, and his affinity for pagan iconography instead of Christian or other modern religious symbols. Left to his own intellectual resources but ignorant of any faith that might help him through just such a crisis as he was facing at that moment, the speaker will succumb to a despair that takes him to the brink of insanity.

The grave and stern decorum of the ebony bird's countenance beguile ("charm" or "trick," a term that recalls the raven's role as trickster in many cultures; line 43) the speaker's "sad fancy" into smiling. Taken aback by the bird's demeanor, he tries to put it in its place by treating it with the exaggerated courtesy he would administer to a human interloper from a much lower class. He starts with veiled criticism of the bird's crest (a tuft of feathers on its head so short that he thinks it looks shaven). This brings to mind the family crests used in heraldry to designate the social position of their bearers, honors that were frequently awarded for courage on a battlefield or other service to a crown. Unsavory conduct in war or peace might lead to such honors being "shorn" (line 45), but the age and attitude of the raven suggest that it was not a coward. Its blackness suggests night and the underworld ruled by Pluto in Roman mythology; hence the speaker asks its "lordly name" on "Night's Plutonian shore" (line 47). The bird responds with the timely answer of "Nevermore."

This apt response pleased and puzzled the speaker, who "marveled [that] this ungainly fowl" (line 49) could understand his discourse (a term implying intellectual discourse and not mere speech; the speaker is still insisting on his superiority not only to the bird but to the bulk of mankind). He dismisses its answer as irrelevant (since few people before then had ever heard of bird or beast with the name of Nevermore sitting on a sculptured bust; lines 52–53) but admires its timing, for it put in its single-word response at precisely the right moment.

The bird sat lonely on the "placid" bust (an unusual adjective for an inanimate object). Since the sculpture depicts the goddess of wisdom, Poe may be suggesting that training the mind provides the intellectual distance that promotes tranquility instead of an emotional response. Thus, although the speaker is becoming uncomfortable with his uninvited guest, instead of taking action he merely comforts himself with the reflection that other friends have "flown" before (left his company). He mutters that the bird will leave in the morning just as his hopes had flown before (line 59), but the bird challenges this assumption with his typical one-word response.

Startled at yet another appropriately placed answer, the speaker attributes the word to some "unhappy master whom unmerciful Disaster followed fast and followed faster" (lines 63–64). Thus his raven picked up the melancholy burden of "Never—nevermore" (note the uncharacteristic stutter as the speaker repeats it; line 66) as "its only stock and store" (line 62; the phrase, mercantile in origin, indicates the goods immediately available in a shop and those which are warehoused more remotely).

Seeking some diversion, the speaker wheeled a cushioned seat before "this grim, ungainly, ghastly, gaunt and ominous bird of yore" (line 71) and, "linking fancy onto fancy" (lines 69–70), engaged in trying to understand the meaning of its "croaking" (here he tries to convey the sound of its voice by comparing it with the raspy call of a frog. The implied comparison with a less-developed animal may have been intended as an insult to the intelligence of his feathered guest).

Although he assumed a relaxed silence, he could feel the fowl's fiery eyes burning into his bosom's core (into his heart, popularly conceived as the seat of love). His head reclined on the velvet cushion upon which, alas, his departed Lenore would "press, ah, nevermore!" (the ejaculation "ah" conveys both his pain and his discovery of a perceived truth; line 78). The air seemed to grow denser and perfumed by a censer (a device typically used in religious ceremonies for dispensing or burning incense), and he can hear the footfalls of angels tinkling on the richly carpeted floor (line 80). The absence of any rational explanation for these sensations, which involve the speaker's touch, smelling and hearing, hasten the poor man's belief that he is in the presence of supernatural forces. Calling himself a wretch (a miserable person who has caused his own misfortune) for wasting so much time on his doubts (line 81), he thinks God has sent angels with respite (a temporary break) from his suffering and would eagerly quaff (gulp down) this nepenthe (a drug offering temporary relief from pain or sorrow, a name with which the speaker would have been familiar because of its appearance in Homer's *Odyssey* and elsewhere in ancient Greek literature. In the 19th century, almost all drugs were unregulated because their deleterious effects were unknown. A popular anodyne [pain reliever] was laudanum, a highly addictive concoction of opium and alcohol) to forget lost Lenore. But the bird ruins this reverie with his "nevermore."

Irate, the speaker calls the bird an evil prophet but nevertheless asks if he will be able to clasp the rare and radiant Lenore in Eden (or "Aidenn," here signifying heaven; line 94). The bird answers predictably, but the speaker is long past the rational thinking that would have allowed him to anticipate its response. Instead, he shrieks at the lying "bird or fiend" and would have him return to "Night's Plutonian shore" (the underworld; line 97) without leaving so much as a feather (the black plume of line 98) as a reminder of his visit. He would prefer his loneliness unbroken and pleads for the bird to "take thy beak from out my heart" and its form from his door. The bird refuses in its accustomed manner.

The raven continued to sit on the bust and still does (a sign that the speaker has internalized its message of hopelessness). Its eyes look like a dreaming demon's, and the lamp throws its shadow across the floor (line 106). This time the speaker, raving mad in the insanity of his grief (hence becoming the "raven," who is the chief study and perhaps even the eponymous character of this poem) states that the shadow will be lifted nevermore.

"THE REAL QUESTION" PAUL LAURENCE DUNBAR (1899) The history of money is long and complicated. In western Europe, coins became acceptable as mediums of exchange as long as both the buyer and seller of a commodity could agree that the value of the minerals they contained were equivalent to their face value. Eventually, paper money replaced actual coins because it was backed by a government's (or a bank's or other private issuing agency's) promise to exchange it for its specified value in gold or silver.

In Britain's American colonies, a variety of foreign coins and currencies circulated until after the American Revolution. In 1785, the new nation promised to back its paper money with silver, and in 1792, the government based the value of its dollar on a set measure of gold. Various financial crises, some directly arising from shortages in precious metals, led to fluctuations in the relative value of gold and silver, and by 1890 there was widespread support for silver-backed currency on the belief that it would make more paper money available. This probably would have made credit cheaper to obtain, and the controversy led to the creation of the Populist Party. People at all levels of society were suddenly given to impassioned debate about federal monetary policy, but gold won out, at least temporarily. In 1933, the government declared that the dollar had to be accepted as legal tender without the backing of precious metals, a system that carried it into the 21st century.

The metals debate reached its apex in the 1892 election when the Populist Party candidate (James B. Weaver) received more than a million votes for president. By the time PAUL LAURENCE DUNBAR's poem appeared, however, the controversy was no longer the hot-button issue that it had been for much of the decade. The speaker in this poem has tired of the debate and fails to see its connection with the hard economic realities of his or her life.

American humorists often like to assume rhetorical positions at the top or bottom of society so they can exploit the comedic potential of the perceived differences between themselves and their audience. The diction used in this poem suggests a speaker of very limited education, and his revelations about his finances place him among the poorest of the poor. The price of coal is rising as winter approaches, and the speaker is already a month behind in his rent. Although some people argue that gold is the only money worth the name (line 5), others say that only silver can save us from the raging goldbug that seeks to devour people.

While the debate over the gold/silver standard gets all the publicity (folks [presumably politicians] keep shouting about it, he notes in line 9), his implicit criticism is that they are doing little to alleviate the real suffering of the people (of whom he can be viewed as an example). Hams (and other meats) are scarce (because of their high price) and fowls are "roosting high" (safely beyond his reach because he cannot afford them, but the phrase also hints that he may not be above stealing chickens, given the opportunity). He is less concerned about the type of money that is circulating than with how he can acquire some money of any kind.

"REARRANGE A 'WIFE'S' AFFECTION"

EMILY DICKINSON (published 1945) This poem reads like a soliloquy by a young woman who is protesting the way that some people change after they get married: they no longer have time for their former friends and no longer share the same interests. The placing of "Wife" in quotation marks in the first line is a reflection of the speaker's confidence that the feelings she shared with the woman she knew before the latter's recent marriage were so strong that they will survive her new identity. The speaker swears that this will be the case; it will only happen when her own brain is "dislocated" (line 2; usually this only happens to bones when an external force pushes or pulls them out of their normal sockets), and when they amputate her "freckled bosom" and beard her like a man. In other words, she is as confident in the married woman's love for her as she is about her own gender identity. The pain of separation is so great for her that she can only compare it to physical mutilation. She may also be arguing that the most important relationship in her life is so independent of sex roles that it has become

a true blending of souls even without the physicality involved in marriage, or even that they might find a way somehow to overcome even the biological limits of their relationship.

In the fifth line she counsels her spirit to blush "in thy fastness" (to take pride in her commitment and perhaps to maintain her regard even to the point of public censure implied by the language of the poem's first line) and in her "unacknowledged clay" (line 6). This may refer to her virginal state (she may be "unacknowledged" in the rather precise sense that Adam "knew" Eve in Genesis 4:1, and "clay" because she had not yet undergone the test of matrimonial fire), but the malleability and physicality of clay as a sculptural medium may also hint at another dimension of their relationship. Noting her seven years of "troth" (line 7; between heterosexual couples, this was historically a more serious betrothal [conveying many more privileges and responsibilities] than the mere engagement of later centuries. Alternatively, the speaker may have appropriated the term for the time and relationship she shared with the new wife. They were more than just friends, but society's lack of a term for their special friendship underscores its failure to recognize it on any level). She argues that their mutual experience taught the wife more than Wifehood ever may (line 8); the argument may be that the wife has been seriously engaged with the speaker for so long that there should not be many surprises left in the wife's interaction with another person, and the hope seems to be that she will also have time for her after the marriage. The speaker may feel that the closeness of the "troth" they shared has taught the wife everything there is to know about relationships.

The third stanza recalls all that the two of them have been through. They maintained their love and trust even in difficult times ("in narrow pain" [line 10]; in EMILY DICKINSON's poetry the adjective implies that only pain existed in those moments), but what was the speaker's reward for her "constancy through fire" (line 11)? Nothing but pain without the benefit of any anesthetic (the painkilling "anodyne" of line 12).

In the fourth stanza she congratulates herself on so triumphantly bearing up under the circumstances that no one suspects their relationship or her suffering. She will continue wearing this "crown of thorns" (one of the torments meted out to Jesus before he was crucified; Mark 15:17 and John 19:2) until after "sunset" (line 15). The term may suggest meetings after dark (when they may secretly resume their intimacy) or after death, when she will be rewarded with a real crown (in acknowledgment of her suffering, but also perhaps a resumption of her connection with the wife is indicated). Until then, her love and loss will be bandaged and hidden, but it will never go away until the day when she (the "Weary Keeper" of her love, line 19) dies. Even then she hopes to be reunited in heaven, a place where open social recognition of their relationship may allow her to replace the crown of thorns resulting from the unacknowledged aspects of their friendship with a diadem, a jeweled crown that all may recognize.

"THE REBEL SOLDIER, OR THE POOR STRANGER" ANONYMOUS (19th century) The speaker in this sentimental folk song is a soldier of the Confederate States of America during the Civil War. After briefly touching on a few of the horrors of the battlefield, he recalls the folks left behind, the uncertainty of his immediate future, his camaraderie with a fellow soldier, and his long-term (perhaps even postmortem) goal of building a castle near his beloved Polly.

In the Civil War, grapeshot consisted of a load of small projectiles that could be fired from cannon at close range as an antipersonnel weapon against a massed infantry attack. Muskets, prized for the relative rapidity with which they could be loaded although notorious for their inaccuracy, were sometimes standard issue but also frequently brought to the war from the homes of those who carried them and might be taken here as representative of all the small arms fire to which soldiers were exposed. To mention the cannon's loud "lumber" recalls their thunderous noise as well as their unwieldy bulk. Thus the first stanza opens with a few of the sights and sounds of a battle, but it is chiefly concerned with its aftermath, the many mangled bodies of the dead men left on the field with only a blanket as their burial shroud. A one-line chorus in which the speaker reveals he is a rebel soldier far from home ends each stanza, but it assumes a special poignancy the first time it is used because it

closely identifies the speaker with the casualties left on the field.

"Polly" (a shortened form of Pauline) was a much more common nickname for girls in that era than it would subsequently become. In the second stanza, the speaker reveals that he left his aged parents, his country and home for the sake of Polly alone. Thus she may either have been a war hawk determined not to associate with a nonsoldier or, a more likely scenario in the context of this song, an idealized construct of a woman who represented all the romantic (not literally love, but more broadly novel and adventurous) experience the war offered.

The third stanza brings the loose narrative to the present, where the speaker finds himself living a hand-to-mouth existence (eating when hungry, drinking when "dry" [and not merely "thirsty," a detail that suggests true hardship; line 9]) and fatalistically expecting little beyond living until the Yankees kill him or he dies. To distance himself from such morbid thoughts, he imagines mourning his own death (line 11), a sentimental indulgence that sets up the last stanza.

In the penultimate stanza, the speaker shares brandy and wine with a comrade. The latter can drink to his true love, but in the 15th line the speaker reveals that he can only lament and mourn, an admission that he has not yet found the Polly for whose sake he went to war. In the last stanza, the speaker imagines building a castle on a high green mountain from which he can view Polly and help her mourn (line 17) the lover that she may never have had a chance to meet.

"RECONCILIATION" WALT WHITMAN (1866) If pressed, WALT WHITMAN's initial readership probably would have interpreted "Word over all," the phrase with which this poem begins, as an indication that everything had happened (or is happening) in accordance with God's will. It is vaguely reminiscent of the biblical account of creation in Genesis, since God created light by *saying* "Let there be light." It may also be viewed as a mild oath, as an indication of the extent of the speaker's involvement with the scene that he is about to describe, as an expression of his sincerity (as a pledge of his word), and as an indication of his true belief in God. It also celebrates the reconciliation of the

two sides at the conclusion of the Civil War, an event of such magnitude to the speaker that he views it as "beautiful as the sky" (line 1). He considers it beautiful that the war and its carnage must be forgotten ("utterly lost" in time; line 2). As if deeply troubled by the experience, he speaks figuratively of Death and Night, the sisters who will eventually wash "this soiled world" (line 3), but notice the emphasis he places on their hands, which "again, and ever again" incessantly labor at their task (line 3). Not since Shakespeare's Lady Macbeth has such a fixation on scrubbing suggested a deep neurosis.

At last the speaker returns to the present, describing the scene before him almost as though he were observing someone else in his role. In identifying the dead man as his personal enemy, he reveals the hatred he harbored during the war. In the same line, however, he embraces the new spirit of reconciliation in recognizing that the deceased was "as divine" as himself (since the Bible assures that we were all made in God's image). Note the deliberate language with which the speaker describes his interaction with the cadaver. At first he looks "where he lies" (line 5) and only gradually directly at him, then—as if his physical movements were a reflection of his mental state—draws near. As an act of contrition and in a show of brotherhood, he "lightly touches with [his] lips" (line 6; the speaker has taken great pains with the description so that his kiss will not be misinterpreted as a sexual or arrogant gesture) the white face in the coffin. Death and Time had already completed some of the work of reconciliation, and it was up to the good hearts of the survivors to finish the process.

"RECORDERS AGES HENCE" WALT WHITMAN (1860)
This poem is remarkable because WALT WHITMAN seems to be telling the critics and biographers of the distant future (whom he addresses as the "recorders ages hence" in line 1) what to say about him. Of course it is always dangerous to blur the distinction between the speaker and the poet, but the speaker includes three important facts that make it seem as though the poet was speaking of himself. For one thing, he imagines that future scholars would be interested in him principally for his songs (men-

tioned in line 4). Whitman was also known for his long walks in the woods (line 6) and, as a great many of his poems bear witness, for frequently thinking of his lovers (line 6).

The speaker apparently has his photograph in front of him, for he invites the reader "underneath this impassive exterior" (line 2); he would have his target audience publish his name and his picture as a representation of the tenderest lover (line 3). Surprisingly, he claims not to be proud of his songs but of his "measureless ocean of love" and his willingness to freely pour it out (line 5). Pensive, sleepless, and dissatisfied away from his lover, he was tormented at the possibility of the lover's secret indifference. His happiest days were spent sharing his long walks hand in hand with this friend, "they twain apart from other men" (line 9) as they often walked the streets with their arms resting on each other's shoulders (line 10).

It was exceedingly rare for Whitman to make such a frank admission of his sexual orientation as the speaker does in this poem.

"REHEARSAL TO OURSELVES" EMILY DICKINSON (published 1951)
In this poem the speaker seems to have gotten in touch with her sexuality and is pondering the implications of that act. Calling it a rehearsal reflects her society's emphasis on heterosexual courtship and marriage, and reference to herself in the third-person plural is less an affectation of royalty than a recognition of her other, darker self, that comes out once she permits such probing behind the veil of Victorian respectability. Reference to a "Withdrawn Delight" (line 2) not only sets the stage (by announcing her focus on the repercussions of the act), it also provides the central image of the poem. Her guilt sets in with all the weight of a church; wanton sex merited the same death penalty as murder in many of the pre-Christian cultures, and even Christ identified lust as adultery in the heart (Matthew 5:27). Thus she can rely on biblical precedent in linking "Bliss" to "Murder" (line 3). That in turn leads her to God (the "Omnipotent" of line 4), and her pain is probably even more "Acute" than her pleasure had been.

That will not keep her from additional exploration, however, since "We will not drop the Dirk" (line 5;

in Dickinson's day a dirk was a short dagger all the more dangerous since it could easily be concealed). In that pre-Freudian era the statement that "We love the Wound the Dirk Commemorate" (lines 6–7) probably seemed even more masochistic than it sounds to a modern audience. In the heady afterglow, the antecedent of "Itself" is the Wound, which continues to "Remind us" that we died (perhaps in the French sense of the small death of a consummated courtship).

"RENUNCIATION—IS A PIERCING VIRTUE" EMILY DICKINSON (1951) With the general decline of torture as an acceptable police procedure in the 17th century and the increased popularity of decorative piercing in the 21st century, the term "piercing" has lost much of its power to induce dread. Dickinson's opening line would have seemed a terrifying oxymoron to most of her contemporaries, schooled as they were in the notion that since man was formed in God's image (Genesis 1:27), it bordered on sacrilege to desecrate the body in such a manner. Only "the [willful] putting out of [one's own] eyes" (line 5) provides modern readers with a similar shock of horror.

On one level, such mortification of the flesh seemed logical to extreme religious penitents since bodily sensations are the chief temptation to focus on this life and disregard the next, but most people viewed it as mere self-mutilation. Thus it can be inferred that the renunciations to which Dickinson refers are extremely severe, perhaps on the order of the vows of chastity taken by the celebrants of some religious orders. These can be viewed as piercings (because of the pain they cause) of such magnitude that they penetrate the heart, at least metaphorically.

Renunciation on that level requires a leap of faith, a "letting go" (line 2) not only of a tangible treat already in one's hands (the "presence" of the third line), but a letting go of the very roots by which one enjoys this life, in exchange for "an Expectation," the promise of everlasting joy. It requires a sacrifice on the level of putting out one's eyes at sunrise (line 6) before the Day (and its blessings) prove too great a temptation to preserve them.

In line 10 Dickinson defines renunciation as the self's choosing against itself, a choice the self must then justify to itself (line 13). Thus the self, or at least the soul, must convince itself that the larger function (living for a purpose, or for Christians, living in accordance with Christ's dictates or by the teachings of his ordained representatives) dwarfs the apparent advantages of immediate gratification of the body's desires. It must argue that the "Covered Vision" (the promise of salvation and a heaven that might seem to beckon only from beyond the grave) is as present here as the obviously more tangible things that might otherwise distract us.

"RICHARD CORY" EDWIN ARLINGTON ROBINSON (1897) EDWIN ARLINGTON ROBINSON's poem's popularity stems from its simplicity, the inevitable moral so easily extrapolated from its surprise ending, and the reassurance it extends to the middle and lower classes that those with more wealth are really no happier than they are. Not coincidentally, it appeared during the Gilded Age, a period of American prosperity marked by the unprecedented accumulation of large fortunes by a few industrialists. Paradoxically, it was also a period with several severe stock market crashes and other unregulated disruptions in the nation's economic life.

The title character evidently lived uptown, a term frequently designating the more fashionable areas of a town or city, because he attracts attention when he went downtown (line 1). Evidently he characteristically rode through the streets, which set him apart from the "people on the pavement," those who lacked the money for a horse or carriage (but the phrase also suggests that, unlike Cory, they led very visible lives close to the earth and lacked the insulation from hunger and other misfortunes that his money and connections provided him). He is described almost as if he were royalty, with the admiring speaker noting everything from his sole (but the real question of the poem deals more with the man's soul and not his shoe leather) to his crown (the top of his head). Unlike those who must work with their hands for a living, he has the leisure to be "clean favored" (well-groomed, clean, and shaved) and "imperially slim" (line 4), a sign that he has not had to make do with the coarse fare that tended to add weight as well as strength to the laborers.

The fact that he was habitually "quietly arrayed" (line 5) meant that he was so comfortable in his status that he did not have to dress for show. The first sign that he was not the great man that the speaker imagined came when he talked; his utterances were "always human" (line 6) although his status was such that his greeting alone caused hearts to beat faster. Though modestly attired, he evidently moved with the refined gait of a gentleman, which made the speaker think even his walk glittered (line 8). He could seem "richer than a king" to a speaker with little firsthand knowledge of royalty. His education (or at least, his manners) made him a source of popular envy.

The most curious phrase of the poem occurs in line 13; the speaker and others of his class worked "and waited for the light." The phrase may suggest that they had to work throughout the daylight hours and had nothing to do after dark than wait to resume working at dawn (labor union guarantees of an eight-hour day were still in the future). It also invokes the Protestant work ethic that not only called for devotion to one's work but also counseled believers to be patient until the "light" of Judgment Day announced the eternal reward awaiting their resurrected souls.

Since one of the earmarks of predatory capitalism is to obtain labor at the lowest possible price, it was not unlikely that some workers would go without meat. Comparison with more fortunate people like Cory could lead them to curse their bread (line 14). Everything changed on a calm summer night (line 15), a time when a workingman's life was typically less arduous because agriculture offered seasonal employment and winter's cold misery was half a year away. Although no reason is provided for Cory's suicide, the speaker describes that tragedy with the same close attention to detail that he brought to other aspects of his idol's life.

"ROBERT OF LINCOLN" WILLIAM CULLEN BRYANT (1855)

The most surprising thing about this poem is how much natural history it accurately conveys, although a modern biologist would dismiss WILLIAM CULLEN BRYANT's tendency to translate the bird's song into human speech as anthropomorphism (the description and interpretation of animal behavior as though it were human), a serious flaw in that science. Bryant's contemporaries would have been more likely to object to his irregular line length, a consideration of far less concern to a modern reader. Bryant, never a whiz when it came to titles, let an exceedingly bad pun serve here: the bird in question is a bobolink, which the poet changed into a formal title such as those enjoyed by European nobility.

The arrangement of this poem is rather unusual. Each stanza contains three lines of description, one line of introduction for the celebrated singer, two lines of transliterated bird song, two lines of rather free translation of the bird song into English, and a concluding line of song such as the bird makes in flight. The first stanza locates the male bird as he swings on weed stalks on a mountainside or meadow over his nesting mate. He takes his name from one of his characteristic calls, and he seems to be either bragging about the safety of their hidden nest or assuring his mate that it is safe.

Like most birds, the bobolinks are sexually dimorphic in their plumage, which means that the males look different than the females of the same species. The male bobolink's feathers bring a black wedding coat to mind. Their brightness is so accentuated by the bird's white shoulders and crest that the bird seems to be definitely bragging that his nice new coat (line 16) makes him finer than any other bird.

The speaker describes the female as a "Quaker wife" (line 19) not only because the clothing of that sect has been stereotyped as drab, but because the Quakers have a tradition of seldom speaking in their congregations unless they are inspired. It is this wife's lot to "brood" (line 22) in the grass while her husband sings, and both meanings of the verb might apply here. *Brooding* covers most of the functions associated with nesting behavior such as incubating eggs and protecting the young, but it also conveys fretting or moping about something. This ambiguity can be rather humorous (to an uninvolved observer) because many marriages also feature only one happy spouse, and a human mate can be just as clueless about his wife's true feelings as this bobolink. This particular bird seems so content with himself that he sees only nesting behavior and encourages her to brood (line 25);

if she seems pensive, he attributes it to fear of thieves and robbers (line 26) and assures her that none will come while he is here.

The fourth and fifth stanzas are devoted to contrasting their behavior. She is as "shy as a nun" (line 28; this stereotype probably arose from the fact that some religious orders insist on maintaining cloistered lives) and has only a weak chirp, which the speaker does not bother to translate. Her mate seems the "prince of braggarts" and his song contrasts his bravado with the cowardly knavery of men. They have six white eggs with purple flecks, and her job is to sit all day while he sings "with all his might" (line 40). He encourages her housekeeping while he frolics about.

When the eggs hatch in the next stanza, he gathers seeds for the chicks. Now he sings of how hard this new life will be for such a gay young fellow (line 53). Sobered by work and silent with care (line 56), he abandons his holiday garment (bobolinks molt twice a year and the male's coloration is much closer to that of the female after the breeding season). His song reveals a new conception of himself; he shares secrets with his spouse (such as the location of the nest) and reassures everyone as to the safety of nest and nestlings.

The last stanza brings the end of summer and an end to the family. The husband, having become "a humdrum crone" (line 66; since a *crone* is a derogatory term for a withered woman, the speaker must again be referring to the bird's non-breeding plumage. If one wanted to be equally hateful about age in offending the opposite sex, he might refer to an older man as a drone, a male bee of no value after the breeding season), knows no more fun and frolic. He flies off, leaving the speaker and others who appreciate the bird to mimic his call as an invitation for him to return when he again feels like singing.

"THE RHODORA" RALPH WALDO EMERSON (1839) This simple poem is a response to the question of where the flower comes from, which the poet chose to use as an epigram ("On being asked, whence is the flower"). This inquiry probably had its roots in the plant's natural history, for it blossoms in the early spring in swampy areas generally unsuited to full vege-

tative cover and even in advance of its own leaves (thus the speaker refers to the "desert" in line 4). Unlike the rose with which Emerson compares its beauty, the individual blossoms tend to spread out like bursting shells, an illusion enhanced by their 10 long stamens. Like a skilled photographer, Emerson used the black water of a brook to set off the flowers, and the effect is so charming that even a cardinal (or other "red-bird") cannot compete with its beauty.

Having thus dispatched with the description of the plant, the speaker devotes the second half of the poem to its philosophical implications. In the epigram the word "whence" provided an adult tone for a question a child would have been more likely to ask. In lines 9 through 12 he provides the Rhodora with a response for what seems an unlikely event: how to answer if the sages ask why its charm is wasted where no one can see it. Why would sages, the wisest of men, ask such a childish question? The answer lies in the 15th line: while staking no claim to sagelike wisdom, the speaker does possess "simple ignorance." This suggests philosophical simplicity; the speaker poses such questions and frames their answers not because he is simpleminded but because attempting to explain the reason for our (or anything's) existence is one of the fundamental exercises of philosophy. Adopting a childlike approach sometimes enables such an enquirer to develop a new perspective on an issue.

Like the man (RALPH WALDO EMERSON) who created him, the speaker can draw his answers to the question of existence from two different sources. As a poet, he responds that "Beauty is its own excuse for being" (line 12). As a philosopher, he provides a rather cosmological answer to the basic ontological question: "the self-same Power" that brought him there also brought the Rhodora (line 16). This does more than just deflect the question back onto the enquirer; it suggests that there must be a godlike prime mover or some other power, since their existence is itself an argument for a creator. That the speaker did not identify the power as the Christian God suggests that, like Emerson (who gave up his post as a Unitarian minister because he no longer believed in the miracle of communion) he may have unconventional ideas about the nature of the deity.

"THE RIVER" RALPH WALDO EMERSON (1827)

This poem unfortunately begins on a sour note: The speaker's description of himself as "awed" violates the principle of showing and not telling, the first rule one should learn about writing. Later writers have proven it far more effective to show or reveal the speaker's awe without being told that he has it, and by starting off with this reminder of adult consciousness (and diction), RALPH WALDO EMERSON has made it more difficult for readers to appreciate the state of childlike rapture for nature that the poet celebrates in this poem.

If one ignores this misstep (a process bringing to mind the necessary retrieval of one's shoe from the marshy spring mud so often experienced on such an outing), the poem begins on much surer ground. "To behold" conveys the speaker's awe at returning to his familiar old haunts (lines 1–2), and his emphasis on the blue hue of the river and its immediate correlation with the "blue wonder" it engenders in the infant's mind are wonderfully evocative. The phrase places the child in that state of development where he began to differentiate colors at the same time that it conveys his innocence. His horizons are not clouded with preconceptions or extraneous ideas about guilt or opportunity, so his infant eye picks up unfiltered perceptions directly from nature.

His infant self is in some respects as miraculous for the speaker as the surrounding environment. He admires the nascent wisdom that sagely entertained doubts about the origins of the river, which he even then personified as a traveler. He was equally curious about the origins of the sunny bubbles in the water, and where the river went after watering the "flag-roots" (perhaps a reference to the sweet flag, an inhabitant of New England wetlands filling much of the same ecological niche as the more common cattails do in other parts of the country) of his father's fields.

Returning to the site, the adult speaker found the river unaltered except for its having flooded the surrounding valleys with "redundant" waves (a distracting word in this context; it is unclear what could be superfluous or unnecessarily repetitious about the waves unless he is thinking of their continually washing the shore or other objects even though the prior wave already had; line 10). He finds the rock from which he caught his first fish on a bent pin (probably a straight pin commandeered from his mother's sewing kit for that adventure since the modern safety pin was not invented until 1849), an occasion of "much triumphing" (as it represented an important developmental step, his use of nature to fulfill his needs). His reference to himself as a "blooming" hunter makes him seem an almost integral part of the landscape as he chased the butterfly (the "fairy fine" of line 15) above the flower blossoms, while overhead ancient crows held their "sour conversation" in the sky.

The scene seemed the same, but the speaker was not the same. He had grown wiser at the cost of growing sadder, because he realized what he had lost as well as what he had gained. The trees, flowers and even stones (!) were audible to him (line 22), for he understood their "fairy syllables" and sad significance. The wind is more eloquent than speech, and he hears sounds of parental admonishment and love from vegetative and inanimate objects. Their message is one of pity for the puny clay "that holds and boasts the immeasurable mind" (line 35). He feels welcomed back by the trees like their son. The trees witnessed the lives of his ancestors in colonial ("primitive") times, and they may soon provide funeral shade for his dust.

ROBINSON, EDWIN ARLINGTON (1869–1935)

The best indicators of the wealth of the poet's family are his birthplace (December 22, 1869) in Head Tide and his early childhood home in nearby Gardiner, Maine. Each of them entered the 21st century as a well-maintained private home, and the latter enjoys the status of a National Historic Landmark. Although the family's wealth was not destined to last, the move to Gardiner proved very fortuitous for their third son as it brought him into contact with a small circle of aspiring poets who could encourage his growth in that direction.

His family was still living high when he graduated from high school and began studying at Harvard, but his father's death was a devastating blow, and the widespread financial panic of 1893 further crippled the family. The sensitive young man was soon back in

Gardiner. Replicating the small circle of friends that had nurtured his early interest led to his production of his first collections of poetry, *The Torrent and the Night Before* (1896) and *The Children of the Night* (1897). From then on he sought out similar group situations, most successfully among the artists of the MacDowell Colony in Peterborough, New Hampshire, where he spent his summers from 1911 until his cancerous death (April 6, 1935) in New York City.

Although the bulk of his poetry (24 of the 26 volumes published during his lifetime, including the books that led to his three Pulitzer Prizes) was written in the 20th century, his most successful earlier work applied the dark determinism of the naturalism that dominated the last decade of the 19th century to the bleak lives he sometimes found among people very like his seemingly prosperous neighbors. Such is the theme of "RICHARD CORY" (1897); the ease of the title character's life poisons that of the speaker until an unforeseen tragedy casts new light on the subject. "The HOUSE ON THE HILL" (1897) ponders the fate of the occupants who abandoned their home, leaving only a shrill wind that blows through the structure and bears an uncomfortable message for those who try to understand it. "CREDO" (1897) represents a departure from the bleak naturalism of its era in that the speaker, although nearly completely isolated, fearful of his failing senses, and perhaps even dead, finds some basis for hope despite his predicament.

Transcriptions of most of Robinson's letters are archived at Colby College of Waterville, Maine. Other important manuscripts are held at the Library of Congress, the New York Public Library, Oberlin College, and the universities of New Hampshire, Harvard, and Syracuse.

BIBLIOGRAPHY

Coxe, Louis Osborne. *Edwin Arlington Robinson: The Life of Poetry*. New York: Pegasus, 1969.

Donaldson, Scott. *Edwin Arlington Robinson: A Poet's Life.* New York: Columbia University Press, 2007.

Gale, Robert L. *An Edwin Arlington Robinson Encyclopedia.* Jefferson, N.C.: Macfarland, 2006.

Robinson, Edwin Arlington. *The Poetry of E. A. Robinson.* Edited by Robert Mezey. New York: Modern Library, 1999.

"ROLL, JORDAN, ROLL" ANONYMOUS (19th century)

For the slave chained to his plantation by hereditary slavery, the notion of a promised land held four meanings, including the biblical promise of heaven, a reward for living a good life and acting in accordance with Christian principles. Mindful of salvation and damnation, the speaker of this song counsels his young sibling or friend to learn to fear the Lord (line 7) and to avoid false and spiteful words (line 10). By thus marching to the angel march (line 4), his soul would arise in heaven (line 5) on Judgment Day, in the year in which the Jordan rolls (when God fulfills His promise to His people; line 6).

Part of the Holy Land on earth, the geographical place where all the biblical miracles happened, was still fed by the Jordan River in which Christ was baptized (Matthew 3:14–17). If that part of the Bible was undeniably true, then there was hope for its entire message, and even slaves could participate in such rites as baptism (even if the ritual had to be improvised without benefit of clergy).

From that promised land came hope of a third; if the Lord freed His people from bondage in Egypt, then there was hope that He would do the same thing here. The angels might march against the institution of slavery with their progress as unstoppable as that of the river's currents. Although few angels would be found in its ranks, the Union Army eventually proved that faith in the destruction of slavery by an outside agency was not entirely misplaced.

The fourth promised land lay just over the Ohio River in the free states, and the song might encourage and counsel those who were tempted to "march de angel march" (run away from the slaveholders). An individual planning such a desperate maneuver would be well advised to appear frightened ("fear de [land]lord"), work hard ("let your days be long," the eighth line advises), avoid talk of his plans (lest his words prove "false" to his own interests) and act perfectly content with his condition (above all avoiding the "spiteful word" of line 10) until he had given the slaveholders a false sense of security.

The phrase "sittin' on de tree of life" (line 1) might only be a fancy way of suggesting that the internal audience had not yet reached the age in which one assumes an active role in life, or it may refer to some-one in crisis. Christians have sometimes referred to the cross as the tree of life since it holds the promise of their salvation; to be "sittin'" on the cross might suggest undergoing crucifixion or similarly excruciating torments. To hear the "angel march" at such a time might refer to a near death experience that reinforced a believer's faith in the afterlife promised by Christianity. Thus this seemingly innocuous song could bring all kinds of hope to an enslaved people.

"ROMANCE" EDGAR ALLAN POE (1845)

In this poem EDGAR ALLAN POE reveals how he grew as a writer as a consequence of early exposure to the easy rhymes of a romantic poetry that did not challenge his intellect. Romance is personified in the first stanza as an almost somnambular singer who "loves to nod" and sing with "drowsy head" (without a fully engaged mind) and "folded wing" (without really engaging or challenging the reader or the poet; lines 1–2). Its preferred habitat is a "shadowy lake" (line 4; this may be a reference to the fondness of early British romantic poets such as Wordsworth for the Lake District in England, but it also implies an objection that their work [marked by the "green leaves" of the easiest time of year in line 3] is far removed from the hard-edged reality that Poe faced throughout much of his life). It seemed a "painted" (colorful, but also artificial) parakeet (such as Poe would often encounter in a drawing room and not in the wild; line 5). He could learn his alphabet from such a tame bird, but even then he realized its inability to stir his emotional and intellectual depths (he inhabited the "wild wood" and already possessed "a most knowing eye" [lines 9–10]).

As he grew older, the years took on the more sinister aspect of the condor, a large New World bird of prey that typically thrives on carrion (line 11). Emblematic of the troubles he faced, the birds seem to shake heaven with tumult "as they thunder by" (lines 12–13) and leave him no time "for idle cares" (line 14). When a rare hour "with calmer wings" (note how carefully he maintains the avian metaphor; line 16) flings its "down" (the softer feathers of more value for insulation than for flight; line 17) upon his spirit, he does not want to waste the little time available for poetry (the "lyre and rhyme" of line 18) on poems that do not cause the strings of his heart to tremble.

"A ROUTE OF EVANESCENCE" EMILY DICKINSON (1891)

As quick as EMILY DICKINSON's eyes were, they were still no match for a hummingbird's wings. Hence they appear as the "revolving Wheel" of line 2, and propel the bird so fast that his emerald green feathers resonate (a musical or aural verb) and his cochineal "rushes" (line 4; cochineal is a bright red dye produced by processing the bodies of certain western American insects. As used here, the description implies that the bird [probably a ruby-throated hummingbird] departs so rapidly that only his red feathers register in a viewer's eyes. The verb "rushes" also conveys something of the enjoyable impact his brilliant colors have on the viewer's mind). They dart so fast that their route seems "evanescent" (as ephemeral as a vapor).

The tubular flowers that hummingbirds seem to prefer probably reminded the speaker of human heads (line 6) and the thoroughness with which they seem to visit most of the blossoms on a bush brings to mind the regularity of the daily mail. It is their speed that most impresses, however, and within a century, supersonic Concorde jets were capable of making the speaker's dream of flying to Amherst, Massachusetts, from Tunis, the modern capital of the north African country of Tunisia, "an easy morning's ride" (line 8).

"THE RUNNER" WALT WHITMAN (1867)

Although this may seem more like a sketch than a finished poem to the modern reader since the same scene can be seen on virtually any urban street in the United States, the sight was still a novelty when this poem appeared. Notice the poet's quick eye: Despite the runner's apparent speed (he is well-trained and leaning forward), Whitman saw his slim physique, muscular legs, and thin clothing (another novelty; specialized athletic gear for joggers lay far in the future).

The runner appears well-trained even to a modern reader because his fists are lightly closed; with relaxed arms and hands, an athlete is able to run much farther.

Similarly, his arms are partially raised to balance his stride, but not so high as to conspicuously require additional energy to power them. A slight lean may help with what would later be called correct footing, but Whitman evidently lacked a clear view of the runner's feet or the time or interest to describe them. He provides a picture of a middle- to long-distance runner with some of the clarity of a photograph but also with a sense of his movement such as would later be captured by motion picture technology.

S

"SAFE IN THEIR ALABASTER CHAMBERS" Emily Dickinson (1890)

The 1859 version of this poem consists of two stanzas that present conflicting images and ideas about the nature of human existence. The first stanza draws on one of the most important New Testament verses that purports to offer the exact words of Christ as he delivers his famous Sermon on the Mount: "Blessed are the meek for they shall inherit the earth" (Matthew 5:5). This probably led to the fourth line of Emily Dickinson's poem, for the entire stanza is focused on "the meek members of the Resurrection" who sleep in their graves awaiting the promised call to glory at the end of time. The poem begins by viewing these chosen inheritors of the world as they lie safely ensconced in their graves untouched by morning, noon, or any other change in the world above them. Their humble circumstances are evident in the materials in which they were buried; alabaster, satin and stone (and not marble or silk) cover them. Notice how the perspective of the viewer shifts in the first stanza from an overview of the bodies to the way things might appear if viewed from within a grave. Looking up from down there, the bunting or lining of the coffin can resemble the rafters of a building that support a roof.

In sharp contrast to the stillness of the tomb, the second stanza presents the changing and merry world of light and nature that plays above the graves. A personified breeze lightly laughs, a bee babbles and the sweet birds pipe their music. Unlike the macabre images of the first stanza, all seems pleasant until one considers that the ear which notes the bee's babbling is described as "stolid" (line 9), which stresses its insensitivity and impassivity, and the bird songs are dismissed as ignorant (line 10).

The poem's last line encapsulates much of its ambiguity as well as its essential mystery. If read ironically, the line scoffs at the foolishness of the deceased, which led them to live cramped and unappreciative lives. In this reading, it is their "stolid ear" that missed the delightful songs of life and continues to do so. An alternative reading would accept the praise of the last line as sincere; the meek were sagacious in living with an eye toward preserving their immortal souls instead of building earthly castles or ignorantly perishing as a consequence of heeding the seductive but ultimately vacuous enticements of nature. Given the general temper of the Victorian age in which she lived and the generally reverent tone evident in most of her early poetry, it seems likely that the author was sincere in her praise. Because the poet was so keenly aware of her region's Puritan origins, she may also have intended the quaint beauty of a grave tended by bees and sweet birds as a sign of divine favor.

Dickinson penned an entirely new second stanza in 1861 that often has been anthologized along with the first version. In place of ephemeral bee babbles and bird pipes, she focused on the timelessness of the heavens, striving with elevated diction to more closely link the first stanza's securely resting chosen souls with the promise of eternal elevation. The new version has the advantage of maintaining the perspective of the destined-to-be-resurrected throughout the poem.

The years pass grandly "in the Crescent" above them (line 6), a phrase that may combine a view of the earth's curvature with the changing phases of the lunar cycle in the same way that saints are thought to have spent half their lives with their eyes fixed on heaven and half fixed on the earth. The speaker's knowledge of planetary motion is evident in her new seventh line, which suggests countless other worlds that still "scoop their Arcs" around their respective suns. Note how the unusual verb focuses the reader's attention on the movement of the planets at the same time that it reminds the viewer of his interred perspective; the dirt must in some way be scooped from the grave before the resurrection can have full effect.

Few things seemed as unchangeable to primitive man as the stars in the sky, hence the word "firmament" (line 8) became synonymous with the heavens. Viewed from the perspective of eternity, however, the stars are not only not permanent but change their positions so constantly that the poet chose the very active verb "row" to convey their constant motion. Slightly deeper metaphysical meanings arise if two other meanings of "row" are considered. The stars' constant jockeying for position may have suggested a "row" in the sense of a boisterous physical altercation. With unlimited time and divine guidance, however, even the movements of the most distant stars may be understood to the point where they slip into the predictable pattern of rows (like the agricultural crops on earth).

To a viewer with such unlimited understanding of the heavens, the affairs of men seem inconsequential. If the stars seem to move like meteorites, such events as the death of kings (represented by the dropping of their crowns, the "diadems" of line 9) and other changes in human governance (such as the surrender of the "Doges," for 500 years the most powerful men in their Italian republics) no longer seem momentous. In fact, such changes register no more than "dots on a disc of snow" (line 20), an image that not only conveys their soundlessness but also their lack of gravity.

"SCENTED HERBAGE OF MY BREAST"
WALT WHITMAN (1860)   Although its title almost drips with a self-absorbed, aggressive virility, in this poem WALT WHITMAN considers the significance of the plants that will grow from his grave (which 32 years later happened to be located in the Harleigh Cemetery of Camden, New Jersey) as a meditation on mortality and the importance of his life's work.

In the second line his speaker transcends time by conflating the future (when he will be able to "glean" [collect or harvest] leaves growing from his grave), the present (when he is writing his letter) and the past (in the sense that "afterwards" someone will read the leaves he is presently writing, thus inferring that his present is already the past for the reader). His delicate written leaves will at least not be frozen in winter (line 4), and on a metaphorical level, he hopes their "perennial roots" have achieved enough depth that his work will still have meaning for successive generations. Every year, he believes, a few will discover his work or inhale "the faint odor" of his leaves (line 6).

With rich ambiguity, the rest of the poem could apply equally to the organic leaves enriched by his decomposing body or to the leaves extracted from his heart (metaphorically) and written on the page. The angst associated with the creative process is evident when he refers to the "slender" leaves of line 7; one could always have written more. Although writing poetry is often a pleasant pursuit, to have devoted as much of your life to it as Whitman did incurred enough opportunity costs (he could have been doing something less mentally strenuous but also enriching) that he might well think of his poems as the "blossoms of my blood" (line 7). He relies on the poetry to tell its own story just as the leaves that are nourished by his grave will translate the remnants of his body into their own message.

Imagining the "faint tinged" roots (not faint-tinged, which would more likely mean "pale" or "weak" only, but also "faint" as in the momentary unconsciousness attendant upon a physical or mental shock, line 10) that will pierce his body is a bitter experience not because he conceives of the body as still sensate (hence capable of being burned and stung; line 9), but because he is forced into that activity because of the aesthetic demands of his art. Hence, in a way, death is beautiful, and only death and love are finally beautiful (line 11).

Oddly, he finds himself engaged in the chant of lovers for the sake of death and not for life, and his soul (like the high soul of lovers perhaps) prefers death (lines 14–16). Thus reconciled with his death because of its inextricable links with his writing, he looks forward to seeing the vegetative growth that will sprout from his chest. He wants it to spring up in "emblematic and capricious blades" (line 22) instead of being stifled and choked like its roots and like he feels. Baring his broad breast, he resolves to say clearly what he has to say (line 23) for his comrades and himself only, which will raise "immortal reverberations" throughout the States (line 25). He will provide examples for lovers "to take permanent shape" (line 26; in his lifetime, the poet was unable to fashion such lasting bonds) and will make death exhilarating (line 27).

He desires not just the tone of death so as to be in harmony with it (line 28), but death itself, for it belongs to him; they are as inseparable as love and death. He will not be forced back (the "balk" of line 30) to what he had been calling life (a declaration of independence that might extend to issues of sexual preference as well), but will embrace death as "the real reality" (line 33). A personified death waits beyond "the mask of materials" and may one day control everything, dissipating "the entire show of appearance" (line 36). Perhaps death is all there is; life is short, but death lasts very long.

"SHALL I TAKE THEE, THE POET SAID" Emily Dickinson (published 1945)

This poem compares the process by which a poet selects a word with the selection of a job applicant. Openly pondering whether to accept it, the poet orders the "propounded" (proposed) word back with the other candidates while s/he searches for one that more closely fits her needs.

She searched Philology (line 5). This is the study of language as it evolves over time, a subject that includes the roots of words as well as shifts in their meanings. To develop the speaker's job interview analogy, she has checked the applicant's work history and references. She was about to "ring for" (line 6; in the mid-19th century this most often meant ringing a small bell by hand to summon a servant) the candidate in question when (breaching all office and domestic protocols) "that portion of the Vision" for which she was hoping to use the word came to her. This leads her to the philosophical reflection about the nature of poetic diction summed up in the last two lines: the "Cherubim" do not reveal their gifts "unto nomination." In other words, the best gifts of inspiration are not willed into being, but come more naturally (or supernaturally).

Some of EMILY DICKINSON's surviving manuscripts reveal that she worked in approximately the same way as the poet who serves as her point-of-view character in this poem. If a word did not fully satisfy her, she typically marked it with an "x" and began a list of alternatives in the margin. Although she remained receptive to additional or alternative images as well as words, perhaps the most important lesson revealed here is that she did not wait for the inspiration that led to her best work but actively pursued her craft.

"SHE CAME AND WENT" James Russell Lowell (1849)

On a camping trip, the speaker in this simple but nice poem by JAMES RUSSELL LOWELL was touched by an evidently brief encounter with a girl, a woman, or an angel. Their time together was evidently as brief as the moment a twig trembles beneath the weight of a singing bird, but she continues to thrill and stir his memory (line 3). As if to convince the speaker or the internal audience that it really happened, the refrain keeps repeating that he "only" knows she came and went (the adverb should forestall any request for additional information about her appearance, disappearance, or other aspects of her mystery. It serves as a continual assurance that he has revealed all he can about her).

Just as the perfectly placid surface of a lake captures the sky's measureless content, so his soul held "that moment's heaven" (line 7). Just as quickly as spring fills the orchards with flowers ("at one bound," he notes in line 9; the phrase puns on "spring" as a verb), so she split (the "clove" of line 11) his wintry sleeps. Literally or figuratively, she was an angel who briefly stood in the doorway of his tent. Although he subsequently took the tent down (the "struck" of line 15), he retains the vision.

Fast-forwarding to the distant future when the room slowly dims and "life's last oil" (line 18; houses were usually lit by candles or with whale oil lamps at the time) is nearly spent (he is nearly dead), he asserts that the thought of her will fill his eyes to the brim with light.

"SHENANDOAH" ANONYMOUS (19th century)

Perhaps because additional verses were added over a number of years, few folk songs approach the level of purely abstract sound as closely as this one. The euphonic bliss twice afforded by the long *O* of "Oh Shenandoah" (line 1) plaintively conveys the mournful spirit of a speaker torn between love of his former home in old Virginia and the love and adventure awaiting him in the American West. Or at least that appears to be the situation in the first stanza; perhaps because he finds himself on the verge of crossing a different river, he longs to again hear the Shenandoah, which he appears to be addressing.

In the second stanza, however, he seems to address the parent of a daughter of the Shenandoah, a river found in present-day West Virginia and Virginia, or the entire region. He plans to take the girl with him across that rolling river (presumably, the Shenandoah; line 7) and eventually beyond the Missouri River. Evidently these plans did not work out, for the next stanza finds him announcing his love for an Indian maiden. Setting out in a canoe laden with "notions" (presumably sundry manufactured goods chosen for their appeal to the feminine eye and perhaps destined for trade with the Indians), he appears to be at long last actually on the wide Missouri. First, however, he pauses to bid adieu and farewell to the Shenandoah, to which he has no plans of returning since he will not "grieve" it with a lengthy good-bye or "deceive" it with a promise to return (lines 16 and 18).

Regardless of how his love for the Indian maiden turned out, the speaker's mercantile endeavors were evidently crowned with success. The last stanza finds him again embarking on the river, but this time in a vessel with sails capable of withstanding gale-force winds (line 21) and sporting "braces" (the horizontal spars to which a ship's sails are attached) and "sheets" (the ropes or lines by which the sailing apparatus of a ship or boat are controlled).

Part of the appeal of the song rests in its rendering of the collective history of the first people who embraced it, the settlers along the Missouri River valley. Among the many reasons they had for heading west, certainly the romance of new adventures (personified here as an Indian maiden) played a crucial role. Like the speaker in this poem, most of them had to bid farewell to the eastern lives to which they had little hope of ever returning.

"SHE ROSE TO HIS REQUIREMENT— DROPT" EMILY DICKINSON (1890)

This is a requiem for the lost girlhoods of those who marry too young to have fully experienced them, and of those who were forced to make all the compromises upon entering the marriage contract.

In an age when there were few professional opportunities for women, dropping the "Playthings of Her Life" (line 2) meant giving up her intellectual and artistic interests to be a full-time wife and mother. Families were large and there were few laborsaving devices available, so such work was far more demanding than it would become in the 21st century. Most women lacked the time and energy for pursuing other interests.

As a literary artist, Dickinson knew the value of amplitude (the magnificence of great things), awe, and novel sensations (the "first Prospective" of line 7). The "Gold" that wives and mothers could wear away by constant use (lines 7–8) could include their health, sweet temperaments, idealism, intellects, and other virtues and assets. Part of being a conventionally good wife in the late 19th century meant that the loss of such things went largely unmentioned so as not to burden the husband with distractions from his "serious" work.

Publicly, a married woman of the late Victorian era was not expected to mourn the growth opportunities she might otherwise have enjoyed (stanza three). Dickinson was wise enough to know that some of what was given up would probably amount to no more than weeds, but great pearls were also lost.

"SHILOH" HERMAN MELVILLE (1866)

Before becoming the nemesis of Robert E. Lee's Army of Northern Virginia, the Union general Ulysses S. Grant proved his mettle (and several times nearly lost his life and an entire army) in the battles of the West. Hailed as a national hero for taking Fort Donelson in Tennessee on February 16, 1862, Grant was ordered to await the arrival of additional forces before furthering his invasion of the South. By April 6, Confederate general Albert S. Johnston was able to send 44,000 soldiers in a surprise attack aimed at destroying the Army of Tennessee before it could be joined by the Army of the Ohio. Individual units retreated before the onslaught or stood and fought while they could, seemingly suicidal tactics that bought time for the bulk of the army to regroup and effectively resist, and the very fortunate arrival of the second Union army in the night brought Grant's strength up to an irresistible 65,000. On April 7, the Southerners were forced to withdraw. Nearly one in four of the participants from both sides had become casualties or missing in the three miles separating Shiloh Church and the deepest Confederate penetration.

HERMAN MELVILLE's poem, announced as a requiem (a hymn for the dead) in the subtitle, begins with a charming portrait of the swallows flying low over the Shiloh field. It then returns to Monday, April 7, 1862, when the rain brought water to the wounded still lying where they fell (lines 6–8). The log church at Shiloh, accurately described as lonely in line 10, was located near the point of initial contact between the armies and commandeered for service as a makeshift hospital. Parting groans and natural prayers (lines 11–12) mixed there just as casualties from the two armies did. Perhaps the speaker overgeneralizes in claiming that the soldiers had begun the day as foes but ended it as friends no longer interested in fame or country (line 15), but like those personally "undeceived" by the bullets at Shiloh (line 16), the battle helped the entire nation to realize just how costly the war was going to be. By 1866 when the poem appeared, the sentiment of reconciliation was widespread among many of the former warriors, but those who died of wounds on the field were resting in their graves beneath the skimming swallows (symbols of life or the resilience of nature, the reappearance of these birds in the penultimate line provides an attractive frame for the poem). That "all is hushed at Shiloh" (line 19) seems a fitting tribute to the sacrifices made by the soldiers for each side, but

the comment on their being undeceived by bullets suggests that on another level the "hush" is an affront to the truth about war that they discovered.

"THE SHIP OF EARTH" SIDNEY LANIER (1868)

Having experienced the social, political, and economic upheavals of the Civil War and its aftermath as they were visited upon the Deep South, it could seem to a member of the formerly empowered classes that God had indeed abandoned them. SIDNEY LANIER's apocalyptic poem mourns the passing of the gentility that had previously kept the grosser aspects of such things as death, birth, life, sex, and desire out of sight.

The first stanza introduces the central conceit of the poem. The earth is envisioned as a ship containing men plagued by the punishments that God brought upon them for the sins of Adam and Eve as recorded in Genesis 3:13–19. As if their predicament was not perilous enough, they also face the worst calamities that are likely to befall a vessel as a consequence of human depravity. The "fires of desires" (line 2; a distractingly facile phrase) are burning in the hold, where even if they are somehow extinguished before consuming the entire ship they threaten the food and water supplies.

The internal audience of the poem is the earth, and the speaker's exclamations suggest that he both fears it and fears its loss (line 3). Men blaspheme as they battle each other on deck, with at least some of them having become wild mutineers (who seem rebels against God as well as against the ship's commander).

The break between stanzas signals a jump in time to the next morning, and at first it seems that nature will cleanse the ship and restore its appearance. The speaker's predicament probably led to his incongruous vision of the dew dropping from "the petal of the sky" (line 5), but this Edenic hope is soon dashed as the dew seems inadequate for the task. Instead of washing away the blood, shed in such quantities that the deck remains wet with it, the dew takes up the "stain" (a word layered with moral as well as physical meaning). This adds another layer of horror to the scene when the refraction of the morning light changes the bloody dew into a red crystal, producing a spot of surreal beauty amid all the carnage.

The speaker's truncated prayer to God for a pilot (line 7) contains some little hope for humanity: At least one of the survivors realizes that without His help, man is doomed. First, however, our attention is turned to the bodies strewn along the deck. In a scene reminiscent of the battlefields of the recently concluded Civil War, the "best sailors" can be found among the dead. This poem reminds us that such fallen flowers of southern gentility provided not only the practical leadership but also the moral guidance of their states.

"SHUT NOT YOUR DOORS" Walt Whitman (1865)

In this poem the speaker addresses the libraries in a boastful tone much in keeping with the brimming confidence of post–Civil War optimism. In less than five years the same forces that threw back the Southern invasion at Gettysburg (and kept their former adversaries from joining in the general postwar economic boom) would throw great bridges across its broad eastern rivers and complete a transcontinental railroad.

Like a good salesman, the speaker points out what the customers lack, what they need, and how his product can satisfy that demand. Since this is a poem and not a sales pitch, however, he stops short of explaining precisely what it is they lack and relies on his external audience of readers and critics to fill in the gaps. Perhaps the most important clue can be found in the speaker's reference to "proud libraries" in the first line; they might pride themselves on being bastions of high culture while most of Whitman's work celebrates common men laboring in their respective trades. Since the huddled masses need a literature accessible to them, Whitman's innovations in free verse would help libraries meet their diverse patrons' needs. His work also promises to be more topical than most of their collections since, like the country, it has just emerged from the war (line 3).

Thus far his pitch has been rather straightforward and mainstream, but beginning with the fourth line the huckster takes over from the conventional salesman. His tone changes from boosterism to become almost confessional: "the words of my book [mean] nothing" he confides, "the drift of it [is] every thing" (line 4). A book that "is not linked with the rest" (line 5) may lack

only referential citations, or it may represent a radical departure in theme or approach from all that has gone before it. Although it will not be "felt by the intellect," that does not necessarily mean that it will not engage the intellect, or be felt emotionally, which is frequently regarded as a higher achievement in poetry.

Having thus dispensed with what the book cannot do, he turns his attention to what it can do: thrill the "untold latencies" (line 6). The phrase probably refers to those desires and tendencies that have been repressed either by an individual or by society. Walt Whitman, in his desire to embrace all aspects of life and to fully explore his own personality in print, thus promises to deliver new experience "on every page" (line 6).

"A SIGHT IN CAMP IN THE DAYBREAK GRAY AND DIM" Walt Whitman (1865)

The situation in this poem is that the speaker has come across three bodies left outside an army hospital tent. They probably died in the night because each has been left on a stretcher and covered with a brown woolen blanket by a medical unit too tired or too overwhelmed with work to do anything else for them at present. It is tempting to criticize the speaker for having the audacity to disturb the dead, but as he is himself a denizen of the camp, he must either be one of their fellow soldiers or, perhaps like Walt Whitman, he is a volunteer nurse. Whatever his status, he is so bothered by something that he cannot sleep out the night (line 2). Such personal involvement in the war may suggest that his is not an idle curiosity, and the reverential tone of the rest of the poem soon establishes that, far from desecrating their bodies, his touch is benedictory.

The first casualty is an elderly man, gaunt, grim, gray, and so old that the flesh around his eyes seems shrunken, yet because he stood with that band of brothers the narrator mourns the loss of this dear comrade regardless of his age (line 10). The second victim was so young he seemed but a "sweet boy with cheeks yet blooming" (line 12), a coincidence that brings out the speaker's paternal side, for he addresses him as a "child and darling." In each case, the speaker wants to know who they are. The moment would have been especially poignant for his audience in 1865, many of whom had lost sons, brothers or fathers in the late conflict. It may not have been a coincidence that the dead the poet describes are each representative of one of the stages of life in which he would have normally been filling one or more of these rolls.

The calm face and attractive yellow-white ivory skin of the third soldier brings to mind innumerable portraits of Christ. This represents a transcendent moment for the speaker; in recognizing Christ in the features of the fallen soldier, he also implies that, like Christ, he is not just "dead and divine and brother of all" (line 15). Like the Savior, the dead soldier may be an inheritor of heaven, and the comparison further implies that he died for a sacred cause.

SIGOURNEY, LYDIA HUNTLEY (1791–1865)
Lydia Huntley was born the only child of working-class parents in Norwich, Connecticut, on September 1, 1791. She was so well educated in the public schools that she began teaching in 1811, a profession she pursued until her marriage to Charles Sigourney, a Hartford businessman, in 1819. Their marriage was blessed with five children, but only two survived childhood. Her husband died in 1854.

In 1815, the title of her first poetry collection revealed the subsequent direction of her literary career: *Moral Pieces, in Prose and Verse*. Although much of her work seems too precious for serious study by later scholars (*Sayings of the Little Ones, and Poems for their Mothers*) or too didactic to long entertain a sophisticated audience (*How to Be Happy [a children's book]*), she was one of the most prominent and prolific writers of her day. On a brief trip to Europe in 1840 she was able to meet such literary luminaries as the romantic British poet William Wordsworth and the Victorian essayist Thomas Carlyle. Her autobiography, *Letters of Life*, was posthumously published in 1866.

Of the four poems discussed in this volume, "INDIAN NAMES" and "The INDIAN'S WELCOME TO THE PILGRIM FATHERS" reveal her sensitivity to the plight of the Native Americans even as the policies of forced relocation, exile, and genocide were gaining widespread public support. "The DEATH OF AN INFANT" can provide an excellent example of the early Victorian sentimentality that later ages found too cloying. "The SUTTEE" demonstrates her empathy for the suffering women were forced to endure in foreign lands; in some districts of India women were often forced to burn themselves alive on the funeral pyres of their husbands as a tribute to their love. The practice became illegal throughout India in 1846.

The poet died in Hartford, Connecticut, on June 10, 1865. Her 54 letters in the George Griffin-Lydia H. Sigourney Papers at the University of Michigan reveal how well she managed the financial side of her career as well as some commentary on creative literary matters.

BIBLIOGRAPHY
Haight, Gordon S. *Mrs. Sigourney, the Sweetest Singer of Hartford.* New Haven, Conn.: Yale University Press, 1930.

"SIOUX GHOST DANCE" ANONYMOUS (19th century)
The dates of the most famous battles of the Indian Wars of the Great Plains, especially those associated with George Armstrong Custer, reveal a fatal weakness in Native American culture when it came time to fight against white intrusion into their ancestral lands. In high summer, entire tribes could outrun and outfight the cavalry units dispatched to suppress them. Hence Custer was unable to make contact with the Sioux and Cheyenne in the summer of 1867 despite having 1,100 men of the Seventh Cavalry under his direct command, although on July 2, a detachment of 10 soldiers and a Sioux Indian guide under the command of Lt. Lyman S. Kidder was ambushed and destroyed on its way to deliver dispatches to Custer. It was a similarly hot summer day when Custer himself rode to his death along with all of the soldiers of the five companies of the Seventh Cavalry he chose to personally lead at the Battle of the Little Bighorn, on June 25, 1876.

There were exceptions (most notably the loss of infantry Captain William Fetterman and 79 other soldiers at the hands of the Sioux and Cheyenne on December 21, 1866, and the defeat of the same Indian warriors by a smaller detachment of better-armed soldiers in the heat of August 2, 1867), but usually, the strategy of attacking the tribes during midwinter devised by Major General Phil Sheridan proved effective. Thus the Battle of the Washita (marked by a Seventh Cavalry charge against a peaceful Indian encampment) took place on November 27, 1868, and the Battle of Wounded Knee, so intimately tied to the Sioux Ghost Dance, occurred on December 29, 1890.

By 1889, it was clear even to the Plains Indians, overwhelmed by the superior numbers and armament of the settlers and soldiers from the East and the near extinction of the buffalo, that they could entertain no hope of a successful military conclusion to the conflict. Demoralizing battlefield reverses had led to the loss of their lands and freedom, and even their spirituality was undermined.

In Nevada, a Paiute Indian named Wovoka had a vision in which adherence to a few principles such as pacifism and the practice of a sacred dance, named the Ghost Dance because it would supposedly lead to the resurrection of all the Indian dead, would bring about a new, white-free, golden age. Several Sioux traveled west to learn the dance, and this new religion invigorated their tribe. Any movement involving significant numbers of the more recently subjugated Plains tribes frightened the white settlers in the area, and the military intervened. Early in December, the South Dakota home guard ambushed and killed about 75 of the Ghost Dancers on their Pine Ridge Reservation. Sitting Bull, the most famous Sioux leader, was killed on December 15 by the Indian police sent to arrest him. On December 29, 1890, at Wounded Knee in South Dakota, around 300 Lakota Sioux men, women, and children had their weapons confiscated by a detachment of the Seventh Cavalry. The encircling army then attacked with murderous intent. Five days later, around 150 of the remaining dead were buried in a mass grave, and with them went any realistic faith in an Indian future independent of white culture on the open plains.

The short poem preserved as the "Sioux Ghost Dance" by United States Bureau of Indian Affairs reveals several of the aims of the movement. The "whole world" prophesied to come includes all the animals in their prior abundance as well as the Native Americans (line 1). Until the 20th century, American Indians identified with their separate tribes in the same way that Europeans identified with their nations, so that the coming "nation" predicted in the second line probably referred

only to the Sioux nation, but other tribes also embraced the hope that led to the Ghost Dance. The mysticism of many western tribes included anthropomorphized animals sometimes capable of supernatural feats including the ability to converse with men, a connection that this poem exploits in its identification of the Eagle as the messenger who brought this news to the tribe (line 3). Reverence for the elderly is combined with a quasi-religious faith in "the father" who confirms the validity of the message in the next line.

The fourth line prophesizes that the whole earth will be changed (thus preventing the return of European civilization). The buffalo will come back in their former numbers, according to the crow who brought this portion of the message and the father who confirms it (lines 6–8).

The repetition of key phrases (especially the most optimistic word of all, "coming") can be viewed as an incantation designed to bring about the desired change, and in its links to the animals (and birds), the poem reached into one of the deepest currents of Native American mysticism.

For more information about the Ghost Dance and the suppression of American Indians from 1860 to 1890, see Dee Brown's *Bury My Heart at Wounded Knee* (New York: Henry Holt, 2001).

"SKIPPER IRESON'S RIDE" JOHN GREENLEAF WHITTIER (1857)

One of the artistic merits of JOHN GREENLEAF WHITTIER's poem lies in its offer to carry the reader through the same emotions experienced by the speaker as he moved from his initial mirth at the thought of tarring and feathering a former ship captain and delight at the bedraggled appearance of that misfortunate to eventual pity for the victim.

Although figures from antiquity were often invoked to inspire and amaze early 19th-century readers, the first three of those cited here are humorous even without knowledge of the classics. The speaker's claim that Ireson's ride was even stranger than these is funny for its exaggeration. Notice that the phrase "out from Marblehead" in line 8 marks the speaker as an inhabitant of a Massachusetts seaport, for it describes Ireson's ride as if he had shipped out on a boat. This is important because it suggests that the speaker would fully understand the implications of the Captain's actions and would be inclined to sympathize with those who punish him. The refrain clarifies the situation, with the gender of the perpetrators adding to its novelty.

The skipper appears in the second stanza, although he scarcely looks human. The lack of flight feathers on his "wings" probably reminded the speaker of a plucked turkey, and a human head covered with feathers most resembles that of an owl. Since their seafaring husbands were often away at sea, the women of Marblehead led self-sufficient lives. This would explain their muscular strength and also the confidence that led to their being "glib of tongue" (line 17). It should not be inferred by the seeming awkwardness with which their speech is rendered that they are unintelligent or even uneducated; rather, the speaker is attempting to phonetically convey the sounds of their New England dialect.

In the third stanza, the speaker shifts his attention to the women, noting the "wrinkled scolds" only in passing. The younger women, or "girls in bloom" as he calls them (line 24), remind him of the uninhibited revelers who surround the god of wine on an antique vase. As if sensing that the humiliation of a sea captain, who held one of the most respected and powerful positions in their society, somehow licensed their own misbehavior, they appeared in public in brief skirts (shocking! Their bare ankles even show!) and loose hair (line 28; most early colonial women wore bonnets in deference to their God). Members of this generally less public gender even blew conch shells and horns, and the appreciative speaker takes in the entire spectacle. Notice the pun on "chase" in line 25; contemporary audiences expected girls to be described as "chaste" even in such exceptional circumstances, but these girls are like those who chased Bacchus!

The next stanza reveals the sordid details of the Captain's crime. Alerted to a crisis by the crew of a sinking ship, he sailed away instead of rescuing them even though they hailed from his own town. That wreck will lie in the depths forever, but the female relatives of the missing crew kept up their vigil until they turned their attention to "the cruel captain who sailed away" (line 52). Those too old to walk tripled the sound of the horns by braying from their windows as the procession passed, and the old grandfathers, metaphorically connected with the missing boat when the speaker calls them "hulks of old sailors run aground" (line 61), add their curses. The younger men were probably still fishing out in the sea.

The skipper takes no apparent notice of the fine day or the taunts that surround him but stood as mute as an Indian idol (line 72). Members of many New England Native American tribes gained reputations for stoicism as a consequence of the deprivations they endured each winter, so to be compared not only to such stereotypically taciturn people but to their manufactured idol is to be extraordinarily silent. A second possible source for this image was the wooden representations of Native Americans, later manufactured in such bulk for use in advertisement as to earn the designation of "cigar store Indians." In Skipper Ireson's time, however, such a carving was more likely used as the figurehead placed over a ship's bow for good luck.

Long exposure to danger and adversity taught the captain to merely weather a storm until it was possible to maneuver out of harm's way, and he uses the same tactic here. Waiting until the storm of the women's fury had dissipated to the point where they would listen to him, in the eighth stanza he speaks at last. Explaining that he suffers from a "nameless horror" in which he constantly sees the sinking ship and hears the cries from its sailors, his fear of God and the faces of the dead render him indifferent to the public shame they are forcing him to endure.

Notice how, in the last stanza, a sense of the shipboard hierarchy becomes evident as soon as the women's rage has begun to subside. First up is the wife of the skipper of the lost boat, and she sounds rather like a captain in her knowledge of men, her reference to God, and the brevity of her speech: "God has touched him! why should we!" (line 90).

Next up is an old wife who mourns her only son, and her comment is remarkable for its nautical content; she would have them cut the tether and "let him run" like an unwanted fish (line 92). The speaker has stressed her age as if to suggest that she is beyond childbearing years, so that the loss of her only son, often the only source of material support for an aging woman, rendered her loss doubly horrible. The essence of life in that village is probably captured in lines 93–95, in which the women's fury passes like a storm at sea, at first still dangerous but gradually settling to the point where the tortured captain is not only released but given a cloak. This may mimic the action on a vessel when, after passing through a patch of the direst weather with minimal sail exposure, the sails are again raised and the danger left behind.

"THE SLAVE" Sarah Louisa Forten (1831) It was common for propagandists for independence during the American Revolutionary War era to argue that continued allegiance to the king must inevitably end in slavery once any of their rights were taken away. For the African-American slaves who joined the American army in order to gain their personal freedom, this was not an empty slogan, and many members of the Philadelphia community to which Sarah Louisa Forten belonged did owe their liberty to the "sires" who risked everything more than half a century before. In the first four lines the poet acknowledges their success and applauds their "deeds of glory" (line 3), but the major argument of this poem is that their sons and grandsons should not pride themselves on merely possessing this hard-won freedom. They owe it to their race to remember the bondage in which their fathers had been held and in which most African-Americans still remained. They must speak for those who must remain silent, the poor wronged slaves who dare not own their freeman's pride (line 16).

As terrible as the whips, chains, and physical scourges of slavery were, this poem suggests that the psychological damage was much more severe. The slave's very soul is darkened by "a cloud of error, doubt and fear" (line 19) from which he cannot escape.

The poet broadens her appeal in the last four lines by asking if her country must still oppose "the despised" (line 26) upon whose behalf justice will soon arise to plead its cause. Although the poem seems aimed at the free African-American community, all readers might ponder its contrast between the rhetoric of freedom and liberty that helped America win her independence and the slavery that denied such things to millions of her people.

"THE SLAVE GIRL'S FAREWELL" Sarah Louisa Forten (1832) As an artistic expression, this poem's weaknesses stem from Sarah Louisa Forten's failure to fully realize the speaker's anguish. In striving to speak for those who could not, the poet chose the theatrical voice of a melodramatic actress. For modern readers, this voice is too genteel and its tone is too measured to be that of a slave girl who is permitted by her owner to bid good-bye to her mother before he sails off across the sea with her.

"Mother, I leave thee" sounds like the preamble of a rehearsed statement such as a new bride might tell her parent before leaving for her new home. Placing it in the mouth of a young girl being forced to abandon her familiar life for an exceedingly uncertain but predictably unpleasant future borders on the farcical. The only justification for such an aesthetic lapse is that the author may hope to shock the reader with the discrepancy between the language of the poem and the circumstances that prompt it.

The sentimentality of the poem knows no limits. The speaker briefly recalls her happy childhood before she knew she was a slave, a time of the utterly conventional murmuring stream and mossy banks of the 15th line. At the time, it seemed only her mother "could bend [her] spirit's pride" (line 19) or silence her. Since then, however, she has experienced weary toil and learned of "the heavy lash" (line 23). Only when she bids adieu to her mother's protection and notes that "tears are the only language . . . a mother's love can speak" (lines 27–28) does the poem rise to the poignancy the situation demands. The author seems incapable of sustaining it, however. The speaker asks her mother to waft her blessing (such stilted diction at such a time!) to the one who prays for her despite her own cares.

For a far better poem with many of the same essential elements, read "The Slave Mother" by Frances Ellen Watkins Harper. At least part of the difference can be attributed to the increasing success of the abolitionist movement in the 22 years between the publishing of the two poems. Perhaps Forten realized that her readership was not yet ready for a more realistic rendering of the horrors of slavery.

"THE SLAVE MOTHER" FRANCES ELLEN WATKINS HARPER (1857)

This poem is filtered through the consciousness of an impressionable young woman who witnesses slavery's cruelest moment, the separation of a child from his mother on the auction block. It is remarkable for its almost exclusive focus on body language, a device that renders eloquent the plight of the otherwise voiceless victims. The only audible sounds are the mother's shrieks, which open and close the poem, and the speaker's asking her Father (probably both her biological parent and God are intended; line 32) if the mother and son must be separated.

Although the gender of the speaker is never announced, it seems likely that she is female because she feels such empathy for the slave mother and so highly values that woman's relationship with her son. The only clothing mentioned is the "kirtle" (a simply designed woman's dress; line 15) worn by the mother, and there is no overt reference to the race of the victims. Such a scarcity of concrete sensory details and the poet's willingness to so constantly focus on the internal instead of the external landscape may hinder a modern reader's ability to fully realize the scene, but it could be argued that FRANCES E. W. HARPER did not want such details to shift the focus from the human dimensions of the tragedy. One of her metaphors effectively conveys subjective impressions of the woman's plight (when a storm of agony sweeps through the woman's brain in line 12), but another is so overwrought that it distracts from the business at hand (the boy's love is artificially described as a gushing fountain amid life's wild desert in line 28). Even less defensible is her reliance on such conditional phrases as "it seemed" and "as if" (lines 3 and 11); notice how much more effective are the cruel hands that threaten to tear the "wreath of household love that binds her breaking heart" (lines 23–24) without such qualifiers.

Later audiences might recognize the broad gestures of the Victorian melodrama in the poem, but a contemporary audience would have been more involved with and shocked at such a dramatic portrayal of an overt attack on one of their most sacred institutions, motherhood. This helped them realize the real pain involved in such tragic scenes, which were an undeniable fact of mid-19th-century American life.

"THE SLAVE'S DREAM" HENRY WADSWORTH LONGFELLOW (1842)

Although it is most commonly associated with cotton farming, American slavery was used for the production of a variety of agricultural commodities as well as for nonagricultural labor in all of the British-American colonies prior to the Revolutionary War. By 1842, slavery had been outlawed in the states north of Maryland, but most Americans were trying so desperately to ignore this explosive issue that even Congress passed gag rules to prevent its members from raising it. With this and similar poems, Longfellow added his voice to those of the other New England poets who supported the abolitionist movement.

The poem begins with an unflattering portrait of the slave asleep on the job. Closer examination would reveal that although he was engaged in harvesting food, he was evidently too hungry, too ill, or too abused to continue. His bare breast and matted hair hint at his poverty (line 3), and the tragic ending of the poem is foreshadowed by the description of his hair as buried in the sand. He is dreaming of Africa.

His dream landscape, which mixes images from both sides of the Atlantic, includes the "lordly" Niger (line 8), a West African river longer than the Mississippi, which touched the native lands of a plurality of the Africans brought to America until their importation was banned in 1808. As a king he strode until he heard "the tinkling caravans" descending the mountain road (lines 11–12); their "tinkling" may have come from the finished wares they hoped to sell or, more sinisterly, the chains of their slaves. Once more he saw his queen and their children. This is a moving sight, but HENRY WADSWORTH LONGFELLOW overdoes it when he describes the sleeper's single "tear burst" (line 17). It somehow fell into the sand despite the sleeper's posture.

Then he rode his horse with its golden reins, and at each leap "he could feel his scabbard of steel" (line 23), a line that begs Freudian interpretation. As his erotic dream continues, he spends an entire day following the blood red flamingoes over plains where the tamarind trees, native to Asia, were growing. Near the ocean, he also passes "Kaffir" huts. Today in southern Africa that is often used as a pejorative term based on race, but at the time it merely indicated that the inhabitants were not Moslem. The point may be that he has left a virtual paradise and is now entering the godless portion of his life. It is now night, and to the darkness are added the terrifying sounds of predatory animals (lion and hyena) and a rampaging hippopotamus. This last creature was so fast and ponderous that it sounded like a glorious drum roll as it passed (line 35) in the "triumph" (think "parade of images") of his dream.

The forests, with the myriad tongues of the innumerable animal as well as human tribes, shout of liberty. The Blast of the Desert might refer to the fierce sirocco winds off the mountains of North Africa (in southern California similar winds are called Santa Anas). This is serious enough to startle him, but he smiles in sympathy with their tempestuous glee.

Because slavery was so inefficient, owners frequently hired overseers to compel as much labor from their slaves as possible. Their weapon of choice was a driver's whip capable of removing flesh and leaving a lasting scar with each lash. On this occasion, the sleeper was not roused by such cruelty because he was already dead. Longfellow's euphemism ("Death had illumined the Land of Sleep," line 45) is interesting for its suggestion of something like an afterlife in which the spirit would be returned to paradisiacal Africa.

Like any good poet, Longfellow drew his final image from the subject at hand; the sleeper's soul had left his body behind like a worn-out and discarded fetter. Rivaling the hated whip in the slavers' arsenal of oppression were the chains in which slaves were marched from Africa, frequently restrained on the ships and often on the New World auction block, and thereafter whenever it was deemed necessary by the overseers as a deterrent against their escaping.

Why was this poem considered controversial? Southern sympathizers before the war would have been troubled by the poem's account of the slave's rich emotional life, including his family relationships, its identification of Africa as a paradise and land of liberty, and the disquieting intensity with which the slave

desires freedom. The penultimate line even states that the slave had a soul, so his humanity cannot be denied. These are uncomfortable assertions to anyone whose livelihood was tied to an institution in which a slave's body could be whipped even after his death (line 43).

"THE SLEEPER" EDGAR ALLAN POE (1845)

The best thing about this is the twist it gives to the traditional love poem by frustrating the early 19th-century reader's expectation of an easily accomplished happy ending. The situation seems to begin conventionally; the speaker has taken up the admirer's usual post outside a beautiful girl's window under the June moon. The facile pairing of these last two words, quite possibly the first two to spring into a novice poet's head since the Norman conquest led to their being rhymed in English, would normally be a clear signal that the poet has not challenged himself. Here, however, the lateness of the hour (it is already midnight, traditionally viewed as the "witching" hour) and the speaker's dwelling not on the fullness of the moon but on its mystical qualities (line 2) suggest that something unexpected may be afoot. Rather than being a mere lamp in the night or a focal point around which two lovers might build a shared experience, this moon is malignant. A dewy opiate ("sleep-inducing," but the term has the sinister background of being derived from opium, a narcotic) vapor exhales from the moon's golden rim (line 4), "dripping, drop by drop" (a phrase that suggests the absorbed fixation of a drug abuser on the delivery of his medication. Before the terrible addictive properties of opium were understood, it was freely sold as a patent medicine [most commonly in a sweetened form known as laudanum] and often taken as a painkiller or sleep aid). Here it drops upon a quiet mountain top, but "steals drowsily and musically" (perhaps an indication of the distorted sensory perceptions in a drug-addled mind: a visual sensation is experienced as an aural one) "into the universal valley" (a probable metaphor for death or sign of the speaker's inescapable [because "universal"] depression; line 8).

In the 19th century, use of the language of flowers (the message sent by the choice of a particular species) was more common than it would be in later centuries. Here, if the rosemary (suggestive of remembrance) "nods" on a grave and the lily (purity) "lolls" upon the wave (lines 9–10), EDGAR ALLAN POE's contemporaries might suspect that such tender emotions were not in play in this scene, or that the object of his affections had passed on to a better life. The next lines seem to solve the mystery; a personified ruin wraps the fog about its breast and "moulders [decays] into rest" (lines 11–12). A nearby lake brings Lethe, a river in the Greek myth of Hades, to mind, and a "conscious slumber" (an oxymoron suggestive, here, of a life after death) takes hold. All beauty sleeps, including Irene and her Destinies (That this Irene had more than one destiny suggests that the speaker was thinking of Irene, the Greek goddess of peace; line 17).

The second section begins with some ambiguity as the speaker addresses "lady bright" (line 18), who might be his lost love, the personified moon, or the goddess Irene. He also finds a window "open to the night" which, because the poem is as much concerned with internal emotional landscapes as with external physical ones, may also imply that his psyche is open to the dark thoughts that may be repressed during the day. There is a suggestion of a sexual element (one definition of the "wanton airs" that drop "laughingly" from the treetop is "licentious attitudes or influences;" lines 20–21), but the first stanza has already established the malevolency of the evening, and the lady's chamber is filled with the "bodiless airs" (or spirits) that flit in and out in their "wizard rout" (line 22). These wave the canopy curtains (a feature on many of the elaborate four-poster beds of the period as well as of the richest tombs) fitfully and fearfully "above the closed and fringed lid" that covers the beautiful woman's coffin (line 26). One senses that for the speaker the phrase "slumbering soul lies hid" is not an empty euphemism for death but an expression of fervid desire for her restoration not in the next life, but in this one. Like ghosts, the shadows rise and fall on floor and wall, and suddenly the speaker sees a phantom "lady dear" (line 30). Noting her absence of fear, he asks why she is dreaming there and the content of her thoughts. Her coloring (the term "pallor" often designates ill-health or death), strange attire, and exceedingly long hair (because decay of a cadaver's scalp and gum loss revealed more of its previously hidden length of hair and teeth, super-

stition held that they continued to grow post-mortem; line 35). But her "solemn silentness" is what really gets to him (his coining of the term "silentness" for "silence" may indicate how shaken he is; line 36).

This lady (the apparition before him) sleeps (line 37), and he wishes her deep sleep to remain enduring and for heaven to keep her in its "sacred keep" (since the "keep" of a castle is its dungeon, the expression is ambiguous. It is unclear whether he is asking for protection for her soul or for his own protection from it; line 39). He would have her change the present chamber for one more holy and her present bed "for one more melancholy" (namely her own tomb; line 41). He prays to God that she may lie "forever with unopened eye while the pale sheeted ghosts go by" (lines 43–44).

The last stanza begins with more ambiguity as his exclamation "My love, she sleeps!" may indicate that the apparition is still asleep (and he invokes "my love" as one might a protective saint), that he has turned his attention back to the woman in the coffin, or that the disquieting adventures of this night have brought closure in the sense that love is no longer his chief thought in relation to the dead. It gradually becomes clear that he is referring to the phantom, for he hopes that the worms will creep so softly about her cadaver that she will not awaken. He hopes that a far-distant burial vault, as richly embellished as befits her noble birth, will call her back. In her youth she may have idly thrown stones against the door of the family tomb, but now no echo from her will penetrate it. As a child, it thrilled her to think that the echo from her stones came from the groans of the dead. Calling her a "poor child of sin" (line 59) not only connected her with Adam and Eve, whose original sin made all their descendents inherently rebellious, it may also lightly condemn her innocent action (throwing stones at a tomb) as immoral. At the time, she did not fully realize the implications for her own mortality that her family's deaths would have insinuated to an older person.

For the first version of this poem (1831), Poe used "Irene" as his title and, as the name of the goddess of peace might suggest, the spirits were allowed their rest. The final version of the work is superior because it is difficult to reconcile the passion that could bring the speaker to such a midnight rendezvous with the cynicism with which the original began. After Love stopped weeping for the dead (it takes but a week or two before "light laughter chokes the sigh"), the spirit rises from the crypt. Returning to a lake where in happier times it may have once bathed with friends, it sinks to the "uncertain, shadowy heaven below" (a probable reference to the reflections of the sky [or "heavens"] one can see in standing water). Thus it can be seen that Poe's updating of the myth of Lethe, which brought forgetfulness to all who drank from it in Hades, probably played a seminal role in the creation of the poem.

"THE SLEEPERS" WALT WHITMAN (1855)

The commentary that follows is based on the 1881 version of this poem, for which WALT WHITMAN divided the text into sections, eliminated 18 lines and replaced the many ellipses that originally separated many of the items in his lists with commas. Since the speaker announces that she has taken a female role (or is a woman) in the opening section (line 46), she will merit female pronouns throughout this essay.

The poem opens with the speaker's confused wandering in her night visions. She stops to look at the generally solemn-looking sleepers and to listen to their quiet breaths. She also sees the wretched faces of the ennui (the terminally bored), the white features of corpses, the livid faces of drunks, the sick-gray faces of onanists (masturbators), gashed battlefield bodies, the confined insane, "sacred idiots" (in many cultures the mentally challenged are considered God's people and protected because of their innocence), the newborn emerging from gates (a rather cold metaphor for the birthing process) and the dying emerging from gates. The night pervades and enfolds them (line 10).

She sees married couples sleeping with their palms on each other's hips, the sisters sleeping together, the men sleeping "lovingly side by side" in their beds and the mother sleeping with her carefully wrapped child. The blind, the deaf, those incapable of speech, the imprisoned and the runaway son sleep. The speaker wonders how the murderer sleeps on the day before he is to be hanged, and how the murdered person sleeps (line 18).

Unrequited lovers, successful money-makers, the enraged, and the treacherous all sleep. (Like a benevolent sandman), she passes her hands over the worst-suffering and most restless and they fitfully sleep (line 25). She can pierce the darkness or fly into space, sleep close with all the other sleepers and dream all the dreams, becoming the other dreamers (line 31).

Calling herself a dance, she describes a fit, a trance-like state in which she whirls (which could be a reference to the Whirling Dervish or Mevlevi Order founded in the old Persian Empire, or to one of the Christian sects in which similar movement was used to achieve religious ecstasy; line 32). She claims to be the ever-laughing (perhaps a pun on "everlasting," one of the adjectives or euphemisms for God). She sees delights (the "douceurs" of line 34; since colonial times, French terms frequently were used by educated Americans to designate things for which the English names might offend) and treasures being hidden deep in the ground and the sea, and ghosts.

Though the divine journeymen may be skilled, they can hide nothing from her, their boss and pet (lines 36–37). They actually delight in revealing things to her, forming a "gay (which only meant "happy" at the time) gang of blackguards with mirth-shouting music and wild-flapping pennants of joy" (Freudians take note; line 41).

She is the actor and actress, the voter and politician, the emigrant and the exile (note the connectedness of each pairing; line 42) as well as famous men of the past and future, one who stammers, an attractive person, and a sick or feeble person.

She dressed herself and her hair in expectation. When her truant lover comes, she asks that the darkness double itself and receive the two of them, for the lover will not let her go alone. She rolls herself upon the internal audience (which, at this point, is the darkness) as upon a bed, resigning herself to the dusk (line 50). She may summon whomever she chooses to replace the lover, and they rise silently from the bed.

Darkness is gentler than her lover, who left her, sweaty and panting, with hot moisture. She presses her spread hands in all directions and would "sound up" (measure the depths) of the shadowy shore to which the darkness is journeying. But darkness must be careful as they are not alone. She hears the heartbeat of the lover she thought had left. Following, she fades away.

The next section anticipates the speaker's declining years, when her muscles are weak and she seems only the wake of the perfume and youth that earlier flowed through her. She identifies with the yellow wrinkled face of an old woman who darns her grandson's stockings and stares at the sparkles of starshine on a winter night like a widow (who lacks someone with whom to share the scene). She becomes a shroud (the clothes in which cadavers were wrapped prior to burial that can be seen as the very symbols of death; line 66). She finds no pain or evil in the grave, but only blank darkness, and feels that everything still in the light and air should be happy. She would have everyone not in the coffin or the grave know that he/she has enough.

The third section presents the wet dream of a gigantic middle-aged naked swimmer in the sea. He has short brown hair, courageous arms that strike the sea, and a white body. The speaker hates the eddies that would dash him on the rocks and chastises the "ruffianly red-tickled waves" for trying to kill him. He struggles long and steady, but eventually his strength gives out. The circling, blood-spotted eddies bear him away, swinging and turning his beautiful corpse until they bear it out of sight.

In the fourth section the speaker continues dreaming. Although touched by the imagery of the prior section, she does not yet want to rouse herself from the dream state. A "razory ice-wind" (line 83) cuts the beach as wreck-guns (life-saving signals that a ship is sinking close offshore) sound. During a break in the tempest the moon "comes floundering" (a verb often used to describe the breakup of a boat or ship against rocks or other hazards) through the drifts (a noun probably chosen to reinforce how cold it is, since it is more commonly used in reference to snow).

The ship is driven stern first toward the shore and breaks up immediately, judging from the "howls of dismay" (line 85) that just as suddenly diminish (since this is a dream sequence one can expect distortions in time, but in this instance that may not have been the case. The ability to swim was far less widespread during the 19th century than in the 20th because of the lessons provided by the Red Cross throughout most of the

latter century. Panic and the shock of sudden immersion in freezing water could account for the rapidity of some of the deaths, and if the water temperature was close to freezing, hypothermia could kill everyone not adequately clothed [preferably in a rubberized survival suit] in less than 15 minutes. Although the dreamer may have felt badly about not being able to rescue the victims, she did all she could by positioning herself in the surf zone to help anyone who made it that far). In the morning she helped pick up the dead and lay them in rows in a barn (but she would have joined their number had she tried to swim to the rescue).

The fifth section deals with two Revolutionary War incidents at opposite ends of the emotional spectrum in the life of George Washington. The first represents the lowest point, a disastrous rout by the British army on the morning of August 27, 1776. The poet focused on the tears on the general's cold and damp face as he looked through a monocular field glass from Brooklyn Heights at the slaughter of young men entrusted to him by their parents (line 94. Most modern military historians think the British could have ended the war had they more vigorously followed up on this victory. Instead, Washington and the remainder of his Long Island forces were able to slip across the river to safety on the evening of August 29, leaving New York City in British hands until the end of the war).

The second scene took place in New York City on December 4, 1783, when Washington bid farewell to his senior officers at the Fraunces Tavern. Men like General Henry Knox who had stoically endured all the privations of war since 1775 openly wept as they embraced their leader and received his kiss. The victorious Washington returned his commission as commander in chief to Congress on December 23, 1783.

In the sixth section, the speaker used the racist language of her mother to relate the early morning visit of a beautiful "red squaw" to her father's homestead (if the speaker shared the same parental history as the poet, the meeting probably occurred on Long Island some time before the marriage of his parents on June 8, 1816). The Native American maiden carried rushes (the sturdy harvested stems of aquatic plants) as a trade or sale item for use in making furniture. The speaker's mother fell in love with her physicality, especially the ease of her step, her "tall-borne face" (an indication of her pride) and pliant limbs (line 107). Although her mother had no work for this guest, she fondly fed and talked with her until the maiden left in mid-afternoon. The speaker's mother often thought of and even watched for her return, but it never happened.

The seventh section deals with the juxtaposition of opposites leading toward their reconciliation, since night and sleep make them equals. The speaker dreams of a summer softness in which she can gallivant (a more elegant term for cavorting or partying) with the light and air, and of autumn and winter. Elements merge in the night (becoming new things) and sailing ships "make tacks" (change direction to continue sailing across the wind while ultimately zigzagging to their goal since they are incapable of sailing directly upwind; line 123) in her dreams. Sailors sail, and exiles and emigrants return home. A poor Irishman returns to his native land and barefoot ways, forgetting he is well off. Various nationalities return home, and loaded vessels enter the ports of England, France, and Spain.

In dreams most of the people identified by their extreme behavior in the opening section return, including an affectionate boy, the voter, and successful and unsuccessful nominees. The great of the past and of the future appear, as does the person who stammers and the handsome as well as the homely. The criminal appears with all the court officials, the laugher, the weeper, and the red squaw. The comsumptive (a victim of tuberculosis, then a terrifyingly common and deadly disease) and the erysipalite (who suffers from erysipelas, thus developing a serious skin rash caused by an acute streptococcus bacterial infection), and the mentally challenged appear, and like antipodes (two opposites points on the earth, like the North and South Poles) and everyone between them, all are averaged and none is better than another in the dreams.

In dreams the speaker declares that everyone is beautiful, as are all sleepers. The "wildest and bloodiest" (line 146) is over, leaving beautiful, heavenly peace. The myth of heaven indicates peace, night, and the soul (lines 148–49). The soul is always beautiful as it comes from the embowered garden (a probable reference to the Garden of Eden; line 151), as are the previously "jetting" (an adjective suggesting a physical angle and

a verb akin to spraying) genitals and the womb. The head, bowels, and joints are also well proportioned.

Everything has its place in the ordered universe of the dream, even the twisted skull and illness (represented by the "watery or rotten blood" of line 157). The child of the glutton, veneralee (a person who has devoted himself entirely to the pursuit of sexual pleasure), or drunkard will also eventually find their place. Sleepers living and dead wait, the far advanced go in their turn, and the far behind come on in their turn (line 159). The diverse remain diverse but unite even now.

The last section begins with the assertion that naked sleepers are beautiful and flow hand in hand. Various races (identified by their continent of origin such as "Asiatic") unite, as do the learned and unlearned, male and female. In sleep, lovers embrace without lust, as do the father and son, and the mother and daughter. The breath of the boy goes with the breath of the man, and friend is "inarmed" (probably "taken in arm") by friend (line 168). Scholars and teachers kiss, and the wronged is made right. The slave's call is equal to the master's, and the latter salutes the former. Felons and the insane leave their respective prisons, and the sick no longer suffer. Even rheumatic joints move smoother than ever. The paralyzed, swelled, convulsed and congested are restored by the invigoration and chemistry of the night (line 176).

The speaker also passes from the night but returns and loves it. She sees no reason to fear entrusting herself to the night although she loves the rich running day (line 181). She does not know how she came of night or where it will take her, but she knows she shall go well. She will stop with the night only for a time and then rise, but will duly return to that mother.

"SNOW-BOUND" John Greenleaf Whittier (1866)

For many modern readers, the prospect of spending a week cooped up in the family home with nine other people sounds anything but idyllic. John Greenleaf Whittier's poem begins with the cheerless observation that the sun at noon gave "a sadder light" than a waning moon (lines 3–4). In addition to its seasonal gloom, the day brought bone-chilling cold that the speaker's homemade clothing (called "homespun" in line 10, a designation suggesting that its fibers were hand-woven on a spinning wheel before being turned into cloth and ultimately fashioned into a garment) could not entirely stop. Thus the poem begins with two of winter's three principal drawbacks (darkness and cold), and the east wind promises the third: tons of snow will fall all along the New England seaboard as the moisture-saturated oceanic air is chilled as it pushes up into the hills.

Although the snow might close the local school, innumerable farm chores prevent the children from complete enjoyment of the impromptu holiday. Exposure to a variety of animals has enriched their lives immeasurably, however. Notice that the speaker understands the animals' situations just from hearing their customary noises and also has the ability to identify various types of wood and their uses (walnut in line 25 and birch in line 27). The children also have variations in weather to enjoy, and the richness of their imaginations is evident in the description of the "whirl-dance" of the falling snow and the comparison of particular drifts to "tall and sheeted ghosts" (lines 34 and 40). Any child raised in snow country has stopped to examine individual flakes, but probably only an adult would think to describe their geometry in terms of the spherule and pellicle of the fourth stanza.

Although it snowed all night, by morning not a single cloud remained in the sky. Layers of snow have transformed the rural landscape into some of the most distinctive architectural features from around the world, including Chinese roofs and the leaning tower of Pisa (lines 62 and 65).

Their father ordered a path to the barn, which the boys eagerly shoveled, including a tunnel named in honor of Aladdin's cave. The speaker marked each type of animal's reaction to their slightly delayed breakfasts, including oxen and sheep. The farm had been so isolated that even in other seasons the brook's sound was almost as welcome as a human voice, but now even that solace was inaudible beneath layers of snow and ice (line 111).

Not all the novelties of that winter occurred outdoors, however. The expertly built fire casts its red hue on the whitewashed walls and even out onto the snowdrifts (stanza seven), and the process of its kindling is recorded with the close attention of one who

is not only fascinated by its sights and sounds, but one whose survival may be dependent upon it. The ornamental heads on the andirons (metal supports upon which the wood is placed to facilitate better oxygen flow to the fire) bring to mind witches, an apt transition to the eerie lighting of the full moon. This once again transforms the landscape, but even as the north wind howls, the family (including the house dog and the cat) loiter as their cider and apples are warmed by the fire (stanza nine).

Although the wind could not touch the family, time and death did, and only the poet and his brother were still alive when the poem was written. Love keeps all of them alive in his memory, however, and faith adds its hope. The 11th stanza recalls the stories, puzzles, and riddles with which they interacted. The children recited poetry, including lines from an abolitionist poem that probably helped inspire Whittier's own antislavery verses. His father's talk of a rugged trip to Canada ended with his memories of a village dance that "mingled in its merry whirl" the oldest woman and the laughing girl (lines 234–235). On another occasion, he used a clamshell to dip the freshest possible chowder from a pot over a beach fire.

For her part, his mother told of an Indian attack and her life story, with an emphasis on her fishing and flower- and nut-gathering. She drew on Quaker books for other tales, which included a skipper's willingness to sacrifice himself to feed his starving crew until porpoises appeared as if by divine decree to save him (by taking his place on the menu; lines 290–306). Although his uncle lacked formal education, the speaker was well versed in woodcraft, natural portents, and all the adventures a hunter and fisherman could find in the immediate vicinity. His aunt, grown but still girlish as a consequence of never having married, told of such community activities as huskings (harvesting and removing the leaves and silk from ears of corn), apple-bees, sleigh-rides, and sailing (lines 361–363).

His older sister, remarkable for her self-sacrificing earnestness and trusting nature, has also passed beneath the grave, here euphemistically described as a "low green tent" (line 390). His younger sister passed into eternity just the year before the poem was written (line 404). He remembers her devotion and companionship on such summer jaunts as her health permitted and is confident of her place in heaven.

The local schoolmaster, so young he lacked whiskers, stayed with the family. During the longer school vacations he would travel as a salesman, which provided him with anecdotes. He played the violin and brought classical mythology closer to home by placing the action in the surrounding hills. Although he seemed but a boy at the fireplace, at his desk he assumed the mantle of an apostle of freedom and enlightenment. Such men had recently overcome the darkness, ignorance, pride, lust, and squalid sloth that sparked the South's treason, murders, and prison tortures (lines 491–496). They would soon, by spreading education and using the latest technological advances like the telegraph (lines 502–505), reconnect North and South and together harvest the fields upon which the recently concluded Civil War had been fought.

A second guest seemed the terror of household, for her demure exterior hid a mercurial temperament. A "woman tropical, intense in thought and act" (lines 531–532), she brought to mind a leopard's treacherous grace (line 523). Since then she has gone on Old-World pilgrimages, fallen in with another eccentric woman and, now gray-haired and stooped, each daydreams, prophecies, and watches for the second coming of the Lord. Her moods swung from sorrow to happiness, but the speaker feels it is not for mankind to understand "the tangled skein of will and fate" that made her so (line 580).

At nine o'clock the household roused themselves from the fireside. The speaker's uncle stirred the fire until ashes covered the smoldering brands, and his mother paused and, motivated by her own contentment, prayed that no one else would lack food, clothing, warmth, and light on that cold night.

Severe winds sometimes shook the house, but everyone soon settled into summer dreams. The next morning men with oxen (called teamsters long before organized labor appropriated that term) worked their way to the house on their road-clearing mission. After tasting the homemade cider of each household they would move on, but not until the younger members of the group had wrestled in the snow and thrown snowballs in the direction of the merry girls they saw in the doorways of the houses.

The first up the newly opened road was the doctor, who asked the speaker's mother to help a sick neighbor. In the face of suffering, Quaker and Calvinist acted in concert without their respective religions making a difference. They had been snowed in for a week and had exhausted their limited supply of reading material to the point where they were forced to read an uninspiring epic poem by a Quaker writer. When the newspaper finally arrived, it transported them beyond the states and across the Atlantic in its topical references to Greek and Costa Rican military adventures. Closer to home, its reports of sales, "the latest culprit sent to jail" (line 705), weddings, and deaths effectively lifted the "chill embargo of the snow" (line 711).

The pressing events of his current life force him to ask the "Angel of the backward look" to close up its book of the spectral past (lines 715–739). Yet he imagines a reader in the hectic urban world to whom his portraits of that winter, and especially the homestead hearth and wood fire blaze, will be as welcome and perhaps as restorative as a fresh breeze.

"SNOW-FLAKES" HENRY WADSWORTH LONGFELLOW (1863)

Although the speaker uses the softest words to convey the slow descent of the snow and personifies the Air as a maiden who softly shakes the precipitation from the clouds (her garments), the bulk of HENRY WADSWORTH LONGFELLOW's poem focuses not on the beauty of winter but on the grief and despair attendant upon the death that inevitably accompanies the season.

The titillating imagery of the opening stanza captures the initial beauty of a storm and its transformation of brown and bare woodlands and lonely, postharvest fields by the silent, soft, and slow descent of the snow (lines 5–6; the cumulative effect of the s sounds is less sibilant [a hissing sound] than soothing because the vowels and consonants that follow that letter are different in each word).

The second stanza challenges such an easy acceptance of the change, however. Only "our cloudy fancies" read some divine expression into the shapes nature assumes (lines 7–8; the convoluted syntax of this entire stanza may have been intended to mirror the chaos of the advancing storm or the confusion confronting the human mind as it struggles to understand the season of death as a manifestation of divine will). Similarly enigmatic is the white countenance (line 10) with which the troubled heart makes a confession (note that its message remains on the physiological level instead of prompting a verbal response. Blanched skin could as easily indicate a variety of physical problems or a general emotional reaction to the stress of a situation, instead of a straightforward confession). The stanza ends with a pathetic fallacy (in which inanimate things such as clouds are seen to act in sympathy with a developing human drama). This constitutes yet another warning against too literally or liberally interpreting natural phenomena as signs from God or nature. In this connection, rain is more conventionally described as representing the tears of nature, and the speaker's more unusual interpretation of snow as symptomatic of the sky's troubled grief reveals the extent of his troubled emotions.

The last stanza interprets snow as the poem of the air (line 13), with individual flakes or moments of the storm representing the syllables of a spoken language. Returning to the image with which the poem began, the speaker is now able to understand the secret of despair that comes whispering from the cloudy bosom of the air until it is revealed to the wood and field. Such a message was evident even in the beginning, however; the poet's chosen Venus and Adonis stanza (six lines rhymed ababcc) tends to emphasize the importance of the rhymed words in its quatrain. Here these include *shaken, bare,* and *forsaken* (lines 2–4); only the provocative beauty of its imagery and the smoothness of its closing couplet kept the speaker from fully realizing the implications of these words.

"THE SNOW-STORM" RALPH WALDO EMERSON (1846)

Perhaps the strong winter winds are "the trumpets of the sky" (line 1); they certainly contribute to "the whited air" (line 3) by keeping the snow in motion. Apparently the storm is approaching the conditions modern meteorologists call "white-out;" when the visibility approaches zero not even hills, woods or houses can be seen. This brings all transportation

(ranging from the horse-drawn sled to the express courier, lines 5–6) to a halt. Eventually almost all motion even inside the house is reduced to a circle around the radiant fireplace (line 8). At this point RALPH WALDO EMERSON's description takes an unexpected turn; the housemates have been driven to the point where they are "enclosed in a tumultuous privacy of storm" (lines 8–9). Although the phrase clearly points to the tempest outside the door, there is sufficient ambiguity to suggest that the inhabitants may be getting on each other's nerves. This reading is reinforced by the coldness of their description as "housemates" and not "family," especially since "all friends" have been shut out by the storm (in line 7).

The storm evidently stopped between stanzas, and now the speaker invites the internal audience to see the north wind's masonry (line 10). Masons typically work with mortar or concrete to bind cinder blocks, bricks, or tiles for the construction of walks, floors, and walls. The rest of this poem focuses on the fanciful comparison of the snow-encrusted features in the landscape with the work of masterful masons in the service of an imaginative architect with no regard for "number or proportion" (line 17), two of the concerns traditionally helping to give architecture its pleasing symmetry. Coated with snow, even stakes and trees appear as massive as "bastions," the protruding portions of castle walls. The most picturesque effects, including marble wreaths, appear on the chicken coop or dog kennel, but the sculpture also works in miniatures, such as the swan that covers a thorn (line 19), and resurfaces the lane from wall to wall regardless of the owner's wishes ("Maugre [notwithstanding] the farmer's sighs," line 21), and finishes with a special ornamental column ("a tapering turret") at the gate. Despite their needlessly convoluted syntax, the last six lines suggest that it will take human architects and masons (since only they have the "Art" required for the service at hand) an entire "age" (perhaps an entire historical era or even geologic period) to mimic the night wind's "frolic architecture of the snow" (line 28).

"SOME KEEP THE SABBATH GOING TO CHURCH" EMILY DICKINSON (1864)

This poem expresses sentiments similar to those of WILLIAM

CULLEN BRYANT's "A FOREST HYMN"; like his/her precursor, the speaker in EMILY DICKINSON's poem finds the contemplation of God to be more appealing in those natural haunts most congenial to her than in a formal religious setting. In each poem parallels are drawn between aspects of the natural world and the church fixtures they resemble. As in Bryant's forest, the trees of an orchard seem a fitting dome, and a Bobolink (also celebrated in Bryant's "ROBERT OF LINCOLN") leads the choir. Each poem answers the criticism that the speakers are not keeping the Sabbath, which for the poets' New England ancestors frequently meant state-mandated church attendance as well as enforced abstinence from work or pleasure.

In the second stanza, the speaker identifies more with the birds (or possibly the angels) when she expresses a preference for "just" wearing "my" wings instead of vestments. Such diction reinforces the simplicity of her devotion and her ownership of her faith. Instead of the intrusive public tolling of the bell (one of the duties performed by a sexton), she prefers the singing of "our little Sexton," presumably a bird that she compares to the menial laborer of the church.

For clergy, she has God (whom she jokingly refers to as "a noted Clergyman" [line 9] whose sermon is never long). Instead of getting to heaven "at last" (after her death and resurrection), she feels as though she is experiencing it all along. The phrasing of the last line ("I'm going, all along") also reveals the speaker's confidence that this approach will lead her to that goal.

"SONG OF EGLA" MARIA GOWEN BROOKS (1820)

This poem reveals why the major poets Robert Southey (the British poet laureate) and EDGAR ALLAN POE were so lavish in their praise of MARIA GOWEN BROOKS and what that poet lacked that led her to be all but forgotten in the following century. As a psychological study, the poem was wonderfully insightful for its time. Modern feminists might bristle at the speaker's need for a lover to save her from herself (or at least from her intolerable loneliness) and chafe at the passivity involved in merely awaiting the lover's arrival instead of developing more proactive strategies, but they can admire the self-awareness she brings to the affair and thus her implied control of the situation.

The opening line, "Day in melting purple dying," remains wonderfully fresh and evocative, but her chosen meter, rhymed couplets of trochaic heptameter, comes across as too mechanically predictable and hence too playful to adequately convey the loneliness of the speaker. The next two lines use the pathetic fallacy (having nature act as if in sympathy with human emotion): Blossoms sigh and lily fragrance strays (diction that may imply the speaker is contemplating doing the same thing). Zephyr (the name for the west wind adapted from Greek mythology) plays with her ringlets (curls of her hair), but this only awakens her distress. She is, she announces, sick of her loneliness (line 6). From her absent lover ("Thou to whom I love to hearken," line 7. "To hearken" is to hear, but it also implies obedience), she requests a visit before nightfall. She sees through his pretenses ("Though thy softness but deceive me," line 9), but admits her complicity with his dodges in stating that she will believe his assertions of devotion. She would have him veil his soul's intent so that she can think it innocent (line 12).

She does not need his "toiling" (perhaps his labored attempts to please her) or his wealth, but only asks for the pleasure of his friendship. She has no desire for gold or gems, but only to look on him and to tell him the "high-wrought feeling" (line 19) that is ecstasy to reveal. She would "paint to thee the deep sensation" and "rapture in participation" (phrases that invite Freudian interpretation; lines 21–2), but is tortured by the same impulses when they remain compressed in a "lone unfriended breast" (line 24).

She yearns for the blessing of his company so that she can caress him with her eyes (line 26). Whereas she once cautiously fled him, she can now deny him nothing and is willing to face death for the privilege of gazing on him.

THE SONG OF HIAWATHA HENRY WADSWORTH LONGFELLOW (1855)

In his introduction HENRY WADSWORTH LONGFELLOW attributes the poem's stories and sensory details (including the odors of the forest and the damp of the meadows) to a great Indian singer named Nawadaha who lived in the valley named Tawasentha in the land of the Ojibwa, the Dakota, and the Great Lakes. He learned these tales directly from the fauna of the region (which are itemized in both English and Ojibwa; for example, the wild goose is called Wawa). The eponymous hero is introduced as a Christ-like figure complete with "wondrous birth and being," prayers, and fasting. He toiled and suffered that the tribes of men might prosper and his people might advance.

The poet recommends this song for those who love nature when the echoes of mountain thunder flap like eagles on their nests, and for those who love national legends. Those with fresh and simple hearts who have faith in God and nature, who believe that every human heart is human, should also listen. Even savages have yearnings they cannot comprehend; although their feeble hands grope blindly they sometimes touch God's right hand in the darkness. This "rude inscription" should also appeal to those who pause at old tombstones to read their homely phrases full of the hope but also the heartbreak of the Here and the Hereafter.

In the first part ("The Peace Pipe"), Gitche Manito, the mighty Master of Life, descended to the Red Pipe-Stone Quarry (a Minnesota site that has been preserved as Pipestone National Monument) and called together all the tribes. A river flowed from his footsteps, for which the Spirit traced a path with his finger in the meadow. He molded and engraved a stone into a pipe-head, and took a long reed from the riverbank for a stem. After filling the pipe with red willow bark, he breathed on the neighboring forest until the great boughs chafed and finally burst into flame. His smoke from this calumet (or peace pipe) rose to heaven, and all the tribes from the Tawasentha valley (near modern Albany in eastern New York) to Wyoming, and from Tuscaloosa (in Alabama) to the Rocky Mountains, beheld the signal. Warriors came to Manito's council from every direction and glared at each other with the feuds of ages in their hearts, but Gitche Manito looked upon them with paternal love and compassion. Chiding his children, the Great Spirit recalled his gifts to them (including the brant [a small goose], the reindeer, and the roe deer, an Old-World species) and asked why they hunt each other.

Tired of their quarrels, he warns them that their strength lies in their union and that discord brings danger. They are to live as brothers, and he will send a prophet to become a deliverer of the nations. If they follow his guidance, they will multiply and prosper; otherwise, they will perish. Manito had them wash their war paint and bloodstain in the stream (which then turned blood red) and bury their weapons. They were to quarry and smoke the calumet together, then live in peace. As they buried weapons, Manito smiled upon his helpless children. They went home, and he ascended through the cloud-curtains and the doorways of heaven, vanishing before them in the smoke ("Pukwana") of the calumet.

The second section celebrates Mudjekeewis. He stole the sacred wampum belt from the neck of the sleeping Mishe-Mokwa (the Great Bear of the Mountains) in the land of the White Rabbit, then clubbed and taunted the dazed animal. The bear whimpered like a woman, and the brave struck him again, breaking his skull as the ice is broken for winter fishing. Thus rid of the terror of the nations, the people renamed the warrior Kabeyun, the West Wind, and gave him control of all winds. He kept the West Wind, but gave the three other winds to his children.

The East Wind went to Wabun, young and beautiful, whose silver arrows chased the dark from the land. He was lonely until successfully wooing a blue-eyed maiden gathering water-flags (which share their name with a European iris) and rushes for him; her blue eyes were two blue lakes. His sunshine smile, sighing, and singing drew her to his bosom. They can still be seen in the heavens, the Sun and the Morning Star.

The fierce North Wind (Kabibonokka) dwelt among icebergs, sent snowflakes hissing, and drove the birds south. He found a diver named Shingebis, who still lingered although his tribe had gone south, and resolved to put out his fire. Well stocked with fish and wood, Shingebis laughed at the wind's ferocity and turned a log so it burnt more hotly. Kabibonokka sweated like spring snow until he could no longer bear the heat and laughter. Shingebis then engaged him in a naked nocturnal wrestling match on the frozen moorlands (or bogs), forcing him back to the North.

Shawondasee, given the South Wind, sent the birds and melons, tobacco and grapes northward. He had once seen a golden-haired maiden in bright green garments on a prairie but was too fat and lazy to woo her.

Finally he saw her covered with snow and accused the North Wind of taking her from him. He breathed his sorrow into the air, and the maiden disappeared, for she had been the prairie dandelion. Thus the four winds stayed divided.

Part three reveals Hiawatha's maternal lineage and childhood. A jealous rival cut the grape vines upon which the beautiful Nokomis was swinging, and she gave birth to Wenonah, her first daughter. Although Nokomis warned her daughter against listening to the West Wind, Wenonah bore him a son, Hiawatha, before dying of anguish at being deserted. Nokomis gave up work and weeping to nurse the boy by the shores of Gitche Gumee (Lake Superior, the Big-Sea-Water). She stilled his wailing with threats of the Big Bear, and taught him the stars, the Death Dance, and the Milky Way (pathway of ghosts). She had a mythological explanation for every phenomenon.

He learned every bird and beast language, including their names and all their secrets. Then Iagoo gave him a bow out of ash, and arrows from an oak, to kill an antlered roebuck. The birds and animals were frightened, but Hiawatha's arrow stung a red deer (an elk) like a wasp. He gained a cloak, a feast, and nicknames from this success.

In part four Hiawatha grows to a skilled and learned manhood. Swift and so strong that he could keep 10 arrows in the air at one time, he also had magic deer-skin mittens enabling him to grind rocks to powder and mile-per-stride moccasins. He became hot "like a living coal" upon learning of his father's treachery and sought him with arrows tipped with jasper.

He journeyed west across Michigan's Escanaba River and the Mississippi River. Eventually he came to the West Wind in the Rocky Mountains, where his father was happy to see such a reminder of his own youth and the beautiful Wenonah. For many days they talked, until the West Wind boasted of his invulnerable body. Hiawatha asked if nothing could harm him and learned the Wind was only afraid of a black rock named Wawbeek. Proud of his son, the West Wind asked the same question, and learned of his fear of the bulrush.

Eventually Hiawatha forced the West Wind to admit his killing of Wenonah. The son grabbed the black rock and ground it into fragments that he hurled at his father. The Wind blew them back and grabbed the bulrushes, but Hiawatha only laughed. They fought as the great war eagle circled over them until the Wind ran west for three days. He stopped at the Sunset, the earth's remotest border, to announce it was impossible to kill an immortal and that he had only been testing the lad's courage. As a reward, Hiawatha was to return to his people to slay all monsters, magicians, and giants and eventually share the West Wind's rule.

Returning home without his anger, Hiawatha met Minnehaha (Laughing Water [or waterfall]), the moody daughter of an arrowhead craftsman. He lingered to see her face and hear the rustle of her garments but did not mention the meeting when he got home.

Part five finds the hero fasting for seven days for the profit of the people. The first three days he observed the animals, plants, and fish and asked the Master of Life if human life must depend upon them. On the fourth day a youth approached in green and yellow garments, with plumes of green over his forehead and golden hair. His name was Mondamin, and he promised to instruct Hiawatha on living by struggle and labor since his prayers had been so unselfish. First, however, they had to wrestle, and Hiawatha felt re-energized every time he touched him. Twenty-four hours later, after sunset on the fifth day, Mondamin called a reprieve. They also wrestled the next two evenings as well, and finally Mondamin announced that the Master of Life would reward Hiawatha for his triumph. Hiawatha was to overcome his adversary, strip his garments, and cover him lightly with dirt. No one and no raven must molest Mondamin until he leaps into the sunshine.

Hiawatha slept well, and Nokomis brought him food on the seventh day to prevent fatal starvation, which he refused. When Mondamin reappeared, the haggard Hiawatha wrestled again although his strong heart leaped like a sturgeon struggles in a net. When Mondamin died, Hiawatha began a daily watch over the grave. Finally a small green feather emerged, and by the end of summer stood the maize (natural Indian corn, which came in a variety of colors). Hiawatha recognized Mondamin, the friend of man. Soon the Indians enjoyed the Feast of Mondamin as a gift from the Great Spirit.

The next part introduces Hiawatha's two good friends, the musician Chibiabos and the strong Kwasind; the three of them talked with naked hearts about how the tribes might prosper. Chibiabos produced such music from reed flutes that the brook and the birds asked for his instruction. He softened men's hearts with songs of Ponemah, in the Hereafter. The devout Kwasind allied his strength to goodness, but drew criticism as a lad for being lazy. Asked to help wring water from the fishnets, he could not help breaking them (and even hunting bows) with his strength. While hunting with his father, he cleared tree trunks from their path. He would not join other youth in quoits (a game similar to horseshoes except circular metal rings are tossed), but he threw a huge rock into the river, where it can still be seen. He also dove and brought back the King of Beavers, dead and dripping on his shoulders.

In part seven, Hiawatha built the first birch-bark canoe, ribbed with trimmed branches, sewn at the ends with larch-root fibers, and sealed with fir-tree resin. He also produced a hedgehog (native only to Europe and Asia; perhaps Longfellow meant porcupine), quill necklace, girdle, and two decorative stars. The hedgehog shot his quills like arrows (normally an impossibility for porcupines, who must come into contact with an assailant), and Hiawatha gathered and stained them. His thoughts alone powered the canoe, and Kwasind cleared logs and sandbars from the water. Thus Hiawatha sailed down the Taquamenaw (perhaps the modern Tahquamenon River in upper Michigan).

In the eighth section, Hiawatha catches the King of Fishes, the sturgeon Mishe-Nahma, on Lake Superior (Gitche Gumee), resplendent in his natural colors and protected by bony plates and spines. Tired of the Indian's verbal challenges, the King told the pike and then the sunfish to break his line, but each failed. Finally the King swallowed Hiawatha and his canoe, but Hiawatha smote the fish's heart. The fish drifted dead upon the shore, and the seagulls freed Hiawatha from the sturgeon's ribs. For this service they were considered friends and allowed to eat their fill until evening, when the remainder of the fish would be boiled for oil. For three days and nights these two shifts alternated until only the skeleton remained.

The next section begins with Nokomis, Hiawatha's grandmother and guardian, sending him west to avenge the murder of her father by the great magician Pearl-Feather (by the pestilential vapors of the white fog of his exhalations), who is guarded by fiery serpents. These the hero dispatched with his jasper-headed arrows. Another night's sailing took him across the black pitch-water despite the war songs of the mosquitoes and the fireflies, which waved torches to mislead him. Arriving at the shining wigwam of Pearl-Feather, he shot an arrow as a herald and a challenge. The mighty Megissogwon, clad in wampum and war paint, threatened to slay him as he slew his great grandfather. Hiawatha countered that deeds are better things than words. The ensuing battle lasted all day, with Hiawatha's arrows, magic mittens, and war club harmlessly landing on the shirt of wampum.

At sunset a woodpecker told him to aim for the tuft of hair on the magician's head. Hiawatha drove each of his last three arrows deeper into that spot, with telling results, and then stained the woodpecker's tuft with crimson feathers in gratitude. Leaving the body half on land and half submerged, Hiawatha took the wampum shirt and all the wealth in furs, wampum, and silver-headed arrows from the wigwam. On his return, the people celebrated his victory over the Magician who had sent the fiery fever, disease, and death among them. As token of his friendship, he decked his pipe stem with the blood-red crest of the woodpecker before sharing all his trophies and plunder equally among the tribe.

Part 10 finds Hiawatha feeling as useless as an arrowless bow without Minnehaha, although his mother urged him to marry a neighbor's girl. Unable to persuade him, she asked for an obedient working girl, and definitely not a warlike Dakota, with whom his tribe often fought. Hiawatha answered that he would unite the tribes, and killed a fallow (wild, but probably not a [Eurasian] roebuck as the speaker claims) deer as he hastened west. Minnehaha sat weaving mats and thinking of a hunter she had once seen as her father made arrows and thought of the past (when hunting and war parties needed all the arrows he made) and of future maidens. The tall wigwam had Dakota gods painted on its curtains (the entrance flaps, perhaps).

Hiawatha told them of his life and asked that he be given Minnehaha to cement the friendship between the Ojibwa and the Dakota. The arrow-maker left it up to her, and Minnehaha announced her acquiescence. They traveled home at her slow pace, which now seemed fast to Hiawatha. The sun advised Hiawatha to rule by love, and the moon urged Minnehaha to rule by patience.

Part 11 tells of the sumptuous wedding feast and its delightful guests. The plates were made of basswood and the black spoons were carved from buffalo horn.

They ate sturgeon, venison, pemmican (a mix of dried berries, wild game meat and processed fat), buffalo marrow and hump, corncakes and wild rice. Hiawatha and Nokomis served the others, then she filled their pipes with southern tobacco spliced with fragrant herbs. The handsome Pau-Puk-Keewis danced the rapid and mystical beggar's dance. Chibiabos contributed a love song, and boastful Iagoo the storyteller took credit for having taught Hiawatha almost everything and promised the tale of Osseo, the Magician from the Evening Star.

The next section begins by connecting the sunset with the death of a red swan, wounded by a magic arrow. Iagoo's tale of Osseo began in a time when the heavens were closer and the gods were on more familiar terms. A northern hunter had 10 daughters, of whom the youngest, willful and dreamy Oweenee, was the fairest and last to marry. She finally married old Osseo, poor and always coughing like a squirrel, but descended from the Evening Star. At a banquet Osseo was heard praying for pity. The eldest daughter wished he had fallen and broken his neck, but Osseo ran into the fallen trunk of an ancient oak and emerged tall, strong, and handsome from its far end. Unfortunately, his transformation rendered Oweenee a tottering old woman at whom all her sisters and their husbands laughed. Only Osseo remained kind, but could not bring himself to eat or drink until a voice came from the empty vastness. Food would remove all evil charms from him, and all the bowls and kettles would become wampum and silver. Women would no longer be doomed dreary laborers, but changed to birds with the beauty of starlight. The lodge trembled, the utensils were changed, and the nine sisters and their

husbands became magpies, thrushes, blackbirds, or jays. Then youth and beauty returned to Oweenee, and the Evening Star alighted as lightly as snowflake falls on snowflake. The god instructed Osseo to hang the birds in a doorway cage, for they had mocked his son and only Oweenee had seen his passionate heart and immortal youth. He also warned against Wabeno, a magician in nearby lodge, who had transformed Osseo into old age.

After many years of peace, Oweenee bore a beautiful son with the courage of his father. For entertainment, Osseo let him shoot at his aunts and uncles, still birds. Great fun, until he hit one and a beautiful young woman fell dead at his feet. He, the birds (transformed now to pygmies, the Puk-Wudjies), and his parents moved to an island in Lake Superior. Iagoo suggested that their fate should caution those who jest at great men. After another love song by Chibiabos, the guests departed.

In part 13, Hiawatha enjoys the fruits of marriage in a time of peace. He has buried his weapons and forgotten the war-cry in favor of songs of the mysteries of Mondamin (the corn) and the Blessing of the Cornfields. Unmolested, the men hunt, fish and trap, and the women make maple sugar, gather rice, and cure the animal skins. After Hiawatha taught them, the women planted the corn in the spring and harvested it in fall. He asked Minnehaha to bless the fields by drawing a magic circle around them (an all-purpose herbicide and pesticide also effective against mildew, blight, and animal raiders except for crows). She is to arise in the night and, covered only by her tresses and the darkness, circumnavigate the field. Although the crows and ravens laughed at hearing these instructions, Minnehaha dutifully obliged. Unashamed and unafraid, she drew the magic circle of her footprints around the field. No one saw her.

Kahgahgee, King of the Ravens, intended to attack the crop, but Hiawatha had spread snares all over the fields. When the crows, blackbirds, jays, and ravens descended "with caw and clamor," their claws became entangled. Destroying them by tens and twenties, he hung up their bodies as scarecrows. Only the Raven King was spared, although he was bound and held hostage against further attacks. From the wigwam's summit he croaked his displeasure and flapped his wings.

Shawondasee, the South Wind, arrived with summer, and the maize (or Indian corn) ripened. Nokomis, Hiawatha's maternal grandmother, told Minnehaha that since the wild rice had been gathered it was time to harvest the corn. They called all the women and young men together for the husking, while the warriors and old men smoked in the shade of the nearby pine forest. The laborers seemed to enjoy their work because they talked like magpies, laughed like blue jays and sang like robins. Discovery of a bright red ear of corn portends a handsome husband for the lucky maiden who finds it. A crooked ear, however, would set the entire party laughingly mocking the old bent man thus predicted to be the finder's husband. A blighted, mildewed or misshapen ear would set them to singing against Wagemin or Paimosaid, the thieves behind these misfortunes.

When the laughter ringing from the fields reached the King of Ravens on his captive perch, he screamed in anger. From the neighboring trees the other ravens cawed and croaked, and the old men all responded "Ugh" from their seats beneath the pines.

In part 14, Hiawatha noted how the great warriors, artists, and thinkers are forgotten after their deaths, and devised a system of hieroglyphics to preserve their memory and thought. It would also enable them to communicate across distance and time. He painted the Great Spirit (Gitche Manito) as an egg with points radiating toward the four winds. A serpent represented Kenabeek, the Spirit of Evil. Life became a white circle, and death a darkened one. Flora and fauna were also painted, and an inverted bow with a point on the right or left represented sunrise or sunset. Footprints indicated welcome, but bloody hands were hostile signs. Each family was to adopt a symbol (or animal) as a totem. Especially imaginative were the headless men walking in the heavens and bodies lying pierced with arrows, and the love song (a scarlet man first standing, then sitting with a drum and finally in a wigwam, then a man and a woman standing together, the maiden on an island, and then sleeping with the lover near, and finally a heart within a magic circle).

In the next section, jealous Evil Spirits tried to undermine Hiawatha's love for Chibiabos (his best friend). Chibiabos went deer hunting alone across Lake Superior and they pulled him through the ice and buried him in the sand at the bottom. For seven weeks Hiawatha lamented with blackened face, and even animals mourned his passing. The medicine men built a sacred lodge beside Hiawatha and brought magic roots and simples (herbal remedies). He washed his face and followed them, then drank their magic spearmint and yarrow drink as they chanted about their unique powers and ability to heal him. He was cured of his madness and melancholy.

They summoned Chibiabos from his watery grave but forbade his entrance to the wigwam. Passing him a coal and a burning torch, they sent him to prepare fires for their encampments on the journey to the Hereafter. Four days' journey brought him to the melancholy river that he crossed on a swinging log, then he crossed the Lake of Silver in the Stone Canoe to the islands of blessed ghosts and shadows. He passed many who were slowed and burdened with things like clubs, robes, and food that their friends had provided for their journey. Hiawatha wandered, teaching simples and antidotes.

In part 16, Pau-Puk-Keewis, the great dancer at Hiawatha's wedding party, went to Iagoo's lodge to hear him tell the story of Ojeeg, the Summer-Maker. He made a hole in the sky, letting out the summer weather. The animals tried to emulate him, and the Wolverine succeeded and disappeared above, and Ojeeg, the Fisher (a weasel-like cousin of the wolverine) jumped after him.

Pau-Puk-Keewis, announcing that he was tired of stories and Hiawatha's wisdom, produced the 13 pieces of Pugasaing or Bowl and Counters, white on one side and painted red on the other. Points are awarded when the pieces are shaken out and land rightside up or down. Iagoo announced he could beat Pau-Puk-Keewis, and everyone gambled until Pau-Puk-Keewis took everything. Finally Face-in-a-Mist (or Meshinauwa), Iagoo's nephew and servant, won.

Pau-Puk-Keewis stopped at Hiawatha's wigwam, and the King of Ravens screamed that all were gone. The mischievous Indian strangled the raven and left it as an insult. Then he trashed the place to insult Noko-mis and taunt Minnehaha. Hiawatha's mountain chick-ens flocked about him as he rested on a hill, and he killed them until a seagull shouted his name and that he should be told.

In the next section, Hiawatha vowed to kill Pau-Puk-Keewis but had difficulty catching up with him. Pau-Puk-Keewis paused on a beaver dam and asked to be made into that animal. The beavers agreed, and he slid into the water. They also made him 10 times larger than the others and their new king. Hiawatha and his hunters arrived and broke the dam and their lodge. Only Pau-Puk-Keewis, swollen like a bladder from pride and feeding, could not escape, and the hunters beat him to death as corn is pounded. They bore him home on poles and branches, but his ghost still lived on as Pau-Puk-Keewis and finally would have vanished into the forest had not Hiawatha given chase. The trickster asked the brant (small geese) to make him one of them, but 10 times larger. They agreed, but warned him against looking down as they flew far north. The next day, a south wind blew them back over the vil-lage. Hearing the shouts, Pau-Puk-Keewis looked down, changing his aerodynamics and whirled down to his death.

Hiawatha almost grabbed him, but his adversary cir-cled, creating a dusty whirlwind, and changed to first a serpent and then to human form. He sped to the Pic-tured Rocks of sandstone (petroglyphs [Native Ameri-can paintings] were once common along the shores of Lake Superior but have largely eroded. The best place to see them today may be at Ontario's Agawa Park. There are none in Michigan's Pictured Rocks National Seashore), where the Manito of the Mountain sheltered him in a cave.

With his magic mittens, Hiawatha created caverns in the stone, then called for the lightning. The crags fell, killing the trickster in his human form. Hiawatha grabbed his soul and changed him into the war eagle, making him chief of all of his chickens.

The 18th section chronicles the death of the famously strong Kwasind at the hands of the Puk-Widjies, the envious little people who thought he could crush them like mushrooms. His strength stemmed from his crown, his only vulnerable spot, and only the seed

cone of the fir tree could hurt him there. The pygmies piled the cones where the rocks overhung the water, and the canoe of the sleeping Kwasind drifted beneath them. Stricken, he plunged into the water like an otter. Whenever trees snapped in the winter, people attrib-uted it to Kwasind's gathering firewood.

In the next section, disasters descended on the peo-ple like a succession of vultures. In snowy winter the hunters roamed in snowshoes, the women pounded corn and cured deerskins, and the boys played ball on the ice. Two female ghosts came uninvited to haunt the wigwam of Nokomis and Minnehaha, and then Hiawatha returned with a deer. He did not question the strangers, but bid them welcome. They ate the choicest bits reserved for Minnehaha but received no rebuke. By day the guests sat silent, but by night they gathered firewood and pinecones (for fuel), and always seized Minnehaha's portions.

One midnight Hiawatha heard their sighing and asked if the women had failed in their hospitality. They were souls of his former acquaintances come from his friend Chibiabos (a fine singer) to warn him. They told him not to sadden the souls of the departed with lam-entations, which they can hear in the Islands of the Blessed, or load them down with possessions for the next world. Only food and fire (to light the way) are useful on their journey, so for four nights a fire should be kindled on a new grave. They had tested Hiawatha by their insulting presence and outrageous actions, and found him noble. They hoped he would remain so in the coming trial.

In part 20, an especially harsh winter has driven the animals from the land. The children wailed, and the air and sky were hungry. The stars glared at them like hungry wolves. Two new guests, famine and fever, came uninvited and sat in Minnehaha's place. Hiawatha rushed into the forest, praying to Gitche Manito for food. Minnehaha began to hallucinate about her old home, complete with father in the doorway, calling her. She called out for Hiawatha, and he returned after she died. Hiawatha sat motionless for seven days and nights. They buried her in ermine (fur from a small weasel still prized for its white winter coat) in a snow grave. For four nights a fire was lit on her grave, and the sleepless Hiawatha kept it burning. Then he bade her farewell, happy that she was beyond famine and fever in the Land of the Hereafter.

In the penultimate section, an old man sat folded in his white-skin wrap as the snowstorm whirled outside. A youth entered with flowers, filling the lodge with sweetness. The old man offered the peace pipe and suggested they tell each other of their adventures. He turned out to be winter, and his visitor was spring. The Spring Beauty, a delicate wildflower, bloomed. The swans flew north, then the snow geese, loon, blue heron, grouse, bluebird, robin, and pigeon. Iagoo returned from the east, having seen a water bigger than Lake Superior but bitter. A great canoe with pinions and wings unloaded hairy-faced men with white painted faces. Most people laughed derisively, but Hiawatha had seen the same in a vision. Gitche Manito said that the stinging fly, the honeybee, would come before the strangers. He told the Native Americans to greet them with the heart's right hand of friendship. Hiawatha saw the future, when the unknown crowded restless nations would fill the land, speaking many languages but feeling just one heartbeat in their bosoms. Their axes and towns scattered Hiawatha's nation, which had forgotten his counsels and warred with each other before sweeping westward, wild and woeful, like withered autumn leaves.

In the last section, honeybees passed in golden swarms. The sturgeon still leaped and the forest still cast shadows on the water, but Hiawatha saw them with a smile of joy and triumph, for his vision was coming true. In a birch canoe came the Black-Robe chief, the Prophet and Priest of Prayer, with his cross, guides, and companions.

Hiawatha welcomed them, claiming that their presence made the lake more tranquil, the tobacco more pleasant, and the cornfields more beautiful. The priest blessed them in the Peace of prayer and Christ, and the joy of Mary. They were seated on furs, and Nokomis brought the peace pipe. All the prophets, magicians, and medicine men bid them welcome.

The Black-Robe chief told of his mission, not sparing the role the "accursed Jews" played in the crucifixion. Christ ascended to heaven. The people spread the tale of how the Master of Life had sent them these strangers, who lingered and slept in Hiawatha's wigwam.

Hiawatha bade farewell to Nikomis, announcing a long journey to the west, but encouraging her hospitality and protection for their guests. He told the warriors to listen to the wisdom and truth of the guests, and sailed west in his magic canoe. The people bade him farewell forever, a sad refrain taken up by the forests, the waves, and the heron. Thus he rode into the sunset, into the Land of the Hereafter.

"SONG OF MYSELF" WALT WHITMAN (1855)

Although its length prevents little more than a summary of its 52 divisions here, this poem may be considered the greatest achievement of WALT WHITMAN's early career. From the outset, the reader seems confronted by a speaker whose grasp is so great that his voice might be that of the earth itself. Coupled with an omniscient perspective is an audacious energy that compulsively (and frequently, compellingly) directs the reader's attention toward a series of innumerable anecdotes that collectively suggest the myriad levels and developmental experience of the American psyche as it stood in 1855.

The first stanza attempts to break the traditional separation between the internal audience toward whom a speaker ostensibly directs his argument and the external audience (the person who reads the poem). With typical American self-assurance, the speaker assumes that the reader must share his assumptions (line 2). Before an objection can be raised, however, the speaker disarms criticism with a show of munificence that takes the traditional Spanish expression of *mi casa su casa* (my house is your house) to its logical extreme: he would share even his atoms (line 3). Although he began by introducing his greatest subject, "myself" (line 1), the earnestness with which he urges the audience to share in this bounty renders the reader complicit with the acquisitive spirit that made it possible.

As if in recognition that his opening has been too aggressive, he assumes the least threatening posture possible: He leans while observing a blade of grass (line 5). Note the unconventional spelling and repetition of "loafe," which suggests a rite of communion ("I loafe and invite my soul" in line 4). In vaguely biblical language he traces his American lineage back to his great grandparents. As if this reminded him of his own mortality, in lines 8 and 9 he shifts to a variation on the traditional opening line of a will. Although he inexplicably states his age incorrectly (he turned 37 on May 31, 1856), he asserts that he is in good health and hopes to continue (writing? living?) until his death.

He states his credo in the 13th line: He will permit Nature to speak with its unrestrained original energy. This will require him to hold "Creeds and schools" (the systems formulated by others to understand and shape experience) in abeyance (line 10).

In the second division, Whitman revels in the animalistic side of his nature. Although he enjoys the artificial "perfumes," the odors he finds indoors, he is especially enamored with the tasteless atmosphere of fresh air. "Mad" for contact with it (line 20), he strips to his undisguised, naked self on a wooded riverbank. Soon he is comparing the landscape of his own body and its respiration with the surrounding elements. An introductory list of the things that give him pleasure ranges from the sexual (the kisses, embraces, and "reaching around of arms" of line 26) to the rush of the streets (line 28). The odors of leaves (both green and dry) and of hay help him recall the other sensations.

The poet seems as unashamedly acquisitive as other Americans of his era, but instead of hoarding material goods, he preserves anecdotes of personal and national experience. Hence he asks if the reader values a thousand acres (an immense property in the days when all farming had to rely on animal and human labor) or the entire earth (line 30). Instead of receiving things secondhand, through reading, he promises to give the reader "the origin of all poems" (line 33), enabling him to "listen to all sides and filter them from yourself" (line 37).

The third part of the poem dismisses talk of the beginning, the end, heaven, and hell in favor of the procreant urge (line 44). Sex is the constant "knit of identity" (line 46), the best-constructed aspect of being human (note how, in line 48 and elsewhere, Whitman uses the construction terminology he learned through his employment as a carpenter).

He will not get caught up in generational conflicts, preferring instead to "go bathe and admire myself" (line 52). He is pleased with every particle of an inch of himself that he finds. Happy, he dances and sings,

sharing the laughter with a "hugging and loving bedfellow" who leaves bread dough rising beneath white towels before he stealthily retires at the first light of day. The awkwardness of the relationship turns him against himself; he wants to "scream at [his] eyes" (line 61) for not continuing to gaze on the road. Instead, they calculate the value of one, of two, and the difficulties that lay ahead.

In part four, the speaker asserts that although surrounded by sales pitches and frenetic commercial activity, he stands apart from the daily vicissitudes even within his family circle. Simultaneously he is "in and out of the game" (line 78), involved in life but also always observing it. Formerly he argued "with linguists and contenders" (line 80); now he just watches and waits.

In the fifth division he addresses his soul, which turns out to be his lover. Recalling rather graphically their interaction as they lay on a "transparent summer morning" (line 87), he felt the hand and spirit of God and kinship with all men and women. He also embraces all of creation down to the brown ants and "mossy scabs of the worm fence" (line 98).

The sixth part is Whitman's paean to grass, which he admires for its ubiquity. Perhaps the Lord dropped it as a scented handkerchief, a token by which he can be remembered (lines 102–105) by humans of every description. It also seems the uncut hair of graves, like that which sprouts over the breasts of young men and the hips of women. Because grass grows from graves, "to die is different from what any one supposed, and luckier" (line 130).

The speaker knows it is just as lucky to die as to be born, for he realizes that all people are immortal even if they do not. Because he is like them, he claims the male and female, children, and the begetters of children. He tells the internal audience (and his remarks seem aimed at the reader as well) to undrape. He will still consider you to be innocent and not stale or discarded (line 145). He can see through your clothes anyway, "and cannot be shaken away" (line 147).

In the eighth division, the speaker flits from scene to scene as if excitedly exploring his newly discovered omniscience. He gains unmonitored access to a baby in its cradle, observes a young couple alone on a hill and finds a suicide and his gun on a bloody bedroom floor. The poem proceeds from a juxtaposition of opposites, and the poet seems to delight in frustrating the reader's expectation that some of incidents will have a causal as well as a temporal link. For example, he sees the fury of aroused mobs in line 157, and the next line begins with someone being carried to the hospital on a curtained litter. It contains a sick man and not the victim of mob violence that one expects, however. He is privy to the darker side of human interaction, witnessing arrests, and adulterous offers made and accepted. He studies people with an artist's eye, effectively capturing the "rejections with convex lips" (line 165) of those who refuse adulterous affairs.

As if the reader needed a breath of fresh air from the urban excitements of the prior section, in the next division the speaker helps with a hay harvest and ends by rolling head over heels with tangles of straw in his hair.

In the 10th section the speaker hunts in the mountains, sails on a Yankee clipper, digs clams with other men and witnesses the marriage of a bearded trapper to a Native American girl whose hair reaches to her feet. Finding a runaway slave by his woodpile, he boards (provides food for) the desperate man for a week until his sores have healed and he again heads north. They sat next to each other at the table. The speaker notes that his flintlock rifle leaned in the corner (line 198). Although he does not explain the significance of this fact, it may demonstrate the level of trust he and his guest shared, for either might have seized the weapon had he mistrusted the other's motives. Alternatively, it may suggest that the speaker was willing and able to take up arms on a moment's notice to defend the freedom of his guest.

Twenty-eight young men bathe together in the 11th stanza. The speaker sees them and also the affluent, handsome, and lonely woman who watches and enjoys them from behind the blinds in her windows. She imagines passing her hands over their bodies, but they are unaware of this 29th bather. They do not know who puffs and arches or "whom they souse with spray" (line 216).

In the 12th stanza the speaker enjoys repartee with a butcher boy and watching the slow, sure movements of blacksmiths. In the 13th, he admires a statuesque drayman and follows him about the stone yard. Always and everywhere he observes and absorbs everything for himself and for this song. He also studies the oxen, wood ducks, a jay, a tortoise and an old bay mare, admiring the attributes of each. In the 14th, he hears the call of a wild goose as an invitation and sees in all the beasts of forest and farm "the same old law" (line 252) that he finds in himself. He loves growing outdoors and men who live among cattle or who taste (some degree of homoerotic ambiguity was probably intentional here) of the ocean or woods (line 256). He could eat and sleep with builders and other manual laborers for weeks. He makes himself "the commonest, cheapest, nearest and easiest" (line 259), ready to bestow himself on the first that would take him and "scattering it freely forever" (line 262).

In the 15th division he continues admiring professional competence and the men (mostly) who possess it, occasionally including less fortunate people (a lunatic and a surgery patient with malformed limbs) for contrast. His diction registers shock when "what is removed drops horribly in a pail" during surgery (line 278) but no horror when a quadroon girl (a person with one black and three white grandparents at a time in American history when a single drop of blood could define your race) is sold as a slave.

It seems as though all America swirls with industry, but in addition to a new mother and a bride-to-be, he sees an opium-eater and hears a taunted prostitute's retaliatory oaths without joining in the merriment of the crowd that jeers her (lines 305–307). The speaker is willing to include everyone from the president to a flatboatman in his "song of myself" (line 329).

In part 16 he asserts his claim to all hues and castes (line 346) of Americans and creates a list of regional types from the woods of Maine to California. He embraces diversity (line 349) and is in his place within all the identities he claims just as moths, fish-eggs and suns are in their places (line 352).

In part 17, he admits that these thoughts are not original with him but belong to all men in all ages and lands (line 355). They are the grass that grows wherever there is water, land, and air. In 18, he marches for the vanquished and slain as well as for the victors, celebrating the generals who lost their engagements and the heroes who fell in battle.

In the 19th division, he speaks of his work as a prepared meal to which all are invited, even the kept woman, thief, and sponger (line 375). He promises to tell the reader things in confidence that he might not tell everyone (lines 387–388). In the 20th, he denounces the snivel that "mouths are vacuums and the ground but wallow and filth" (line 395). Instead, he celebrates his humanity, having found no sweeter fat than that on his own bones (line 400). He feels a complete world unto himself and cares not whether his existence came now or in 10 million years. He laughs at dissolution for he knows "the amplitude of time" (lines 420–421).

In part 21, the speaker asserts that he is the poet of the body and of the soul, heaven and hell, and man and woman. He asserts that it is equally great to be a man or woman and that being the mother of men is the greatest. He appreciates night, stars, and the entire earth. He would have the earth smile, for her unspeakably passionate lover has come. In the next section, he invites the sea to come feel of him and dash him "with amorous wet" (line 453), a courtesy he is confident he can repay. Just as the sea carries things in and out, he is a poet of both good and evil, choosing to "moisten the roots of all that has grown" (line 466). He feels that some celestial laws are still being developed, but he wonders (since life is so wonderful) how there can be a mean man or an infidel.

Section 23 celebrates time and the practical sciences, but the latter do not interest him unless they yield insights into himself. He does not want his words to signify properties, but to celebrate life and freedom. He prefers fully equipped men and women and not neutered ones, and will beat the "gong of revolt" with fugitives and conspirators.

The speaker insists that he is the same as the author in the next section, and as Walt Whitman he would have the locks unscrewed from the doors (line 501). He will lend his voice to the dispossessed and forbidden. His belief is "in the flesh and the appetites" (line 522), and his senses are miracles. His embrace of life seems inherently (and here, rather explicitly) sexual.

In section 25, he retains the right to withhold his voice so that he can never be fully possessed, and in the next section he announces that he will only listen. He hears natural sounds, but the best is the human voice. He experiences music as sexual tension and it takes his breath away.

The speaker celebrates the "instant conductors" of his nervous system in section 27. Touch brings happiness, and to touch someone else's flesh with his own "is about as much as [he] can stand" (line 617). In the next section, touch leads him to a new identity. The other senses are shut down or become subservient, and he thinks himself a traitor for letting it happen. In division 29, he appears to have reached orgasm through "blind loving wrestling touch" (line 642). In the 30th division, he would admit no truth but that upon which everyone can agree. Everyone would then be united on the basis of the most elemental urges and feelings, and take delight in everyone else.

As if in the afterglow of some profound experience, his omniscience is restored in the next section. Neither a single ant nor even the razor-billed auk of Labrador is beyond his vision or his appreciation. In section 32, he admires animals for their self-contained placidity. They have no lives beyond the present, and do not make him sick with talk of God (line 688). Not one owns anything or kneels to another of his species that lived thousands of years before him (line 690). Aspects of them remind him of himself, and he wonders if he did not lend them these tokens in the far distant past (lines 694–695). There is a gigantic stallion, for example, that responded to his caresses (line 701). His nostrils dilate as the speaker heels him, but the speaker leaves him behind as he can outgallop him on his own.

Section 33 is one of the longest and one of the best in the poem. Although it tends to read like the artist's notebook instead of a finished work, some of the lines approach the disciplined imagery (and approximate length) of Japanese haiku. Vigorous action verbs aid Whitman's depiction of a continent being transformed by irresistible human energy. Although principally concerned with the most dramatic human actors in this drama, he also pauses to vividly depict the individual animals whose habitats are quickly being transformed. Hence a rattlesnake "suns his flabby length" and an alligator "in his tough pimples sleeps" (lines 723–725). These southern animals quickly give way to agricultural crops like sugar, cotton, and rice, and other domestic crops replace the wild lands in other parts of the country. Industry, represented by trip-hammers of heavy industry and the whirling cylinders of the press (line 738) is already present. Balloons have begun man's conquest of the air (line 740), and only the sea (where the fin of the shark cuts the water like a black chip in line 744) appears to stymie his progress. Americans join regiments, community work projects, or merrymaking groups.

Through it all, Whitman observes and absorbs, pleased with everything that is true to itself. Imaginatively, he is already speeding through space in and beyond the planets (lines 791–794) and into the ocean ("below the soundings of plummets," the weights lowered from ships for the purpose of measuring the depth of the water beneath them; line 801). He goes to the Arctic as well as the battlefield, and into the past (or is that the future?) in the form of a ruined city (line 815). He sleeps with someone else's bride (line 818), but also embraces altruistic heroism.

His empathetic responses are so great that he claims "I am the man, I suffer'd, I was there" (line 832). He is the witch burned in front of her children and the "hounded" slave bitten by a dog (line 835; the painful pun had to have been intentional). He is the mashed fireman rescued by his comrades, a combat artillerist (lines 847 and 858), and the dying general who still wants the entrenchments manned despite his personal fate.

The 34th section mentions the Alamo but focuses on Goliad, another Texas battle after which prisoners were executed. Several individual executions are dramatized, and all the bodies were burned.

Although John Paul Jones is not mentioned by name, his courage in his successful fight with the British ship *Serapis* is covered in the 35th and 36th sections. That Revolutionary War engagement remains the only time in American history that a captain lost his own ship but successfully transferred his command to the vessel he had just defeated. Whitman also mentions the horrors of surgery that followed the battle.

In the 37th division, the speaker identifies with the more dangerous convicts, a dying cholera patient and a beggar. In the next, he steps back from the usual mis-take of forgetting all the painful humiliations people endure, including his own crucifixion. Like a restored spirit on Judgment Day, however, he emerges from the grave with all gashes healed and encourages "eleves," students of his work (line 974), to continue their notes and questioning. In part 39, he imagines a new man, "the friendly and flowing savage." Simple, naïve and common, he is desired wherever he goes.

In the next two stanzas, he comes on like a new savior and embraces even the cleaner of privies (line 1003). He cures the sick and stands guard over the sleeping. He has heard philosophies several thousand years old, and outbids Jehovah and all the huckstering old gods who "bore mites . . . for unfledg'd birds who now have to rise and fly and sing for themselves" (line 1035). The human life he sees around him reveals just as much as religion. He dismisses the supernatural and becomes a creator through putting his semen in "the ambush'd womb of the shadows" (line 1053).

By section 42 he has attracted a crowd. He would awaken everyone to the life around them and prefers real life to representations of it. He cherishes the "fath-omless human brain" and asks the meaning of reason, love, and life (lines 1094–1095). In the next section, he announces that he does not despise priests, but joins in all the world's processionals. He drinks from a skull-cup and sacrifices humans with the Aztecs, but believes in the Gospels and accepts Christ's divinity. His beliefs cannot fail anyone or anything down to the jellyfish, "the sacs merely floating with open mouths for food to slip in" (line 1130).

In section 44, he explains himself: He is the end result of a something like evolution. In the next, he feels so much in love with everything that he feels smothered. His is an expanding universe, and his imagination is similarly unlimited. He will die and meet the Lord and the great Camerado, the "lover true" for whom he pines (line 1200).

Judging that he has shown his students the road and that they are now ready to see for themselves, he is ready to stand aside. Like a swimming instructor, he wants them to boldly strike out on their own (line 1233). The same self-reliant message is expressed throughout section 47 with the assurance that the speaker and his teachings will always be with those who hear him.

He counsels his followers to forget about God. Although he finds God in everything he sees and does, he advocates studying man instead. He argues that it is better to enjoy the present hour than to worry about forever. He is at peace about God and death (line 1280). In section 49, he embraces death just as he embraces birth and thinks of each in terms of feminine imagery. He probably died 10 thousand deaths before (line 1298).

Section 50 celebrates the afterglow following bodily exertion and a good sleep. The speaker considers it eternal life and happiness instead of death. The penultimate section deals with his twilight reflections. He agrees that he has contradicted himself, explaining that "I am large, I contain multitudes" (line 1326). He asks who wants to walk with him after supper, if it is not already too late.

In the last division, a spotted hawk swoops by to complain of the speaker's loitering. Despite this apparent reference to his imminent death, he is still untamed: "I sound my barbaric yawp over the roofs of the world" (line 1333). Although he bequeaths his body to the dirt for his beloved grass (he kept reissuing expanded editions of his poetry under the title *Leaves of Grass* throughout his career), the reader is advised to keep looking for him underfoot and elsewhere.

Since the poem was divided into 52 sections, Whitman may have wanted to show how the cycles of life mimic the seasonal patterns of a 52-week year. Reinforcing this interpretation are his mentions of his birth in the first section and his own death in those sections preceding the last one. Since the speaker claimed to have had innumerable lives, there is something reassuring in the way that each new year replaces the old, yet time transcends the division.

"SONG OF THE REDWOOD-TREE" WALT WHITMAN (1873)

The breathtaking dimensions of the two best-known species of California redwood trees overwhelm the visitor who stands at the base of the record 379.1-foot (115.55 meters) coast redwood or before the 36.5-foot (11.1 meter) base diameter of the largest tree in the world in terms of volume, a giant sequoia. When gold was discovered in California in 1848, redwood forests covered around 2 million acres.

The relatively primitive logging technology of the 19th century slowly but inexorably cut into their range because the trees take centuries to grow (the oldest Giant Sequoia, based on the annual growth rings visible only when the tree had been harvested, had lived for more than 3,200 years). This poem features two speakers, a chorus who introduces the main speaker, and a coast redwood (based on its location in Mendocino County, line 11) that sings as it is being chopped down. Perhaps unsurprisingly, they both come to echo the poet's praise of the acquisitive impulse in the American psyche that was rapidly changing the landscape by its harvesting of natural resources. Conspicuous by its absence is any regret at the tree's passing. The nascent American conservation movement had its first striking success in the creation of Wyoming's Yellowstone, the world's first national park, in 1872, but Whitman, most at home on the pavement of New York City, still preferred industrial progress.

The introductory speaker's lack of sentiment is apparent when he calls the tree's song a chorus of departing dryads (female Greek spirits [called nymphs] associated with groves of trees) or hamadryads (each of whom lived as long as a specific tree; line 3). He does not believe in such pagan myths, but his inclusion of such classical references can be viewed as a poetic justification for his subject and approach. He issues a prophecy in the death chant of the tree, but neither the diction nor the content of the tree's song (set off in italics throughout the poem to distinguish it from the speaker's voice) connect with Greek mythology.

The tree begins by bidding farewell to its brethren, earth, sky, and water, and announcing its "term" (a word emphasizing vocalization as well as a particular period of time; it is also an abbreviation for "termination;" line 8).

The chorus resumes with more background information, establishing a specific California location so close to the sea mists and surges that the low and hoarse surf can be heard. Onomatopoeia provides the crackling blows of the axes as the tree is "riven" deep ("split apart," line 14). Neither the choppers nor their "shanties" (rough wilderness cabins or work songs [a variant spelling of "chanteys"]; line 16) echo its death chant. Neither the teamsters (those who managed the teams of horses who hauled the logs away) nor the chain and jack-screw men (those who winch the bigger logs into accessible positions; line 17) heard the wood-spirits join the refrain, but the speaker heard it in his soul. From the treetop 200 feet high and from the foot-thick (and fire resistant) bark (line 22) came a chant of the past and the future.

Reflecting on its untold life, the tree recalls its "venerable and innocent joys" (line 25), all the seasons, and the "great patient rugged joys" of which men have no reckoning, for it also has consciousness and a soul (line 29) like the rocks, mountains and rest of the earth. It announces that the term also has come for all his brothers (a gender designation that further distinguishes his voice from that of the ancient dryads). Although they have filled their time with Nature's "calm content" and with their own "tacit huge delight" (line 35), they [should] welcome the "superber" (redwood jargon for "more superb") race whose time has come. The new kings of the forest will absorb and assimilate Mt. Shasta and the Sierra Nevada peaks, and the Yosemite Valley (and perhaps be themselves absorbed and assimilated into these landscape features; line 43 is grammatically ambiguous).

In a miracle announced by the first speaker, the chant grows prouder and more ecstatic as if the lumbermen and other new deities of the West were joining in.

The western shore comes not weary or melancholy from Asian fetishes (mystical attachments or beliefs; line 48) nor bloodied by Europe's "dynastic [ruled by hereditary kings] slaughter-house" in which murder achieves thrones and is perpetuated by those on them, with the odor of wars and scaffolds everywhere. Instead, the virgin lands come to the "new culminating man" (line 53) from "Nature's long and harmless throes" (line 51), and the trees pledge their dedication to the new empire.

In lines sounding far more Whitmanesque than arboreal, the tree praises "the occult deep volitions," "average spiritual manhood," "womanhood divine, mistress and source of all," and the unseen moral essence of all the vast American materials including the work of past ages (lines 55–57), that still shapes and molds the New World. The trees are dedicated to

the deeply hidden national will, the past and present purposes tenaciously pursued regardless of passing errors or surface disruptions, and the "vital, universal, deathless germs" (that is, seeds that germinate) that lie beneath all creeds, arts, laws, literatures, permanent homes, and all the western lands.

Here the "man of you" may grow to a gigantic, hardy tower proportionate to nature (line 67), laughing with storm or sun (as the trees have done in their turn). Here man may unfold himself and fill his time until he also will fall, disappear, and serve.

The original speaker heard the tree's ecstatic, ancient, and rustling voices amid the echo of teamsters' calls, clinking chains, and chopping axes. The dryads (probably representing the mysticism that flees before the rational [and commercial] principles of the New World) sing as they depart from the Cascades (Oregon and Washington mountains), the Wasatch Mountains of Utah, and Idaho. The speaker caught their chorus, along with indications and vistas of the future settlements.

In the second section, the speaker views the golden pageant of California along with the entire West from Washington's Puget Sound to Colorado, including the now fallow (undeveloped; line 87) land and still developing ore fields. A swarming, organizing, and busy race will receive ships from around the world and dispatch ships to India, China, Australia, and a thousand Pacific island paradises. Steam-powered riverboats and trains will pass mechanized farms in this land of wool, wheat, grapes, and yellow gold (line 94).

In the final section, the speaker sees the promise of thousands of years fulfilled by "our common kind, the race" (line 98) on the western lands. The new society will create a new man of more substance than mountains or imperial trees, and a new woman far greater than all the gold, vines, or even vital air. The "genius of the modern, child of the real and ideal" (line 103), will clear the ground for the broad humanity that represents the grand future of the true America.

"SONNET—TO SCIENCE" EDGAR ALLAN POE (1845)

Can science progress to the point where it destroys poetry? The speaker in EDGAR ALLAN POE's poem seems to fear that it might, but notice how heavily his conception of poetry relies upon classical mythology. His are the aesthetics that dominated American art for much of the 18th century and still lingered into the beginning of the 19th, an era when artists frequently were expected to demonstrate their knowledge of the ancient classics and express themselves within the narrow limits and traditional proprieties of a relatively few time-honored forms.

To call science the true daughter of Old Time (line 1) places her near the beginning of Greek mythology, for that was the moniker of Cronus (or Saturn, his Roman name). Fearful that he would be supplanted by one of his children, he ate them, until the mother of Zeus succeeded in shielding her son from this fate. In this way the ancient Greeks recognized the destructive power of time, and the poet argues that science is equally destructive to all things, since it seems to deprive the poet of his mythological tools. The second line provides some evidence that the speaker knows something about science, for it echoes the scientific maxim that observation inevitably alters its subject.

The speaker mistakenly argues that science has violently overthrown the Roman demigods from their haunts: the Hamadryad had been driven from the woods, while the Naiad and the Elfin had been torn from the water and the grass respectively (lines 10–13). Even Diana, one of the most important gods, had been dragged from her "car" (line 9; just as the sun was thought to be Apollo driving his chariot across the sky, this goddess was identified with the moon). Christianity, not science, played the largest role in overthrowing the ancient gods, a battle begun a couple of decades after the birth of Christ and largely finished when Constantine the Great became the first Roman emperor to publicly embrace Christianity a little more than three centuries later.

Even the speaker acknowledges that the ancient religion, and the necessity of citing its mythology, are dead when he calls science a vulture. Although that bird can be considered repugnant because of its diet, in this poem the carrion upon which it feeds is the poet's heart (line 3). In the 1829 version of the poem, *Vulture* was set off by commas, a grammatical configuration (one might classify it as an appellative used as a vocative) of vital importance to the meaning of the

poem, not only because it identifies the internal audience but also because the phrase that follows it would modify "the poet's heart" (line 3), "whose wings are dull realities" (line 4). Some modern editors change the second comma to an exclamation point, thus raising the possibility that Poe intended to stick science, and not the poor speaker's heart, with dull wings. This reveals their reverence for the poet, whom they would protect from himself. It seems a far greater kindness to differentiate between the author and the speaker in this instance.

The speaker's methodology as a poet is highly questionable and quite at odds with those of the author, as Poe revealed them in his PHILOSOPHY OF COMPOSITION. To wander "seeking treasure in the jeweled skies" (line 7) on an undaunted wing might lead to ecstasy, but it is unlikely to lead to poetry without the discipline required to acquire and practice the craft. That we last see the speaker roused from his "summer dream beneath the tamarind tree" (line 14) is a further indication of his dilettantism. He is so out of touch with nature that he names a tropical Asian evergreen instead of focusing on the American materials that surrounded him. The author may have been implying that the time for an erudite poetry predicated on pagan myths and conservative aesthetics has passed. His title, a virtual celebratory dedication of the poem to Science instead of a mere announcement of its subject (as "Sonnet—on Science" would have been) may have been sincere.

Can science destroy poetry? That battle is probably still being fought for, like the Hydra that grew two new heads every time one of its old ones was destroyed, every new discovery provides a new subject, an enhanced vocabulary, and perhaps even a new approach for poets not bound by classical mores. While a poet, especially one whose beloved mythology has heretofore been the stuff dreams have been made of, may see the advance of science as the end of magic in the world, poetry, including new poetry that speaks directly to the heart of each succeeding age, will always retain its emotional appeal.

"THE SOT-WEED FACTOR; OR, A VOYAGE TO MARYLAND, ETC." EBENEZER COOKE (1708)

Much of the tension in EBENEZER

COOKE's satire comes from the discrepancy between the educated voice of the speaker and his inability to succeed on either of two continents. His classical references identify him as a member of Albion's (Britain's) educated class, but unkind friends and unfortunate fate (notice how he attempts to distance himself from personal responsibility for his failures) have given him plagues worse than Pandora's Box (line 3). In Greek mythology, Pandora violated a divine sanction against opening a particular box and, in so doing, released all the evils on the world). He has come to Maryland as a company representative (the tobacco "factor" of the title) to barter English goods for good tobacco.

The British society from which he had to fly put great stock in its upper class, providing them with all possible advantages and instilling in some of them an unshakable faith in their own superiority. Hence the speaker describes the ship that carried him from Plymouth (in southwest England) to Maryland as "freighted with Fools" (line 10; the original American audience would have chaffed at such an implied putdown of themselves or their immediate predecessors). The storms (lines 15–19) they encountered were merely par for the course and the three months required for the voyage constituted a slightly better than average time for the crossing. They raised the ship's anchor (the "weighing" of line 20) and sailed from their first anchorage to Piscataway Bay, where the speaker put his goods ashore in hopes of opening a store. Immediately a crowd of tobacco planters in their blue linen homespun trousers and shirts appeared, lacking stockings, hats and shoes but resplendent in their Moorish tans (line 28. The Moors are a northwestern African nation who ruled Spain from the eighth to almost the 16th centuries. At the time in England, fair skin was thought particularly appealing because it signified that the possessor was a person of leisure who did not have to work in the fields). Their strange appearance brought to mind the land of Nod, where Cain hid after killing his brother (Genesis 4:16). Calling Cain the first to deal in furs and tobacco (line 40) raises ethical questions about the entire history of the industry.

Perhaps thinking of Cain made the speaker mindful of his own safety; judging the planters by appearance alone, he thinks them desperate men. He finds good sense (as he views it), conversation, and manners lacking (lines 54–55; these are priorities for his class, and probably serve one well in London). He crossed a river in a canoe, and its resemblance to a hog trough (line 64) probably encouraged him to assume the perilous posture of standing erect in it. Discovering wolves prowling on the far shore, he would have panicked had he not heard a female voice calling for a peasant to herd the cattle home. He asked for a room, but when the peasant asked from whom he had run away (thus mistaking him for an indentured servant; line 85), he drew his sword (a sign of his noble birth). Surprisingly, the lad apologized as formally as one might expect in court (lines 92–95).

He enjoyed the planter's hospitality without payment, explaining it was customary in that land for planters' tables to be free for all (lines 110–112). This does not prevent his complaining about the coarse food (corn pone and milk, cider, and mush sweetened with molasses). The planter produced a tobacco pouch and a pipe no longer than a finger or a penis ("that for which the ladies linger," line 125. High-class Englishman thought their language above reproach and modesty an affectation of the lower classes). The planter brought out a keg of rum and "bending backwards strongly drew" (line 142; note the speaker's fine eye for the telling gesture).

After duplicating his host's effort, the speaker must be helped to his bed (lines 146–147). To the disgrace of not being in control of his liquor, he quickly adds another by taking a rather prurient interest in the chambermaid. Her loose dress reminds him of an inmate of Bedlam (line 150), an insane asylum in London, and he presses her for her name and condition. She, too, is eloquent beyond her station. Becoming an indentured servant for four years (a deal often made in exchange for transportation to the New World, but occasionally women in desperate straits were judicially ordered into emigration) has reduced her to living barefoot "at the hoe" (laboring on a farm; line 162). Kidnapped and tricked into an unfortunate marriage, she fled but soon realized that her life here was worse. Of course his speculation about her misfortune puts it in the worst possible light: "She was supping [dining] before the Priest said Grace" (line 173; in other words, she had probably engaged in matrimonial relations without benefit of clergy).

He tried to sleep, but a fray between a cat and a grunting pig kept him up despite the efforts of the barking dog to quiet them (lines 182–185). Then a fox chased ducks and geese into the room, and he chased them all away with his sword (lines 187–199). He wandered out to the orchard, but the frogs kept him awake. Then he heard a rattlesnake and rode out the night on a tree limb to defy the devil and the snake, but mosquitoes feasted on him. He had bear cub strips for breakfast, and borrowed a horse and the farmer's son as guide to view the county court in Battle-Town. First, however, he came upon an Indian on a deer hunt, and marked his bear-greased hair and natural musculature. As they rode on, they speculate on how the Indians came to inhabit the New World, whether they descended from the Chinese or the Phoenicians. The speaker held for the latter, reasoning that the Chinese lacked the skill to sail the oceans (line 345–349). Neither was converted by the other's logic, leaving them in a stalemate like that of the Catholic priests and Protestant ministers who argue over the literalness of the miracle of Communion.

Arriving at the open-air court, they sat among the rabble before the drunken court, (lines 381–389) and finally the lawyers broke the peace (line 390). The judge could write his name, but most of his trade could not. He quickly lost control of the proceedings, and the sheriff seized stray hats and wigs for the queen. Drunken planters infested the local inn, and some burned their clothes to save mending (line 425). He finally slept in an old corn loft, but in the morning his shoes, hat, wig, and stockings were gone (line 445–446). He searched until he found them in the fire. His guide was completely naked, but the speaker was able to rouse him by twisting his bloody nose. While that lad was searching for his horse, the speaker found only jests instead of sympathy until given more rum, new clothes, and a rather spirited horse (line 493). Finally they arrived at an old cedar house whose wood had withstood hurricanes that leveled buildings made of more substantial materials as if they had been muskmelon vines. Here his new-found friend supplied him

with punch and apple juice until he retired at midnight and slept until noon, when the bedbugs roused him (line 517). Along with exquisite wild game (venison and turkey), they enjoyed imported Madeira wine until he slept out the day.

The next night at the house a "jolly Female Crew" (line 543) lounged in white nightgowns and played cards. At length one began to curse, calling the other a four-year slave fit only for the hoe. The other charged the first with kissing the captain to pay for her voyage, saying that she was a streetwalker familiar with British jails. They fought. The wine continued flowing the next day, but he was by then feverish. His care depended upon his purse (line 602), and he recovered. Recalling his trade mission, he returned to his goods but met a Quaker en route "who neither swore nor kept his word" (line 617). That merchant fled his debts "by light within" (line 620; Quaker services were conducted without a minister and were sometimes completely silent unless someone was moved to speak by "an inner light"). They traded 10,000 pounds of English goods for 500 pounds of the best tobacco. Cheated, the speaker sought counsel and settled for an apothecary turned lawyer, adept at making pills and forging wills (line 642). The lawyer, although no wiser than a crow in a steeple, so gouged the speaker that he'd have poisoned half the parish and hanged his father for another such fee (lines 646–652). He mixes several medicinal and legal terms, finally swearing that he could win as easily as he could cure the yaws (a tropical childhood disease).

They proceeded to Annapolis, capital of the colony, where the drunken judges lack the heart to give a favorable verdict to a stranger (line 683). Finding for the speaker, they ordered that he accept produce from the country in payment rather than the bargained tobacco. He hastened back to present-day Hampton, Virginia, glad to escape back to England but wishing cannonballs for those slaves who had practiced on him so sorely. He would have no merchant visits but leave them to starve or turn as savage as the wild Indians. He hopes they lapse into paganism so as to invite divine wrath (line 711); no man (excepting English gentlemen, he qualifies in a note) is faithful there, and no woman is chaste.

"THE SOUL SELECTS HER OWN SOCIETY" EMILY DICKINSON (1890)

Few love poems have ever achieved the power, clarity, profundity, or universality of this one. Note that it is the soul that makes the choice and that it is not based on such variables as the intellect, the heart, physical attraction, or any clear combination of these. Even more remarkable is the ambiguity of the amazingly solid opening line; the chosen can be numerous (even an entire society), a few people, a single individual, or no one else at all.

Shutting the Door (line 2) was a much more powerful metaphor when this poem was written than it is today. For the initial audience, the physicality of that act is matched by its domesticity and its finality. It is clearly willful, and because in the poem it comes from the soul, the very essence of the person, it can represent an impenetrable barrier. To fully understand the forcefulness of the image for its contemporary audience, it may be necessary for a modern reader to imagine the narrowly circumscribed lives of many 19th-century women. Just as vigorously as American society encourages a woman's choice to pursue a professional career outside the home in the 21st century, Dickinson's contemporaries were instructed to find happiness behind the doors of their families' houses. Since houses are small and families were relatively large in that era, shutting the door to a room meant the inhabitant needed one of those moments of quiet contemplation or occasional solitude that are essential to our species. Intruders who violated this space not only imperiled their own boundaries but could also face the considerable wrath of a woman who felt as though she were being hounded to the very limits of her existence.

In seeking an apt metaphor to convey the soul's dominion over a person's entire life, Dickinson drew on the old notion of the divine right of kings. Since their kingdoms were inherited, the individual kings were sometimes thought to have been chosen by God for their roles even before they were born. After American independence, the right to rule passed to the majority, a change that must also have been in accordance with God's will, since it came to pass. Although few people would take the resulting notion of a "divine Majority" (line 3) seriously, in this poem that phrase is applied to a woman's right to choose her soul mates. Thus we hear the voice of the absolute ruler in the fourth line: "Present no more" is her cold command against additional suitors.

She will not be moved by the obvious wealth of potential suitors in their "chariots" (a specific type of fashionable buggy in the 19th century) even if, as the "low gate" of line 6 suggests, she lacked comparable wealth. Even a kneeling emperor would be turned away.

The speaker has firsthand knowledge of a soul's choosing a single person from an entire nation and then closing off her heart until it seems like stone to the rest. Note the use of synecdoche in the penultimate line: the valves of the heart are used to represent the entire heart. This is an excellent example of how a part of something can represent the whole.

The glorious self-sufficiency of the soul examined in this poem may extend to all matters in life and not just romance. If the soul's choice is "her own Society" and not someone else's, she is free to devote her life to whatever she chooses.

"THE SOUL'S GROAN TO CHRIST FOR SUCCOR" EDWARD TAYLOR (published 1939)

In this poem EDWARD TAYLOR used his relatively unchallenging "Venus and Adonis" six-line stanzas (rhymed ababcc) to express the greatest challenge of his life, his inner struggle with the temptations of the archfiend and his soul's unrest because of the compromises he feels forced into. Although the speaker provides no information about the triggering incident, it is clear that the good minister found himself possessed of evil thoughts, for his soul finds many faults in itself (line 4). Although he is able to justify himself to his tormentor (line 5), he knows that the Lord can see through his rationalizations. In Puritan theology, all people are regarded as inherently sinful as a consequence of the original sin, and only those whom Christ through His grace (it is His choice, in other words, but the term also refers to His willful sacrifice on the cross for the sake of humanity) chooses for salvation are redeemed. Thus Taylor freely (albeit painfully) condemns himself (line 6) by admitting his sinful nature and relies on Christ's grace to save his soul.

Although Taylor mentions the devil's "fierce assaults" (line 2), it is unclear whether he imagines the opening situation as a military battle or a personal duel. What matters most is his terror at this critical moment (he mentions his trembling in line 2 and his fear in line 3). Outmatched, he calls on Christ for help even though he is admittedly unworthy of His aid.

In the second stanza the speaker outlines the enemy's strategy: He tries to combine all the speaker's sins until they would make Christ's gifts seem inconsequential, or at least inadequate to cover such an enormous bill, or such an imposition on His grace that His enhanced wrath (line 9) will be a certain outcome. Although the speaker sees through the way the enemy has undervalued both Christ's merits and His penchant for clemency, he confesses that his heart has been tempted to sin by these arguments (line 12).

In the next stanza, the enemy finished his biased accounting arguments by questioning the worth of the virtues Christ's grace has created in the speaker. Evidently he implied that since man is inherently sinful, grace that would turn him away from his essential nature is essentially cruel. Grace might be thought of as the honeycomb upon which, like an industrious bee, the believer may store the fruits of his labor, creating a metaphorical nectar that will be pleasing to Christ as well as to the individual and his colony. The enemy seizes on this apiarian metaphor to remind the speaker that bees sting as well as make honey, implying that his supposed good works may in fact be unnatural acts leading to his undoing. Reminded of the pain that an angry swarm can inflict, the speaker would instinctively run from the honeycomb, but intellectually he knows that running from the Lord can only have negative consequences.

By the last stanza, the speaker is nearly in control of the situation. What had seemed overwhelming odds and a most ferocious attacker now is revealed as little more than a barking dog, a revelation that leaves the speaker somewhat perplexed at his own reactions. He would have the Lord discipline the cur to the point of breaking its teeth (line 22). No longer as fearful, he first asks the Lord to remember him (hopefully as one of the elect, the chosen few designated by grace for salvation), and asks that the cur be haltered (this may imply more than being muzzled or secured by a rope; the halter was a contemporary euphemism for hanging).

Many modern readers may marvel at the fervency of Taylor's faith in divine intervention, but even those who do not share his beliefs must admire the rich emotional and imaginative life that they have engendered. It should be noted that the speaker's battle was essentially won at the point when he called on Christ for aid. On a psychological level, it seems as though just being able to express his concerns returned the speaker's self-control. It never hurts to have Jesus (whose divinity Taylor fully accepted) in your corner as well, however, and His response is provided in a sister poem, "CHRIST'S REPLY."

"STARTING FROM PAUMANOK" WALT WHITMAN (1881)

This lengthy poem presents not so much an accurate autobiography of the poet as it does the autobiography of the perfect American as WALT WHITMAN conceives him. Although the speaker shares the poet's birthplace (Long Island, or the "fish-shape Paumanok" of the first line) and lengthy residence in Manhattan (line 4), he simultaneously suggests alternative backgrounds such as military experience ("with knapsack and gun," line 5), mining in California and homesteading in the Dakotas that Whitman could only imaginatively embrace. Although the poet preferred the "clank of crowds" (line 8), like the speaker he was at least "aware" (line 9) of the Missouri and Niagara Rivers, the buffalo herds, and the hirsute (hairy) bull buffalo, as well as the herd, earth, and rocks, "experienced" in May flowers, and amazed by stars, rain, and snow (line 11). Instead of a formal education, he studied the birds (especially when a species exhibited exceptional gifts, such as a mockingbird's vocal range, a hawk's flight, and a hermit thrush's dawn song from the swamp cedar trees (lines 11–13). With either the thrush or the speaker (the grammar of line 14 permits either possibility, a pleasing ambiguity suggesting the possibility that the latter's singing grew out of and is intrinsically linked with the former [as well as everything else listed in the first section]) solitary and singing in the West, the speaker "strike[s] up" (commences singing; line 14) for a New World.

The second part begins by combining some of the intangible elements that contributed to America's ascendance with more universal mysteries in a short list that ends by juxtaposing eternal progress and the cosmos with "the modern reports" (line 17). This could read like a humorous punch line because the last item is so prosaic whereas the other elements tend to build in grandeur until arriving at this (anti)climax. However, as the speaker points out, life is what has risen to the surface after all the convulsions of the past (line 19). Divine soil is underfoot, the sun is overhead and, as if by divine plan, the "ancestor-continents" (Africa, Europe and Asia) are grouped together and so are the present and future continents (North and South America, respectively). Countless masses have filled the formerly trackless spaces, creating for the speaker/artist a never-ending audience. One hundred million Americanos march on, generation after generation, with faces turned sideways (by his contemporaries) or backwards (by the generations to follow) to listen to and learn of him (line 36).

The third section celebrates Americans as conquerors and liberators with whom humanity progresses, and for whom the speaker offers a series of chants of the upper midwestern states and the center of Kansas (which was the center of controversy before the first version of the poem appeared in 1860 because of its pro- and antislavery violence and eventual statehood). The "pulses of fire" shot from there (line 44; the reference might be to the heated emotions generated by the emancipation question or the actual fighting) vivified everyone in the years leading up to the Civil War.

The fourth part offers the speaker's leaves (a reference to the poet's *Leaves of Grass*, the constantly revised collection of his most important poems) to all sections of America, identifying them as the nation's offspring in that they connect lovingly with all the precedent literature and history. The speaker studied old times and old masters, and his leaves are the children of their work and justify it. In the next section he continues his appreciation of those individuals and even entire nations he credits with shaping the present, but although he intently regarded them, he finally must stand in his own place in his own day (line 61). Everything has come down to the male and female inheritors

of the world (those individuals currently alive), with spirituality being invested in this finale of visible forms (evidently, the present generation). Here, "the satisfier" joins "my mistress the soul" (lines 67–68).

In the sixth division the speaker predicts that the soul will last longer than the soil and the water. Paradoxically, he will use material substances, his body and mortality to create spiritual poems of his soul and immortality (lines 71–73). He will make a song of social harmony (the "comity" of line 75) for the States and a song "full of weapons with menacing points" (line 76) for their president, and another for the "fanged and glittering" One whose head is over all (lines 78–81; this may refer to the United States [since the One is described as "formed out of all" in line 78]). He will also acknowledge every city on earth and the heroism displayed on land and sea "from an American point of view" (line 85).

He will also sing of companionship, especially those who are "to found [create] their own ideal of manly love" (line 91) and let flame the burning fires that threatened to consume him (line 89). He will write the "evangel-poem" (line 92; evidently a poem calculated to enlist followers for this ideal), considering himself the best able to understand love with its joys and sorrows, "the poet of comrades" (line 94).

In the seventh part he presents himself as a "credulous" man (one who will believe anything) who "sings unrestricted faith" (lines 95–98). He begins with "Omnes!" (the Latin word for "all"), a mantra that will let him sing of evil since he (and his nation) is just as much evil as good (line 100). Then he denies that evil exists, but if it does, he states that it is as necessary as everything else. In inaugurating a religion, he will "descend into the arena" (perhaps entering public life or fighting for his beliefs like a gladiator with a purpose; line 102) where he may win the loudest acclaim. Perhaps, he suggests, "they" (his followers) rise from him to "soar above everything" (line 104).

Waxing philosophic, he proclaims that "each is not for its own sake" (line 105), and that earth and stars are for religion's sake. No one has ever adored or worshipped half enough, or thought how divine he is and how certain the future is. Closing on a patriotic note as if to distract from what some might consider blasphemy, he states that "the real and permanent grandeur of these states must be their religion" (line 110). There can be no life, land, man, or woman without religion (line 111).

In the eighth section he questions those young men who devote themselves to literature, science, art, and/or amours, and those who make such superficial realities as politics their ambition or business. Although he is also the poet of these things, he feels that those interests (or the young men who pursue them; his grammatical constructions and meaning become increasingly cloudy as the section proceeds) will soon be burnt up "for religion's sake" (line 119) because not all matter is "fuel to heat, impalpable flame, the essential life of the earth" (line 120) any more than all matter is fraught with religious significance. He may be implying that those young men who should be interested in his new religion (of the love of comrades, as identified in the sixth section) who do not openly devote themselves to (or at least acknowledge) his new religion will be destroyed by conventional religion.

It is not until the ninth section that the poet clarifies the situation of the poem and its internal audience, who was probably representative of his ideal audience. By addressing his internal audience as "son" and "camerado" (line 124), the speaker identifies his "comrade" as a "pensive and silent" younger man who may have love on his mind (line 124). The speaker cautions that it is painful to love to excess, and that while it satisfies and is great, there is something else very great. He talks about "it" in cryptic terms; magnificent "beyond materials" (line 128), it sweeps and provides for all "with continuous hands."

As if to plant the seeds (or "germs") from which his new religion will grow, in the 10th part the speaker introduces his comrade to the three "greatnesses," Love, Democracy, and Religion (lines 131–133). In his own mixture (the French-derived "mélange" of line 134) of a seen and unseen ocean containing a mystical and prophetic spirit, materials in which he lives hourly make their presence known to him, whom they have selected and into whom they drop hints of their demands (lines 134–139; these lines are murky not only because the speaker wishes to hide something

about himself but also presumably because they deal with the mystical roots of his new religion). His condition arose not from being twisted by the daily kiss he received from childhood onward until he was bound to the kisser; he asserts that he is no more bound to that friend than he was to the heavens and the spiritual world "after what they have done to me, suggesting themes" (line 143; he is asserting that nature and not nurture is responsible for his feelings and identity). He accepts such themes with their emphasis on equalities and the "divine average" but mainly for their "reckless and composite chords" to which he adds before passing them forward.

In the 11th section the speaker relates how he has walked in Alabama and seen the female mockingbird hatching its brood on the nest, and also the he-bird that inflated his throat and sang not only for what was there, including his mate and the echoes, but for a subtle and clandestine something "away beyond" (line 154), passed like an electrical charge as an occult gift for those being born.

Cohesiveness is a major concern whenever a poet breaks a poem into sections, and the 12th division offers clear examples of the ways Whitman overcame this handicap in this poem. The "inflating throat and joyful singing" (line 156) refer back to the mockingbird of the prior section, but in this section the speaker seems to take over that role. Similarly, he writes of "threading a thread" (line 170), a metaphor that suggests that thematic links as well as images unify the poem. The speaker's voice, often self-absorbed and as frequently messianic, and his willingness to jump from one point-of-view perspective to another like a skilled musician on a triangle, also unify not just this poem but the poet's entire oeuvre.

The speaker sees his role as preparation for those who will follow with stronger and haughtier carols than have ever been heard on earth (line 159). He will make "the true poem of riches" (line 162) that will celebrate those parts of the body and mind that survive death, his own egotism ("I will be the bard of personality;" line 164), gender equality, sexual organs and acts (which he promises to prove illustrious [line 166]), the perfection of the present, and that "nothing is more beautiful than death" (line 169).

Contrary to the prevailing religious thought of his era, he argues that the present holds no imperfection (line 167; modern western religions tend to view permanent perfection as one of the attractions waiting only in heaven) and universal miracles, that anything might produce beautiful results, and that time and events are "compact" (line 170). He will make only those poems that reference the ensemble rather than separate parts (lines 172–173), all days instead of a single day, and the soul. He believes that every particle of man "has reference to the soul" (line 176).

In the next section, Whitman advances a rather unique interpretation of the link between the body and the soul by claiming that the latter can be seen in the human form as well as in animals and inanimate objects. The speaker's love for the body leads him to believe that one's real body will elude the corpse-cleaners and "pass to fitting spheres" (line 182) with all that it has gained during its former life (The notion of a bodily resurrection is rather problematic but not without its biblical basis [see Job 19:26 and Romans 6:5, but elsewhere the biblical evidence implies a spiritual but not bodily resurrection]). The speaker compares the body to a printer's types, which do not "return their impression, meaning or main concern" (line 184; perhaps he is considering the disassembly of the types following the completion of a printing run. He may be imply that the real body and soul of the edition may lie in the printed page rather than in the reusable type that produced it). Similarly, he argues, "the body includes and is the meaning [and the] main concern" of the soul (line 187). He would have you appreciate the divinity of your body and all its parts (line 188).

In the 14th division the speaker seems to reach out to the external audience with a promise of endless announcements (line 189). To the "Daughter of the lands" (line 190) he implies that he is the poet for whom she has been waiting (or he may only be encouraging her to take heart, for such a poet will come). To male, female, and the lands of Democracy, he sends exalting words. He celebrates by listing the agricultural and mineral products of the land from the Columbia River in the northwest to the Colorado River of the southwest (including hemp [line 196], a cash crop cultivated because its fibers could be woven into durable ropes.

An adobe structure is made from sun-dried bricks of mud and straw). He also lists eastern rivers, the Great Lakes, the 13 original states, the oceans, and mountain peaks. Of its human complement, he mentions the fisherman, the "clutched together," the passionate (line 205), and the side-by-side elder and younger brothers with their bony limbs. He also celebrates the great women's land and the experienced and inexperienced sisters (line 207).

The land takes its breath from the Arctic and Mexico. Although death awaits him, he walks New England and dips his feet in Paumanok's ripples. He lives everywhere and observes shows, births and orators, and is near to those of the southern states as well. He annexes new shores and new leaves, welcoming every new brother (line 225). He "enjoins" (line 228; "forbids." *Enjoins* probably should be edited to "encourages") acts, characters, and spectacles.

Returning to his internal audience again in the 15th division, the speaker encourages him to "haste on" (an unusual verb to be repeated again in the last section of the poem). The context of this section suggests it is only an encouragement to persist, for like nature the speaker may have to be persuaded many times before consenting to give himself to the audience. If that comes to pass, the recipient should expect no tender dainty sweetness but a grizzled, forbidding, bearded foe well aware of his own merit ("I have arrived," he states in line 234) who must be wrestled before he will yield "the solid prizes of the universe" to "whoever can persevere to win them" (line 236).

In section 16, he extends his celebration of America's present and future to the "red aborigines," the Native Americans whose breaths echoed the sounds of rain, winds, and birds. His list of 15 of the names they gave the land and water begins with Okonee (a lake in Georgia) and ends with Walla-Walla (a river in Oregon and Washington). "After "charging" (like static electricity) the water and land with such names, the Native Americans "melt, they depart" (line 245; rarely did Whitman so blatantly display such insensitivity to the displacement of their nations and the racism and genocide that in many cases facilitated it).

In the next section he turns to the future, predicting a return to the primal (line 248) with expanding "vistas of glory" in which a new race will dominate and surpass previous ones, creating new politics, literatures, religions, inventions and arts. Aroused by his own announcements, he feels the oceans stirring within him, "preparing unprecedented waves and storms" (line 252).

Section 18 returns to the poet's era, and the speaker points out the steamboats, immigrants, backwoods scenes, corn leaves, mining claims, and rude fences. In a self-reflexive moment (an instance when an artist insists on drawing attention to the artificiality of his work), the speaker points out that the western and eastern seas (the Pacific and Atlantic Oceans) advance and retreat in his poems as they do on their shores (line 256). His skill is such, and his innovative production of lists of closely observed scenes is so conducive to the illusion, that he can conjure buffalo feeding on the short curly grass of Kansas in the very next line.

He points out the solid iron and stone buildings of the cities with their paved streets and active commerce, and such 19th-century engineering marvels as a steam-cylindered printing press, the transcontinental and transatlantic telegraph cables (the latter provided uninterrupted service from 1866 until the technology became obsolete; line 260), and the powerful steam locomotives. His landscape features farmers, miners, and blue-collar craftsmen engaged in their specialties, such manly, productive occupations as to offer marked contrast to the judges, philosophers, and presidents who emerge in their "working dresses" (line 263). There, "lounging through" the States, is the well-beloved, "close-held by day and night" speaker (and the distance separating the poet and speaker is as narrow at this point as it ever gets in poetry) who will, among the loud echoes of his songs, at last get to the hints that are of such paramount importance to him.

In the last section, the speaker salutes his close "camerado," an affectionate term Whitman coined for those who share manly love. The two of them are alone at last and need but a single word ("something ecstatic and undemonstrable [intangible or not provable]," the speaker exclaims in line 268) to clear the path to "music wild." They shall each triumph hand in hand, a wholesome pleasure. The speaker rejoices in having found an additional desirer and lover, and would haste ("haste, haste on with me," he instructs) the two of them into "firm holding" (line 271).

"STEAL AWAY TO JESUS" ANONYMOUS (19th century)

To the African American in bondage, to "steal away" usually meant to run away from slavery to the free states of the north, and to "Steal away to Jesus" could also mean to escape this life through death. The delightful ambiguity of this song resides in its combining these two possibilities with a third, the absurdity of literally stealing one's way to salvation. All three interpretations shed light on the immorality of slavery, and the singing of such songs in a plantation congregation would have been a show of community support for the first option, of empathy for the second, and of approval for the conventionally moral resolution of the third.

As encouragement for trying to escape, the song's title implies that Jesus is not present on the plantation but awaits elsewhere, and the second line suggests that "home" is not "here." The fifth line suggests that the Lord (and/or nature) favors that option by interpreting the thunder as His call, and the 11th line suggests that it is a sin not to obey. The speaker's repeated assertions that "I ain't got long to stay here" strengthen his/her resolve, and by the last line she is ready to declare her intention to the Lord.

As an exposition of the good Christian's anticipation of heaven as a well-earned reward, the song identifies heaven as "home" and looks forward to the meeting with Jesus. The thunder and trumpet of the Lord's call to this reunion sound around and in the speaker's soul, offering further proof that she is not long for this world. The gathering storm reminds the speaker of Judgment Day, when the winds will bend the trees and the poor sinner will "stand a-trembling" (line 11). The speaker, however, hears the trumpet within her soul, a sign that she will soon be leaving the company of sinners.

As a morality tale, the song establishes the pattern of theft upon which the speaker is commenting but abruptly brings those activities to a halt in the presence of Jesus (line 1). Using reverse psychology, the speaker does not directly condemn the sinner, but points out the brevity of this life (even she has not long to stay here, she asserts, and the trumpets of heaven seem as close as the thunder) and the cumulative erosion of "home" which the life of crime hastens. She contrasts the specter of the poor sinner's trembling wait for Judgment with her own response to His call and her personal relationship with God. On a personal level, she also may be asking the thief to abandon his crimes out of deference to her advanced age or ill health.

STOCKTON, ANNIS BOUDINOT (1736–1801)

The poet was born July 1, 1736, in Darby, Pennsylvania, into a family just returned from Antigua, a Caribbean island, where her father had managed a plantation (see James Grainger's SUGER-CANE to understand what this meant in regard to slavery). His success as a silversmith and merchant brought his family into the elite circles of New Jersey, and Annis Boudinot married a wealthy attorney named Richard Stockton at the age of 21. Together, they (and their slaves) developed their property in Princeton. Her husband became a delegate to the Continental Congress and signed the Declaration of Independence, but he was captured on November 30, 1776. Thrown into irons, he was released in a prisoner exchange after six weeks of privations that seriously undermined his health. At one point, his mansion was commandeered by the same British general, Charles Cornwallis, whose surrender at Yorktown was instrumental in ending the Revolutionary War, and many of their personal possessions were burned. Stockton died in 1781.

The poet survived her husband by two full decades. She was important enough in her own right to merit lengthly letters from such notables as George Washington (such as the one dated September 2, 1783, on the draft held by the Library of Congress) and to host Washington when he came to Princeton. Her brother, Elias Boudinot, was elected president of the Continental Congress in 1782 and stayed at her mansion when the Continental Congress met in Princeton for six months in 1783 (thus making it the de facto capital of the nation).

The gender biases of her age were not only evident in the poetry of Annis Stockton, where she defers to men, but also in the financial arrangements of her family. She named the estate Morven and helped build it up, shared her husband's political philosophy, and entertained their many guests. The property was not left to her after her husband's demise, however, nor to the three girls who were their three oldest children, but to her oldest son. Annis continued entertaining the Washingtons and other important guests after the war, but when her son married, she yielded her role as mistress (hostess and manager) of Morven to his wife, and went to live in a less fashionable house. She died on February 6, 1801.

Boudinot wrote elegies about nature (separate poems explore a wheat harvest, a garden pavilion, and the destruction of trees by icicles, for example) and odes to political figures (including General Washington and the dauphin [crown prince] of France, whose birth many Americans celebrated as an expression of gratitude for the French king's essential financial and military support during the Revolutionary War). Her devotion to her husband is evident even in the title of "An extempore [spontaneous] ode in a sleepless night by a lady attending on her husband in a long and painful illness." She also wrote elegies following his death on February 28, 1781, and on the first, second, and seventh anniversaries of that event. "A POETICAL, EPISTLE, ADDRESSED BY A LADY OF NEW JERSEY, TO HER NIECE, UPON HER MARRIAGE" combines timeless insights into human nature with very dated advice on willingly making her husband's pleasure the study of her life.

Morven, the Stockton home in Princeton dating from 1754, has been preserved as a museum after having served as the New Jersey Governor's Mansion from 1945–81. The New Jersey Historical Society holds a copybook with manuscript copies of many of Stockton's published poems, and Princeton University also holds important manuscripts.

BIBLIOGRAPHY

Boudinot, Elias. *The Life, Public Services, Addresses, and Letters of Elias Boudinot.* Edited by J. J. Boudinot. New York: DaCapo Press, 1971.

Boyd, George Adams. *Elias Boudinot: Patriot and Statesman, 1740–1821.* New York: Greenwood Press, 1969.

Greiff, Constance M., and Wanda S. Gunning. *Morven: Memory, Myth and Reality.* Princeton, N.J.: Historic Morven, Inc., 2004.

Stockton, Annis Boudinot. *Only for the Eye of a Friend: The Poems of Annis Boudinot Stockton.* Edited by Carla Mulford. Charlottesville: University Press of Virginia, 1995.

"SUCCESS IS COUNTED SWEETEST"
EMILY DICKINSON (published 1978)   EMILY DICKINSON's antiwar poem not only focuses on a dying soldier in the aftermath of a battle but also attacks the jingoism of those whose advocacy of such violence promises an easy victory.

The poem begins with an emphatic statement about human nature; it is metaphysical in its claim that an amorphous abstract concept (success) can not only be counted but also tasted (line 1). The first two lines may have been intended to separate those who will actually do the fighting (since only they can be victorious) from those who will never succeed (because they will not actively engage in the conflict). It seems a clever aphorism delivered in almost a singsong voice, but the next two lines deepen the tone of the poem by making the "sorest need" (line 4) a prerequisite for truly understanding all that success implies. The speaker of the poem uses some of the jargon and technique of a wine taster to judge the nature of military success, here distilled to a nectar (line 3).

Describing the victorious host as "purple," traditionally the color of royalty, may indicate their association with the overwhelming power of a king, or their success in having formed a new kingdom as a consequence of the battle. It may also recall the color of their faces during their recent exertions and signal their transformation into something akin to monsters, as they were exposed to the inhuman conditions of the battle. The color is also used in association with purple prose, an overly ornate rhetorical style that can hide unpleasant realities behind bombastic appeals and abstractions.

To deal with the confusion on battlefields even as late as the Civil War, army units typically entrusted their battle flags to particularly strong or aggressive individuals who would coordinate troop movements by carrying the emblem forward. Since his comrades were trained to orient their own movements in accordance with its progress, and because it was frequently deemed especially meritorious to be accorded the honor of flag bearer, a battle flag would typically not be surrendered while the battle raged unless by a rout. Because in this poem "a purple Host" and not a single soldier or small group of men takes the flag (lines 5–6), the implication is that the victors easily overwhelmed their foes.

After the surging battle imagery of the first half of the second stanza, the speaker returns to focusing on the clarity of the victory (line 8) with the cold detachment (and same vocabulary) as a wine taster. Just as it takes an experienced palate to determine the quality of wine, the dying, defeated soldier knows more of the true nature of military victory than those who so easily overcame him. His is the "forbidden ear" (line 10) in the sense that it will never hear the sound of triumphant victory, but note how closely his ear is attuned not to the triumph, but to the "strains" of triumph. Filtered through the sensory perceptions of a mortally wounded man, the distorted sounds can be at once distant (line 11) and loud (the "bursting" of line 12). His physical pain is combined with the emotional pain attendant upon the loss with agonizing clarity (line 12).

SUGAR-CANE: A POEM IN FOUR BOOKS
JAMES GRAINGER (1764)   In his preface, JAMES GRAINGER expressed a desire to be thought a good man on the basis of the educational value of this poem, "the nobler end of all poetry" in his opinion. He cites various classical authors and several of his contemporaries who also wrote didactic compositions. When in the course of describing sugarcane agriculture he happens to recommend the medical properties of other plants, he does so as a physician.

Each book begins with an "Argument," a prose summary of its contents. The first book is devoted to the soils and microclimates of St. Christopher (modern St. Kitts) with an eye toward determining which best support the cane. The second part describes the vermin and hurricanes that can destroy it, and the third book tells how to refine the sugar. The fourth book is devoted to labor issues; more specifically, it discusses the selection and use of slaves.

In the first book, after a lengthy invocation that is not without art, Grainger advises planting in a good soil. Avoid rocky slopes, clay and sandy soils; ideally, cedar and locust forests can be leveled for the plantation although stands of particularly fruitful or medicinal plants should be preserved. Cane likes a deep black soil, and Grainger thanks Columbus for discovering a region rich in it, including St. Kitts and its neighbors. By avoiding planting on the mountain tops and too close to the sea, the cane and its industry will prosper, ultimately permitting British vessels to convey the harvest while the lilies on the French flag are kept away (the English who colonized the center of the island in 1623 were joined by French two years later. Each found sugar cultivation so lucrative that by the mid-17th century they began forcing the other off whenever they could. In 1713, a treaty confirmed English possession, which was maintained except for a year and half beginning in 1782, when the French again prevailed. Political independence came in the 20th century). Wind, monkeys, and rats threaten the crops, while mosquitoes, cockroaches, lizards, and crabs invade houses, but it is easy to imagine varieties of mythical nymphs among the heavy foliage in the hills. Citrus fruits and bananas offer their own enticements, and taken as a whole, the richness of the land brings a variety of classical myths to the poet's mind.

The second book suggests active patrols with dogs against the marauding monkeys of the uplands, a troop that reminds him of the recent French invasion. The lowland rats can be controlled with cats, snakes, arsenic, and nightshade, but care must be taken to avoid the water in the area until the poison has been washed away. Weeds can also overwhelm the crop, and only the medicinal plants and those producing ample birdseed (birds being valued for their colorful plumage and song) should be spared. These include a useful purgative and a sovereign remedy for a particular type of fish poisoning.

Timely rains will keep some insects under control, but others can appear more numerous than the shells on a virgin beach. At such times it is better to burn the crop with an eye toward the following year's success, just as sailors throw merchandise overboard in the roughest seas in order to survive to take additional voyages.

Hurricanes have their own season and buildings should be barred against them. Increased waves, darkened skies and unwonted animal behavior provide clues, and soon thunder, lightning, and rain (water thus yoked with fire) fill the air. The eye of the hurricane offers such a respite as Indian warriors enjoy when they pause to regroup on the bloodiest battlefield before fighting even more fiercely. Calm days can be so hot as to scorch man and cane. Earthquakes consume buildings and intimidate horses, cows and even the bravest dogs.

Junio, an islander sent to school in England's famed Eton, fell in love with Theana, the girl whom in his youth he had presented with coconuts for their nectar. On meeting him in England later, she accepted his hand but his father did not approve. They had to part until that parent's death; she returned to the island, and he traveled in Europe. He found semblances of his lover in the best art, and the best songs seemed unequal to her voice. Two years passed before he learned of his father's death, and despite a French attack on the ship that Junio played a key role in repulsing by killing their chief, he was soon back on the island. Alas, on that very day lightning had struck Theana as she was walking off her amorous frustration on the beach. She lingered long enough to thrust her arms around him. He gave her corpse 10,000 kisses and died from the thousand pangs that had torn his breast. They share a single grave, and the island still talks of their love.

The third book finds the Muse celebrating January as a traveler greets civilization after a hazardous journey. The sun keeps winter out, and the cane's juices are ready to run; the plants have resisted all the hazards including fire to get to this point. One midnight, however, great bells announce a fire in the fields, and men scurry to save the plantation house and the already harvested cane. They also get to savor the fresh-cut cane as they work, which they normally would be prevented from doing, but the account is not rendered with all its due terror.

The cane cutting is a joyous affair enlivened by song, and the driver, an "Ethiop [African] authorized, [and therefore] more inhuman" still cracks his horrid whip from malice and the wantonness of power. The large boiling cauldrons present an industrial hazard, and the speaker, recognizing that slaves are human, recommends accommodation for those who are maimed in one's employ instead of merely turning them out.

Both the field hands and those feeding the mill should weed out the bad cane from the good, and a mule-powered upcountry mill can squeeze the juice from it. Mules should be shielded from the noon sun and from nightly dews, and rubbed down after their labors. Waterwheels provide more dependable power. Lord Romney and the force of arms have kept the profitable islands under English instead of French rule.

The boilers should be kept hot, but care must be taken when adding water for fear of bursting the metal. The sugar should not be overheated or it will crystallize, and the slaves should be encouraged to partake of a nightly drink to keep them in the best health and spirits.

French planters feloniously add sand to their sugar to increase its weight, but English planters are above that. One of them tried it once and succeeded enormously, but the next year no one would buy his sugar.

Grainger praises the islands' rum, which helps him forget the friends he left behind in England (or "Albion"). The tropical islands and the ocean are beautiful, and they offer freer advancement that would be checked in England by those whose inherited titles giver them preferment. Seafood is also better than the old country's cuisine. Nature can be found here in its spectacular wildness, and if he can spend his days in worshipping her and at the same time produce something to prolong, soften, or adorn human life, he will not regret a lonely grave on the island.

The fourth book deals with the major labor issue of the plantation: how to exploit slaves for maximum return. He invokes the "Genius" (evidently, the spirit) of Africa to serve as his muse for this section, and in so doing he encounters the chief problem of this work: an advanced education makes the poem possible, but at the same time it sensitized the poet to the immorality of slavery. Thus he can imagine a muse who pities the distressful state and grieves at the sight of her sons in fetters, but he does nothing toward fulfilling her wish of freedom for the human race. This muse is inadequate; he requests the aid of those who helped him earlier in the poem for the task of describing how to care for the black African.

First one should consider their nature, and he admits that they differ in their aptitude for various types of work. Unfortunately, he ascribes these differences not to their individual characters, but to their places of origin and/or tribes in Africa. Thus he describes the people from a given region as if they shared common traits such as one might find in a particular breed of domesticated animal (for example, German shepherd dogs are intelligent and highly trainable). The distinctions he makes will not be repeated here since they constitute a slander on the various countries and tribes he names. His greatest praise is that the people from a particular region make good slaves for field work, a recommendation that sounds more like a reproach to readers of a more enlightened age. Those from one region are prone to worms, those from another tribe cannot be prevented from eating dirt, and slaves from another place are more likely than others to stab the slaveholder with his own knife at midnight. Buy the women if they perform all the agricultural tasks in their tribe while the men hunt, as they will soon adapt to sugar cultivation work that would kill the men.

Regardless of their origins, however, he advocates buying the young and strong. The elderly cannot work or learn English or refuse to do so, and are prone to suicide. One should look for clear eyes, red tongues, wide shoulders, broad chests, and strong legs and arms. After purchase, they should be bled and their bowels purged by medicinal plants (two procedures prevalent in Western medicine as late as the first half of the 19th century). Restore their appetites by replicating African cuisine, and work them so lightly (perhaps gathering grasses for animal fodder) as to almost indulge them with play until they adjust to the new climate. This process is referred to as "seasoning."

Students of medical history may value this text as a record of 18th-century practice. Modern medical ethicists have qualms about the administration of drugs without the consent of the "patients," but it made financial sense for an 18th-century planter to keep his "investments" as healthy as possible. Grainger informs the slaves that their open-air work is healthier and less strenuous than that undertaken by certain enslaved miners in South America, for example, but his real audience remains the planter whose painful con-

science is thus assuaged (it seldom comforts to realize that one's torments are less excruciating than those
of someone somewhere else in the world). He would
have them prove worthy of their masters' solicitude for
their health!

The good master treats his slaves like individuals
by studying their reaction to the hoe (an implement
of serious labor in that climate). He then uses encouraging words, threats, and blows, depending on the
level of force it takes to make them work. Yet, the poet
urges humanity; perhaps the slaves had been masters
in Africa, and miss their homes and wives. Perhaps
they had been war prisoners or innocents swept up in
a slaver's raids. Even if they had been forced into slavery as a penalty for some crime, however, he counsels
letting mercy soften rigid justice (laborers were being
imported in such numbers as to suggest that very few
of them were convicts, but the fiction of their somehow
having deserved slavery helped ease the conscience of
the slaveholders).

If the tender muse had the power of monarchs, she
would "knock off the chains of heart-debasing slavery,"
giving freedom to men of every color and climate. Servants and not slaves should cultivate the cane islands.

To deal with the dragon worm, a parasite native to
some African regions, wind the lengthy adult around
a lead cylinder to pull it from under the victim's skin,
taking care not to break it or lameness will ensue.
Chiggers can penetrate hands and feet, and their offspring soon destroy flesh unless cleansed away. Good
food, sulfur and "smoking niccars" will cure the yaws
if mercury is also judiciously administered. Still other
worms torture the most, and often disguise their presence with symptoms (such as spasms, shivering, or
bloated features) of other afflictions, but a plant called
cow-itch can cure them. He praises seafaring commerce, which brings prosperity in the form of gold,
diamonds, and slaves.

Some slaves will pine if they believe themselves
bewitched, losing their appetite and consequently
their health unless a spiritual healer (an Obia-man) can
intervene with magic. Their charms may include fern
root, teeth from a white man's skull, lizard skeleton,
serpent's head, salt, and water, over which the native
doctor will mutter jargon and form wild circles. The

potion secures one from poison, demons, diseases, and
thieves (whose feet will become blotched if they do
manage to steal from a protected home). Possession of
the potion also shields a thief from detection.

Slaves should only begin work at six A.M., break from
11 or noon (when the broom-bush flowers fully open)
until two, and work until sunset, when the snakes, lizards and insects come out. If you must ask them to
do more, reward them with double food for the day.
An African is not without intelligence and feelings, and
will labor ("for his lord," Grainger fallaciously states, as
if to make slaveholders more acceptable by suggesting
that slavery elevated them into the peerage enjoyed by
medieval knights over their fiefdoms) at night if compelled by necessity.

The good manager will not starve his slaves during
the half year when they are not needed in the fields.
Every week he should dispense English beans, Carolinian rice, imported beef, Pennsylvanian flour, Newfoundland cod or Scottish herrings [a list that reveals
the international aspect of slave-based Atlantic commerce as well as its prosperity]. Prepare food for those
too lazy to cook as well as the young, old, and ill.

Also give them plots on waste ground and allow
them to cultivate yams, cassava, okra, potatoes, kale,
coffee, cotton and sundry other plants one day each
week. A trusted old slave should be encouraged to
live nearby with an alert dog, loaded gun and cutlass
to ward off those fugitive slaves who would consume
such produce. A variety of trees, including figs, will
provide shade, fruit, and beauty.

Build slave huts surrounded with coconut palms on
the beach or on a gently sloping hill alongside banana
trees, but not so close that their fronds or leaves can
spread fire to the roofs. Indian millet and nuts can also
be grown.

Slaves should be allowed to dance on festival days,
or when their work is finished. They might form a great
circle of dancers in which the more talented can caper
with intemperate joy. Some may plant a stolen kiss on
a dancer's neck despite her semblance of scorn. Drink
and drums should not be allowed or such occasions
could turn into violent bacchanalian frenzies. Slaves
should be compelled to marry others on the plantation instead of wearing themselves out on distant jour-

neys at untimely hours. Yearly give each slave a woolly cloak for the rainy season and strong coarse linen that can ward off heat and fevers.

He praises the King Louis XIV of France (1638–1715) for the Code Noir (1689). (Although it banished Jews from French colonies, it mandated Roman Catholic baptism for all slaves and all slaveholders. It offered some legal protection against sexual exploitation and required slave as well as slaveholder consent for marriages. It standardized penalties for offenses such as striking the slaveholder or a member of his family [death] and escape [loss of ears and branding for first offense; execution for third]. It specified that slaves could be chained and beaten but not tortured). Grainger considers the author of these "mild laws" to have been a wise man, and would have the English sugar colonies adopt them.

He also has praise for the Thames, the river of commerce that collects tribute from around the globe, but prophesies (beneath thunderous dark heavens) that the colonies will one day surpass its preeminence in trade. No fleets will grace its waves and no bards will sing of them unless wisdom guides England and its sugar colony policy. Then England will forever triumph over the oceans.

"THE SUTTEE" Lydia Howard Huntley Sigourney (1827)

This poem serves as an early example of a 19th-century woman writer, Lydia H. Sigourney, lending her talent to the cause of social protest when empathy led her to identify with the suffering of others of her gender regardless of international boundaries. Until the British, who then ruled India, outlawed the gruesome practice in 1829, in some Hindu communities a surviving widow was expected to throw herself into the flames to be burned to death on her husband's funeral pyre.

The omniscient speaker is close enough to examine the facial features of the condemned but makes no attempt to understand her culture. This gives her an outsider's perspective, enabling her to describe things objectively as events unfold before her without having her impressions filtered through a cultural or religious lens. This tends to rob the ceremony of its majesty; the victim sits upon a "pile" (line 1) instead of a pyre and

the "infuriate priests" hoarsely chant instead of pray (line 5).

The reader's sentiments are manipulated by the discrepancy between the victim's youth and her late husband's age, her love for her infant (lines 7–12), and her feeding of the child from the "full fount of infant happiness" (lines 18–19) atop her funeral pyre. In a move demonstrating his love for both parents and possibly foreshadowing his own demise, the innocent also embraces his "bloated sire" (line 23).

Up to this point, the tone of the poem has been close to that of a newspaper account. Lacking knowledge of the native religion and mindful of the reader's probable background, the speaker compares the innocence of the infant with that of Adam and Eve ("our parents") and those who pull him from his mother's grasp with the devil (the "Spirit malign" of line 27). Moved by the pathetic struggle unfolding before her, the speaker ungrammatically registers her moral protest with language that distracts from the crisis: the fibers of the mother's nerves that rack her inmost soul "uprooted seemed" (line 33).

The mother, evidently possessing more self-control than the speaker, commanded them to again bring her son and immediately tried to escape with him. She was tied to "her loathsome partner" (line 39), and burning wood was showered onto the pyre accompanied by the demonic yells "of priest and people" and an infernal gong. Three times her death shrieks were heard above the noise. Her fearful cries turned those closest to "the red pile" (line 45) to their idol-gods and would often disturb their sleep.

Today the suttee is best remembered for its appearance in *Around the World in Eighty Days* by the French author Jules Verne in 1873. In that novel, the hero pauses in India to rescue a woman condemned to death after her husband died.

"SWING LOW, SWEET CHARIOT" Anonymous (19th century)

Since Jesus lived in an age when the fastest way to travel was by horse-drawn chariot, this spiritual imagines His return (or at least the return of someone or some angel from that era) in such a vehicle to convey the speaker to heaven, his/her "home." In line 3 the speaker looks over the landscape of the Holy Land, distilled here to the single country of Jordan so often mentioned in the Bible, and finds "a band of angels" coming after him/her to carry him home. If the internal audience gets there before the speaker, he wants him to tell all his friends that he is also coming. It is a rather physical view of an afterlife in which not only the personality (or at least the essential spirit) of the saved will be transported rather bodily to heaven, but even their relationships with their friends will survive the transition.

T

TAYLOR, EDWARD (1642–1729) The future poet's decision to leave his native England was made easier when the death of the Puritan Oliver Cromwell provided the royalists with the opportunity to regain the throne in 1660. Cromwell had been a crucial figure in the overthrow and execution (January 30, 1649) of King Charles I, and had ruled England since assuming the title of Lord Protector in 1653. Revenge was not slow in coming once Charles II, son of the executed king, found himself fully in control. There were bloody retributions and repressive measures such as the Conventicle Act of 1664 that prohibited non-Anglican religious meetings of more than five people.

Fortunately for Taylor, the Puritans still ruled the Massachusetts colony. He arrived in 1668 and began studying theology at Harvard. After graduating in 1671, he served the people of Westfield, Massachusetts, as their minister. A frontier town around 100 miles distant from the college, Westfield sat squarely in harm's way during King Philip's War (a murderous conflict that almost succeeded in ridding western Massachusetts of its white settlements in 1675). Even their church had to be fortified against attack. It would take Taylor until 1679 to have his congregation formally recognized and himself ordained. In addition to serving the community, he farmed, married twice (Elizabeth Fitch in 1674 and, after her death, Ruth Wyllys in 1692), and fathered 14 children. He died on June 29, 1729.

Poets frequently seek the company of other poets as a perceptive audience and sometimes even as mentors, but Taylor settled into a backwoods community that lacked such possibilities. Instead of talking about his craft with his peers, he substituted an active interest in the minutiae of daily colonial life (as evidenced by his poem "HUSWIFERY"), searching for homespun truths and organic metaphors that could help him reach his congregation and, privately, that could help him fully understand and develop all the dimensions of his relationship with God, who replaced his human audience.

In 1682, Taylor began quietly writing his preparatory meditations in verse with a discipline similar to that with which medieval monks were able to make multiple copies of the Bible. As he explained in his "PROLOGUE," such poems were meant to get him in touch with God and, although he recognized his own inadequacy as a writer, he could hope that God could transform both the poet and his message into something that would not displease Him. For more than 40 years he added one such poem each month, probably relishing the necessity of carefully measuring each word as a vehicle for his sacred communion with God. He may also have delighted in the possibility that the rhythms and rhymes realized by his efforts could be interpreted as a sign of divine pleasure, as could his own ability to create them. He was soon expressing himself in other poems (grouped as *God's Determinations in Touching His Elect*) in addition to his sacramental meditations.

Content in his belief that the Lord had heard and appreciated him, Taylor never published his volumes of poetry during his lifetime. His manuscripts eventually found their way to the Yale Library, where they languished for more than two centuries after his death before a scholar named Thomas H. Johnson rediscovered them in 1937. Yale University is still the most important archive for Taylor documents although the Redwood Library and Athenaeum (Newport, Rhode Island) owns an original copy of his *Metrical History of Christianity*. Two of his short diaries have also been preserved.

The Bible and religious tradition represented the primary ways in which God could reach a Puritan's intellect, and Taylor's eventual collection of more than 200 books, many of which were his own laborious handwritten copies, offer further evidence of his devotion. A good Puritan tended to think of his free will as the battlefield upon which God and the devil fought over the ultimate prize, possession of a human soul for eternity. This invited a great deal of soul-searching: one's conscience and impulses could offer important clues as to whether one was destined to spend eternity in heaven or hell.

Of the Taylor poems discussed in this volume, "The Soul's Groan to Christ for Succor" provides one of the best introductions to a Puritan's tortured struggle with his own sense of unworthiness. The speaker may be Taylor himself or an unnamed Christian, but there is little doubt about the adversary's identity. The archfiend has seized on the soul's doubts about his own worth and attacked this soft spot with the chief weapon in his arsenal, a sophisticated knowledge of Puritan theology that stresses the innate depravity of man. He questions why the speaker thinks he would merit salvation, an argument that holds sway until the speaker relies on his faith in Christ. Suddenly able to keep things in perspective, he calls for Christ to weaken and punish the tempter. "Christ's Reply" is so simple that it initially sounds condescending: Man must have faith because his intelligence is too limited to understand God's design. Instead of punishing the archfiend like a wayward cur, Christ wants the soul to think of him as a sheepdog whose seeming ferocity serves to keep His flock in line. Similarly, the soul should accept suffering in this life as part of the process by which souls are refined for heaven. The real danger lies in the soul's own capacity for sin, which if unleashed would perpetrate such enormities as to dwarf the sins that now seem so troubling. Recognizing the soul's true sanctity, Christ promises pardons for all but the most egregious sin.

While the soul addressed in the above poems might belong to any Christian, the speaker in "The Ebb and Flow" should be considered one of the most devout. He is troubled not by disbelief, but by his own inconstancy; he would have his love for God remain always at its most passionate, a human impossibility. Only God can restore his passion.

Since God created nature as well as man in their theology, Puritans tended to pay close attention to natural phenomena in hopes of obtaining additional information about Him. Poems such as "Upon a Wasp Chilled with Cold" suggest that lessons for human behavior could be ascertained even from the beauty and apparent gratitude of an insect. God was also able to signal his displeasure with the Christian community by sending such scourges as Indian attacks and natural catastrophes like that which inspired "Upon the Sweeping Flood."

BIBLIOGRAPHY

Gatta, John. *Gracious Laughter: The Meditative Wit of Edward Taylor*. Columbia: University of Missouri Press, 1989.

Guruswamy, Rosemary Fithian. *The Poems of Edward Taylor: A Reference Guide*. Westport, Conn.: Greenwood Press, 2003.

Keller, Karl. *The Example of Edward Taylor*. Amherst: University of Massachusetts Press, 1975.

Rowe, Karen E. *Saint and Sinner: Edward Taylor's Typology and the Poetics of Meditation*. New York: Cambridge University Press, 1986.

Taylor, Edward. *Edward Taylor's God's Determinations and Preparatory Meditations: A Critical Edition*. Edited by Daniel Patterson. Kent, Ohio: Kent State Press, 2003.

"TELL ALL THE TRUTH BUT TELL IT SLANT" Emily Dickinson (c. 1868) Emily Dickinson's poetic creed has often been thought to be compressed into these eight seemingly simple lines. Condensed into the first four words alone is a powerfully ambiguous statement: Is she counseling the reader (or herself) to tell everyone the truth, or to always tell every bit of the truth, or both? As most of the rest of the

poem addresses the inadequacy of various audiences to receive the Truth, the first interpretation seems more probable, but the second half of the line seems to favor the latter. And who or what is the "All" she wants to tell? If her poetry is her window to the world, then the line may be her summons to the herald's role: her art will carry her message to all the world. On the other hand, the capitalization of the word may connect it with the similarly capitalized Truth, suggesting that they are inseparable, but the entire line advocates withholding information or purposely misleading the reader.

Yet another complication arises from the notion of *Truth*. Can the Dickinson line be completely understood if it is separated from the emphasis Christ placed on the word? Pressed by his tormentors to proclaim himself a king, Christ instead emphasized his truth (John 18:37). Like Dickinson, on that occasion He understood that "Success in Circuit lies," but does the last word of Dickinson's second line also imply lying? If the second line is not viewed as a continuation of the first—the dash Dickinson used to separate them is deliberately (and for a lover of poetry, deliciously) ambiguous—the line might be an admission that it is impossible to tell the Truth with a slant.

The biblical implications of the question at hand are enhanced by the poet's inclusion of herself in "our" infirm Delight (line 3). The line suggests that because the delights of heaven are beyond our ability to comprehend them, a superb surprise awaits. In the meantime, we must be like the children who accept easy explanations of such complex natural phenomena as lightning without fully conceiving their nature. The Truth as it will be revealed is so extraordinary that we must only gradually acquire the capacity to apprehend it, or like lightning, it could render us senseless.

"TELLING THE BEES" JOHN GREENLEAF WHITTIER (1858)

The speaker in this poem points out the features of the farmstead before him with an attention to detail that indicates something of momentous import must have happened there. This is an excellent strategy for two reasons: it enables JOHN GREENLEAF WHITTIER to thoroughly describe the landscape and it prolongs the suspense, since the poet's footnote makes it clear from the outset that someone has died.

Such signs as the tall poplars, the length of the barn, and the large cattle whose white horns can be seen "tossing above the wall" (line 8) indicate the prosperity of Fernside farm (the name is provided in line 20), and its red-barred gate and flower garden suggest its good maintenance. Even the beehives have been "ranged in the sun" (line 8), evidently placed to maximize their health and productivity but perhaps also with a view towards maximizing the farm's aesthetic appeal. The bees, however, and pansies and daffodils (or perhaps a single blossom of each, the line is ambiguous) remind the speaker of what had been one of the farm's chief attractions. Note how their colors, "rose and pink" (line 12) suggest the femininity and beauty of the person who tended them, but the fact that they are overgrown with weeds on a farm where everything else is picture perfect is the first solid clue in the poem of precisely who has died.

How deeply the speaker was touched by the loss is evident in his statement that the intervening year passed as heavy and slow as a tortoise (lines 13–14). Although he now sees the same sun, rose, brook, and clover that he saw then (lines 13–20), they are now fraught with different meanings. All these items trigger memories of the fateful day when, having no clue as to the staggering blow he was about to receive, he paused at the brook to properly groom himself (lines 21–24) before returning to the girl from whom he had parted (under what circumstances, the reader is left uninformed) a month before.

Everything seemed perfect, including the reflection of the sunset on her window and the roses under the eaves. Only the beehives had an ominous appearance; a servant girl was draping them in black and informing them of a death in the family. He thought that Mary's decrepit grandfather had passed until he found him still in the doorway. The horrible truth was revealed by the servant's song, for Mistress Mary was dead and gone.

"Telling the bees" may seem an awful contrivance to an audience of the 21st century, but the minute care with which the family managed their farm suggests that they would not overlook this important detail even in the hour of their sorest trial, especially as the task could be relegated to a chore-girl who might otherwise have been underfoot.

Part of the poignancy of the poem stems from the speaker's implicit identification with the bees, for the message intended for them seems uncomfortably suited to his own circumstance as well. A country lad finding himself in such a circumstance would probably feel culpable or at least complicit in the death of a lover whom he had not visited for a month. Lacking any formal recognition of his relationship with the girl, he cannot avoid looking as inconsistent as a bee that seems to court all the blossoms in a neighborhood without true feeling for a single one of them. Now a true outsider, he stands on the public road beyond the gate wishing he had followed the delightful steps so easily traced with the eye.

"TERMINUS" Ralph Waldo Emerson (1867)

In Roman mythology, Terminus was the god of physical boundaries, and in Ralph Waldo Emerson's poem the speaker acknowledges that age and infirmity can alter one's powers to the point that even physical boundaries have to be inwardly adjusted. One takes in sail (line 2) to avoid winds heavy enough to topple a vessel; metaphorically, the phrase implies a need for the speaker to adjust his ambition to accommodate his changed circumstances.

Terminus becomes the second speaker in the poem, and his message is not a good one. Beginning with a vegetative metaphor, he counsels against shooting broad ambitious branches (beginning vast new projects; line 8). Fancy has departed from the speaker's root (depriving it of necessary nutrients), so he should look to the heavens (the firmament of line 10) no higher than a tent ceiling. His forced economies include choosing between two options since he lacks the energy for both. He should still revere the Giver, but pursue only a few interests. Instead of striking out forcefully, he should soften his footsteps, planning and smiling a little while, but focusing on ripening the fruit still on the tree (projects nearly completed) instead of entertaining "novel germs" (thus germinating new ideas; line 21).

If he wants to find fault, he should blame his ancestors for not bequeathing sturdier stock. Formerly as robust as a Berserker (an enraged Norse warrior who fought without regard for his personal safety; line

28), he is left with ebbing veins, inconstant heat and nerveless reins (probably slow reflexes but perhaps an inability to perfectly control his body). He is insensate among the Muses (representing the arts) and incapable of expressing himself. Crippled and unfeeling, he is also unsuited for combat.

The speaker takes this advice to heart, trimming his effort as a bird adjusts the surface area of its wings to combat the winds of a storm. He will continue guiding the vessel (his life) with reefed sails (sails rolled and tied up to greatly reduce their surface area) in accordance with the voice he obeyed in his prime: faithful to his beliefs, he should banish fear and drive forward, for the port (evidently an afterlife "well worth the cruise"; line 40) is near, and every wave is charmed (helps him toward that goal).

TERRY PRINCE, LUCY (c. 1724–1821)

Much of our knowledge about the early life of this very minor poet but important spokesperson for her race comes from a newspaper obituary. She was either kidnapped as an infant or lawfully taken from her parents somewhere along the chain of misery that extended from the shores of Africa to Bristol, Rhode Island. Although through her infancy and earliest childhood she may have been kept in Connecticut, at approximately four years of age she was resold to Ebenezer Wells. He brought her to Deerfield, Massachusetts, a frontier town frequently decimated in wars against the French and the local native tribes. She was baptized in 1735 and eventually gained full fellowship in the local church. At some point she also gained her freedom; her marriage to Abijah Prince, on May 17, 1756, resulted in seven children and made them the only freed family in a community where others were still enslaved. They lived in Guilford, Vermont.

The various legends about Terry's eloquence that have survived include her arguing passionately but ultimately unsuccessfully for her son's admission to college and her successful argument before the Vermont Supreme Court. Although little corroborating evidence for the first of these feats survives, such stories suggest what might have been had Lucy Terry Prince and others of her century not been denied the chance to achieve their full human potential. It is clear that the woman could ably use her eloquence to defend her family's rights under the law.

After Terry Prince died in Sunderland, Vermont, on July 11, 1821, her obituary put her age at 97. Her only surviving poem chronicles the aftermath of an ambush by the local Abenaki tribe on a haymaking party of settlers on August 25, 1746. It is impossible to know exactly when Terry wrote the poem because "BARS FIGHT" remained in the oral history of the region until it was published in 1855 in Josiah Gilbert Holland's *History of Western Massachusetts* (Springfield: S. Bowles and Company), but tradition has identified her as the first black American poet.

The Georgian mansion belonging to the Wells family the poet served was being expanded to its present size around the time of her wedding. It has been preserved as the Wells-Thorn House in Deerfield, Massachusetts.

BIBLIOGRAPHY

Katz, Bernard, and Jonathan Katz. *Black Woman: A Fictionalized Biography of Lucy Terry Prince.* Juvenile historical fiction. New York: Pantheon Books, 1973.

Merriam, Robert L. *Lucy Terry Prince.* Conway, Mass.: R. L. Merriam, 1983.

Proper, David R. *Lucy Terry Prince: Singer of History.* Deerfield, Mass.: Pocumtuck Valley Memorial Association, 1997.

Williams, Stephen West. *A Biographical Memoir of the Rev. John Williams.* Greenfield, Mass.: Imprints, 1837.

"THANATOPSIS" WILLIAM CULLEN BRYANT **(1821)** Few poems suffer more from an uninviting title than this "Meditation on Death" or "View of Death," to use alternative English translations of its Greek. It begins joyously enough as a communion with Nature, briefly but charmingly personified as a smiling elegant young beauty. The rapture is exceedingly short-lived, however; part of being human is the understanding that you must die. The problem of WILLIAM CULLEN BRYANT's poem is how to live with this certainty.

The answers, for the speaker at the start of the poem, are to learn from nature and to fully embrace your faith to the point where it transcends mortality. The achievement of the poem lies in its suggestion of several of the insights that later came to prominence in America with the transcendentalists of the mid-1840s: a belief that Nature provides innumerable hints at the essence of existence, which humanity can profitably study (the Puritans also held this belief); an awareness of common humanity with people from other cultures and belief systems; a striving for an awareness of reality beyond its surface features; and an implicit acceptance of what late-20th-century America would come to embrace as cultural relativism.

Nature, in this poem's conceit, is more teacher than companion; personified, she becomes the speaker of the poem in line 17 as the original speaker is relegated to the role of internal audience. Nature gathers a pupil's interest with the varied beauties of her visible forms (line 2), and intercedes when he faces emotional as well as intellectual difficulties (lines 5–8). Foremost among the problems each human must face are morbid thoughts of mortality. At the author's age, a robust 27 when the poem was first published in its entirety, death is still something that happens to other people, and his visions of his own demise are romanticized to the extent that the speaker fixates on the trappings of a rather sanitized, abstract death. A sad procession of images is presented chronologically, beginning with the physical suffering attendant upon the hour of death, here condensed to a single bitter hour of an abstract "stern agony" (line 11). Aspects of the traditional American funeral take up the rest of the line; in preparation for burial, a cadaver is wrapped in a shroud and placed in a coffin; the word *pall* can refer to the black covering of the coffin as well as the coffin itself. The problem of burial in the morbid imagination lies in empathy; the sufferer imagines the breathless darkness and confined space of the "narrow house" (line 12) as the coffin is placed in cold ground (line 19), whereas the deceased is insensate.

The speaker at this point in the poem can also be viewed as representative of his age (such British romantic poets as Lord Byron and William Wordsworth were very popular in America) in cherishing the uniqueness of his individuality; he is troubled by the thought that (as Nature teaches) first his image and then every human trace of his existence will perish (lines 21–26). This reaches its zenith in a fear of dying friendless and unmourned (lines 58–60), while the gay (the term had nothing to do with sexual orientation at the time this poem was written) will laugh, the solemn will plod on, and each will chase his favorite phantom despite the death of an individual (lines 61–64). If such lines suggest the sensibility of the Byronic hero, his melancholic brooding might therefore be dismissed as a popular pose. A major difference lies in the eventual optimism expressed in the closing lines of this poem.

The poem's first alternative to the inevitable gathering darkness of the tomb is to turn to limitless nature under the open sky, but everywhere Nature reinforces the lesson of mortality, especially the eventual corruption of all flesh into mold and dust. The poet, in the guise of Nature, briefly offers a modicum of philosophical resignation: once dead you eventually will be on terms of total equality with the richest, wisest, and most beautiful people who ever lived, and the whole earth in all its glory can be viewed as your collective crypt. This insight, however, leads to the gloomy reflection that the dead are buried everywhere, and it is as impossible to escape their presence as it is to escape their fate.

A turning point in the poem occurs when Nature begins to list the various stages of man at the time of death. This roll call reinforces the poem's theme of the universality of death, but it could also carry the initial speaker past brooding over the unfairness of his own demise. Note that each successive stage moves him further from his own circumstance; when he first began writing the poem the author could be viewed as a "youth in life's green spring" (line 68). He next considers the death of the aged man (which he would in time become) before crossing gender lines. The list also advances by the juxtaposition of opposites, hence the death of the aged is combined with "the infant in the smiles and beauty of its innocent age cut off" (lines 70–71). The sharpness of the last two words of that line is especially poignant.

Perhaps the realization that at least he did not die as an infant returns the speaker to the important question of how to live one's life; it certainly moves him from his fixation with his own grave to the abstract euphemism of joining "the innumerable caravan" of the dead on their way to their final chambers "in the silent halls of death" (lines 75–78).

At this point, Nature begins speaking like a didactic secular humanist, encouraging auditors to live in their (religion unspecified) faith. Such devotion will help you accept death as naturally and as snugly as you lie down to nap on your couch, a rather pat solution to the central problem of the poem, except for those whose faith is so strong that they can achieve an unfaltering trust in their beliefs.

"THAT BOY, THE FARMER SAID, WITH HAZEL WAND" Frederick Goddard Tuckerman (1860)

This is a poem about that crucial point in someone's life when he figures out he is better off following his own interests, instead of doing what someone else would have him do.

The image of the farmer wielding a hazel stick like a military officer's baton sets the tone of the poem and reinforces its meaning. On a working farm, such a tool would be used to poke or prod recalcitrant animals into motion, but here it is wielded as a "wand" (line 1), as if it could magically transform the speaker into a more diligent worker. The farmer uses it to direct the speaker's attention to a 16-year-old boy who can work at harvesting hay from sunrise to sunset. This is barely veiled criticism of the speaker's efforts, for the prior day he had taken time off to gather a few flowers. Possibly unaccustomed to farm labor, but definitely unaccustomed to criticism, he does not know if he smiled or frowned (line 5), or if it meant nothing ("aught") to him.

All the prior day the boy had held the plow steady or kept up with the adult mowers, while other fingers (the speaker's) gathered flowers not from the meadow or field, where work was being done, but from the forest (line 12). He had been literally caught red-handed, for either a thorn had caused his hand to bleed, or the pokeberries he had gathered dyed it. Although the farmer would prefer single-minded devotion to his assigned tasks, the playful language of Frederick Goddard Tuckerman's last line ("[perhaps] the pokeberry spit purple on my hand") suggests that the speaker still retained a sense of joy in life.

"THERE ARE TWO RIPENINGS" Emily Dickinson (published 1951)

This homage to the bur oak (its eponymous feature is named in line 6) focuses on the contributions its foliage makes to the fall landscape and its production of acorns. Its leaves turn from green to shades of yellow in the fall, a first "ripening" for the eye (line 1). The poet evidently designed this poem as a puzzle, for the second line offers the reader several alternative clues depending on the pronunciation of the word *wind*. It can refer to either the breeze or a curling motion, and one of the pleasing aspects of this poem is that both meanings can play a role in the process (mystified by EMILY DICKINSON's diction, "Whose forces Spheric wind," in the second line) by which the Velvet product (a probable reference to the distinctively fuzzy caps on each acorn) drops "spicy" (a comment on the acorn's flavor; line 4) to the ground. The term "Spheric wind" may refer to those winds belonging to the earth, or it may refer to the twisting applied to the leaves (the "forces" of the tree) by the wind until they fall.

The burr's maturing is "homelier" because the acorns grow where its flowers flourished earlier, but the adjective may also suggest that the edible product that results is less splendid than the feast afforded the eye by the fall foliage. The fall frosts make the acorns more visible because they finish off the last of the leaves and because the acorns fall to the ground afterward.

"THERE CAME A WIND LIKE A BUGLE"

EMILY DICKINSON (published 1951)   Storms in the eastern United States can bring high winds (responsible for the loud noise of the first line and the quivering grass of the second). The most ominous clouds can turn the sky a distinctive green and greatly reduce the temperature, two phenomena combined in the single phrase of "Green Chill" (line 3) and responsible for the subsequent human reaction of barring doors and windows against the "Emerald Ghost," an acknowledgment of how spooky the eerie light and changing air pressure can make everything seem. To help the reader understand the sense of danger pervading the air, EMILY DICKINSON's speaker compares the lightning with a poisonous snake in the sixth line's reference to "Doom's electric [water] Moccasin." The "panting" trees (a description suggesting the sounds the wind makes as it whistles through them as well as an indication of the stresses placed upon them) bend and bow until they

suggest "a strange Mob" (line 9). Many of them fled away like the fences, and rivers ran where the houses used to stand. Such were the things witnessed by the survivors (recipients of a new identity, having become those who "looked and lived;" line 12).

Appropriately, the church bell, which traditionally warned of grave dangers and the passing of townspeople as well as announcing church services, wildly told the "flying tidings" (lines 13–14). This leads to the speaker's philosophical comment (appropriately ending with a biblical-sounding phrase): much can come and much can go (repetition of such simple words is yet another way of mimicking biblical syntax and diction), and "yet abide the World" (lines 15–18). The last phrase echoes Ecclesiastes 1:24: human generations succeed each other, "but the earth abideth forever."

Because tornadoes and hurricanes tend to happen to other towns most frequently located in other states and because modern Americans trust in their weather service to provide warnings far enough in advance to take preventive measures such as evacuating low-lying areas, mere thunderstorms have lost their terror for most readers. For those who have had firsthand experience with the full fury of nature's unbridled destructive forces, the experience can be as unforgettable, life-changing, and horrifying as the poet tries to make it here.

"THERE'S A CERTAIN SLANT OF LIGHT"

EMILY DICKINSON (published 1951)   As she did for other seasonal poems (such as "A LIGHT EXISTS IN SPRING"), EMILY DICKINSON gave herself the difficult task of describing the quality of light as it appeared at its most representative moment. For winter, she sought the afternoon sun, but in this poem she abandoned any attempt to describe it directly or objectively. Instead, she treats the reader to a subjective rendering of the emotional experience of the weak sunlight.

In other seasons, sunlight tends to invigorate human nature, but the speaker finds its winter slant oppressive like the "Heft of Cathedral Tunes" (lines 3–4), a doubling up of the trope by which the perceptions generally received by one sense are described in terms of another. In this case, the slant of light (normally perceivable only by the eye) is described in terms of the "heft" (normally only felt by lifting) of tunes (normally only heard), and yet the meaning is perfectly clear to anyone who has heard a full-throated organ set the mood for a funeral.

The second stanza begins with the apparent oxymoron of "Heavenly Hurt." Although this lacks a physical component (hence it leaves no visible scar, line 6), it nevertheless changes things internally, "where the Meanings are" (it affects one both mentally and emotionally). It also reminds us of the brevity of this life and its grave ramifications for the afterlife, a "Heavenly Hurt" brought upon the human race by the transgressions of Adam and Eve.

It affects the mental state but cannot be reached by teaching. Her addition of the word *Any* (separated from the surrounding text by dashes; line 9) provides a medical context for any attempt to alleviate the suffering it causes. Colloquially, the term is used as an adverb to convey the notion of "at all" as in the sentence "Did that help any?" That such usage is substandard not only evokes the regional voice of New England in the poet's era, it may also suggest that any attempt to alleviate the suffering is likely to be conducted by relatively uneducated amateurs who lack the professional tools to effectively intervene. Properly diagnosed as "Despair" (line 10; the modern term would be "depression"), it is described as an "imperial" affliction (line 10; the adjective implies that the depression so completely takes over as to merit its own "Seal" of state; line 10) delivered by the Air (or at least by the depressingly dull winter light).

When it (ostensibly the afternoon sun, but also depression) comes, the mental landscape "listens" (an example of one sense being trained to react to the stimulation of another, in this case sight; line 13). Like the listening landscape, Shadows are also personified (they "hold their breath" in the next line). When it goes (when the sunlight departs as night falls, or when full-scale, clinical depression sets in), the phenomenon reminds the speaker of "the Distance on the look of Death" (lines 15–16), a phrase not only recalling the nonresponsive stare of the dead, but also anticipating that dread state which, nearly a century later, Second World War veterans referred to as "the thousand-yard stare" of shell-shock victims (those suffering from post-traumatic stress syndrome, to use the language of the 21st century). Modern psychology would be tempted to diagnose the core problem in this poem as "seasonal affective disorder," however, and prescribe, among other things, daily exposure to ultraviolet light.

"THERE'S BEEN A DEATH, IN THE OPPOSITE HOUSE" EMILY DICKINSON (published 1951)

In an age before care for the sick and dying were outsourced to hospitals and their professional staffs, most families were intimately acquainted with death because it occurred in a bedroom of the house in which they lived. In EMILY DICKINSON's poem, however, the speaker's voice is so remarkably cold that it completely lacks sympathy, let alone empathy. The opening line may reveal a possible explanation for his cold tone: referring to the "opposite house" not only indicates its location (across the street from the speaker's own), it also may imply a degree of enmity between the residents of the two buildings. The speaker is also so accustomed to deaths that he not only recognizes "the numb look" of the houses in which they have occurred, but can even make an educated guess as to the time of death, as "lately" as today (line 2. Was the term chosen as a macabre pun on *late,* an adjective often used to indicate that the subject in question has died? More idiomatic diction would have chosen "recently").

Like mice, the neighbors "rustle" in and out of the house (line 5) and the doctor, having failed at driving away the disease, drives away himself. Death, especially when it follows a lengthy illness, has its own stench, and like clockwork someone mechanically opens a window "like a pod" (as naturally as a vegetable pod opens when the enclosed peas or beans become too large for it to continue enclosing them; line 7). Acting on much the same impulse, someone "flings" (a verb choice accurately conveying their disgust; line 8) a mattress outside. Children hurry by, but the speaker recalls that when he was a boy, he wondered if "it" (line 10; dehumanizing the dead man with this impersonal pronoun distances a child from the fact of his own mortality) died on "that" (therefore making the mattress an object to be avoided like a trap).

The minister arrives "stiffly," an adverb that stresses his formality while it also connects him with the rigidity of the corpse. He takes charge as if the house, mourners, and little boys were all his property. Next comes the milliner (a hatmaker probably keen on selling his/her wares from a funerary line to the bereaved), and an undertaker (who works in the "Appalling Trade," line 18). He "takes the measure of the house" (he not only considers how to arrange the funeral within its confines, he may also be judging the wealth of its occupants so as to calculate his most profitable sales strategies). The "Dark Parade" (line 20) of such officials, neighbors, friends, and family dressed in mourning will accompany the deceased to the grave, frequently walking behind the horse-drawn hearse decorated with black tassels, or riding in their own similarly adorned coaches.

All of these things have happened so often before in such country towns that the speaker can read them as clearly as a sign in advance of the public announcement (in "Intuition of the News," line 23). Only in this diction of the last stanza does the speaker hint at some possible awareness of a spiritual meaning in the death and the human rituals surrounding it. A "Sign" might come from heaven in the form of an "Intuition" about the "News" of Resurrection and eternal life, for example, but the prosaic realism of his cold rendering of the facts as he perceives them suggests that he is not a fervent believer in such outcomes.

"THERE WAS A CHILD WENT FORTH"
WALT WHITMAN (1855) Perhaps the most beautiful things about this poem are its celebration of a child's growth by accretion and its sense that nothing is lost on the artist even before he discovers his voice. There is a very faint echo of Alfred Tennyson's famed poem "Ulysses" (1842) in the opening stanza. Like the ancient Greek king who, in Tennyson's rendering, fancied himself part of all he had met, Whitman's child became the first object he looked upon. It became a part of him for a day or perhaps for "stretching cycles of years" (line 4). Anyone who has watched an infant study an object in its crib must at some point wonder what is going on in that tiny brain, and Whitman provides one possibility.

By the second stanza the child has progressed outdoors and from inanimate objects to living nature, with "lilacs" (line 5) serving as a transitional term because it introduces both biology and color (*lilac* denotes a pale purple hue as well as a flower), the child's two most important discoveries in the second stanza. It seems especially fitting for a poet who named his life's work *Leaves of Grass* to plant that grain as the first exclusively outdoor object in the poem (line 6), although the child evidently has yet to learn the name of its color. He can distinguish red and white, however, and by the sixth line comes to understand that such hues are not unique to one object, but that different things (such as morning glories and clover) can share them. He has not only begun to notice sounds but to associate a particular bird song with the species that creates it.

With its March lambs, "pink-faint" piglets (note how his struggle to find the precise color combines the two pigments already mentioned), foal (technically a colt is a male foal and a "filly" is a female foal. This is an important distinction because it suggests that the child may not yet be distinguishing between genders), and calf, nature seems as young as he is. He can grasp the similarities and differences between chickens and ducks (the "noisy broods" of the barnyard and the pond mire in line 7), and the magic of water with its curiously suspended fish and graceful plants.

One of the happy consequences of the poet's Quaker background stems from that sect's unwillingness to honor pagan gods (*Wednesday* derives from Woden's Day and *Thursday* from Thor) and Roman rulers (*July* and *August* honor Julius and Augustus Caesar) in the names of the days of the week and the months. Hence the "fourth- and fifth-month" observations at the beginning of the third stanza may refer to April and May, but may also refer to the child's developmental age; he may now be almost halfway through his early childhood just as May is almost halfway through a year. He has learned that, like the animals, plants also have their stages of infancy (the "sprouts" of line 12), growth and maturity (apple blossoms become fruit), and that some are edible (the "esculent" of line 12) whereas others are mere weeds. This introduces classification by utility, a principle he quickly applies to humanity (hence "the old drunkard staggering home from the outhouse of the tavern" [a wonderfully detailed description; line 14] is juxtaposed with the schoolmistress on her way to school. Note that these are both events of the early morning, which corresponds to that period of the child's life). While boys can either be friendly or quarrelsome and girls remain "tidy and fresh-cheeked" mysteries, the child's notice of the bare feet of the black children suggests he has learned to make a connection between race and privilege, race and economic deprivation, or perhaps race and freedom. By line 18 he is already traveling from city to country and beyond.

In the fourth stanza the child considers parents. His studies of nature enable him to understand the biology that led to his creation (line 19), but he also recognizes the vital role his parents daily played in his development. In the next stanza he contrasts the quiet, mild, and busy mother's "wholesome odor" (line 23) with the manly strength and self-sufficiency of the sometimes unjust and violent father, armed with blows, loud words, tight bargains and crafty lures (line 25). The family culture, including its customs, language, and furniture, shapes his "yearning and swelling heart" (line 26), and their mutual affection cannot be denied (the "gain-say'd" of line 27). Thus far everything has seemed real, but now doubts (both "day-time" [presumably based on logic] and "night-time" [probably more emotional in nature]) begin to arise about the very nature of existence.

The pace of his life advances to the point where even people appear to be only "flashes and specks" (line 29). There seems no end to the physical phenomena seemingly so substantial around him, and their appearance predictably changes as the lighting changes, yet there are still shadows, mists, and "aureolas" (the coronas [circles of light] around the sun or other light sources when viewed through mists, but also a similar effect crowning the heads of people in religious art [and sometimes naturally, with the right lighting]). As if listing various visual phenomena in some way forestalled questions about the reality of all things, but also to show how rich the child's life has become, the poem ends with a ferry trip such as so often inspired the poet's other poems. What seems to matter most is the impression all these things have on the former child (now, his knowledge and wonderful sensitivity suggest, a poet or other artist who has maintained his innate sensitivity to color [he mentions a cloud's forming a long bar of maroon tint against "the purity" of its background in line 37], motion [the schooner "sleepily dropping down the tide], sound [the waves' "slapping"], and odor [from the salt marsh and shore mud in line 38]). Through the miracle of his art, everyone who catches his attention that day will go forth every day.

"THESE ARE THE DAYS WHEN BIRDS COME BACK" EMILY DICKINSON (1890) Carefully attuned to such aspects of nature as she could encounter in her backyard, EMILY DICKINSON was so moved by a particularly warm fall day that she wrote this poem. It begins happily enough, with superficial notice of the arrival of a bird or two (the speaker is not so interested as to make an exact count), and the pleasant enough but too easy rhyming of "few" and "two" in the first stanza. The trouble begins with her suggestion that the birds are taking a "backward look" (line 3), for the unseasonable warmth might remind them of their easy early summer lives.

Unfortunately, the "backward look" reminded her of several biblical personalities such as Lot's wife, who was turned into salt for looking back as she left the evil city of Sodom (Genesis 19), and the followers of Moses, who were denied the promised land after they looked back to their primitive gods while their leader Moses was off receiving the Ten Commandments (Exodus 20 and Deuteronomy 5). Similarly, it is tempting on such a day to believe in the "old sophistries of June" (line 5), chief among which is the notion that the fair skies, good health, and bright prospects of spring and youth will last forever, and that life on this earth is such a paradise that we need not prepare for eternity.

Calling this "a blue and gold mistake" (line 6) suggests that it erroneously mixes secular and religious concerns, for the color choices combine the blue of the heavens with the golden (but earthbound) fields of ripening grain. The poet was also aware that a thousand years of Western art have depicted the Virgin Mary in blue, a color associated with celestial glory, whereas gold has not only been used for halos and auras in religious paintings but also has been associated with the metal that has diverted men's eyes from heaven for so long.

The third stanza continues to combine natural observation with metaphysical concerns. Just as the bees are not fooled by the warm weather into abandoning their hives for the nectar harvests of the false spring, the human who busily attends to his proper business of grooming his soul will not be tricked into believing in the impermanent things of this world. Characteristically, the speaker continues enjoying the day; it is so fine that it almost seduces her into mistaking its magnificence for that of paradise.

Then all the seeds that surround her in autumn and a falling leaf (called "timid" in line 12 because it keeps turning away in its flight and soon hides in the grasses) remind her of the true season and that all things on earth must die. But if nature can lead her to such apprehensions of the saddest fact of religious truth, it also can suggest the happiest Christian promise of Resurrection and eternal life. Thus reassured that enjoying nature is not worshiping it, she proceeds to appreciate the day for its intimations of heaven and its reinforcement of her beliefs.

She now views the unseasonably warm day like a sacramental wafer (stanza five). Just as the wafer is symbolically supposed to represent the body of Christ (and some sects believe that through a miracle of metaphysical transformation it *is* the body of Christ), a warm day in very late fall in Massachusetts reminds one that there had been a summer and promises that there will be a summer again. Thus relieved of the tensions visited upon nature by an adult view of its association with sin, she asks to commune with nature as innocently as a child.

The last stanza borders on sacrilege, even though she has prepared the reader for it by establishing the religious framework through which she views the day. Some religious readers may wince at her use of the most sacred emblems of their church (those relating to the communion services in which the body and blood of Christ are at least symbolically consumed) to suggest the fervor with which she will enjoy nature on this choicest of days.

"THEY SHUT ME UP IN PROSE" EMILY DICKINSON (**published 1935**) To be "shut up in prose" implies that the speaker was either denied access to poetry or denied an appreciative audience for her own verse. Either approach, if administered with a draconic siege mentality, would have eventually silenced her just as effectively as the horrific practice of placing a little girl in a closet could make her "still" (lines 3–4).

As if the memory of her confinement reduced her to the developmental stage at which it occurred, her speech becomes more childish in the second stanza. The use of "themself" (line 5) conveys a childlike awkwardness with grammar. The playful verb "peeped" and the image of her brain "go[ing] round" (line 6) might also have been a child's. As if the word "peeped" reminded her of a baby bird, the image provides her with a transition to her presumably full-fledged state. Her diction brings the intelligence of her jailers into question when she uses "as wise" in place of the more idiomatic phrase "as well" (line 7); she has progressed to an age when she can defend herself. In place of the dark closet, she imagines a bird "lodged" (instead of caged) in an open-roofed pound. As an indictment of the injustice of her incarceration, she implicitly suggests that only a crime as serious as treason should merit such a penalty (line 8). Her ambiguous phrasing may question the motives as well as the judgment of her elders; grammatically, they may have acted "for treason" (treasonously), but even if they were punishing the speaker's treason instead of revealing their own, the notion of punishing a bird for that offense is ludicrous.

The speaker's use of the pronoun "Himself" (line 9) might be read as a further emblem of her strength; instead of thinking of herself as a powerless little girl, she has mentally switched genders to identify with the might and authority enjoyed by men in her Victorian society. Like the God of Genesis she may have encountered in her Sunday school lessons, she "has but to will" to gain "as easy as a Star" the perspective from heaven. As a bird might laugh at the ineptitude of those who sought to confine him in the open air, but even more potently, as a god with unlimited power as well as omniscience, she can laugh at her punishment.

Her ambiguous final statement "No more have I" (line 12) suggests that she can escape from the closet as easily as a bird can fly, but it also suggests that she has no more fear of that punishment or (fortunately for all concerned) any need of revenge. Like a god who can laugh at the foibles of men, she forgives her transgressors because she understands their relative weakness. Her statement suggests that she has effectively closed the door on that part of her past.

Of course, no one prevented EMILY DICKINSON from eventually writing and experiencing poetry, but the poem may have a much wider application than that. It is thought to have been written in 1862, the historical moment when women were on the very verge of making their voices heard on a wide range of public issues. The notion that women as well as children were best kept still behind the staid doors of domesticity might be celebrated in the prose of the newspapers and other media and echoed by the men in their lives, but this poem asserts that they were already recognizing their new poetry of power.

"THIS COMPOST" WALT WHITMAN (1856)

The 19th century was the golden age of the indescribable trope: If a writer waxes eloquent about the effect an object or experience has had on him without revealing much information about it, he can rely on the reader's imagination to supply the missing details about the thing too horrible (or too wonderful) for words. In WALT WHITMAN's poem only the locale is provided: the still woods where the speaker thought he was safest. At first the triggering incident seems minor; it "startles" the speaker instead of horrifying him, and he "withdraws" from the scene, a verb suggesting an orderly retreat. Evidence that he is deeply troubled soon surfaces, however, when he changes his behavior as a consequence of the experience. Gone are his long walks on pastures, naked swims ("to meet my lover the sea," a phrase that suggests how much that pastime meant to him, line 4), and touching the earth as he would other flesh ("to renew me," wording that stresses the sexual aspect of his communing with nature).

The second stanza introduces the central theme of the poem, a celebration of nature's ability to cleanse itself. How can the "blood" of herbs and other food plants (line 8) not be contaminated by the sour dead, the distempered corpses interred in every continent? The third stanza introduces a moral dimension into the equation by focusing on the foul liquid and meat of buried drunkards and gluttons (lines 12–13). The speaker does not see it but is sure that plowing and spading the ground will expose it.

The second section of the poem focuses on a compost of which every bit may once have been part of a sick person. Action verbs ("covers," "bursts," and "pierces") describe how domestic crops spring from the mould, and, with a pale visage (like a ghost), "the resurrection of the wheat" (line 23) emerges from its graves. The "tinge" (a gradual change of hue signaling new growth) appears all over certain trees, the "he-birds" carol and the "she-birds" sit on nests (line 25). The next generation of farm animals take their first breaths, the potatoes and corn (the "maize" of line 29) raise from their little hills, and the summer growth "is innocent and disdainful" (line 30) above all the sour dead.

Trusting such chemistry, in the fifth stanza the speaker again returns to the "transparent green-wash" (line 33) of the amorous sea, finding it safe to let it lick his naked body "with its tongues" (line 34). Like the earth, the sea is "clean forever and forever" despite all the fevers deposited in it. He also enjoys drinking from a well, eating fruits, and lying on the grass, confident that they will not poison him even though the grass grows from what was once a catchable disease.

In the last stanza, the speaker is terrified because the patient Earth "grows sweet things out of such corruptions" (line 43). Harmless and stainless despite its "endless successions of diseased corpses" (line 44), it distills "exquisite winds" from "infused fetor" (bacteria- and germ-laden odors; line 45). The Earth annually bestows its prodigious, divine gifts on man, and accepts their corpses at last (line 47).

"THIS IS MY LETTER TO THE WORLD"

EMILY DICKINSON (1890) As a statement of the poet's intent written near the start of her career, this rather simple poem was prescient in several telling ways. The first line seems to indicate that EMILY DICKINSON's ambition extended to reaching the world, but the second line acknowledges that the world was unlikely to take much interest during her lifetime. This was largely a consequence of her decision to publish so few poems before her death, so the slightly whining tone is misleading. Under the circumstances, her poetry had about the same chance of achieving immediate recognition that a note in a bottle thrown into the ocean has of generating a timely response. This implies that she was not writing to gain a reputation.

The next two lines suggest that she felt compelled to write not only because she recognized Nature's majesty but also because of its tenderness. If the human world beyond her intimate circle took no interest, that left her more receptive to the "simple News" (line 3) conveyed by Nature, with which she communed all the more readily.

Dickinson began the second stanza with the self-effacing implication that her poetry is chiefly important because it conveys Nature's message. Not only is her role as the poet not mentioned, she implies that the poems were merely in her care, as her chief concern is that she does not know to whose hands they will eventually be committed after her death (when she "cannot see," line 5). In the tradition of female American poets dating from ANNE BRADSTREET's "PROLOGUE," she asks that she be judged tenderly because of the reader's love of Nature; only in the 21st century would a female poet's request for indulgence not automatically ensure a more sympathetic reading.

The poet's use of dashes in this poem adds a modicum of artistic ambiguity to the last two lines. If more conventional commas were used in line 7, for example, it would be clear if the poet is parenthetically commenting that the love of Nature is sweet, if she is addressing her own sweet countrymen, or if it is Nature's countrymen (her fauna) that are sweet. As it stands, the line may indicate any or all of these possibilities. Rather paradoxically, the last line reveals that the speaker expects the poet as well as the poetry to be judged. Thus the poem ends with the poet's confident assertion that her poetry will attract the attention of the world, for she openly addresses her countrymen in the penultimate line. The reader can almost feel her satisfaction at the thought that if this does indeed come to pass (as of course it did), the world will regret not taking more notice of her. The word "Sweet" brack-

eted by dashes in line 7 invites the reader to join her in savoring this thought of ultimate triumph. Success is the best revenge.

"THIS WAS A POET—IT IS THAT"

EMILY DICKINSON (published 1951) This poem celebrates the great services poets provide for the rest of humanity: awakening us to the miracles that surround us in the physical objects we encounter on a daily basis, and fathoming the depth of meaning of individual words and phrases so that we can realize the latent power of language (the "distilling" of "amazing sense [with an important pun on "scents"] from ordinary Meanings" [lines 2–3]).

Like an especially skilled perfumer (a maker or purveyor of perfumes), the Poet can demonstrate how powerful attars can be made from the familiar summer flowers the rest of us admire but allow to perish (lines 4–5). Thus having shown the way (and because language is our common birthright and ideas alone do not constitute intellectual property), the new ways of seeing that the Poet provides can seem so natural that the common person can take that gift for granted, wondering that s/he did not realize it before (lines 6–7).

In revealing the secrets ("disclosing") of pictures as well as of the objects represented in them, the Poet entitles nonpoets to "ceaseless poverty" (line 12); that is, s/he can enlighten them to the poverty of their existence and thus awaken them to the necessity of appreciating life (and art) more fully.

The Poet is so wealthy in images, insights, and ideas, that "robbing" (not only the theft of his physical property [since he has a better sense of his true wealth] but also perhaps the adoption of His best lines for use as unattributed commonplace phrases) does him no harm. The Poet's "Portion" is so great that His Fortune can withstand such losses to the rest of mankind, and to Time.

"THIS WORLD IS NOT CONCLUSION"

EMILY DICKINSON (1862) The emphatic assertion of the first line ultimately has only faith to back it up, but the poem presents a very brief overview of the history of man's attempts to prove the existence of an afterlife. The second line echoes the creation myths of those religions that believe in man's special place in the divine scheme of things; for them, humanity is a species standing beyond those natural laws that indicate that eventually everything must completely perish. The major distinction Western man drew between his own species and the rest of creation is that the former has an indestructible soul.

The images at this point in EMILY DICKINSON's poem invite a pause to consider the intuitive nature of primitive men and women as they stood together on the African plain. There were quite often other species beyond the tight circle of their fire, and human survival was dependent upon the closest possible coordination of their efforts with other members of their clan. They developed music and listened for every sound, though they scarce understood most of them. Everything seemed magical, including the death of those people upon whom their lives depended. Eventually the thought of something like heaven beckoned and baffled. At least as early as the ancient Greeks, a few advanced thinkers began focusing on Philosophy, and Dickinson conflates about two and a half millennia of philosophical thought on such problems as the nature of man and the possibility of an afterlife into the two succinct words "don't know" (line 6). Even the wisest men and ablest scholars (grouped here under the general heading of "Sagacity") have had to go "through a Riddle" when they died.

To gain their due in the afterlife, Men have "borne the Contempt of Generations and Crucifixion" (lines 10–12), a reference that moves the chronology into the early Christian era of two millennia ago. Since then Faith has slipped, laughed, and rallied innumerable times and survived countless scandals (lines 13–14). For centuries men venerated anything associated with Christ and the more helpful saints as sacred relics, thus plucking "a twig of Evidence" (line 15). The advent of science is represented by the weather vane (line 16; note the deliberate pun on "vain"), an entirely useless instrument when it comes to determining the best way to achieve the afterlife since it points a new way each time the wind shifts. Theatrics from the pulpit and even the loudest "Hallelujahs" can offer no better backing than faith in support of their guarantees.

Whether or not the reader believes this poem is ultimately despairing depends on how sensitive one is to the nuances of its last two lines. Dickinson begins with a reference to the use of narcotics (line 19), a cutting-edge development that brings the poem's chronology almost up to the very day it was written, probably in the year 1862. The 19th century was a golden age for opiates, and ether anesthesia had been taking some of the pain out of medical procedures since its development in 1846. The American Civil War was the first time that field hospitals adopted the practice of anesthesia on a wide scale. Even narcotics, Dickinson might have said, cannot stop the "Tooth" (in addition to being a bad pun on "Truth," the term connects with the use of the popular drug laudanum, a concoction of alcohol and opium often prescribed for everything from toothache to calming hysteria and other mysterious symptoms) "that nibbles at the soul" (line 20). It remains an open question whether that image symbolizes the destruction of whatever doubts one may have about the possibility of an afterlife or suggests the erosion of faith in such things as heaven, hell, eternity, and Salvation because of a lack of any concrete evidence or irrefutable proof of their existence. It is only safe to say that all of the evidence gathered and all the work and thought devoted to this problem have not proven the existence of God, supernatural forces or the eternal life of the soul. It is equally true that the existence of any of these has not been disproved. Ultimately, the only thing upon which both doubters and affirmers can agree is the line with which this poem began, although it holds a different meaning for each.

THOREAU, HENRY DAVID (1817–1862)

Thoreau is justly famous for an eccentric life that permitted him close contact with the nature he loved, but it all would have been wasted were it not for his writing. In addition to his published books, he produced 30 volumes of journals from which scholars continue to produce thematic studies on whatever aspect of Thoreau's studies most interests them. Since these journals are the only source of most of his poems, few of which were published in his lifetime, some of them can seem like mere studies without the polish one expects of work meant to challenge the ages.

He was born (July 12, 1817) and died (of tuberculosis on May 6, 1862) in Concord, Massachusetts. He studied at the Concord Academy and graduated from Harvard in 1837 but chose to return to nature instead of pursuing a more likely career. In that age before forestry, botany, and similar fields had produced recognizable career paths, he supported himself temporarily with teaching, tutoring, and day labor. On Independence Day in 1845, he took up residence on Walden Pond in a small hut he had built himself from a recycled building. He emerged after 26 months (including the time spent on a trip to the Maine woods) with a draft of his first book, *A Week on the Concord and Merrimack Rivers,* and the experience that he would craft into his enduring legacy, *Walden, or Life in the Woods* (1854).

As presented in this book, Thoreau's poetry gives the illusion of growing as naturally and substantially as one of his beloved trees. "I MARK THE SUMMER'S SWIFT DECLINE" (1842) turns on the poet's frustration that his art is not up to the level of beauty that his subject displays, a common enough lament among beginning writers.

"FOG" (1843) is as concerned with the resources of the speaker's mind as with its ostensible subject, and while it illustrates the capricious nature of each, it lacks polish. The posthumously published "The FALL OF THE LEAF" (1863) reveals a poet more judicious in building a poem for a specific end, and the resulting coherence is even more evident when the first four stanzas are recognized as the separate poem they were before an editor combined them with "The Soul's Season," as the last 12 stanzas were titled.

Because he lived in a place where writers were revered, much of Thoreau's work (and even the fixtures of his Walden cabin, now housed in the Concord Museum) has been preserved. A reasonable facsimile of his cabin has been built on the shore of the water he made famous, and his true home there (the woods and waters) are now protected as the Walden Pond State Reservation, which also enjoys the status of a national historic landmark. The poet's birthplace (Thoreau Farm) is still standing, as is the RALPH WALDO EMERSON house where he occasionally lived. Two journals, the *Thoreau Society Bulletin* and the *Concord Saunterer,*

are devoted to his work. Important collections of Thoreau manuscripts and letters include those at the Concord Free Public Library and at Harvard's Houghton Library. The Thoreau Institute is also devoted to preserving his memory.

BIBLIOGRAPHY

Bly, Robert, ed. *The Winged Life: The Poetic Voice of Henry David Thoreau.* Includes wood engravings by Michael McCurdy. New York: HarperPerennial, 1992.

Cain, William E. *A Historical Guide to Henry David Thoreau.* New York: Oxford University Press, 2000.

Thoreau, Henry David. *Collected Poems,* edited by Carl Bode. Baltimore: Johns Hopkins Press, 1964.

———. *Poems of Nature.* Edited by Henry S. Salt and Frank B. Sanborn. Boston: Houghton Mifflin, 1895.

"THREE SONGS OF MAD COYOTE"

ANONYMOUS (19th century) A visit to the Visitor Center of the Nez Perce National Historical Park in Spalding, Idaho, reveals the importance of the coyote as the most potent mythical force in their traditional culture, able to fling a bear up a mountainside and turn insects to stone. Investing such a ubiquitous animal with supernatural abilities can have interesting repercussions.

In the first song Coyote appears with several human traits (sporting a necklace and hands instead of paws), several natural attributes (a red mouth, perhaps bloodied by a recent kill, and a voracious, "ravening" appetite) and several supernatural aspects (red [bloody?] hands and a eyeball necklace). It all makes for a terrifying image, a nightmarish combination suggestive of a powerful yet wholly destructive god. Belief in such a being must sharpen one's senses in the wild for fear of donating an eye to its trophy necklace, or perhaps being spotted by one of those already in his collection.

The second song takes a natural attribute of the coyote, its frequent nocturnal serenades, and invests it with supernatural powers (in this case, the ability to make the west wind roar). Here, too, Coyote is destructive ("Mad" in attitude and "madly" singing), and the force of the raging winds can be felt as well as seen.

The third song pulls the two other songs together. Daybreak brings the meaning of the song: Mad Coyote comes into view with his bloodstained mouth. Repetition of the phrase "Daybreak finds me" may indicate that the cultural weight given the mythical Coyote combined with frequent interaction with real animals of that species may have unsettled the singer's nerves. His happiness at having survived the night is tempered by his realization that at least the myth is literally true; his statements can be taken as an eyewitness account that the mythological creature exists just as he has been portrayed, or, on a more figurative level, that all life must eventually fall victim to the destruction of which Mad Coyote is both an emblem and an agent.

"THRENODY" Ralph Waldo Emerson (1847)

This "lamentation" (or elegy) memorializes the death of Ralph Waldo Emerson's six-year-old namesake son in 1842. Although the poem begins in spring, the south wind has no power over the dead (line 5). This leaves the speaker mourning despite the season's promises of renewal. Although his trees repair their boughs (again covering them with foliage), his house is empty. The "silver warble wild" (line 12) of that wondrous child held more value than every living sound in the earth's atmosphere (or everything under the "cerulean [azure, the hue of the clear sky on a sunny day] round;" line 14). The "hyacinthine" (or "lovely," line 15) boy adorned the world and repaid the loving Day that favored him (line 20), but nowhere does the budding man appear among the budding birches despite the searches of Nature, Fate (which let him fall but cannot restore him) and men (line 29).

Like a truant, the boy is absent from his place, and his father wonders what he did to forfeit the right to see him or if a new delight lured him away (lines 30–36). In both his person and his voice, the child was eloquent (in the sense of being persuasive). Although his age and understanding limited his influence to toys, neither fair ladies nor bearded men could refuse his sweet request. They turned from the world's affairs to share his "cordial game" or mend his wicker (woven from plant stems or slats in that era of homemade toys; line 49) wagon frame while plotting how to hear his voice again. His simple words could be persuasions.

Every morning a little convoy performed the school march as if to music played by fairies, with the boys spread out (rather like cavalry escorts). It pleased

the father that his "little captain innocent" (line 70) appeared to take a leading role and march on to noble works as if he alone heard that music (lines 77–79). Love and Pride now find the boy's sled, the dog kennel, the sticks he gathered to reinforce the walls of a snow tower in anticipation of the snow, and the ominous (because the lad so soon wound up in the earth) hole he dug (line 86). His father sees the lad's daily haunts as hallowed ground, but the "deep-eyed boy" (line 97) is gone.

On an exceptionally dark cloudy day, the boy yielded his innocent breath "in birdlike (because of his small size) heavings unto death" (line 101).

"THE TIDE RISES, THE TIDE FALLS" Henry Wadsworth Longfellow (1880)

Henry Wadsworth Longfellow's seemingly simple poem presents the reader with three basic questions concerning the situation of the poem and the identities of the speaker and the traveler.

The speaker evidently lives (or stays) close enough to the beach to see the footprints a traveler leaves on the sand and the froth of the little waves that efface them (line 10). He (or she) is also close enough to an inn to hear the hostler call to the horses as well as their stamping and neighing in response. Evidently he has much time on his hands since he must spend slightly more than twenty-four hours in the same place in order to note the rising and falling of three high tides (he does not necessarily see the six high and low points of each tide, which would require 30 hours since a tide reaches such an extreme point only once every six hours). He has spent enough time on the coast to recognize the evening call of the curlew, one of the fair-season migratory avian visitors to the New England shore. Because he takes no active role in life beyond observing the waterfront, it is tempting to think of him as an invalid, and perhaps an elderly person (since the poem is more concerned with evening and night sensations than those of daylight). He is sensitive to changes in light and texture, especially those occurring in his beloved sands, and seems rather resigned to his fate. Unlike his inland peers who stereotypically sit on their front porches to watch the world go by (a euphemism for the traffic passing on the road in front of their houses), he watches the coast. Alternatively, he may be an emotionally troubled individual of almost any age who may be pondering a way to escape from his problems.

The most noteworthy event on the particular day in question was the hurried twilight passing of a traveler. The speaker fails to note even the gender of this person, who may have been a traveler only from the relatively disadvantaged perspective of an invalid. The traveler carries the speaker's attention toward the town, which fails to hold it for long. One senses that the darkness settling on its roofs and walls (line 6) may be a subjective indication of the speaker's growing lack of interest in human affairs as well as an objective description of the failing light as night descends.

The traveler may have but one journey left to take, following a short path into a sea of oblivion. This is the message that reaches the speaker from the sea during his long dark night of the soul. He has apparently reconciled himself to the fact that the few remaining steps before him will be so inconsequential that no monumental catastrophe will be needed to obliterate any trace of them. Instead, only the soft white hands of the littlest waves (line 8) will almost soothingly remove all traces of whatever physical pain or mental anguish is tormenting him.

Morning breaks (line 11) the spell, and the horses suggest the possibility of future travel. Identifying the hostler (a label that signals his connection with his fellow man, especially travelers) reattaches the speaker to the living world of men, but note that the designation suggests at best a professional or business connection with the speaker, whose essential isolation on a more personal level remains unchanged.

Although the speaker survived this particular night, his subsequent fate remains ambiguous. One on level, the certainty with which he proclaims that the traveler never returned to the shore (lines 13–14) implies that he lived on to maintain his vigil over the now trackless sand for some time into the future. A second alternative is that, having survived this night of severe depression, the speaker has himself returned to his travels among the rest of mankind and (now having assumed the role of traveler) never again visited the melancholy

shore. A third, less auspicious interpretation suggests that no traveler again arrived to draw the speaker back to the world of men, leaving him vulnerable to the self-destructive despondency for which the deserted beach and irresistible ocean are the pervasive symbols. An indifferent nature will maintain its diurnal cycles regardless of the outcome.

TIMROD, HENRY (1828–1867)

Although born (December 8, 1828) the son of a bookbinder in Charleston, South Carolina, the future poet's troubles were complicated by his family's poverty and his own ill health. He attended the University of Georgia and began studying law but then taught school and experienced plantation life by becoming a tutor. He volunteered for service in the Civil War, but poor health spared him to serve as a reporter for the Charleston *Mercury* and later as an editor on the Columbia *South Carolinian*. He married Kate Goodwin, a former student, in 1864, but their only son preceded the poet in death.

Timrod's "CHARLESTON" (1862) celebrated the martial spirit of the city (with special attention paid to the ladies, who in normal times would weep over an injured hound but who wholeheartedly supported the war despite its inevitable casualties) even as a gunboat could be seen enforcing the federal blockade of all southern ports beyond the barrier of Fort Sumter, where the active fighting of the Civil War had begun a year earlier. In perhaps his most famous poem, "ODE" (1866), Timrod publicly commemorated the burial grounds of the soldiers killed defending the same city, accurately predicting that future monuments would be raised over their humble graves. He again tips his hat to the ladies, whose tears for their dead brothers on that occasion should be viewed as greater tributes than the future monuments will be.

The poet died of tuberculosis in Columbia, South Carolina, on October 7, 1867. It was symptomatic of the poverty of his family and of the war-torn state that his grave went unmarked in the Trinity churchyard until 1901. He fared better in the South Carolina statehouse, where his portrait hangs, and in Charleston, where a bust of the poet was eventually erected in the city's Washington Park.

Poems (1860) was the only book the man later hailed as the "Laureate of the Confederacy" and "The Harp of the South" (titles of two early Timrod biographies) saw published in his lifetime. He drew enough inspiration from his wife to merit posthumous publication of *Katie* (1884), a small book of poems in her honor, and slim volumes of his collected works have been published several times since the first in 1872. In 1911, the State of South Carolina did him the honor of adopting his "Carolina" as its official state song.

The small school where he once taught has been preserved in the Timrod Park of Florence, South Carolina. The Military Order of the Stars and Bars (a social club for descendents of Confederate officers) has honored his memory with the Henry Timrod Southern Culture Award. The Henry Timrod Papers are located in the South Caroliniana Library, and additional manuscripts have been preserved by the University of Alabama, the University of Georgia, and Princeton and Duke Universities.

BIBLIOGRAPHY

Cisco, Walter Brian. *Henry Timrod: A Biography.* Madison, N.J.: Fairleigh Dickinson University Press, 2004.

Hubbell, Jay Broadus, ed. *The Last Years of Henry Timrod, 1864–1867.* Durham, N.C.: Duke University Press, 1941.

Timrod, Henry. *Poems of Henry Timrod with Memoir and Portrait.* Reprint, Whitefish, Mont.: Kessinger Publishing, 2004.

"TITLE DIVINE—IS MINE!" EMILY DICKINSON (1924)

This poem protests the treatment of women who, like EMILY DICKINSON, choose never to marry. In the opening line, the speaker seems to exult in proclaiming her status, which she identifies in the second line as "The Wife without the Sign." The situation (and her true feelings on the issue) soon become apparent, however. As the recipient of the "acute" (definitions for this adjective include "excruciating" and "piercing") degree conferred on her, she has become "Empress of Calvary" (line 4). Since Calvary was the site of Christ's crucifixion (see Luke 23:33 and elsewhere), the speaker found herself in a very painful position.

She now had two names for the same status. Being regarded as a wife meant social recognition as a mature woman sure of herself and equal to all around her. For modern readers this might seem her birthright regardless of her marital status, but age, experience, and even talent could go uncrowned (unrecognized) for women of Dickinson's era who lacked the requisite marriage certificate. They could be "betrothed" (line 6) in the sense of being in committed relationships or experienced in life, but without the "swoon" (without the fainting, ultimately self-effacing participation in the rites of marriage; line 6), they would never be fully valued.

All women are equal at birth, since "God sends us all," the speaker argues (line 5). If held garnet to garnet (line 8; although the poet was born in December, the speaker may have chosen the birthstone of January to represent everyone born throughout the year) and gold to gold (up to the point when they acquire marriage rings, line 9) they are still heralded as equals. Their brief lives (that can seem but a single day, line 11) might be reduced to the three major events during which things happen to them, but which the women do not, in the way the speaker presents them, really control: they are born, "bridalled" (wedded, but with a pun on "bridled" [prepared to be guided like a horse regardless of their will], and "shrouded" (prepared for burial).

Women say "My Husband" and stroke the Melody (embellish the sound of the words as if proud of their own achievement, or as an implied criticism of those who have not yet married; line 14). The speaker questions whether this is the best way for women to act (line 15).

An alternative interpretation might uncover the similarity between the taking of vows by the nuns of certain religious orders and the language at the start of this poem; in some orders the nuns are considered brides of Christ and given silver bands as symbols of their vows. Their spiritual wedding entitles them to the divine title of "Sister" and the embrace of all that Christ means, including His uncrowned royalty, death, and promise of redemption at Calvary. The speaker implicitly contrasts the enduring spirituality of that marriage with that of those who pride themselves on being wedded to ordinary men despite their knowledge of the brevity of all things in this life. The ending chastises those women who forget their religion as they immerse themselves into their roles as wives.

"TO A COMMON PROSTITUTE" WALT WHITMAN (1860)

In "One's-Self I Sing," WALT WHITMAN claims to embrace the female as well as the male, but in this poem Whitman seems more intent on coming to her as a savior than as a client. To gain her confidence, he not only tells her to remain composed and at ease, he brags about his virility ("I am . . . liberal and lusty as Nature," line 1), so that she can feel in control of the situation in a rather conventional manner.

His real message is one of inclusion, however. He will not exclude her until the sun does, and will act as naturally toward her as the waters and leaves do with their nondiscriminatory glistening and rustling (line 3). He proceeds to appoint her with an appointment, but instead of setting up an illicit liaison, he seems to be appointing her worthy of the same consideration that he would extend to all humanity. This interpretation is reinforced by the last half of line 4, in which he charges her with making preparation to be worthy to meet him on equal terms based on their shared humanity. For her part, she is to work on such virtues as being as patient and true to her nature (a type of perfection) as she can be. Until such time as they can meet as moral equals, he salutes her with a significant look (line 6) so that she will not forget him. Although the lines are filled with suggestive action verbs and rather simple double entendres, it seems evident that Whitman is more turned on by his verbal acuity and his generosity in treating the girl as a social equal than he is by the thought of consummating their relationship in a biblical manner. To avoid any confusion on this key issue, he twice states that he will charge her for his services, which is contrary to the usual practice.

"TO A LOCOMOTIVE IN WINTER" WALT WHITMAN (1876)

On May 10, 1869, the transcontinental railroad was completed at Promontory Point in northern Utah. In the year that this poem first appeared, an express train traveled from New York City to San Francisco in less than three and a half days. American financiers and civil engineers had captured the eyes of the world with their remarkable achieve-

ments, but it remained for the Great Singer of America to create a poem worthy of the engine that powered this transportation revolution.

In referring to the poem as a "recitative" (line 1), WALT WHITMAN revealed his approach to the poem: he would produce an oration that schoolchildren and others could commit to memory and recite on public occasions (although the term usually refers to the narrative part of an opera). The internal audience is the locomotive, not only personified but addressed by the familiar "thee." To indicate its power over nature, the speaker places it near nightfall in a driving winter storm. Within its armor (the "panoply" of line 3) reside the "measured dual throbbing" and convulsive beat. The rest of the first stanza focuses on its appearance ("black cylindric body, golden brass and silvery steel," line 4), its size (it features ponderous sidebars and a great protruding front headlight; lines 5 and 7), the movement of its working parts (described with such novel action verbs as gyrating and shuttling), and its sound (a "swelling pant and roar, now tapering in the distance" (line 6). Note that each item in this list is placed according to the order in which one would encounter it on an engine sitting idle on the tracks until it pulled away.

With his trained eye, the speaker notes the long vapor pennants tinged with delicate smoke (produced by heat, condensation, and steam) as well as the murky clouds belched from the smokestack. His ear seems to have failed him in that he describes the sound of the wheels as the "tremulous twinkle" (line 10). The cars obediently, merrily follow as the engine steadily careers through gale or calm (line 12).

The speaker celebrates the engine as "the type of the modern—emblem of motion and power—the pulse of the continent" (line 13); he would have it join his verse just as he sees it. By day it warns with bells and by night with swinging lanterns.

While the opening stanza delivered a straightforward objective description, the second stanza uses subjective details to convey the emotions the "fierce-throated beauty" (line 18) stirs up in the speaker. His description of its rumbling rousing lawless music, swinging lamps and "madly-whistled laughter" (lines 19–20) makes it sound like the ultimate party machine.

While it lacks the refined sweetness of a harp or piano, its trilling shrieks are echoed by rocks and hills and launched over prairies, lakes, and to the free skies.

"TO A NEW ENGLAND POET" PHILIP FRENEAU (1823)

Few people have so bitterly chastised America's early disregard for its writers. PHILIP FRENEAU, the first American whose wealth, education, and connections enabled him to attempt a full career as a professional poet, here expresses his regret that it could not pay him more.

The opening stanza recalls Freneau's brief tenure as a schoolteacher and the discrepancy between his classical education and his low salary. He bemoans the fact that the teachers of his day were paid as poorly as unskilled labor. The problem was aesthetic as well as financial, as the second stanza indicates. The American public, nourishing the egalitarian spirit of the revolutionary and early national periods in the nation's history and still priding themselves on their political and social equality, did not like to make distinctions among themselves for personal achievements in something as esoteric as poetry. For celebrating and even insisting on their commonality, they are criticized as tasteless (line 7), and aesthetic growth is viewed as an individual choice. Ironically, Freneau's attack on Washington Irving in this poem is as unprincipled and tasteless as the judgments of his less educated peers.

The sarcastic tone of the poem is typical of Freneau's propagandizing work. He characteristically impugns an individual opponent, often imagining him in an indelicate moment. Hence Irving, best remembered today as the author of such short stories as "The Legend of Sleepy Hollow," is unfairly criticized for kissing a monarch's—hand (line 15). If read aloud, a well-timed pause at the dash in that line will permit a listener to substitute the monarch's ass for his hand, thus completing a phrase that remains a vernacular cliché two centuries later. For Freneau, a confirmed patriot who had been held as a British prisoner of war during the American Revolution, the American Irving's celebrations of the British past could seem like betrayal.

From a mere economic standpoint, however, Freneau's advice to his announced audience (the New England poet of the title) was sound. In 1823, it was far easier for an excellent writer to establish an international reputation in England, the literary and cultural center of an empire, than to achieve wide exposure and the possibility of wealth and fame in New England. It was also easier for work originating in England to be published in America than vice versa, and poets and poetry generally enjoyed a much more genial reception on that side of the Atlantic.

"TO A PRESIDENT" WALT WHITMAN (1860)

James Buchanan's distinguished governmental career included 10 years in the House of Representatives, 10 years in the Senate, four years as secretary of state, and four years as the American ambassador, first, to England and much later to Russia. It is important to remember his contributions prior to his becoming president of the United States from 1857 to 1861 because his presidency is generally dismissed as a great failure. He hoped to keep the Union intact by a series of compromises on the question of slavery, and perhaps he did manage to delay the inevitable by four years. The nation had become so polarized by 1859 that the antislavery Republicans were able to seize control of the House of Representatives in the midterm elections while the old southern Democrats maintained control of the Senate. Thus Congress could do nothing about slavery, and the vitriolic propagandists on both sides pushed the nation ever closer to a war that even the strongest of presidents would have been powerless to prevent. As this poem demonstrates, sentiment in the North had reached the point of vilifying not just the abominable institution of slavery but even those who would compromise with it in order to maintain the peace.

Chief among Buchanan's "dangled mirages" (line 1) was his unsuccessful attempt to admit Kansas as a slave state in order to maintain the political balance between northern and southern interests. Nature meant a great deal to WALT WHITMAN, so his accusation that Buchanan did not learn "of" Nature (line 2; the prepositional phrase could mean either "learn about Nature" or "learn from nature"), while unsupported and vague, was probably intended as a grave insult. The speaker's reference to "the politics of Nature" in the same line is similarly misguided; aside from the fact that politics as it needs to be practiced at the presidential level is a strictly human affair, the phrase conjures up rules like "only the strong survive," which few modern Americans would care to see enforced as domestic policy.

It is fair to state that Buchanan did not learn "great amplitude" from nature, if that phrase means that he lacked the acumen to see things from Whitman's perspective and to force his will upon the body politic. Slavery was such an emotional issue that the president's failure to oppose it led Whitman to challenge his "rectitude," his moral code or standards of decency. Whitman's charge that Buchanan was ignorant of "impartiality" might seem the weakest of his three accusations given the president's desire to somehow accommodate both sections of the country, but the poet may have been thinking that the people held as slaves deserved the same protection under the law as the slaveholders.

When the speaker claims that only "such as they are for these States" (line 4), he may be crossing racial lines to identify with the plight of the slaves as fellow laborers, the class to which he evidently believes the future must belong.

"TO A WATERFOWL" WILLIAM CULLEN BRYANT (1818)

Some aspects of avian migration still remain mysteries nearly 200 years after WILLIAM CULLEN BRYANT penned this short poem, although modern scientists tend to attribute the birds' unique navigational abilities to an extraordinary sensitivity to the earth's magnetic fields, perhaps in combination with such visual cues as seasonal variations in the angle of the sun. Like the Puritans nearly 200 years before it was written, however, the author of this poem examined a natural phenomenon and then tried to apply its apparent meaning to the human condition. The poem might read like a parable; the devil may be lurking for the unwary like the fowler (a devilish pun for "fouler" in the sense of one who fouls?) of the second stanza, but adherence to God's will leads to the Promised Land. How does one know what God intended? This optimistic poem suggests that it might be as instinctively subconscious as the migrating bird's instinct.

The internal audience of this poem is a passing waterfowl, and the speaker asks where it is bound. The bird is already out of gun range; in fact, it is so far away

that it seems to be floating in air (line 8). The speaker wonders if it is bound for the edge of a lake, river, or ocean. A Power seems to be guiding the lone wanderer, for the bird is not lost.

The speaker seems omniscient: In the fifth stanza he knows (or speculates) that the fowl has flown all day at considerable height but is not weary enough to land despite the approaching darkness. In the sixth stanza, he can see into the future; the bird will land at its summer home, scream its calls, and build a sheltered nest among the reeds. By this time the bird has flown out of sight, but the speaker has taken a lesson from the bird to heart. He seems confident that the same power that guides the bird will also guide the speaker on his own lonely road.

In addition to its religious implications, the poem is interesting for its landscapes with waterfowl. The poet loaded his canvas with a picture of the rosy sky in the first stanza, and the second stanza presents an even more complex picture combining the fowler in the foreground with an almost abstract bird "darkly painted on the crimson sky" (line 7). Also note how the poet's unconventional diction in line 9 attracts the reader's attention. A large part of the power of the phrase "the plashy brink of weedy lake" lies in the visual, aural and haptic appeal of the word "plashy." When a bird splashes down, its sight, hearing, and touch must register abrupt changes, and the same senses would be engaged by anyone standing in the lake very near the bird's entry point. The term is just unusual enough to perhaps trigger some of these same sensations in the memory of any reader lucky enough to have experienced them in the past.

"TO COLE, THE PAINTER, DEPARTING FOR EUROPE" WILLIAM CULLEN BRYANT (1830)

This poem throbs with the pride of an emerging American nationalism. Much of its charm lies in the poet's turning of his nation's markedly inferior infrastructure to rhetorical advantage. Note its implied contrast between New World optimism (bright with unlimited prospects) and a European pessimism largely grounded in its abundant ruins, ubiquitous reminders that all civilizations eventually collapse and that, as a consequence, all human endeavor may be ultimately futile.

In addition to being a friend of the poet, Thomas Cole belonged to the Hudson River School, an informal grouping of painters whose reaction to the unspoiled grandeur of America's eastern mountain ranges led them to create enormous, richly detailed landscapes. WILLIAM CULLEN BRYANT sometimes joined Cole as they sought out the most picturesque locations, which typically included bare granite boulders, tumbling waters, and dense forestation. In this sonnet he insists on the vast difference between the raw force of nature as it shaped the wilderness on the American side of the Atlantic and the highly human-engineered tracts of the Old World.

He stops just short of claiming that even the skies will be different, contenting himself with the observation that they are distant (line 1). He is certain, however, that New England's scenery will leave as indelible an image on the painter's heart as it has on his canvases. In the second quatrain, he lists some of the distinct attractions of the western plains, including isolated lakes, bison, deserts so vast and uninhabited that one can hear an eagle's screams, and seasonal variations in the boundless vegetation.

In the third quatrain the speaker admits that Europe also has fair scenes but notes how the artist's backwoods jaunts have led to extraordinary beauty, while the Old World paths lead to homes, graves, and ruins (line 11) from (Bryant imagines) the deepest valleys to the uninhabitable alpine regions. His closing couplet encourages Cole to gaze on European scenes until they bring him to tears (probably not tears of joy at their beauty, given the images of European decay that Bryant described in the prior quatrain), but to keep bright his "earlier" (Bryant mistakenly thought that Cole was born in America), "wilder" image. Note the skill with which the couplet refers to the scenes of wild America but also to the painter's concept of himself, for the last line directs his attention back to the "living image" within his heart mentioned in the first quatrain.

"TO HELEN" EDGAR ALLAN POE (1831) The subject of this poem is the speaker's adulation from afar for a lovely woman, but his chief focus is on his own reaction to her beauty. He may think she merits comparison with the Helen of Troy for whose recov-

ery, according to Homer's *Iliad,* the Greeks went to war in a thousand ships, but his own story is closer to that of Odysseus, the hero of the *Odyssey*. His ancient predecessor certainly earned the title of "weary, way-worn wanderer" (line 4) for the 10 years it took him to return to "his own native shore" (line 5) following the end of the Trojan War. Such an interpretation would explain the reference to the Nicaean barks (ships built in the Nicaea region of Turkey, close to where Odysseus would have left Troy at the end of the war). Only the end of Odysseus's voyage could be described as progressing "gently, over a perfumed sea" (he slept for the entire last leg of the trip on a Phaeacian ship [and not, alas, a Nicaean vessel, although no one knows the location of the mythical Phaeacia] until the sailors softly put him and their gifts ashore in his native Ithaca; line 3).

Although like Odysseus, the speaker claims long acquaintance with roaming desperate seas (line 5), the second stanza leads one to suspect that his tempests had been mostly emotional in origin. Helen's upswept hair (perhaps he calls it "hyacinth" because that flower at a distance brought to mind the tightly curled hairstyle that is more easily rendered in marble representations of female figures than straight hair would be), classic face and "Naiad airs" (presumably conveying something of the buoyant spirit of the water nymphs [spirits] of Greek mythology) have brought him "home" (to perhaps the two most famous lines in all of EDGAR ALLAN POE's poetry):

> "To the glory that was Greece
> And the grandeur that was Rome"

Such lines may imply that adoration of her beauty unites him in spirit with the similar admirers throughout Western history, inspires him to attempt greatness, and/or leads him to discover that greatness in aspects of himself.

The last stanza reveals the situation of the poem: the speaker is viewing "Helen" at night through a "brilliant window-niche" (presumably a well-lit small window) where she resembles a statue and holds an (elegant and expensive) agate lamp (presumably with a base made of agate, although some lampshades also have slices of that translucent mineral stuck in them for an effect like a stained glass window). He deems her "Psyche" (after a mythical woman so beautiful that even Cupid fell for her) from "the regions which are Holy-Land" (which in this context probably refers only secondarily to the people, places, and things that possess an ethereal, transcendent beauty and primarily to the state to which exposure to such beauty can transport an admirer).

"TO HIS EXCELLENCY, GENERAL WASHINGTON" Phillis Wheatley (1775)

In the letter (October 26. 1775) to General Washington accompanying this poem, Phyllis Wheatley addressed him as "your Excellency," an honorific term more typically used for colonial governors, and congratulates him on being named "Generalissimo [an Italian term] of the armies of North America" although he was actually elected "commander in chief to take supreme command of the forces . . . raised for the defense of American Liberty" by the Continental Congress on July 15, 1775. Asking for his approval (and mindful of the fact that poets often obtained the patronage of rich and influential people in less troubled times), she praises his virtues and wishes him success. Her closing, although conventional, could not have been more deferential as she called herself his most obedient servant.

In place of the invocation of the muse that so frequently began classical Greek poetry, Wheatley invoked a celestial choir (a choice that may imply a certain saintliness in her subject). She also personifies the colonies as Columbia, an important step toward independence in that it claims an identity for America that was distinct from its British roots. (As in a painting), Columbia is portrayed as being filled with anxiety and alarmed at the threat to freedom. She also "flashes dreadful" in her shining (the "refulgent" of line 4) armor.

As Mother Earth bemoans her offspring's fate (this is another point of disconnect from the mother country since most of the colonists were not born in England proper and large numbers had no roots there), Columbia's "glorious toils" are illuminated by "bright beams of heaven's revolving light" (the sun; line 7) despite sorrows and the veil of night.

Divinely beautiful, Columbia has bound her hair with sprigs of olive (symbolizing peace) and laurel (symbolizing honor). In the 13th line, the muse (probably Euterpe, who inspired lyrical poetry) is rather unceremoniously summoned as almost an afterthought and ordered to "bow propitious" (to bring luck). The speaker will write of Columbia's armies pouring through a thousand gates with the threatening demeanor of Aeolus (god of the winds) when he brings tempests to the heavens and tidal surges (rendered less threatening by the adjective "refluent," which means receding or ebbing) beat the ocean shore.

Columbia's warriors are as numerous as autumn leaves (this was perhaps not the best analogy since it might suggest that an abrupt end awaits the soldiers; line 19), but her audience (General Washington) knows them so well that she need not praise them or their grace and glory. Instead, she will focus on Washington's prominence. Already famous for his courage and other virtues (or: famous for courage but even more so for other virtues), Washington is the man whose guardian aid everyone seeks (like a secular saint).

The French (finally driven from British colonial America at the close of the Seven Years' War in 1763) once faced Columbia's fury, and so will any other attacker of freedom's "heaven-defended race" (line 32). The eyes of nations watch the balance of power in the current struggle in hopes that Columbia will prevail, and now Britannia droops her brooding head while the hills of the dead rise around her (this was written in the year before Britain responded to the revolutionaries with a full-scale military campaign. Very dark days filled the coming years before independence was secured). The speaker rather pities Britain's blindness to the glory and power of Columbia; Britannia will lament its thirst for boundless power too late (to prevent its embarrassment).

The speaker encourages the great chief to proceed with virtue and the goddess Columbia on his side. Washington will gain a crown, a mansion, and a throne that shines with gold unfading (that is, he will earn a place in heaven for leading a righteous cause, but the line also captures the sentiment of the historical moment when many people would have favored George Washington as their new king. Fortunately, Washington was not interested in acquiring that honor).

"TO MAKE A PRAIRIE . . ." EMILY DICK-INSON (1896) EMILY DICKINSON'S seemingly simple poem radiates meaning on many levels. It sounds like a recipe in the nonchalant form one housewife would share information with another; notice how kindly she repeats the ingredient list as if her internal audience was trying to take notes, or as if she were making sure she remembered all of them. She also suggests an alternative approach if one of the ingredients is missing.

The complexities of the poem become evident when one tries to understand more about the speaker's identity. Who but Mother Nature could provide a recipe for making a prairie? Although she personally would probably not experience a shortage of bees, she may have included the alternative instruction because of her realization that her internal audience may not have her powers. Thus the internal audience becomes an important question for understanding the situation of the poem. Who, other than a demigod or some other mythical figure, could use a prairie-making recipe?

One answer would be a poet; the internal audience could be a less accomplished poet learning directly from nature, or perhaps from an accomplished master of the poetic arts. On this level, the poem begins with a lesson in synecdoche, the familiar trope in which a part of something is used to represent the thing as a whole. However, in the third line the poet adds "revery" (the modern spelling is *reverie*) as the most important element. The term denotes a daydream, but its more interesting connotations suggest a state of rapturous contemplation capable of transporting the poet (and with luck, her audience) to the point where she can imaginatively embrace a prairie or other locale without being physically present at that scene. Such an approach places more emphasis on the poetic experience as it is embraced by the author and her audience than on the subject (the thing being described) in the poem.

An entirely different approach would be to examine the poem from a biographical perspective. Dickinson may be informing her audience that it is not necessary to travel to the prairie to experience the marvels of life or to find fit subjects for poems. This helps explain why she was willing to live a relatively sequestered life in her father's home with a few relatively brief exceptions.

"TOM DEADLIGHT" HERMAN MELVILLE (1888) Like "JOHN MARR," another late HERMAN MELVILLE poem, this one derives much of its meaning from a headnote supplied by the author. The speaker is a petty officer dying of fever on a British warship, and occasionally delirious, he relies on "Spanish Ladies," a sea ditty, to communicate with his attendants. That song recalls the various sites visible as one proceeds up the English Channel, but his version suggests a passage to the afterlife. The point of it all may be that he has so thoroughly become a sailor that he has scarce a thought for any life on land.

After bidding adieu to the noble "hearties" (good fellow sailors) and the ladies of Spain (brought to mind by the ditty, from which the dying man's second line is lifted in its entirety), he announces his orders to sail for the Deadman (line 3). That is the first English land visible on the voyage of the original sea ditty, but for the speaker may be implying that he is bound for the land of the dead. In the original the speaker sails with the grand fleet, but here he hopes to join it (line 4).

Like the cautious sailor advancing over unknown waters, he has "hove to" (steered his ship directly into the wind to stall its forward motion, a maneuver also known as "sailing into irons," and lowered its mainsail; line 5). Similarly, he has taken soundings to insure that there is enough water under the boat to avoid bottoming out, but he will fly up the channel despite the heavy weather (indicated by the "black scud [dark rain clouds] a'flying," line 7).

On earlier voyages he has experienced the "Doldrums" (calm days without the wind to power the vessel) and the "Sargasso" (tropical seaweed that can get wrapped around anything propelled through the water). On a metaphorical level, he may have experienced days of boredom and/or depression, and coped with his declining energy (lines 9–10). Now his sight is failing (a mist hides the lightship), but he sees the *Flying Dutchman* off the Cape of Good Hope (this famous ghost ship appears to desperate sailors during storms near the southern tip of Africa). On a metaphorical level, the sailor seems to be facing a mixed future in the afterlife.

He mistakes a messmate's fanning him with a raincoat for the wing of a "goney" bird (the albatross is also known as the gooney bird, but the speaker [almost a "goner"] may be enjoying a poor pun on that name; line 14). He directs that his belongings be given to those who share his shift ("mess" is nautical jargon for "meal" and "dining room," hence messmates are those who share his mealtimes). He wants "Holy Joe" (evidently a particularly religious sailor) to stop ("avast") with the "crape" (gloom; line 16).

Joe answers that "dead reckoning" (navigating without instruments, or in this case, dying without Jesus [presumably] as a guide) "won't do" (line 17). The speaker answers that the rain put out the candles (the "glims," but perhaps also any guiding light from heaven) a few nights before, and that "dead reckoning" is the best way to sail "for the Deadman" (line 19).

He hears trumpets and other signals, a sign for the grand fleet to anchor. Everyone should quickly (one meaning of "for blue-blazes" [line 23], another might suggest a heavenly or devilish vision) "stand by" (cease work but remain in a stationary but alert posture) and "mind the shank-painters" (be careful that the anchor ropes do not ensnare you on their way to the bottom) because the Lord High Admiral (presumably God) is studying you (even "squinting" to get a better look).

In the last stanza he asks for his "tot" (presumably his allotment [perhaps of grog, a daily dose of an alcoholic beverage]) before he rolls over (before he dies like a sinking ship; the reference to turning up his keel [the center bottom of the boat, often ridged for stability] in the last line conveys the same image). Being entirely of a nautical turn, he asks for Jock's flipper instead of his hand (line 26) and reminds them not to sew him up (in canvas, preparatory to burying him at sea) without putting a little tobacco (the "baccy" of line 27) in his mouth. He also asks them not to cry like landlubbers (nonsailors) at his burial ceremony.

"TO MY DEAR AND LOVING HUS-BAND" ANNE BRADSTREET (1678) The language of the traditional marriage vow stipulates that the sacrament unites the participants in one flesh, and in this poem ANNE BRADSTREET asserts to her husband that she feels that close. In her happiness, she cannot imagine any woman ever being happier in her man. She values his love more than gold mines or the riches of the East; by the 17th century, oceanic trade routes were supplementing the overland caravans that had been bringing spices, silks, and other treasures from Asia to Europe for centuries.

The comparison of love with an unquenchable thirst (line 7) hints at the physicality of their relationship, but the poet quickly returned to a safer, more abstract concept of reciprocity in only asking for his love in exchange for hers. His love is so valuable that only the heavens can reward it, and she prays that his rewards will be many and varied. She wants them to love throughout their lives with such persistence that it becomes transcendent; in some way their love could give them immortality even after they die.

"TO MY DEAR CHILDREN" ANNE BRAD-STREET (published 1867) Near the end of her life the poet penned a private letter to her children to which she fixed a short poem as an epigraph. The poem bequeaths her unread book (although she may be referring only to the letter; line 1) to them that they may "find" their mother's mind (lines 3–4; note how her careful phrasing may refer to their learning of her thoughts and to their discovery of their own faith [they would then be of their mother's mind]). Assuming the role of their spiritual guide, she assures them that God will bless them for using her suggestions.

The accompanying letter reveals the poet's practical as well as spiritual side. Recognizing the power of a parent's last words, she set her thoughts in writing because she might not be able to talk at the end, or all the children might not be present. She relates how her conscience developed at the age of six or seven, and that confession to God soothed it. Around age 15, her heart grew more carnal, and she entertained vanity and the follies of youth until God smote her with smallpox. Confession led Him to restore her. Perhaps the most memorable line in terms of secular colonial history concerns her reaction to arriving in America in 1630: "I found a new world and new manners, at which my heart rose."

Throughout her life, God chastised her straying by sickening a child or weakening her finances, and in retrospect she considers the times of such afflictions to have been the most advantageous to her and the most indicative of God's love. She found herself at times like an unruly child and was grateful for the application of the corrective rod. She sometimes had doubts, but the wonders of the world convinced her that God exists, that His word proves the correctness of the Trinity and that the accuracy of the biblical prophecies reveal their divine authorship. Since Roman Catholics share the same core beliefs, she privately wondered if their way might be correct, but the "vain fooleries" of their popish religion, their "lying miracles" and cruel persecution of the saints (the Puritans who were persecuted in England during Queen Mary's short rule) convinced her that her sect was the correct one. She would have her children build their faith in Christ.

"TO MY DEAR GRANDCHILD SIMON BRADSTREET, WHO DIED ON 16 NOVEMBER, 1669, BEING BUT A MONTH, AND ONE DAY OLD" ANNE BRADSTREET (1678)

The loss of three children in a single family in one year was a bitter blow even in 17th-century New England, where mortality rates were very high compared to modern standards. This grandchild lived but 32 days, and Bradstreet's personification of God as the gardener who cropped Simon's two sisters in their first flowering ("scarcely blown") and Simon while still a bud hints at a slight wavering in the speaker's belief in a benign God. She must remind herself that He is good and counsel herself to remain silent before His power. The internal audience of the poem appears to have been at least as close to the child as the speaker; she acknowledges that they feel as if their faces were being pushed into the dust, yet they will be compensated for their losses when He returns with a smile on his face (this time!) and the deserving dead are redeemed on Judgment Day. In the meantime, she entrusts the infant to his sisters' company and the blessing of endless joys.

"TO MY MOTHER" EDGAR ALLAN POE (1849)

EDGAR ALLAN POE's life was so uniquely and surreally stressful that even his most sweet and sincere poem can seem bizarre. It was his misfortune to consider three different women his mother. His biological mother, an itinerant actress abandoned with three children by her husband, died before his third birthday. His stepmother, although he was never formally adopted, died when he was 20. In this poem, he bestows the honor of that title on Maria Clemm, the sister of his father and the mother of his wife (who was 13 years old when the 27-year-old poet married her in 1836). Clemm would live with the couple until her daughter's death.

The poem begins with a reference to heaven and angels that would not have been lost on Mrs. Clemm, in mourning since her daughter's death on January 30, 1847. Poe's heaven is a place where angels whisper burning words of love to each other, and because "Mother" is their most "devotional" term (calling it "devotional" in such a setting imbues love for the parent with religious meaning), Poe has called Mrs. Clemm by that name (line 5). Now she is more than a mother to him since she fills the space Death vacated in his "heart of hearts" by setting free his wife's spirit.

His biological mother died early and was but his mother. Maria Clemm, on the other hand, was the mother of Virginia, whom Poe dearly loved. Thus his mother-in-law is dearer to him "by that infinity" (line 13) with which his wife was dearer to him than his own soul.

"TO ONE IN PARADISE" EDGAR ALLAN POE (c. 1833)

In keeping with his belief that the death of a young woman is the most poetical topic in the world (an opinion he advances in "The PHILOSOPHY OF COMPOSITION"), in this poem EDGAR ALLAN POE exploits such a passing to explore the meaning of loss as viewed from a lover's perspective.

In the first stanza the speaker establishes the beauty of his relationship with the deceased by announcing that she was everything for which his soul pined. Poe's approach seems rather cinematic although this poem was written before the invention of the motion picture camera. The girl seemed a "green isle in the sea" (line 3) where he found love, a fountain, and a shrine (note how the succession of images forms a natural progression from virginal island nature to the propagation of a sustaining love [as nourishing as a fountain] and eventually to the speaker's considering her a virtual shrine). It is important to the meaning of the poem that the reader sees a connection between these images because without it the speaker would appear to be too easily making such comparisons. Any love might seem wreathed with "fairy fruits" and flowers (line 5) if it is not tested by time or the challenges of life, and modern feminists might be troubled by the possessiveness apparent in his assertion that "all the flowers were mine" (line 6).

The second stanza announces a paradigm shift. Although the imagery of the first stanza was as substantial as its concrete nouns (flowers, fruits, and the sea) could make it, the second stanza emphasizes abstract nouns like hope, future and past. Gone is the lightness in both imagery and tone; the former prospect of happiness now seems as distant as the stars, and as easily beclouded (Poe is not above a pun: like the night sky, the speaker's Hope is "overcast" in line 9). Although a voice from the future urges him on, his stunned spirit hovers in the past.

Like a tormented soul, the speaker wails that "the light of Life" is over (line 15). With a touch of purposeful ambiguity, he thrice repeats "no more," a cry that might be either a lament for his vanished vision or a plea for the end of his torture (line 16). Equally ambiguous is his claim that such language holds the sea to a shore's sands (line 17–18; it is unclear whether the sand or the water is the beneficiary or the victim of such an embrace). Because he is no longer capable of seeing beyond his pain, his prospects seem as limited as those of the "thunder-blasted" tree (probably destroyed [or at least stricken] by lightning) or the incapacitated ("stricken") eagle.

The last stanza finds the speaker in a trancelike state, really living only at night when he is reunited with his lover in his dreams. He feels dead in the day, but at night he indulges in ethereal dances by eternal streams where his beloved's footstep gleams.

"TO SIR TOBY" PHILIP FRENEAU (1784)

Although a subtitle identifies Sir Toby as a sugar planter living near the city of San Jago de la Vega (then a colonial capitol located 10 miles west of modern Kingston) in Jamaica, PHILIP FRENEAU probably was thinking of the toby, a popular Revolutionary War–era drinking mug, when he chose the name. A very common version featured an elegant older gentleman with his own pot of brew, an exceedingly long-stemmed pipe and the latest fashionable wig, tricornered hat and greatcoat with broad lapels. He appears on the verge of uttering something, and his obvious wealth would have accustomed him to being taken very seriously in those cash-strapped times. He sits with all the solidity and self-possession of a king on his throne, but as the poem advances the speaker will challenge this smugness by connecting it with the slavery that made his comfort possible. An epigram from Shakespeare's *Merchant of Venice* (Act 5, scene one, line 79) hints at the spiritual bankruptcy of such a man so clearly on his way to hell.

Freneau spent two years in the West Indies from 1776 to 1778. Although attracted to the tropical blossoms and endless spring of Jamaica (mentioned here in line 43 but celebrated more fully in other of his poems from the period), he was appalled by the conditions the island's slaves were forced to endure. His wit is clear from the opening lines of the poem: although as a child of the Enlightenment he questions the literal existence of hell, he asserts that Sir Toby's slaves "enjoy that portion here" (line 2). The notion of enjoying hell is pure sarcasm except that its proven existence would substantiate at least one of the tenets of fundamentalist Christianity. Thus the whole of which that "portion" is a part might be construed as the promise of an eternity in which one's deeds in this lifetime are punished or rewarded, and it is within this tradition that the speaker asks what the slaves have done to merit such a fate (line 20). He also hints at the pains that await Sir Toby for using such infernal means to obtain his wealth (line 38). The term "portion" also designates a share, especially of food and drink, and thus serves as a segue to the question of the rum for which Jamaica was already famous in Freneau's time. While it is true that the Jamaican hell contained no "blazing brimstone lakes," Freneau notes that kindled rum burns as blue (lines 3–4). The image of burning brimstone comes from biblical passages such as Psalms 11:6 (in the King James version). That verse is especially relevant to the present poem because it mentions fire and brimstone as the *portion of their cup* that the wicked will be served. Brimstone was the name by which sulfur was known, and it does burn with a blue flame. Rums can consist of 80-percent alcohol or even more, which explains why they can burn. In Freneau's poem, burning rum is used to heat Toby's brand prior to branding a slave's breast with it, a West Indies custom practiced here by "some fiend who nature must detest" (line 5) since he would so willingly mar the features of a "natural" man.

The middle section of the poem itemizes the means by which the slaves were terrorized into submission, beginning with "whips on whips" (line 6) that crack like pistols (line 18. This noise can occur on the back swing when, in the hands of an expert, the end of a bullwhip can break the speed of sound). The "mingled howlings" (line 8) vibrating in the speaker's ears originate in the breasts of those actually experiencing the physical suffering of a whipping and in their loved ones. Other tortures include hunger in the presence of an abundance of food that they see but cannot taste and dare not steal (lines 22–24). With few legal restrictions on his authority, an exceptionally sadistic slaver maintained gallows (the "gibbet" of line 25) from which he could hang those luckless enough to fall under his power. Other slavers preferred to inflict humiliating and excruciating corporal punishments ranging from nailing someone to a windmill by his ears, starvation, submersion in brine or suspension by the thumbs (lines 25–29).

All of the above occurs in a land already plagued by heat (referenced in the "burning soil" of line 15), "snakes, scorpions, despots, lizards [and] centipedes" (line 10). Modern science has determined that there are no poisonous snakes or lizards in Jamaica, but the slaves lacked this knowledge. Scorpions and fanged centipedes (one species grows up to 10 inches) do flourish there, as did despots (Freneau learned the technique of placing a human object of derision in a list of vermin from his fellow Revolutionary War propagandists for whom the indignity of such an honor typically fell on King George's head).

The slaves all have their dues and "are paid in cash" (line 11). British currency was in such short supply even before the American Revolution that sundry moneys from other countries circulated in the North American colonies and simple bartering was common. For Freneau's immediate audience, to be paid in cash meant to receive the full price of a commodity in ready money and thus to receive its full value. In the context of this poem, however, the phrase means that the slaves received the full impact of the driver's unstinted cruelty.

Freneau was so intimately acquainted with Jamaican slavery that he could pinpoint the origins of many slaves. Angola (line 41) and Guinea (line 50) were among the southernmost and northernmost of the heavily populated West African states most commonly visited by slave ships on Africa's Atlantic coast. Eboe (more commonly spelled Ibo or Igbo; line 21) was a small kingdom in modern Nigeria that was roughly halfway between them. From a distance the slaves could appear a black herd (line 14), but up close the speaker has seen 24 women, each with a gourd, an infant, a hoe and an iron collar. Chained together, they were driven by an overseeing devil (lines 31–36), an image that reminds him of the pictures of hell drawn by the Italian poet Virgil (Publius Vergilius Maro, 70–19 B.C., whose hero of the *Aeneid* [c. 19 B.C.] visited hell). Like Charon, who ferried the dead over the River Styx in Greek myths, the slavers deliver their human cargoes to the devilish scourges and despotic lords of the West Indies (lines 47–52).

Those slaves intent on freedom must scale the Liguanea Mountains (the tallest of which is Blue Mountain at just over 7,400 feet) and then run a gauntlet of former slaves who, having won their own freedom, gladly turn the new arrivals over to the British officials for a fee.

"TO S. M., A YOUNG AFRICAN PAINTER, ON SEEING HIS WORKS" Phillis Wheatley (1773)

After the invention of the cotton gin in 1793 resulted in a fiftyfold increase in the need for field workers, slavery was usually depicted in New England popular culture as the ruthless coercion of plantation laborers under the most inhumane circumstances imaginable. Prior to that time, however, slaves north and south who showed any penchant for skilled labor were as likely to be employed in crafts or trades if their holders could see a chance for profit from such an indulgence. Thus Scipio Moorhead came to be trained in the visual arts by Sarah Moorhead, a professional art teacher whose advertisement in the *Boston Evening Post* on April 18, 1748, offered lessons in drawing, japanning (varnishing wood, metal, or glass to obtain a lustrous finish similar in gloss to the lacquered objects of Japan), and painting (Dow 267). His holder, John Moorhead, was so prominent that he was among the seven ministers who joined the colonial governor, lieutenant governor, and nine other worthies (including the subsequently famous John Hancock and John Wheatley, PHILLIS WHEATLEY's master) in attesting to Wheatley's background and authorship of her poetry. At a time when most slaveholders were entertaining the comfortable (for them) notion that the people they kept in bondage were somehow less human than themselves, such testimonials were crucial in dispelling the myth that a slave was incapable of such virtuosity as Phillis Wheatley exhibited in her poetry. Both a letter to the public from John Wheatley and this testament were published as front matter to her *Poems on Various Subjects, Religious and Moral*. They were joined by, remarkably, a portrait of the poet by Scipio Moorhead. Today the artist is chiefly remembered for that engraving (thought to be among the first attributable works of visual art produced by an American slave) and for this poem.

From this poem, it is difficult to say whether the poet was more charmed by Moorhead's drawing or exhilarated by a nascent racial pride that recognized another black artist's having overcome the same barriers that she faced. Her praise begins with notice of his skill in capturing the deep intent of her heart (the "laboring bosom" of the first line) and thought. His pencil and paints brought breathing figures to life and delighted her soul. She encourages him to always (the "still" of lines 7 and 9) pursue noble paths and to focus on deathless glories. Apparently he also wrote poetry (which has not survived), for she wishes him the painter's and the poet's fire (line 9). She hopes the charms of his angelic themes will lead him to immortal fame; he should elate his soul and raise his eyes to "the blissful wonders of the skies" (heaven, line 13). He will be "thrice happy" (a formula that may echo the many biblical references to the "thrice blessed;" line 15) when

"exalted" to view heaven (or Jerusalem, the 12-gated "Salem" of line 18, a name chosen for its importance in the life of the Savior who she believed provided the key to taking him there [Jerusalem was the site of much of Christ's preaching and healing, and later of his arrest, trial, crucifixion, burial, resurrection and ascension]) crowned with endless day and the blooms of endless spring.

The last stanza begins by noting Scipio Moorhead's calm and serene manner. Wheatley hopes that the muse will inspire his future songs, that his soul will be blessed with "the sweets of contemplation" (line 21), and that peace will invest his mild (or "balmy") wings. She anticipates heaven (when the shades of time are chased away [by death and resurrection]), an eternity of everlasting day in which they will soar to view the landscapes on angel's wings. His tongue will flow in heavenly murmurs, and her muse will glow "with heavenly transport" (she will be divinely inspired, but the line also may suggest that she will be rendered even more angelic or saintly by the things she will be inspired to compose there).

She follows this with a remarkable assessment of the differences in discourse communities between Enlightenment America and heaven. No longer will audience expectations dictate the use of such classical references as the sighs of the shepherd Damon created by the Roman poet Virgil for his *Ecologues* or the use of the Greek myths that once explained natural phenomena (as Aurora was once considered the goddess of the dawn). Nobler themes (such as those appropriate in heaven) demand a nobler strain and a purer language appropriate to those lofty heights. This may imply some dissatisfaction on the poet's part that she was forced to write for her current audience, a possibility that would illustrate some frustration with the poetic voice she has been forced to assume by virtue of her circumstances and the demands of the marketplace.

The poem ends with her asking the muse to stop inspiring her, for "the solemn gloom of night" (either of the night during which she was writing or, a more exciting possibility, the limitations of her life [or life in general]) now removes the vision of "the fair creation" (heaven, but the line may possibly be a veiled revelation of a desire to write a poem not so limited by the aesthetics of her age and further dictated by her enslaved condition).

BIBLIOGRAPHY
Dow, George Francis. *The Arts & Crafts in New England 1704–1775.* Topsfield, Mass.: Wayside Press, 1927.

"TO THE DANDELION" James Russell Lowell (1845)

One of the great services poetry can perform is to enliven readers by making them aware of the miracles that surround them. Here, JAMES RUSSELL LOWELL undertakes the momentous task of rehabilitating the reputation of the scourge of every manicured urban lawn. He begins by noting the plant's most outstanding traits, its commonness, the vibrant hue of its flowers, which he likens to gold, and its typical habitat, "fringing the dusty road" (line 2) of high summer.

Like a good publicist of a century later, Lowell realized that the problem was not with the plant, but with our perception of it. Calling it "harmless gold" not only contrasted it with the metal for which so many lives have been ruined, but it also contrasted the values adults place on things for their commercial potential with the innocent appreciation of children. As a flower of spring (subtract a month or more if you live in a more temperate horticultural zone, but New Englanders like Lowell associated it with May [line 3]), it provides proud trophies for the children who pluck it with the pride of buccaneers. This makes the dandelion more dear (more expensive, which continues the poem's play with the notion of commercial value, but also more cherished) than all the other summer blossoms (line 9).

Because it continues blooming throughout the summer, the speaker considers it his window to warmer climes. By mid-June, he appreciates the flower as much as the "golden-cuirassed bee" (line 23). A cuirass was the piece of armor that protected the trunk of a soldier and allowed greater mobility than full armor. One might find it employed by the pirates in the glory days of the Spanish Main, a connection that again touches on the recurrent image of buccaneers in the poem. The speaker completes his description of the blossom by recalling that its yellow circles burst from amid its dark green leaves (line 27).

The plant reminds him of the delights of summer, when the weather permits travel to a woodland lake. He remembers a single white cloud that crossed the sky like a stray lamb (line 36). It recalls the time when a robin's song seemed that of an angel, when birds, flowers, and he were happy peers (line 45). Dandelions can also symbolize "those meek charities" (line 46) that count for half the nobleness of life. Wise men appreciate small signs of cheer, friendship, and love; such things can provide a "glimpse of God" (line 54) for a starving heart.

The winged seeds of the plant might, like the words of poets and philosophers, go unheeded until they take root in another age (or at least season). Their work can inspire more words and deeds, ultimately blooming into stars that can guide the earth (or at least its human complement). Dandelions are full of deep love that, if we listen for it, can soothe life's ache and guide us to heaven and away from "the gates of Ill" (line 72). Nature seems prodigal in making dandelion gold so common, which might teach us to value the similarly plentiful human hearts around us and appreciate the living pages of the Bible (stanza nine).

The speaker is sure of one great gift from the plant: he will never grow old as long as the dandelion comes each year to remind him of his childhood. We owe more than half of "life's holiness" (line 87) to our first exposure to nature's influence. The mere thought of them can burst open the heart's glad doors to peace and hope (line 90).

"TO THE FRINGED GENTIAN" William Cullen Bryant (1832)

Like WILLIAM CULLEN BRYANT's other flower poems, this one opens with the plant's natural history. It is remarkable for blooming in the fall, when the night is "keen" (line 4; the term suggests a certain eagerness on the night's part to unleash its piercing frosts). The plant copes with this threat by closing its blue blossoms at dusk and reopening them at dawn, when the autumnal light might be considered "quiet" (line 3) both in contrast to the more intense lights of summer sunshine and because the frosts have killed most of the insects that earlier filled the woods with sound.

This flower does not bloom in the spring or early summer when the violets and columbines do, but comes alone when the shortening days signal that "the aged year is near his end" (line 12). This serves as a transition to the application of the observed phenomenon to the human condition: like a graceful person mellowed by age and no longer as active (now viewing life through the "sweet and quiet eye" that the flower brings to mind in line 13), the plant turns its cerulean (a dark sky-blue) blossom to the sky. In the last stanza the speaker interprets this as a hopeful sign and prays that he may similarly look to heaven as his hour of death draws near.

"TO THE MEMORY OF MY DEAR AND EVER HONORED FATHER THOMAS DUDLEY ESQ. WHO DECEASED, JULY 31, 1653, AND OF HIS AGE 77" Anne Bradstreet (1678)

For most 21st-century readers, the principal interest of this poem lies in the light it sheds on the poet's formative years, but her father's prominence in the Massachusetts Bay colony was such as to interest historians even without his famous daughter.

In the opening lines, the poet anticipates and deflects any criticism her poem might engender in her staunchly religious community. She takes pains to differentiate her heartfelt effort from that of those speakers upon whom it customarily fell to praise the deceased; filial devotion and not custom prompts her speech. She is even an unwilling witness; her mournful mind was "sore pressed" (line 3), a phrase drawn from the quaint practice of extracting confessions by placing increasingly heavy stones upon the accused. The practice was very irregular even in New England, but the most famous incident occurred nearly four decades after the death of Thomas Dudley. In nearby Salem, Massachusetts, Giles Corey was pressed to death on September 19, 1692, for refusing to confess during the infamous witch trials. Although the torture of prisoners was the furthest thing from the speaker's mind in this poem, the vivid picture this phrase could have brought to mind in her initial audience reminds us that many of even our most clichéd metaphors were once fresh and vital.

Along with the tremendous pressures attendant upon mourning the death of one's father in general, the situation of this poem placed the speaker in the funeral train, which usually meant walking directly behind the casket from the deathbed or the church to the graveyard. Although as a four-time governor of the colony, her father merited a hearse (line 4), whatever pomp could be mustered for the funeral would have been lost on such a close mourner as the deceased's beloved daughter. In identifying the poem with the lamentations sometimes wailed in those circumstances, the speaker forestalled those deeply religious critics who would in calmer times have counseled her to rejoice in his ascension from this world to a better one.

She begins her praise by listing the roles her father filled in her life and states that she owes everything to him. Far from feeling disqualified to speak on his behalf by their close kinship, she asserts that she is the one who not only knew him best (line 8) but also the one who owed him the most. She resolves to continue with her plan regardless of the malice and envy her actions may generate (line 11).

Because he was such an important public figure, she need not fear that other speakers may distort his memory by exaggerating his praise in the absence of any evidence to the contrary. She can rely on his friends both in England (his native coast; line 18) and New England to make his true merit known, but she owes it to him ("I must pay my sum") to speak her piece. She will not be silent ("dumb," line 22). She evokes the perils of the Atlantic crossing to establish her father's importance as a founder of New England; he bolstered ("stayed") the colony when it was as imperiled as a ship or boat that rode low in the water. He invested his finances, his strength, and years of his life so that the colony would not flounder. The author's use of the unidiomatic term "after-comers" (line 26) denotes more than merely later immigrants or even his own descendents; it suggests that the intended beneficiaries of his efforts were his coreligionists. His only flaw was his zeal; this would hardly seem a sin in that theocracy, but in guarding the truth, he was heavily criticized by apostates (line 30). These included, in his opinion, Anne Hutchinson; Bradstreet's father was instrumental in her banishment from the colony for forming what 21st-century faithful would more likely see as a Bible study group with other women than as heresy. Ironically, Bradstreet's father was thus a central figure in creating a climate so hostile to women's voices that his daughter had to spend 22 lines of this eulogy defending her right to deliver it.

The rest of the poem is less devoted to relating the edifying anecdotes from his life designed to render her father's memory more vividly and more centered on enumerating the many ways in which he can be viewed as a perfect Puritan. He did not live to feather his nest but took a pilgrim's attitude towards worldly wealth (lines 33–34). Ambitious to attain heaven, he retained his humility and loathed honors and titles. In his speeches, he often gave other leaders the "rich jewel" (line 42) of reminding them to be similarly humble. He was modest in attire as well as in demeanor; he despised the vanity of those who wanted to publicly demonstrate their greatness. Full of longing for the heavenly mansion, he cheerfully exalted in the thought of death instead of fearing it.

In a wonderfully agricultural simile, Bradstreet compared his death to the mowing of fully ripe wheat with a sickle. Although this may seem an appropriately more humble instrument than the scythe with which death is more commonly caricatured in popular culture, its use suggests the more careful handling accorded one who was on his way to the celestial barn (line 57) where he would be safe from storms, showers, and damnation.

With his work finished on earth, his happy soul will rest among the saints, angels, and his fathers, with the last term probably meant to indicate God, Jesus, and perhaps the church fathers in addition to his biological fathers (Bradstreet probably did not mean to imply that only males could attain salvation). The speaker presumes that he was found righteous and calls for earthly praise to match the joy this judgment occasioned in heaven. Describing his head as "hoary" (line 63) not only provides the only physical detail of the late man the poem provides, it also suggests that his white hair may have prefigured the aura of glory that will surround his head in heaven. Achieving the wealth of experience that advanced age implies was so venerated at that point in American history that this manifestation of the aging process fits in well in this list of virtues.

The poet's prayer is that her father's memory will not be forgotten; he blessed posterity with a pious example of how to live in order to achieve heaven, the happy place where the redeemed are reunited with their loved ones and never again separated by death. Having finished with this eulogy, the poet appends an epitaph for her father. On one level, the effect is like having the funeral train arrive at the gravesite, where this epitaph can be read on the tombstone.

It would have seemed very appropriate to her father's peers if Bradstreet's epitaph were inscribed in stone; her father was that adamant in his beliefs. Unlike the more subjective, often apologetic voice of the speaker in the poem proper, the tone of the epitaph is more objective, as if the poet were assuming the voice of society. Although the second line of the epitaph (line 72 of the poem) seems ungrammatical in following the word "both" with three items instead of two, the distinction Bradstreet probably had in mind was between Dudley's religious beliefs (he was pious) and his governing role (he was just and wise). His religious certitude was such that he shielded its truth from distortion and protected it like a wall. To say that he was a "whip and a maul" to sectaries (line 74) refers to the colony's reliance on corporal punishment to stifle dissent within its own sect, an approach which was also applied to such interlopers as the Quakers.

Less controversially, Dudley loved history and good company, but these lines are immediately followed by the most chilling of the entire poem: in manners, he was both pleasant and severe. Which end of this spectrum you encountered depended on if you were one of the good people or the bad (line 78), as defined by the colony's theocrats. Clearly, Thomas Dudley was a controversial figure at whose death some rejoiced while more lamented (lines 79–80).

"TO THE MEMORY OF THE BRAVE AMERICANS" Philip Freneau (1781)   As the Revolutionary War dragged on into its last years, the British still held New York City and the chief American army hovered in the surrounding states as a counterbalance. The capture of Savannah, Georgia, on December 29, 1778, encouraged the British high command to shift their focus to the south, where they were thought

to enjoy stronger popular support. In South Carolina on May 12, 1780, they captured Charleston, and on August 16 of that year they routed the Americans at Camden. Patriot victories reversed the trend at King's Mountain (October 17, 1780) and at Cowpens (January 17, 1781). In North Carolina, a costly British victory at Guilford Courthouse (March 15, 1781) opened the way for an invasion of Virginia, and Lieutenant General Charles Cornwallis (second in command of all the British armies in the colonies) pushed all the way to Yorktown.

He expected to be supplied and reinforced by the British navy, with additional possible support coming up by land from the south. On September 8, 1781, the Battle of Eutaw Springs cut off the best chance Cornwallis had of receiving additional troops overland. As the headnote indicates, the patriots on that South Carolina battlefield were commanded by Major General Nathanael Greene, an officer so competent that he was able to untangle the logistical nightmares of supplying the army at Valley Forge during its terrible winter of 1777–78. After taking command of the southern army (on December 2, 1780) after the debacle at Camden, he had been wise enough to yield ground to the better trained and equipped British regulars, thus replicating the strategy that had kept Washington's troops in the war for six years. Finally pressed by the British in North Carolina, he gave up ground so grudgingly at Guilford Courthouse on March 15, 1781, that Cornwallis turned north instead of continuing his pursuit, and Greene was able to concentrate his forces in South Carolina.

Cornwallis soon found himself under siege at Yorktown when a French fleet kept the British from supplying him by sea, and on October 19, 1781, he surrendered to the combined French and American armies that had been marched down from the north to seize this opportunity.

The poem begins after the dust had settled at Eutaw Springs, and PHILIP FRENEAU called on the springs and the tide to weep for the fallen heroes, the "friends of freedom" (line 8) who now slumber on the battlefield. He asks the poem's internal audience, a subsequent visitor to the "bloody plain," to sigh for the shepherds who "sunk to rest" there (line 12). That stranger should

adorn their humble graves because s/he may also fall and "ask a tear" (desire mourning), for beautiful mornings do not always indicate clear evenings.

The patriots saw their injured country's flaming town and wasted field and rushed forth with the spear but not the shield. Under the "Conquering genius, Greene" (line 21), they compelled the Britons to fly; none viewed the battle from a distance but charged in without grief at the prospect of death.

Unfortunately, the poorly equipped continentals stopped to ransack the British supplies, a reprieve that enabled the British to reform and counterattack. Like the Parthians of antiquity, the British thus proved deadly on the retreat (line 28. Centered in modern-day Iran, the Parthians controlled much of the Near East from Turkey to the Persian Gulf of Saudi Arabia from 150 B.C. to A.D. 224. Their famed cavalry would sometimes feign retreat and then whirl to release a volley of arrows into their exposed attackers).

Freneau closes with the wish that the fallen patriots should rest in peace. Although they had been thrown "far from nature's limits" (killed at a very young age; line 29), their supporters trust they will find a happier land "with a brighter sunshine of their own" (in heaven, where they will shine as radiantly as saints).

Although the British reclaimed the field that day, it was a Pyrrhic victory (one that cost more than it gained). They were forced to withdraw to Charleston, leaving Greene to regain control of the South. This limited British hopes of ultimate victory to their secure hold on New York City and the invasion of Virginia led by Cornwallis. The Battle of Eutaw Springs commemorated in this poem was an important milestone on the way to the ultimate American victory in the war.

"TO THE UNIVERSITY OF CAMBRIDGE, IN NEW ENGLAND" PHILLIS WHEATLEY (1773)

In her opening stanza, the poet introduced herself to the Harvard undergraduates (the university is in Cambridge, Massachusetts, just across the Charles River from Boston) by stressing the things they have in common. These include a love of writing that she refers to as the "intrinsic ardor" that prompts her (line 1) and familiarity with classical Greek literature, which she demonstrates by calling on the muses to aid her. Harvard had been founded (in 1636) to train Puritan and Congregationalist ministers, so Wheatley reached out to her fellow Christians by referring to her native Africa as "the land of errors" because it lacked exposure to the biblical truths. She also considers it a place of "Egyptian gloom" not only because of the darkness Moses cast on the land (Exodus 10:22) but also because its inhabitants were doomed without exposure to her religion. Finally she offers her life as a testament to God's mercy, for His gracious hand brought her safely from those foreign shores.

She then turns to flattery, telling the students (in language that anticipates that of the transcendental optimist RALPH WALDO EMERSON in the next century) that they are "to scan the heights" and "traverse the ethereal space" (lines 7–8). As "sons of science" (women were not allowed Harvard educations until separate classes were started for them at Radcliffe in the 1870s; the university did not become fully coeducational until World War II), they were to "mark the systems of revolving worlds" (line 9) and receive the blissful news from heavenly messengers that Jesus' blood flows for their redemption. She reminds them of His hands outstretched on the cross and the immense compassion that glows in his chest. With His matchless mercy, He is indifferent to reviler's (or "tormentor's") scorn. When by sin the human race had fallen, He died that they might rise again and share the most sublime skies, life without death, and endless glory.

The final stanza encourages them to use their privileges and to redeem each hour's chance to send a good or bad report to heaven. They should shun sin and never let down their guards, thus "suppress[ing] the deadly serpent in its egg" (line 26). They are the "blooming plants" of the divine human race, and an Ethiope (an African, not specifically an Ethiopian; Shakespeare frequently used the same name for people with descendents from that continent, a tradition that was continued by American poets, including WALT WHITMAN and EMILY DICKINSON, throughout the 19th century as well) tells them that sin is their greatest foe. Sin's temporary sweetness turns to endless pain, and an "immense perdition" (hell; line 30) sinks the soul.

TRANSCENDENTALIST POETRY

American transcendentalism can conveniently be dated from the publication of RALPH WALDO EMERSON's *Nature* in 1836. It reached its intellectual zenith when Margaret Fuller and Emerson published *The Dial* from 1840 to 1844. That organ offered a voice to the leading lights of the informal movement, which was centered in the small village of Concord, Massachusetts, where many of them lived, and Harvard's Cambridge. It perished when age dimmed those lights, and death began removing them. The Civil War finally killed off the idealism that had sustained the transcendentalists, but their writings helped the nonconformists of the counterculture of the mid-20th century formulate their ideals. They still bolster those individuals who would rather live philosophically simple lives instead of trying to upstage everyone else in a headlong pursuit of material goods. They also offered equal public voice to the women who held similar beliefs, acknowledged the values offered by religions and cultures far remote from those of mainstream America, and generally opposed the country's involvement in imperialistic wars like the Mexican-American War of 1846–48.

The general aims of American transcendentalism were outlined in a lecture ("The Transcendentalist") that Emerson, the leading poet, theoretician and one of the founders of the movement, delivered in Boston's Masonic Temple in January 1842. Emerson divided human thought into two sects, materialists who would have all knowledge begin with sensory perceptions and ultimately verified by that source, and idealists, who base their theories on consciousness. He places the transcendentalists in the latter group because they value the power of thought, will, inspiration, miracle, individual culture, and ecstasy. The transcendentalist accepts the physical objects of this world but focuses his attention on the spiritual facts that led to the creation of such things. It is evident, for example, that a seemingly solid commercial bank, a cornerstone of capitalistic grandeur, is ultimately grounded on the earth's fiery molten core, so Emerson's idealist starts with his consciousness, discounts the world of appearances, and accepts his mind as the only reality. He does not accept government or other social organizations (thus there can be no Transcendental party,

Emerson argues) except insofar as they reveal or touch the Unknown Center in each individual. It follows that he will not try to change the distant evils of the world, but will focus on obtaining harmony within himself. He does, however, admit the existence of some facts beyond his knowing, and a spiritual principle.

In the same essay, Emerson acknowledges two of his many debts to German philosophy by quoting "[Friedrich Heinrich] Jacobi, the Transcendentalist moralist" (1743–1819)," and Immanuel Kant (1724–1894), who coined the term "Transcendental." He also draws on the Asian philosophy of Buddhism, which admires things and people acting in accordance with their true natures. He states that transcendentalists are repulsed by vulgarity, frivolity and political activity in general, even when it is for such a good cause as the antislavery movement. Instead, they stay focused on their own paths.

The transcendentalist message of self-sufficient independence probably helped EMILY DICKINSON renounce any pursuit of worldly notoriety and the compromises it would entail in favor of furthering her family relationships and privately perfecting her poetry. WALT WHITMAN also drew strength from the same source, along with very practical poetic guidance from Emerson at a critical point in his young career.

A survey of Emerson's most commonly anthologized poems offers a brief overview of his own career and reveals many of the characteristic traits of the movement. "The PROBLEM" introduces the crisis of faith that led him to abandon his ministry even as he continued to admire some aspects of the church and other expressions of inspiration both within religious settings and in nature. In "The RIVER," he revisits a scene important to his youth and is reminded of the brevity of human life while nature presses on. His fascination with nature is also evident in "The HUMBLE-BEE" and "The RHODURA." "WALDEINSAMKEIT," a name reminiscent of the pond made famous when HENRY DAVID THOREAU built a cabin and experimented with a life of philosophical simplicity on land owned by Emerson, suggests that a feeling of peace can be fostered in a wilderness environment and carried with you everywhere.

In "DAYS," however, the speaker chastises himself for not making more of his life. Emerson's ideal tran-

scendentalist is not a loafer, but chooses to work on what he values instead of what seems more acceptable to society. In "The APOLOGY," Emerson provided a few clues as to his own industry for his neighbors who worked their fields while he strolled by with flowers in his hands. Much later he penned an "ODE INSCRIBED TO W. H. CHANNING" celebrating that Unitarian minister's willingness to fight for his beliefs, many of which Emerson shared, but apologizing for not feeling adequate to personally join the battles.

In "The POET" and other essays, Emerson argues for self-reliance in literature as well as in life. Some exposure to the trilogies prevalent in eastern as well as western religions may have led him to postulate on the three basic belief systems, for which the poet serves the important role as the announcer of new things. "EACH AND ALL" argues that every element is essential to the overall beauty of a place, and that the absence of a part would diminish the whole.

Two other Emerson poems pay homage to the Hindu philosophies that he studied. "BRAHMA" introduces the Hindu god who ultimately will recreate the universe regardless of how it turned out last time. In "HAMATREYA," the earth mocks those who pride themselves in ownership of its parcels, because it will soon hold them. Both poems mock human ambition in the face of cosmic indifference.

Thoreau's poetry has been widely anthologized because of the author's importance as a cultural figure rather than for its own merits, but it is not without interest. "I MARK THE SUMMER'S SWIFT DECLINE" combines the trained eye of the naturalist with a poet's feel for language. "FOG" is the most transcendental of his poems in the sense that its subject constantly changes shape (as does everything on earth), but the mind of the speaker is ultimately of greater interest. "The FALL OF THE LEAF" also turns on the mind's ability to reconstruct nature; Thoreau recalls other seasons and other places even as he carefully delineates the subtle changes he finds in the landscape.

BIBLIOGRAPHY

Buell, Lawrence, ed. *The American Transcendentalists: Essential Writings.* New York: Modern Library, 2006.

Emerson, Ralph Waldo. "The Transcendentalist." In *Nature: Addresses and Lectures,* constituting the first volume of *The*

Works of Ralph Waldo Emerson. Boston: Phillips, Sampson, 1909.

Wayne, Tiffany K. *Encyclopedia of Transcendentalism.* New York: Facts On File, 2006.

TUCKERMAN, FREDERICK GODDARD (1821–1873)

It is perhaps fitting that a Renaissance man (one who takes an intellectual interest in a broad range of subjects) would be best remembered for his work in the sonnet form that was so popular in that bygone Elizabethan era, when Shakespeare and his contemporaries were perfecting their sonnets. Born the son of a wealthy Boston merchant on February 4, 1821, the future poet attended Harvard and for a short time became a practicing lawyer. Family wealth enabled him to pursue his interests in botany, astronomy, and poetry at his leisure, and he published only one volume of poetry (*Poems,* 1860) in his lifetime.

After settling in Greenfield, Massachusetts, he married a local girl (Anna Jones) and informally studied the stars and local trees. It was characteristic of the man that, on an 1869 trip abroad, he collected and preserved (by pressing) leaves from Ireland, England, France, Germany, Greece, Jerusalem, and Damascus so well that they still remain in the Harvard University archives. He might well have lived the life of a quiet country gentleman, never bringing the full force of his manhood to bear on anything, were it not for the death of his wife of 10 years in 1857. That trauma is credited with inspiring the more than 100 sonnets he wrote before his death.

In addition to the herbarium (plant collection) mentioned above, Harvard holds manuscript poems, several of his letters, a scrapbook and commonplace book, and his astronomical and meteorological journals. The Greenfield Public Library annually sponsors a local poetry competition in his honor, and the nearby Poets Seat Tower, erected in Tuckerman's honor, offers a view of the nature trails the poet liked to frequent.

Since Tuckerman chose not to name his sonnets they are typically identified by their first lines. "DANK FENS OF CEDAR, HEMLOCK BRANCHES GRAY" shows the poet at his moody best, somehow extrapolating hope for future happiness from a desolate natural landscape. The nostalgic "AND CHANGE WITH HURRIED HAND HAS SWEPT THESE SCENES" misses the vitality of the wilderness even as it recalls that everything in its natural state is not always pleasant. The poet's legal training and patrician background are evident in the argument advanced in "NO! COVER NOT THE FAULT." In "THAT BOY, THE FARMER SAID, WITH HAZEL WAND," the speaker is chastised for his poor work habits but implies that a capacity to appreciate beauty is more worthwhile. "YET VAIN, PERHAPS, THE FRUITS OUR CARE APPLAUD" questions the value of work in a world determined by fate. "An UPPER CHAMBER IN A DARKENED HOUSE" presents a nightmarish world dominated by a single threatening image, while "AS ONE TURNED ROUND ON SOME HIGH MOUNTAIN TOP" presents a surreal view of life. As even the small sample of his poems discussed here demonstrate, Tuckerman brought a wide variety of intellectual gifts to his poetry.

BIBLIOGRAPHY

Bean, Jonathan, ed. *Three American Poets: Melville, Tuckerman, Robinson.* London and New York: Penguin, 2003.

England, Eugene. *Beyond Romanticism: Tuckerman's Life and Poetry.* Provo, Utah: Brigham Young University. Distributed by State University of New York Press, 1991.

Tuckerman, Frederick Goddard. *Complete Poems.* Edited by N. Scott Momaday. New York: Oxford University Press, 1965.

"THE TUFT OF KELP" HERMAN MELVILLE (1888)

Kelp are fast-growing seaweeds typically anchored to the ocean floor until uprooted by storms, when they can be washed ashore in large clumps (a "Tuft"). Such deposits are so common that most beachgoers soon learn to ignore them, but something in the speaker's past in HERMAN MELVILLE's poem has drawn his attention to the tuft that he addresses. His understanding of how the thing got stranded ("Cast up by a lonely sea," line 2), his diction ("O Weed" and "ye" hint at a salty background, as does his romanticized reference to the lonely sea), affection for sea life (which prompts a close enough examination that he describes it rather lovingly as "dripping in tangles green," line 1), and empathy with its plight (he anticipates its bitterness at being trapped ashore) suggest that he is a sailor. As such he may have been struck by what is almost a role reversal; instead of the tufts of hair on a dead sailor's head adrift in the sea, he finds tufts of seaweed ashore.

The seaweed is "purer" (line 3) in the sense of being more concentrated because all the saltwater and most of the marine life it supported would have drained away or abandoned it, but the term is also reminiscent of the religious notion (not unique to Christianity) that a person, soul, or spirit must undergo frequently painful purification rites or rituals in order to achieve the next stage of enlightenment or a higher state of grace. Perhaps only someone forced into a similar "purification" would realize how bitter that experience could make him. Thus the principal interest in the poem lies not in the situation or its nominal subject, but in the personality of the producer of such laconic speech.

"'TWAS LIKE A MAELSTROM, WITH A NOTCH" EMILY DICKINSON (published 1951)

This tribute to EDGAR ALLAN POE begins with a reference to his short story "A Descent into the Maelstrom" and combines it with the mechanized terror of another story, "The Pit and the Pendulum." The maelstrom is a whirlpool in the ocean, capable of pulling down ships. Like clockwork (hence the "notch" of line 1, a device to prevent the springs from releasing all their pent-up power at once), the maelstrom keeps bringing the certain doom of "its boiling Wheel" (line 3; both the Poe story and EMILY DICKINSON's homage revel in concrete sensory details) nearer every day like the slowly descending swinging blade of the second Poe story.

The second stanza insinuates that reading Poe has a fantasy element not unlike a sexual dream. When the "Agony," which this poem suggests derives mainly from the delay of the seemingly inevitable and irredeemable, "toyed coolly" with the final inch of the "delirious Hem" (line 6) of "your" (the speaker's shift to the second person may indicate her eagerness both to share the pleasurable experience and to distance herself from any moral qualms she may have about it) dress, the reader is transported into the realm of pleasurable passivity, a world of the masochistic delights of a bondage game so heady that you dropped, lost, until something broke (line 7) and released you from this dream.

Poe's imaginative world was peopled with human demons, the most frightening of whom served as narrators (see "The Cask of Amontillado" and "The Tell-Tale Heart"). "Goblins" are much less scary, more the stuff of folklore than a real elfin menace, and a "goblin with a gauge" (line 9) is a more surreal rather than terrifying image, an aesthetic choice that reinforces the dream quality of the third stanza. Anyway, the little guy keeps measuring the hours (a difficult task with a "gauge" rather than a clock) until you felt your second "weigh" (line 12; a pun on "way" that nevertheless recalls the two pendulums typically used on the most expensive mechanical clocks of the era); the speaker clarifies that the "second weigh" makes you feel helpless in his paws.

That she is a willing participant can be inferred since "not a sinew—stirred—could help" (line 13) implies that she never moved a muscle to try to escape. Her "sense" (the normal rational ways she conducted her life) was "setting numb" (was held in abeyance). Then she remembered God (at an inopportune time, if she were enjoying the fantasy as much as her description suggests) and the Fiend let go, "Overcome" (by, a Freudian scholar might suggest, her own sense of guilt).

If you were sentenced to death and led, with all your thought and emotions frozen by the enormity of immediately facing your fate, from the "Dungeon's luxury of Doubt" (maybe they won't really kill me, one probably rationalizes) to the Gibbets (or gallows, the structures from which condemned criminals were hanged) and the Dead (line 21; the dash ending this stanza serves roughly the same function as an ellipsis, the three dots signifying the lapse of time or a change in circumstances).

Just as your eyes were glazing over (the speaker's choice of "when the Film had stitched your eyes" [line 22] is more horrifying because the phrasing is so new and the damage so irretrievably permanent), a Creature (since this is another surreal landscape, the inhabitants are not human) "gasps (as if barely able or unwilling to deliver such a disappointing message) 'Reprieve!'" (Thus so luckily being recalled from the point of death figures heavily in several of Poe's tales, and the fear of safety's too late arrival is the subject of his "The Premature Burial"). When the speaker concludes by questioning which Anguish was more severe, to perish or to live (to return to a world peopled with such monsters, or to move on to your reward), on one level she is asking whether it is more desirable to return to her normal reality, or to continue reading about Poe's fictional accounts of alternative mental states and to experience the dreams they foster.

"THE TWO GRAVES" WILLIAM CULLEN BRYANT (1832) WILLIAM CULLEN BRYANT loved nature so much that he wanted the relationship to continue for eternity, or at least until Judgment Day. Although this poem's title most directly refers to the forgotten graves of an elderly couple on their former homestead, it invites the reader to contrast their resting place with the plots in a city cemetery. As was so often the case when Bryant compared aspects of life in the two settings, he found the less civilized alternative preferable.

If the chief concern is the impact of the scene on a visitor's frame of mind, the wilderness grave wins hands down. Drawn to a "bleak wild hill" (line one) in hopes of again finding the two graves s/he had evidently happened upon 18 years earlier, the speaker finds himself surrounded by vibrant high-summer nature. His occasional use of onomatopoeia (the bee's hum and wren's chirp; line 3) helps the reader imaginatively reconstruct the scene. So do the sound of a bell (line 5), which can help herders round up their grazing flocks at day's end if they are placed around the sheep's necks, and his description of the difference in temperature as the shade passes over a rock. The last line of the first stanza reinforces the central argument of the poem: nothing in this bucolic scene speaks of death.

Human births and deaths occur in the distant urban environment, where the "populous graveyard" (this mild oxymoron contains one of the central images of the poem) "lightens the bier" (line 12; a bier is a coffin stand). Close proximity is chief among "the ties that bind" (line 13) all the people buried there, although the dead do not complain because friends and foes have been so crowded together. Each is calm in his "winding-sheet" (line 20; early American cadavers were frequently wrapped in white linen shrouds prior to being placed in a pine box or a more elaborate casket

prior to burial). The description of their "sullen home of peace and gloom" (line 21) implicitly contrasts it to the vitality surrounding the less crowded graves on the old homestead.

In the third stanza, the speaker turns his attention back to searching for the two graves. The farmer and his wife had been buried for 50 years, but the speaker somehow knew that their children had preceded them in death and that they had no close relatives when they were interred. Thus the final prayer was delivered coldly (line 34) by a nonrelative, a chill prospect in keeping with the speaker's referring to the lapsed time as 50 winters in line 27.

On his prior visit, he had found that even 32 years after their burial their graves had been marked by slight rises in the ground (the "low green hillocks" of line 35) and small memorial stones. Now he cannot discover where the aged couple "sleep" (line 40). He considers this appropriate since the deceased must have been among the earliest pioneers in the area. The country had been so new that even the sky was unknown (line 50), and the old man's crops of gourds (which yielded edible squash), beans, maize (corn), and rye (which could be used as animal feed or processed to make flour or whiskey) were the first in that virgin ground.

The penultimate stanza questions the happiness of the traditional vision of heaven, arguing that it would feel like banishment for a spirit to be carried to "a distant sphere" (line 52) so far from the familiar rock and stream.

He asks the reader to reject this cruel creed and to replace it with how he would treat the "harmless pair" of spirits (line 63). "They are here" he exclaims twice, ecstatic with either finally having found their graves or, more likely, with his own vision of their sitting or walking around their old haunts. To avoid confusion with the infernal spirits that might harm those who encounter them (an outcome some believers might consider a more distinct possibility since their burial place was not connected with a church), the speaker asserts that the sunny couple is "patient, peaceful and passionless" (line 71). They wait for Judgment Day, when some Christian sects promise a bodily Resurrection (hence the claim that "their bodies shall leave the ground" in line 74).

"TWO RIVERS" RALPH WALDO EMERSON
(1867)   As a transcendentalist, RALPH WALDO EMERSON brought a sensitivity sometimes strikingly similar to that of the earliest Puritans to the observation of nature. Both hoped to discern the origin of the forces behind a natural phenomenon, although his New England predecessors referred to it as the hand of God whereas Emerson searched not for signs of a deity, but for clues relating it to a less anthropomorphized but no less permanent and universal order or power.

By referring to the Concord River by its Native American name of Musketaquit (line 1), Emerson has already implied that there were at least two ways of looking at it based upon its historical use by two different cultures. He also personified the river by giving it a voice and having it repeat "the music of the rain" (line 2). Thus he classified it by sound with another natural phenomenon of the same substance, an observation that leads him to seek a "sweeter river's" pulsing within the physical river just as the river pulses through Concord Plain (line 4; had the poem ended at this point, the speaker would have exposed himself to the charge of creating a mysticism grounded in obscurity, but he has only begun introducing his subject).

The second stanza contrasts the narrow limits imposed on the river by its banks with the unbounded stream (line 6) the speaker loves finding not just in water (including the flood and sea) but also in the air (the "firmament" of line 7). It flows "forward" (Emerson's optimism is evident here) through light and life (line 8).

The speaker claims that he can see the "inundation sweet" and hear "the spending of the stream" (lines 9–10) through years, men, "Nature fleet" (a term possibly referring either to animal and vegetative life because it has the power of movement, or to the changes observable in all of nature), love, thought, power, and dream.

The last stanza begins with the spirit of Musketaquit (a "goblin strong," line 13) making gay jewels of the shard and flint found in its bed. His song has the power to take away grief, and being in his presence makes for an exceptionally good day (the "day of day" of line 16). The speaker's stream flows similarly but even brighter, and can produce the even more astonishing trick of forever satiating the consumer's thirst (line 18). Although just by itself the phrase "shall not thirst again" suggests the finality of death, it echoes Jesus' promise to a Samaritan woman (John 4:13–14) that the water He offers will last forever. The spiritual river in this Emerson poem is uniformly bright, light, and more permanent ("ages drop in it like rain," line 20).

It is tempting to conceive of this poem as an elaboration of a biblical event, with the speaker's mystical powers (he sees and hears things other people cannot) finally being explained when he identifies himself (by so closely echoing a biblical speech) as (or at least, "with") Jesus. However, since Emerson famously (or infamously) publicized his challenge to the unique divinity of Christ (a "noxious exaggeration," he called it in "The Divinity School Address" of 1838), this poem probably should not be viewed within such a narrowly conventional religious frame. Thus, although the speaker perceives an eternal force acting within nature, Emerson's insights from the Divinity School Address suggest that the speaker need not be thought divine for possessing the power of discernment. Then again, this poem may represent a softening in the poet's attitude toward conventional religious belief as he aged.

U

"AN UNINSCRIBED MONUMENT" HER-
MAN MELVILLE (1866) In May of 1864, the Army
of the Potomac, rebuilt to its full strength of approximately 120,000 men, renewed its push toward Richmond, Virginia. In their way were two major obstacles,
the entrenched defenses of the Southern capital and
about 62,000 men in Robert E. Lee's Army of Northern
Virginia. On May 5, the two armies collided on ground
of Lee's choosing, terrain so rugged as to be dubbed
"The Wilderness." Within 48 hours the South had lost
an eighth of their men and the North had lost about
one for every 6.7, or around 8,000 and 18,000 men,
respectively. On the third day the fighting could not be
resumed because of forest fires, a calamity that charred
the dead and burned alive those wounded who could
not be reached or drag themselves to safety. Under
General Ulysses S. Grant's energetic command, the
Northerners pressed forward the next evening, engaging the enemy in yet another battle, Spotsylvania, with
even worse casualty ratios and even more dead.

In commemorating one of the battles of The Wilderness, as its subtitle indicates, HERMAN MELVILLE's poem
recognizes the limited scope of the Virginia terrain over
which armies fought in each of the five calendar years
of the war. The speaker in this poem assumes the voice
of the monument not yet raised on the site and begins
with the solemn reflection that Silence and Solitude
better honor the fallen than words on any monument
could (thus providing yet another example of the 19th
century's indescribability trope). S/he touches on the

noise (the "din" of line 4) and movement (the "striving
of the multitude," line 5) of the battle before moving to
a striking visual effect: because the poem has taken us
into the battle, the "iron cones and spheres of death"
seem airborne in line 6. By line 7, however, they lay
rusting in the ground around the monument (the iron
cones originated in either the rifles or the cannon of
both sides; such primitively shaped charges were constantly being tried alongside the spherical Minnie balls
and cannonballs of earlier design). Like the monument,
these relics "speak with more than animated breath"
(each tells a vivid story of the battle even after their
brief role in it; line 9).

Addressing future spectators whose view of the
landscape will not be tinted by thoughts of their own
personal cheer (lines 10–11), the speaker focuses
attention on the meaning of the "quiet, the after-quiet,
and the calm full fraught" (a trio of states which might
be associated with the actual deaths as they occurred
on the field, the quiet that descended on the field after
the battle [with a tip of the hat to whatever beliefs the
spectator may hold about the afterlife], and that state
of calm reflection in which the full freight of meaning
of the battle, the war, and the individual lives lost can
be properly felt and acknowledged). Such thoughts
will render the spectator as silent as the uninscribed
monument, and as "lonesome as the land" (line 15).

"UPON A WASP CHILLED WITH COLD"
EDWARD TAYLOR (published 1943) By describing a

wasp as if its body were human (it has hands, toes, and fingers in lines 5–6) and closely observing its apparent grooming rituals as it warmed up in the morning light, the Puritan divine may be implying that the distance between that lowly creature and man is very slight whereas the distance between man and God is incomprehensibly greater than even the physical distance separating the insect from the sun. The first two lines conflate an aboriginal understanding of the stars (the harsh north wind originates as the breath of the "great bear" [Ursa Major] visible in the northern sky) with a less mystical understanding of a different natural phenomenon: the cold has numbed the wasp like a torpedo, a cousin of the more familiar stingray. Instead of a venous barb in a whip-like tail attached to a circular body, however, the torpedo's pectoral fins form a second, smaller disc and pack an electrical charge on the dorsal fins emanating from them. The effect of this feature has led to this electric ray's alternative names of numbfish or crampfish, identifications that the poet echoes in the verbs "numb" and "encramped" (lines 2–3). In this most pantheistic of EDWARD TAYLOR poems, the wasp is saved by the warm breath of a personified sun.

Because his pronoun choice implies that the insect is female, Taylor's account of her "rubbing her legs, shanks, thighs, and hands" takes on an almost voyeuristic quality (line 6). He luxuriates in describing how she extends her "petty toes and fingers . . . in great desire" to warm herself at the sun's fire (lines 7–10). Like a human, she stretches her small body and seems to comb her "velvet capital" (the top of her head, a description that not only combines the insect's color with the texture of fine human hair but may also pun on the notion that her hair could constitute a source of a woman's wealth; line 14). The insect acts as if her little brain "pan" (the space enclosing the brain) may hold "a volume of choice precepts" (lines 15–16) and her "hot" satin jacket (note how "hot" may refer to the warm color of the insect's thorax, the temperature at which its chemicals have greatest effect, and possibly even its sexual attractiveness) may contain an apothecary's shop (a drugstore, line 18) full of nature's remedies. She may even act as if her "velvet helmet" (the pleasing rhyme of line 21) contained "rationality"

(the capacity of human reasoning). Finally warmed to the point where flight is possible, she fans her wings (revealing her petticoat or undergarment in line 24) and "hoists sails" (takes off) back to the light grayish-brown ("dun") curved walls of her nest (here elevated to a "palace hall") and offers warm thanks for all (probably not just for the other wasps she meets, but for all the blessings [including the sun, the gift of flight and her own extraordinary being], line 28).

The second stanza of the poem is devoted to the application of the lesson of the wasp to the speaker's own condition. He asks the Lord to clear his "misted" sight (thus recognizing the limitations of human perception; line 29) that he may view His divinity. The characteristic Puritan attitude toward nature is revealed in lines 31–35; as a manifestation of divine intention, even the body of a small wasp can prove instructive. Noting the bravery with which her "nimble spirit" (line 36) attends her tasks and the "vital grace" with which she conducts herself, he hopes to similarly conduct his own affairs regardless of how small his role may be (line 39). Then this ladder (evidently consisting of devoted actions in accordance with God's will) will facilitate his elevation into heaven. It is also the product of divine grace since he may only ascend it "into the Godhead" when "enravished" [inspired and otherwise prepared by God]; line 41). Then all his "pipes" (a reference to the pipe organ usually found only in churches, but also perhaps to his windpipe; thus the term may refer to a life devoted to God and his praise of that divinity as well as his anticipated role in the divine chorus; line 43) will be filled with heavenly music decorated (or "furred") with praise (line 44). In this impossible image of music trimmed with fur, Taylor suggests a metaphysical mystery that transcends human understanding.

"UPON THE SWEEPING FLOOD, AUGUST 13–14, 1683" EDWARD TAYLOR (published 1943)

For a staunch Puritan like EDWARD TAYLOR, a natural catastrophe like a flood could have come directly from God as a token of His displeasure. In this poem the speaker laments not having recognized their perilous state before it required a divine corrective. Even a single tear of contrition might have quenched God's anger. Instead, that "flame" (line 1) dissolved the heavens into a deluge to "drown our carnal love" (this does not refer to illicit sex but to loving this physical world to the extent that we lose sight of God; line 4). Perhaps as a consequence of having grown too confident of His love, our dry cheeks and eyes meant that we were forgetting our essentially sinful nature. The pain that this gave Him caused the tears to burst down the "sky's dark cheek" (line 6). Thus the flood can be seen as restoring our proper respect for the condition of our souls at the same time it cleanses the world, a "sweeping" such as that provided by the biblical flood of Noah's time (Genesis 6:17).

Reversing roles in the second stanza, Taylor asks if the heavens were sick and if we were their doctors. Seventeenth-century medicine believed in purging the body of its bad blood and other chemical imbalances, and often achieved these results with laxatives and other purgatives. Thus our sin acted as a corrective dose, making the heavens purge by vomiting and flinging out excrements (line 10). We so grieved them that they "shed their excrements upon our lofty heads" (line 12).

Such powerful images were probably brought to mind by the garbage carried by the floodwaters and perhaps even mudslides, but they would have seemed less alien in that age of home remedies and familial responsibility for sick care. The poet may also have sought out an apt metaphor that would illustrate how repugnant our sin is to God.

"AN UPPER CHAMBER IN A DARK-ENED HOUSE" Frederick Goddard Tuckerman (1860)

This poem sounds like an impact statement by a victim of violence. The central speaker of the poem evidently endured a childhood experience (before "his footsteps reached ripe manhood's brink," line 2) so traumatic that it still haunts him. To the modern mind, only such crimes as incest, rape, or child abuse seem likely to cause such lingering pain that "I cannot rid the thought nor hold it close" (line 4), which means that he cannot forget the incident or face up to it.

A minor technical problem with point-of-view could have been avoided by enclosing the fourth through

14th lines in quotation marks. Thus separated, the first three lines would introduce the situation with a sophisticated, third-person authorial voice ("Terror and anguish were his lot to drink," line 3), and in the rest of the lines the victim would speak for himself in first person. The first line designates the setting where the horrific acts occurred, but metaphorically, they may also allude to the darker recesses of the victim's psyche; he may generally protect himself by compartmentalizing the events in the mental equivalent of "an upper chamber in a darkened house." It is also possible that the speaker shifts point of view as a means of further distancing himself from what may have happened to him at a much younger age. It usually feels much safer to relate something that happened to "him" instead of to "me."

A problem with compartmentalizing trauma is that the brain often still has to work it out; thus "[I] dimly dream upon that man alone" (line 5) suggests that the repressed memory is so emotionally powerful that it increasingly forces itself back to the surface. Although the "autumn clouds" of line 6 may suggest that speaker has entered the third quarter of his life, the cricket is probably chiding him (line 7) for not taking full advantage of the opportunities that still present themselves, like the grass growing "greener than the season" in the next line. In "The Cricket," another poem by the same author, the insect is celebrated for bringing "dim accents from the grave." The implication is that the unresolved issues arising from his childhood trauma may be keeping him from getting on with his adult life.

By choosing to write sonnets, Frederick Goddard Tuckerman created certain expectations in his contemporary audience. Centuries of exposure to its two chief forms led them to believe that, in addition to 14 lines of 10 syllables each, a sonnet must use either of the two rhyme schemes available. For them, the poet began on the right foot with the first four lines rhyming *abba,* although many would bristle at the pairing of "close" with "house," at best almost an eye rhyme that failed to produce the harmony they desired. Instead of following up with another four lines also ending in an *abba* rhyme scheme, as tradition dictated that Petrarchan sonnets must, Tuckerman struck off into a *cdcd* which belonged, if anywhere, in a Shakespearean sonnet, and finished with an even more disappointing *efgehi,* which leaves the last line unrhymed as if he were determined to rob them of what they considered one of the chief pleasures of poetry.

Modern readers, thanks in no small part to the work of WALT WHITMAN and EMILY DICKINSON in schooling the American audience to appreciate poems for their content regardless of deviations from traditional forms or no rhymes at all, do not have these hang-ups. They may miss the point of Tuckerman's audacious experiment, however, for his fourth-line variation in rhyme scheme apparently signals a shift to a second speaker and to an inner, more subjective reality. This second speaker, as one more affected by trauma, seems unable to follow the pattern established in the first three lines or even to continue his own rhyme scheme. Perhaps this breakdown demonstrates how his prior trauma keeps the speaker from realizing such opportunities as they present themselves.

Although the poet did not maintain a traditional rhyme scheme, he may have been relying on his readers' familiarity with the Petrarchan sonnet for yet another effect. Such sonnets have traditionally been divided into an eight-line octave followed by a six-line sestet, which the rhyme schemes clearly delineated. A skilled practitioner might choose to introduce a problem or situation in the octave and its solution or resolution in the sestet just as in this poem Tuckerman shifts to an even more subjective exploration of the effects of the trauma in the last six lines.

Whereas in the past, compartmentalization or other protective strategies evidently enabled the speaker to continue living an outwardly normal life, the ninth line suggests that his defenses are breaking down. Whereas the appearance of his oppressor used to plague his nightmares, it has begun to intrude into his waking moments. Now he appears in his most threatening aspect whenever the speaker closes his eyes or merely shades his brows. His placement beside the "lifted sash" not only situates the perpetrator in the place where the violence occurred, it indicates that the window is open and thus presents no barrier between them. The "swooning" of the speaker's heart (line 11) may be a figurative expression of

how he feels, but it also suggests the onset of physical symptoms.

The dark imagery of the 12th line suggests a trap, for the tree boughs present an additional barrier even if one could climb up or down on the black shingles' slope. In sharp contrast, the final image of the poem consists of the tiny petals of mountain ash scattered on the roof like the smallest, most transitory snows. They might be taken as emblematic of the speaker's lost innocence, irretrievably shattered by the man who violated him.

"URIEL" RALPH WALDO EMERSON (1845) This poem examines the implications of the sad role the title character played in the British Puritan poet John Milton's *Paradise Lost* (1667). In book 3 of *Paradise Lost,* Uriel, Regent of the Sun and one of the seven archangels kept closest to the throne of God, revealed Adam and Eve in their paradise to the dishonored but disguised and jealous Satan. Satan's chief advantage was hypocrisy, which neither man nor angel could detect (line 684). In book 4, Uriel realized his mistake, but Satan was soon tempting the parents of mankind to eat the forbidden fruit despite the efforts of the angels sent to warn them.

Emerson's poem begins before "wild Time coined itself" (line 3) into the calendar divisions of months and days. While walking among the Pleiades (part of the constellation of Taurus, visible in the winter months in the Northern Hemisphere), the famed 13th-century Persian poet Saadi (celebrated in "Saadi," another Emerson poem) overheard young gods talking about physics and metaphysics: "laws of form, and meter just, orb, quintessence and sunbeams" including "what subsisteth, and what seems" (what exists, and what only seems to exist; lines 10–14). One argued that a line is not found in nature (perhaps because any seemingly straight line can be seen, upon greater magnification, to contain many deviations; line 20). Extrapolation from this fact leads him into the dangerous premise that, since "unit and universe are round" (line 22), eventually polar opposites will lead to the same thing (so evil will bless, and ice will burn; line 24).

Line 25 identifies the speaker of that contrary idea as Uriel, whose behavior here represents a radical departure from Milton's Uriel. This one's blasphemy shakes the sky, boding ill to all and bending the balance-beam of Fate (not a gymnastics apparatus, but the balancing arm of a scale; line 31). Hades could not keep the dead in their world, and all slid to confusion (line 34). Thus sad self-knowledge withered the beauty of Uriel (line 36; note that his fate led directly to the similar fall of Adam and Eve). A celestial wind kept angels from speaking of his secret, but the truth remained like a live coal deep within the ashes. Sometimes "truth-speaking things" would shame the angels' veiling wings (lines 47–48). Metaphysical miracles (related to solar, water, or chemical power, "the procession of a soul in matter" [as a consequence of the existence of man], or the good that comes from an evil event [lines 49–53]) would follow. Uriel's "voice of Cherub scorn" (line 54) would again shake the gods and tinge the upper sky with a blush.

"A UTILITARIAN VIEW OF THE MONITOR'S FIGHT" HERMAN MELVILLE (1866)

Looking back at the most famous naval battle of the Civil War led Melville to create his most prescient poem. On May 9, 1862, the *Monitor* of the United States Navy engaged her Confederate counterpart, the *Merrimack,* in a slugfest that forever changed naval warfare. For several centuries prior to their engagement, combat at sea had largely favored the ship with the heaviest effective fire. This led to rows of guns being mounted along the sides and sterns of the vessels, with additional decks being added to accommodate even more guns. Size mattered a great deal because it allowed heavier weapons as well as more of them; since the ships relied on the wind for propulsion, as much sail as the masts and spars could handle was added to offset the added weight.

The *Merrimack* represented an advance in naval armament because its low profile made it a difficult target, and the cannon of the era had great difficulty penetrating its sheet metal. Its primitive steam engine left it so underpowered that it had to be towed into position, but it took advantage of the narrow confines and currents of a river to approach and destroy two much larger wooden warships with relative ease. It soon met its match in the *Monitor,* a similarly ironclad

vessel, and their ineffectual volleys against each other further demonstrated the effectiveness of their innovations. Each easily survived the encounter.

A battle poem might, like the "Star-Spangled Banner," thrill the reader with its pyrotechnics and bristling patriotism. The appeal of this poem, however, is intellectual rather than emotional. Its announced philosophical stance is utilitarian, which asks the reader to bring a rather prosaic practicality to any decision or appraisal. At its most altruistic, in accordance with a popular catchphrase among the followers of Jeremy Bentham, the inventor of the concept, the trick behind wise decision making was to consider the greatest good for the greatest number of people. Bentham's notion of enlightened self-interest encouraged his followers to consider the broader societal implications of their actions as well as their immediate personal benefit.

The title promises an entirely pragmatic view of the encounter stripped of its bombast, a theme repeated in the first stanza. The capitalized War is personified, but describing it with the unidiomatic word "grimed" (line 3) suggests less a stain from human blood than something closer to the message of the poem, the grease and dirt attendant upon the functioning of an industrial machine of the 19th century. The word *Orient* (an adjective as it is used in line 4) suggests the exotic and gaudy opulence of an imperial court at the apex of an East Asian dynasty, as such things were imagined in Europe and America at the time. Note that the "here" of line 3 not only refers to this point in the poem but may also refer to the time and place of the battle; viewed this way, the line implies that war became a depersonalized, entirely mechanized affair at this very point in history. The second stanza welcomes the change because the new emphasis on mechanical power deglamorizes the warriors, displacing them from society's elite to the more mundane level of working men and women.

The reduced status of war is further indicated by a shift in diction from the elevated "strife of fleets heroic" (line 14) to "calculations of caloric" (line 18), a technical term from mechanical engineering referring to the amount of energy required to realize a desired change. The new practice of war is less dependent upon the courage of individual participants (the "fans of banners") than on the timely application of common workshop tools (crank, pivot, and screw are listed in lines 16–17). The fourth stanza evokes the new sound of battle, a "ringing of plates on plates," and implicitly contrasts this "blacksmith's fray" (line 22) with a more heroic moment in American history. The line "Still ringeth round the world" recalls the most famous line of RALPH WALDO EMERSON's immensely popular "Concord Hymn," which commemorated the embattled farmers who "fired the shot heard round the world" to begin the continuous warfare of the American Revolution. The musketry of that battle is implicitly contrasted with the advanced weaponry of modern warfare.

In the guise of the Fates, HERMAN MELVILLE ends the poem with a prophecy that partially came to pass in the stalemated gunnery and mechanized butchery of the 20th century's two world wars. The days of lace, feather, and war-paint, at once symbolic of the proper accoutrements donned in anticipation of direct, even hand-to-hand, contact with the enemy and the first opportunity for an individual to render conspicuous his personal gallantry on the battlefield, were quickly passing. Melville's reference to weathered war-paint (line 26) makes Native American culture seem almost as antiquated as Greek mythology, although the warrior spirit still flourished among the tribes of the American West. The "lace and feather" of the last line are not specifically Native American;

they were still popular adornments of the dress uniforms of ambitious officers hoping to be noticed in the ranks of European and American armies until the First World War. Military attire was becoming more uniform, however, and at least in matters of dress, warriors had already become less grand than the newly rich railroad magnates and other business tycoons in the drawing rooms of late 19th-century America. The optimism inherent in the claim that "War's made less grand than Peace" (lines 28–29) strikes much deeper chords than the poem's surface preoccupation with military finery.

Avid readers of Melville's fiction may feel that this poem represents a missed opportunity. Its author sailed halfway around the world on a whaling voyage, which provided material for his three most important novels, and he also wrote *White Jacket,* a fictionalized account of his brief service on a U.S. Navy ship. One might expect such an old tar to fill such a poem with concrete sensory details gleaned from his firsthand experience on the seas. His assumption of a Utilitarian voice may have been critical to the creation of the poem; its limited perspective could provide an author with a way to reduce his impressions from that rich store of experience to the manageable dimensions required by short poetry. On the other hand, its strict objectivity deprives the reader of an opportunity to imaginatively recreate the battle as he reads this poem.

V

"THE VALLEY OF UNREST" EDGAR ALLAN POE (1831)

This poem visits a small valley (the "dell" of line 1) that once smiled but has been uninhabited and haunted since its people left for the wars or were consumed by them (the phrase "gone unto the wars" could admit either possibility). They trusted to the "mild-eyed stars" (line 4) to keep nightly watch from their sky-blue (the "azure" of line 5) towers (but the fourth line may also vaguely hint that the missing people committed themselves to the war in accordance with favorable astrological signs). All day the red (the color of blood, a connection that suggests the people may have come to a violent end) sunlight lazily lies among the flowers.

Now the sad dell is continually in restless motion except for the brooding airs that linger over its magic solitude (lines 11–12). Note how the term "airs" in reference to the valley's emotional atmosphere pleases almost like a subtle pun because it comes so close to offering an environmental explanation (the winds) for the ceaseless movement. The term "magic" more clearly transitions to the supernatural aspects of the poem, and the locale's solitude implies that no human agent is responsible.

No wind stirs the trees that "palpitate" (a term usually used to describe a racing heart, a connotation that suggests a living animal spirit inhabits the trees; line 15) like the chill seas around the Hebrides (an archipelago [a chain of connected islands] that juts out into the North Atlantic from western Scotland. EDGAR ALLAN POE was probably aware that the isolation and eerie mists of the Hebrides may have contributed to their rich mythical lore, including such things as witches, the production of fairy music emanating from its rocks, and enchanted trees). No wind drives the clouds that continually rustle uneasily through the "unquiet Heaven" (line 17) over the violets (often taken as symbols of faithfulness but probably also mentioned here for their coloration often matching the cloudless sky), and lilies (representing loyalty) that weep and wave over a nameless grave (line 23). As is common in the best ghost tales, an alternative, more realistic explanation is provided for at least some of the seemingly unnatural occurrences: the illusion of their weeping can be attributed to the eternal dews that come down in drops (line 25) from the surrounding mists. The speaker repeats that they weep, however, and focuses on the "perennial tears [that] descend in gems" from their delicate stems.

"VIGIL STRANGE I KEPT ON THE FIELD ONE NIGHT" WALT WHITMAN (1865)

The situation of WALT WHITMAN's poem is revealed in the second line: the speaker and his son were fighting in the same military unit when the younger man was wounded at the father's side. The vigil is strange because of the dual nature of the relationship and because, instead of being a deathwatch, a vigil kept by a care provider (usually a close family relative in the mid-19th century), the son had already died by the

389

time the speaker was able to leave the battle and return to his side.

In the heat of battle father and son were able to exchange a meaningful look (acknowledging that the wound was fatal? recognizing that the speaker must temporarily desert his comrade? pledging his return? apologizing for the state of affairs that brought them to this pass?). The possibilities are endless and include any combination of such feelings or all of them together, and the speaker will have the rest of his life to consider them. The dying man reached out to touch his father's hand, then the speaker rushed back to the battle, where he would remain until relieved (replaced in the frontline by fresh troops) late that night. He found the cold body of his son, who would never again respond to his kisses. Baring the fallen man's face to the starlight, he began his "wondrous" and "sweet" vigil (line 10) in the fragrant night. He neither shed tears nor sighed but passed "sweet . . . immortal and mystic hours" (line 13) remembering his love and care for this dearest comrade and hoping that they will meet again.

As dawn came he carefully wrapped the boy in his blanket and deposited him in his rudely dug grave (line 21) on the spot where he fell. He never forgot that night, his vigil over his dead son's body, or the burial.

It is tempting for a post-Freudian critic to read much into the speaker's repeated emphasis on the younger man's "responding kisses" (lines 7 and 23) and his use of a possessive pronoun in reference to "my son" (lines 2, 14, and 21), "my comrade" (lines 2, 7, 13, and 19) and "my soldier" (lines 14 and 25) and to suggest a possible sexual link between the two men, as if the dead man was not a biological son but only a much younger soldier. The speaker's exclamation of "O boy" when the dying man reaches up to touch his hand in line 4 is also suggestive, as is Whitman's use of the word "comrade" which, in his Calamus poems such as "IN PATHS UNTRODDEN," refers to those who can appreciate songs of "manly attachment." A mid-19th-century American audience, many of whom would have lost close family members in the Civil War, would have shared many of the noble sentiments expressed in this poem without picking up on such seemingly mixed signals.

"A VISION OF HANDSOME LAKE" HANDSOME LAKE (19th century)

The Seneca were the westernmost of the five tribes of the Iroquois Confederation, which dominated upstate New York. By 1800, pressure from white settlement and an increasingly strong American national government made many of the tribe receptive to the message of Handsome Lake, one of their religious prophets who had a vision of a more settled, less aggressive, more agricultural existence. The portion of his teaching presented here endows the domestic corn crop with some of the mysticism more often associated with unusual land formations in the past.

On a bright day in high summer (the time of the second hoeing, line 3, but a more telling detail is that the corn reached the speaker's neck, lines 8–9), the speaker was alone in a cornfield when a maiden appeared and, clasping him around the neck, said that "we" want to follow him to the next world. He looked for her, but found only the corn leaves wrapped around his shoulders.

Native American prophets not only had visions but also sometimes interpreted them. In this instance, the speaker understood that the spirit of the corn, "the sustainer of life," had spoken. He responded that the corn should stay on earth and remain faithful to its purpose, feeding the children of women. This is only the beginning of his teaching.

Although Handsome Lake died in 1815, the alternative religion he founded helped his people more peacefully transition into the changing political and economic landscape of their native region.

"VOLCANOES BE IN SICILY" EMILY DICKINSON (published 1914)

EMILY DICKINSON disliked travel, and although she had enough background in world geography to know that volcanoes can be found in Sicily (where Mt. Etna has been periodically erupting for around half a million years) and South America (where almost all the countries with a Pacific coast have active volcanoes), she did not yearn for firsthand experience with them.

Instead, she looked inside herself and, within her geography (line 3), found volcanoes, or at least forces that seemed as powerful. The carelessness with which she discusses the similarity ("A Lava step at any time/

Am I inclined to climb," lines 5–6) may convey her own lack of interest at the same time that it increases reader interest in her volatile nature. A complete lack of punctuation adds a layer of playful yet distracting ambiguity to the poem; sentence portions are tumbled together like volcanic debris. By examining herself or perhaps the frictions in her intimate circle, she may contemplate Vesuvius, the most famous volcano in Europe. Of special interest is the location of a crater (line 7) in that home environment; it suggests a prior explosion or active volcanic activity instead of the mere potential for such destruction.

W

"WALDEINSAMKEIT" Raph Waldo Emerson **(1858)** Although Walden Pond in rural Massachusetts will forever be associated with the book by Henry David Thoreau covering the months beginning in 1845 that he spent in the small cabin he constructed there, Ralph Waldo Emerson owned the land and frequented its shores. *Walde* is the German word for "forest," and the title of this poem might be translated into English as "Forest Isolation" or "Forest Solitude." This poem is not about Walden Pond (references to the sea and mountain crests disqualify it as the specific locale), but instead celebrates the restorative power of communing with wild nature almost anywhere you can find it. The subject probably struck Emerson as sufficiently philosophical to suggest the use of common meter: as in many hymns, the quatrains (usually) alternate lines of eight and six feet, and every other line rhymes.

The poem begins at the sea, where the speaker reveals much in the simple declaration that he does not count the hours he spends wandering (lines 1–2). This implies that he does count the hours he spends elsewhere, probably because his working life demands such accounting and/or because he finds life so tedious. To refer to the forest as his loyal friend suggests that he may have had difficulties with humans in that role. He turns to nature to heal these or other wounds, and the antiquated verb form "useth" implies that he views the wilderness with the same reverence and with many of the same expectations that other people might turn to God.

The syntax of the second stanza is convoluted as if the speaker were just beginning to unwind from the pressures of his normal life. The plains offer room for the shadows of the surrounding hills to lie (on a metaphorical level, the hills could represent the speaker's troubles and the wide-open spaces temporarily remove the weight of their shadows from his soul). Streams not only serve as protective boundaries from the pressures of the civilized world, they also awaken the speaker to the transcendent beauty of nature as it manifests itself in the colors they reflect from the sky. They might literally take on such hues, but with the exception of mists and related phenomena, they are unlikely to actually give color to the sky (line 7). Metaphorically, the speaker may be suggesting that the presence of streams may change one's emotional realization of his surroundings.

Mountains and oaken glades are also conducive to recuperation, and by line 11 the speaker is wondering why he bothers with the artificial restraints of time when the day was made to escape such pressures. Cities of miserable people (the "woe-begone" of line 13) mock the "fantastic care" (healing) available in such serious, isolated landscapes, but the things they treasure will tarnish as they become surfeited with pleasure (represented by nauseatingly sweet or "cloying" honey in line 17). They may seem merry to mask their sadness, but true joy is found in the sober heart of the woods.

Such considerations bring to mind "the great Planter" (line 21), a euphemism for God since he plants worlds of grain and enchants "the souls that walk in pain" (humanity; line 24). The rose of beauty still burns on all his creation just as immortal youth returns (presumably in successive generations) despite trying times and formal changes.

The eighth stanza celebrates birds in their respective habitats: the black duck (a regionally common color variant of the mallard) flying up from the lake, the pigeon in pines, and the bittern producing his characteristic call (for which the species acquired the local name of "boomer") each make a "desert" (a place facilitating meditation and relaxation) that can not be refined by human artistry.

By the middle of the 19th century, urban New England had become so alienated from nature as to actually fear it, a situation that Emerson tries to confront in the ninth stanza by dredging up myths so old that no one believed in them any more. Hence he points out the "watery nook" with "bearded mists" (line 34) that hides the "gray old gods whom Chaos knew." This refers to the earliest moment in Greek mythology when only Chaos existed; the inference is that there are no evil spirits in the wilderness. In the next stanza, he argues that "the sweet breath of song" can be found only in the breezes of the uplands where only the brave visit even though they belong to everyone (his point is two-fold: only in solitude can one connect with the natural impulses informing the best creative endeavors and only those brave enough to try something new in their art can achieve universal acclaim). In the 10th stanza, he advises leaving the books behind. You should develop your own eyes and directly experience nature instead of adopting perspectives from authors.

Wisdom, thrift, and temporary relief ("sleep") from the usual worldly cares can be found in such oblivion (as solitude in nature brings; lines 45–46). Such a "proud idleness" crowns (surpasses but at the same time elevates) all your "mean" (as in average, everyday, and normal) affairs.

WAR AND ANTIWAR POETRY Four
centuries of intermittent warfare between European colonists who turned into American pioneers and the Native Americans who sought to preserve their livelihoods, their ancestral lands and, finally, their

lives inspired very little poetry by the greatest American writers in English prior to 1900. One of the best accounts of a small-scale raid is LUCY TERRY's " BARS FIGHT," which chronicled a raid near Deerfield, Massachusetts, on August 25, 1746. By examining the disposition of the killed and wounded on the battlefield, Terry's seemingly objective report effectively conveyed the suddenness of the attack and its apparent atrocities without the burden of the didactic pronouncements a sentimental poet of the mid-19th century would have felt compelled to add.

Two hundred and thirty years later, WALT WHITMAN's account of the Battle of the Little Bighorn ("From Far Dakota's Canyons") reads more like the newspaper accounts of Custer's last stand upon which it was based than an eyewitness account of a battle or its aftermath. Correctly judging that his initial audience would be familiar with the events of June 25, 1876, he begins with a few details that, despite their paucity, manage to embody the spirit of a life-or-death struggle in what habitués of an eastern metropolis would view as the great American desert: "Land of the wild ravine, the dusky Sioux, the lonesome stretch [and] the silence." His depiction of the cavalry company's "fighting to the last in sternest heroism" in tight circles behind the horses slaughtered for breastworks resembles a popular visual artist's rendering of the fight instead of the more disordered rout that modern historians have reconstructed based on forensic evidence. Whitman embraced the romanticized image of "the loftiest of life upheld by death" as "the old, old legend of our race," a modern proof of the supposed superiority of the American spirit. Custer, in Whitman's rendering, was a lightning flash who "ended well in death;" his tawny hair flowing in battle like that of Samson, or some other biblical warrior, offers a vivid contrast to the "dusky" Sioux whose primitive treachery (an ambush! Whitman implies, although modern historians acknowledge that it was Custer who planned a surprise attack) overcame Custer's nobility. Like Christ, Custer "yielded up [him]self," leaving "a memory sweet to soldiers" (for a more balanced view of the battle and an account of the varied ways successive generations have dealt with the Custer myth, see Evan S. Connell's *Son of the Morning Star*).

By the early 19th century, what had been viewed as an Indian menace to the frontier towns of the eastern states had been reduced to the point where such poems as PHILIP FRENEAU's "The INDIAN BURYING GROUND" and WILLIAM CULLEN BRYANT's "An INDIAN AT THE BURIAL-PLACE OF HIS FATHERS" could begin marveling at a few of the less threatening aspects of Native American culture. That changed with the publication of the first of five of James Fenimore Cooper's widely popular Leatherstocking novels (a series including *The Last of the Mohicans,* 1826), when both the warrior and the frontiersman were romanticized to the point where they resemble supermen. The most numerous of the tribes east of the Mississippi River had by that time become thoroughly dispossessed and displaced, a process culminating in the Indian Removal Act of 1830, which exiled the Cherokee from Georgia to Oklahoma territory. Within that historical context, LYDIA SIGOURNEY's "The INDIAN's WELCOME TO THE PILGRIM FATHERS" (1835) can be viewed as a more inflammatory protest poem that it might seem in a later century. FRANCES OSGOOD crossed cultural and religious lines to embrace an example of self-sufficient womanhood in "The INDIAN MAID's REPLY TO THE MISSIONARY" (1850). Later, Walt Whitman could admire a warrior's stoic acceptance of death in "OSCEOLA" and adopt an Iroquois term (in "YONNONDIO") as an appropriately dour lament for the passage of all cultures, a lesson he applies to his own. By the end of the 19th century, the Bureau of Indian Affairs had begun translating and preserving NATIVE AMERICAN POETRY, including the exceptionally beautiful "AT THE TIME OF THE WHITE DOVE," but such gestures of appreciation of tribal cultures came too late to preserve their traditional ways of life in the uninterrupted forests and on the open plains.

The most commonly anthologized poem about the American Revolutionary War was the "CONCORD HYMN" created by RALPH WALDO EMERSON in 1836 for the dedication ceremonies of a monument to the citizen soldiers who first repulsed an attack by the British regulars in 1775. The poems written during that war were often slanderous satires or rhymed chronicles. The popular "Yankee Doodle" was initially a rather nonsensical refrain to which additional lyrics could be penned by anyone who cared as a means of showing support for the rebellion. Propagandists were quick to use the day's events as fodder for their poems. On the Loyalist side, "Burrowing Yankees" satirized the patriots' effective use of breastworks. Despite the fact that they proved so effective in the Battle of Bunker Hill on June 17, 1775, and led to the British withdrawal from Boston in March of 1776, the anonymous poet predicted that the cause would fail as soon as the Yankees discovered the effects of British steel in the hands of well-disciplined soldiers. The most famous of the Loyalist poets, Jonathan Odell, contrasted the former prosperity attendant upon peaceful obedience with the certain failure of the rebellion in "A BIRTHDAY SONG" for the king in 1777.

For the Patriots, Francis Hopkinson could turn a largely unsuccessful attempt in 1777 to mine the Delaware River with floating kegs of gunpowder into a farcical poem "The Battle of the Kegs," which revealed some fear in the disorganized response of the British navy and some amusement at those enemies' reports of how bravely they all acted in the face of this overblown threat. The early satires of PHILIP FRENEAU poked fun at the British commanders, but by 1781 he could add an account of his own captivity in "The British Prison Ship" and mourn the dead in "TO THE MEMORY OF THE BRAVE AMERICANS."

Although the War of 1812 produced a string of military defeats for the young nation's arms, one of which led to the occupation of the nation's capital and the burning of the White House (August 24, 1814), it also produced Francis Scott Key's "The Battle of Fort McHenry." It is clearly among the best war poems ever written in America and has the distinction of being penned by an eyewitness to an important battle (the fate of the nation was imperiled by the prior success of the enemy) on the day after it occurred. The poem commences with the moment when the speaker first returns to the main deck following the British fleet's bombardment of Fort McHenry in the Battle of Baltimore (September 12–15, 1814). Having witnessed the prior evening's rockets and bombs, he is predictably anxious about the outcome of the battle and presses a fellow prisoner for information. The issue is still in doubt at the conclusion of the first stanza, the only one commonly sung, and the speaker ends by rephrasing his initial question in a way that so memorably ties in the flag as a symbol with the country's values of freedom and courage. Slight variations in the last two lines of the first stanza serve as the refrain for the other stanzas.

The second stanza refers to the British army besieging the fort as a haughty host, and captures the very moment when the morning sun first disclosed the flag, a revelation beautifully reflected in the water. It is interesting how in the next stanza, with the outcome of the battle increasingly certain, the enemy troops are described with increasing vehemence. The speaker searches in vain for the band of hirelings and slaves (the British soldiers) who swore they would take the country. They have nor refuge but terrified flight or a gloomy grave, but first their blood must wash away "their foul footsteps' pollution." The last stanza prays to heaven always to rescue the land as long as free men stand between their home and war. It is a testament to the perceived power of religion in the new republic that the speaker trusts in the nation's devotion to God to insure conquests in just causes and that the banner will continue to wave in triumph. Key began the poem while still in British custody and finished it after his release on September 16. A publisher changed the title to its present form later that month, and "The Star-Spangled Banner" was made the national anthem in 1931.

The War of 1812 also gave the USS *Constitution* a fair chance at poetic immortality. Commissioned in Boston in 1797, it performed admirably in an undeclared naval war with France (1797–1800) and in the War with the Barbary Pirates (1801–05; it was later referred to as the Tripolitan War so as not to infuriate the former foes). Its greatest glory came in the War of 1812, however, when it overcame the British frigates *Guerriere* and *Java* and several smaller vessels. It was scheduled for demolition until it caught the eye of OLIVER WENDELL HOLMES in 1830, and "OLD IRONSIDES," his poetic tribute, led to the preservation of the ship.

That second war with England ended when that foe finally overcame Napoleon, a victory that rendered unnecessary its prior assaults on American shipping that had largely precipitated the war. Before the final exile of the French emperor in 1815, however, an American poet had died in the aftermath of Napo-

leon's disastrous Russian winter campaign of 1812. JOEL BARLOW's final poem, "ADVICE TO A RAVEN IN RUSSIA," conveyed his disgust with the emperor's military adventures.

The war with Mexico (1846–48) produced no poetry deemed worthy of inclusion by the editors of the major 21st-century anthologies of American literature. Half a century later, the Spanish-American War (1898) produced several jingoistic songs, but none of them has found their way into the general literary anthologies of the current century.

The long buildup to the American Civil War can be seen in the increasingly abundant antislavery poetry of the northern states. Early on, such poets as SARAH LOUISA FORTEN tried to humanize the suffering of an oppressed people in poems like "The SLAVE" and "The SLAVE GIRL'S FAREWELL." By midcentury, poets like FRANCES ELLEN WATKINS HARPER could be more directly inflammatory in their protests, as such poems as "An APPEAL TO THE AMERICAN PEOPLE," "BURY ME IN A FREE LAND" and "FREE LABOR" attest. The entry on AFRICAN-AMERICAN POETRY in this book hints at some of the lasting damage that racism caused, and ANTISLAVERY POETRY discusses some of the efforts by numerous poets to overcome this injustice.

War seemed increasingly inevitable despite the implied threats by major poets such as HENRY WADSWORTH LONGFELLOW's "The ARSENAL AT SPRINGFIELD" and the less veiled threats of JOHN GREENLEAF WHITTIER's "MASSACHUSETTS TO VIRGINIA." In "ICHABOD," Whittier castigated Daniel Webster for his role in the Compromise of 1850, by which the Massachusetts statesman tried to avert war by endorsing the Fugitive Slave Act and other pernicious laws. New states were allowed to vote on whether to enter the Union as either slaveholding or free, a development that had the unforeseen consequence of sectarian violence as waves of northerners and southerners inundated Kansas in hopes of securing it for their side. Whittier's "LETTER FROM A MISSIONARY" presented a jaundiced analysis of the situation supposedly from the southern point of view. The country quickened its pace on the path to war when the militant abolitionist John Brown tried to free the slaves by starting a violent revolt in Virginia. Northern poetry such as Whittier's "BROWN OF

OSSAWATOMIE" and HERMAN MELVILLE's "THE PORTENT" lionized the captured freedom fighter even though he was put to death by the order of a criminal court. Brown was such an important symbol that his fate led to one of the two most important songs to come from the war. JULIA WARD HOWE heard Union soldiers singing a rather ghoulish song ("JOHN BROWN's BODY") and was inspired to write "The BATTLE HYMN OF THE REPUBLIC" to the same tune.

Equally famous but frequently controversial in later centuries because it came to be viewed as a rallying cry for slavery is "Dixie," created by Dan Emmett in 1859 and adopted as the unofficial anthem of the Confederacy. No poetry books were printed in the South during the war, but topical poems flooded the newspapers on both sides of the Mason-Dixon line. Southern poetry is rarely presented in general literature anthologies, however, although the common soldier's plight is evident in a folk song, "The REBEL SOLDIER." HENRY TIMROD's "CHARLESTON" dates from the second year of the war, and the city that began the conflict with a barrage on the Union's Fort Sumter in its harbor was still well fortified and prosperous. By 1866, as Timrod's "ODE" to the Confederate dead indicates, the city lacked even the funds to erect a memorial to its fallen heroes. The other widely anthologized southern poet, SYDNEY LANIER, is usually remembered in general anthologies for "The SHIP OF EARTH," a postapocalyptic vision perhaps inspired by the devastation he witnessed in the wartorn South.

Northern perspectives on the Civil War are far more frequently anthologized, and the two writers whose anthologized poems give the most complete view of the Civil War are HERMAN MELVILLE and Walt Whitman. Melville's war poetry begins with "MISGIVINGS," a comparison of a destructive thunderstorm with the dark clouds of political unrest gathering on the prewar horizon. He studied the strangely joyous mood of the Union army in "The MARCH INTO VIRGINIA," but the picnic spirit was dashed when they ran into a waiting Southern army of approximately equal numbers at Bull Run in 1861. Death frequently comes as a surprise to individual soldiers in poetry (as in Longfellow's "KILLED AT THE FORD" and STEPHEN CRANE's "WAR IS KIND"), and Whittier focused on the bees his speaker finds on a

battlefield (in "The HIVE AT GETTYSBURG") instead of the two fully engaged armies that had so recently clashed on that hallowed ground. Melville and Whitman are unique among the popularly anthologized poets in that several of their poems present an entire battlefield.

Melville's "MALVERN HILL" follows the war into its second year, when a Northern army slugged its way south to within 80 miles of the Southern capital of Richmond, Virginia, in the Seven Days Battles. The speaker in the poem is a veteran who returns to the battlefield in the following May, repopulating it with the mutilated bodies of his fallen comrades in his imagination but proud of the fact that the bulk of the army was able to retreat in force instead of in a rout. In April of 1862, a Southern army almost overran Ulysses S. Grant's Army of Tennessee, a battle remembered in Melville's "SHILOH." Once again the speaker is a returning veteran who appreciates the natural beauty of the area and the silence he finds over the graves of his fallen comrades. As they died, he suggests, individual soldiers made a separate peace with their former enemies.

The subject of "COMMEMORATIVE OF A NAVAL VICTORY," one of the two popular Melville poems covering the war at sea, finds no such peace, as he is tormented by the destruction his vessel wrought on his brother sailors even though he is celebrated in postwar society. The internal evidence of that poem does not indicate a specific battle. "A UTILITARIAN VIEW OF THE MONITOR's FIGHT" covers the slugfest between two ironclad vessels on March 9, 1862. Melville's unique take on the battle is that it ushered in a new age of warfare dominated by ponderous machines that challenged the prominence that individual warriors sometimes had had in previous conflicts.

The third year of the conflict brought the only violence of the war that Melville personally witnessed; on July 13, 1863, a New York City riot against the military draft escalated into a murderous race riot that had to be suppressed by Union veterans of the Gettysburg battle. The poet preserved his thoughts on the ship and wharf rats who terrorized the city in "The HOUSE-TOP: A NIGHT PIECE." Imaginatively returning to the front lines, in "An UNINSCRIBED MONUMENT," Melville offered the suggestion that the silence one finds in the wilderness area near Richmond in which the Southern army continued to hold the line in 1864 was in some way a greater tribute to the memory of the fallen soldiers than a physical monument could be.

If the former naval officer in "Commemorative of a Naval Victory" is haunted by his memories, the speaker in Melville's "The COLLEGE COLONEL" can only wonder at the changes a soldier's experience must have made in the officer who rides so inscrutably through a victory parade with his wounded arm and missing leg.

Walt Whitman's war poems were informed not only by his personal experience as a volunteer in the military hospitals but also by the accounts of battle he heard from the soldiers he met there. The speaker in "The WOUND-DRESSER" had much in common with the poet; both initially supported the war (see Whitman's "BEAT! BEAT! DRUMS!"). Their attitudes changed as they commenced their service. Unlike the poet, the speaker saw active service as a soldier and can recall a forced march before charging into battle. One of the poet's best battlefield scenes can be found in "The ARTILLERYMAN'S VISION;" it includes a description of the classic Civil War battle in that skirmishers are used for reconnaissance and then a succession of artillery and small arms fire marks the approach of the opposing line. The unique perspective afforded artillery units (which profit from placement upon whatever elevated ground could be found so as to maximize their range) enabled him to witness the deployment of infantry, cavalry (also see "CAVALRY CROSSING A FORD") and other artillery units. Only after a battle, or during a lull in the fighting necessitated by the darkest night, does the speaker in "LOOK DOWN FAIR MOON" have time to really see the human carnage that surrounds him. As if in rebellion against God for permitting such savagery, he prays only to the clouds for a rain that would alleviate the thirst of the wounded still laying in the field and cleanse the spilled human blood from the earth. In less threatening times, a similarly elevated perspective sometimes exposed soldiers to landscapes of exquisite beauty (such as that described in "A BIVOUAC ON A MOUNTAIN SIDE") that they would have never seen in civilian life.

Some signs of a battle are not so easily erased either from the fields or from the memory, however, and in "AS TOILSOME I WANDER'D IN VIRGINIA'S WOODS," the speaker, by then so familiar with an army's movements that he can recognize the speed with which it was sometimes forced to move, discovers a hastily dug grave with a quickly penned note attesting to the fallen man's courage and devotion. For the speaker in "THE WOUND-DRESSER" and for the poet as well, a chance exposure to a field hospital like that described in "A MARCH IN RANKS HARD-PREST, AND THE ROAD UNKNOWN" revealed a hellish scene that he forced himself to observe in its many painful details so as to serve as a witness for humanity. In "A SIGHT IN THE DAYBREAK GRAY AND DIM," the speaker encountered three unavoidable products of the war and the hurried surgery that followed so closely on its heels. A soldier in "VIGIL STRANGE I KEPT ON THE FIELD ONE NIGHT" found his deathwatch over his wounded comrade, brother, or perhaps biological son interrupted by the urgent necessity of fighting off the enemy.

Like the newspaper accounts almost daily conveying casualty reports from the war, Whitman's war poems were steeped in death and blood. Even after four years of fighting so intense that 10,000 men could die in a single afternoon, however, the assassination of President Lincoln still managed to shock the nation. The title of Melville's "THE MARTYR" reveals the prevailing Northern sentiment for the fallen leader, and eulogies by William Cullen Bryant ("ABRAHAM LINCOLN") and Walt Whitman ("WHEN LILACS LAST IN THE DOORYARD BLOOM'D") are frequently anthologized. After the war, many of the nation's soldiers (like the speaker in Whitman's "RECONCILIATION") were ready to embrace their former enemies as fellow sufferers in the great tragedy. The war had taken hundreds of thousands of lives, but only by such a sacrifice could the nation lift a terrible curse from its head. Harper's jubilation at the death of slavery is evident in her poem, "FIFTEENTH AMENDMENT." Whittier expressed similar although more subdued sentiments in "LAUS DEO."

BIBLIOGRAPHY

Anonymous. *National songster; or, A collection of the most admired patriotic songs, on the brilliant victories, achieved by the naval and military heroes of the United States of America, over equal and superior forces of the British. From the best American authors.* Hagerstown, Md.: John Gruber and Daniel May, 1814.

Barrett, Faith, and Cristanne Miller, eds. *Words for the Hour: A New Anthology of American Civil War Poetry.* Amherst: University of Massachusetts Press, 2005.

Browne, Francis F., ed. *Bugle-Echoes: A Collection of Poems of the Civil War, Northern and Southern.* New York: White, Stokes & Allen, 1886.

Brownlee, James Henry, comp. *War-time Echoes; Patriotic Poems, Heroic and Pathetic, Humorous and Dialectic, of the Spanish-American War.* New York: Werner, 1898.

Connell, Evan S. *Son of the Morning Star.* New York: Harper & Row, 1985.

Eggleston, George Cary, ed. *American War Ballads and Lyrics: A Collection of the Songs and Ballads of the Colonial Wars, the Revolution, the War of 1812–15, the War with Mexico, and the Civil War.* New York: Putnam, 1889.

Goldensohn, Lorrie. *American War Poetry: An Anthology.* New York: Columbia University Press, 2006.

Hubner, Charles William. *War Poets of the South and Confederate Camp-Fire Songs.* Atlanta, Ga.: University Press Byrd, 1896.

Mason, Emily V., ed. *The Southern Poems of the War.* Baltimore: J. Murphy & Co., 1867.

Moore, Frank, ed. *Rebel Rhymes and Rhapsodies.* New York: G. P. Putnam, 1864.

Moss, William. *Confederate Broadside Poems: An Annotated Descriptive Bibliography Based on the Collection of the Z. Smith Reynolds Library of Wake Forest University.* Westport, Conn.: Meckler, 1988.

Wilson, Edmund. *Patriotic Gore: Studies in the Literature of the American Civil War.* London: A. Deutsch, 1962.

"WAR IS KIND" Stephen Crane **(1896)** The effectiveness of Stephen Crane's antiwar poem stems from its seeming objectivity, but its argument and its imagery have been so well crafted that a reader's logic and emotion usually arrive at the same conclusion, a refutation of its title. It appeared at a time when American jingoism was at its highest; many people were seeking a pretext for grabbing Puerto Rico, Cuba, the Philippines, and other islands from the overextended Spanish empire so that their own country would be recognized as a great nation in that imperialistic age. The militarily successful if morally questionable Spanish-American War of 1898 represented the culmination of their desires.

The title and refrain (a phrase that reappears at predictable intervals) of this poem challenged the aggressive mood of the nation by summing up all the benefits its advocates advanced for the war in a single, untenable maxim (logicians call this tactic, much beloved by satirists, *reductio ad absurdum*). The first stanza juxtaposes two interrelated scenes, the consolation of a weeping maiden and the death of her lover on a battlefield. The omniscient speaker is so objective that his indifference seems an affront. Instead of attempting to comfort the woman (significantly, he calls her "maiden" instead of using her name) with more suitable aphorisms, he uses his catchphrase. He exhibits even less feeling as he reveals the details of her lover's death, savoring the dramatic image when the soldier "threw wild hands" (line 2) toward the sky instead of considering the negative effect the image could have on the woman. He might argue that war is kind (soothingly repeating the phrase as one might repeat a nursery rhyme to an infant he considered too undeveloped to comprehend anything), but the speaker is definitely not kind. His gaze followed the soldier's horse (glamorized as the "affrighted steed" of line 3) as an object of more interest than the dying man.

In the third stanza he comforts a baby in his accustomed manner. Without the distraction of a gallivanting horse, the speaker was able to keep his attention focused on the dying gestures of its father in the infantry: a raging "at his breast" (line 14; an area of the body commonly spoken of as the source and storehouse of the pride, courage, patriotism, and whatever else may have brought him to the war, as well as of the love he will now be unable to shower on the child), a "gulp" (this term for the last physical act of the dying man that the speaker will describe conveys the possibility of the soldier's desperate awareness of his plight, or it may have been a mere reflexive action), and the moment of death (evidently a phenomenon with which the speaker is so well acquainted that he does not describe it here). The "yellow trench" (line 13) into which the man had fallen not only prefigures his grave, it reveals the deft touch of an artist who is able to render a scene vividly with the barest minimum of concrete sensory details. Like a masterstroke by the impressionist painters who were ensuring their enduring popularity at that time, it anticipates the abstract focus on color and line that fascinated later artists. The poet's choice of yellow (which is a slang term for cowardice as well as one of the primary colors) may suggest that the speaker found this death less heroic than that of the mounted man of the first stanza. It seems a singularly unhealthy hue, perhaps ever linked with jaundice and the deadly yellow fever. Similarly revealing may be the description of this soldier's "tumbling" (line 13; the verb can imply a lack of dignity) and the contrast between his downward physical movement and the first soldier's upraised arms.

That he would end up in a trench reflects the evolution of warfare to the point of individual anonymity; weaponry had become so advanced by the time of the American Civil War that battles could sometimes be stalemated for months with only a small killing field (appropriately called a *no man's land*) separating the two sides. Individual gallantry is less apparent under such conditions, and trenches were often used as communal graves for the many deaths that such continual contact with the enemy (or a single ill-advised frontal assault) could bring.

Interspersed between the three stanzas in which soldiers' relatives are informed of their deaths are two stanzas that further challenge the conventional portrayals of heroic battlefield deeds. Even those little-souled men "born to drill and die" who thirst for a fight are reduced to "hoarse, booming drums" (lines 6–8). Above them "the unexplained glory flies" (line 9); although on one level the phrase suggests that some people actually do receive distinguishing honors on the battlefield, the deeds for which they gain fame would invite censure in any other sphere of human action. On another level, the American flag bears the epithet of Old Glory; referring to such a venerated object as "unexplained" questions whether the nation's policies have been sufficiently examined. To the speaker, it represents the kingdom of the battle god, a field of a thousand corpses.

Although the fourth stanza deals with a battle flag instead of the national flag, it is emblazoned with the eagle that has been a symbol of national power since the Revolutionary War. Under this "swift blazing flag" (line 17) the soldiers are schooled in the virtue of slaughter and the excellence of killing (lines 20–21), ideally being exposed to the field of a thousand corpses as an example of what might be accomplished. By withhold-ing even the names of the three soldiers whose kin are notified in this poem, the poet has suggested the relative meaninglessness of their sacrifice. No one in their army of men "who thirst for a fight" (line 7) will suffer their deaths as will the members of their families.

In the last stanza the speaker consoles the mother of a dead soldier. In sharp contrast to the colorful ribbons and medals awarded by the military, the artist Crane imagines her heart "hung humble as a button" (line 23) on her son's splendid shroud.

"THE WARNING" HENRY WADSWORTH LONGFELLOW (1842)

The depth of New England sentiment against slavery can be measured in the willingness of its most popular poets to lend their voices to the cause. To defend themselves against charges of immorality, slaveholders turned to the Bible for Old Testament precedents and (far less successfully) justifications for the abominable institution. To counteract that trend, in this poem the speaker draws on the story of Samson (Genesis 10:20–30) to suggest the danger that slavery posed to the nation.

Samson, so strong that he killed a lion with his bare hands (lines 2–3), warred against the Philistines so determinedly that he killed hundreds of them using only the jawbone of an ass. His fatal weakness was his love for Delilah, who persuaded him to reveal that the key to his strength was his hair. She cut it while he slept, and the Philistines blinded the newly vulnerable man before making him their slave and subjecting him to all the humiliations the surviving relatives and countrymen of his victims could devise.

Unfortunately for thousands of Philistines, Samson's strength returned as his hair grew out, and as described in the second stanza, he was able to bring down their temple by pushing on its columns.

Slavery is like the poor blind Samson in that it has the potential to shake the pillars of the American commonwealth until the "vast Temple of our liberties" (line 17) is reduced to rubbish. Note that the American Samson in this poem is one of the slaves. A widespread slave rebellion was the worst fear of many southerners.

"WAR SONG" ANONYMOUS (published 1935)

The plains of northern Wyoming upon which Crow

Indians lived until their displacement by white settlers were also frequented by other warlike tribes. This war song had the important advantage of brevity, a hint of metaphysical permanence (since the heavens and the earth were perceived as eternal), and a disparaging glance at the poverty-stricken decrepitude faced by those elderly who did not fall on a battlefield in the fullness of their youth. At first glance the last line may seem counterintuitive because of its tacit admission that fear is the natural emotion in a battle, and the entire song seems predicated on the calculation that a rational consideration of an even less desirable alternative will make possible dismemberment or death in battle appear less undesirable.

On the other hand, for their intended audience these three short lines may have touched on beliefs deeply held by the entire Crow nation. If, for example, they believed in an afterlife in which fallen warriors would become as eternal as heaven and earth, the short reminder of this promise in the first line may have been all that was needed. Regardless of its content, however, the ritual of singing such a prescribed song in the face of adversity probably went a long way toward achieving the desired calming effect.

"THE WAYFARER" Stephen Crane (1899)

This simple but effective poem presents STEPHEN CRANE's corollary to the maxim that the truth hurts: That is why everyone avoids it. The speaker observes a man whom he identifies only as a "wayfarer" (a traveler) who happens to perceive the path to truth (line 2). Astonished, the man followed it until he realized that each weed was a knife. Then he mumbled that there are other roads.

Crane's speaker delivers the anecdote in a succession of short declarative sentences as though he were merely relaying this information as the events unfolded before him. The effect of this seemingly objective approach is enhanced by his refusal to supply the reader with any logical connections that would aid her in processing the information he provides; the events are simply narrated in chronological order. This also leads the reader to question the traveler's perspicacity: Has he truly found the path to truth or merely perceived that he has? Is he astonished because of his find, or because

such a seemingly important path was covered with weeds (line 4)? Is his unwillingness to persist on the path to truth a result of his flawed character, or does the poem suggest that truth is beyond human capacity? Does he mumble because he is a traveler and hence a mere dilettante who gives up, whereas great discoveries and true leadership are the natural province of the men and women who persist? There is little evidence in any of Crane's poetry to suggest that he believes in such superior people.

The poem refutes the optimism of those who would argue, for example, that the road to heaven is straight and true.

"WE TWO" Sarah Morgan Bryan Piatt (1874)

In the biblical book bearing his name, Job is a God-fearing, extraordinarily prosperous, truly good man whose chief fear was that his sons were not sincere in their piety. His fears in this regard were perhaps not unfounded, because Satan showed up when the sons came into God's presence. Satan had evidently been investigating at God's command, because the Lord asked for his consideration of Job (Job 1:8). Satan had nothing bad to report but pointed out that Job's faith, like that of the internal audience of Piatt's poem, had not been tested by adversity.

The opening stanza establishes the internal audience's beauty, wealth, and easy piety, which makes her content with God's will. Like the devil's representative, in the second stanza the speaker asks if that audience would be so content if God's will included famine, flood, death (with a hint at the horror of premature burial because the coffin shuts in her face, line 6), and disease (represented by a worm in the bud of a rose she wears in her hair). What if she lost her looks, her picture-perfect life, her guiding light (her faith or, perhaps, her sight), and lace?

Thus far the speaker has used simple rhymes like "hair/fair" and "face/lace" as if to mimic the lack of critical thinking by the internal audience. The third stanza implicitly challenges such complacency by using biblical verb forms and presenting two of the dangers of Psalms 91:5–6 (although here, as if to illustrate the speaker's challenge to gospel truth, it is the arrow that flies in the dark and the pestilence that walks by day.

Perhaps this version better illustrates the will of God since it diminishes the role of the human archer. Any shot hitting its mark in the darkness has traditionally been attributed to either blind luck or divine guidance). Similarly, the clods in the valley as well as the rocks on high (line 11; a reference to Job 21:33, where the point is that the soil might seem sweet to the man whose mental and spiritual life are centered in this world but that such worldly men will perish) might be viewed as representative of those things which Job was denied as he was tested by the Lord. The speaker asks if the internal audience could maintain her faith in the face of similar trials.

Because the internal audience has been getting everything she wants, the speaker contends that God's will and hers seem to have the same aims (lines 13–14). She should take no more credit for appearing to act in accordance with God's will than should a lily that keeps His dew (line 15; "dew" may pun on *due,* with the point being that instead of priding herself on acting in accordance with what she perceives is God's will, the internal audience should realize that God has yet to exact his due).

Unlike her audience, the speaker fully feels the weight of her devotion to God. Apparently feeling inherently sinful, in the fifth stanza she reveals meeting His reproach with desolate tears (line 19). Although the speaker apparently feels that the promise of heaven awaits her, she also feels that she will be no better than dust until she dies (line 20). God's will is not her will (line 20), but at the end of the world (when she meets the Lord, lines 21–22), the Lord will accept the speaker precisely because she follows His will and not her own.

"WE WEAR THE MASK" Paul Laurence Dunbar (1895)

Among the most painful of all the survival strategies imposed on an oppressed minority by the presence of an overwhelmingly hostile majority is maintaining the pretense that problems do not exist. In a nation that denied basic civil rights to a people whose ancestors were kidnapped from their native land, where open bigotry often proved the decisive advantage in political campaigns, and where an ill-timed smile could lead to a lynching, the ugly face of oppression dissolves the fraternal bonds that naturally occur among men.

Part of being human is that we all have to wear masks at various times as a necessary means of getting along in society. The profound difference in the speaker's experience in this poem by Paul Laurence Dunbar is the depth of his/her suffering. He is exceedingly uncomfortable with the role he feels forced to play as part of a marginalized group and resents the painful compromises he must make in adopting a persona that "grins and lies" (line 1). To "hide our cheeks" means to stiffen the face so as not to reveal genuine emotion, and to "shade our eyes" has the triple meaning of adopting an indirect or deferring manner, of avoiding the eye contact that implies a shared understanding of the situation, and of internalizing society's artificial barriers so that an individual will not embarrass himself or others by appearing to desire things that are clearly beyond his reach. This results in a "debt" that has economic, political, and (most important) personal implications, and the incredibly sad thing is that it must be paid to "human guile" (line 3). To the severest pain (hearts are "torn and bleeding" in line 4) is added the insult of the forced smile and the myriad subtleties the victim is forced to mouth.

The second stanza admits that there are some benefits to wearing the mask. It shields the pain from a (sadistic) world that would count the "tears and sighs" (perhaps with an eye towards increasing them; line 7). Thus the world is best kept from becoming "overwise," a term that may consciously register against the notion of an "overseer," the plantation boss who was frequently charged with whipping the slaves under the old system. Such a reference would bring special significance to "the world's" counting of the pain it inflicts just as the lashes were frequently counted in the old slave system.

In the third stanza, the speaker drops the mask to curse but catches himself in time to turn it to a prayer to Christ from the tortured souls (line 11). They sing, but the earth (he uses "clay," a reference to the creation of man in Genesis) is vile beneath their feet and the mile is long (their lot in life is repellent, their work is arduous, and their torments are many). He would have "the world" dream otherwise (line 14) as they wear the mask, which by this point has become a powerful weapon they can use against their oppressors.

The dominant rhythm is iambic tetrameter, but the chorus (the phrase repeated in lines 9 and 15) is only half as long as if to highlight its central point by suggesting that much is left unsaid when "we wear the mask." Another part of the poem's perfection lies in its rhymes, which are good except for the eye rhyme (the use of words that look as if they should sound alike, but do not) of "subtleties" (which rhymes with "bees" instead of "lies" and "eyes"). This variation occurs just after the most painful point in the poem, as if the speaker were unable to maintain the mask of rhyme. Note that the painful word *mask* also goes unrhymed.

"WHAT MYSTERY PERVADES A WELL!"

EMILY DICKINSON (1896) In an age when many people still raised their water with buckets dropped into an open well, numerous mysteries surrounded that potentially deadly source of life. The water could seem to have a life of its own since nothing could keep it from rushing to the sea at every opportunity. Thus EMILY DICKINSON's speaker comes to think of it as a neighbor (line 3) even though it can be made to inhabit a jar.

The well in question need not be considered as naturally occurring; it could be argued that until the well fills with water, it is just a hole in the ground, and hence even the men who dug it could not be said to have seen its limit (line 5). The water's surface forms a lid of "glass" (as mirrors were often called), and so, looking into the well is like looking in the face of a bottomless abyss (line 8). This is so frightening that the speaker wonders how the grass can stand so close and yet appear unafraid. The grass must therefore somehow be related to the sedge that displays the same boldness even though it stands "floorless" (line 15) on the edge of a precipice over the sea.

Nature remains a stranger, however, and those that most "cite" her (refer to her teachings) are the least aware of her spirit (mystified here as an "unsimplified" [e.g., not discredited or rationally explained] ghost inhabiting a haunted house, lines 19–20). Pity for those unacquainted with nature should be balanced by regret for those who "know her less the nearer they get" (probably those scientists who tend to collect and categorize specimens or study her minutiae instead of entire ecosystems, and those who travel to the wilderness for the sake of exploiting its resources).

"WHAT SOFT—CHERUBIC CREATURES"

EMILY DICKINSON (published 1951) In EMILY DICKINSON's poem the speaker marvels at the soft, angelic personalities of "gentlewomen" (line 2; presumably these are women of such wealth that they are insulated from the more sobering aspects of life, such as personal finance and daily interaction with the less affluent members of society). One would as soon "assault a Plush" (an expensive fabric with a velvety or thick pile, or something [a throw pillow springs to mind] covered with that material) or "violate" (a term used for all manner of serious sexual assault or other defilement; line 4) a Star. What is there about them that so fills the speaker with vitriol?

Their ideas are so poorly conceived that the speaker must coin a new phrase, "Dimity Convictions," to describe them (although the speaker's usage may suggests a meaning derived from "dim" and "diminutive," dimity is a type of fabric with raised striped patterns. She is not so directly condemning their lack of intelligence, but their adherence to the ideals of a certain class, the habitués of homes where such expensive fabrics can be found). Because of their sheltered existence, they possess such a horror of "freckled" (spotted, or slightly irregular) human nature that they are ashamed of the God that created or allowed such things (lines 5–8).

The speaker hurls the worst possible insult at such pretentious beings, calling their behavior (their assumed "Glory," which elevates them above everyone else) "common" (line 9), and no better than that of a fisherman. They are so "brittle" (inflexible in their opinions) that Redemption (line 11; this could refer either to Christ the Redeemer or the process during which souls will be called to account for their behavior on Judgment Day) will be ashamed of them.

WHEATLEY, PHILLIS (c.1754–1784) Born in West Africa, Phillis Wheatley was given the same Christian name as the slave ship upon which she

arrived in Boston on July 11, 1761, and the family name of the people who purchased her. People were treated like animals in the slave trade: A potential purchaser would carefully examine the teeth of a victim to determine that person's age and general condition. The adults who surrounded her were poked, prodded, chained and rechained before being led away in small groups and sometimes alone to meet whatever destiny awaited them on a strange continent with a completely alien language and culture.

In that era clothing meant more to society in general than it does even in a modern urban high school. A man had to dress like a gentleman in order to be treated like one, so it is likely that John Wheatley came to the wharf in the imported hat, waistcoat, vest, fashionable wig, breeches, and shoes of the finest leather that would have distinguished him as a man of considerable means. Suddenly he came upon a young girl covered only with a piece of old carpet, as he later liked to tell the story, among the slaves for sale. Perhaps it was the girl's teeth that prompted him to buy; a proud father, he may have been reminded of his own accomplished and beautiful 18-year-old daughter at an earlier age. Her missing front teeth made him think that Phillis was then eight years old. At that time, the address of the mansion on King Street to which he took her could not have been fashionable for a merchant, nor more welcoming for the girl.

Fortunately she had fallen into the hands of Susannah and John Wheatley, and Phillis quickly astonished them with her intelligence. They decided to raise her as almost one of their family; she learned English at their table and literature from their daughter and the Bible. The family also owned other slaves, but she was kept from them. Although she was eventually invited into the fashionable homes of her patrons' peers, probably dressed as well as their own daughters, and frequently astonished them with her recitations, she had to respectfully decline any offer to eat at the main table of her surrogate parents' friends. In time, her ability to produce high-quality poetry could be viewed as evidence of the basic humanity of slaves at a time in American history when this right was being denied for the sake of the commerce in international kidnapping.

Her first published poem, celebrating a narrow escape by two men she met at her father's table, appeared in the *Newport Mercury* in 1767 (Shields 298). "On Messrs. Hussey and Coffin" is interesting for its use of classical references to represent the forces of nature (a storm at sea nearly shipwrecked them) from which the eponymous characters were saved by God.

Already well-known in the Wheatleys' social circle, Phillis gained a wider audience with the publication of "ON THE DEATH OF THE REV. MR. GEORGE WHITEFIELD" in 1770, and an even wider reputation with the publication of *Poems on Various Subjects, Religious and Moral* in London in 1773. The printing of this book necessitated bringing together the leading men of Boston, including the governor, lieutenant governor, religious leaders, and Paul Revere, to attest that Wheatley was the author of her verses despite being a slave. The power of the Wheatley family can be seen in their ability to summon such men to interview the poet, and they used their influence in the community to solicit adequate subscriptions (prepublication book orders) to make the subsidized printing feasible. Additional funds and upper-class influence were needed to find a British publisher after the Boston printers turned down the project (American poetry books did not sell during that era, and this book raised race and gender issues that even the most progressive must have viewed as additional impediments against sales). Thus Phillis Wheatley was permitted to accompany the Wheatley's son to Britain to see the book through its printing and to meet the Countess of Huntington, who wisely counseled having a print of the author adorn the book. Remarkably, an African-American painter had been chosen for the honor of creating the likeness, and Phillis Wheatley showed her appreciation with the poem "TO S. M., A YOUNG AFRICAN PAINTER, ON SEEING HIS WORKS." Arriving in England after five weeks on the *London,* her itinerary included visits to the Tower of London, Westminster Abbey, and the Royal Observatory at Greenwich. Her social calendar included visits to Benjamin Franklin and other distinguished gentlemen. Susannah Wheatley fell ill, however, a misfortune that required Phillis to return to America even before she got to meet with the countess. The same letter (October 18, 1773) that announced her return to America informed her British patron that, "at the desire of [her] friends in England," she had been released from slavery (in a letter of October 30, 1774, she attributed her manumission to John Wheatley's kindness in accordance with his wife's desire). She was also allowed to keep the proceeds from the sales of her book, a prospect that encouraged her to ask her powerful English patroness to prevent pirated American editions that would not profit her.

American poets were still more than half a century away from being able to support themselves exclusively by their literary work, and very few people had Wheatley's early opportunity to devote themselves so completely to their art. In 1774, her chief patroness, Susannah Wheatley, died. Before the approximate age of 21, Phillis had been emancipated but continued to live with the family.

In 1775 her poem celebrating George Washington, "the Generalissimo of the Armies of North America," led to an interview with the general in Cambridge (across the river from Boston) the next year. Her political poems, often addressed to the powerful people they commemorated, typically surrounded their subjects with references from the Greek and Latin classics as if to imply that these men were as great and as worthy of admiration as those of antiquity had been.

Wheatley produced an even larger volume of poetry, but without the full support of both Wheatleys she was unable to obtain enough subscribers in that war-strapped economy to finance its printing. Most of the poems she had produced for the volume have been lost.

Marriage to John Peters, a black businessman, in 1778 brought an end to her emotional isolation, but her happiness was short lived as the couple found themselves running out of money. It was an era in which the American dollar came close to losing all its value, and the Revolutionary War would not officially end until 1783. Her Christianity prepared her to accept such reverses in the material facts of her life, as evidence of "the uncertain duration of all things temporal," as she wrote to a friend on May 29, 1778 (Shields 185). She died on December 5, 1784.

Of the Wheatley poems discussed in this volume, "ON BEING BROUGHT FROM AFRICA TO AMERICA" celebrates the Christianity that prompted her benefactors to rescue her from the devastating fate of becoming an ordinary slave and to nurture her talent. "An HYMN TO MORNING" reveals her training in the classics (ancient Greek and Roman literature) and a rare suggestion of her humor. Its fraternal twin, "An HYMN TO EVENING" celebrates the triumph of Christianity.

The John and Susannah Wheatley mansion, wrecked by British bombardment in 1776, no longer exists. Archival collections of Wheatley's work are typically limited to first editions. These include the Charles L. Blockson Afro-American Collection at Temple University and the W. E. B. DuBois Library at the University of Massachusetts, Amherst. The Massachusetts Historical Society and the Library of Congress have a few additional items.

BIBLIOGRAPHY
Jensen, Marilyn. *Phyllis Wheatley*. Scarsdale, N.Y.: Lion Books, 1987.
Renfro, G. Herbert. *Life and Works of Phillis Wheatley*. 1916. Reprint, Miami, Fla.: Mnemosyn Press, 1969.
Robinson, William H. *Phillis Wheatley and Her Writings*. Boston: G. K. Hall, 1984.
Shields, John C. "Phillis Wheatley's Struggle for Freedom." In *The Collected Works of Phillis Wheatley*. New York: Oxford University Press, 1988.
Wheatley, Phillis. *The Collected Works of Phillis Wheatley*. Edited by John C. Shields. New York: Oxford University Press, 1988.

"WHEN I HEARD AT THE CLOSE OF DAY" WALT WHITMAN (1860)

WALT WHITMAN'S poem finds the happiness of public acclaim ("my name had been received with plaudits in the capital," line 1), of carousing, and of accomplishing a plan to be less complete than that of three days begun with perfect health and spent in anticipation of the arrival of the speaker's true love. Evidently unable to focus on anything else, the speaker spent the first dawn watching the moon and then wandering and swimming at the beach, reveling in sensory pleasure ("laughing with cool waters" as he bathed, line 5). Just thinking of the dear friend and lover coming on his way made him happy, each breath sweeter, and his food seem more nourishing. The second day brought equal joy, and on the evening of the third day the friend came (line 8).

That night the speaker heard the "hissing rustle of the liquid and sands" (line 10) as if the waves were whispering their congratulations on the speaker's sleeping with the lover under the same cover. In the autumnal moonlight the speaker could see the lover's face and felt his arm lightly around the speaker's breast, and that night the speaker was happy.

Whitman chose to use a first-person speaker, and care has been taken here to preserve the distinction between the poet and the speaker (whose gender is not specified). The poet may have preferred to think of the poem as a celebration of the "manly love" he mentions in "I Saw in Louisiana a Live-Oak Growing" or the "athletic love" of "manly attachment" of which he sings in "In Paths Untrodden."

"WHEN I HEARD THE LEARN'D ASTRONOMER" Walt Whitman (1865)

Major stars such as Ralph Waldo Emerson and Mark Twain were able to earn a comfortable living from the 19th-century lecture circuit, an important mass medium that frequently aimed at enlightening an audience as well as entertaining them. "The Learned Astronomer" to whom this poem refers evidently tried to overwhelm his audience with statistics about the size of the solar system and the surrounding galaxies. Such an application of mathematics to the stars would have seemed like a foreign language to a rock-solid humanist like Walt Whitman. If the astronomer used his numbers to point out the relative insignificance of our planet, our species, and any individual human, it should come as no surprise if the greatest celebrator in poetry of individual American independence would become tired and sick as the speaker (the voice one hears in this poem and not the lecturer) does in line 5.

Whitman, who much preferred the company of blue-collar workers and hands-on experience to the theories of intellectuals, let the speaker in this poem retain his romantic isolation as well as his mystical appreciation of the stars. The silence is "perfect" (line 8) only because he will not listen; rarely does such a major poet imply that ignorance is bliss.

"WHEN I READ THE BOOK" Walt Whitman (1871)

Although the thought behind this poem is rather simple, Walt Whitman apparently chose to express its opening lines unconventionally to mimic the difficulties and inadequacies of his subject. Although the biography he read was famous, Whitman felt that the book failed to deliver on the implied promise of its genre (and perhaps of its title) to present the life of a man. When he wonders if someone will "write [his] life" after he is dead (line 3), his phrase emphasizes the inescapable discrepancy between the reality of a subject's life and a literary recreation of it.

He argues that no one else really knows anything about his life (line 4). Even he often thinks he knows at best just a little about his real life. For his own purposes, he will try to record (he uses the word "trace," which emphasizes his sense of discovery; line 7) a few hints, faint clues, and indirections in the rest of the book (*Leaves of Grass*) that follows this inscription.

His point is that the mental and moral lives of other men and women must forever remain a mystery to us except as they reveal themselves in public acts or publication, and that an individual's personal experience of life is so incomparably and impossibly rich that no biography can do it justice. His announced goal of recording his own thoughts and impulses for his own use promises to be of more interest than a biography because it suggests an unfiltered look at the mental and emotional processes that create the fabric of an individual's real life.

"WHEN LILACS LAST AT THE DOOR-YARD BLOOMED" Walt Whitman (1866)

The assassination of the president on April 14, 1865, proved that four years of intense civil war and the deaths of more than 600,000 soldiers had not exhausted the nation's capacity for grief. In this poem, Whitman struggles to convey the impact of Lincoln's murder by revealing how deeply personally he felt the loss. For him, the forces of life and his artist's need for self-expression, represented by the call of a thrush, initially seem overmatched by the triumph of tragedy and death.

In the first section, the speaker associates Lincoln's death with the perennial natural events of spring, asserting that the changes of Venus (the great evening star), the blooming of lilacs, and his mourning for "him

I love" (line 6) form for him a trinity that will remain connected with that season. The purposeful ambiguity of the next section combines the speaker's anguish with the setting of the evening star; only shades of tearful black murk dominate both the inner and outer landscapes. A "harsh surrounding cloud" (line 11) imprisons his soul.

In the third section the poet's power of close observation illuminates his love of nature. The old farmhouse with its whitewashed picket fence (the "palings" of line 12) can connect with the antebellum nation, a study in rural tranquility in which one had time to appreciate the heart-shaped rich green leaves of the lilac and its delicately colored, perfumed, pointed blossoms. The speaker breaks a sprig from the bush.

In the next part, a thrush (one of a large family of migratory songbirds whose appearance is yet another signal that spring is in the air. Perhaps it is a Hermit Thrush, although the term "hermit" in line 21 describes its reclusive behavior instead of identifying its species) warbles from a secluded swamp. The speaker thinks its plaintive, descending notes ("song of the bleeding throat") are "death's outlet song of life" (line 24). Like the bird, the speaker feels he would die without the privilege of singing.

The surprise at the end of the fifth section is that a coffin is being carried day and night past signs of spring and life: violets, grass, emergent wheat, and apple blossoms. From April 21 to May 3, 1865, the president's coffin was carried by a special train from Washington, D.C., to Springfield, Illinois, with stops in major cities to facilitate oration and public mourning. The sixth section marks the passing of the train "like a great cloud darkening the land" (line 34) at night through an informal (hence many people attended with "unbared" [still covered] heads, forgetting to doff their hats as the customary token of their respect; line 38), silent sea of faces. Dirges were sung by thousand-voice choruses, accompanied by "shuddering [church] organs" and tolling bells. The speaker quietly presents his sprig of lilac to the coffin.

The seventh section consists of the speaker's parenthetic statement that he brings blossoms (roses, lilies, and sprigs from bushes) and songs for "sane and sacred death" and not for a single coffin. In the next

part, he remembers the "transparent shadowy night" of the prior month when, unable to sleep, he walked until the Evening Star set. His troubled and dissatisfied soul sank like the planet. The ninth section returns to the thrush that calls from the swamp. The speaker promises to attend him, but lingers a moment for the lustrous star, his dear departing comrade.

The 10th division finds the speaker worrying about how to warble, deck his song, and perfume the grave of the "large sweet soul" (line 72) now gone. Sea winds from both coasts will meet on the prairies and, with the perfume of his chant, perfume the grave (in less figurative language, the entire nation will mourn).

As though he were a carpenter or interior decorator, in the 11th section he gives some thought to the best pictures to adorn the burial house. As if thinking Lincoln would be most at home in an agrarian landscape, the speaker imagines a farm at sunset in April with sweet herbage underfoot, a river and a city in the distance, and workmen returning home. This vision seems to help him recover from the tragedy, for in the next part he celebrates Manhattan's spires, tides, and ships, the North and South "in the light" (a phrase that may recall the late war; line 91), the Ohio and Missouri Rivers, and finally the distant prairies with their grass and corn. The spring sun bathes the land and the cities, enveloping man and land in its shining.

Section 13 encourages the gray-brown thrush to continue its singing. The reedy, woeful song seems so in keeping with the times that the speaker calls it human. He also relates to its liquid, free, and tender spirit that comes wild and loose to his soul, but is still in the spell of the sinking star and the lilac's odor (two things that remind him of the recent tragedy).

The next section finds the speaker looking back on the day. The farmers prepared crops, and he heard the voices of women, children, and the tides. Ships sailed. Households continued their meals and "minutia of daily usages" (line 115), and among them all appeared the cloud of death. He walked with the knowledge of death on one side and the thought of death on the other, until fleeing into the night by the shore. There the thrush received the three comrades (the speaker and his knowledge and thoughts of death) and sang the carol of death and a verse for the dead president. Enraptured, the speaker held the hands of his comrades.

In italics, he translates and interprets the song of the thrush. Lovely, soothing, and delicate death comes to all. The fathomless universe, life, joy, and objects are praiseworthy, but he wants more praise for the "sure-enwinding arms of cool-enfolding death" (line 142). None have chanted for this dark mother, but the thrush glorifies her above all. It sings for death when it must come, and it will come unfalteringly. The bird would have the strong "deliveress" (death) approach and joyously sings of the dead, lost in death's "loving floating ocean" and "laved" in the flood of her bliss (lines 149–150). Over all life, the fields and the sea, the soul turns to well-veiled death and the body (possibly Lincoln's, but the application is far broader), gratefully nestling close to her. The bird joyfully floats this carol to her.

In the last two sections, the major images of the poem are brought together. The speaker's soul keeps tally by the bird's deliberate notes as he stands amid the swamp perfume with the knowledge and thought of death. In noiseless dreams he saw hundreds of battle flags (carried by units to coordinate their movements on the field) pierced with missiles until only a few shreds were left on the staffs, and the staffs splintered (since each 1,000-man infantry regiment [at full strength] had its own flag, the implied human cost associated with such destruction is phenomenal). He saw multitudes of battle corpses and "the white skeletons of young men" (line 178) amid the debris of war, but they were fully at rest without suffering. Only their living mothers, wives, children, comrades, and armies suffered.

The poet's five rapid repetitions of the word "passing" (a very common euphemism for death) has temporal ("passing the night," line 185), spatial (the visions he passes in the same line are associated with the swamp where he stands), creative (he is passing the visions and songs to his external audience), and psychological (the unloosening of his comrade's [two personified aspects of death] hands suggests he is getting past the nightmarish scenes of the war) dimensions. Victorious songs, which are also death's outlet song (although they celebrate success they also bring the horrendous costs of the war to mind; line 188), flood

the night with warnings, yet burst with joy. Despite the speaker's passing (line 193), he leaves his readers an inheritance, a new association for the lilacs that bloom each spring, a reminder not only of Lincoln's death but also of all the tragedies of the Civil War.

Thus he ends his chant "for thee" (a pronoun for which the antecedent is unclear; it might be spring [as in line 4]), Lincoln (line 45), all the dead and death itself, the external audience, the evening star, the thrush, or his own soul). He will keep the memory of death (personified as the two comrades who facilitated the vision of the war) as well as the memory of Lincoln and of the speaker's fallen comrades. Lincoln, lilac, star, and bird are entwined (but also "twined" in the sense of being doubled) in the chant of his soul (line 205).

"WHEN LOVELY WOMAN" Phoebe Cary (1855)

The myths of mid-19th-century urban American society encouraged men to make their mark in the business world, a priority that left wives in charge of running their homes. This could leave a couple at cross-purposes in the financial arena if she were entirely dependent upon his income, as was usually the case. As nominal head of the family, a man was frequently expected to take his wife's happiness as a sacred charge and ideally tried to support her with at least a promise of the level of comfort her father had provided.

Phoebe Cary's poem suggests that one of the ways a woman could win an argument is by bringing out the big guns in her emotional arsenal. Note how objectively the speaker presents the situation: The argument is over "a favor" (line 1) and not a necessity, and the disappointment is so slight that instead of the wife's being crushed by his decision, the speaker suggests trying an additional "experiment" (line 6). The wife's behavior may strike readers of a later century as anything but "lovely," since she seems so willing to manipulate her man over a relative trifle. It is largely a question of whose will is stronger, and the only ambiguity in the poem lies in the wife's finding out "too late" (line 2) that her husband would not bend. This could either imply that she found out too late to approach her present goal more indirectly, or that she has only just become aware of how stubborn her mate is now that she is stuck with him.

The only "earthly circumstance" (line 3) that can save her is the reputed weakness of her gender. She can cry, which the poem presents as a rather childish gesture since it seems so out of touch with any real feelings. Unfortunately, many women of the era had no recourse except to ineffectual tears when their mates proved unfeeling. Instead of producing strong, assertive women, such scenes reinforced their dependency on the men in their lives.

WHITMAN, WALT (1819–1892)

Whitman's poetry tends to celebrate the laboring men in whose collective hands the landscape of America was being rapidly transformed. As a consequence of his refusal to conform to traditional patterns of rhyme and meter, he created a reading public receptive to the free-verse experiments that have come to dominate poetry since the 20th century. Much of his work may seem autobiographical, but the first-person speaker in many poems speaks less for the author and more as a celebrant of his nation's self-reliant spirit. In Whitman's panoramic vision of the American landscape, the speaker tends to dominate the foreground like a seasoned old bison bull, a hoary specimen representative of the herd even as it insists on asserting its individuality.

On May 31, 1819, the future poet was born in a house built by his father, the carpenter whose name he shared. When he was four years old, the family moved to Brooklyn, where Whitman finished his formal education at the age of 11. In 1831 he found a job as a printer setting type in a newspaper office, thus beginning a career in an industry that exposed him to a wider variety of people than he might otherwise have known and that solidified his love of the printed page. Although he had become a journeyman printer in 1835, he was thrown out of work by a major fire that consumed New York's publishing district in that year. He briefly taught school before eventually working as a reporter and editor for several newspapers in Brooklyn and even, briefly in 1848, in New Orleans. The influence of this training can be seen in the topicality of his poems and in the precision with which he preserved the most salient details of the scenes he

presents. The chief difference between his newspaper articles and his best poetry is that the audience for the latter rarely encounters a voice other than Whitman's own. His subjectivity is paramount; he insists on narrowing the distance between the voices of the speaker and the poet to the point where the author seems to be "a man speaking to men," to use a definition of poetry advanced by the famous British romantic poet William Wordsworth just before the start of the 19th century.

In 1855 Whitman published the first edition of *Leaves of Grass,* a collection of 12 poems to which he continued to add new selections for the rest of his life and upon which his reputation rests. In the years immediately prior to its appearance, he had worked at a variety of relatively short-term jobs ranging from carpentry to shopkeeping, and even wrote a short temperance novel, *Franklin Evans,* in 1842. *Leaves of Grass* gave such meaning and purpose to his life that he seemed to be living for it as well as in it, but it was not until after the Civil War that he began earning the respect of the nation that he so earnestly craved. His poem "As I Ebbed with the Ocean of Life" hints that he had begun to feel played out by 1860, but the war refueled his passion for life and reinvigorated his poetry even as it undermined his health.

In 1862, upon receiving word that his younger brother George had been wounded in the disastrous battle of Fredericksburg, the poet set out from Brooklyn to find him. His brother had been only slightly wounded, but Whitman's search among the field hospitals and subsequent nine-day sojourn in the army camp led to his volunteering as an attendant at the understaffed military hospitals in Washington, D.C. He continued this practice throughout the rest of the war, probably saving a very few lives but alleviating the suffering and tedium of many convalescing soldiers by conversing, reading poetry, and distributing the small gifts that his friends had donated for them.

During the war, the poet had supported himself as a part-time copyist, and he briefly served as a clerk in the Bureau of Indian Affairs until either his neglect of his official responsibilities or (the true cause) the immorality of his poetry as judged by the standards of the day led to his dismissal in 1865. He was promptly hired by the attorney general's office, a clerking job he held until 1874. In 1865 he published, first, *Drum-Taps* and then *Drum-Taps and Sequel,* poems incorporating his experience in army camps, hospitals, and the nation's capital during the war, including frequent observation of Abraham Lincoln as the president rode through the streets and at his second inauguration. The war poems were added to the fourth edition of *Leaves of Grass* in 1868.

Whitman suffered a crippling stroke in 1873 but had recovered sufficiently by 1879 to deliver his first public lecture on Abraham Lincoln, a success he duplicated every year until further incapacitated in 1887. He frequently experimented with the order in which the poems of *Leaves of Grass* appeared and sometimes even left out a few of them. By the ninth and final edition in 1891, he had written more than 400 poems. A collection of his best prose works, *Specimen Days and Collect,* appeared in 1892. Although the occasional recipient of much-appreciated charity and growing celebrity in his later years, he managed to continue writing until he died on March 26, 1892, of pneumonia.

Of the numerous poems discussed in this volume, among the most interesting are those exploring Whitman's development as a poet. The process begins with his arrival, in "OUT OF THE CRADLE ENDLESSLY ROCKING," a poem taking him from infancy to his discovery of nature and its inescapable facts of loss and death as well as beauty. "THERE WAS A CHILD WENT FORTH" describes how a poet should open himself up to the world immediately around him. As a mature poet, he announced his poetic credo in "ONE'S SELF I SING," a pledge to sing at full voice of all aspects of life, including his own sexuality. "SONG OF MYSELF" takes his growth as an individual to the point where it transcends personal experience, and he begins drawing on the collective experience of the nation. "CROSSING BROOKLYN FERRY" focuses on the sublime elements of what could have been a mundane river crossing and conveys the poet's desire to immortalize that moment by providing future readers with enough sensory stimulation to make it come alive in their imaginations. His consciousness that this, in a very limited way, brings the poet as well as the poem to life is also evident in "WHOEVER YOU ARE HOLDING ME NOW IN HAND."

A sampling of his Civil War poems might reveal his initial enthusiasm for the cause in "BEAT! BEAT! DRUMS!" and his beautiful portrait of a "CAVALRY CROSSING A FORD." Poems like "A MARCH IN RANKS HARD-PRESSED" present the horrors of a field hospital and the impact of its harrowing sights on those whose duty demands that they soldier on. His observation of and sympathy for Abraham Lincoln throughout the war led to "WHEN LILACS LAST IN THE DOORYARD BLOOMED," his most eloquent expression of the loss he felt when the president died.

No introduction to the life and work of Walt Whitman would be satisfactory without recognition of his autoerotic and homoerotic imagery. Many references to the love of comrades permeate his poems, and in the 1860 edition of *Leaves of Grass* he devoted an entire section (the *Calamus* cluster of 45 divisions and/or individual poems, depending upon how they are viewed) to this important aspect of his life. Two of his poems not in that section, "FROM PENT-UP ACHING RIVERS" and "AS I LAY WITH MY HEAD IN YOUR LAP," provide rather explicit reminders of Whitman's groundbreaking work in making sexuality an acceptable subject in mainstream, serious literature.

Two of the houses in which Whitman lived have been preserved as historic sites: his birthplace in Huntington (on Long Island), New York, and the Walt Whitman House in Camden, New Jersey, in which he died. Additional archives are held by the New York [City] Public Library, the Library of Congress, and Brown University. The University of Iowa Press has published several collections of his letters as well as numerous biographical and interpretive studies as the Iowa Whitman Series. Shorter articles make their way into the *Walt Whitman Quarterly Review.*

BIBLIOGRAPHY

Callow, Philip. *From Noon to Starry Night: A Life of Walt Whitman.* Chicago: Ivan R. Dee, 1992.

Epstein, Daniel Mark. *Lincoln and Whitman: Parallel Lives in Civil War Washington.* New York: Ballantine Books, 2004.

Kaplan, Justin. *Walt Whitman: A Life.* New York: HarperCollins, 1980.

Loving, Jerome. *Walt Whitman: The Song of Himself.* Berkeley: University of California Press, 1999.

Morris, Roy, Jr. *The Better Angel: Walt Whitman in the Civil War.* New York: Oxford University Press, 2000.

WHITTIER, JOHN GREENLEAF (1807–1892)

The best starting point for information about Whittier is an autobiographical letter dated Fifth Month (as Quakers refer to May), 1882. The future poet was born into a pious family on December 17, 1807, on a subsistence farm near Haverhill, Massachusetts. The chief inconvenience of the isolation imposed by blizzards like the one made famous by his poem "SNOW-BOUND" was that it kept his parents from their 16-mile round ride to the meetinghouse in Amesbury and back on First-Days (Sundays). His formal education centered on a small public school only half a mile from their home which, because its students were needed for labor on their family farms, held classes only three months each winter. His early reading consisted of family copies of "about twenty" journals of Quaker pioneer ministers, a yearly almanac, the Bible, a local weekly newspaper, and such books on biography or travel as he could borrow from neighbors.

His first exposure to poetry came from the Bible, and the second (at the age of 14) came from a schoolmaster's visit to their home with a book of poems by the Scottish poet Robert Burns. Whittier borrowed the volume and was soon creating rhymes and imagining adventures. William Lloyd Garrison, the future firebrand best remembered for his abolitionist lectures and editorship of *The Liberator,* chanced to open the *Newburyport Free Press* only 15 miles from Haverhill, and Whittier's father promptly subscribed. Like many papers of the day, the *Free Press* devoted a poet's corner in each edition to such local work as was submitted, and on June 1, 1826, Whittier saw his first poem in print after his sister surreptitiously submitted "The Exile's Departure" (penned in 1825). Equally thrillingly, the young editor stopped by the farm to meet the poet, and Garrison encouraged him to seek additional education. The frugal poet, with a lifelong aversion to borrowing money that grew from exposure to his parents' debts, managed to finance a term at the Haverhill Academy with savings from the manufacture of ladies' slippers and shoes, a craft he had learned from a summer farm laborer. The following year, he financed an additional term by teaching school in Amesbury. In the meantime, he continued submitting poems to the paper, and found a job editing the *American Manufac-*turer in Boston in the winter of 1828. Hoping to return to the farm in the spring, he was instead hired as editor of the *Hartford Review* in Connecticut. He worked there for two years until the fatal illness of his father necessitated his return to the family farm.

It was partially through Garrison's influence, but very much in keeping with the Quaker tradition that had issued its first abolition declaration at the end of the 17th century, that Whittier wrote his first abolitionist pamphlet, "Justice and Expediency," in 1833 and had the first 500 printed at his own expense (other men paid to have more than 10 times that number printed). He was a delegate to the National Anti-Slavery Convention in Philadelphia that same year, helped draft their Declaration of Sentiments, and was elected to the Massachusetts legislature. On the downside, a mob in Concord, New Hampshire, nearly turned him into a martyr for the cause, an end for which a Boston mob also voiced their support. The year 1837 found him in the New York offices of the American Anti-Slavery society, and the next year he edited the *Pennsylvania Freeman* even though another mob burned his office. When his health failed, he returned to Amesbury, where his family had moved to be closer to the meetinghouse. As he edited the definitive edition of his collected poetry far later in his life, he regretted the lack of polish evident in the more than 90 poems in which he attacked slavery, but he ultimately defended them as "protests, alarm calls to action, [and] words wrung from the writer's heart." Slavery, and a compelling need to resist its evil, made him a public poet, empowering him with the will to overcome his shy nature.

Although he had managed to publish his first book, *Legends of New England,* in 1831 (a fact which he does not mention in his short autobiographical letter), he had earned only a few dollars from his poems and literary articles until his complete poems was published in 1837, by Ticknor and Fields (the poet may have become confused on this point. The Library of Congress holds copies of *Poems Written During the Progress of the Abolition Question in the United States* published by I. Knapp in 1837, and *Poems, by John G. Whittier,* published in Philadelphia by J. Healy and in Boston by Weeks, Jordan and Company in 1838. The Boston publisher Ticknor and Fields did not publish *The Poetical Works of John Greenleaf Whittier* until 1863). For almost three decades he had produced an additional book of either poetry or prose each year, but he skips to *In War Time and Other Poems* (1863) and "Snow-Bound" (1866) in his autobiographical letter. He served on the Board of Overseers at Harvard from 1858 to 1871, and as a trustee of Brown from 1869 to 1892 but declined offers to become a political candidate because, he stated, he was unwilling to add his own example to the greed of office. He remained an active member of the Society of Friends (the Quakers) throughout his life.

Although he abhorred violence as much as slavery, two of his poems, "SONG OF SLAVES IN THE DESERT" and "MASSACHUSETTS TO VIRGINIA" demonstrate his empathy with the oppressed and his willingness to inflame the regional antagonisms that led to the Civil War. Although unlucky in love and forced by poor health to return periodically to Amesbury, Massachusetts, after editorial stints elsewhere, he was a loving son (his mother lived with him until her death in 1857), a gracious host and friend to many. Although he did not travel the world, the world (or at least such important literary and cultural figures as RALPH WALDO EMERSON, HENRY WADSWORTH LONGFELLOW, and the leading antislavery men) came to visit him. For his 70th birthday in 1877, Mark Twain, OLIVER WENDELL HOLMES, JAMES RUSSELL LOWELL, and others joined Emerson and Longfellow in honoring him at a celebratory dinner in Boston. At the time of his death he was one of America's most famous writers.

Of the poems discussed in this volume, none capture the warmth of the Whittier family circle as well as "Snow-Bound." His "TELLING THE BEES" demonstrates his skill in turning the New England landscape and its customs into literature. "BROWN OF OSSAWATOMIE" and "ICHABOD" reveal the poet's hatred of slavery, but "The HIVE AT GETTYSBURG" reveals his opposition to violence even when it was wedded to a good cause.

The farmhouse in which Whittier was born was built by Thomas Whittier in 1688 and served the family for five generations until the poet sold it. This setting for the winter idyll of "Snow-Bound" has been preserved as the John Greenleaf Whittier Homestead.

In 1836, the poet moved to a house in Amesbury, Massachusetts, where he wrote his major poems and lived until his death (in Hampton Falls, New Hampshire) on September 7, 1892. This structure has been preserved as the John Greenleaf Whittier Home. The Amesbury Friends Meetinghouse, for which Whittier served on the building committee in 1850, continues serving as a house of worship. The largest Whittier archives are at Swarthmore. Additional material can be found at Whittier College, Yale, Harvard, and the Library of Congress.

BIBLIOGRAPHY

Higginson, Thomas Wentworth. *John Greenleaf Whittier.* New York: Macmillan, 1911.

Mordell, Albert. *Quaker Militant: John Greenleaf Whittier.* New York: Macmillan, 1911.

Pickard, John B. *The Letters of John Greenleaf Whittier.* 3 vols. Cambridge, Mass.: Harvard University Press, 1975.

Pollard, John Albert. *John Greenleaf Whittier: Friend of Man.* Hamden, Conn.: Archon Books, 1969.

Wagenknecht, Edward. *John Greenleaf Whittier: A Portrait in Paradox.* New York: Oxford University Press, 1967.

Whittier, John Greenleaf. *The Complete Poetical Works of John Greenleaf Whittier.* Boston: Houghton Mifflin, 1894.

Woodwell, Robert H. *John Greenleaf Whittier: A Biography.* Haverhill, Mass.: Trustees of the John Greenleaf Whittier Homestead, 1985.

"WHOEVER YOU ARE HOLDING ME NOW IN HAND" WALT WHITMAN (1881)

The situation of this homoerotic poem is that the speaker has been approached from behind by somebody who has placed his hand(s) on the speaker's shoulder(s). Choosing to interpret the gesture in a playful manner, the speaker reacts as if an apparent variation on the children's game of "guess who" had been intended. The speaker quickly turns the tables by asking if he really realizes who it is he has in his hands. He invites an additional level of intimacy with a riddle about the one thing without which all will be useless (line 2) and with language that interprets the opening gesture as sexual: he declares that he is not the man he seems, knowledge that his friend should possess before deciding to "attempt me further" (line 3).

Maintaining the charade in the second stanza, he pretends to be pondering the identity of the other man while suggesting the terms by which the relationship might proceed. He wants to dominate, relegating his friend to the status of a follower and a pursuer (lines 5–6). While recognizing the uncertainty of the road they would travel, he nevertheless would require complete devotion as the "sole and exclusive standard" (line 8). Like someone entering a nunnery or monastery (the term "novitiate" can refer to the studies, by one of either gender, that lead to full acceptance by a religious order; line 9), the friend would have to put aside all aspects of his former life. This seems like enormous presumption on the speaker's part since the triggering incident (especially if only one hand and one shoulder was involved) resembled a casual gesture, but the proof that he is addressing a receptive audience lies in the friend's having kept his hand in place thus far. If he is unwilling to accept the speaker's terms, he should "put me down" (line 12; the phrase not only suggests the speaker's subsequent dejection but may also contain a vague sexual insinuation) and leave.

Since he still has an audience, the speaker suggests that they go to some open space "for trial" (line 13). He would not be as comfortable in a room (where "I emerge not," line 15) or in a public place like a library (where his performance would be inhibited). Instead, he suggests a high hill, a sailing vessel or a remote island, all vantages from which an interloper could be spotted. There, he would permit the "long-dwelling" (line 20) kiss of the comrade or the equally passionate kiss of the new husband. He is willing to accept either or both roles.

Lest he seem too forward, he backtracks in the fourth stanza. Mere thrusts beneath the clothing (line 22) and indeed, merely touching, would be enough to whisk him off to dreamland and eternal bliss.

Thus far the poem has seemed rather straightforward, but in the fifth stanza Whitman retreats into an ambiguity probably designed to keep his sexual orientation veiled. The speaker now implies that he was talking about poetry all along, that he was addressing the reader in the opening stanza and not a male friend, and that it is impossible to imply anything about him based on "conning" (line 27; the verb conveys deceit but also can mean study or careful examination) the lines on the leaves of the book in which the poem appears. It is

an artful dodge; he could claim that the second stanza refers to submission to the muse undertaken when one seriously takes up the practice of poetry, and the third stanza merely suggests the most congenial places for reading his work. Thus he eludes the reader (especially those agents of repression in society who might be seeking to do the poet harm) even when the reader feels most confident about his understanding of the poem.

The last stanza is a further disclaimer. He did not write the book for the sake of the things that appear in it, nor can you learn his intent by reading it. Neither his admirers nor his lovers have the answer. His poems may do as much evil as good, but all is useless without the thing that he hinted at, but which both his internal audience and the reader may never guess. He finishes by instructing both audiences (for he appears to have directly addressed each in turn as the second person "you" in the poem) to release him and go away. Like a good salesman (or potential lover), he has brought closure to his pitch and waits for a commitment on the audience's part.

WIGGLESWORTH, MICHAEL (1631–1705)

The future physician, minister, and poet was born in England on October 18, 1631, and christened three days later in the parish church of Wrawby in Lincolnshire. Michael Wigglesworth was only seven years old when his family moved to the colonies and settled in New Haven, Connecticut. He graduated from Harvard (as have so many of his direct descendents) in 1651, married and began to preach in Malden, Massachusetts (today a suburb of Boston) in 1655. He received his master's in 1656 and remarried in 1679 and 1691.

In 1663 he made a voyage to Bermuda in search of health, a consideration that probably led to his interest in medicine. He did not return to the pulpit until 1686, when he labored for the health of his congregation during the week and for their souls on Sunday (and as needed).

The work for which he will always be remembered was the authorship of "The DAY OF DOOM" in 1662. Essentially he collected a number of warnings about Judgment Day from various books of the Bible, translated them into New England vernacular speech, arranged them in chronological order as they would occur on a single night, and frightened the second generation of Puritans back to the faith of their fathers. The text is so central to our understanding of early New England's religious history that it has been included in almost every early American literary anthology. The length and importance of this seminal tome has largely elbowed his other work out of the public eye, but the full title of his second most important work reveals much about his approach to poetry and to life: *Meat out of the eater: or, Meditations concerning the necessity, end, and usefulness of afflictions unto God's children. All tending to prepare them for, and comfort them under the cross.*

He died in Malden, Massachusetts, June 10, 1705; his 73 years nearly doubled the average life expectancy of the time. Despite the popularity of "The Day of Doom" during the poet's lifetime, very few of his letters and manuscripts have been preserved. Harvard University has early editions of his poetry and the notebook he kept as a master's student. Indiana University holds two of his letters to his wife. Elsewhere, collections of original Wigglesworth manuscripts are scant.

BIBLIOGRAPHY

Crowder, Richard. *No Featherbed to Heaven: A Biography of Michael Wigglesworth, 1631–1705.* East Lansing: Michigan State University Press, 1962.

Wigglesworth, Michael. *The Diary of Michael Wigglesworth, 1653–1657: The Conscience of a Puritan.* Edited by Edmund S. Morgan. Gloucester, Mass.: Peter Smith, 1970.

———. *The Poems of Michael Wigglesworth.* Edited by Ronald A. Bosco. Lanham, Md.: University Press of America, c. 1989.

"THE WILD HONEY SUCKLE" PHILIP FRENEAU (1786)

In late 18th-century America, botany was concerned mainly with collecting and cataloging. Such broader interests as PHILIP FRENEAU expresses here were still largely considered the purview of poetry instead of the natural sciences. The pattern of the poem is one of discovery, description, consideration of the subject's place in the immediate ecosystem, and finally an attempt to understand its characteristic life history. To elevate his subject, the poet ties it in with a biblical myth and finally draws a universal lesson from the experience.

In the first stanza, the plant is discovered in full bloom in a secluded spot. The poet evidently assumes that the reader already has some familiarity with the plant because he does not mention the distinctive tubular shape of its flowers. Its blossoms are "honeyed" (line 3) because each produces enough sweet nectar that a tasty drop (the "tear" of line 6) can be enjoyed when the flower is carefully pulled apart.

The plant is described as a moisture- and shade-loving forest dweller in the second stanza. It lives out its summer in tranquil seclusion. The poet compares it with the flowers of Eden (line 16), a biblical paradise of such ease and enjoyment that even the flowers are honeyed, but the reference also serves as a reminder that all nature was affected as a consequence of the transgressions of Adam and Eve.

When the plants die, they leave no vestige of their flowers behind (line 18). This seems to remind the poet of the frailty of human existence as well, especially if, like Freneau, you question the notion of an eternal soul. His argument that if you were once nothing and you return to nothing, then you have lost nothing (lines 21–22) is easily refuted; unless he believed that the plant appeared through some miracle of spontaneous generation, it was not once nothing. His memorable last lines point to the transience of all life, however. Earlier (lines 11–12) he pointed out that the plant lives for days, perhaps even an entire summer. Subjectively, this can seem "but an hour" (line 23). Even the far lengthier period of a human life can seem so short, lasting no more than, as Freneau so beautifully expresses it, "the frail duration of a flower" (line 24).

"WILD NIGHTS" EMILY DICKINSON (1891)

This is the poet's flirtation with the wild side of human experience although it seems necessary to the speaker that whatever happens occurs within the framework of a committed relationship. The absence of the internal audience is indicated by the speaker's use of the hypothetical mood in the second line, but whoever this absent intimate may be, he or she would probably be titillated by the speaker's thrice-repeated promise of wild nights. Only in the fourth line does a potential problem arise; referring to the Wild Nights as a "luxury" conveys a sense of the completeness of the relationship since it suggests all their primary needs have been met and serves as a further invitation for the couple to luxuriate in each other's company. "Luxury" is almost always used pejoratively in Christian texts, however, since it suggests a selfish superfluity acquired by excessive hoarding that may prevent other people from obtaining the necessities of life and an idleness that can lead to temptation. On this level, the first stanza may faintly suggest that indulgence, however tempting and potentially pleasing, ends in vice.

In the second stanza, the speaker figuratively expresses her willingness to put such concerns behind her. Content that, like a harbored ship, her heart has been safely anchored in the secure port (line 6) of another's similarly committed heart, she is willing to abandon her usual inhibitions. Part of the fun of this poem is figuring out what each of her nautical renunciations might imply when applied analogously to a relationship. The Winds described as futile in line 5 might represent the rumors and innuendos spread by gossipmongers, any number of the other outside forces that might damage a relationship (including such passions and lusts as the speaker seems to be unleashing here), or even such natural concerns as pregnancy. Announcing that she is "done with the compass" may mean that she will no longer consult her moral compass and/or it may also imply that she will no longer apply her intellect when it comes to their relationship, since use of a compass involves one's mental faculties. Renouncing the chart (line 8) could mean that she will ignore such counsel as experience (perhaps her own, as well as that of others) might bring. It would appear that from now on (or at least for this one blessed night), she will be acting on instinct alone.

She looks forward to the euphoria ("Ah, the Sea!" she exclaims in line 7) stemming from the physicality (the vigorous verb "rowing" has perhaps never been used so fortuitously as a euphemism for another strenuous activity) and transcendent potential (the rowing of line 9 takes place in Eden) of the sex act.

Feminist and Freudian critics (strange bedfellows!) seem fond of interpreting the last two lines as if they presented a literal image of a sex act with the important distinction that, because the speaker of the poem is imagined as female, the lines must contain yet another example of the poet's cross-gender identification. A less literal reading would recall the sixth line of the poem and connect "Might I but moor . . . in Thee" with the charming conceit of the speaker's heart safely anchored to another. Either way, the recipient of such sentiments as this poem professes is likely to rue his or her absence if the feelings it professes are reciprocal.

"THE WITCH IN THE GLASS" SARAH MORGAN BRYAN PIATT (1889) The speaker in SARAH MORGAN BRYAN PIATT's poem is a young girl who shares with a friend the enigmatic warning her mother gave her. This situation lets readers feel as though they are overhearing a private conversation.

Much of the humor for the initial audience lay in their mental juxtaposition of the young girl's innocent good looks with the features of the demoniacal crone that the word "witch" conjures. It is predicated on the assumption that women and girls are base creatures with an innate predilection for destruction, a prejudice that extends at least as far back as the biblical Eve. Notice how carefully the mother used three additional aspects of the stereotypical witch to give force to her warning. Mirrors (like the "glass" of line 2) can seem magical as they permit the seeing of things that otherwise could not be seen, but they are also unreliable because they reverse the image placed before them. The scariest witches also possess shape-shifting or identity theft potential, a supernatural ability in evidence here as the witch appears as a mirror image of the girl (line 4). Stereotypical witches may also engage in satanic rituals sometimes involving the consumption of blood, which may explain her "red, red mouth" (line 5).

Because distrust of the female gender permeates American society, it is easy for the girl's friend to play along with the mother's conceit. Instead of directly solving the riddle, in the second stanza the friend produces an even more severe warning before teasing the girl with even more confusing clues. Despite all her mother's care, the girl will receive the same message from a bird "of the air" (line 8), a wistful wind, or a rose. Part of the fun is that the dreaded "very thing you should not know" (lines 6 and 12) essentially places the girl in Eve's predicament; her curiosity may lead to the forbidden knowledge of good and evil and the end of her innocent paradise, but it may not be humanly possible to resist such an enticement.

Although the poem succeeds largely on the basis of its humor, it raises serious issues as to the proper nurturance of girls and a serious question about what a girl should and should not know. What was it that the mother so feared that made her willing to so gratuitously undermine her daughter's self-confidence at the very age when many girls undergo an identity crisis? Perhaps a major clue lies in the witch's "red, red mouth." If only the lips were described as so red, she may most have feared a precocious sexuality in the child. Instead, the image hints that the mother may most fear that her daughter will be so consumed by her own image that she might base her entire identity on her prettiness alone.

Such vanity is mostly self-destructive, however, and the most dreaded thing about witches is their ability to wreak havoc in other people's lives. If the daughter discovers the premium which society places on beauty before her moral development is complete, she may well turn into a destructive force. The resulting catastrophes might well poison her life and that of those unlucky enough to come within her influence.

Unfortunately, the riddle with which the mother chose to convey her concerns not only confuses the child, it instills hatred of her gender and passes a harmful stereotype to the next generation. The more one empathizes with the daughter, the less inclined one is to appreciate her mother's joke at her expense.

"A WORD IS DEAD" EMILY DICKINSON (published 1951)

Taboos are typically irrational. The speaker in this short poem found herself among those who evidently were afraid to say something either, because like primitive people elsewhere, they believe in a supernatural connection between uttering the names of things and what happens to those things in the tangible world, or because, as often happens in modern societies, to name a thing forces people to admit its existence and to deal with it. Still other people pronounce it unlucky to talk about good luck, happiness, and love, half-jokingly suggesting that even

these good things can become unlucky, sad, and lost if they are talked about too much.

The optimistic tone of EMILY DICKINSON's poem suggests that a belief in the magic of silence is not deeply held by the speaker or her social set, and that she considers the thing in question to be so good that she wants it to live and grow. As a surrogate speaker for a great poet, her stand in favor of putting things into words should come as no surprise.

"A WORD MADE FLESH IS SELDOM" EMILY DICKINSON (published 1951)

EMILY DICKINSON's poem challenges the complacency with which many people go through rituals without bothering to understand or deeply feel their significance. The opening stanza focuses on Holy Communion, the most compelling of Christian rites in that it forces communicants to take an active role in the services and to acknowledge, by one of the most basic and yet personal of acts, that the Word of God can transcend the limits of the physical world. With their act of consuming the sacramental wafers and wine, they ingest the body of Christ transmuted by the miracle of the Word. While this does not render them complicit in His crucifixion, it should make them aware that His sacrifice was for their direct benefit.

It is a miracle grounded in faith, which the speaker claims is "seldom and tremblingly partook" (lines 1–2) and "rarely reported" (which would be an instance of the Flesh being turned back into word. There would be little divine about this second transmutation, a fact in which the skeptical speaker secretly delights). Because the speaker believes that most people do not believe in the miracle, s/he feels that they have shared her "ecstasies of stealth" (line 6) to the extent "to our specific strength," line 8) that they are aware of their true feelings and capable of reveling in them.

The second stanza begins with enumerating three miracles of the Word: It creates or embodies life, it is immortal, and it is as cohesive (as indivisible) as the Spirit (lines 9–11). Once Word becomes flesh, however, it becomes as mortal as the flesh of Christ and as likely to perish. A similar process occurs with language; it symbolizes and embodies the miracle, but this "loved Philology" (generally, the study of how time changes languages, but also in this instance the changes that occur in the meaning of the Word; line 16) tends to lose its power when the words become commonplace, or when a skeptical audience refuses to see or understand its magic, or when a shift in meaning or state changes it.

"THE WOUND DRESSER" WALT WHITMAN (1865)

The situation of this poem is presented in the opening section: At some point in the future, children will ask a Civil War veteran to tell about the war. Like WALT WHITMAN (see, for example, "BEAT! BEAT! DRUMS," a veritable recruiting poem from the start of the war), the speaker initially supported relentless war, but he soon devoted himself to caring for the wounded and the dead. His audience wants scenes of the furious passion of unsurpassed heroes, and he states that both sides were equally brave. They want him to again "paint" (a verb suggesting artifice, as if they did not entirely believe his tales, but it also implies that he can make the scenes as tangible as a picture; line 9). Familiar with his stories of rapid and wondrous armies, they specifically request the scene, perhaps a curious panic, hard-fought engagement or tremendous siege (lines 11–12) that has stayed with him longest and deepest.

In the second part, he recalls arriving in the nick of time after a long sweaty march, plunging into the fight, and loudly shouting in a successful charge. That image, prompted by the children's request, fades "like a swift-running river" (line 17); he does not dwell on the many perils or few joys of soldiering other than to remark that he was content despite the hardships. In his dreams, while the daily business of civilian life washes most of the memories away as if they were imprints in sand, he recalls again entering the doors (identified as "doors of time" and hospital doors in the third section) "with hinged knees" (line 25; this vague phrase might suggest that he was already tired from his labors at the time, or it may indicate his respect, or he may be comparing his present condition with his former fitness) as he silently counsels those on the upper story to follow (his progress down the ward) without noise and with strong heart (he will tend their wounds soon).

In the next stanza he recalls carrying bandages, water, and a sponge to his wounded as they lie on the ground after a battle, his rounds in the hospital tents and, eventually, a roofed hospital; his memories have duplicated the experience of a wounded soldier as he moves through the army's casualty system. His attendant cares a pail that he fills and refills with clotted bandages.

Although he brings a steady hand and a firm demeanor to the dressing of their wounds, the unavoidable pangs (for both the wound-dresser and the patient) are sharp (line 38). When he sees the appeal for help in the eyes of one young soldier, he thinks he would agree to die if that would save the lad.

In the third stanza he recalls the worst cases: a crazed hand that tears at the bandage covering a crushed head, and the cavalry soldier with a terminal bullet wound in the neck who lingers on even when his eyes are glazed and his breathing rattles. In the face of such irremediable suffering he can only pray to sweet, beautiful death to come mercifully, quickly.

He must deal with the matter and blood on the stump of an arm even though the wounded soldier has not yet dared to look at it. He dresses a deep wound in another patient's side but can already tell from his wasted frame and "yellow-blue" coloring that he is also doomed. He dresses the "perforated" shoulder (possibly from a saber, bayonet, or knife wound such as might occur in ferocious hand-to-hand combat) as well as the foot with the bullet wound (which might have been self-inflicted as a dodge to escape the more deadly dangers of the front line). He cleans a wound with gangrene, an extremely deadly infection that emits a putrid odor unlike any other on earth, and finds that the attendant stands "behind aside me" (line 57) an ungrammatical phrase that may convey some of the speaker's surprise when he learns that his assistant has moved. If the odor prompted him to move, the attendant offers a pointed contrast with the speaker's focus on his patient.

The speaker stayed at his post through other wounds (thigh, knee, abdomen), which he dresses with an impassive hand despite the "burning flame" (line 60) he feels deep in his breast.

In the last stanza, the old soldier relates that he returns to the hospitals in his dreams, "pacifying" (line 63) the wounded (bringing peace to them) with his soothing hand. The experience remains both sweet (some patients are very grateful) and sad (some cannot be saved). In his dreams, many of the soldiers lovingly rested their arms around his neck, and many kissed his bearded lips.

Y

"THE YELLOW VIOLET" William Cullen Bryant (1821)

One of the great services poets provide is to make their readers aware of the miracle of the mundane. In this poem, William Cullen Bryant calls our attention to one of the less pretentious lights of the floral community, and it turns out to be rather special after all. For one thing, it makes its appearance on the forest floor before the other flowers appear, making it as great a herald of the New England spring as the buds on the beech trees and the return of the bluebird mentioned in the first two lines. Notice how carefully the poet observed the flower's natural history; the modest bell he describes in line 3 represents the flower in its immature growth state. He also informs us that it is found in wooded areas and not in cultivated fields, and can grow beside a lingering snow bank. Like most people, the poet is more attuned to visual than olfactory sensations. Although he mentions its scent to signal the plant's growth to maturity, he makes no attempt to differentiate its odor from that of other flowers aside from noting that its faint perfume (line 7) precedes their scents.

To artificially raise his humble subject in our esteem, the poet turns to personification: Spring is a gardener who plants the violet and the sun is its nurturing parent. In midspring the flower reaches its fullest expression when its yellow seems to match the sun and the effect is heightened by its deep "jet" black streak. Now, however, the speaker begins to distance himself from the plant, which has also turned its eye away from him (flower blossoms are often likened to faces in poetry, but the speaker's commonplace remark that the yellow violet blossom resembles an eye describes a pattern which is typical of this species).

The surprise of this poem lies in its shift from natural history to a personification of the flower to the extent that the speaker has a relationship with it. He is an inconstant lover, however, and is distracted by loftier, more gorgeous blossoms. With other options available, he cannot fail to again return to considering its shortcomings, including a spindly stalk and retiring manner. Symptomatic of his cooling ardor is the way in which, in the penultimate stanza, he compares the relationship to a mere friendship among business associates.

The major difference between this and other, less accomplished poems, is its transition from close observation of the flower to a revelation about human nature. The speaker focused on the plant through its early growth, but, easily distracted, he so far lost sight of it that he did not mourn its passing from his acquaintance. The seasons in the poem have again changed by the last stanza, for the flowers, cheerfully referred to as "the painted tribes of light," have yet to be awakened by the genial light of spring. Like an inconstant lover, the speaker will return to his modest first love until he again sees other options, and his pride tells him he can do better.

"YET VAIN, PERHAPS, THE FRUITS OUR CARE APPLAUD" Frederick Goddard Tuckerman (1860)

This sonnet is Frederick God-

DARD TUCKERMAN's poetic meditation on such things as free will, fate, and the insignificance of man. The influence of the transcendentalists can be seen in the speaker's references to the Forefate and the Giver (lines 2 and 5), an attempt to create universal euphemisms that could encompass non-European as well as European divinities. His use of the word "perhaps" (line one) probably stems from the same source; just as he would deny any single religion a monopoly on the truth, he inserts this conjectural term to demonstrate his awareness that his own theories are also speculative.

The word "vain" in the first line contains a twofold indictment against those who would take undue credit for "the fruits" of natural phenomena that would probably occur with or without human labor. It questions whether pride (or "vanity") provokes such presumption while at the same time it suggests that such claims are useless ("in vain"). The first four lines introduce the central question of the poem: why work at all if only fate will determine the success of the harvest?

Curiously, the next four lines recommend faith as an answer. Perhaps it is useful to treat this sonnet as a dialog between two speakers, with the first speaker providing the first four and last six lines, which question the more traditional beliefs expressed by the second speaker.

The second speaker evidently relies on the Bible or one of the more strict New England religious sects as his ultimate authority, for his speech is cast in the imperative mood and sprinkled with the archaic pronouns "thee" and "thy." Although he is willing to use the euphemism of "the Giver," he leaves little doubt that his God will reinforce the Protestant work ethic. He evidently believes in an inevitable Judgment Day when a judicious God will know if you have provided anything but your best labor and will reward or punish you in accordance with your merit.

The first speaker answers by demonstrating his familiarity with the other's language and tone in counseling him to "Behold" the breaking waves of the sea and the stars (the "rolling zone and zodiac" of line 9). What can a single individual do, whose impotence can be demonstrated by his incapacity to hasten dawn by a single hour or stop the motion of a planet (lines 11 to 12)?

All the questions and answers provided in the poem could have occurred to a single individual who is working out these problems for himself. If that is the case, the poem consists of an interior monologue in a dialectic format. Either way, it questions the efficacy of the Protestant work ethic because of the relative impotence of an individual.

"YONNONDIO" WALT WHITMAN (1887) This bleak lament covers one of the great themes of poetry, the passage of time. Great poets are often drawn by the sounds of words quite apart from their meanings, and lacking the precise meaning of the Iroquois term, WALT WHITMAN associates its sounds with the harshness of primitive death in a wilderness unmarred by the numerous generations that have preceded the passing one. The speaker is less concerned with nature—seemingly dismissed as inhospitable wilds offering little protection against the wintry night (line 2)—than with the passing of entire tribes and their swarms of powerful men of various types. They have vanished without leaving art like the pictures, poems, or literature that the speaker values as the highest expression of culture. He considers these former inhabitants of the woods to be as insubstantial as ghosts, since they have created nothing permanent for subsequent generations to remember them by.

In keeping with the somber tone of the poem, the speaker associates the habitats of the vanished people with the night, the darkness of the mountains, and twilight. Their world has given place to the relatively open farms, factories, and cities (line 10) of his culture. Even before creating lasting works of art, European settlement seems to have changed the landscape with its structures and engineering; even the first pioneers did not perish without leaving some trace of their passing on the land. Ultimately, however, everything his civilization produces will prove to be as ephemeral as the temporary changes wrought by the more primitive culture that preceded it. Thinking about Yonnondio brings him to the realization that, in time, his culture's landmarks will also fade. A wail like *Yonnondio* or some similarly sonorous sound will momentarily fill the air, then European/American culture will also fall silent, and all traces of it will be lost.

"A YOUTH IN APPAREL THAT GLITTERED" Stephen Crane (1895)

The Civil War was much on STEPHEN CRANE's mind during the year he wrote this poem as his most famous novel, *The Red Badge of Courage,* appeared just a year later and dealt with a raw recruit's impressions of a battle in that conflict. It had been the first modern war in the sense that advancements in defensive weaponry gave a decisive edge to any entrenched troops facing a frontal assault by the enemy. When it first started, soldiers by the tens of thousands rushed forth with the panache of medieval knights, very conscious of their role in the spectacle they were making. Unfortunately, improvements in the accuracy and firing rates of infantry rifles exposed them to deadly fire, and battles frequently became bloodbaths. For months on end the fighting between two great armies could come to a virtual standstill as each waited for the enemy to make the fatal error of attacking them.

This poem examines the indomitable spirit of a youth whose idealistic fervor prompts him to expose himself "in a grim forest" (line 2). With his apparel glittering (like a newly issued military uniform), he was struck first by the medieval garb of an assailant who rushes upon him (line 7) and then by that assassin's knife. Despite facing certain death, he is still so enraptured by the enchantment of his boyhood legends that he apparently offers no resistance, as the passivity of line 14 indicates: "he took the wound." The expression of joy that constituted his last words and his smiling acceptance of his fate indicate that, for him at least, death came before disillusionment.

The poet's fatalistic pessimism led him to remove all the glamorous patriotic jingoism with which a nation summons its youth to sacrifice in its army. In its place is a suggestion that these attitudes are embedded in such broader cultural phenomena as children's literature, where young readers encounter "the best" legends (line 12).

By 1898, the hard lessons learned about modern war by the Civil War veterans had been forgotten, and the glamour of the short-lived Spanish-American War with its triumphant charge up San Juan Hill did much to rekindle the hawkish spirit of the nation.

Z

ZOPHIEL, A POEM Maria Gowen Brooks

(1825) This essay is based on the first published version of the poem (Boston: Richardson and Lloyd, 1825). The title page identifies the poet as "Mrs. Brooks," but by the 1831 edition she was identified as "Maria del Occidente." It is divided into 64 parts (each identified by a roman numeral) and includes numerous footnotes that should be avoided if the reader wants to fully engage the dreamscape of the poem.

Although seldom anthologized due to its length, outmoded aesthetics, and wafts of immorality, *Zophiel* can be viewed as somewhat typical of the fantasies concocted during the romantic period. Some of it is timeless, however; later generations can still enjoy Maria Gowen Brooks's charmed tale of a daughter's resistance to her parents' pressure to marry. In form, it is an epic, complete with a lengthy "Invocation" to "Poesy," personified as a Daughter of God with wild tresses, a "dark blue eye upturned to heaven," and robes of "loosened flow." The speaker is interesting as the female equivalent of the brooding romantic hero, sighing from some unspecified sorrow but reveling in that persona as a sign of her own individuality.

The speaker would have Poesy appear not as a "just-formed maid," but at the age of Cleopatra, when she could repay death and infamy with a smile (the Egyptian queen was 38 years old in 31 B.C. when Mark Antony led their combined navies against Rome, of which he was one of the ruling triumvirate, in the battle of Actium. He died a suicide as his would-be captors approached in the following year). Alternatively, she could appear as Sappho (a legendary female Greek poet born 600 years before Christ and famous for her tragic life and mature love poems addressed to other women), but the speaker would also welcome Poesy as a fair dame "ripe, but untouched by time." The poet's point may be that the gains women make with age and experience are too important not to be included as emblematic of the power of a goddess. Sappho also represents an independent woman who chose an unconventional life and succeeded as a poet.

In mythology, the muses were the daughters whom Zeus brought forth to soften the pain human innocents are born to bear, as the speaker explains in the fifth stanza. Poesy (one could substitute "inspiration" at this point) comes at midnight on the lightning's flash, opening new scenes and unknown worlds to those she loves. She can inspire amid fallen temples or appear before a troubled maid (the "love-reft fair" of the ninth stanza) on an ocean cliff, soothing the latter as no other power can. She can touch a pale youth on his low bed of boards (the "pallet" of the tenth stanza), shaping some kindred maid in his imagination who helps him temporarily forget his suffering and desires. That Homer is believed to have composed in a cave is taken as proof of Poesy's preference for dark grottoes instead of thoughtless grandeur and as a consequence of her inspiration, Homer's dust remains adored while kings "decay untraced" (stanza 14).

The speaker has known poesy as a "Husher of secret sighs" in her own childhood, and turned to her whenever her heart has bled (stanza 16), an acknowledgment of the way some writers create poetry almost as therapy (a means of thinking through or gaining perspective on their problems). She sings not for the crowd, but urges Poesy to abandon her not. A single one of Poesy's tears or glimpse at her person will let the speaker scorn life's ills. She would even welcome every pain if it helps her inspiration, actively chasing even the deadly (the "fell" of the 20th stanza) despair that always watches for her victim, the speaker.

The poem proper begins with the ghastly thought of banished spirits malignantly wandering the earth at night. Their pranks included talking to monarchs from marble statues, but in that era even angels lingered to help some justice-loving mortal or to meet the aspiring love of a high-gifted maid. These days, the infernal host is chained in the darkling depths, but "who would not brave a fiend to share an angel's smile," Stanza IV).

The second part introduces a captive Hebrew couple later identified as Sephora and Raguel. They passed their youths in woe, but eventually they produced a daughter, Egla, as fair as a rose, the loveliest of their line. Although the last two stanzas are unclear, their implication may be that Egla may have looked like a goddess but is subject to the same brevity of existence as all men and worms. The next section claims that she knew neither envy nor hate, and was less troubled by any injury to herself than its effect on the perpetrator. If she sensed anything amiss in her makeup, her pride crushed it before it could grow. The fifth section asserts that youth must learn to armor itself, since the sweetest singing bird can least endure the storm.

The sixth part praises her hair (more golden than the sands of Pactolus; the reference is to a river in Turkey, where traces of real gold can still be found and where the mythical Midas cleansed himself from the curse of his golden touch) and blue eyes. The next section finds Sephora anxious to see Egla married and her race renovated by the arrival of grandchildren.

Section eight tells of the marriage offers her father received from strangers, but their gifts and promises meant less than her tears, and he left her free. Sephora extracted a vow from Egla that if her fancy (her dream of an alternative future) did not come true, she would marry ("hearken" to the voice of her "light-giver" [her mother]) in her 20th year. Egla would then yield her life and love, "hush each idle wish and learn to be a wife."

Sephora's persistence is demonstrated in the next 15 sections. Having finished her daily chores, Egla liked to repair to the woods, where the burning noon sun was filtered like twilight. Reclining, she was soon given to reverie, the mother of the muses. One day she meant to tune her lute, but threatening images had kept her from sleeping the prior night. Then her mother intruded on her haven. Egla rose to meet her even as her heart sank. The matron, "not yet marred by time" (section X), soothingly explained her purpose with a "gently serious air."

Sephora began by pointing out her own patience despite the pain of suppressing her heart's desire. She observed that when Raguel broached the subject, Egla's rebel blush revealed what her tongue would not. Sephora asks if she wastes the day alone, or comes to her retreat to bathe a pagan youth. Egla retorts that Sephora may doubt her wisdom but she should have some regard for her truth.

When 12 years old, Egla had sat in the same spot with dreams of desolate Judea. She had listened to her mother's weeping exile tales while still on her knee, but a piteous moan interrupted her daydream. She discovered a wretched old man in the bushes who begged for food and water. She fed him the bread, figs, and honey-sweetened wine that her mother had sent for her, and with her garment wiped away his tears mingled with the remnants of the drink.

Revived, he blesses her with the wish that she would be "a crown to him who weds thee" (XV) and a story: On the banks of the Euphrates (probably in modern Iraq), a child escaped its youthful nurse and playfully tried to balance over the torrent. The onlookers wailed and tore their hair, but "a stranger boy" flung down his bow and quiver and made the sparkling billows sing as he swam. The boy disappeared beneath the curling waters, but the stranger climbed out on a rock with the child (XVIII).

That child was the son of the king of Nineveh, but his rescuer only wanted a place among warlike men.

He was left with the buoyant hope of paternal blessings and the court's pleasures. His mother only wept, for who would eventually bury his parents if he were stationed far away or killed in battle. Selflessly he put away his ambition, and stayed to comfort her.

The old man stopped the story, and his face grew fair. A mellow light mantled him, and he vanished from the young Egla's sight (XXI). She has since been faithful to the notion of the youth for fear that he might show up and find her married. Her mother answers that he was probably killed in the distant wars, but even if he lives, he has no notion of the "phantom's bride" who is wasting "love, life and charms." She compares this to a vine of Galilee that would wait for support only from a Euphrates palm (XXIII; a distance of hundreds of miles, depending on the starting points on the sea and the river, respectively. The ancient kingdom of Galilee may have come slightly closer to the river but still represented an impossible distance for a plant to cover). She is fruitlessly waiting for an angel's love, and days on earth like those of heaven.

Sephora has chosen a worthy man for her. On an earlier occasion, a sacrificial dove escaped when they took Egla to an altar, and a handsome man from Media (from the region of modern Iran) with black curly hair offered them a replacement (we later learn his name is Meles). He has adopted their religion, and her parents would accept him. She agrees out of filial devotion, but with tears (XXV). Sephora holds her until, whimpering, she falls asleep using her soft arm as a pillow.

Left alone, Egla lies indolent except that the "cool velvet turf" touched one cheek too rudely. The wind (Zephyr) blew her ringlets around her narrow ribbon headband (the "fillet" of section XXVII) and kissed her brow. Although her emotion had passed, it still was visible just as the waves continue on the Caspian Sea, even though the winds have passed. An occasional sob escaped her sleeping lips as it sometimes might from a small napping child.

The glade attracted Zophiel, a fallen angel. He paused in awe before the altar Raguel had erected, painfully reminded of heaven's forfeited joys. Though a rebel, he had merely complained when others howled and now was free to roam the earth and even kept his blissless harp. He sang against the wild ambition that

led to the creation of hell. The angels had taken up positions beneath their banners and became fiends, but were hurled from the shrinking field. They woke in agony, and took the earth down with them: death was introduced. Each was tormented by a thousand wild desires. They mourn, but not for inconsequential man, and death proves his mastery on earth. The fallen angels unfurled their wings in earth's cool night, and Zophiel crossed deserts and mountains in search of a faint likeness of his lost heaven. He sustained his mystic nature by feeding on the scent of sacrificed flowers (XXXIV), and amused himself by giving out oracles through shrines or through a fair Sibyl's lips (the name comes from the ancient Greek prophetesses).

He mistakes Egla for a resting angel and would have fled, fearful of having his misery observed. Thoughts of paradise lost (or *Paradise Lost,* the masterpiece by the 17th-century British poet John Milton whose version of rebel angels and the subsequent fall of man informs this poem) cause him to writhe in pain. Then he heard her sleeping sigh.

Convinced of her mortality, he thought of the sweet Eve corrupted by first sin's sovereign (Satan), and he would drink up her sweet breath for eternity, even though he realizes that even the brief bliss of a human lifetime ("poor insect man;" XXXVI) cannot be his. Past experience has taught him that mortal women mildew in his arms. No matter how attractive they are initially, they wither to hideousness and, with muttered word and harmful drug, force him to their will.

Yet he sees a recent tear stain on her cheek. Noting her unhappiness, he postulates that she had been chided or wronged by a rude mortal. This presents an opportunity to heal her heart as a means of claiming it for himself. He calculates her present beauty and sweetness will last a year, but even that little time would give him respite from his despair. Although acknowledging the grievance he will bring her, it seems nothing compared to his eternal doom. Calling her a "pretty fly," he attempts to waken her from sleep and to her new role—of being his. He is ready as the fond bird to be entrapped in her snare, to work her robes and "twine amidst her hair."

That higher power that watches over slumbering innocents repelled him momentarily, just long enough for Sephora to return. He followed them, and saw the noble Meles receive his new bride with golden rings for her arms symbolic of her charms' forever enslaving and clasping his captive heart (XL). In black glances, his eyes revealed his approval, while she "shrunk reluctant" from his ardency.

They seemed a goodly pair, almost the same height, although she was fair and curvaceous, and he was manly with black curls. His attire was rich, and she had to admire him. She often looked into his face, but found it lacking in what was most required.

Section 44 cuts to Egla at her window, where she has been left alone to pray in the moonlight. She envies the girl who lives in blessed obedience; she can tell her earthly lord (her father, and after her marriage, her husband) that God is his law, and her husband is her law. He is her protection; she need not turn faint at "thoughts befitting his superior mind" (XLV). The dutiful wife protects his heart. For such "soul's food," the heathen molds a golden idol or shines his smiling marble goddess. Such a girl is at peace with God. Egla, on the other hand, can only pray to bear her fate well.

The next section is the most romantic—or at least the most operatic—of the entire poem. Egla's eyes were fixed on heaven as if she still hoped to find her phantom lover. After a starburst, a brilliant cloud filled the room. A youth, his "beauty bare" save for a slight scarf and a diamond crown, appeared like a flowering narcissus and began fanning Egla with his transparent wings. Their hue changed like the prismatic tints on a bubble, and he held out a little golden vase as a gift.

He calmed her fears by calling her "sister" (as a coreligionist might) and claims he has come over mountain and stream to serve her. He asked if her soul rushes to the bridegroom, and if she yields to the loathed caress despite her heart's protest. He also reminds her of the wretched forsaken maid who wasted "wild complaints" against Meles on the banks of the Tigris. The winged stranger offers Egla knowledge of earth and heaven and promises to become her messenger and slave.

She sensibly asks if heaven sent him to charm her pains away and tells him to inform her father about Meles, for only he can release her from her oath. The stranger offers an alternative: he will hurl Meles to the Lybian deserts if she gives the word (LI). He will expose the bridegroom's frauds and reveal the hearts he has unstrung. All the pain inflicted "for his own vile joys" will rend him. But first, as she wishes, the stranger will visit her father.

He hands her the vase full of jewels, pausing to praise each and recount how he dove for the pearls and plucked a ruby from a mountain top. Amethyst, sapphire, opals, emeralds, and a diamond from India complete his offering, but Egla has remained focused on each harmonious limb of her visitor.

Egla contained parts of everything beautiful in nature and epitomized their charms. Thus she represented a perfect dower for all who could feel such beauty (LVI). The stranger, comprehending her beauty, "spoke in more melting music to her soul" (LVII), drawing it in like the rose draws in the nightingale (this would appear to be poor science, but all of nature's truths are not yet known). His words moved like the lilies disturbed by two sister-fawns who like to lick the morning dews from them.

A "warm carnation glow" flushed her cheek still wet from the tears shed when she had confessed her inmost soul. Thus a little reptile uses its "fixed bright eye of fascinating flame" to lure a dove within range (since snakes lack eyelids and hence never blink, a popular superstition credited them with hypnotic powers whereas modern science attributes their hunting prowess to camouflage, patience, and surprise. Rodents are their most common prey, but various types of crocodilians, snakes, turtles, and even the bigger lizards [such as Komodo dragons] have been known to consume birds). Bride and spirit came closer.

The next section (LIX) breaks the frame of the story; the author addresses the reader in her own voice to comment on the morality of the action. Few poetic devices so completely place a work in its time as the fortunately outmoded convention of authorial comment that identifies this poem as Victorian. Later poets (and writers in all genres) learned to let readers draw their own inferences about their characters. Here, Gowen would have some force shield her "peerless mortal" from the "invidious" (odious) sprite. He will exult in his power tonight—but why does his "beauteous charge" (Egla) yield?

An alternative reading of the same section might attribute it to whatever dim moral sense still flickered in the fallen angel. Either way, he held out a bracelet and, with his "light" half enfolding the maiden, reached with the other half—the dubious half, the author asserts—for her lily hand (not just white, but also pure, if one subscribes to the traditional meaning associated with those flowers). Its phrasing is convoluted, but the sense of this section (LX) is that his sweet words (a vestige from his prior, angelic state) enfolded the maiden while his corrupt side reached for her hand (and by extension, the rest of her body). The last line is ambiguous: "the dubious half" may refer to her body, whereas she may be keeping her soul pure, or it may suggest that she still remains somewhat dubious. Alternatively, he may have only succeeded in getting his pearly bracelet (a symbol of his figurative possession of her) halfway on.

Just when success seemed certain, however, his pride expressed itself when an unguarded "infernal light shot from his eye" with all its guilt and treachery suddenly apparent. Thus Nature bestows intuitive perception. While artifice overtasks with guile, intuition discloses "the dark soul in the eye, to warn the overtrusting heart" (LXI).

Zophiel was foiled, and torments burned in his breast. Her trembling hand recoiled, for the wily fiend's confession had been in his "wild, exulting glance." He still had a faint hope, which he advanced in asking if she still would take her husband even though Meles had been guilty. Fearful, she nevertheless managed to answer that she would.

Suddenly the room again was dark except for the melancholy flame of the moon and the spark from a burning perfume's uneven flame. Shuddering, she crept to her couch, and Meles stepped through the door. Alas, before he could hastily discard his embroidered belt and sandals, he groaned, gasped and fell.

Morning found him lying next to the couch where his widow convulsively clasped her hands in prayer. A cold black corpse was all that was left of him.

BIBLIOGRAPHY

Alexander, Eleanor. *Lyrics of Sunshine and Shadow: The Tragic Courtship and Marriage of Paul Laurence Dunbar and Alice Ruth Moore, A History of Love and Violence among the African American Elite.* New York: New York University Press, 2001.

Allen, Gay Wilson. *American Prosody.* New York: Octagon Books, Inc., 1966.

Ames, Mary Clemmer. *A Memorial of Alice and Phoebe Cary, with some of their later poems.* Ann Arbor: Scholarly Publishing Office, University of Michigan Library, n.d.

Anonymous. *National songster, or, A collection of the most admired patriotic songs, on the brilliant victories, achieved by the naval and military heroes of the United States of America, over equal and superior forces of the British. From the best American authors.* Hagers-town, Md.: John Gruber and Daniel May, 1814.

Arnold, A. James, ed. *A History of Literature in the Caribbean.* 3 vols. Amsterdam and Philadelphia: John Benjamin Publishing, 1994–2001.

Austin, Mary Hunter. *Medicine Songs.* Charlottesville: University of Virginia Library, 1996.

Axelrod, Jacob. *Philip Freneau: Champion of Democracy.* Austin: University of Texas Press, 1967.

Axelrod, Stephen Gould, et al. *The New Anthology of American Poetry.* New Brunswick, N.J.: Rutgers University Press, 2003.

Balm, Nina, et al. *The Norton Anthology of American Literature.* 4th ed. New York: Norton, 1994.

Barlow, Joel. *The Works of Joel Barlow.* Edited by William Buttorff and Arthur Ford. 2 vols. Gainesville, Fla.: Scholars Facsimilies, 1970.

Barrett, Faith, and Cristanne Miller, eds. *Words for the Hour: A New Anthology of American Civil War Poetry.* Amherst: University of Massachusetts Press, 2005.

Barth, John. *The Sot-Weed Factor.* Garden City, N.Y.: Doubleday, 1960.

Basker, James G. *Amazing Grace: An Anthology of Poems About Slavery, 1660–1810.* New Haven, Conn.: Yale University Press, 2002.

Bender, Louis Prosper. *Literary Sheaves, or la littérature au Canada français: The Drama, History, Romance, Poetry, Lectures, Sketches, Etc.* Montreal: Dawson Brothers, 1881.

Bennett, Paula Bernat. *Poets in the Public Sphere: The Emancipatory Project of American Women's Poetry, 1800–1900.* Princeton, N.J.: Princeton University Press, 2003.

Bernstein, Samuel. *Joel Barlow: A Connecticut Yankee in an Age of Revolution.* New York: Routledge Books, 1985.

Bloom, Harold, ed. *African-American Poets: Phillis Wheatley through Melvin B. Tolson.* Philadelphia: Chelsea House Publishers, 2003.

Bly, Robert, ed. *The Winged Life: The Poetic Voice of Henry David Thoreau.* Includes wood engravings by Michael McCurdy. New York: HarperPerennial, 1992.

Bolland, O. Nigel. *Struggles for Freedom: Essays on Slavery, Colonialism, and Culture in the Caribbean and Central America.* Belize City, Belize: The Angelus Press and Kingston, Jamaica: Ian Randle Publishers, 1997.

Brooks, Cleaneth. *American Literature: The Makers and the Making*. New York: St. Martin's Press, 1973.

Boudinot, Elias. *The Life, Public Services, Addresses, and Letters of Elias Boudinot*. Edited by J. J. Boudinot. New York: Da Capo Press, 1971.

Bowden, Mary Weatherspoon. *Philip Freneau*. Boston: Twayne Publishers, 1976.

Boyd, George Adams. *Elias Boudinot. Patriot and Statesman, 1740–1821*. New York: Greenwood Press, 1969.

Boyd, Melba Joyce. *Discarded Legacy: Politics and Poetics in the Life of Frances E. W. Harper, 1825–1911*. Detroit, Mich.: Wayne State University Press, 1994.

Bradstreet, Anne. *Woman's Inner World: Selected Poetry and Prose of Anne Bradstreet*. Edited by Adelaide P. Amore. Lanham, Md.: University Press of America, 1982.

———. *The Complete Works of Anne Bradstreet*. Edited by Joseph R. McElrath, Jr., and Allan P. Robb. Boston: Twayne Publishers, 1981.

Brown, Charles H. *William Cullen Bryant*. New York: Charles Scribner's Sons, 1971.

Brown, Dee. *Bury My Heart at Wounded Knee*. New York: Henry Holt, 2001.

Browne, Francis F., ed. *Bugle-Echoes: A Collection of Poems of the Civil War, Northern and Southern*. New York: White, Stokes & Allen, 1886.

Brownlee, James Henry, comp. *War-time Echoes; Patriotic Poems, Heroic and Pathetic, Humorous and Dialectic, of the Spanish-American War*. New York: Werner, 1898.

Bryant, William Cullen. *The Letters of William Cullen Bryant*. Edited by William Cullen Bryant II and Thomas G. Voss. New York: Fordham University Press, 1993.

Buell, Lawrence. *Emerson*. Cambridge, Mass.: Harvard University Press, 2003.

———, ed. *The American Transcendentalists: Essential Writings*. New York: Modern Library, 2006.

Cady, Edwin H. *Stephen Crane*. Boston: Twayne Publishers, 1980.

Cain, William E. *American Literature*. New York: Pearson Longman, 2004.

———. *A Historical Guide to Henry David Thoreau*. New York: Oxford University Press, 2000.

Calhoun, Charles C. *Longfellow: A Rediscovered Life*. Boston: Beacon Press, 2004.

Callow, Philip. *From Noon to Starry Night: A Life of Walt Whitman*. Chicago: Ivan R. Dee, 1992.

Carlson, Eric W. *Introduction to Poe: A Thematic Reader*. Glenview, Ill.: Scott, Foresman, 1967.

Cary, Alice, and Phoebe Cary. *The Poems of Alice and Phoebe Cary*. Ann Arbor, Mich.: Scholarly Publishing Office, University of Michigan Library, n.d.

Chichetto, James William. *Reckoning Genocide: Poems on Native Americans*. Morristown, Tenn.: Indian Heritage Council, 2002.

Cisco, Walter Brian. *Henry Timrod: A Biography*. Madison, N.J.: Fairleigh Dickinson University Press, 2004.

Clavel, Stanley. *Emerson's Transcendental Etudes*. Edited by David Justin Hodge. Stanford, Calif.: Stanford University Press, 2003.

Clymer, Theodore, comp. *Four Corners of the Sky: Poems, Chants and Oratory*. Boston: Little, Brown, 1975.

Cohen, Edward H. *Ebenezer Cooke: The Sot-Weed Canon*. Athens: University of Georgia Press, 1975.

Connell, Evan S. *Son of the Morning Star*. New York: Harper & Row, 1985.

Cooke, Ebenezer. *Early Maryland Poetry: The Works of Ebenezer Cooke, Gent. and Laureate of Maryland*. Edited by Bernard C. Steiner. Baltimore: John Murphy Company, 1900.

Coxe, Louis Osborne. *Edwin Arlington Robinson: The Life of Poetry*. New York: Pegasus, 1969.

Craig, Raymond A. *A Concordance to the Complete Works of Anne Bradstreet*. Lewiston, N.Y.: Edwin Mellen Press, 2000.

Crane, Stephen. *The Works of Stephen Crane*. Vol. 10: *Poems and Literary Remains*. Charlottesville: University Press of Virginia, 1975.

Crowder, Richard. *No Featherbed to Heaven: A Biography of Michael Wigglesworth, 1631–1705*. East Lansing: Michigan State University Press, 1962.

Cushman, Stephen. *Fictions of Form in American Poetry*. Princeton, N.J.: Princeton University Press, 1993.

Davis, Linda H. *Badge of Courage: The Life of Stephen Crane*. Boston: Houghton Mifflin, 1998.

Dickinson, Emily. *Emily Dickinson's Selected Letters*. Edited by Thomas H. Johnson. Cambridge, Mass.: Harvard University Press, 1971.

———. *Open Me Carefully: Emily Dickinson's Intimate Letters to Susan Huntington Dickinson*. Edited by Ellen Louise Hart and Martha Nell Smith. Ashfield, Mass.: Paris Press, 1998.

————. *The Poems of Emily Dickinson, Including Variant Readings Critically Compared with All Known Manuscripts.* Edited by Thomas H. Johnson. Cambridge, Mass.: Harvard University Press, 1955.

————. *Poems: Variorum Edition.* 3 vols. Edited by R. W. Franklin. Cambridge, Mass.: Harvard University Press, 1998.

Donaldson, Scott. *Edwin Arlington Robinson: A Poet's Life.* New York: Columbia University Press, 2007.

Douty, Ester Morris. *Hasty Pudding and Barbary Pirates: A Life of Joel Barlow.* Philadelphia: Westminster Press, 1975.

Dow, George Francis. *The Arts and Crafts in New England 1704–1775.* Topsfield, Mass.: Wayside Press, 1927.

Dudley, John. *A Man's Game: Masculinity and the Anti-Aesthetics of American Literary Naturalism.* Tuscaloosa: University of Alabama Press, 2004.

Dunbar, Paul Laurence. *The Collected Poetry of Paul Laurence Dunbar.* Edited by Joanne M. Braxton. Charlottesville: University of Virginia Press, 1993.

————. *In His Own Voice: The Dramatic and Other Uncollected Works of Paul Laurence Dunbar.* Edited by Herbert Howard Martin and Ronald Primeau. Athens: Ohio University Press, 2002.

Duberman, Martin B. *James Russell Lowell.* Boston: Houghton Mifflin, 1966.

Edelberg, Cynthia Dubin. *Jonathan Odell: Loyalist Poet of the American Revolution.* Durham, N.C.: Duke University Press, 1987.

Eggleston, George Cary, ed. *American War Ballads and Lyrics: A Collection of the Songs and Ballads of the Colonial Wars, the Revolution, the War of 1812–15, the War with Mexico, and the Civil War.* New York: Putnam, 1889.

Elliott, Emory, et al. *American Literature: A Prentice Hall Anthology.* Englewood Cliffs, N.J.: Prentice Hall, 1991.

Emerson, Ralph Waldo. "The Transcendentalist." In *Nature: Addresses and Lectures,* constituting the first volume of *The Works of Ralph Waldo Emerson.* Boston: Phillips, 1909.

Epstein, Daniel Mark. *Lincoln and Whitman: Parallel Lives in Civil War Washington.* New York: Ballantine Books, 2004.

Fleissner, Jennifer L. *Women, Compulsion, Modernity: The Moment of American Naturalism.* Chicago: University of Chicago Press, 2004.

Foshay, Ella M., and Barbara Novak. *Intimate Friends: Thomas Cole, Asher B. Durand and William Cullen Bryant.* Hensonville, N.Y.: Black Dome Press, 2001.

Foster, Frances Smith. *A Brighter Coming Day: A Frances Ellen Watkins Reader.* New York: Feminist Press at the City University of New York. Distributed by the Talman Co., 1989.

Gabin, Jane S. *A Living Ministrelsy: The Poetry and Music of Sidney Lanier.* Macon, Ga.: Macon University Press, 1985.

Gale, Robert L. *An Edwin Arlington Robinson Encyclopedia.* Jefferson, N.C.: Macfarland, 2006.

————. *A Henry Wadsworth Longfellow Companion.* Westport, Conn.: Greenwood Press, 2003.

Gatta, John. *Gracious Laughter: The Meditative Wit of Edward Taylor.* Columbia: University of Missouri Press, 1989.

Gentry, Tony. *Paul Laurence Dunbar.* New York: Chelsea House Publishers, 1989.

Gibian, Peter. *Oliver Wendell Holmes and the Culture of Conversation.* New York: Cambridge University Press, 2001.

Gilmore, John. *The Poetics of Empire: A Study of James Grainger's The Sugar Cane.* London and New Brunswick, N.J.: Athlone Press, 2000.

Goldensohn, Lorrie. *American War Poetry: An Anthology.* New York: Columbia University Press, 2006.

Golding, Alan. *From Outlaw to Classic: Canons in American Poetry.* Madison: University of Wisconsin Press, 1995.

Gordon, Charlotte. *Mistress Bradstreet: The Untold Life of America's First Poet.* New York: Little, Brown and Co., 2005.

Granniss, Ruth Shepard. *An American Friend of Southey.* New York: De Vinne Press, 1913.

Grant, Mary Hetherington. *Private Person: An Account of the Life of Julia Ward Howe from 1819–1868.* Brooklyn, N.Y.: Carlson Publishing, 1994.

Gray, Janet. *Race and Time: American Women's Poetics from Antislavery to Racial Modernity.* Iowa City: University of Iowa Press, 2004.

Greene, Roland Arthur. *Unrequited Conquests: Love and Empire in the Colonial Americas.* Chicago: University of Chicago Press, 1999.

Greiff, Constance, and Wanda S. Gunning. *Morven Memory, Myth and Reality.* Princeton, N.J.: Historic Morven, Inc., 2004.

Guruswamy, Rosemary Fithian. *The Poems of Edward Taylor: A Reference Guide*. Westport, Conn.: Greenwood Press, 2003.

Habegger, Alfred. *My Wars Are Laid Away in Books: The Life of Emily Dickinson*. New York: Random House, 2001.

Hall, Florence Howe. *Julia Ward Howe and the Women Suffrage Movement*. Boston: D. Estes, 1913. Reprint, New York: Arno Press, 1969.

Hammon, Jupiter. *America's First Negro Poet; the Complete Works of Jupiter Hammon of Long Island*. Edited by Stanley Austin Ransom, Jr. Port Washington, N.Y.: Kennikat Press, 1970.

Harper, Frances E. W. *Minnie's Sacrifice, Sowing and Reaping, Trial and Triumph: Three Rediscovered Novels*. Edited by Frances Smith Foster. Boston: Beacon Press, 1994.

Higginson, Thomas Wentworth. *John Greenleaf Whittier*. New York: The Macmillan Company, 1911.

Hillway, Tyrus. *Herman Melville*. Boston: Twayne Publishers, 1979.

Hintz, Howard W. *The Quaker Influence in American Literature*. Port Washington, N.Y.: Kennikat Press, 1965.

Hodge, Gene Meany, comp. *Four Winds: Poems from Indian Rituals*. Sante Fe, N.M.: Sunstone Press, 1972.

Hoffman, Daniel G. *The Poetry of Stephen Crane*. New York: Columbia University Press, 1957.

Hoffman, Frederick J., Charles Allen, and Carolyn F. Ulrich. *The Little Magazine: A History and Bibliography*. Princeton, N.J.: Princeton University Press, 1946.

Holt, Edwin P. *The Improper Bostonian: Dr. Oliver Wendell Holmes*. New York: Morrow, 1979.

Howard, Leon. *The Connecticut Wits*. Chicago: University of Chicago Press, 1943.

Howe, Julia Ward. *Reminiscences*. Boston and New York: Houghton, Mifflin, 1900.

Hubbell, Jay Broadus, ed. *The Last Years of Henry Timrod, 1864–1867*. Durham, N.C.: Duke University Press, 1941.

Hubner, Charles William. *War Poets of the South and Confederate Camp-Fire Songs*. Atlanta: U.P. Byrd, 1896.

Huff, Randall. *Popular Culture of the American Revolutionary Era*. Westport, Conn.: Greenwood Press, 2004.

Hutchisson, James M. *Poe*. Jackson: University Press of Mississippi, 2005.

James, Louis. *Caribbean Literature in English*. New York: Longman, 1999.

James, Elisabeth Sheryl. *All Black Voices Count*. Jackson, Miss.: Town Square Books, 1998.

Jensen, Marilyn. *Phyllis Wheatley*. Scarsdale, N.Y.: Lion Books, 1987.

Johnson, Greg. *Emily Dickinson: Perception and the Poet's Quest*. University: University of Alabama Press, 1985.

Kaplan, Justin. *Walt Whitman: A Life*. New York: HarperCollins, 1980.

Katz, Bernard, and Jonathan Katz. *Black Woman: A Fictionalized Biography of Lucy Terry Prince*. Juvenile historical fiction. New York: Pantheon Books, 1973.

Keller, Karl. *The Example of Edward Taylor*. Amherst: University of Massachusetts Press, 1975.

Kelley, Wyn. *Melville's City: Literary and Urban Form in Nineteenth-Century New York*. Cambridge and New York: Cambridge University Press, 1996.

Kennedy, J. Gerald. *A Historical Guide to Edgar Allan Poe*. New York: Oxford University Press, 2001.

Kettell, Samuel, comp. *Specimens of American Poets*. 3 vols. Boston: S. G. Goodrich, 1829.

Kirby-Smith, Henry Tompkins. *The Origins of Free Verse*. Ann Arbor: University of Michigan Press, 1996.

Lauter, Paul, et al. *The Heath Anthology of American Literature*. 3rd edition. Boston: Houghton Mifflin, 1998.

Lazarus, Emma. *Selected Poems*. Edited by John Hollander. New York: Library of America, 2005.

———. *Selected Poems and Other Writings*. Edited by Gregory Eiselein. Orchard Park, N.Y.: Broadview Press, 2002.

Leary, Lewis Gaston. *That Rascal Freneau: A Study in Literary Failure*. New Brunswick, N.J.: Rutgers University Press, 1941.

Leonard, Keith D. *Fettered Genius: The African American Bardic Poet from Slavery Civil Rights*. Charlottesville: University of Virginia Press, 2006.

Link, Eric. *The Vast and Terrible Drama: American Literary Naturalism in the Late Nineteenth Century*. Tuscaloosa: University of Alabama Press, 2004.

Longsworth, Polly. "The 'Latitude of Home': Life in the Homestead and the Evergreens." In *The Dickinsons of*

Amherst. Photographs by Jerome Liebling. Essays by Christopher Benfey, Polly Longsworth, and Barton Levi St. Armand. Hanover and London: University Press of New England, 2001.

Loving, Jerome. *Walt Whitman: The Song of Himself*. Berkeley: University of California Press, 1999.

Low, Dennis. *The Literary Protégées of the Lake Poets*. Burlington, Vt.: Ashgate Publishing, 2006.

Marcotte, Gilles. *Le Temps des poètes: description critique de la poésie actuelle au Canada français*. Montreal: Editions HMH, 1969.

Marsh, Philip Merrill. *The Works of Philip Freneau, A Critical Study*. Metuchen, N.J.: Scarecrow Press, 1968.

Marshall, Tom. *Harsh and Lovely Land: The Major Canadian Poets and the Making of a Canadian Tradition*. Vancouver: University of British Columbia Press, 1979.

Mason, Emily V., ed. *The Southern Poems of the War*. Baltimore: J. Murphy & Co., 1867.

Maxwell, Obediah Craig. *Our Favorites: Our Favorite Poets and Poems, Old and New, Their Homes Fully Described*. Jersey City, N.J.: Star Publishing, 1891.

May, John. *Poe and Fanny: A Novel*. Chapel Hill, N.C.: Algonquin Books of Chapel Hill, 2004.

McAleer, John. *Ralph Waldo Emerson: Days of Encounter*. Boston: Little, Brown, 1984.

McGlinchee, Claire. *James Russell Lowell*. New York: Twayne Publishers, 1967.

McLean, Alfred F., Jr. *William Cullen Bryant*. New York: Twayne, 1989.

McMichael, George, et al. *Anthology of American Literature*. 2nd ed. New York: Macmillan, 1980.

———. *Concise Anthology of American Literature*. 5th ed. Upper Saddle River, N.J.: Prentice Hall, 2001.

McQuade, Donald, et al. *The Harper American Literature*. 2nd ed. New York: Harper & Row, 1994.

Merriam, Robert L. *Lucy Terry Prince*. Conway, Mass.: R. L. Merriam, 1983.

Meyers, Jeffrey. *Edgar Allan Poe: His Life and Legacy*. New York: Charles Scribner's Sons, 1992.

Michaels, Larry. *That New World: The Selected Poems of Sarah Piatt 1861–1911*. West Liberty, Ohio: Mac-A-Cheek Foundation for the Humanities; Toledo, Ohio: Bihl House Publishing, 1999.

Mims, Edwin. *Sidney Lanier*. Port Washington, N.Y.: Kennikat Press, 1968.

Moore, Frank, ed. *Rebel Rhymes and Rhapsodies*. New York: G. P. Putnam, 1864.

Mordell, Albert. *Quaker Militant: John Greenleaf Whittier*. New York: The Macmillan Company, 1911.

Morgan, Kenneth. *Slavery, Atlantic Trade, and the British Economy, 1660–1800*. New York: Cambridge University Press, 2000.

Morris, Roy, Jr. *The Better Angel: Walt Whitman in the Civil War*. New York: Oxford University Press, 2000.

Morton, Sarah Wentworth. *My Mind and Its Thoughts, in Sketches, Fragments and Essays*. Boston: Wells and Lilly, 1823. Reprint, Delmar, N.Y.: Scholars' Facsimiles and Reprints, 1975.

Moss, William. *Confederate Broadside Poems: An Annotated Descriptive Bibliography Based on the Collection of the Z. Smith Reynolds Library of Wake Forest University*. Westport, Conn.: Meckler, 1988.

Mott, Frank Luther. *American Journalism,* 3rd ed. New York: Macmillan, 1962. Republished, London: Routledge/Thoemmes Press, 2000.

———. *A History of American Magazines*. 5 vols. Cambridge, Mass.: Harvard University Press, 1938–68.

Odell, Jonathan. *The New Brunswick Poems of Jonathan Odell*. Kingston, Ont.: Loyal Colonies Press, 1982.

Oliver, Charles M. *Critical Companion to Walt Whitman: A Literary Reference to His Life and Work*. New York: Facts On File, 2006.

O'Neale, Sondra Ann. *Jupiter Hammon and the Biblical Beginnings of African-American Literature*. Metuchen, N.J.: Scarecrow Press, 1993.

Parker, Hershel. *Herman Melville: A Biography*. 2 vols. Baltimore, Md.: Johns Hopkins University Press, 1996, 2002.

Pendleton, Emily, and Milton Ellis. *Philenia: The Life and Works of Sarah Wentworth Morton*. Orono, M.E.: The University of Maine Press, 1931.

Perkins, George, and Barbara Perkins. *The American Tradition in Literature*. 9th ed. New York: McGraw Hill, 1999.

Piatt, Sarah Morgan Bryan. *Palace Burner: The Selected Poetry of Sarah Piatt*. Edited by Paula Bernat Bennett. Urbana: University of Illinois Press, 2001.

Pickard, John B. *The Letters of John Greenleaf Whittier*. 3 vols. Cambridge, Mass.: Harvard University Press, 1975.

Poe, Edgar Allan. *The Letters of Edgar Allan Poe*. 2 vols. New York: Gordian Press, 1966.

———. *The Collected Works of Edgar Allan Poe*. Vol. 1: *Poems*. Edited by Thomas Ollive Mabbott, et al. Cambridge, Mass.: Harvard University Press, 1969.

Pollard, John Albert. *John Greenleaf Whittier: Friend of Man.* Hamden, Conn.: Archon Books, 1969.

Porter, David T. *The Art of Emily Dickinson's Early Poetry.* Cambridge, Mass.: Harvard University Press, 1966.

Proper, David R. *Lucy Terry Prince: Singer of History.* Deerfield, Mass.: Pocumtuck Valley Memorial Association, 1997.

Rand, Theodore Harding, ed. *A Treasury of Canadian Verse.* Toronto: W. Briggs, 1900.

Rasula, Jed. *The American Poetry Wax Museum.* Urbana, Ill.: National Council of Teachers of English, 1995.

Renfro, G. Herbert. *Life and Works of Phillis Wheatley.* 1916. Reprint, Miami, Fla.: Mnemosyn Press, 1969.

Richards, Eliza. *Gender and the Poetics of Reception in Poe's Circle.* New York: Cambridge University Press, 2004.

Richardson, Robert D., Jr. *Emerson: The Mind on Fire.* Berkeley: University of California Press, 1995.

Robertson-Lorant, Laurie, *Melville: A Biography.* New York: Clarkson Potter, 1993.

Robinson, Edwin Arlington. *The Poetry of E. A. Robinson.* Edited by Robert Mezey. New York: Modern Library, 1999.

Robinson, William H. *Phillis Wheatley and Her Writings.* Boston: G. K. Hall, 1984.

Rowe, Karen E. *Saint and Sinner: Edward Taylor's Typology and the Poetics of Meditation.* New York: Cambridge University Press, 1986.

Sacks, Kenneth. *Understanding Emerson: "The American Scholar" and His Struggle for Self-Reliance.* Princeton, N.J.: Princeton University Press, c2003.

Sharpe, J. Ed, ed. *American Indian Prayers and Poetry.* Cherokee, N.C.: Cherokee Publications, 1985.

Sherman, Joan R. *African-American Poetry: An Anthology, 1773–1927.* Mineola, N.Y.: Dover Publications, 1997.

Shields, John C. "Phillis Wheatley's Struggle for Freedom." In *The Collected Works of Phillis Wheatley.* New York: Oxford University Press, 1988.

Shucard, Alan. *American Poetry: The Puritans Through Walt Whitman.* Boston: Twayne Publishers, 1988.

Smith, Elihu Hubbard. *American Poems.* 1793. Reprint, Gainesville, Fla.: Scholars' Facsimiles & Reprints, 1966.

Smith, Harmon. *My Friend, My Friend: The Story of Thoreau's Relationship with Emerson.* Amherst: University of Massachusetts Press, 1999.

Spinden, Herbert Joseph, trans. *Songs of the Tewa.* Sante Fe, N.M.: Sunstone Press, 1976.

Starke, Aubrey. *Sidney Lanier: A Biographical and Critical Study.* N.Y.: Russell & Russell, 1964.

Stockton, Annis Boudinot. *Only for the Eye of a Friend: The Poems of Annis Boudinot Stockton.* Edited by Carla Mulford. Charlottesville: University Press of Virginia, 1995.

Streeter, N. R., comp. *Gems from an Old Drummer's Grip.* Grotten, N.Y.: N. R. Streeter, 1889.

Taylor, Edward. *Edward Taylor's Gods Determinations and Preparatory Meditations: A Critical Edition.* Edited by Daniel Patterson. Kent, Ohio: Kent State University Press, 2003.

Taupin, René. *The Influence of French Symbolism on Modern American Poetry.* Translated by William Pratt and Anne Rich Pratt. New York: A.M.S. Press, 1985.

Tebbel, John. *The American Magazine: A Compact History.* New York: Hawthorn Books, 1969.

Tebbel, John and Mary Ellen Zuckerman. *The Magazine in America, 1741–1990.* New York: Oxford University Press, 1991.

Thompson, Slason, comp. *The Humbler Poets: A Collection of Newspaper and Periodical Verse, 1870–1885.* Chicago: A. C. McClurg, 1890.

Thoreau, Henry David. *Collected Poems.* Edited by Carl Bode. Baltimore: Johns Hopkins Press, 1964.

———. *Poems of Nature.* Edited by Henry S. Salt and Frank B. Sanborn. Boston: Houghton Mifflin, 1895.

Tifflin, Helen. "The Institution of Literature." In *A History of the Caribbean,* Vol. 3, edited by James A. Arnold. Amsterdam and Philadelphia: John Benjamin Publishing, 2001.

Tilden, Eleanor Marguerite. *Amiable Autocrat: A Biography of Dr. Oliver Wendell Holmes.* New York: Henry Schuman, 1947.

Timrod, Henry. *Poems of Henry Timrod with Memoir and Portrait.* 1901. Reprint, Whitefish, Mont.: Kessinger Publishing, 2004.

Vallier, Jane E. *Poet on Demand: The Life, Letters and Works of Celia Thaxter.* Camden, Me.: Down East Books, 1982.

Vincent, Thomas B., ed. *Narrative Verse Satire in Maritime Canada, 1779–1814.* Ottawa: Tecumseh Press, 1978.

———. *Jonathan Odell: An Annotated Chronology of the Poems, 1759–1818.* Kingston, Ont.: Loyal Colonies Press, 1980.

Vines, Lois Davis. *Valéry and Poe: A Literary Legacy.* New York: New York University Press, 1992.

Vining, Elizabeth Gray. *Mr. Whittier.* New York: The Viking Press, 1974.

Vitzthum, Richard C. *Land and Sea: The Lyric Poetry of Philip Freneau.* Minneapolis: University of Minnesota Press, 1978.

Young, Bette Roth. *Emma Lazarus in Her World: Life and Letters.* Philadelphia: Jewish Publication Society, 1995.

Wagenknecht, Edward. *Henry Wadsworth Longfellow: His Poetry and Prose.* New York: Ungar, 1986.

———. *John Greenleaf Whittier: A Portrait in Paradox.* New York: Oxford University Press, 1967.

———. *James Russell Lowell: Portrait of a Many-Sided Man.* New York: Oxford University Press, 1971.

Walsh, John Evangelist. *Plumes in the Dust: The Love Affair of Edgar Allan Poe and Fanny Osgood.* Chicago: Nelson Hall, 1980.

Wayne, Tiffany K. *Encyclopedia of Transcendentalism.* New York: Facts On File, 2006.

Wertheim, Stanley, and Paul Sorrentino. *The Correspondence of Stephen Crane.* New York: Columbia University Press, 1988.

Wheatley, Phillis. *The Collected Works of Phillis Wheatley.* Edited by John C. Shields. New York: Oxford University Press, 1988.

White, Elizabeth Wade. *Anne Bradstreet: The Tenth Muse.* New York: Oxford University Press, 1971.

Whitman, Walt. *Selected Poems 1855–1892.* Edited by Gary Schmidgall. New York: St. Martin's Press, 1999.

Whittier, John Greenleaf. *The Complete Poetical Works of John Greenleaf Whittier.* Boston: Houghton Mifflin Company, 1894.

Wigglesworth, Michael. *The Diary of Michael Wigglesworth, 1653–1657. The Conscience of a Puritan.* Edited by Edmund S. Morgan. Gloucester, Mass.: Peter Smith, 1970.

———. *The Poems of Michael Wigglesworth.* Edited by Ronald A. Bosco. Lanham, Md.: University Press of America, c. 1989.

Williams, Gary. *Hungry Heart: The Literary Emergence of Julia Ward Howe.* Amherst: University of Massachusetts Press, 1999.

Williams, Stephen West. *A Biographical Memoir of the Rev. John Williams.* Greenfield, Mass.: Imprints, 1837.

Wilson, Edmund. *Patriotic Gore: Studies in the Literature of the American Civil War.* London: A. Deutsch, 1962. Reprint, London: The Hogarth Press, 1987.

Winch, Julie. *A Gentleman of Color: The Life of James Forten.* New York: Oxford University Press, 2002.

Wood, Marcus, ed. *The Poetry of Slavery: An Anglo-American Anthology, 1764–1865.* New York: Oxford University Press, 2003.

Woodress, James. *A Yankee's Odyssey: The Life of Joel Barlow.* Philadelphia: Lippincott, 1958.

Woodwell, Robert H. *John Greenleaf Whittier: A Biography.* Haverhill, Mass.: Trustees of the John Greenleaf Whittier Homestead, 1985.

INDEX